June 21–23, 2017
Indianapolis, IN, USA

I0054774

**Association for
Computing Machinery**

Advancing Computing as a Science & Profession

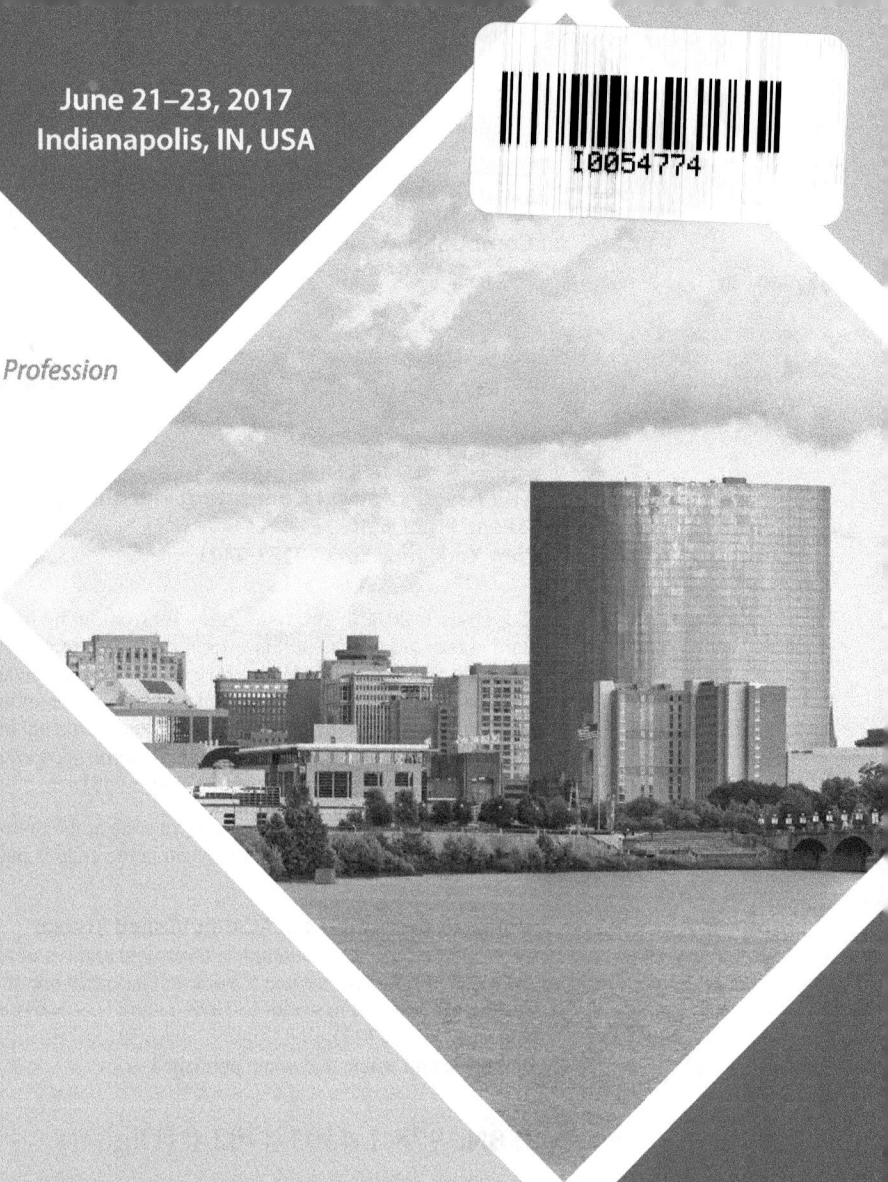

SACMAT'17

Proceedings of the 22nd ACM

Symposium on Access Control Models and Technologies

Sponsored by:

ACM SIGSAC

Supported by:

**Cyber2Slab
& IUPUI, Department of Computer and Information Science**

Association for Computing Machinery

Advancing Computing as a Science & Profession

The Association for Computing Machinery
2 Penn Plaza, Suite 701
New York, New York 10121-0701

Notice to Past Authors of ACM-Published Articles
ACM intends to create a complete electronic archive of all articles and/or other material previously published by ACM. If you have written a work that has been previously published by ACM in any journal or conference proceedings prior to 1978, or any SIG Newsletter at any time, and you do NOT want this work to appear in the ACM Digital Library, please inform permissions@acm.org, stating the title of the work, the author(s), and where and when published.

ISBN: 978-1-4503-4702-0 (Digital)

ISBN: 978-1-4503-5594-0 (Print)

Additional copies may be ordered prepaid from:

ACM Order Department
PO Box 30777
New York, NY 10087-0777, USA

Phone: 1-800-342-6626 (USA and Canada)
+1-212-626-0500 (Global)
Fax: +1-212-944-1318
E-mail: acmhelp@acm.org
Hours of Operation: 8:30 am – 4:30 pm ET

General Chair and PC Chairs' Welcome

It is our great pleasure to welcome you to the *22nd ACM Symposium on Access Control Models and Technologies (SACMAT 2017)* taking place in Indianapolis, IN, USA on June 21-23, 2017. The SACMAT symposium series is the premier forum for presentation of research results and experience reports on leading edge issues of access control in terms of models, systems, applications, and theory. The symposium aims to share novel access control solutions that fulfill the needs of heterogeneous applications and environments, and to identify new directions for future research and development. This year SACMAT introduced a special focus on access control technologies for Internet of Things. We hope to expand this focus in the next editions of SACMAT.

The call for papers attracted about 50 submissions from a variety of countries around the world. Submissions were anonymous; each paper has been reviewed by at least three reviewers who are experts in the field. Extensive online discussions took place to make the selections for the symposium. The program committee finally accepted 14 papers as full papers and 4 papers as short ones for presentation at the symposium. The topics covered include network and mobile access control, access control in applications including IoT and medical devices, policy engineering, access control specification and access control enforcement. The program is complemented by poster and demonstrations sessions, and by a panel discussion focusing on access control in mobile operating systems. We are also very proud to present as part of the program two exciting keynote talks by Seraphin Calo (IBM Research), and Marten van Dijk (University of Connecticut).

Putting together *SACMAT 2017* was a team effort. We first thank the authors for providing the content of the program. We are grateful to the program committee members who worked very hard in reviewing papers and providing feedback for authors. We also acknowledge the poster co-chairs, Dan Lin and Robert Koch, the demonstrations chair, Jianwei Niu, and the panel chair, Ninghui Li, for their contributions to SACMAT 2017 program. Finally, we thank all the conference officers involved in the different organizational aspects of SACMAT 2017: Hongxin Hu – proceedings chair; Yulong Shen – publicity chair; Xukai Zou – local arrangement chair; Basit Shafiq – treasures; Dongwan Shin –webmaster. Last but not least we would like to thank the SACMAT steering committee, chaired by Elena Ferrari, for the constant guidance throughout the process of organizing SACMAT 2017.

We hope that you will find this program interesting and thought-provoking and that the symposium will provide you with a valuable opportunity to share ideas with other researchers and practitioners from institutions and organization around the world.

Elisa Bertino
SACMAT 2017 General Chair
Purdue University, USA

Ravi Sandhu
SACMAT 2017 Program Co-Chair
University of Texas at San Antonio, USA

Edgar Weippl
SACMAT 2017 Program Co-Chair
SBA Research, Austria

General Chair and PC Chairs' Welcome

Table of Contents

Keynote Address I
Session Chair: Ravi Sandhu *(University of Texas at San Antonio)*

Session: Authorization and Authentication
Session Chair: Elena Ferrari *(University of Insubria)*

Session: Applications
Session Chair: Axel Kern *(Beta Systems Software AG)*

Session: Policy Models and Frameworks
Session Chair: Hongxin Hu *(Clemson University)*

Posters
Session Chairs: Dan Lin *(Missouri University of Science and Technology)*
and Robert Koch *(Universität der Bundeswehr München)*

Keynote Address II
Session Chair: Edgar Weippl (*SBA Research*),

Session: Formal Techniques I
Session Chair: Edgar Weippl (*SBA Research*)

Session: Demonstrations
Session Chair: Jianwei Niu (*University of Texas at San Antonio*)

Session: Formal Techniques II
Session Chair: Xukai Zou (*Indiana University-Purdue University Indiana*)

Short Papers
Session Chair: Elisa Bertino *(Purdue University)*

SACMAT 2017 Symposium Organization

General Chair: Elisa Bertino (Purdue University, USA)

Program Chairs: Ravi Sandhu (University of Texas at San Antonio, USA)
Edgar Weippl (SBA Research, Austria)

Panels Chair: Ninghui Li (Purdue University, USA)

Demonstrations Chair: Jianwei Niu (University of Texas at San Antonio, USA)

Poster Co-Chairs: Dan Lin (Missouri University of Science and Technology, USA)
Robert Koch (Universität der Bundeswehr München, Germany)

Proceedings Chair: Hongxin Hu (Clemson University, USA)

Local Arrangements Chair: Xukai Zou (Indiana University-Purdue University Indiana, USA)

Publicity Chair: Barbara Carminati (University of Insubria, Italy)

Treasurer: Basit Shafiq (Lahore University of Management Sciences, Pakistan)

Webmaster: Dongwan Shin (New Mexico Tech, USA)

Steering Committee Chair: Elena Ferrari (University of Insubria, Italy)

Steering Committee: Gail-Joon Ahn (Arizona State University, USA)
Barbara Carminati (University of Insubria, Italy)
James Joshi (University of Pittsburgh, USA)
Axel Kern (Beta Systems Software AG, Germany)
Ninghui Li (Purdue University, USA)
Indrakshi Ray (Colorado State University, USA)
Bhavani Thuraisingham (University of Texas at Dallas, USA)

Program Committee: Ehab Al-Shaer (University of North Carolina at Charlotte, USA)
Vijay Atluri (Rutgers University, USA)
Adam Aviv (US Naval Academy, USA)
Barbara Carminati (University of Insubria, Italy)

SACMAT 2017 Sponsor & Supporters

Sponsor:

Supporters:

Distributed Intelligence – Trends in the Management of Complex Systems

Seraphin B. Calo, Dinesh C. Verma
IBM Research
Yorktown Heights, NY, USA

Elisa Bertino
Purdue University
West Lafayette, IN, USA

ABSTRACT

The ability to incorporate intelligence in even small devices and to make use of contextual information from widely deployed sensors has already begun to change management paradigms. As edge computing and IoT become more prevalent, systems will increasingly consist of cooperating, heterogeneous, distributed, autonomous elements. Architectures for cognitive, collaborative systems are evolving to deal with such complex environments. Concepts from multi-agent systems and autonomic computing are being applied to cope with the scope and breadth of large collections of interacting devices and services. Technologies for security and access control must evolve as well. Policy-based mechanisms are widely used and have been very successful in protecting information and controlling access to systems and services. They tend to rely, however, on a centralized infrastructure and on the automated enforcement of directives. Newer paradigms are being investigated that allow policy structures to be more dynamic and contextual, while still preserving the desired levels of control. We will present trends in the evolution of architectures for distributed, federated systems, and the technologies for managing them.

INTRODUCTION

The Internet of Things (IoT) has become increasingly important due to its great potential for providing ubiquitous services based on real time contextual information. It represents not only the use of simple sensors and actuators, but also the application of sophisticated software and complex systems to data-driven processes. Thus, there is the opportunity to evolve interoperable networks of devices and systems producing large amounts of data and providing a plethora of distributed services.

One of the technologies being explored for overcoming many of the problems being faced in the development of an infrastructure for IoT environments is that of Multi-Agent Systems (MAS) [1], which are based on distributed intelligence and an architecture for supporting cooperating components.

SACMAT'17, June 21-23, 2017, Indianapolis, IN, USA
© 2017 Association for Computing Machinery.
ACM ISBN 978-1-4503-4702-0/17/06...$15.00
http://dx.doi.org/10.1145/3078861.3078881

Independent software agents represent the goals of their actual counterparts (e.g., sensors, hardware devices, operating software) and take actions autonomously. These agents form collaborative units to execute complex processes. They can incorporate learning mechanisms and cognitive analytics. Such agent based approaches offer a promising alternative to more centralized or hierarchical architectures for IoT software that have difficulties coping with the management of huge numbers of devices and the volumes of data that they produce.

Another key technology for dealing with distributed, autonomous systems is that of policy based management. It has proven to be an invaluable element in simplifying the management and operations of complex distributed environments in many different domains. Due to their wide applicability, several policy management frameworks have been developed, and many policy specification languages and information models have been defined [2].

Despite the benefits and usefulness of policy based management, currently deployed technologies have followed an approach in which the management system provides relatively constrained instructions to a managed device. These instructions are typically specified by a central authority and are meant to be explicitly followed by all elements to which they apply. However, in distributed systems, the local context may change or there may be some uncertainty in the values of certain attributes of the system. The directed policies may thus no longer apply or their applicability may have become ambiguous. Further, they incorporate no cognitive mechanisms for learning from past experiences. A policy management system that allowed local modifications or adaptations of globally defined policies might thus be better able to effectively support local autonomy.

In the next section, we present some thoughts on the architecture needed for building cognitive collaborative systems. Then we describe the technologies currently being applied to policy based management, and some extensions being explored for adaptive policy inferencing. Next, we present the overall generative policy approach that further extends the functionality of such systems to include the influences of local context. This would significantly advance the attainment of the capabilities needed for the operation and management of collaborative, autonomous systems. We illustrate the use of generative policies with examples in the two subsequent sections. Finally, we state our conclusions and mention some future investigations.

COGNITIVE COLLABORATIVE SYSTEMS

In order to accommodate the huge numbers of objects that will be part of the Internet of Things (IoT) a suitable management paradigm with appropriate technological foundations must be developed. Internet-connected sensors, actuators and other types of smart devices need an infrastructure for association and control if they are to be coordinated effectively to provide situational awareness and actionable intelligence. The management functionality must overcome the dynamic, heterogeneous, distributed nature of such systems, while providing high reliability. The idea is to enable seamless and interoperable connectivity among heterogeneous devices and systems, while hiding their complexity and providing sophisticated services.

A promising direction for the organization of such complex environments is to make the constituent elements of the system self-managing, and to create an architecture where knowledge mechanisms are tightly coupled with the computing elements. We imagine a collection of autonomous operational units that collectively form a collaborative system. There are several related technologies that have been proposed, and their characteristics are being investigated. These include: Multi-Agent Systems (MAS) [1], Self-Managed Cells (SMC) [3], Autonomic Managers (AM) [4], and the infrastructure developed for Mobile Edge Capture and Analysis (MECA) [5]. Our intent is to also include more recent advances in cognitive computing and generative policy management.

At a high level, the characteristics of the elements of the system (hardware, software, datasets, etc.) would be captured in Virtual Objects (VOs) that would represent them within the software environment. The VOs would track the status of the assets they represent, and would be able to communicate with them and control them to the extent that the actual asset can be externally controlled. Composite Virtual Objects (CVOs) would represent collections of semantically interoperable Virtual Objects (VOs) that provide federated information services.

Autonomous Operational Units (AOUs) would represent collections of hardware and software assets that jointly can perform an operation or process. The AOUs include a management system with cognitive capabilities, and maintain rules, process flows and policies associated with their operational domain as in Figure 1. They can be goal driven, discovering VOs and other AOUs that can provide necessary capabilities for carrying out their responsibilities. They can predict the expected behavior of physical assets, and would incorporate learning mechanisms for improving their effectiveness and performance.

The AOUs would maintain relationships with other AOUs, so that their collection forms a (logically) distributed collaborative system. These collections would establish patterns of behavior, provide mechanisms for continuously optimizing the functioning of their associated physical systems, and would enforce complex policies and workflows associated with multiple interacting organizations, e.g., coalitions. They are self-organizing and self-configuring, coming together to accomplish cooperative tasks.

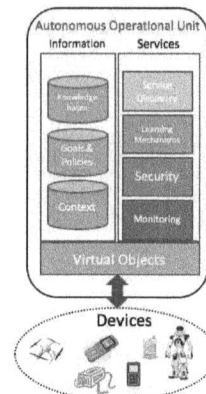

Figure 1: Autonomous Operational Unit

POLICY BASED MANAGEMENT

Policy Based Management Systems (PBMS) typically follow the policy model defined by the Internet Engineering Task Force (IETF) and the Distributed Management Task Force (DMTF) [6]. This framework consists of four basic elements: a policy manager (PM), a policy repository (PR), a policy enforcement point (PEP), and a policy decision point (PDP). Policies themselves are defined as declarative event-condition-action (ECA) rules. A Boolean condition is defined over a set of run-time data provided to the policy at evaluation time by the managed environment. When an event triggers the evaluation of the condition, if it evaluates to *true*, then the action is executed. Policy management frameworks based on this model may provide additional capabilities that make it easier for system administrators to policy enable their applications, middleware, and services.

The human operator or policy administrator specifies objectives for the functioning of the managed devices. The management system translates these higher level policies into a machine view of policy through the process of refinement or policy transformation as in Figure 2. The machine view of policy is provided to entities known as policy decision points (PDPs) either directly or through a policy repository. Entities known as policy enforcement points (PEPs) represent managed resources with respect to particular decisions. When a PEP needs to make one of these decisions, it calls out to its associated PDP, which obtains the relevant policies, interprets them and communicates appropriate actions back to the PEP. This allows decisions to be made based on the current state of the system and the active set of policies, rather than being hard coded in the application. The behavior of the system can then be changed by changing the policies rather than rewriting or extending the software code itself.

The elements of the policy infrastructure can be configured in several different ways, depending upon the desired architecture of the system under management. The PEP is associated with the managed resources and will usually be co-located with them, while the policy refinement process is usually embedded in the policy management tool. The PDP could be embedded in the policy management tool in systems that are meant to be centrally managed, or it could be co-located with its associated PEPs in systems that are meant to be distributed. In the latter configuration policies would be pushed to appropriate PDPs when they are specified or changed, and stored locally. When the PDP is embedded within the managed environment the managed system can exhibit a greater degree of autonomic behavior, since it does not have to go back to a central point to determine which of a set of alternative actions should be taken at specified decision points.

Beyond methods for policy specification, mechanisms for learning applicable policies within the confines of higher level constraints are being investigated. There are efforts to develop techniques for policy mining that serve to: automatically learn security policies from historical examples and granted exceptions; and, infer roles that help compact and simplify security management. Earlier work used data logs to infer policies directly from system usage [7]. This allows the finding of RBAC models which reflect the observed usage of entitlements and the attributes of users. These models are thus causally associated with actual usage of entitlements and combinations of user attributes.

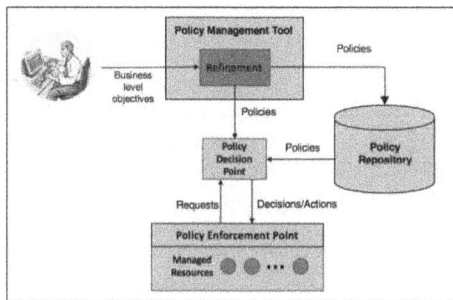

Figure 2: Policy Based Management System

Continuing research applies Behavioral Analytics for anomaly detection to derive policies for operational control [8]. Such techniques, as well as classical machine learning techniques like transfer learning are also being investigated. In transfer learning, the knowledge gained from the creation of policies in one context can be stored and applied to the learning of policies in other related contexts.

A general architecture for dynamic policy adaptation is shown in Figure 3. The policy decisions at various PDPs would be monitored and that knowledge would be used to modify the deployed policies, as well as to provide input to the refinement process so that it could be leveraged in the specification of subsequently defined policies. Only relatively simple instances of the general approach have so far been studied, mostly with respect to the incorporation of history data [9].

Generative policy architecture

A key concept in the generative approach is that local elements will generate their own operational policies within the bounds of higher level policy structures supporting collaboration and meant to assure compliance with high level constraints and the pursuit of common goals. The formal model of a generative PBMS must thus provide constructs for specifying both the higher-level policy structures, the operational policies that are locally generated, and the relationships between the two.

In the generative policy architecture, the policy refinement process (PRF) is separated into two parts, one associated with the global management system (PRFM) and one associated with the managed system (PRFD). The PDP is embedded within the managed system, and it gets its policies from the PRFD module as shown in Figure 4. The PRFM is responsible for sending the overall coordination guidelines to the PRFD. The PRFM provides two types of information to each PRFD. One is an interaction graph, that contains an abstract description of the various entities within the environment with which the PRFD needs to interact.

The interaction graph is defined as a relationship between entities in different roles in the system, not as an exhaustive listing of all the different devices in the system. The role of each PRFD in the interaction graph is defined by the PRFM. The PRFM also associates a set of attributes with each link in the interaction graph. These are the attributes whose values can be obtained via the indicated link.

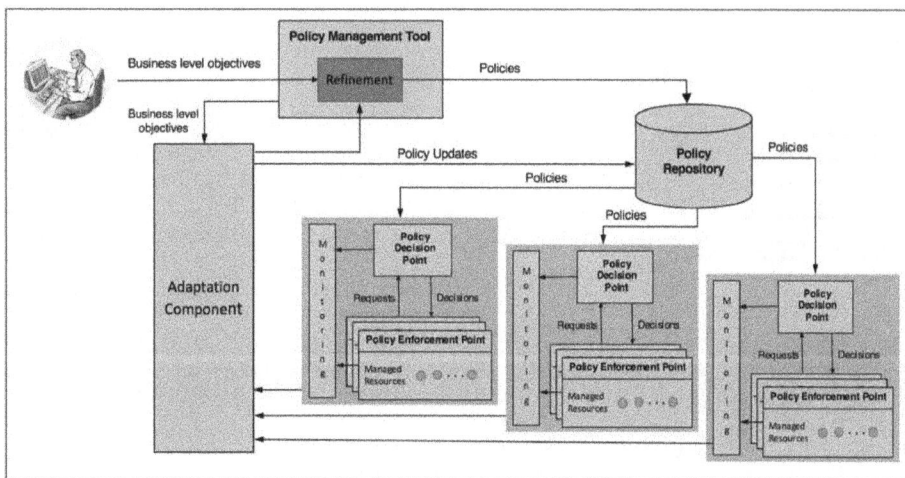

Figure 3: Dynamic Policy Adaptation

Each PRFD receives the interaction graph from the global management system and uses it to generate the policies for its local PDP. This provides each PDP with the attributes of the connecting links that can then be resolved by the policies that require them. To generate these policies, the PRFD can use different mechanisms. One approach is that of utilizing a grammar (either a Context Free Grammar, CFG, or an Attribute Grammar) for capturing the set of allowable policies, and having the distributed elements generate and employ operational policies only if they are derivable from that grammar. Another approach would be to specify a State Machine that indicates the expected operation of the managed system from the point of view of the global management system. This description would typically indicate certain goal states that the local systems should achieve. A third alternative would be for the PRFD to receive policies at a higher level in terms of more abstract concepts, and utilize a refinement hierarchy to produce operational policies pertinent to the local context.

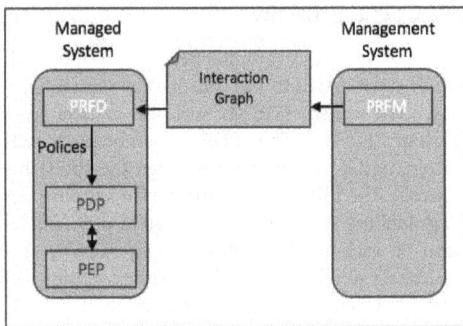

Figure 4: Generative Policy Architecture

Such policy mechanisms can also be provided to the PRFD by an independent management system. As an example, in a military coalition, a U.S. operator may provide the mechanism agreed to for a particular mission to the drones under its control, while in the context of the coalition operation, the management system PRFM may belong to another coalition partner. For each distinct domain to which the policy architecture is applied, the set of valid roles, the attributes which define the mapping of the nodes in the interaction graph to the values referenced in the policies, and the specific policy structures are specified.

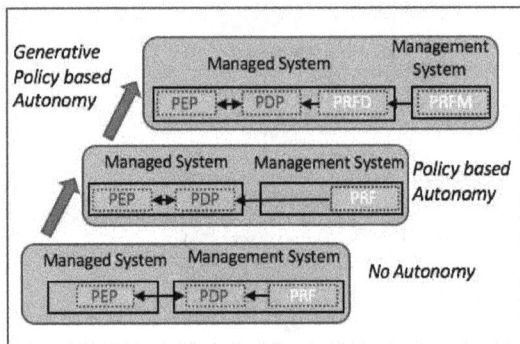

Figure 5: Evolution of Policy Based Management

As mentioned earlier, the current model for policy based management has the semantics that the machine view of policies is determined by the refinement process, and the managed system with the embedded PDP has no ability to define its own policies. Our goal is to enable a situation where the managed system can derive its own policies, which means embedding a part of the policy refinement process within the device itself. Embedding policy refinement within the device has the most significance when modular design principles are used, enabling the same refinement process within the device to be used across multiple management domains. Our view of the evolution of policy based management is depicted in Figure 5.

The broad approach for generative policy based management can be illustrated in an intuitive manner using an example from a common security management situation in data centers and cloud sites as discussed in the next section.

ILLUSTRATIVE PROBLEM SCENARIO

Maintaining secure access to documents is a common problem in any data center/cloud site. We consider a situation where we have a set of documents, some of which are treated as sensitive, and others that are not. A set of users have access to sensitive documents, which can be obtained either using a web-based application or via a secure shell based system. A packet filtering firewall is provided to safeguard access to both systems. The configuration is shown in Figure 6. The scenario is a common one encountered in almost any site requiring access control to a set of documents.

The current practice in securing such systems is for a human administrator to manually configure filtering and access control policies for the firewall, web-server, secure shell server and the document server. In a typical scenario, the ports on a firewall need to be configured to allow access to the web server. However, if we provide more autonomy to the web-server, e.g., assume it is using a moving target defense [10], and changes its port for the web-server at some regular periods, the configuration of the packet filter firewall needs to be repeated manually every-time such a change happens. The management tool will have to create the appropriate policies for each of the devices.

Instead of a manual reconfiguration of access control policies after each change, it would be highly desirable if the human operator simply specified the access requirements on the documents. Based on those access control requirements, the packet firewall, the web server, the SSH server, and the document server would each derive their own policies to comply with those specifications. If the web-server switched its port as part of the moving target defense, the packet firewall would automatically adjust its filtering policies accordingly. In these cases, the policy refinement process happens within the devices themselves, and does not require any human intervention until access control on specific documents are changed.

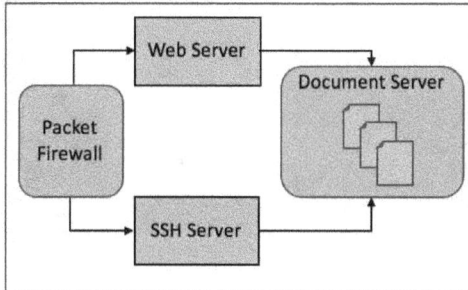

Figure 6: Illustrative Problem Scenario

Note that a similar policy refinement process would be desirable if the devices were to be managed not for access control, but for fault management, configuration management or performance management. When a fault happens in one of the components, we would want all the components impacted by the fault to generate new policies to deal with the fault situation. Similarly, for performance management, the different components should be able to determine their policies for managing performance, e.g., by increasing the number of parallel instances. In all aspects of autonomic behavior, we would like the devices and components to define their policies on their own.

Let us consider the application of the generative policy architecture to the access control scenario. In this case, three roles for different entities can be identified, a network protection role(N), a protocol protection role(P), and a document protection role(D). In the scenario instance shown in Figure 6, the web server and the SSH server both have the protocol protection role. The firewall has the network protection role and the document server has the document protection role. The global interaction graph is shown in Figure 7 with the letters N, P and D indicating the different roles, and the attributes required for each link. The specific interaction graph that will be provided to the PRFD in each of the devices is also shown, with the role of the device marked in black circles in each device specific interaction graph.

When the PRFD for each of the devices receives the interaction graph, it searches for the other nodes that are associated with adjacent roles. The discovery module finds the other devices in those roles, and finds out the attributes identified by the devices in those roles in the interaction graph. Then, the PRFD uses the grammar available with it to generate its own set of policies to be used for its PDP.

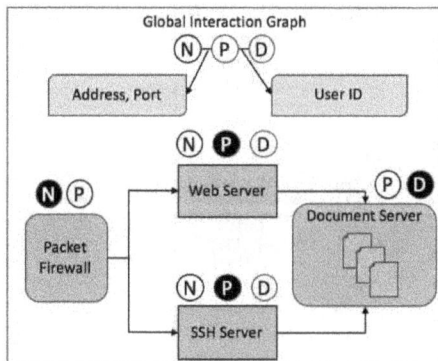

Figure 7: Roles and Interaction Graph

In the illustrative scenario, once the address and port for the protocol protection role are identified, the packet firewall can generate the appropriate packet filtering policies for the firewall. Similarly, the web-server can receive the set of user-ids that are authorized to access the document server, and install its protection policies to only allow those user-ids to access the document server. Note that the document server will provide several user-ids to the protocol protection servers, while each of the web-servers and SSH server will only provide a single network address and port for itself to the packet firewall. Eventually, the document server would need to have its document protection policies. In this case, these policies come directly from the PRFM.

The grammar for policy generation for the packet filter firewall will generate the 5-tuple (source and destination addresses, source and destination ports, and the protocol) that determine whether or not a packet is allowed within the network. The address and port numbers of each protocol protection device (the web-server and SSH server in this scenario) will provide this information to the firewall which it can use to create its network packet filtering policies. When the attributes for the web-server and SSH-server change, e.g., due to a scheme such as moving target defense [10] changing those attributes, the discovery process will again be triggered and the policies in the packet filtering firewalls will be regenerated.

While the previous example was for access control, the same scheme can be generalized for other aspects for the same system setup, e.g., increasing the number of instances of each node in Figure 6 dynamically for performance management.

In the next section, we describe a common situation that arises in coalition operations, and how the generative policy architecture can be applied in that context.

SOFTWARE DEFINED COALITIONS

In coalition operations, e.g., when joint missions need to be undertaken by soldiers belonging to different countries, it is frequently essential to establish a dynamic community of interest. A dynamic community of interest (CoI) is a group of individuals that come together for a specified period to perform a particular mission, and the group dissolves after a specific time has elapsed or the mission has been completed [11]. Such dynamic communities of interest may also be formed in non-military contexts, e.g., when different civilian agencies come together to fight a fire or deal with the aftermath of a hurricane. In a dynamic CoI, not all members are necessarily trusted equally, so policies related to information sharing may differ between groups of coalition members.

When dynamic CoIs are formed, they require supporting IT infrastructure to conduct their operations more effectively. The assets can come from all the different coalition members, and they need to interoperate. Software Defined Coalition (SDC) technologies provide such support. They combine and extend concepts from software defined networking to operate in the context of coalition operations. A more detailed description of software defined coalitions can be found in [12].

Let us consider the situation where some drones from the U.S. and the U.K. are part of a coalition mission where the mission commander is from a third coalition nation. In order to conduct the mission efficiently, the drones have to comply with the commander's instructions. At the same time, the two countries may not want to provide complete control of operations to the commander who is only partially trusted, and may be concerned about the safety of their assets during operations.

The assets in the SDC are subject to dual management, and must be able to deal in an autonomous manner with the instructions and commands from both types of managers. Furthermore, for a significant part of the actual operation, assets may have to work independently in a mode where they may be disconnected from their respective managers. The U.S. asset (drone) needs to be prepared for participation in the CoI by the U.S. operator using a U.S. management system. Analogously, the UK operator would be preparing the UK drone. Once the assets are assigned, the CoI commander needs to prepare them for the mission. At this stage, the asset may only have connectivity to the commander, and have no connectivity to other management systems. The assets belong to more than one nation, and together they perform the actual mission, e.g., surveillance of some geographical area.

Movement Control

One of the constraints the U.K. forces may have on their drones is that they can only be operated in areas considered safe for them. US forces may have their own constraints on the operation of their drones. When the drones are given over to a commander from a separate country, the two countries may still want the drones to conform to their policies.

The waypoint approach is a common method to control the flight of autonomous drones. In this approach, the path of a drone is determined by means of a set of predefined waypoints which the drone follows to complete a path. Figure 8 shows a typical waypoint defined path.

The CoI commander will define a set of waypoints which can be used to instruct the drones how they should fly for any specific mission. As a simple example, let us assume that there are six regions A-F of which three regions, A, B, C are safe and three regions, D, E, F are unsafe. Further, the UK may have a policy which requires them to avoid any of the areas that are considered unsafe. The U.S. may be more permissive, but requires that no two consecutive waypoints be in unsafe areas.

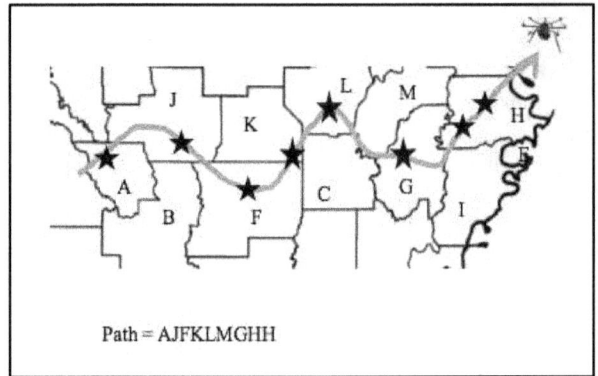

Path = AJFKLMGHH

Figure 8: A sample path for drones specified using waypoints

In this example, we will consider an alternative way to send the high-level policy information. Instead of a grammar, the coalition commander will send the drone the region map and a corresponding transition diagram as in Figure 9, along with the characteristics of each region, in this case whether the region is considered "safe" = {a, b, c} or "unsafe" = {d, e, f}. It also indicates that the goal is to move the drone from an initial state $s_0 = a$ to an end state $c \in F$, following the conventions of a formal state machine.

A state machine is a quintuple $(\Sigma, S, s_0, \delta, F)$ where: Σ is the input alphabet (a finite, non-empty set of symbols); S is a non-empty set of states; s_0 is an initial state, an element of S; δ is the state-transition function: $\delta: S \times \Sigma \rightarrow S$; and F is the set of final states. In this example, the states will be determined by the regions covering the mission theatre {a, b, c, d, e, f}. With $\lambda_x \in \Sigma$, $x \in$ {a, b, c, d, e, f}, we assume that an event that issues λ_x will cause a transition to state x.

Each drone will have local context variables that were either set initially by their owning coalition member or reflect encountered operating conditions, $\mathbf{w} = \{w_1, w_2, \ldots w_R\}$. We assume that w_1 = identity of owning coalition member. The drone will calculate the set of possible trajectories without cycles: T = {abc, aec, abec, aebc, aefc, adfc, adec, aedfc, abefc, adfec, adebc, adefc, abedfc, adfebc}.

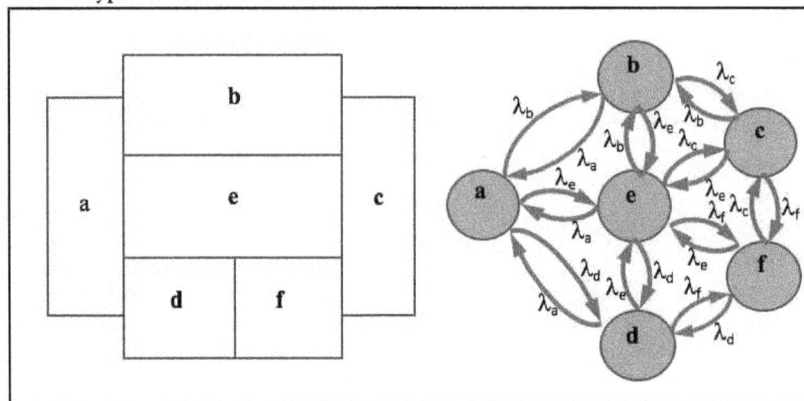

Figure 9: Regions and State Transitions

If w_1 = UK, only the subset of trajectories where all the states are safe will be considered: U = {abc}. If w_1 = US, then only the subset of trajectories in which any unsafe state is followed by a safe state will be considered: U = {abc, aec, abec, aebc}.

These constitute the locally generated policies for choosing an appropriate path. Note that if a suggested path is sent by the coalition commander, it will be checked against these allowable paths. It will be followed if it is in the acceptable set, or a reconciliation must be pursued. Otherwise, the drone can calculate its own path from the information provided and its local context.

CONCLUSIONS

In this paper we have considered how the management of computing systems is evolving due to the increasing ability to include intelligence in the devices comprising them. In particular, the influence of edge computing and IoT devices is leading to more distributed architectures for more autonomous elements. The mechanisms for operating complex systems, protecting information, and controlling access to them must also evolve.

For policy based technologies, we describe a number of efforts at making them more adaptable, contextual and cognitive. The new area of generative policies seems quite promising. A key concept in the generative approach is that local elements generate their own operational policies based upon their local context, but within the bounds of higher level policy structures supporting collaboration and meant to assure compliance with high level constraints and the pursuit of common goals.

Examples of the use and advantages of the generative policy approach have been given, and we will continue to explore its application to different domains. Some basic mechanisms that can be used to develop such generative policy systems have also been presented. There are several alternatives that could be pursued, and algorithms must be developed for checking the validity and effectiveness of generative policies to ensure that they are following the overall intent of the collaborative system.

ACKNOWELDGEMENTS

This research was sponsored by the U.S. Army Research Laboratory and the U.K. Ministry of Defence under Agreement Number W911NF-16-3-0001. The views and conclusions contained in this document are those of the authors and should not be interpreted as representing the official policies, either expressed or implied, of the U.S. Army Research Laboratory, the U.S. Government, the U.K. Ministry of Defence or the U.K. Government. The U.S. and U.K. Governments are authorized to reproduce and distribute reprints for Government purposes notwithstanding any copy-right notation hereon.

REFERENCES

[1]   Y Shoham, K Leyton-Brown, *Multiagent systems: Algorithmic, game-theoretic, and logical foundations,* Cambridge University Press, 2008.

[2]   W. Han, and C. Le, A survey on policy languages in network and security management. Computer Networks, 56(1), pp.477-489, 2012.

[3]   Dulay N., Lupu E., Sloman M., Sventek J., Badr N., Heeps S., *Self-managed Cells for Ubiquitous Systems.* In: Gorodetsky V., Kotenko I., Skormin V. (eds) Computer Network Security. MMM-ACNS 2005. Lecture Notes in Computer Science, vol 3685. Springer, Berlin, Heidelberg.

[4]   J. O. Kephart, D. M. Chess, *The vision of autonomic computing,* Computer, Volume 36, Issue 1, 2003.

[5]   F. Ye, R. Ganti, S. Calo, R. Dimaghani, K. Grueneberg, *Meca: mobile edge capture and analysis middleware for social sensing applications,* Proceedings of the 21st International Conference on World Wide Web, Pages 699-702, Lyon, France, April 16 - 20, 2012.

[6]   B. Moore, Ed., RFC 3460, Policy Core Information Model (PCIM) Extensions, http://www.rfc-editor.org/rfc/rfc3460.txt

[7]   Ian Molloy, Youngja Park, Suresh Chari, *Generative models for access control policies: applications to role mining over logs with attribution,* SACMAT '12 Proceedings of the 17th ACM symposium on Access Control Models and Technologies, Pages 45-56.

[8]   Maroun Touma, Elisa Bertino, Seraphin Calo, Brian Rivera, Dinesh Verma, *Framework for behavioral analytics in anomaly identification,* SPIE DS 2017 (to appear).

[9]   Jorge Lobo, Jiefei Ma, Alessandra Russo, Emil Lupu, Seraphin B. Calo, Morris Sloman, *Refinement of History-Based Policies,* In Logic Programming, Knowledge Representation, and Nonmonotonic Reasoning, *Springer-Verlag, Berlin, Heidelberg 280-299 (2011).*

[10] S. Jajodia et. al., eds., *Moving Target Defense: Creating Asymmetric Uncertainty for Cyber Threats,* Advances in Information Security, Springer, 2011.

[11] E. Asmare, N. Dulay, E. Lupu, M. Sloman, S. Calo, J. Lobo, *Secure Dynamic Community Establishment in Coalitions,* IEEE Military Communications Conference, (MILCOM 2007), Orlando FL, Oct 2007, Pages 1-7.

[12] V. Mishra, D. Verma, C. Williams and K. Marcus, Comparing Software Defined Architectures for Coalition Operations, submitted to International Conference on Military Communications and Information Systems, 2017.

A Flexible Authorization Architecture
for Systems of Interoperable Medical Devices

Qais Tasali
Department of Computer Science
Kansas State University
Manhattan, KS 66506, USA
qtasali@ksu.edu

Chandan Chowdhury
Department of Computer Science
Kansas State University
Manhattan, KS 66506, USA
chandanchowdhury@ksu.edu

Eugene Y. Vasserman
Department of Computer Science
Kansas State University
Manhattan, KS 66506, USA
eyv@ksu.edu

ABSTRACT

Robust authentication and authorization are vital to next-generation distributed medical systems – the Medical Internet of Things (MIoT). However, there is yet no good authorization model for real-time multi-channel data from systems of heterogeneous devices providing multiple physiological parameters for clinicians who may change on a minute-by-minute basis. We present a flexible authorization architecture for interoperable medical systems, and an implementation and evaluation in the context of the Medical Device Coordination Framework (MDCF) high-assurance middleware.

Our framework is based on the well-studied Attributed Based Access Control model, but we introduce a new method of attribute inheritance that provides more fine-grained access control, supporting multiple different authorization levels for multiple physiological data channels from the same device, and rich and expressive policy specification which facilitates plug-and-play connectivity of devices – most do not require pre-specification of individual permissions. Our architecture is standards-compliant and modular, using the eXtensible Access Control Markup Language (XACML), and Axiomatics Language for Authorization (ALFA) for policy specification, and standalone authorization modules which can be integrated with other platforms such as OpenICE. We stress-test our implementation in a realistic distributed system configuration, and show that the unoptimized system introduces negligible network and storage overhead, and minimal memory and CPU overhead.

CCS CONCEPTS

•Security and privacy →Access control; Authorization; •Applied computing →Health care information systems; •Computer systems organization →*Embedded and cyber-physical systems*; Client-server architectures; Sensors and actuators; •Hardware →*Safety critical systems*;

SACMAT'17, June 21–23, 2017, Indianapolis, IN, USA

© 2017 Copyright held by the owner/author(s). Publication rights licensed to ACM.
ACM ISBN 978-1-4503-4702-0/17/06. . . $15.00.
DOI: http://dx.doi.org/10.1145/3078861.3078862

1 INTRODUCTION

Future interoperable medical systems hold the promise of improved patient care through aggregation and manipulation of multiple physiological parameters simultaneously, as well as closed-loop control and automation of common clinical tasks. An early standard for such interoperability is the Integrated Clinical Environment (ICE) [21], first introduced in 2008. ICE is a medical system environment created by combination of interoperable heterogeneous medical devices and other integrated equipment. ICE allows controlling and monitoring of devices connected to a patient from a centralized location through medical applications, which allows better service toward the patients as clinicians can monitor all of their patients from their office and need not visit each patient as often. The systems allow medical device coordination through applications (apps), scripted medical workflows which orchestrate the action of one or more connected medical devices, and can operate either in closed-loop or open-loop control mode [16]. By automating common tasks, apps go beyond the functionality of checklists and increase safety and efficiency of clinician workflows. For a more detailed treatment of the benefits of medical apps we refer the reader to King et al.'s case study of rapid prototyping one such application [27].

Although the Medical Application Platform (MAP) [16, 46] and ICE concepts carry the potential for improvement of accuracy, consistency, and reliability in the practice of medicine, they also introduce new concerns – novel risks to patients' safety and privacy [8, 27]. For example, unauthorized access to the device(s) connected to a patient or an app controlling these devices could result in patient harm, or even death [21, 29]. Although access control concepts are well researched and mature in traditional medical systems, the same is not true when applied to new and emerging standards. There are few current systems claiming compatibility with the ICE standard, including OpenICE [33] and the Medical Device Coordination Framework (MDCF) [29]. Only one of these has implemented authentication [41]. Most research conducted in this area so far has been focused on how to control access to Electronic Medical Records (EMR) and Electronic Health Records (EHR) [9, 17, 22, 35, 45, 48], which are static data collected from doctor-patient interaction in healthcare facilities. Among the access control models used in medical domain, Role Based Access Control (RBAC) [12] and Attribute Based Access Control (ABAC) [18, 19] mostly dominate. However, RBAC lacks flexibility and dynamic access control capabilities [18], leading to the development and use of richer and more granular methods, such as Relationship-Based

Access Control (ReBAC) [38] and Role-Centric Attribute-Based Access Control (RABAC) [24], which are extensions of RBAC rather than entirely different models [15, 30, 37].

The proposed solutions are not entirely generalizable to newer system concepts such as Medical Application Platforms (MAPs) [16, 46]. The ICE standard (ASTM F2761) defines essential safety requirements for equipment comprising the patient-centric care network, but barely covers authentication and authorization. Other challenges in new systems include the high number of physiological data channels, the real-time nature of the communication, and the sheer number of clinicians, each of whom generally only interacts with the system for a few minutes. Moreover, it is less common now to grant permission based on evaluating a single static attribute or role of the user. Instead, an authorization request is evaluated using several different attributes, such as type of action, access time and location, the relation between subject and object, etc. Because some or most of these attributes do not become static once defined, access decisions must be made dynamically as well. For example, time- and location-aware access control systems may allow a clinician to access patient data during their shift while in the hospital, but may not be able to access the same patient data after their shift is over or if they try to access the data remotely. Dynamic authorization management not only allows organizations to react quickly to changing healthcare regulation but offer other benefits such as up-to-date centrally managed authorization policies, consistency in authorization policies, and reduced administrative work.

In this paper we present a new flexible authorization architecture for real-time "plug-and-play" [1] interoperable medical systems [16, 21]. We use ABAC as a basis for its flexibility, but find ourselves with a novel challenge, requiring a new type of solution. Apps are a fundamentally different type of principal – there is always an app intermediary between the clinician and the patient, so we need to reason about the roles and permissions of the clinician and app simultaneously. The app and clinician have differing permissions, and different access patterns: the app is a long-running clinical workflow, but clinicians may come and go while the app operates. For instance, while the clinician who launches and initially configures the app may have one set of permissions, a later operator may have a completely different permission set. At any given time, an arbitrary operator may need access to some or all of the data used by the app, requiring evaluation of the operator's role separately from that of the app, since the operator may hold a subset or a superset of permissions for the app's data and functionality. We solve this problem through **attribute inheritance**: at app launch time, if the app lacks permissions to access some device(s) that are needed for proper functionality, the permissions are reevaluated by combining the app's and requesting operator's permissions. If the combined permissions allow the app to function properly, it *inherits the permissions of the operator who started the app*. More precisely, the app now runs with permissions which are the union of the app's inherent permissions and the permissions of the operating clinician. In a traditional access control workflow, all that is needed is a single check, at app launch time, whether the operator has permission to use *all* data, devices, and functions provided by the app. In our case, the app is its own subject, and requires authorization to access any device providing patient's physiological data. **Inheriting an attribute is done for the purpose of**

temporarily expanding permissions, so attribute inheritance is a mechanism to achieve temporary permission elevation, and may be thought of as permission inheritance.

This work makes the following contributions:

- We show the first proof-of-concept implementation of authorization for systems of plug-and-play interoperable medical devices.
- Our system is sufficiently rich and fine-grained to accommodate principals in the form of devices, apps, and clinician of numerous arbitrarily-defined roles.
- We augment traditional ABAC with a novel method of attribute inheritance that not only achieves fine-grained access control and separation of duty requirements, but also helps in creating genericized policies that support plug-and-play of medical devices for immediate authorized use by clinicians, such as during an emergency.
- We show that our authorization system performs sufficiently well to support very frequent authorization events, such as for protecting dynamically produced data generated in real time.
- Out architecture is flexible-enough to support integration into most implementations of device interoperability standards, such as the Integrated Clinical Environment (ICE).

2 BACKGROUND

We are aware of only two open implementations which claim compatibility with the ICE standard, including OpenICE [33] and the Medical Device Coordination Framework (MDCF) [29]. OpenICE was developed by the Medical Device Plug and Play Interoperability Program (MD PnP) [1] to automate peer-to-peer node discovery, data publishing and subscribing between nodes, and proprietary medical device protocol translations [33]. OpenICE allows users to convert heterogeneous medical device data from supported devices into a common structure and protocol and exchange the data on a different machine using demonstration clinical applications. Like the MDCF, OpenICE does not have an authorization system. We choose the MDCF over the OpenICE to implement our proof-of-concept system solution. This is due to several factors, the most important being that MDCF has a pluggable communication protocol layer, and therefore does not rely exclusively on a particular third-party network protocol (DDS, in case of OpenICE [34]). We also use the modularity of the MDCF security framework to assist in our design and integration [40, 41]. A detailed comparison of the benefits and downsides of the two implementations is beyond the scope of this paper, but it is worth noting that our proposed authorization architecture is designed for any ICE-like architecture, and therefore it should be possible to integrate into OpenICE. Verifying the exact difficulty of integration into OpenICE, and thus testing the generality of out design, is left for future work.

2.1 MDCF

The Medical Device Coordination Framework [27, 29] is an open testbed for medical device integration and coordination. The MDCF is a Medical Application Platform (MAP) [16], architected in logical units that closely follows the Integrated Clinical Environment (ICE) standard [21]. It allows medical devices to be controlled by scripted medical workflows – apps. The system is divided into two large sub-components according to the ICE architecture: 1) Supervisor (the app and user interface host), and 2) Network Controller (the communication abstraction layer). Communication is abstracted as "channels", allowing the MDCF to use different network communication library implementations, such as MIDdleware Assurance Substrate (MIDAS) [28] and Data Distribution Service (DDS) [34], as message-oriented publish/subscribe middleware.[1] Each component is described briefly below and illustrated in Figure 1.

Supervisor Components

- *The App Manager* manages the lifecycle of apps. It starts and stops the execution of apps, manages interactions (communication) between apps, and notifies clinicians of any medically adverse architectural interactions, if applicable.
- *The Clinician Service* provides an interface for configuring, instantiating, and selecting supervisor apps that are used with the clinician graphical user interface (GUI).
- *The Administrative Service* is the control provider for installation and management of apps.

Network Controller Components

- *The Channel Service* is the function set for direct interaction with the communication substrate, and contains code for interfaces used between the MDCF publish/subscribe middleware and any connected components. It contains interfaces for the messaging server, message senders, receivers, and connection listeners, as well as hooks for pluggable authentication providers.
- *The Connection Manager* is the means to create, manage, and destroy connections (abstracted as channels).
- *The Device Manager* configures devices for use with apps and maintains an internal view of device status.
- *The Device Registry* is the known device information store API. These may be device models for which information has been preloaded, or individual devices which are currently connected or have connected in the past.
- *The Component Manager* is analogous to the Device Registry, but is responsible for apps instead of devices.

2.2 Representing Access Control Policies

The design of the Medical Application Platform concept [16] like the MDCF, and the devices meant to interoperate within it, implies the expectation of generic but preassigned device and app attributes that can easily be transformed into access control attributes in authorization policies [41]. These attributes can be preassigned by device vendors, app developers, and/or the defaults can be overridden by the clinical facility for use in the environment where devices and apps are deployed. A facility administrator, creating policies for use by the clinical environment, generates a set of authorization rules in a machine-readable, but human-*usable*, language, creating device and clinician/operator attributes (which can be modified at any time, even as the system is running). Runtime changes to these attributes can result in decision changes between two access requests without the necessity to change the device, app or user relationships

---

[1]Within the Java code, components that have a registered sender/receiver object for a channel are the only components that can send or receive messages in that channel, limiting access to the channel by permitting or denying subscription requests [41].

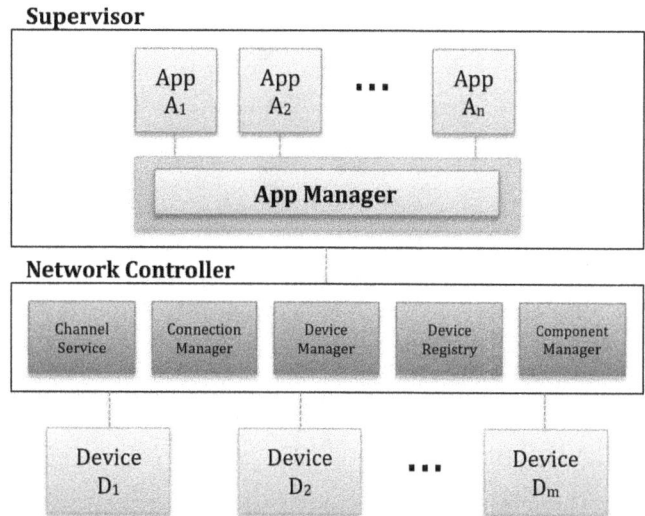

Figure 1: The architecture of the MDCF and its components

defining any underlying rule-sets. To make the process as easy as possible for the policymaker, not only are there predefined defaults for common roles and property sets, but authorization policy generation can be partially or fully automated for common classes of devices and apps – device instances do not require dedicated policies, and in many cases devices with analogous functionality or new models or product lines, even from different manufacturers, can reuse policies written for similar devices. Moreover, policies implemented in ABAC are only limited by the language used to express them, and the richness of the available attributes [18]. Therefore, there is no need to specify individual relationships between each device (or even device class) and each potential operator without sacrificing granular user permissions. We use the eXtensible Access Control Markup Language (XACML) [31, 32] as our back-end, due to its standardization (OASIS) and wide acceptance and portability (it is one of the most widely used policy language).

XACML. The eXtensible Access Control Modeling Language [32], written in XML, is used to define a fine-grained attribute-based access control policy. It can also be used to express an architecture and a processing model that describes how to evaluate access requests according to the rules predefined in access polices. XACML is designed to be suitable for a variety of application environments, such as social networks [8], home automation gateways [25], healthcare domain [10, 37, 44], distributed systems [31], etc.

ALFA. A major goal of XACML is to promote common terminology and interoperability between authorization implementations by multiple vendors. It is very general and expressive, but is verbose and hard to read. The Abbreviated Language for Authorization (ALFA) [2] is a Domain Specific Language (DSL) for XACML. In contrast to policies written in XACML, ALFA provides a friendlier and more usable syntax, similar to C#. Access control polices written in "raw" XACML are complex, and make it difficult to find faults which may be inadvertently introduced [47]. Therefore, we chose ALFA as a high-level policy language due to its increased user-friendliness over XACML, but kept the XACML back-end to

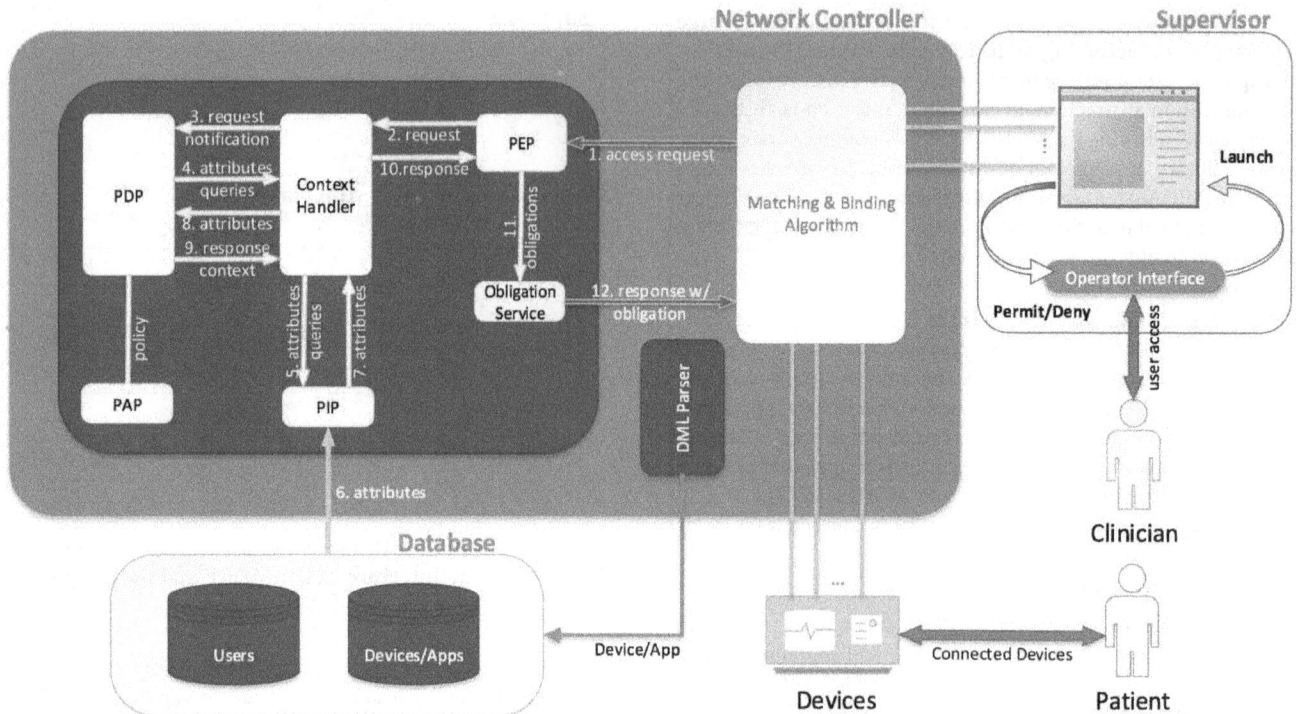

Figure 2: The basic architecture of the new authorization system after integration with the MDCF. Numbering represents the order of operations.

maximize portability. For a quantitative comparison, one of our ALFA policies is 30 lines, while a XACML policy generated from *one line* of code (***target clause app.role == "aR1"***) taken from the ALFA policy is 16 lines. On average, the policies which we wrote consisted of 3903 non-whitespace characters in XACML, while the same policies in ALFA had 528 non-whitespace characters.

2.3   Current Workflow

To better illustrate the workflow of the authorization system, we introduce patient Pamela and her primary nurse Nick. Pamela has had surgery, and is now on pain relief medication (opioid delivered through a PCA pump). Nick wants to access real-time telemetry from sensors monitoring Pamela to watch her vital signs for indications of an accidental opioid overdose, and to change the dosage (set the PCA Pump level). To do so, Nick opens the Clinician Console and launches the PCAShutoff app [6] that displays Pamela's SpO2 (Blood Oxygen Saturation), EtCO2 (End-Tidal Carbon Dioxide), and RR (Respiratory Rate).

The MDCF workflow for setting up a PCA pump interaction with the PCAShutoff app is:

(1) Clinician accesses the Clinician Console
(2) Console connects to the App Manager to fetch and display the list of available apps
(3) Clinician selects and launches the PCAShutoff app from the list of available apps
(4) Console relays the request to the App Manager
(5) App Manager launches the app

(6) Now-running App requests the list of required devices from Device Manager
(7) Via the Connection Manager, the App requests the Device Manager to connect to devices and request physiological data (and displays it to the clinician)
(8) Clinician changes the infusion dose (PCA pump level) in PCAShutoff app
(9) App forwards the new level to the PCA pump
(10) PCA pump changes the dose to the new value
(11) App requests updated values from the devices (and displays them to the clinician)

Without authentication or authorization, all these steps can be performed by anyone at any access level, such as any app, any clinician, etc. For example, anyone can access the Clinician Console and request a change to the PCA pump level. Anyone on the network can even connect to the PCA pump and directly request that it increase the medication level. We detail the workflow with added authentication and authorization in Section 3.

3   DESIGN OF THE AUTHORIZATION SYSTEM

Figure 2 shows the main architectural components of the authorization system. All XACML requests for access are sent to the Policy Enforcement Point (PEP). It forwards the request to the context handler in its native request format, which may include attributes for subjects, resource, action, environment and/or any other custom categories. Once the context handler receives the request for access, it generates a request context, which may include attributes, and forwards the request context to the Policy Decision Point (PDP). The context handler will also handle queries for any additional attributes requested by the PDP. When additional attributes are requested, the context handler retrieves the requested attributes from the Policy Information Point (PIP). It is responsible for obtaining the requested attributes and returning the requested attributes to the context handler. After receiving the requested attributes, the PDP evaluates the policy and returns the response context to the context handler, where the response context is translated to the native response format of the PEP. After the response context is translated, it is sent to the PEP to fulfill the obligation. Obligations are additional constraints to an authorization decision and if PEP cannot fulfill any given obligations then it disallows access. The response context also contains the authorization decision and if the access is permitted, the PEP permits access to the resource. Otherwise, the PEP denies the access to the resource. The Policy Access Point (PAP) is responsible for policy creation.

The MDCF provides a channel abstraction for communication. To control access to the data in the MDCF communication substrate, we need to restrict access to channels, making decisions before either the user-app (clinician accessing an app) or app-device (app subscribing/publishing to a device) connection is created. Since the Network Controller is the component of the MDCF that manages all channel services and connections including creation and destruction of channels, it is the clear choice to host the authorization engine. When a clinician starts interacting with the console and launches an app, the App Manger within the Supervisor generates a user-app access request and forwards it to the Network Controller for evaluation. Only after the authorization engine within the Network Controller returns "permit" are the connections created.

There are two different phases of access control evaluation which take place before a clinician receives access to some features of an app or to physiological data from device(s) in the MDCF. The first phase is evaluation of clinician's access request for accessing app(s). When a clinician launches an app, a XACML launch access request is generated and forwarded to the Network Controller and is evaluated by the authorization engine. Once a "permit" decision for app launch is returned, the second phase is invoked to obtain authorization to access the device(s) that is/are required by the app. The app's requirements are identified internally and automatically by the MDCF's Matching and Binding algorithm. Authorization requests for required devices are generated and forwarded to the authorization engine. Note that the second phase comes into play only if the first phase returns a "permit" decision – if a clinician does not have access to an app, then there is no need to check if the app is authorized to subscribe/publish to required device(s) – the request is simply denied.

3.1 Authorization Policies

Authorization policies in the MDCF can be one of two categories: user-app authorization policies and app-device authorization policies. While access control rules for user-app authorization require use of several different categories of attributes, the app-device rules only requires subject and action attributes, and/or some conditions. For example, the below given rule will allow the PCAShutoff app having role **aR** (subject attribute) to set the data interval rate for a

multimonitor device. (In this access control rule, app is a subject and the data interval rate – from a device – is a resource.)

```
Allow access to resource
  with attribute "dataIntervalRateForPCA"
    if Subject "app" has role "aR"
    and action is "set"
```

The authorization policies created for app access by clinicians have more complex rules. Each has several categories and conditions. The access rule in the example below will allow a clinician to access a patient's SpO2 reading only if 1) the clinician is a nurse who 2) is assigned to the primary physician of the patient, 3) has active role **nR**, and 4) is working during his or her assigned shift.

```
Allow access to resource
  with attribute "SpO2"
        if Subject "clinician" has role "nR"
        and action is "get"
conditions:
  Subject "clinician" is "PrimaryPhysicianOfPatient"
  and Subject "clinician" is in their "shift"
```

3.2 Plug-and-play Support

The proposed authorization architecture can also support "plug-and-play" connectivity of new devices [1] by encouraging reuse of policies for other, similar device and app *types*. Administrators at a clinical environment with the MDCF deployment can define authorization polices for common classes of devices and apps, categorized based on common functionalities and components (capabilities). In order for the authorization system to restrict access to plug-and-play medical devices only to authorized users, all devices and apps are required to carry a set of attributes predefined in their Device Modeling Language (DML) schemas and to be parsed by the MDCF built-in DML parser [26]. Once a device or app is connected to the MDCF, the device registry and component manager in the Network Controller retrieve the DML (configuration) schema for the device or app and store it. The DML parser also retrieves access control attributes within the schema and automatically generates authorization policies based on the access control attributes. If automatic policy generation fails due to a new component or feature of the device or app not being recognized by the system, or errors resulting from missing or improper access control attributes, the administrator will receive a notification regarding the failure of the policy generation. They will then be asked to generate a custom policy for the device or app. More details on this can be found in Section 3.3, but an extensive discussion of the plug-and-play in the MDCF is beyond the scope of this paper.

3.3 Attribute Inheritance

Our design is unique in treating clinicians and apps as distinct and independent actors, and therefore they may have differing permissions for accessing devices. Our solution to this challenge, attribute inheritance, not only improves permission granularity without exposing the policy writer to additional complexity, but also allows **authorized** plug-and-play support *with only a few simple additional policies*. User role inheritance, has been in use for decades, first introduced in the RBAC framework [42]. Relationship among roles in a given organization are defined by a role hierarchy. In a typical healthcare facility, if we pick a specialist surgeon who is

```
namespace edu.ksu.santoslab.mdcf {
  import edu.ksu.santoslab.mdcf.mAttributes.*

  rule allowGet {
    target clause action.actionId == "GET"
    permit
  }

  rule allowSet {
    target clause action.actionId == "SET"
    permit
    condition exchange.exchangeTime >= user.shiftStart &&
              exchange.exchangeTime <= user.shiftEnd
  }

  policyset polMultiMonitorSample {
    target clause resource.resourceId == "*.pulserate.alerts.
        seperation_interval"
    apply denyUnlessPermit
    polMultiMonitorSampleSET
    polMultiMonitorSampleGET
  }

  policy polMultiMonitorSampleSET {
    target clause app.role == "aR1" or app.role == "aR2"
      clause user.role == "Critical_Care_Nurse"
    apply denyOverrides
    allowSet
  }

  policy polMultiMonitorSampleGET {
    target clause app.role == "aR2" or app.role == "aR3" or app.role
        == "aR4"
      clause user.role == "Cardiothoracic_Surgeon" or user.role == "
        Agency_Nurse"
    apply denyOverrides
    allowGet
  }
}
```

Figure 3: An example written in ALFA, a subset of the policy used in evaluating our implementation

```
<xacml3:Target>
  <xacml3:AnyOf>
    <xacml3:AllOf>
      <xacml3:Match MatchId="urn:oasis:names:tc:xacml:1.0:function:
      string-equal">
        <xacml3:AttributeValue
          DataType="http://www.w3.org/2001/XMLSchema#string">aR1</
        xacml3:AttributeValue>
        <xacml3:AttributeDesignator
          AttributeId="edu.ksu.cis.santos.mdcf.app.role-attrID"
          DataType="http://www.w3.org/2001/XMLSchema#string"
          Category="urn:oasis:names:tc:xacml:1.0:subject-category:
            access-subject"
          MustBePresent="false">
      </xacml3:Match>
    </xacml3:AllOf>
  </xacml3:AnyOf>
</xacml3:Target>
```

Figure 4: The XML generated from one line code (*target clause app.role == "aR1"*) in Figure 3

senior in position to a resident surgeon, then the specialist inherits any roles held by the resident. However, this type of role inheritance is not only impractical, but actually impossible in a system like the MDCF, where apps can also be actors (subjects) at certain times. On other hand, the relationships among clinicians, apps, and devices can be captured by using their attributes – yet another reason why we need Attribute-Based Access Control (ABAC).

To explain why user *role inheritance* (attribute inheritance) is needed, it is worth first understanding the main entities of the authorization system. A device in the MDCF is always considered a resource (object).[2] On the other hand, a clinician is always an actor (subject). An app can be an actor or a resource depending on the access scenario. It is a resource when a clinician tries to access it, but that same app can later assume the role of an actor (subject) when it tries to access data from device(s), e.g. patient physiological parameters. Therefore, an app inheriting a user role does not suggest the app will replace its own role with it. Instead, the user role is added as an extra attribute in the access request.

The app always plays the role of an interface between a user and a device, so it is illogical for an app to hold more than one role – there is no way of changing the active role for an app during a single session, unlike a clinician. Instead, based on the set of components and features offered by an app, it will be assigned to a specific role. Thus, all apps are categorized into common classes of features. In contrast, clinicians may be assigned more than one role, but can only have one active role at a time – we refer to this as the clinician's *active role*. Clinicians can switch between roles whenever needed. The clinician is always expected to have access to more resources than an app because an app is always restricted to certain attributes (e.g. one pre-assigned role based on the app's type, category, or feature set). Since neither an app nor a clinician can replace each others' roles, we will not benefit from permissions from user's active role unless the app inherits the clinician's role as an extra attribute when needed (in the second phase of our two-phase access control evaluation design). Note when we say the permissions set for a clinician's active role, we mean the resources to which the clinicians is granted access when the clinician's role is added to a XACML request as a required attribute in the second authorization step. Splitting the access control decision into two phases in this manner is a way to limit having to invoke attribute inheritance, using it only when it is needed, and allowing us to define a more fine-grained access control model without writing more complex policies. **This achieves separation of duty**.

This method of user role inheritance, or in general attribute inheritance, not only provides least privilege to both user and app but also can drastically cut the time required to make newly installed devices available for use (e.g. during an emergency). Note also that this *does not require bypassing the authorization system* – devices are available for authorized use.

To examine this concept in detail, consider the example wherein a clinician discovers the need for some physiological data to be collected from a patient, but none of the already-connected medical devices is able to provide the data due to lack of features or incompatibility with the app. The clinician connects a new plug-and-play medical device to the system that can collect the data from the

---

[2]This may change in future work, as devices and apps become increasingly similar.

patient and is compatible with the app. Since this is a new device, there is a high probability that it will not be available for immediate use due to lack of authorization policies. There are two possible ways to handle access permissions for a newly installed device in the MDCF, and we analyze both options below:

(1) *Use generic predefined authorization policies:* The administrator needs to generate a set of generic policies based on common features sets offered by each device. Similarly, the administrator ensures that apps which are fully or partially compatible with these devices are authorized to access these common features. However, we believe that, for safety, generic predefined authorization policies should only be limited non-safety-critical features of devices, so apps would not be authorized to access all features, but rather a conservative, safe subset. *Generic policies* which allow apps full device access may, in certain specific cases, violate the goals of the authorization system.

(2) *Generate new custom authorization policies:* The administrator introduces a new set of attributes, which will require generation of new authorization policies for each feature each device offers.

In option 1, a newly installed device becomes automatically available for use, but it is expected that any safety-critical features of the device, such as setting infusion rate for a PCA pump, will *not* be available until explicitly authorized by the system administrator since these features can only be used by explicitly authorized apps. This prevents their use in an emergency. Moreover, creating policies that explicitly authorize apps to use safety-critical features of a device defeats the purpose of *generic* predefined policies. Alternatively, in option 2, all features of the newly-installed device can be made available for use by an app if an administrator explicitly pre-authorizes the app to access these features by generating custom authorization policies. However, this requires time and deep understanding of healthcare facility-specific access control rules for these device-specific (often unique) features. Thus, neither option 1 nor option 2 is very effective in an emergency. Regardless of which option is chosen, the safety-critical features (capabilities) of a device – the ones most needed in an emergency – will not be available for immediate use after first-time device connection. *Attribute inheritance* provides the solution to the above problem in two steps, one addressing the clinician and the other the app. They are addressed in turn below.

If a clinician meets the access requirements for the use of some safety-critical features offered by a newly-connected medical device, or any devices that may be connected to the system at a later time (e.g. during an emergency), then authorization policies for all features (including critical features) can be governed by simple, generic policies written in advance, and the clinician will gain authorization for these features dynamically, as needed. For clinicians, administrators write policies based on a per-facility understanding of the clinician's role (responsibilities), and authorize clinician access to known devices. While this seems identical to option 2, apps introduce a layer of complexity which is still unresolved, and are less-well understood by administrators.

Clinician authorization alone does not solve the problem, since an app intermediary is still needed to access the data from a device,

and the app may lack permission to interact with the device. Detailed per-app policies are more complex to write than per-clinician role policies, since app features, capabilities, and data access requirements are not as well understood, and may not even be known in advance. Nonetheless, if a clinician has been previously authorized to access safety-critical features of a device that just connected to the system (through per-clinician role policies), but the clinician is trying to access these features using an app that lacks access permissions, then if apply *attribute inheritance* again so the app *inherits the user role as an extra attribute* and therefore receives authorization to access the data from the device, both the device and app become available for immediate use. In other words, attribute inheritance allows authorized interaction in a new way: **even though neither the clinician nor the app *alone* are authorized, the clinician-app *pair* is authorized**.

Policies generated for attribute inheritance purposes do not fit into either option 1 nor 2 above, since we are neither writing custom policies at the time of device connection, nor we are generating generic policies that will allow any *single* actor full access to the new device. Instead, our approach is a hybrid third option and allows for full authorized access to the resource while maintaining the principles of least privilege and separation of duty. The sample access control rule below shows how user and app roles, with attribute inheritance, are combined to allow authorized access to a device with safety-critical features.

```
Allow access to resource
  with attribute "medicationInfusionRate"
    if Subject "app" has role "aR"
      and action is "set"
conditions:
      Subject "clinician" has role "nR"
```

The above policy shows how to merge clinician and app roles in order to allow the clinician-app pair to access the given resource, and also provide separation of duty. The rule tells us that an app with role (subject attribute) *aR* is authorized to set the infusion rate for a device (infusion pump) connected to the patient only if a clinician with role (subject attribute) *nR* is issuing the command. Authorization policies generated for an app that is compatible with (capable of connecting to) a given medical device should include app (subject) attributes, (in this example, *aR*).

A far more extensive authorization example, written in ALFA, is given in Figure 3. It showcases policy-level details on usage of user and app roles (for the purpose of attribute inheritance). In the policy called "polMultiMonitorSampleSET", the user role "critical care nurse" needs to be inherited by any app having either role "AppSpO2" or "AppPulse", in addition to other required attributes, for the app to set the separation interval for pulse-rate alerts of a multimonitor device.

3.4 Break the Glass

Attribute inheritance should not be considered a substitute for Break The Glass (BTG) features [7, 14], but it does help achieve safe BTG. While the authorization system in a healthcare facility ensures the system is only accessed by authorized users, it may also prevent a clinician from delivering potentially life-saving care to patients during an emergency due to lack of permissions. In this case, saving the patient outweighs any risks associated from overriding access controls, which can be partially deactivated by using BTG features of the system.

BTG allows overriding access controls and provides full (or sufficient) access to the system during an emergency, but attribute inheritance is a step in eliminating the need for a "global" override. Instead, it can be used to allow controlled, authorized access to medical resources (e.g. devices) during emergencies. This is achieved using a hybrid of dynamically and automatically generated app-device interaction polices (at the time of device access) and pre-defined clinician-app interaction polices.

We understand the importance and challenges of controlled BTG in the medical domain, but the scope of this work is deliberately limited to attribute inheritance and lacks a full treatment of BTG. Detailing the design of a Break The Glass feature within our proposed authorization architecture is future work.

3.5 Modified Workflow

Here we show the new workflow, *with authentication and authorization*. Steps which are modified or added to the original workflow from Section 2.3 are italicized. Figure 5 provides a visual aid.

(1) Clinician accesses the Clinician Console
(2) *Console asks for username and password*
(3) *Clinician enters username and password*
(4) *Console forwards the request to Shiro (PEP)*
(5) *Shiro verifies the entered credentials against the stored value and returns yes or no to the Console*
(6) *If yes is returned, the clinician is successfully authenticated and is logged in*
(7) Console connects to the App Manager to fetch and display the list of available apps
(8) Clinician selects and launches the PCAShutoff app from the list of available apps
(9) *Console receives the app launch request and forwards it to Shiro, along with the users' details*
(10) *Shiro takes the request, adds context (user's active role, type of request, timestamp etc.), and forwards it to Balana for an authorization check*
(11) *Balana checks the request against stored XACML policies and returns "yes", "no", or "not applicable"*
(12) *Shiro receives the authorization result from Balana*
(13) *If Shiro receives "no", it forwards it to the Console, and the clinician is denied app launch permission, ending the workflow (otherwise the workflow continues)*
(14) Console relays the request to the App Manager
(15) App Manager launches the app
(16) Now-running App requests the list of required devices from Device Manager
(17) *The access request is forwarded to Shiro*
(18) *Shiro forwards the request to Balana to confirm if the app has been authorized to connect to devices*
(19) *Balana checks the request against stored XACML policies*
(20) *If "yes" is returned, the app is allowed to connect to devices*
(21) *If "no" is returned, the request is reevaluated with the clinician's active role appended [3]*

---
[3]This step is not yet implemented

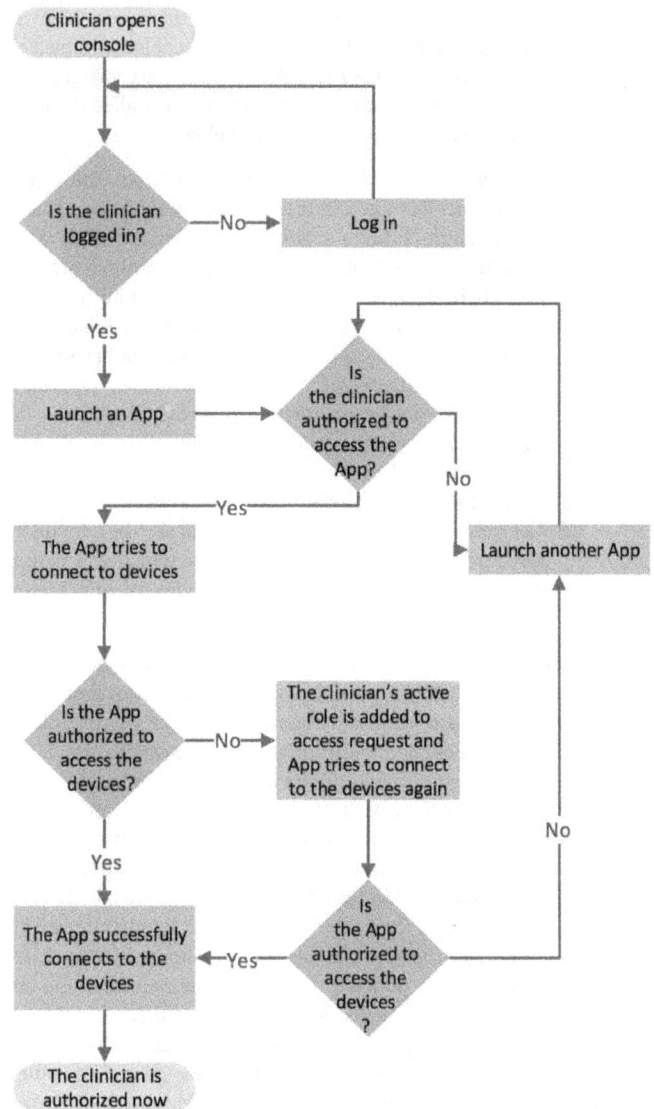

Figure 5: The workflow for a clinician accessing patient physiological data in the MDCF

(22) *If "no" is returned from request reevaluation, the final decision (deny) is returned to the Supervisor and the clinician is denied access (the app can start, but cannot perform useful work), ending the workflow (otherwise the app is allowed to connect to devices and the workflow continues) [3]*
(23) *The final decision (permit) with obligation(s) is returned to the Supervisor, and the clinician is allowed to launch the app*

If the clinician chooses to view physiological data for a patient or tries to make changes to either device or app parameters, the requested access request must be evaluated. For example, after the clinician has successful been authenticated and authorized to launch the application, the clinician may try to change the infusion rate for the PCA pump connected to a patient. The steps to authorize the clinician to change the infusion rate are:

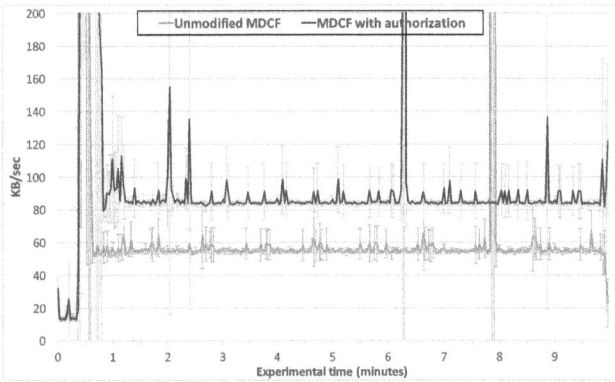

(a) Network (total-read) usage

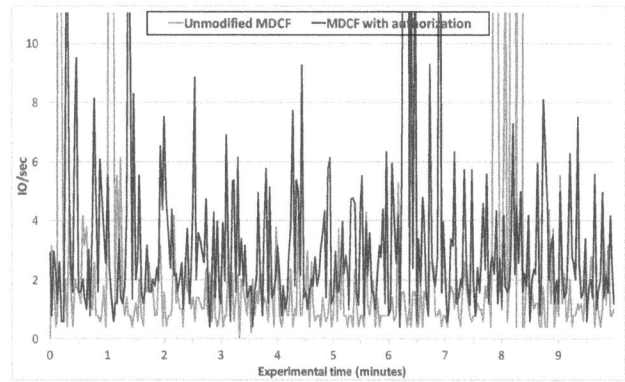

(b) Disk I/O with error bars omitted. The variability between baseline and modified versions is *not statistically significant*.

Figure 6: Disk and network I/O of the baseline versus authorization-enabled MDCF without Shiro caching

(1) Clinician changes the infusion dose (PCA pump level) in PCAShutoff app
(2) *The app requests for access to change the level*
(3) *An access request is generated*
(4) *Shiro adds context to the request and forwards it to Balana*
(5) *Balana checks if the clinician is allowed to change the level*
(6) *If "no", the app discards the change and displays a denied message to the clinician*
(7) *If "yes", the dose change request is sent to the PCA pump*
(8) PCA pump changes the dose to the new value
(9) App requests updated values from the devices (and displays them to the clinician)

Each action is checked for proper authorization. Authentication prevents malicious access to the Clinician Console, and authorization prevents users from doing things they are not authorized to do. For example, another nurse can be given permission to launch the PCAShutoff app to monitor the PCA pump and SpO2 level, but not to change the PCA pump level. An unauthenticated intruder in the network can send request to the PCA pump to change the level, but the message will be rejected as they are not authenticated. Authenticated malicious actors can likewise request the PCA pump to change the level, but the message will be rejected as unauthorized.

3.6 Implementation Details

We chose Apache Shiro [5] as our Policy Enforcement Point (PEP) framework and WSO2 Balana [43] for the Policy Decision Point (PDP). Balana was a natural choice due to its maturity, rich feature set and flexibility for XACML. For the Policy Information Point (PIP), which stores details like usernames, passwords, groups, user-group relations etc., our requirements were that it be open source and compatible with Balana. Cost was also a significant consideration. We considered several options for PEP, such as Spring Security [36], OACC [3] and Shiro. We looked into Spring Security, but we are not currently using the Spring framework. OACC offers native Java compatibility, but it is relatively new (compared with Shiro) and does not come with pluggable authentication protocols, such as for LDAP. For PIP, as per our requirements, we decided

on a simple SQLite database to store the PIP information. In a future version, the database will be replaced by a enterprise class user-management systems like LDAP or Kerberos. This will be a relatively easy change, since Shiro provides out of the box support for these kind of systems via configuration file parameter (for example, securityManager.realms). Also, we found it easier, at the proof-of-concept state, to use Shiro only for authentication, and delegate all authorization tasks to Balana. In future we may rethink our strategy and try to implement authentication using OACC.

The MDCF project already has a graphical Clinician Console for local or network access. Chromium-based and implemented in Dart, the code-base had pre-existing hooks for authorization calls – this is where we integrate our new code. As the PEP, Shiro receives all such requests from the Clinician Console. Shiro handles the authentication requests itself and acts as a mediator for authorization between the front-end and Balana. To keep the logic simple, we implemented two custom classes, MDCFAuthenticator and BalanaAuthorizer, by extending the AuthorizingRealm class of Shiro. MDCFAuthenticator is only responsible for authentication, and BalanaAuthorizer is only responsible for authorization.

MDCFAuthenticator performs password-based authentication. If successful, an active role is assigned to the user. For simplicity, we currently use the first role found in the list of the user's available roles rather than ask the user. In future work, we will assign a role based on a saved user preference. After initial role assignment, the user can always change the active role using the Clinician Console.

When an action requires authorization, e.g. launching an app, the MDCF front-end sends the user details and action attributes (e.g. which feature of the medical application the user is trying to access) to the PDP, which performs the authorization check against available XACML policies and returns a response. Authorization is implemented as the BalanaAuthorizer Java class which

- Is initialized with a set of XACML policies,
- Takes as input the attributes of the app or device, and the details of the user requesting access, and
- Returns true if the user has access via any of the user's available roles.

(a) CPU usage

(b) Memory usage. Error bars are too small to be visible in some places.

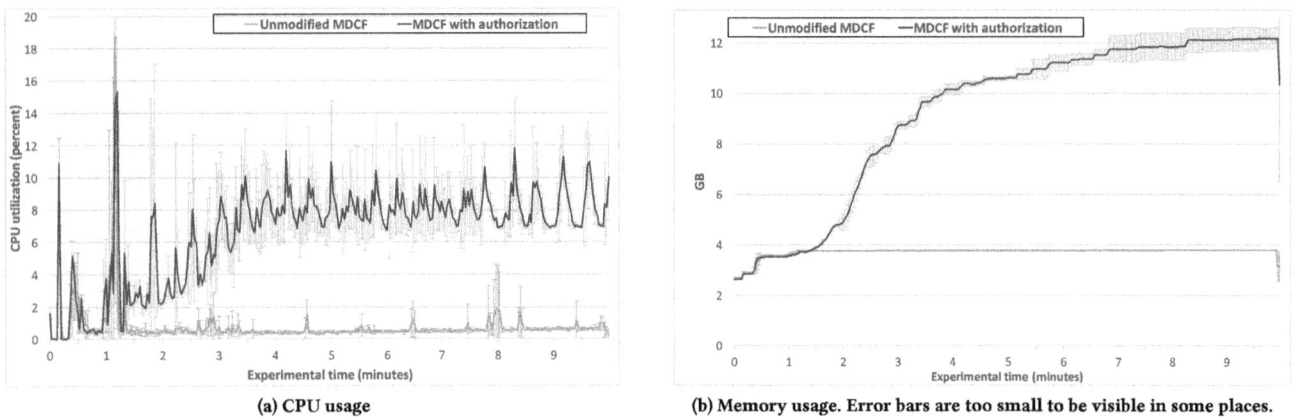

Figure 7: CPU and memory usage of the baseline versus authorization-enabled MDCF without Shiro caching

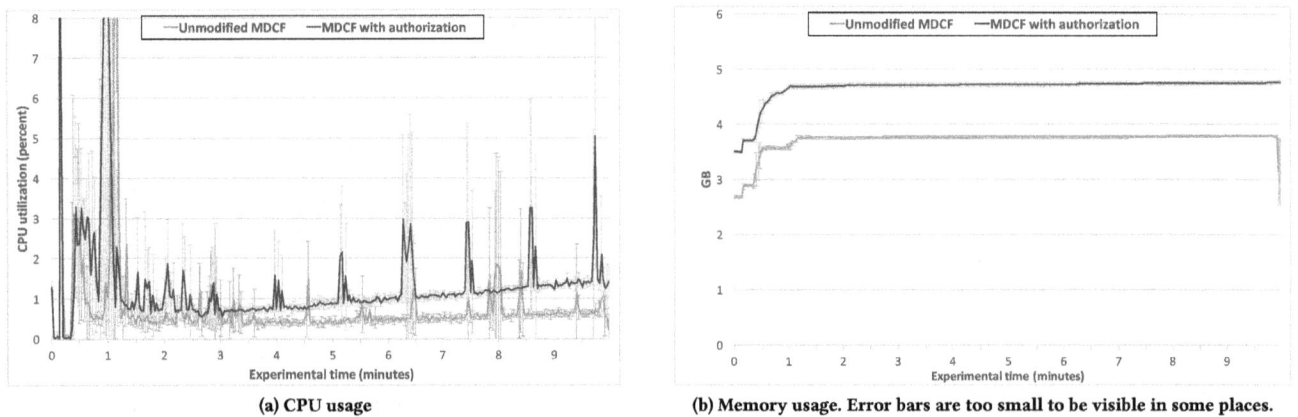

(a) CPU usage

(b) Memory usage. Error bars are too small to be visible in some places.

Figure 8: CPU and memory usage of the baseline versus authorization-enabled MDCF with Shiro caching

4 EVALUATION

In this section we describe the testing methodology and results for the authorization system as integrated into the MDCF. The tests were designed to exceed the normal expected operational capacity of the system (also called stress-testing) to confirm safe usage limits and given specifications are met. Our goal was to maintain the same level of system performance (of the unmodified implementation of the MDCF) for the MDCF with authorization. (Note that phase two of the two-phase authorization design, including attribute inheritance, is not yet implemented and was thus excluded from the evaluation.) We compared the unmodified and modified (authorization-enabled) implementations of the MDCF with 64 medical devices, and observed the system for usage limits, particularly CPU, memory, network, and disk I/O. Since the intended use of the MDCF is for a single patient (as specified in the ICE standard [21]), our tests involved far more than the number of devices expected to be used simultaneously.

We used simulated (virtual) devices for our testing of the system to get around the lack of readily available medical hardware and the incompatibility of current physical medical devices with the

MDCF [27], and due to the exceptional computing power afforded by our test harness when compared to physical devices. We used three different types of virtual devices: capnography (CO2), pulse oximetry (SpO2) and patient-controlled analgesia (PCA), each with multiple physiological output channels and control (input) channels. The clinician workflow also included use of a PCAShuttoff medical workflow script (app), which requires simultaneous use of three devices, one of each type. During the test, each running instance of the app was subscribed to a different set of virtual devices to simulate simultaneous treatment of multiple patients, each with an associated set of devices and a controlling PCAShuttoff app.

For consistency of testing environments between the pre-authorization and authorization-enabled versions of the MDCF, testing was partially automated. We ran the MDCF server using a Linux server (dual octa-core 64-bit Intel Xeon E5520 CPUs at 2.27 GHz, with 8 MB/core cache and 64 GB memory). The 64 devices were ran from two different machines with an identical configuration to the MDCF server. This allows stress-testing of the server without local interference from devices, i.e. devices and server computing resources are distinct and do not interfere with each other except through communication. The 64 devices started connecting to the server after 20 seconds from the time the server began running. The initial peaks in the performance graphs are the result of 64 devices connecting to the sever simultaneously. Each device begins sending physiological data after successfully connecting and authenticating to the MDCF server. Once all devices were connected successfully, the user launches an app after successfully authenticating and verifying authorization. User interaction with the MDCF clinician console was timed, with the launch command issued at the 60th second of the experiment. The test was repeated 5 times for each version of the MDCF.

Figure 6 shows the difference(s) in network and I/O usage between the two implementations. The authorization-enabled MDCF (modified implementation) performed as expected, within normal parameters, even under stress testing. Furthermore, authorization imposed no statistically significant I/O overhead, and minimal to no network overhead (one standard deviation, or 68% confidence). The initial peak (between 0 and 1 minutes) results from the sudden connection of all 64 devices, as intended for stress testing. The average network usage for the unmodified and modified MDCF was 78.97 ± 28.91 KB/s and 116.52 ± 30.89 KB/s, respectively. Similarly, the average I/O usage for the modified and unmodified MDCF was 3.23 ± 4.15 IO/sec and 3.41 ± 1.00 IO/sec, respectively.

Figure 7 shows the CPU and memory utilization for the modified and unmodified versions of the MDCF, showing statistically significant overhead: 95% confidence interval for CPU and > 99% for memory. CPU utilization for the unmodified and modified MDCF averaged 0.77 ± 0.05 % and 6.63 ± 0.04 %, respectively. Note that the CPU visualization in Figure 7a is somewhat misleading, as it accounts for only a 5.86% (on average) overhead from the inclusion of authorization. Memory usage shows the unmodified MDCF using on average 3.62 ± 0.02 GB of the 64 GB available memory, whereas the modified system used on average 9.02 ± 0.12 GB, an increase of 5.4 GB: almost 250%. The reason for this (unexpected) memory overhead was the undocumented excessive use of JDBC connections to the authorization server: each authorization request created a new, *persistent* connection. Since the authorization engine needs to access the database for each access request, we end up with far too many JDBC connections, which persist throughout the experimental run, accounting for not only the memory overhead but also its steady increase over time. In fact, the Clinician Console requests data update from the server at the rate of 16 queries per sec, resulting in about 1000 new JDBC connection objects per minute, which also explains the unexpected CPU overhead.

Figure 8 shows a significant reduction of both CPU and memory overhead due to several simple optimizations: using the built-in Shiro caching API [4], and limiting JDBC to one persistent connection, brought CPU usage to within statistical indistinguishability from the unmodified MDCF (< one standard deviation difference), as shown in Figure 8a, and memory overhead to 20%, also removing the memory growth over the time of the experiment, as shown in Figure 8b. CPU utilization and memory usage for the cache-enabled modified MDCF averaged 1.32 ± 0.05 % and 4.55 ± 0.35 GB of the 64 GB available memory, respectively. Our initial experiment resulted in overhead of 5.8% CPU utilization and 5.4 GB memory (on average) from the inclusion of authorization, whereas the optimized

modified MDCF resulted in an overhead of 0.55% CPU utilization and 0.93 GB memory, on average.

5 RELATED WORK

The differences between healthcare facilities and their individualized, unique access control requirements have resulted in many proposed access control models, all suitable for healthcare. Though a detailed discussion of the access control models themselves is not in the scope of this paper, here we provide several examples of how some of these models work.

Most research on access control in medical domain has focused on Electronic Health Record systems (EHRs), storing data which is accessed or changed only occasionally. The variety of EHRs makes it unlikely that a one-size-fits-all access control model will be used. A small sampling of proposed access control models for distributed EHRs can be found in [11, 20, 23, 37]. Each proposed solution uses different methods to achieve patient privacy. Ray et al. [37] use ABAC to ensure the disclosure of Protected Health Information (PHI), in response to requests from researchers, conform to various policies imposed by patients. Hupperich et al. [20] discusses the problems with some current proposed solutions for privacy, such as the use of smart cards for EHR authorization, and propose a flexible secure architecture based on attribute-based encryption and scalable authorization secrets to enable patient-controlled security and privacy. Moreover, availability of resources during emergencies is an active area of access control research [39]. Various solutions have been proposed [7, 13] to override access restrictions in a controlled manner.

None of the proposed models provides a solution and/or addresses the need for an access control model for real-time patient data generated by medical devices within a heterogeneous, interoperable environment such as standardized by the ASTM Integrated Clinician Environment (ICE) standards or one following the concepts of Medical Application Platforms (MAPs) [46]. Authorization within ICE-compliant medical middleware has been not been studied, nor are the concepts covered in the associated standards [21], which do not provide any authentication or authorization requirements or specifications. Salazar discusses authentication and authorization requirements for MAPs, and designs out a proof-of concept authentication framework scheme within the MDCF [41], but does not present an authorization architecture, except for a high-level design rooted in the Role-Based Access Control (RBAC) model [40]. Salazar's main contribution are limited to ensuring the trustworthiness of medical devices connecting to the MDCF, creation and integration of a flexible authentication system into the MDCF, and evaluation of the implemented system. We show that RBAC is insufficient to fulfill the requirements for dynamic access control required for an ICE-compliant system, and provide an alternative design based on ABAC.

6 CONCLUSION

In this paper, we presented the design, architecture, and evaluation of a flexible authorization architecture for systems of interoperable medical devices with a proof-of-concept implementation within the Medical Device Coordination Framework (MDCF). Our work is a first attempt to implement an authorization system within an

ICE standards-compliant medical middleware and provide access control to real-time data generated by the systems of interoperable medical devices. Our unique approach to attribute inheritance makes our access control model significantly different from prior models used in medical domain to protect mostly static electronic medical records, without sacrificing granularity or expressive power. Attribute inheritance also provides clinicians with authorized emergency access to medical devices, especially interoperable "plug-and-play" devices. Evaluation results show that our authorization architecture performs well, scales to many devices with many distinct physiological data channels, and is sufficiently flexible to integrate with other implementations of the ICE standard or Medical Application Platforms (MAPs). A more thorough and rigorous comparative analysis of our architecture with other flavors of RBAC/ABAC, e.g. RABAC, as well as with different performance characteristics of alternate design choices for the PEP, PDP, and policy languages, is left for future work. Additional future work includes a more complete exploration of the benefits of attribute inheritance, including how it can contribute to implementing a controlled Break The Glass procedure (along with "Fix The Glass").

ACKNOWLEDGMENTS

This work was funded by NSF grant 1253930. The authors also wish to thank Matthew French for his patience in explaining the inner workings of the MDCF.

REFERENCES

[1] Medical device "plug-and-play" interoperability program. http://mdpnp.org. (Accessed on 2/20/2017).

[2] Axiomatics language for authorization (ALFA). https://www.axiomatics.com/solutions/products/authorization-for-applications/developer-tools-and-apis/192-axiomatics-language-for-authorization-alfa.html, 2015. (Accessed on 2/21/2017).

[3] OACC — Java application security framework. http://oaccframework.org/, 2016. (Accessed on 2/21/2017).

[4] Apache Shiro — Simple. Java. Security. https://shiro.apache.org/caching.html. (Accessed on 4/25/2017).

[5] Apache Shiro — Simple. Java. Security. https://shiro.apache.org/documentation.html. (Accessed on 1/12/2017).

[6] S. Barrett. The MDCF PCA Shutoff App 0.3 Documentation. http://people.cs.ksu.edu/~scbarrett/pcashutoff-doc/, 2015.

[7] A. D. Brucker and H. Petritsch. Extending access control models with break-glass. In SACMAT, 2009.

[8] A. Carreras, E. Rodríguez, and J. Delgado. Using XACML for access control in social networks. In W3C Workshop on Access Control Application Scenarios, 2009.

[9] R. Chandramouli. A framework for multiple authorization types in a healthcare application system. In ACSAC, 2001.

[10] A. A. El-Aziz and A. Kannan. Access control for healthcare data using extended XACML-SRBAC model. In ICCCI, 2012.

[11] J. Eyers, David M.and Bacon and K. Moody. OASIS role-based access control for electronic health records. IEEE Proceedings – Software, 153(1), 2006.

[12] D. F. Ferraiolo, R. Sandhu, S. Gavrila, D. R. Kuhn, and R. Chandramouli. Proposed NIST standard for role-based access control. TISSEC, 4(3), 2001.

[13] A. Ferreira, D. Chadwick, P. Farinha, R. Correia, G. Zao, R. Chilro, and L. Antunes. How to securely break into RBAC: The BTG-RBAC model. In ACSAC, 2009.

[14] A. Ferreira, R. Cruz-Correia, L. Antunes, P. Farinha, E. Oliveira-Palhares, D. W. Chadwick, and A. Costa-Pereira. How to break access control in a controlled manner. In CBMS, 2006.

[15] P. W. Fong. Relationship-based access control: Protection model and policy language. In CoDASPY, 2011.

[16] J. Hatcliff, A. King, I. Lee, A. MacDonald, A. Fernando, M. Robkin, E. Y. Vasserman, S. Weininger, and J. M. Goldman. Rationale and architecture principles for medical application platforms. In ICCPS, 2012.

[17] J. Hu and A. C. Weaver. A dynamic, context-aware security infrastructure for distributed healthcare applications. In Workshop on Pervasive Privacy Security, Privacy, and Trust, 2004.

[18] V. C. Hu, D. Ferraiolo, R. Kuhn, A. R. Friedman, A. J. Lang, M. M. Cogdell, A. Schnitzer, K. Sandlin, R. Miller, and K. Scarfone. Guide to attribute based access control (ABAC) definition and considerations (draft). NIST Special Publication 800-162, 2013.

[19] V. C. Hu, D. R. Kuhn, and D. F. Ferraiolo. Attribute-based access control. IEEE Computer, 48(2), 2015.

[20] T. Hupperich, H. Löhr, A.-R. Sadeghi, and M. Winandy. Flexible patient-controlled security for electronic health records. In SIGHIT, 2012.

[21] Medical devices and medical systems-essential safety requirements for 5 equipment comprising the patient-centric integrated clinical environment 6 (ICE)-part 1: General requirements and conceptual model 7. ASTM F2761, 2008.

[22] J. Jin, G.-J. Ahn, H. Hu, M. J. Covington, and X. Zhang. Patient-centric authorization framework for sharing electronic health records. In SACMAT, 2009.

[23] J. Jin, G.-J. Ahn, H. Hu, and X. Covington, Michael J.and Zhang. Patient-centric authorization framework for electronic healthcare services. Computers & Security, 30(2), 2011.

[24] X. Jin, R. Sandhu, and R. Krishnan. RABAC: Role-centric attribute-based access control. In International Conference on Mathematical Methods, Models, and Architectures for Computer Network Security, 2012.

[25] M. Jung, G. Kienesberger, W. Granzer, M. Unger, and W. Kastner. Privacy enabled web service access control using SAML and XACML for home automation gateways. In ICITST, 2011.

[26] Y. J. Kim, S. Procter, J. Hatcliff, V. P. Ranganath, and Robby. Ecosphere principles for medical application platforms. In ICHI, 2015.

[27] A. King, D. Arney, I. Lee, O. Sokolsky, J. Hatcliff, and S. Procter. Prototyping closed loop physiologic control with the medical device coordination framework. In ICSE/SEHC, 2010.

[28] A. L. King, S. Chen, and I. Lee. The middleware assurance substrate: Enabling strong real-time guarantees in open systems with OpenFlow. In ISORC, 2014.

[29] A. L. King, S. Procter, D. Andresen, J. Hatcliff, S. Warren, W. Spees, R. P. Jetley, P. L. Jones, and S. Weininger. An open test bed for medical device integration and coordination. In ICSE Companion, 2009.

[30] M. Li, S. Yu, K. Ren, and W. Lou. Securing personal health records in cloud computing: Patient-centric and fine-grained data access control in multi-owner settings. In SECURECOMM, 2010.

[31] M. Lorch, S. Proctor, R. Lepro, D. Kafura, and S. Shah. First experiences using XACML for access control in distributed systems. In ACM Workshop on XML Security, 2003.

[32] OASIS. eXtensible access control markup language (XACML) version 3.0. http://docs.oasis-open.org/xacml/3.0/xacml-3.0-core-spec-os-en.html, 2013.

[33] OpenICE User Introduction. https://www.openice.info/docs/1_overview.html.

[34] G. Pardo-Castellote. OMG data-distribution service: Architectural overview. In International Conference on Distributed Computing Systems, Workshops, 2003.

[35] M. Peleg, D. Beimel, D. Dori, and Y. Denekamp. Situation-based access control: Privacy management via modeling of patient data access scenarios. Journal of Biomedical Informatics, 41(6), 2008.

[36] Pivotal Software, Inc. Spring security. https://projects.spring.io/spring-security/, 2017. (Accessed on 2/21/2017).

[37] I. Ray, T. C. Ong, I. Ray, and M. G. Kahn. Applying attribute based access control for privacy preserving health data disclosure. In IEEE-EMBS BHI, 2016.

[38] S. Z. R. Rizvi, P. W. Fong, J. Crampton, and J. Sellwood. Relationship-based access control for an open-source medical records system. In SACMAT, 2015.

[39] L. Røstad. Access control in healthcare information systems. PhD thesis, Norwegian University of Science and Technology, 2008.

[40] C. Salazar. A security architecture for medical application platforms. Master's thesis, Kansas State University, 2014.

[41] C. Salazar and E. Y. Vasserman. Retrofitting communication security into a publish/subscribe middleware platform. In FHIES/SEHC, 2014.

[42] R. S. Sandhu, E. J. Coyne, H. L. Feinstein, and C. E. Youman. Role-based access control models. IEEE Computer, 29(2), 1996.

[43] M. Siriwardena. Balana. https://github.com/wso2/balana. (Accessed on 1/12/2017).

[44] S. Sucurovic. An approach to access control in electronic health record. Journal of medical systems, 34(4), 2010.

[45] S. K. Tzelepi, D. K. Koukopoulos, and G. Pangalos. A flexible content and context-based access control model for multimedia medical image database systems. In Workshop on Multimedia and Security: New Challenges, 2001.

[46] E. Y. Vasserman and J. Hatcliff. Foundational security principles for medical application platforms. Information Security Applications, LNCS, 8267, 2014.

[47] D. Xu, Z. Wang, S. Peng, and N. Shen. Automated fault localization of XACML policies. In SACMAT, 2016.

[48] L. Zhang, G.-J. Ahn, and B.-T. Chu. A role-based delegation framework for healthcare information systems. In SACMAT, 2002.

Uncoupling Biometrics from Templates for Secure and Privacy-Preserving Authentication

Aysajan Abidin, Enrique Argones Rúa, and Roel Peeters

imec-COSIC KU Leuven, Belgium

firstname.lastname@esat.kuleuven.be

ABSTRACT

Biometrics are widely used for authentication in several domains, services and applications. However, only very few systems succeed in effectively combining highly secure user authentication with an adequate privacy protection of the biometric templates, due to the difficulty associated with jointly providing good authentication performance, unlinkability and irreversibility to biometric templates. This thwarts the use of biometrics in remote authentication scenarios, despite the advantages that this kind of architectures provides. We propose a user-specific approach for decoupling the biometrics from their binary representation before using biometric protection schemes based on fuzzy extractors. This allows for more reliable, flexible, irreversible and unlinkable protected biometric templates. With the proposed biometrics decoupling procedures, biometric metadata, that does not allow to recover the original biometric template, is generated. However, different biometric metadata that are generated starting from the same biometric template remain statistically linkable, therefore we propose to additionally protect these using a second authentication factor (e.g., knowledge or possession based). We demonstrate the potential of this approach within a two-factor authentication protocol for remote biometric authentication in mobile scenarios.

CCS CONCEPTS

•Security and privacy → Cryptography; Biometrics; Multi-factor authentication; Privacy-preserving protocols;

KEYWORDS

Biometrics; multi-factor authentication; template protection; unlinkability; irreversibility;

ACM Reference format:

Aysajan Abidin, Enrique Argones Rúa, and Roel Peeters. 2017. Uncoupling Biometrics from Templates for Secure and Privacy-Preserving Authentication. In *Proceedings of SACMAT'17, Indianapolis, IN, USA, June 21-23, 2017,* 9 pages.

DOI: http://dx.doi.org/10.1145/3078861.3078863

1 INTRODUCTION

Biometrics is a way to measure personal features, having the potential to authenticate individuals with a high degree of assurance while offering convenience to the user. Consequently, the use of automated biometric-based frameworks has become increasingly popular in both governmental and commercial services for user authentication. However, the use of biometrics also poses serious threats both to privacy and security of the users. It was shown by Pagnin et al. [25] that leakage of biometric data in a remote setting is hard to avoid. Leakage of biometric data may lead to the disclosure of personal information, e.g., demographics (for instance age, as shown by Han et al. [14]) or medical information (for instance as shown by Bolling [8] and Penrose [22] for the case of iris and fingerprint patterns, respectively). Furthermore, the leaked biometric data may be used to create spoofed biometric samples, thus thwarting the secure use of biometrics for authentication. These difficulties have slowed down the adoption of biometrics in remote authentication schemes, where the risks of information leakage are high.

The main goal of designing a biometric protection scheme is to provide irreversibility and unlinkability, as defined in the ISO/IEC 24745:2011 standard [16]. Irreversibility means that it should be computationally hard to reconstruct the original biometric template from the stored reference data, i.e., the protected biometric template, while it should be easy to generate the protected biometric template. Unlinkability means that different versions of protected biometric templates can be generated based on the same biometric data (renewability), while protected biometric templates should not allow cross-matching (diversity).

In literature, several approaches were proposed for protecting biometric data, including the use of biometric template protection schemes, such as those based on fuzzy extractors [12], or through the use of homomorphic encryption schemes. However, most of the proposed biometric template protection schemes suffer from degradation of verification performance, partial reversibility or linkability. Recently, research moved towards a new direction, taking the wider context of authentication into account and leverage multi-factor user authentication. In multi-factor user authentication, the user is verified by a combination of different authentication factors that belong to one of the following categories: (a) *possession factor*, e.g., a token stored on the user's mobile phone; (b) *knowledge factor*, e.g., a PIN or password that the user remembers; and (c) *inherent factor*, e.g., a biometric attribute. This new direction does not only result in increased security, since the user has to provide more than one type of authentication evidence, but it can also be used for improving the privacy protection of biometric data.

In this work, we introduce the first sound procedure to decouple the biometrics from their binary representation *before* using biometric protection schemes. Furthermore, we build further on the latest direction in biometric protection research by proposing a privacy-preserving and secure two-factor authentication protocol for remote scenarios.

1.1   Related Work

Recently, biometric protection research is moving into the direction of combing biometrics with other (knowledge-based or possession-based) authentication factors. Given the shear amount of related work, we limit ourselves to the most relevant related works.

Zheng [32], Zhu [33] and Wua *et al.* [31] presented different approaches that rely on the encryption of the biometric template. However, these schemes need to decrypt the biometric template, which is solely protected by means of the encryption, and do not deal with unlinkability of template.

Syta *et al.* [29] proposed a combination of two factors, but the privacy of biometrics would be disclosed if the token is obtained by the authentication server. Fan *et al.* [13] designed a privacy-preserving scheme using three-factor authentication. However, biometric unlinkability is not achieved if the token is disclosed. Meenakshi and Padmavathi [23] suggested a password-hardened fuzzy vault. The password is directly combined with the biometric binary representation and a uniform distribution of the samples is assumed in order to avoid any information disclosure. Nevertheless, the disclosure of the password would expose the biometrics, and renewability is only achievable by continuously changing the user's password, which is not a real biometric renewability. More recently, Abidin *et al.* [1, 2, 4] proposed privacy-preserving biometric authentication protocols secure against malicious (as opposed to semi-honest) adversaries. These protocols also use a second authentication factor which is used to enhance the privacy of biometric templates, but do not consider revocability and/or renewability of biometric templates.

Abidin *et al.* [3] presented a modification of an earlier protocol presented by Bringer *et al.* [9], which relies on homomorphic encryption. In their modified version, the authors improve the protocol to achieve security against malicious but not colluding insider adversaries, utilising additional secret keys. As in the original protocol, the Abidin *et al.* protocol also stores the reference biometric templates in the clear. Although this approach is secure against malicious adversaries, it comes with more complexity and requires the storage of additional cryptographic keys, and it only protects the link between biometric data and their original owners.

BioHash [17], introduced by Andrew Teoh Beng *et al.*, was a first attempt at decoupling the biometric representation from the original biometric sample. Even though this feature transformation approach asymptotically preserves distances between genuine and impostor biometric samples in the original and transformed domains, the statistical assumptions on the biometric sources (intra-class and inter-class scatter matrices must be known) and the size of the obtained metadata can thwart its practical adoption. Moreover, the use of the stored information (the transformed template) and the metadata (can be stored locally) allows for reconstruction of the biometric representation, posing a serious threat to privacy and security.

Monrose *et al.* [24] presented an approach for generating long-term secret keys from passwords and keystroke dynamics. This approach is similar to ours in the sense that it encrypts a metadata table with the password. The approach proposed by Monrose *et al.* only takes into account the most reliable biometric features provide biometric-dependent information for reconstructing the secret key and it is not taking advantage of the information provided by features with low reliability, which makes the system not useful when the biometric trait exclusively provides a huge number of unreliable feature. The scheme is adaptive in the sense that the changes in the reliability of the features are smoothly taken into account. However, in order to provide the same secret key, all the reliable features have to agree, which results in a trade-off between a high entropy of the secret key and a low false rejection rate. Moreover, the stored metadata related to non-reliable features contains information that can be used to reconstruct the secret key even without access to an original biometric sample.

1.2   Contributions

We propose a procedure that decouples the original biometric samples from their binary representation and use this result to construct a new biometric protection method for two-factor authentication in remote settings. Furthermore, the security and privacy properties of the resulting method are formally analysed. Concretely, our contributions are:

- In Sect. 2, we present our adversarial model and security definitions. We assume malicious external adversaries for security and even allow for an malicious Service Provider (the party where the user authenticates to) for privacy. This adversarial model is stronger than the ones commonly used in related work, i.e. honest-but-curious.

- Our proposed biometric decoupling procedure is presented in Sect. 3, with a concrete example for the case of IrisCodes. The choice of iris biometrics for a mobile user authentication application is motivated by the existence of several commercial and academic systems using this modality (e.g., Wang and Liu [30]) and the camera as a biometric capture device being generally and openly available. The latter in contrast with other commonly used mobile biometrics such as fingerprints, where the biometric capture behaviour is fixed, and its security usually relies on industrial secrecy [5, 26]. We also discuss the application of our biometric decoupling procedure to other biometric modalities in Sect. 3.2, including behavioural and dynamic biometrics. The proposed decoupling procedure provides increased reliability of the binary features by using user-specific information, thus improving security and biometric authentication performance. It also enables us to choose an arbitrary binary representation for the biometrics, thus facilitating unlinkability.

- The feasibility of the proposed decoupling procedure in the context of remote authentication is shown in Sect. 4, by presenting a protocol for secure and privacy-preserving remote user authentication, based on the biometric treat and a second factor based on either knowledge or possession. The metadata, generated by the biometric decoupling procedure, is encrypted using a cryptographic key, which is derived from an independent authentication factor to avoid linkability between metadata. It should also be noted that we do not rely on homomorphic encryption (such as, e.g., [9] and [3]), resulting in reduced complexity.

- In Sect. 5, we show that the proposed protocol is secure against malicious external adversaries and that the overall construction provides privacy both against malicious Service Provider and external adversaries.

2 BACKGROUND

Cryptographic schemes relies on keys, which are chosen uniformly at random and then remain fixed. This means that, in order to use biometrics as keys for cryptographic primitives, one first needs to transform these inherently noisy sources into a stable string which is indistinguishable from a random distribution. A common approach for doing this is using *fuzzy extractors*. A fuzzy extractor is a construction that allows to characterise noisy information sources with fixed random strings. Juels [18] presented a practical construction, which is based on the use of Error Correcting Codes, PseudoRandom Generators and Hash functions. A formal definition can be found in [12]. In our case, we use a binary Error Correcting Code ECC $(n, k, t) \subset \{0, 1\}^n$, where n is the length of the codewords, k is the length of messages, $k < n$, and t is the number of errors that can be corrected in the received codewords. The two associated functions are denoted as ECC_{encode} and ECC_{decode}.

For the proposed protocol we make use of a secure key derivation function (KDF) to derive cryptographic keys using a secret input data, e.g., a password, with sufficient min-entropy. In particular, we use a KDF to generate keys for an IND-CPA-secure symmetric encryption and a strongly-unforgeable digital signature scheme. We denote by ENC and DEC the symmetric key encryption and decryption algorithms, and by SIGN and VER the public key digital signature signing and verification algorithms, respectively.

Definition 2.1 (Adapted from [21]). A key derivation function is said to be secure with respect to a source of input with a min-entropy greater than or equal to λ if no probabilistic polynomial time (PPT) attacker $\mathcal{A}$ can distinguish its output from a random output of equal length, except with a non-negligible probability $\text{negl}(\lambda)$, where negl is a negligible function.

2.1 Adversarial model

We consider two types of adversaries: adversaries that aim to break security and those that aim to break privacy. We assume that the adversary is in full control of all communication between Service Providers (SP) and user devices (D) and can hence eavesdrop, modify, re-order, replay, inject and drop messages at will. We assume that the user and the user's device are fully trusted, i.e., users abide by the protocol specifications when authenticating as themselves and trust their own device only in the sense that the device is not compromised.

The security adversary will try to impersonate an uncompromized user to SP potentially having access, in addition to all protocol transcripts, to all available input of parties involved with the exception of at least one of the authentication factors of the legitimate user it is trying to impersonate.

Definition 2.2 (Security). $\Pi = (\text{Enroll}, \text{Authenticate})$ is a secure multi-factor authentication system if no PPT adversary $\mathcal{A}$ can successfully authenticate itself to the verifier as the legitimate user it impersonates, even when given all protocol transcripts and all inputs of the verifier and all provers with the exception of at least one authentication factor of the user it tries to impersonate.

The privacy adversary will try to link users across enrollments (possibly at different possibly colluding service providers) for which we only consider the linkage of information that is derived from the user's biometric template Q as this cannot (easily) be changed (as opposed to other knowledge-based and possession-based authentication factors). The adversary provides two biometric templates, Q_0 and Q_1, from which one will be used for enrolling user U, after which the adversary can authenticate poly-many times as this user using any input as the other authentication factor(s). We do not consider privacy in the sense that multiple authentication attempts by the same user (for the same enrollment) might be linked.

Definition 2.3 (Privacy). For $\Pi = (\text{Enroll}, \text{Authenticate})$ as before, consider the following game played between a PPT adversary $\mathcal{A}$ and a challenger:

$$
\begin{aligned}
&\text{Exp}_{\Pi, \mathcal{A}}^{Priv}(\lambda): \\
&\quad (Q_0, Q_1) \leftarrow \mathcal{A}(\lambda) \\
&\quad b \xleftarrow{R} \{0, 1\} \\
&\quad \alpha \leftarrow \text{Enroll}(U, Q_b, auth\_factor^*), \text{with} \\
&\quad\quad \alpha \text{ the storage at the verifier and } * \text{ meaning 1 or more} \\
&\quad \text{For } i = 1, \cdots, \text{poly}(\lambda): \\
&\quad\quad \beta_i \leftarrow \text{Authenticate}(U, Q_b, auth\_factor^*), \text{with} \\
&\quad\quad\quad \beta_i \text{ the protocol transcript } i \\
&\quad b' \leftarrow \mathcal{A}(\lambda, Q_0, Q_1, \alpha, (\beta_i)_{i=1}^{\text{poly}(\lambda)}) \\
&\text{Return 1 if } b == b', 0 \text{ otherwise}
\end{aligned}
$$

We define the adversary's advantage in this game as

$$
\text{Adv}_{\Pi, \mathcal{A}}^{Priv}(\lambda) = \left| \Pr \left\{ \text{Exp}_{\Pi, \mathcal{A}}^{Priv}(\lambda) = 1 \right\} - \frac{1}{2} \right|.
$$

Π is privacy-preserving if $\text{Adv}_{\Pi, \mathcal{A}}^{Priv}(\lambda) \leq \text{negl}(\lambda)$, for all PPT adversary $\mathcal{A}$.

3 DECOUPLING BIOMETRIC REPRESENTATIONS

The fuzzy commitment approach does not provide any mechanism for guaranteeing unlinkability of the protected templates. It is easy to determine that two templates have been generated using the same biometric sample, as shown by Simoens et al. in [27], therefore this cryptosystem does not provide unlinkability when the secret (the binary biometric representation) must remain the same.

Furthermore, the number and robustness of biometric features are not usually appropriate for being protected using a fuzzy commitment scheme, and this is a critical issue. On one hand, the fuzzy commitment scheme needs that the number of protected bits coincides with the length of the used error correcting code. And on the other hand, the reliability of these bits (the probability to remain unchanged among different biometric samples from the same individual) determines the required error correcting capability of the code: the higher this reliability, the lower the required error correcting capability, and the higher the message length, or equivalently the security parameter of the fuzzy commitment scheme.

We propose to decouple the binary representation from the biometric data, producing a target binary representation with increased robustness from the biometric features, thus circumventing these problems in the fuzzy commitment. The target binary representation can be chosen during the enrollment stage, making possible that the final binary string is completely independent from the biometric data, thus guaranteeing unlinkability between protected templates generated from the same biometric features. This is achieved by using two intermediate functions. The first one takes as inputs the biometric enrollment samples and the desired random binary representation, and returns a set BM of binarization metadata as output, $BM = f(Q^E, b)$.

This is the binarization metadata extractor function, and must be used during the enrollment phase. The second function takes as inputs the biometric verification samples and the set of binarization metadata produced by the first function. Its output is the binary representation of the verification biometrics. This intermediate function is called the parameterised binarization function, defined as $\widetilde{b} = g(Q^v, BM)$.

It is important to underline that the binarization metadata establishes a relationship between the biometric samples and the binary representation, therefore this binarization metadata have to be protected in order to avoid a leak of information. As a remark, in this work we do not present a general approach for computing these functions, since the paper is focused on the possibilities that such an approach offers for designing authentication protocols providing both the highest security and privacy protection. However, in the next section an example of these two functions for the IrisCode case is illustrated, and the application of this approach to other biometric modalities is then discussed.

3.1 Specific Case: IrisCode

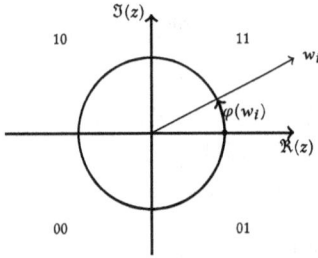

Figure 1: Binary encoding of phase information in IrisCode.

3.1.1 Feature extraction. In the specific example of iris, bits conforming the Daugman's IrisCode [10] encode the phase of complex Gabor wavelets' responses as a vector $\mathbf{w} = [w_1, ..., w_N]^t$. Biometric measurements can be written before the binary encoding step as a vector of phase measurements:

$$Q = \boldsymbol{\varphi}(\mathbf{w}) = [\varphi(w_1), ..., \varphi(w_N)]^t$$
$$= [\varphi_1, ..., \varphi_N]^t,$$

where $\varphi_i = \arctan(\Im(w_i)/\Re(w_i))$, $i \in \{1, ..., N\}$. Two bits are extracted from each phase value, as portrayed in Fig. 1, and formally

defined by the following IrisCode coding function,

$$\mathbf{b_i} = \text{IC}(\varphi_i)$$
$$= \begin{cases} [1,1]^t, & \text{if mod}\{\varphi_i, 2\pi\} \in [0, \pi/2) \\ [1,0]^t, & \text{if mod}\{\varphi_i, 2\pi\} \in [\pi/2, \pi) \\ [0,0]^t, & \text{if mod}\{\varphi_i, 2\pi\} \in [\pi, 3\pi/2) \\ [0,1]^t, & \text{if mod}\{\varphi_i, 2\pi\} \in [3\pi/2, 2\pi). \end{cases}$$

3.1.2 Proposed randomized binarization process. The bit values $\mathbf{b_i}$ can be decoupled from the corresponding biometric phase measurement φ_i by using shifted versions $\phi_i = \varphi_i + \theta_i$ in the binarization in Eq. 3.1.1, where θ_i are phase shift terms. We could simply choose these phase shift terms for each phase measurement as:

$$\theta_i = k_i \frac{\pi}{2}, \tag{1}$$

with $k_i \in \{0, ..., 3\}$, obtaining a binarization metadata $BM = [\theta_1, ..., \theta_N]$ completely independent from the original biometric representation Q. However, phase measurements near the decision thresholds will provide low reliability, i.e., new biometric samples from the same individual could produce different bits. A further improvement can be done for increasing the reliability (resilience to change) of the bits in the resulting template, making the phase $\phi_i = \varphi_i + \theta_i$ to be centred in its corresponding quadrant, i.e. $\phi_i = k_i\pi/2 + \pi/4 + j(\pi/2)$, with $k_i \in \{0, ..., 3\}$ and $j \in \mathbb{Z}$. Let us define $j_{\varphi_i} = \text{minarg}_{j \in \mathbb{Z}} \{|j(\pi/2) + \pi/4 - \varphi_i|\}$. Then, the phase shifts producing robust binary features can be defined as:

$$\theta_i = \text{mod}\left\{ k_i \frac{\pi}{2} + \left[\frac{\pi}{4} - \varphi_i + j_{\varphi_i} \frac{\pi}{2} \right], 2\pi \right\}, \tag{2}$$

with k_i chosen from the set $\{0, ..., 3\}$.

Given a binary representation for the i-th phase term $\mathbf{b_i} = [b_i^0, b_i^1]^t$, we remind that it holds the IrisCode binarization, i.e. $\mathbf{b_i} = \text{IC}(\phi_i) = \text{IC}(\varphi_i + \theta_i)$. Therefore, the k_i indexes can be computed as $k_i = \{k \in \{0, ..., 3\} \mid \mathbf{b_i} = \text{IC}(\varphi_i + \theta_i)\}$, with θ_i computed using Eq. 1, or Eq. 2 for increased binary reliability.

The complete *metadata extractor function* is defined as the randomised function $BM = f(Q, \mathbf{b}) = [\theta_1, ..., \theta_N]^t$, where θ_i is computed using Eq. 1, or alternatively Eq. 2. For the binarization of a biometric phase measurement $Q' = [\varphi_1, ..., \varphi_N]$, the phase shifts stored in BM are applied to Q'. This is done by the *binarization function*, defined as $g(Q', BM) = [IC(\varphi_1' + \theta_1)^t, ..., IC(\varphi_N' + \theta_N)^t]^t$. It can be checked that $g(Q, f(Q, \mathbf{b})) = \mathbf{b}$, in both cases when Eq. 1 or Eq. 2 are used for calculating the phase shift terms.

The phase shifts obtained using this approach carry information about the original representation, since $\text{mod}\{\theta_i, \pi/2\}$ is the distance of the original phase measurement to the closest phase bin centre. However, this metadata does not carry information about the original bin, and therefore it does not pose any risk to security, keeping a 2-bit uncertainty on the corresponding biometric phase. As long as these metadata are encrypted, the privacy risk posed by the distances to phase bin centre can be assumed for the sake of both (a) improved feature reliability, and thus increased security parameter in the biometric template protection scheme and improved biometric authentication performance, and (b) protected template unlinkability.

Further increasing robustness. The procedure described in the previous section can be modified to also reduce the binary representation length n and further improve binary features reliability. This length must not depend on the number of biometric features N. Instead, n can be imposed by other criterion, such as available code lengths when using a fuzzy commitment scheme. In the previously explained procedure, $n = 2N$. We present here how to proceed for $n < 2N$. Some biometric features will be contributing to the same couple of bits, thus increasing the reliability of these bits. This is specially useful in the case of iris, where occlusions of large parts of the iris pattern is a very usual situation.

Let us define the set of biometric features contributing to a given couple of bits $\mathbf{b}_i$ as $\mathcal{F}_i = \{\varphi_{i_1}, \ldots, \varphi_{i_{|\mathcal{F}_i|}}\}$, with $i_j \in \{1, \ldots, N\}$, and $j \in \{1, \ldots, |\mathcal{F}_i|\}$. Then, all the corresponding phase shifts are calculated using the same target bit values $\mathbf{b}_i$, i.e.

$$k_{i_j} = \left\{ k \in \{0, \ldots, 3\} \mid \mathbf{b_i} = \text{IC}\left(\varphi_{i_j} + \theta_{i_j}\right) \right\},$$

and θ_{i_j} is calculated using Eq. 1 or Eq. 2 alternatively. The sets describing which phase measurements contribute to each bit should be mutually exclusive to avoid undesired correlations between bits, and become part of the binarization metadata:

$$BM = \{\{\mathcal{F}_1, \ldots, \mathcal{F}_n\}, \theta\}.$$

Describing an exact procedure for partitioning the phase measurements into these sets in an optimal way is out of the scope of this paper, though we provide here an intuition. This partition must be aimed at minimising the mean number of bit errors in the verification phase for genuine users. Therefore, it must take into account the following factors:

- Inter-session user-dependent distribution of the biometric features. This will allow for designing partitions where the resultant bits are equally reliable.
- Feature occlusion model, to distribute the occluded features in an uniform way through all the bits.

In the case of the binarization function, it relies on the available biometric measurements in each set. If the user-dependent distribution model assumes the same inter-session noise distribution and independence between the phase features, this function can simply be the arithmetic mean.

3.2 Application to other biometric modalities

The derivation of the parameterised binarization and metadata extractor uncoupling functions depends on the nature of the biometric features. Similar derivations to the one presented in the previous section could be done for other biometric modalities, as long as biometric features are presented in a fixed-length vectorial form. In general, the proposed approach can be applied to any modality where a fuzzy extractor can be derived, with the advantage that user-specific information can be easily integrated in the uncoupling process, as shown in the iris case, for increasing biometric authentication performance. This covers most of the biometric modalities:

(1) Face recognition, where textural descriptors and eigenspace representations are usually fixed-length. Examples of the successful application of fuzzy extraction schemes to face biometrics can be found for instance in [19] and [28].

(2) Speaker recognition, where the state-of-the-art i-vector representation presented by Dehak et al. in [11] is also a fixed-length vector representation. Feasibility of fuzzy extraction for the speech modality has been shown by Billeb et al. in [7].

(3) Dynamic biometrics, such as online signature recognition, where fixed-length representations can be obtained using eigen-model representations and successfully used for building fuzzy extractors, as shown by Argones Rúa et al. in [6]. Other fixed length descriptions for dynamic biometrics, such as the global features presented by Ibrahim et al. in [15] for online signature, or the ones used by Monrose et al. in [24] for keystroke dynamics, are also well suited.

(4) Textural-based fingerprint recognition, such as the scheme presented by Khalil et al. in [20].

4 USER AUTHENTICATION

We now present our two-factor secure and privacy-preserving user authentication system, consisting of an enrollment and an authentication protocol. One factor is the biometric data, from which we extract an uncoupled random binary representation as explained in the previous section. The second factor is used to protect the binarization metadata. The random biometric binary representation is transformed into a signing key sk with a corresponding verification key pk. Authentication is done by signing a challenge from the verifier. Intuitively, our authentication system is secure because in order to impersonate a legitimate user, an attacker needs to correctly sign the challenge, where the signing key is protected by both factors.

Authentication takes place between a user through his or her device and a service provider. The device mainly acts as a proxy for the user, being able to do the necessary computations and setting up communication with the service provider. The protocols are designed such that no storage is required on the device. This has two major benefits: (1) users can use any trusted device to authenticate to the service provider, and (2) losing the device does not lead to security or privacy issues as there is no secret information stored. On the downside, it is generally acknowledged that users tend to choose passwords with low min-entropy. This has an impact on the maximal achievable security and privacy, where security can be maintained at the same level as long as the adversary has no access to the biometric data of the user, the privacy-preserving properties of the system go down to the min-entropy of the password. Another reason for opting for a possession-based second factor is user convenience as the user is not required to type the password. For this reason, we leave both options open to which second authentication factor to use.

4.1 Enrollment Protocol

The enrollment protocol is illustrated in Fig. 2 and involves the following:

- The device asks the user to provide a (unique) username for the service provider and in a second phase a set of biometric samples together with a second authentication factor. In case of a possession-based second authentication factor, this could be generated by the device itself.

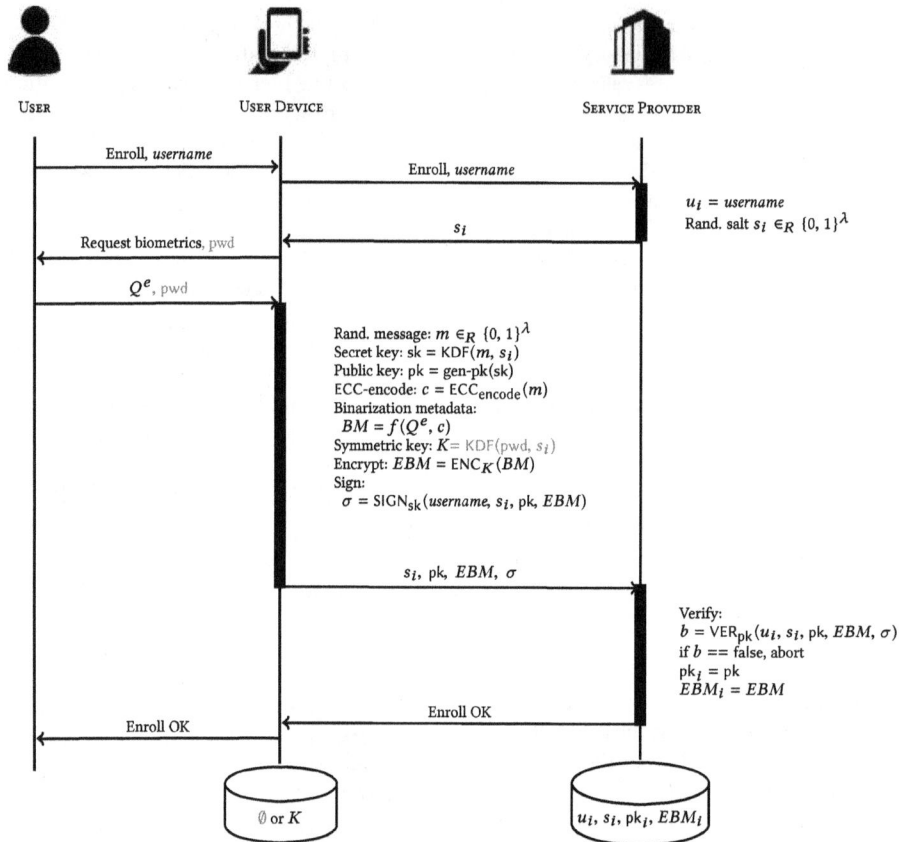

Figure 2: Two factor user enrollment protocol.

- The service provider supplies the device with a unique salt for the given username. This salt will be used for deriving both the symmetric key (when having a knowledge-based second authentication factor) and the signing key, ensuring that there is sufficient randomness as input for the key derivation function for both keys. It also ensures that if the database of the server gets compromised, one cannot efficiently precompute the symmetric keys derived from the most frequently used passwords.
- The device generates a random message that serves as input to the KDF for generating the signing key and corresponding public verification key. To ensure that one can later-on recover this message from the randomised binary representation, it is first encoded with an error correcting code.
- The binarization metadata is generated and protected by a symmetric key encryption scheme to ensure the privacy of the user.
- The device sends the public key and the encrypted binarization metadata back to the service provider, together with a signature over these data and the username. With this signature, the device proves knowledge of the secret key corresponding to the public key. The signature also

effectively ties the entire protocol transcript together, ensuring matching conversations between device and service provider. The salt being a unique identifier, is also used as session identifier for the service provider to link the messages.

4.2 Authentication protocol

The verification protocol is illustrated in Fig. 3 and involves the following:

- The device asks the user to provide his or her username for the service provider and in a second phase a fresh biometric sample together with a second authentication factor. In case of a possession-based second authentication factor, the user is only asked for a biometric sample.
- The service provider supplies the device with the salt, encrypted binarization metadata for the given username. Additionally the service provider also supplies a challenge to the device to ensure freshness of the authentication.
- The device reconstructs the message that was chosen at random during the enrollment protocol from the received inputs. Thanks to the error correcting code, one can decode errors due to the biometric sample being slightly different from the ones supplied during the enrollment protocol.

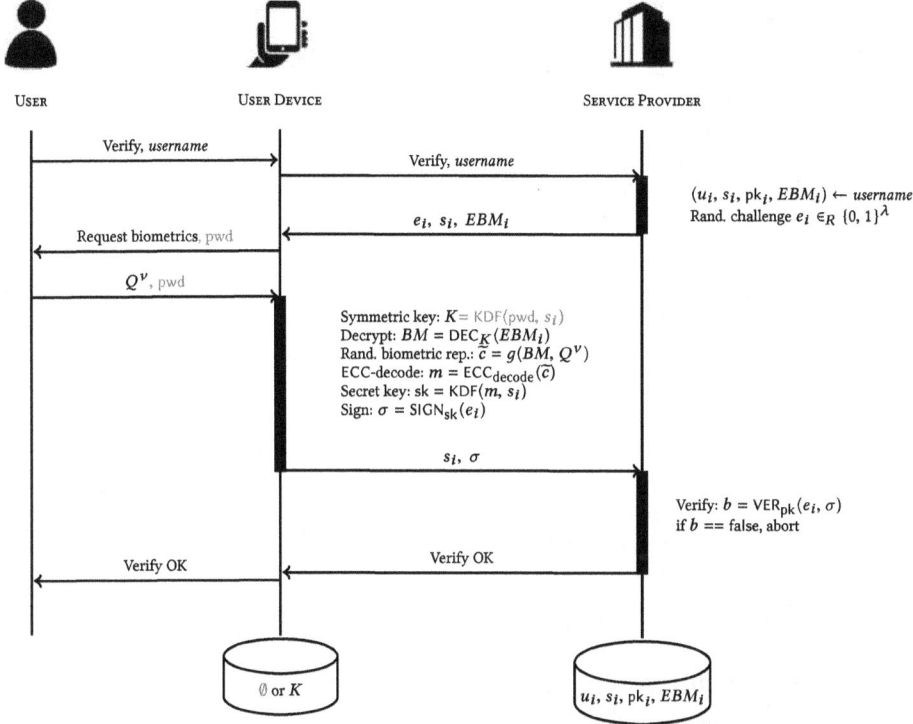

Figure 3: Two-factor user authentication protocol.

From the decoded message the signing key is derived as in the enrollment protocol.

- The device signs the service provider's challenge and sends the signature back to the service provider. Again the salt is used as a session identifier.
- If the signature verifies with the stored public key, the user is authenticated.

5 SECURITY AND PRIVACY ANALYSIS

We show that the proposed scheme is secure and privacy-preserving. The security and privacy analysis are performed for the worst case, i.e. assuming a knowledge-based second authentication factor with min-entropy $\ell << \lambda$. When using a possession-based second authentication factor, $\ell = \lambda$.

5.1 Security

THEOREM 5.1 (SECURITY). *The proposed user authentication scheme is a secure two-factor authentication scheme in the security parameter ℓ according to Definition 2.2, assuming a secure KDF, IND-CPA-secure encryption scheme and an universal unforgeable signature scheme.*

PROOF. The adversary $\mathcal{A}$ is given a complete copy of the server's database and one authentication factor of the user it tries to impersonate. The proof consists of two cases: in the first $\mathcal{A}$ is given the user's password pwd while in the second it is given the user's biometric feature vector Q^v.

The adversary succeeds in impersonating a user if it can produce a valid signature on a given challenge. Without knowledge of the

user's signing key sk, this implies $\mathcal{A}$ breaking universal unforgeability of the signature scheme of which the probability of success is negl(λ). We will now show for both cases, that the adversary cannot recover the message m and hence not sk. m can be recovered using the binarization metadata BM_i and a valid biometric data Q^v by means of the function g and the error-correction code.

- *Case 1:* Given the user's password pwd, $\mathcal{A}$ can decrypt EBM to obtain the binarization metadata BM. However, without knowledge on the biometric data Q^v, $\mathcal{A}$'s probability to recover $\tilde{c}$, and hence m, is negl(λ).
- *Case 2:* Given the user's biometric data Q^v, $\mathcal{A}$ needs BM to recover m. Without knowledge of the secret key K, this implies $\mathcal{A}$ breaking IND-CPA security of the encryption scheme of which the probability of success is negl(λ). The KDF is secure with respect to the source min-entropy, being ℓ. Hence $\mathcal{A}$'s probability of success of recovering K, hence BM and m, is negl(ℓ). □

5.2 Privacy

THEOREM 5.2. *The proposed user authentication scheme is privacy-preserving in the security parameter ℓ according to Definition 2.3, assuming a secure KDF and IND-CPA-secure encryption scheme.*

PROOF. The proof is based on a series of hybrid games.

- Game$_0$: This is the original privacy game $\text{Exp}_{\Pi,\mathcal{A}}^{\text{Priv}}(\ell)$. Let X_0 be the event that $b' = b$ in this game.

- Game$_1$: This is the same as Game$_0$, except that now the symmetric encryption key generated from $\mathsf{KDF}(\mathsf{pwd}, s_b)$ is replaced by a uniformly distributed random key of equal length. Let X_1 be the event that $b' = b$ in this game.
- Game$_2$: This is the same as Game$_1$, except that the secret signing key generated from $\mathsf{KDF}(m, s_b)$ is replaced by a uniformly distributed random key of equal length. Let X_2 be the event that $b' = b$ in this game.

Claim 1: $|\Pr\{X_0\} - \Pr\{X_1\}|$ is $\mathsf{negl}(\ell)$.

Proof: (by reduction) An adversary $\mathcal{A}$ with an advantage $\epsilon > \mathsf{negl}(\ell)$, can be used to construct another adversary $\mathcal{B}$ against the security of the KDF with advantage ϵ for the source's min-entropy of ℓ, which contradicts the definition of a secure KDF.

Claim 2: $|\Pr\{X_1\} - \Pr\{X_2\}|$ is $\mathsf{negl}(\lambda)$.

Proof Similar to the proof of claim 1.

Claim 3: $|2\Pr\{X_2\} - 1|$ is $\mathsf{negl}(\ell)$.

Proof In Game$_2$, both the symmetric encryption key and the signing key are replaced by uniformly random keys. Therefore, the claim follows from the assumption that the symmetric encryption scheme is IND-CPA secure (in the security parameter λ). □

5.3 Unlinkability and Irreversibility

In our protocol, we achieve unlinkability by uncoupling the biometrics from its binary representation (cf. Sect. 4 for details). So if the binary representation is somehow compromised, then the user can just revoke it and re-enroll, knowing that a new random binary representation will be generated. A compromised binary representation cannot be linked to a user biometrics. Regarding linkability due to the disclosure of the stored metadata, this is avoided by encrypting it using a second authentication factor.

Regarding irreversibility, the binarization metadata provides some information about the original biometric features in the case that this metadata is designed to increase the reliability of the binary features. The binary representation is not present in the stored metadata, impeding the recovering of the original biometric features. As our protocol protects both the binarization metadata and the binary biometric representation, no information is disclosed about the original biometric template to the considered adversaries.

6 CONCLUSIONS

We presented a method for decoupling biometrics from their protected binary representation. The usefulness of this construction for biometric template protection is demonstrated by incorporating it in a multi-factor authentication protocol in a remote scenario, based on an inherent factor (biometric) combined with either a possession factor (token stored on the smart phone) or a knowledge factor (password inputted by user). The proposed protocol uses the decoupling primitives for providing unlinkability to biometrics and relies on a minimum of two authentication factors to provide resistance against malicious adversaries both regarding security and privacy. The proposed solution provides irreversibility and unlinkability of the biometric template. Comprehensive security and privacy analysis demonstrate the effectiveness and robustness of the design.

ACKNOWLEDGMENTS

The authors would like to thank the anonymous reviewers for their valuable feedback. The work was supported by the European Commission FP7 project "EKSISTENZ" grant number: 607049. In addition, this work was supported in part by the Research Council KU Leuven: C16/15/058, and by imec through ICON Diskman.

REFERENCES

[1] Aysajan Abidin. 2017. *On Privacy-Preserving Biometric Authentication.* Springer International Publishing, Cham, 169–186. https://doi.org/10.1007/978-3-319-54705-3_11

[2] Aysajan Abidin, Abdelrahaman Aly, Enrique Argones Rúa, and Aikaterini Mitrokotsa. 2016. *Efficient Verifiable Computation of XOR for Biometric Authentication.* Springer International Publishing, Cham, 284–298. https://doi.org/10.1007/978-3-319-48965-0_17

[3] Aysajan Abidin, Kanta Matsuura, and Aiketerini Mitrokotsa. 2014. Security of a Privacy-Preserving Biometric Authentication Protocol Revisited. In *International Conference on Cryptology & Network Security (LNCS)*, Vol. 8813. Springer, 291–304.

[4] Aysajan Abidin, Enrique Argones Rúa, and Bart Preneel. 2016. *An Efficient Entity Authentication Protocol with Enhanced Security and Privacy Properties.* Springer International Publishing, Cham, 335–349. https://doi.org/10.1007/978-3-319-48965-0_20

[5] Apple. 2015. *KeychainTouchID: Using Touch ID with Keychain and LocalAuthentication.* https://developer.apple.com/library/ios/samplecode/KeychainTouchID/Introduction/Intro.html

[6] E. Argones Rúa, E. Maiorana, J. L. Alba Castro, and P. Campisi. 2012. Biometric Template Protection Using Universal Background Models: An Application to Online Signature. *IEEE Transactions on Information Forensics and Security* 7, 1 (Feb 2012), 269–282. https://doi.org/10.1109/TIFS.2011.2168213

[7] S. Billeb, C. Rathgeb, H. Reininger, K. Kasper, and C. Busch. 2015. Biometric template protection for speaker recognition based on universal background models. *IET Biometrics* 4, 2 (2015), 116–126. https://doi.org/10.1049/iet-bmt.2014.0031

[8] J. Bolling. 2000. A window to your health. *Jacksonville Medicine, Special Issue: Retinal Diseases* 51 (2000).

[9] Julien Bringer and Hervé Chabanne. 2008. An Authentication Protocol with Encrypted Biometric Data. In *AFRICACRYPT '08 (LNCS)*, Vol. 8813. Springer, 109–124.

[10] John Daugman. 1998. Recognizing people by their iris patterns. *Inf. Sec. Techn. Report* 3, 1 (1998), 33–39.

[11] Najim Dehak, Réda Dehak, Patrick Kenny, Niko Brümmer, Pierre Ouellet, and Pierre Dumouchel. 2009. Support vector machines versus fast scoring in the low-dimensional total variability space for speaker verification. In *INTERSPEECH '09.* 1559–1562.

[12] Yevgeniy Dodis, Rafail Ostrovsky, Leonid Reyzin, and Adam Smith. 2008. Fuzzy Extractors: How to Generate Strong Keys from Biometrics and Other Noisy Data. *SIAM J. Comput.* 38, 1 (2008), 97–139. https://doi.org/10.1137/060651380

[13] Chun-I Fan and Yi-Hui Lin. 2009. Provably secure remote truly three-factor authentication scheme with privacy protection on biometrics. *IEEE Transactions on Information Forensics and Security* 4, 4 (2009), 933–945. https://doi.org/10.1109/TIFS.2009.2031942

[14] Hu Han, Charles Otto, and Anil K. Jain. 2013. Age estimation from face images: Human vs. machine performance. In *International Conference on Biometrics - ICB 2013.* IEEE, 1–8.

[15] M. T. Ibrahim, M. Kyan, and L. Guan. 2009. On-line signature verification using global features. In *Electrical and Computer Engineering, 2009. CCECE '09. Canadian Conference on.* 682–685. https://doi.org/10.1109/CCECE.2009.5090216

[16] ISO/IEC 24745:2011. 2011. Information technology – Security techniques – Biometric information protection. (2011).

[17] Andrew Teoh Beng Jin, Alwyn Goh, and David Ngo Chek Ling. 2006. Random Multispace Quantization as an Analytic Mechanism for BioHashing of Biometric and Random Identity Inputs. *IEEE Trans. Pattern Anal. Mach. Intell.* 28, 12 (2006), 1892–1901.

[18] Ari Juels and Martin Wattenberg. 1999. A Fuzzy Commitment Scheme. In *ACM CCS'99.* ACM Press, 28–36.

[19] Tom A. M. Kevenaar, Geert Jan Schrijen, Michiel van der Veen, Anton H. M. Akkermans, and Fei Zuo. 2005. Face Recognition with Renewable and Privacy Preserving Binary Templates.. In *AutoID.* IEEE Computer Society, 21–26.

[20] Mohammed S. Khalil, Dzulkifli Muhammad, and Qais AL-Nuzaili. 2009. Fingerprint Verification Using the Texture of Fingerprint Image. *Machine Vision, International Conference on* 0 (2009), 27–31. https://doi.org/10.1109/ICMV.2009.18

[21] Hugo Krawczyk. 2010. Cryptographic extraction and key derivation: The HKDF

scheme. In *Advances in Cryptology–CRYPTO 2010*. LNCS, Vol. 6223. Springer, 631–648.

[22] L. S. Penrose. 1965. Dermatoglyphic Topology. *Nature* 205 (February 1965), 544 – 546. https://doi.org/doi:10.1038/205544a0

[23] V.S. Meenakshi and Dr.G. Padmavathi. 2010. Security analysis of password hardened multimodal biometric fuzzy vault with combined feature points extracted from fingerprint, iris and retina for high security applications. *Procedia Computer Science* 2 (2010), 195 – 206. https://doi.org/10.1016/j.procs.2010.11.025

[24] Fabian Monrose, Michael K. Reiter, and Susanne Wetzel. 1999. Password Hardening Based on Keystroke Dynamics. In *ACM CCS '99*. ACM, 73–82. https://doi.org/10.1145/319709.319720

[25] Elena Pagnin, Christos Dimitrakakis, Aysajan Abidin, and Aikaterini Mitrokotsa. 2014. On the Leakage of Information in Biometric Authentication. In *INDOCRYPT 2014 (LNCS)*, Vol. 8885. Springer, 265–280.

[26] Samsung. 2016. *Pass Programming Guide*. http://developer.samsung.com/resources/pass

[27] Koen Simoens, Pim Tuyls, and Bart Preneel. 2009. Privacy Weaknesses in Biometric Sketches. In *IEEE Symposium on Security and Privacy 2009*. 188–203.

[28] Yagiz Sutcu, Qiming Li, and Nasir Memon. 2009. Design and analysis of fuzzy extractors for faces. *Proc. of SPIE* 7306 (2009), 73061X–73061X–12. https://doi.org/10.1117/12.820571

[29] Ewa Syta, Michael J. Fischer, and Abraham Silberschatz. 2012. *Strong Theft-Proof Privacy-Preserving Biometric Authentication*. Technical Report. Yale/DCS/TR-1455.

[30] Shuo Wang and Jing Liu. 2011. Biometrics on mobile phone. In *Recent Application on Biometrics*. InTech.

[31] Fan Wua, Lili Xu, Saru Kumari, and Xiong Li. 2015. A novel and provably secure biometrics-based three-factor remote authentication scheme for mobile client-server networks. *Computers and Electrical Engineering* 45 (2015), 274–285.

[32] Jian De Zheng. 2011. A Framework for Token and Biometrics Based Authentication in Computer Systems. *JCP* 6, 6 (2011), 1206–1212. https://doi.org/10.4304/jcp.6.6.1206-1212

[33] Hongfeng Zhu. 2015. One-time identity-password authenticated key agreement scheme based on biometrics. *Security and Communication Networks* 8, 13 (2015), 2350–2360. https://doi.org/10.1002/sec.1182

On Risk in Access Control Enforcement

Giuseppe Petracca
The Pennsylvania State University
School of Electrical Engineering and Computer Science
gxp18@cse.psu.edu

Frank Capobianco
The Pennsylvania State University
School of Electrical Engineering and Computer Science
fnc110@cse.psu.edu

Christian Skalka
The University of Vermont
College of Engineering and Mathematical Sciences
skalka@cs.uvm.edu

Trent Jaeger
The Pennsylvania State University
School of Electrical Engineering and Computer Science
tjaeger@cse.psu.edu

ABSTRACT

While we have long had principles describing how access control enforcement should be implemented, such as the *reference monitor concept*, imprecision in access control mechanisms and access control policies leads to risks that may enable exploitation. In practice, least privilege access control policies often allow information flows that may enable exploits. In addition, the implementation of access control mechanisms often tries to balance security with ease of use implicitly (e.g., with respect to determining where to place authorization hooks) and approaches to tighten access control, such as accounting for program context, are ad hoc. In this paper, we define four types of risks in access control enforcement and explore possible approaches and challenges in tracking those types of risks. In principle, we advocate runtime tracking to produce risk estimates for each of these types of risk. To better understand the potential of risk estimation for authorization, we propose risk estimate functions for each of the four types of risk, finding that benign program deployments accumulate risks in each of the four areas for ten Android programs examined. As a result, we find that tracking of relative risk may be useful for guiding changes to security choices, such as authorized unsafe operations or placement of authorization checks, when risk differs from that expected.

CCS CONCEPTS

•**Security and privacy** → *Operating systems security;* Access control; Software security engineering;

KEYWORDS

Risk, Access Control Enforcement

ACM Reference format:
Giuseppe Petracca, Frank Capobianco, Christian Skalka, and Trent Jaeger. 2017. On Risk in Access Control Enforcement. In *Proceedings of SACMAT'17, June 21–23, 2017, Indianapolis, IN, USA, , 12 pages.*
DOI: http://dx.doi.org/10.1145/3078861.3078872

1 INTRODUCTION

Access control restricts the subjects (e.g., users and programs) that may perform operations (e.g., read and write) over objects (e.g., files and records). It has long been recommended that the software that implements access control should separate the access control mechanism from the access control policy. Access control mechanisms should satisfy the requirements specified by the reference monitor concept [6], such as complete mediation, to enforce access control policies correctly. Access control policies should express the access control requirements to be enforced.

In practice, the design and implementation of both access control mechanisms and policies is a manual process, which leads to risks that adversaries may circumvent the access control goals. First, access control policies may allow unsafe operations. While multilevel security (MLS) policies, such as Bell-La Padula [7] and Biba [8], block risky information flows, MLS policies often result in many trusted subjects (i.e., trusted readers and writers) that are outside the policy [27]. In addition, least privilege policies [43], which favor functionality over blocking risky operations, are more popular today. Also, authorized subjects may be compromised by adversaries, introducing risk even for accesses that would have been safe for the uncompromised subject. Second, errors in implementing access control mechanisms may produce risks. For example, programmers may misplace the access control policy checks, which are often called *authorization hooks*, in their programs. To reduce the number of authorization hooks needed, programmers may allow subjects to access more objects or perform more operations, possibly including risky operations with authorized operations. For example, one hook may allow two objects to be read, one of which may be used to create an information flow from other subjects. At present, there are no methods to track risks in overly coarse authorization hook placements.

Current research does not track the risk created by manual access control system design and implementation. Risk has generally been explored in two ways: (1) to identify undesirable permissions in access control policies statically and (2) to produce access control models that integrate risk estimates into the authorization decisions. First, researchers have proposed static analysis tools for mandatory access control policies to identify permission assignments that may impact the secrecy and integrity of the system [3, 10, 18, 28]. For example, Jaeger *et al.* identify permission assignments that violate Biba integrity as unsafe [28]. The point of such work to motivate changes in the policy design, but sometimes unsafe permissions are deemed necessary for functional reasons.

More recent work focuses on how applications may misuse the permissions assigned to them [20, 21, 30], such as when a mobile phone app leaks data [19]. Second, researchers have proposed access control models that integrate risk into the access control decision process [9, 11, 13, 31, 37, 42]. Bijon *et al.* [9] examine which relationships in the RBAC model may be made risk-aware and examine constraint-based and metric-based expressions of risk. Chen and Crampton [11] propose to leverage an estimate of the risk that a subject is not trustworthy or a permission assignment is not appropriate in authorizing an operation. However, estimating risk values or defining risks constraints on such concepts involves a significant amount of subjectivity regarding trustworthiness and appropriateness.

In this paper, we explore the problem of tracking the accumulation of risk in access control enforcement. Toward this goal, we are motivated by three types of efforts. First, researchers have demonstrated methods to compute trusted and untrusted resources for each subject [49]. By identifying trusted resources for each subject, we can identify operations that risk integrity for each subject. We will have to develop analogous principles for identifying resources that are secret to a subject. Second, researchers have demonstrated the value of auditing to enforce retrospective policies [50]. Access control cannot produce false positives, which implies that some risky operations may be allowed, but auditing may be leveraged to enforce such operations retrospectively to reduce risk. We explore auditing the risk of authorized, unsafe operations. Third, researchers have shown that risk may accumulate systematically for unsafe operations, as for differential privacy [16]. For each query to a differentially private database, an estimate on the privacy loss incurred by that query operation increments a risk that an adversary may infer the presence of a particular record in the database. In this work, we explore ways to estimate accumulated risk in the context of access control decisions. However, relating accumulated risk to security properties remains future work, as we explore different types of risks that may accumulate due to access control.

Based on these insights, we identify four different types of risks taken in access control: (1) risk due to authorizing unsafe operations; (2) risk due to abuse of authorized permissions; (3) risk due to lack of program context; and (4) risk due to the granularity of authorization hooks. We explore how to identify such risks, ways we may associate risk estimate values with such risks, and issues in computing such risk estimates in practice. We would then envision that access control mechanisms would record risk estimates as they accumulate using auditing both within the programs (to collect inputs for computing risk) and within the access control mechanism (to collect risks regarding enforcement) to enable risk computation. Ideally, accumulated risk may either lead to a denial or at least some change in access control enforcement, such as changes in policies or authorization hook placements, along the lines of preventing violations in differential privacy. Formalizing properties related to risk in access control enforcement in a manner analogous to differential privacy remains future work.

We evaluate our proposed approach to risk estimation in Android systems. First, we use the Android Compatibility Test Suite (CTS) to study risks due to unsafe operations and permission abuse in an Android 6.0.1 system protected by its SEAndroid policy. We find that high integrity Android system processes take only a modest number of risky operations to access data modified by untrusted apps, but each high integrity process accesses some risky objects. Also, we found that no program uses more than 12% of its permissions in CTS operation, indicating that detecting permission abuse may be practical. Second, we computed the risk estimates for ten Android system processes on the same Android system based on events generated by the Android UI/Application Exerciser Monkey. We found that all these processes accumulate a modest amount of risk along each risk dimension (less that 0.1 for our equations), indicating that risk estimates may be useful for comparing relative risks.

In summary, this paper makes the following contributions:

- We identify four risk areas in access control enforcement related to weaknesses in access control policies and weaknesses in how access control is enforced.
- We outline an approach for computing risk estimates and logging such estimates as security-sensitive operations occur that aims for monotonicity of risk over time for each subject and proportionality with respect to impact.
- We evaluate the four risk areas on programs in Android systems, finding that programs generally run with a small, but tangible, risk, which may be used to compare relative risks of programs.

The remainder of the paper is structured as follows. Section 2 describes the four types of risk we identify in access control enforcement. Section 3 specifies the security model we assume when assessing risk. Section 4 outlines our objectives for tracking risk. Section 5 examines runtime risk estimation, proposing techniques for risk estimation and identify challenges in gathering information necessary for risk estimation. Section 6 examines risk estimation in Android systems. Section 7 discusses some issues found in risk estimation. Section 8 concludes the paper.

2 RISKS IN ACCESS CONTROL

The fundamental problem is that choices in both access control enforcement mechanisms and access control policies introduce risk, and that at present we neither track nor react to such risk. As a result, adversaries may be allowed to perform operations that exploit such risks with impunity. Thus, if an adversary can find an exploit for the risks taken in a system deployment, then they may be able to abuse such an exploit persistently, as a so-called *Advanced Persistent Threat* (APT), possibly across many hosts.

We examine four classes of risks in this paper: (1) risk due to the authorization of unsafe operations; (2) risk due to the possible compromise of subjects; (3) risk due to enforcement context; and (4) risk due to the granularity of mediation. While these classes of risk are not entirely independent (e.g., allowing unsafe operations may be a result of the reference monitor design), we examine each class separately in this paper.

2.1 Access Control Enforcement

Before delving into the risks, we review the relevant principles of access control enforcement. Traditionally, access control restricts which subjects (e.g., users and processes) can perform which operations (e.g., read and write) on which objects (e.g., files and database

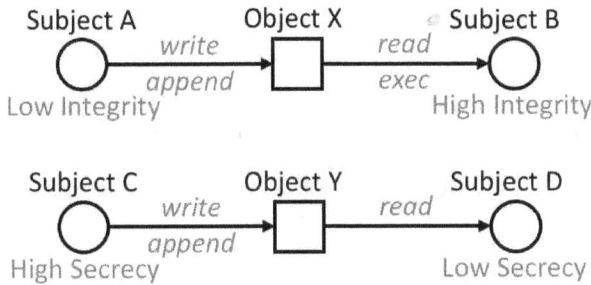

Figure 1: Illegal information flows for integrity and secrecy

records). Programs (e.g., operation system or database) are said to enforce access control using a *reference validation mechanism*. A reference validation mechanism consists of three components: (1) *authorization hooks*, which mediate security-sensitive operations in the program and produce authorization queries identifying the subject, object, and operation to be authorized; (2) *authorization mechanism*, which compares authorization queries to the access control policy to determine the authorization result; and (3) *access control policies*, which define the granted authorization queries.

The *reference monitor concept* [6] proposes three requirements for correct reference validation mechanisms. First, a reference validation mechanism must be non-bypassable. That is, the authorization hooks must mediate access to all security-sensitive operations, which is also called *complete mediation*. Second, the authorization mechanism must be verifiable. That is, it must be possible to test that the reference validation mechanism enforces the expected security policy. Third, the reference validation mechanism and access control policy must be tamperproof to prevent attacks on access control itself. Finally, although not explicitly stated by the reference monitor concept, the access control policy must correctly define the expected security requirements.

One challenge is to identify security-sensitive operations in programs. Researchers have proposed identifying security-sensitive operations via program data flows [15, 36] and control flows [22, 23, 34, 35, 44]. Using data flows, security-sensitive operations occur when a program data flow violates the program's information flow policy. For example, an assignment of a variable with secret data to a variable sent to the public network would be a security-sensitive operation because that data flow would violate an information flow requirement that secret data not be made available to public subjects. Using control flows, researchers have proposed using both syntactic and semantic features of programs to identify security-sensitive operations. One semantic approach [34] identifies security-sensitive operations by data-flow and control-flow "choices" that programs make with untrusted input. For example, if a program uses untrusted input in a conditional, the program makes a control-flow choice based on such untrusted input that should be mediated. Neither approach is perfect, as we would like to proactively mediate operations before information-flow violations (for data flow), but heuristics are currently necessary to identify security-sensitive operations before such violations occur (for control flow).

2.2 Risks of Authorizing Unsafe Operations

While an aim of computer security has long been to prevent the execution of unsafe operations by restricting *information flows* [15] for secrecy [7] and integrity [8] as shown in Figure 1. However, in practice, systems deployments take risks with respect to information flows. When information flow policies are employed, risks are taken in the ad hoc design of declassifiers and endorsers [36] or choice of trusted readers and writers. Most commercial systems employ *least privilege* [43], where the permissions available to each subject are determined by the functionality required of the subject. Researchers have shown that even mandatory access control policies based on least privilege produce integrity risks [28], even for highly privileged processes [10]. We will refer to a permission that violates an information flow constraint as a *unsafe permission*.

Unfortunately, static analysis of access control policies to highlight possible risks has not had a tangible impact on the design of access control policies. We have found that the stock Android policy for the Android 6.0.1 (kernel 3.4.0) version system allows all the high integrity subjects (i.e., those started directly or indirectly by Android kernel subjects) to read, and in some cases even execute, objects that can be modified by low integrity subjects, according to the default SE Android policy. For 57 high integrity subjects identified, they can read or execute 57 object labels that may be written by low integrity subjects in this policy and have over 22,000 permissions that are not available to low integrity subjects. Thus, to prevent unauthorized access by low integrity subjects, we must ensure that high integrity subjects are not compromised when utilizing an object assigned one of these 57 labels controlled by low integrity subjects. However, no systematic approach is taken either to protect the high integrity subjects that use such objects or track the risk created by their use.

In addition, vendors extend the stock Android policy for their own devices. In one vendor's system[1], the number of low integrity object labels accessible to high integrity subjects increases to 240 from 57, and over 100,000 permissions are available to high integrity subjects only. Thus, simply shaming policy designers regarding violations of information flow appears to be an insufficient approach.

More recently, researchers have developed risk models based on a variety of properties of applications, such as application ratings [12, 14] and descriptions [38], in addition to static permission assignments [18, 30, 39]. Such techniques tend to focus on differences between individual applications and average applications, sometimes limited to a specific class of applications. While some malicious applications may be identified as outliers, applications' normal least privilege policies often include permissions that enable a variety of attacks, as described above. Thus, closer tracking of applications' use of their permissions is necessary to detect malice. However, fine-grained tracking, such as dynamic taint tracking [19], incurs an overhead that prevents wide deployment.

2.3 Risks of Permission Abuse

Another problem is that processes may be compromised, and adversaries may utilize the compromised process's permissions freely. In addition, insiders may misuse their authorized permissions to leak information or embed malice in a system. Researchers identified

---

[1]We anonymize the vendor system.

this problem in defining role-based access control (RBAC) models that reason about risk [9, 11]. For example, Chen and Crampton integrate risk thresholds into access control decisions, enabling administrators to utilize knowledge of the trustworthiness of users, competence of users in roles, and the appropriateness of a permission for a role. However, a challenge is to quantify risk for these cases objectively.

An interesting analogue for this problem is the problem of differential privacy. Differential privacy is a method for limiting the risk associated with allowing authorized subjects access to sensitive data [16]. In this case, the sensitive data is a database of individuals' anonymized records, and the intuitive goal is to make the database indistinguishable from another database missing any one individual's records. Functionally, systems that enforce differential privacy [25, 33, 41] limit the queries that may be executed to a total privacy budget. Interestingly, researchers have proven the "cost" of a set of queries in terms of information leaked is bounded by the sum of the costs for each query.

While preventing information leakage is a common goal for both differentially private databases and access control enforcement, our ability to measure when the requests to an access control system have exceed a bound has not yet been formalized. However, methods have been proposed to estimate data leakage. McCammant and Ernst [32] define a method for estimating the amount of information leakage in a program statically, although one must identify which leakages are important.

2.4 Risks in Authorization Context

One challenge in access control enforcement is to restrict subjects to appropriate permissions for the individual requests they make. Typically, access control treats each subject uniformly for all requests. For example, the operating system grants each subject the same set of permissions for any request made.

Such a "black box" approach can lead to two kinds of problems. First, an adversary may try to attack the system using their available permissions, and we may want to limit the adversary to a subset of their permissions based on some contextual knowledge related to the request. For example, ContexIoT [29] aims to limit the permissions available to processes on IoT devices based on the control flow and data flow that led to the request being submitted. In this case, the authors instrument untrusted programs to gather control and data flows that are used in access control enforcement. Second, victims may be protected from compromise if access control enforcement limits the permissions they may use when processing their requests. For example, Jigsaw [47] limits the permissions available to a process when it opens a file to prevent *confused deputy* attacks [26, 40]. If a victim uses input from an adversary to build a file name, the victim is restricted to only access objects available to untrusted parties. Again, knowledge of data flows (e.g., to constructing file names) are used to restrict access.

We find that risk occurs because subjects may have too many permissions available for a particular context. Risk of authorization context occurs because we do not know enough about the program context to reduce the subject's permissions. For example, without program context, we cannot identify the two cases above, where subjects may maliciously or accidentally misuse their permissions.

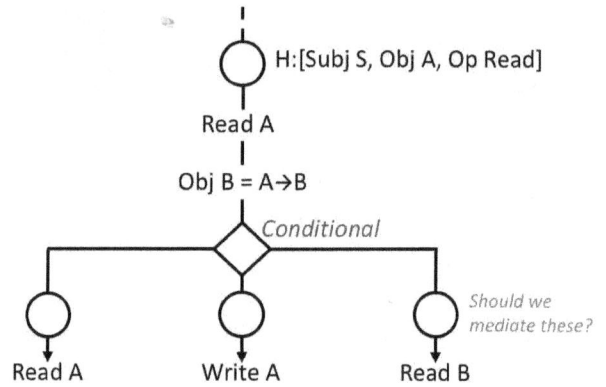

Figure 2: Risks in placing authorization hooks that do not mediate every security-sensitive operation

2.5 Risks in Mediation Granularity

Finally, the assumption that the authorization system mediates all the security-sensitive operations correctly may be flawed, leading to additional risks. A major concern is that an authorization system does not satisfy the *complete mediation* property of the reference monitor concept [6]. When one considers failures in complete mediation, one normally thinks of a security-sensitive operation that may not be mediated by any authorization hook in some execution trace. Such errors have occurred in the deployment of authorization systems [17, 46], but some operations may not require mediation and even mediated operations may be incorrect.

In particular, we find that risks occur because programmers may understand whether operations may allow unauthorized access. Even when an operation is mediated by an authorization hook, this problem may occur for two reasons. First, programmers aim to minimize the number of authorization hooks (e.g., for performance or to keep the policy simpler), so they may only mediate the first security-sensitive operation and assume subsequent operations are protected. Figure 2 shows an example. Suppose that an authorization hook checks whether subjects can read an object A. However, subsequent statements may write to that object or may operate on different objects, such as object B extracted from a field of object A. In general, no subsequent authorization hook is necessary as long as all the subjects authorized for the mediated operation (e.g., read of the object in the example) are also authorized to perform all security-sensitive operations that may directly dominated by that hook [35]. In the example, should some of the authorized subjects for reading object A not be allowed to write object A or not be allowed to access all the objects that may be assigned to object B, then other authorization hooks would be necessary to block those unauthorized accesses while allowing the read operation.

Second, mediation may only be intended to allow limited access to an object. Consider a database where some fields contain secret data. We may authorize a subject to access a record, and even allow updates to a secret field based on such accesses. However, we would want to prevent the values in that secret field from being released publicly (e.g., sent over the network) [4]. Typically, programmers add authorization hooks and sanitizers independently, meaning that there may be a risk of a missing sanitizer even after authorization. In addition, for integrity, Amir-Mohammadian and Skalka [5] prevent victims from using adversary-controlled data without sanitization to augment access control.

3 SECURITY MODEL

In this work, we assume that programmers and system administrators are benign. They may make mistakes in the configuration of access control policies (administrators) or in the enforcement of access control policies (programmers), but they are not active adversaries in the system. We further assume that the systems upon which programs enforcing access control run are able to prevent compromise.

On the other hand, all the processes that make access control requests may be compromised. Some processes may aim to escalate their current privileges by trying to compromise another process with greater access. Others may simply want to exploit permissions already assigned to them (e.g., insiders).

4 RISK MODEL OBJECTIVES

In this paper, we explore the requirement for a system that reasons about the risk incurred during access control enforcement, which covers the four sources of risk described in the problem section: (1) risk due to authorizing unsafe operations; (2) risk due to abuse of authorized permissions; (3) risk due to lack of context; and (4) risk due to the granularity of authorization hooks. To do so, we have to overcome several challenges. First, we aim to capture *real* risks. Static analysis shows possible risks, but does not tell us whether risks actually appear. Second, we aim for risk to be *monotonic* [39]. That is, we aim to identify risks in access control enforcement that add attack options for adversaries, such that the risk value computed must be greater if the risk was taken than if it was not taken. Third, we envision that risky behaviors must be *proportional* to its impact. For example, an action that does not enable any privilege escalation must create a lower risk than an action that does enable privilege escalation. Ideally, we could compute a risk cost for each operation and determine whether that cost is within a risk budget, analogous to differential privacy [16]. Unfortunately, we presently lack the formal foundations of differential privacy in evaluating access control, but perhaps studying how risk may accumulate may lead to insights in the future.

To capture real risks, we propose to compute risk by tracking the dynamic behaviors in program executions. To capture unsafe operations and abuse of authorized permissions, we propose to collect risks associated with these operations as they are authorized. To capture risks from security-sensitive operations that are not explicitly authorized, we collect risks associated with those operations when they are run.

To capture risks monotonically, we propose to separating the accumulation of threats from the risks actually taken by targets. As shown in Figure 1, there is both a threatening operation (e.g., writing to an object used by a high integrity party) and a risky operation (e.g., reading the object by the high integrity party). A *threatening operation* creates a potential for risk by propagating threats from untrusted subjects to objects. The potential risk created by threatening operations accumulates in objects, which we call *object risk*. A *risky operation* occurs when a target subject accesses

(reads or executes) an object that has been threatened, transferring the risk from the object to the target subjects. That is, a threat is not truly a risk until at least one target subject performs a risky operation on a threatened object. Thus, if an object if threatened, but the risk never is taken (e.g., the object is deleted before being accessed), then the threats are not turned into risk for any subject. However, if a risk is taken by a subject, that risk is maintained with the subject even if the threatened object is removed later (e.g., to hide the attack).

To capture risks proportionally, we propose to estimate the value of the risk based on how the risk may impact the victim. For example, we explore estimating risk based on three factors: (1) *the scope of the threat created by adversaries*; (2) *how unique the risk is*; and (3) *how much an adversary may gain from the risk*. First, an adversary may create a larger risk by controlling more data used by the victim. Also, for each threat, we increase the potential for risk based on the uniqueness of the unsafe operation. For example, if very few low integrity subjects can write to a particular object, then we envision that the potential for risk of this subject writing to the object is greater than if many subjects may have the same permission. Third, we assume that a threat that may enable an adversary to gain access to more new privileges should be a higher risk than one that only grants fewer new privileges.

Finally, to compute risk, we propose to collect risk estimate information at runtime. We find that access control enforcement allows many risks to be taken, but if such risks are expected (e.g., receiving a network packet) and infrequent then the risk estimate for the subject should be low. However, modifying programs in an ad hoc manner is complex and error-prone. We envision that program code to collect information for risk estimates at runtime should be generated from declarative specifications, as proposed for auditing code [4]. One concern is the overhead incurred by runtime logging, so we suggest exploring optimizations to compute information statically, such as proposed for ContexIoT [29].

5 RUNTIME RISK ESTIMATION

5.1 Computing Risk Estimates

The idea of computing risk is to record for each threatening operation how much risk is created by the threat. The risk created by threatening operations is accumulated at the object for each threatening operation. Then, when a target subject performs a risky operation, the risk transfers from the object to the subject that invoked the risky operation. A subject's risk then is an accumulation of the risks collected from the threatened objects that that subject accesses.

In theory, if an object utilized (i.e., read or executed when considering integrity) by a subject is fully controlled by an adversary, then the risk faced by that subject is *complete* for that object. However, a complete risk may or may not provide an advantage to an adversary, depending on what an adversary gains from the risk. For integrity violations, we consider the privilege escalation that an adversary may gain from the permissions available to the subject, such as by compromising the subject completely or exploiting its permissions as a confused deputy [26, 40].

Thus, we envision a risk estimation method where a complete risk incurs a risk estimate of 1 and no risk incurs a risk estimate of

0. Given information flow as a motivation, a risk estimate of 0 for a subject would occur if the subject only reads objects that have never had a threatening operation. On the other extreme, a subject that only performs risky operations on objects whose data is fully threatened would incur a risk value of k, where k is the number of objects read and each object has a risk value of 1. To estimate risk between these two extremes, we propose equations that relate the adversary control of an object to the risk of accessing it. The equations presented are strawmen, so the focus should be on the elements that constitute risks.

To capture the proportionality of risk, we modulate the risk estimates by the uniqueness of the threatening operation and the advantage to be gained by the adversary through that operation. First, if a risk can rarely be created, i.e., very few subjects could perform the threatening operation, then we propose that the risk estimate should be increased. Second, if a risk may have a big payout, i.e., enables an untrusted subject to gain access to many or critical privileged permissions, we also propose to increase the risk estimate based on the fraction of privileged permissions that are available to the target subject performing a risky operation. In this paper, we say that *privileged permissions* are permissions not available to any low integrity subject.

Example: Risk Flows between Subjects and Objects. We now demonstrate the proposed approach for risk estimation with a simple example based on Figure 1. Suppose that (low integrity) Subject A contributes 10 bytes to Object X, which consists of 100 bytes altogether. If the remaining 90 bytes are from writes from high integrity subjects, then one could say that Object X's risk estimate is 0.1 (10 bytes out of 100 bytes). When (high integrity) Subject Y reads from Object X, the risk estimate of Subject Y is updated based on the risk estimate of Object X. Suppose that Subject Y only reads or executes Object X, then the risk estimate of Subject Y will be the value of Object X at the time of read (risky) operation, which could be 0.1. We will examine the specific approaches proposed for computing risk estimates for objects and subjects in the remainder of this section.

5.2 Risk Estimation for Unsafe Operations

Unsafe operations are authorized by the existing authorization hooks, so we can update risk estimates when such unsafe operations are authorized. The main challenge is to determine whether an operation is unsafe, and hence either a threatening or risky operation. To do this, the system must have identified the low integrity (high secrecy) and high integrity (low secrecy) subjects in the access control policy. For example, researchers have used knowledge of how system's boot [28] or which subjects may attack the kernel [49] to estimate low and high integrity subjects. Identifying high secrecy subjects is more difficult because a wider variety of subjects and objects contain secret information. We assume that some choice of trusted and untrusted subjects has been made a priori and utilize this knowledge to identify unsafe operations.

However, a second challenge occurs if other threatening operations change the risk estimate of an object while it is in use. Suppose that a high integrity subject and a low integrity subject have a file open concurrently. Thus, if the low integrity subject continues to write the object after the first time the object is read by the high integrity subject, we may compute the risk estimate incorrectly if we only update risk when the open operation occurs. Although authorization may occur at the open operation, we need to be able to update the risk estimate each time an object is used (e.g., read operations).

To compute a risk estimate for unsafe operations, we propose that the risk estimate account for: (1) the *scope* of the threat; (2) the *uniqueness* of the threat; and (3) the *gain* for the adversary in terms of the privilege escalation possible via compromise. For a threatening operation, the scope of the threat may be reflected by the amount of threatening data contained in the object,

$$scope(obj) = x(obj)/d(obj) \tag{1}$$

where: (1) $x(obj)$ is the amount of threatening data (i.e., data written by threatening operations) written to the object and $d(obj)$ is the total amount of data for the object. Presumably, the more adversary-controlled data that a program must process, the greater the risk, although the risk may not be linear as reflected here.

However, the threatening operation may be common, which should reduce the threat of any individual operation, as the more common a threat, the more likely it is to be addressed. Thus, we may want to adjust the risk caused by an unsafe operation in an inverse relationship to the number of subjects who may perform it,

$$uniqueness(obj) = f(potentialThreat(obj)) \tag{2}$$

where f is a function and $potentialThreat(obj)$ is the fraction of threatening subjects that are authorized to write to the object. This term aims to adjust the risk estimate based on the uniqueness of the adversary's ability to create the threat from $f(potentialThreat(obj)) = 0$ (if common) and approximately $f(potentialThreat(obj)) = 1$ (if rare). f could be linear (i.e., $1 - potentialThreat(obj)$), but alternatives may reflect that risks emerge mainly from rare permissions (higher order) or that risk only reduces if a permission is very common. We will explore these alternatives.

Thus, for each object its associated risk is estimated by,

$$risk_{un}(obj) = scope(obj) \times uniqueness(obj) \tag{3}$$

For a subject, we want to produce a risk estimate that reflects the impact of the risky unsafe operations that the subject has performed. For example, a subject's risk estimate may depend on the combination of the risk estimates for the objects that the subject has accessed,

$$risk_{un}(subj) = \sum_{i=1}^{n} max(risk_{un}(obj_i)) \tag{4}$$

where n is the number of objects accessed by the subject. The maximum value is used here for each object to account for the fact that the risk associated with an object may change at each access of the object by the subject. Thus, by using the max we account for the access with the higher risk. An alternative would be to have n be the number of operations, where risk would be summed using the current object risk value. However, that approach may enable an adversary to hide risk, if an object is accessed many times in a safe form.

Finally, the risk to a subject should also factor in the benefit of exploiting the permissions available to the subject. Thus, we suggest multiplying the risk estimate resulting from risky operations by the privilege escalation possible via compromise $potentialGain(subj)$,

$$risk_{un}(subj) = \sum_{i=1}^{n} max(risk_{un}(obj_i)) \times potentialGain(subj) \quad (5)$$

where $potentialGain(subj)$ is the fraction of privileged permissions accessible to the subject. The fraction of the privileged permissions available to a subject indicates the amount of privilege escalation that may be achieved by an adversary, which justifies an adversary trying to exploit the subject. Privileged permissions may include high secrecy and high integrity permissions for resources that must be protected in the system.

These risk equations leave open the question of which bytes in a file currently may have originated from a threatening operation or a safe operation. The problem is that both threatening and safe data may be overwritten, so all the prior threatening (or safe) data may have been removed or at least reduced. Tracking file taint per byte may be expensive, but simply tracking the amount of data written can be straightforward since we can simply log these operations. We will conservatively assume that all the threatening data written remains in the file, and explore this problem further in future work.

5.3 Risk Estimation for Permission Abuse

In this section, the challenge is to map the threatening and risky operations to operations performed by a subject with their own permissions. In this case, the threat is due to sensitive data defined by or protected by a high integrity subject that may be tampered with or leaked should that subject be compromised or be a malicious insider. Thus, we must identify threatening and risky operations, and determine how to compute risk estimates for each.

In this case, we view threats as being the operations that cause data to be sensitive. If some subject adds sensitive data to an object that can be accessed by a target subject, then we want to measure how much of this sensitive data each target subject may put at risk by accessing those objects. However, programmers do not explicitly identify sensitive information, so we need a way to detect operations that cause an object to become sensitive. A simplistic approach is to assume that all the data of each object available to a subject is sensitive. We can mitigate the impact of the threat by determining if adding data to the resource is a common operation. If so, it is likely the data is less sensitive.

As a result, the risk estimate for objects related to permission abuse is calculated as follows,

$$risk_{ab}(obj) = scope(obj) \times actualThreat(obj) \quad (6)$$

where: (1) $scope(obj)$ is again the fraction of sensitive data written in the object (which may be assumed to be 1 in some cases) and (2) $actualThreat(obj)$ estimates the sensitivity of the object based on the fraction of subjects that wrote (read) the object for integrity (for secrecy). We plan to track the amount of data produced by threatening operations x as described above, but the challenge is to estimate which operations produce sensitive information. To do this we propose to leverage the commonality of access to the data, where a higher commonality reduces the risk of permission abuse. For integrity, the higher the fraction of subjects that can write to the object, then the lower the sensitivity of the object. Since few objects may be written (read) by all subjects, the estimate for $actualThreat(obj)$ may be normalized to fill more of the range between 0 and 1 (e.g., use the maximum fraction of subjects).

Risky operations occur when a subject uses its permissions to access a threatened object. We propose that the risk estimate for subjects abusing permissions is calculated as follows,

$$risk_{ab}(subj) = \sum_{i=1}^{n} max(risk_{ab}(obj_i)) \times actualGain(subj) \quad (7)$$

where $max(risk_{ab}(obj_i))$ is the maximum value of object i's risk estimate across all accesses so far by the subject upon this object. The function $actualGain(subj)$ adjusts the risk sum by the fraction of sensitive permissions that the subject has utilized. The $actualGain$ term captures the level of abuse across all the sensitive data in a system.

5.4 Risk Estimation for Authorization Context

Other risks occur because of the difficulty in predicting which permissions to authorize in which program execution contexts. First, malicious programs may abuse the permissions that they are granted and request permissions that are not relevant to the execution context to spy on users or leak information. Second, programs may fall victim to attacks that trick them into using their privileged permissions on behalf of adversaries, in the so-called *confused deputy attacks* [26, 40]. Finally, the party performing authorization (e.g., operating system or server program) typically does not track the execution context of a program requesting permissions. Thus, traditional access control does not identify such abuses.

In general, risks of malicious programs or confused deputy attacks because access control enforcement does not consider program context occur because the program may access different objects through the same system call invocation. Researchers have found that while programs may access lots of different objects, several system calls only access a small number of objects and only access objects with similar properties. Vijayakumar [48] found that 67% of the statements that invoked system calls to retrieve an object (e.g., calls to the libc function open) retrieve only one object in the programs in a LAMP stack (i.e., Apache, MySQL, and PHP). 78% of the statements retrieved objects of only one SELinux label. Thus, risk estimate due to the objects retrieved $risk_{re}(subj)$ should be based on the variance in security properties of objects retrieved,

$$risk_{re}(subj) = \sum_{k=1}^{m} classes(subj, stmt_k) \times actualGain(subj) \quad (8)$$

where m is the number of system call statements and *classes* is the fraction of classes of objects associated with a particular statement that retrieves objects for that subject ($stmt_k$). Classes of objects can be based on the object name (one or more), label (one or more), secrecy and integrity classification. In general, the worst case occurs when a subject has a single statement that may retrieve a variety of objects that differ in their security classifications (e.g., high and low integrity as well as high and low secrecy). In such a case, the program has to determine how to enforce a variety of security requirements itself, creating more risk.

Another aspect of risk is the way that the program gathers the information that leads to system calls that retrieve or access system objects. Researchers have explored methods that collect control flows and data flows, as well as detect particular operations, such as filtering, to judge whether to allow a program to perform a particular system call [29, 47]. For example, the complexity of the control and data flows that lead to a particular system call statement in terms of the size of these flows may be indicative of risk,

$$risk_{flow}(subj) = \sum_{k=1}^{m} flow(subj, stmt_k) \times actualGain(subj) \quad (9)$$

where *flow* computes a risk estimate based on the complexity of the control and data flows that produced the inputs to the statement. The complexity should be normalized (between 0 and 1) to be consistent with other risk values. Computing risk estimates from flows will require the application of static analysis tools to collect such information at runtime. Thus, we will defer calculation of such risk to future work.

5.5 Risk Estimation for Mediation Granularity

Recall that risks due to mediation granularity are caused because a programmer chooses not to directly mediate some security-sensitive operations. We find that computing risk estimates related to mediation granularity is essentially the same as computing the risk estimate for unsafe operations, as described above. The difference is that the administrators do not specify policy for unmediated operations, so the main challenges are to identify which unmediated security-sensitive operations are unsafe and how many untrusted subjects can perform threatening operations. In addition, identifying security-sensitive operations is itself an imprecise process that induces risk.

An operation is unsafe if it causes an illegal information flow as shown in Figure 1. Threatening operations occur when untrusted subjects actually access objects that may be accessible to trusted subjects. Although we lack a policy to determine whether a trusted subject may be able to access an unmediated object explicitly, we can record risk estimates for all unmediated objects accessed by untrusted subjects. We envision that programs would record risk estimates for objects accessed in unsafe, unmediated security-sensitive operations in the same way as described in Section 5.2.

Risky operations transfer the objects risk estimate to the subject that has taken the risk, as for unsafe operations. One question is how to estimate the impact of privilege escalation given that we are tracking objects for which there is no explicit authorization policy. One simple approach would be to simply use the privilege escalation possible in the specified access control policy alone, although this misses the possible escalation in unmediated security-sensitive operations. Researchers need to develop methods to extrapolate policies for unmediated operations to estimate where escalation is possible.

Finally, as mentioned in Section 2.1, identifying security-sensitive operations itself induces risk. First, both data-flow and control-flow methods require programmers to manually identify untrusted and secret inputs, which itself is error-prone [34, 45]. Second, the computation of security-sensitive operations using control flow involves heuristics and the resolution of information-flow violations using data flow involves possible imperfect sanitizers. Again, we must log information necessary to compute risk estimates and determine how such inaccuracies may impact risk estimation.

We propose to estimate the risk for mediation granularity as follows,

$$risk_{me}(subj) = \sum_{i=1}^{n} max(risk_{un}(obj_i)) \times SSO_{unmed}(subj) \quad (10)$$

where $SSO_{unmed}(subj)$ is the fraction of unmediated security-sensitive operations (SSOs). We identify three types of unmediated SSOs: (1) "open" SSOs that are not control-flow dominated by any authorization hook on any control-flow path leading to those SSOs; (2) "partial" SSOs that are control-flow dominated by an authorization hook on some, but not all, control-flow paths leading to those SSOs; and (3) "dominated" SSOs that are control-flow dominated along all control-flow paths leading to those SSOs. We consider the dominated SSOs to be the least risky, although because these operations are not directly associated with an authorization hook they may still incur risk. Interestingly, we consider "open" SSOs to be less risky than "partial" SSOs, because an open SSO may legitimately be accessible to all subjects or not actually access security-sensitive resources. On the other hand, a "partial" SSO is expected to be mediated along some paths. Thus, we propose to compute $SSO_{unmed}(subj)$ as a combination of the three types of unmediated operations, where their fractions are augmented by multiplicative factors α, β and γ, for dominated, open, and partial, respectively. In addition, we require that $\alpha < \beta < \gamma$ to account for their relative levels of risk.

6 EXPERIENCES WITH RISK

In this section, we examine experimental results in computing risk estimates for access control enforcement. Primarily, we evaluate use of the risk estimate equations proposed in Section 5 on Android systems. The main question that we aim to answer is whether the inputs to risk estimation described above may actually be computed in practice and what the inputs currently look like for benign system operation.

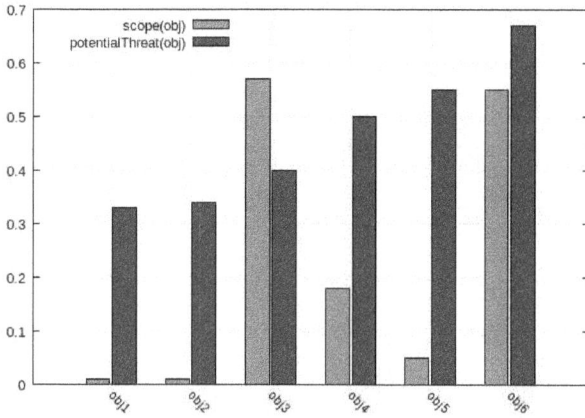

Figure 3: Scope and fraction of threatening subjects (potential threat) for the six untrusted objects accessed by the `mediaserver`

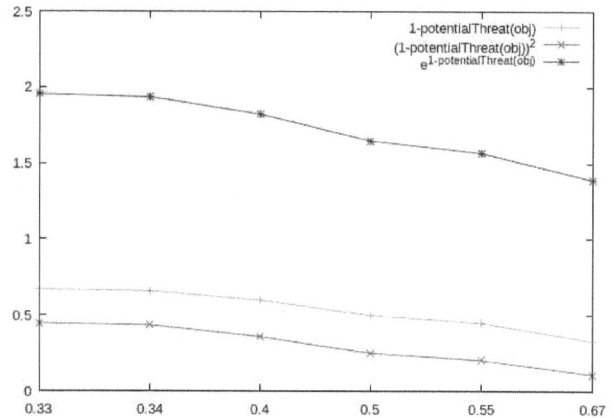

Figure 4: Uniqueness values for the six untrusted objects accessed by the `mediaserver`, plotted for three different choices of the f function: $f_1(obj) = 1 - potentialThreat(obj)$, $f_2(obj) = e^{1-potentialThreat(obj)}$, and $f_3(obj) = (1-potentialThreat(obj))^2$

6.1 Experiences with Unsafe Operations

Regarding tracking unsafe operations, we examined a stock Android policy for the Android 6.0.1 (kernel 3.4.0) version. To determine how many unsafe operations are performed, we utilize the Android Compatibility Test Suite (CTS) [2]. CTS is designed to reveal functional incompatibilities between applications and the Android system. CTS runs unit tests to test for incompatibilities. Using CTS, we ran 127,058 tests over 20 hours and 44 minutes. The access control policy is enforced by SEAndroid.

What we see in Android is that for 1,264,978 operations there are 926,491 operations that are threatening operations, but only 445 operations that are risky operations. While this may appear surprising, CTS creates a factor of 10 more write-like operations than read-like operations. That is, while the untrusted subjects may perform a wide variety of operations that may threaten privileged, high-integrity subjects, the high-integrity subjects only use risk operations for a very small fraction of their authorized operations. Thus, most of the risk estimate computation effort would apply to threatening operations. Future risk estimation methods should focus on low-overhead for threatening operations and put more effort for assessing risky operations.

Furthermore, we examined a macrobenchmark of 15 system apps shipped with the stock Android operating system for the Android 6.0.1 (kernel 3.4.0) version. We used the Android UI/Application Exerciser Monkey [1] to target sensitive operations and automatically generate sequences of input events.

From the data collected via the UI/Application Exerciser we calculated the risk taken by 10 Android processes selected among those implementing core features of the operating system. The selected processes are listed in column 1 of Table 1, whereas the corresponding calculated risk for unsafe operations ($risk_{un}$) is listed in column 5 of Table 1.

To calculate such values of risk we adopted equation (5). In particular, we started by measuring the scope of all untrusted object accessed by each process as per equation (1), and the fraction of subjects that are authorized to write to such object. For example,

Figure 3 plots the measured values for the 6 untrusted objects accessed by the `mediaserver` process, as reported in column 2 of Table 1. As one can see, adversaries often control a small amount of data in threatened objects (scope), but few enough subjects can exercise the threat to make that estimate significant (potentialThreat).

For our experimental measurements, we have considered as untrusted objects all files that can be written by low-integrity processes, which were identified as the complement of the transitive closure of transition rules for subject types starting with the `kernel` label. Such choice is motivated by the fact that after the kernel is loaded during the boot process, the initial process is assigned the predefined initial SELinux ID `kernel`, which is used for bootstrapping before the policy is loaded.

We then proceeded with the calculation of the uniqueness value, which we used to calculate the risk reported in column 5 of Table 1, for such objects by adopting equation (2). Figure 4 plots the measured values for the 6 untrusted objects accessed by the `mediaserver` process by considering three alternative choices for the f function to model a linear, a polynomial, and an exponential dependency of the uniqueness factor from the potential threat.

6.2 Experiences with Permission Abuse

As shown in Table 2, using CTS again over the stock Android policy we found that no trusted subject uses more than 143 of their permissions (su) or greater than 12% of their permissions (system_server). As a result, permission use greater than about 20% may be considered unusual. Thus, we may want to adjust the risk estimation approach from a linear approach to one that accelerates risk at lower fractions. Alternatively, we may compare permission use to an average over a period of time.

Furthermore, from the data collected via the UI/Application Exerciser, we calculated the risk taken by 10 Android processes when considering possible permission abuse ($risk_{ab}$) as listed in column 6 of Table 1. To calculate such values of risk we adopted equation (7). In particular, we started by measuring the fraction

Table 1: Risk measurements for the ten core Android processes. We report the untrusted objects and the unmediated security sensitive operations (SSOs) as fractions of the total number of objects and total number of SSOs respectively

Subject	Untrusted Objects	Call Sites	Unmediated SSOs	$risk_{un}$	$risk_{ab}$	$risk_{re}$	$risk_{me}$
mediaserver	6/115	6	17/334	0.0246	0.0031	0.0626	0.0417
init	2/96	18	5/145	0.03	0.0164	0.0299	0.0259
main	8/1,122	8	18/2,511	0.0234	0.035	0.0039	0.0028
activitymanager	9/7,650	11	45/27,552	0.012	0.0057	0.0013	0.0005
servicemanager	1/568	8	2/1,018	0.0105	0.0053	0.0005	0.0007
surfaceflinger	1/5	4	4/55	0.0019	0.0002	0.008	0.0705
keystore	1/24	5	8/129	0.0077	0.0019	0.002	0.0477
netd	8/48	10	7/130	0.0176	0.0039	0.0667	0.0473
rild	1/3	2	1/10	0.0297	0.0002	0.03	0.099
sdcard	1/104	8	4/409	0.008	0.0098	0.0023	0.0039

Table 2: Permissions usage information for a run of the Android Compatibility Test Suite for the top ten subjects (by number of permissions)

Subject	Used Permissions	Total Permissions	Fract. of Used Permissions
su	143	1,983	0.07
dumpstate	96	1,237	0.08
system_server	92	787	0.12
system_app	26	468	0.06
radio	18	531	0.03
nfc	16	406	0.04
bluetooth	15	497	0.03
mediaserver	14	655	0.02
shell	5	1,272	< 0.01
surfaceflinger	5	329	0.01

Table 3: Evolution in authorization hook counts for X Windows. Manually placed hooks are compared to "Automated Hooks" generated using a proposed method [34]

XServer versions	Automated Hooks	Manual Hooks
1.7	278	186
1.8	280	186
1.9	276	181
1.10	272	180
1.11	284	180
1.12	312	207
1.13	333	206
1.14	333	206
1.15	317	207
1.16	310	207
1.17	334	207

of sensitive data in each object $scope(obj)$ again calculated as the amount of data written by low-integrity subjects to the object. We then measured the sensitivity of the object $sensitivity(obj)$ as fraction of subjects that can write the object. By following equation (6) we obtained the risk estimate for each object related to permission abuse. We then used such estimate to calculate the corresponding risk for each of the subjects accessing the object by following equation (7).

6.3 Experiences with Authorization Context

The data collected via the UI/Application Exerciser also allowed us to calculate the risk taken by the 10 Android processes when considering their authorization context while retrieving objects ($risk_{re}$). The measurements are listed in column 7 of Table 1. To calculate such values of risk we adopted equation (8). In particular, we identified all the call sites (or system call statements) used by each of the 10 processes when accessing untrusted objects. We enumerated them in column 3 of Table 1. We then calculated $classes(subj, stmt_k)$ as 1 plus the fraction of trusted object labels times the fraction of untrusted object labels (over the total objects labels specified in the policy) seen at call site k when retrieving untrusted objects. This is in line with the intuition that the risk increases if the subject access

a higher number of untrusted objects, and increases even further if the subject also accesses a set of trusted objects.

Also, our findings are in line with previous research [29] reporting that the number of operations requested per application in a particular context on average is only 3.5 with no more than 30 contexts being seen. Again, this runtime analysis may be prone to false positives. However, one can see that while restricting permissions available in individual contexts may lead to program failures (due to blocking necessary permissions), risk may be limited to only a small number operations because only a few program contexts require risk and only a small fraction of the program contexts are complex and/or variable.

6.4 Experiences with Mediation Granularity

As shown in Table 3, developers often have difficulty determining the correct placement of authorization hooks for their programs. As can be seen, the actual number of authorization hooks in X Windows varied slightly with each version, excepting between versions 1.11 and 1.12 where a significant change was made to the program. Also, we compare the number of hooks placed manually to the number of security-sensitive operations computed using a control-flow method [35]. As one can see, there is not a clear correlation between changes in the number of hooks placed manually and changes in the number of security-sensitive operations identified automatically.

Additionally, we calculated the risk taken by the ten core Android processes when considering their mediation granularity in security sensitive operations, shown as the $risk_{me}$ column in Table 1. We define the security-sensitive operations in this study as those operations that operate on data types considered security sensitive, such as files, sockets, and databases. Using data types to identify security-sensitive operations has been a common approach [24].

In our study, such operations are said to be "unmediated" if they were not preceded by a permission check (either SELinux or Android permission check) in the most enclosing control block. We then classify the unmediated operations using a static control-flow analysis to detect whether the operation is mediated along all control-flow paths (dominated), no control-flow paths (open), and some control-flow paths (partial). We set the risk factor of each type, α, β, and γ to the values 1, 2, and 3, respectively, for application of equation (10).

7 DISCUSSION

We note that the risks computed in this evaluation are examples of "baseline" risks, not risks under attack conditions. Programs are run in a benign manner, so the risk values computed are modest in many cases. None of the programs evaluated in Table 1 incur a risk estimate of over 0.1 for any of the four categories.

An aim of using risk estimates would be to use accumulated risk to motivate changes in security posture, analogous to using accumulated privacy cost to block queries in differential privacy. However, at present, we lack a definition of security risk that precisely describes a security property as meaningful as differential privacy. We advocate comparing accumulated risk of one system or program to that system or program under conditionals that comply with safe, expected use to identify when risk estimates differ by more than an expected amount as a basis for adjusting security decision-making. By identifying dimensions upon which risk may be tracked and proposing strawman risk estimates that accumulate, we hope to further investigate how risk estimates may relate to security properties in the future.

Finally, the focus of this research should primarily be on the types of risk related to authorization, one type of security mechanism. We propose simple equations for each type of risk, but much more work will be necessary to devise equations that capture expected security properties.

8 CONCLUSIONS

In this paper, we present a study of risk in access control enforcement. While we have long had principles describing how access control enforcement should be implemented, imprecision in access control mechanisms and access control policies leads to risks that may enable exploitation. We identify four types of risk in access control enforcement, two that relate to access control policies and two that relate to access control mechanisms. We propose an approach for estimating risk as subjects perform operations. At a

high level, the approach aims to leverage tracking of information directed at risk estimation and the development of risk estimation approaches that are monotonic and account for the impact of risks proportionally. We examine challenges in implementation such risk estimation for the four types of risks. Our evaluation shows that in normal use programs due not take excessive risks for the programs we investigated directly under benign use conditions. Thus, it may be possible to use such risk estimation to gauge when defenses should be added (e.g., more authorization hooks) and/or operations should be blocked or audited more carefully (e.g., tighter access control policies) when seeing an excessive or increased accumulation of risk. We propose using the scope, uniqueness, and gain possible via risk as principles underlying risk estimation, although a formal definition of a risk property for access control remains future work.

ACKNOWLEDGEMENTS

This research was sponsored by the Army Research Laboratory and was accomplished under Cooperative Agreement Number W911NF-13-2-0045 (ARL Cyber Security CRA). The views and conclusions contained in this document are those of the authors and should not be interpreted as representing the official policies, either expressed or implied, of the Army Research Laboratory or the U.S. Government. The U.S. Government is authorized to reproduce and distribute reprints for Government purposes notwithstanding any copyright notation hereon.

This research is also based in part upon work supported by the National Science Foundation (NSF) under Grant Numbers CNS-1408880 and CNS-1408801. Any opinions, findings, and conclusions or recommendations expressed in this material are those of the author(s) and do not necessarily reflect the views of the National Science Foundation.

REFERENCES

[1] Android UI/Application Exerciser. https://developer.android.com/studio/test/monkey.html.
[2] Compatibility Test Suite — Android Open Source Project. https://source.android.com/compatibility/cts/.
[3] Tresys. SETools - Policy Anakysis Tools for SELinux. https://github.com/TresysTechnology/setools3/wiki.
[4] Sepehr Amir-Mohammadian, Stephen Chong, and Christian Skalka. 2016. Correct Audit Logging: Theory and Practice. In *Principles of Security and Trust (POST)*.
[5] Sepehr Amir-Mohammadian and Christian Skalka. 2016. In-Depth Enforcement of Dynamic Integrity Taint Analysis. In *ACM Programming Languages and Security Workshop (PLAS)*.
[6] J. P. Anderson. 1972. *Computer Security Technology Planning Study, Volume II*. Technical Report ESD-TR-73-51. Deputy for Command and Management Systems, HQ Electronics Systems Division (AFSC), L. G. Hanscom Field, Bedford, MA.
[7] D. E. Bell and L. J. LaPadula. 1976. *Secure Computer System: Unified Exposition and Multics Interpretation*. Technical Report ESD-TR-75-306. Deputy for Command and Management Systems, HQ Electronic Systems Division (AFSC), L. G. Hanscom Field, Bedford, MA.
[8] K. J. Biba. 1977. *Integrity Considerations for Secure Computer Systems*. Technical Report MTR-3153. MITRE.
[9] Khalid Zaman Bijon, Ram Krishnan, and Ravi S. Sandhu. 2013. A framework for risk-aware role based access control. In *IEEE Conference on Communications and Network Security*. 462–469.
[10] Hong Chen, Ninghui Li, and Ziqing Mao. 2009. Analyzing and Comparing the Protection Quality of Security Enhanced Operating Systems. In *Proceedings of the Network and Distributed Systems Security Symposium (NDSS)*.
[11] Liang Chen and Jason Crampton. 2011. Risk-Aware Role-Based Access Control. In *Proceedings of 7th International Workshop on Security and Trust Management*. 140–156.

[12] Ying Chen, Heng Xu, Yilu Zhou, and Sencun Zhu. 2013. Is This App Safe for Children?: A Comparison Study of Maturity Ratings on Android and iOS Applications. In *Proceedings of the 22nd International Conference on World Wide Web*. 201–212.

[13] Pau-Chen Cheng, Pankaj Rohatgi, Claudia Keser, Paul A. Karger, Grant M. Wagner, and Angela Schuett Reninger. 2007. Fuzzy Multi-Level Security: An Experiment on Quantified Risk-Adaptive Access Control.. In *Proceedings of the 2007 IEEE Symposium on Security and Privacy*. 222–230.

[14] Pern Hui Chia, Yusuke Yamamoto, and N. Asokan. 2012. Is This App Safe?: A Large Scale Study on Application Permissions and Risk Signals. In *Proceedings of the 21st International Conference on World Wide Web*. 311–320.

[15] D. Denning. 1976. A Lattice Model of Secure Information Flow. *Commun. ACM* 19, 5 (1976), 236–242.

[16] Cynthia Dwork and Aaron Roth. 2014. The Algorithmic Foundations of Differential Privacy. 9, 3 (2014), 211–407.

[17] Antony Edwards, Trent Jaeger, and Xiaolan Zhang. 2002. Runtime verification of authorization hook placement for the Linux security modules framework. In *Proceedings of the 9th ACM Conference on Computer and Communications Security*. 225–234.

[18] William Enck, Machigar Ongtang, and Patrick McDaniel. 2009. On lightweight mobile phone application certification. In *Proceedings of the 16th ACM Conference on Computer and Communications Security*. ACM, New York, NY, USA, 235–245. DOI:http://dx.doi.org/10.1145/1653662.1653691

[19] W. Enck et al. 2010. TaintDroid: an information-flow tracking system for realtime privacy monitoring on smartphones. In *Proceedings of the 9th USENIX conference on Operating systems design and implementation*.

[20] Adrienne Porter Felt, Erika Chin, Steve Hanna, Dawn Song, and David Wagner. 2011. Android permissions demystified. In *Proceedings of the 18th ACM Conference on Computer and Communications Security*. 627–638.

[21] Earlence Fernandes, Jaeyeon Jung, and Atul Prakash. 2016. Security Analysis of Emerging Smart Home Applications. In *IEEE Symposium on Security and Privacy*. 636–654.

[22] V. Ganapathy, T. Jaeger, and S. Jha. 2005. Automatic placement of authorization hooks in the Linux security modules framework. In *Proceedings of the 12th ACM Conference on Computer and Communications Security*. Alexandria, VA, USA.

[23] V. Ganapathy, T. Jaeger, and S. Jha. 2006. Retrofitting Legacy Code for Authorization Policy Enforcement. In *Proceedings of the 2006 IEEE Symposium on Security and Privacy*. To Appear.

[24] Vinod Ganapathy, David H. King, Trent Jaeger, and Somesh Jha. 2007. Mining security-sensitive operations in legacy code using concept analysis. In *Proceedings of the 38th International Conference on Software Engineering*. 458–467.

[25] Andreas Haeberlen, Benjamin C. Pierce, and Arjun Narayan. 2011. Differential Privacy Under Fire. In *Proceedings of the 20th USENIX Security Symposium*.

[26] N. Hardy. 1988. The Confused Deputy. *Operating Systems Review* 22 (1988), 36–38.

[27] Boniface Hicks, Sandra Rueda, Trent Jaeger, and Patrick McDaniel. 2007. From trusted to secure: building and executing applications that enforce system security. In *Proceedings of the USENIX Annual Technical Conference*. USENIX Association, Berkeley, CA, USA, 1–14.

[28] T. Jaeger, R. Sailer, and X. Zhang. 2003. Analyzing Integrity Protection in the SELinux Example Policy. In *Proceedings of the 12th USENIX Security Symposium*. 59–74.

[29] Yunhan Jack Jia, Qi Alfred Chen, Shiqi Wang, Amir Rahmati, Earlence Fernandes, Z. Morley Mao, and Atul Prakash. 2017. ContexIoT: Towards Providing Contextual Integrity to Appified IoT Platforms. In *Proceedings of the 21st Network and Distributed System Security Symposium (NDSS'17)*.

[30] Yiming Jing, Gail-Joon Ahn, Ziming Zhao, and Hongxin Hu. 2014. RiskMon: Continuous and Automated Risk Assessment of Mobile Applications. In *Proceedings of the 4th ACM Conference on Data and Application Security and Privacy*. 99–110.

[31] Savith Kandala, Ravi S. Sandhu, and Venkata Bhamidipati. 2011. An Attribute Based Framework for Risk-Adaptive Access Control Models. In *Proceedings of the Sixth International Conference on Availability, Reliability and Security*. 236–241.

[32] Stephen McCamant and Michael D. Ernst. 2008. Quantitative information flow as network flow capacity. In *Proceedings of the ACM SIGPLAN 2008 Conference on Programming Language Design and Implementation*. Tucson, AZ, USA, 193–205.

[33] Frank D. McSherry. 2009. Privacy Integrated Queries: An Extensible Platform for Privacy-preserving Data Analysis. In *Proceedings of the 2009 ACM SIGMOD International Conference on Management of Data*. 19–30.

[34] Divya Muthukumaran, Trent Jaeger, and Vinod Ganapathy. 2012. Leveraging "Choice" to Automate Authorization Hook Placement. In *Proceedings of the 19th ACM Conference on Computer and Communications Security*. ACM Press, Raleigh, North Carolina, USA.

[35] Divya Muthukumaran, Nirupama Talele, Trent Jaeger, and Gang Tan. 2015. Producing Hook Placements to Enforce Expected Access Control Policies. In *Proceedings of the 2015 International Symposium on Engineering Secure Software and Systems*.

[36] Andrew C. Myers and Barbara Liskov. 1997. A Decentralized Model for Information Flow Control. *ACM Operating Systems Review* 31, 5 (Oct. 1997), 129–142. http://www.cs.cornell.edu/andru/papers/iflow-sosp97/paper.html

[37] Qun Ni, Elisa Bertino, and Jorge Lobo. 2010. Risk-based Access Control Systems Built on Fuzzy Inferences. In *Proceedings of the 5th ACM Symposium on Information, Computer and Communications Security*. 250–260.

[38] Rahul Pandita, Xusheng Xiao, Wei Yang, William Enck, and Tao Xie. 2013. WHYPER: Towards Automating Risk Assessment of Mobile Applications. In *Proceedings of the 22nd USENIX Security Symposium*. 527–542.

[39] Hao Peng, Chris Gates, Bhaskar Sarma, Ninghui Li, Yuan Qi, Rahul Potharaju, Cristina Nita-Rotaru, and Ian Molloy. 2012. Using Probabilistic Generative Models for Ranking Risks of Android Apps. In *Proceedings of the 2012 ACM Conference on Computer and Communications Security*. 241–252.

[40] Giuseppe Petracca, Yuqiong Sun, Trent Jaeger, and Ahmad Atamli. 2015. Audroid: Preventing attacks on audio channels in mobile devices. In *Proceedings of the 31st Annual Computer Security Applications Conference*. ACM, 181–190.

[41] Indrajit Roy, Srinath T. V. Setty, Ann Kilzer, Vitaly Shmatikov, and Emmett Witchel. 2010. Airavat: Security and Privacy for MapReduce. In *Proceedings of the 7th USENIX Conference on Networked Systems Design and Implementation*.

[42] Farzad Salim, Jason Reid, Ed Dawson, and Uwe Dulleck. 2011. An Approach to Access Control under Uncertainty. In *Proceedings of the Sixth International Conference on Availability, Reliability and Security*. 1–8.

[43] J. H. Saltzer et al. 1975. The Protection of Information in Computer Systems. *Proc. IEEE* (1975).

[44] Sooel Son, Kathryn S. McKinley, and Vitaly Shmatikov. 2011. RoleCast: finding missing security checks when you do not know what checks are. In *Proceedings of the 2011 ACM international conference on Object oriented programming systems languages and applications*.

[45] Sooel Son, Kathryn S. McKinley, and Vitaly Shmatikov. 2013. Fix Me Up: Repairing Access-Control Bugs in Web Applications. In *Proceedings of the 20th Annual Network and Distributed System Security Symposium*.

[46] Lin Tan, Xiaolan Zhang, Xiao Ma, Weiwei Xiong, and Yuanyuan Zhou. 2008. AutoISES: automatically inferring security specifications and detecting violations. In *USENIX Security*.

[47] Hayawardh Vijayakumar, Xinyang Ge, Mathias Payer, and Trent Jaeger. 2014. JIGSAW: Protecting Resource Access by Inferring Programmer Expectations. In *Proceedings of the 23rd USENIX Security Symposium*.

[48] Hayawardh Vijayakumar and Trent Jaeger. 2012. The Right Files at the Right Time. In *Proceedings of the 5th IEEE Symposium on Configuration Analytics and Automation (SafeConfig 2012)*.

[49] Hayawardh Vijayakumar et al. 2012. Integrity Walls: Finding attack surfaces from mandatory access control policies. In *ASIACCS*.

[50] Wen Zhang, You Chen, Thaddeus Cybulski, Daniel Fabbri, Carl Gunter, Patrick Lawlor, David Liebovitz, and Bradley Malin. 2014. Decide Now or Decide Later?: Quantifying the Tradeoff Between Prospective and Retrospective Access Decisions. In *Proceedings of the 2014 ACM SIGSAC Conference on Computer and Communications Security*. 1182–1192.

FACT: Functionality-centric Access Control System for IoT Programming Frameworks

Sanghak Lee
POSTECH
uzbu89@postech.ac.kr

Jiwon Choi
POSTECH
wldnjs7@postech.ac.kr

Jihun Kim
POSTECH
jihun735@postech.ac.kr

Beumjin Cho
POSTECH
beumjincho@postech.ac.kr

Sangho Lee
Georgia Tech.
sangho@gatech.edu

Hanjun Kim
POSTECH
hanjun@postech.ac.kr

Jong Kim
Pohang University of Science and
Technology (POSTECH)
jkim@postech.ac.kr

ABSTRACT

Improvement in the security and availability is important for the success of the Internet of Things (IoT). Given that recent IoT devices are likely to have multiple functionalities and support third-party applications, this goal becomes challenging to achieve. Through an in-depth investigation of existing IoT frameworks, we focused on two inherent security flaws in their design caused by their device-centric approaches: (1) coarse-grained access control and (2) lack of resource isolation. Because of the coarse-grained access control, IoT devices suffer from over-privileged applications. Furthermore, the lack of resource isolation allows the possibility of Denial-of-Service attacks.

In this paper, we propose a functionality-centric approach to managing IoT devices, called FACT, which has two design goals, namely, the principle of least privilege and the availability in terms of device functionalities. FACT isolates each functionality of the device using Linux Containers and grants a subject the privilege to access for each required functionality. We provide the overall framework and detailed working procedures between components that constitute FACT. We built a prototype of FACT on IoTivity and show that it accomplishes secure and efficient linkages between applications and functionalities of IoT devices through analysis and experiments.

CCS CONCEPTS

• **Security and privacy** → **Trust frameworks**; **Access control**; Denial-of-service attacks;

SACMAT'17, June 21–23, 2017, Indianapolis, IN, USA
© 2017 ACM. ACM ISBN 978-1-4503-4702-0/17/06. . . $15.00
DOI: http://dx.doi.org/10.1145/3078861.3078864

KEYWORDS

Internet of Things; Functionality-centric; Access control; Over-privileged application; Denial-of-Service

ACM Reference format:
Sanghak Lee, Jiwon Choi, Jihun Kim, Beumjin Cho, Sangho Lee, Hanjun Kim, and Jong Kim. 2017. FACT: Functionality-centric Access Control System for IoT Programming Frameworks. In *Proceedings of SACMAT'17, June 21–23, 2017, Indianapolis, IN, USA*, , 12 pages.
DOI: http://dx.doi.org/10.1145/3078861.3078864

1 INTRODUCTION

The Internet of Things (IoT) has emerged as a leading technology, and the scale of its expansion is overwhelming. It is only a matter of time until connecting every device to the Internet would become natural. The International Data Corporation (IDC) forecasts that 28 billion IoT devices (or things)[1] will be installed by 2020 [19]. Many companies (e.g., Google, Samsung, and Qualcomm) establish their frameworks and standards (e.g., AllJoyn, Android Things, IoTivity, and SmartThings), and release various IoT devices to dominate the IoT market [27].

Security is one of the most important requirements of the IoT systems. Among the 184 requirements issued by Internet of Things Architecture (IoT-A), 52 requirements (roughly 30%) are relevant to security [28]. In practice, however, IoT devices hardly support existing security mechanisms originally designed for servers, personal computers, or even smartphones, because of not only their constrained resources but also their diverse features (e.g., smart TVs with payment and social networking supports). Accordingly, IoT devices are becoming easy and attractive attack targets [8]. Thus, security mechanisms that consider the features of IoT devices have become imperative.

Furthermore, we observe the following two trends in the recent IoT developments. First, the number of supporting

---

[1]We use the terms 'device' and 'thing' interchangeably throughout this paper.

functionalities of IoT devices are increasing. Second, IoT devices tend to interact with third party applications. For example, a healthcare IoT device can have many sensors (e.g., pace and pulse sensors) and interact with diverse third party applications to for logging or alarming. Previous IoT frameworks adopt a device-centric approach that gives a user or an application either *all or no* permissions to use IoT devices because they usually have single or a few functionalities. Without selectively controlling accesses to each functionality (i.e., without satisfying the principal of least privilege), IoT devices would suffer from over-privilege and Denial-of-Service (DoS) attacks performed by third-party applications. We need a new access control approach for IoT devices to come up with their recent development trends providing and controlling *multiple* functionalities.

In this paper, we first conduct a case study to know how two popular IoT frameworks, SmartThings and IoTivity, implement access control mechanisms. We confirm that they suffer from the over-privilege and DoS problems we mentioned since their access control mechanisms are based on a device-centric approach. Motivated by the case study results, we propose FACT, a functionality-centric access control system to manage IoT devices securely.

In FACT, the basic unit of control and usage is not the device, but the *functionality*. This functionality-centric approach resolves the security problems of the existing IoT frameworks. First, FACT examines whether an application has the privilege to access the functionalities it requests to prevent unauthorized access. Users no longer have to worry about security problems derived from unprivileged applications. Second, FACT isolates each functionality of IoT devices to maximize the overall availability of the functionalities. Despite the attack of a malicious or compromised application to a functionality (e.g., DoS attack), the isolation prevents the attack from affecting the remaining functionalities such that the functionalities can be provided to other applications.

We implement a prototype of FACT on IoTivity, which is one of the popular open-source IoT frameworks. The evaluation results confirm that FACT satisfies our security goals with minimal overhead.

This work makes the following contributions:

- **Novel study.** To the best of our knowledge, FACT is the first functionality-centric approach to protecting IoT devices from third-party applications. Given that recent IoT devices are likely to have many functionalities and interact with third-party applications, our approach is necessary for fostering a secure IoT environment.
- **Fine-grained access control.** FACT prevents unauthorized applications from using any disallowed functionalities of IoT devices. Malicious or compromised applications are restricted from accessing the unauthorized functionalities of IoT devices.
- **Functionality Isolation:** FACT separates each functionality, which restrains the functionalities from

affecting each other. Thus, resource exhaustion attacks on a functionality cannot harm the availability of the other functionalities.

This paper is organized as follows. Section 2 provides the investigation of existing IoT frameworks and their problems. Section 3 presents the security flaws in the existing IoT frameworks, threat models, and our design goals. Section 4 presents the overview and detailed working procedures of components that constitute the proposed FACT framework. We present the implementation and evaluation results in Section 5. Sections 6 and 7 provide discussion and related works. Finally, we conclude in Section 8.

2 EXISTING IOT FRAMEWORKS

In this section, we investigate how the existing IoT frameworks establish a connection between a host and an IoT device. We classify the IoT frameworks into two types: commercial IoT frameworks and open-source frameworks. For each type, we select the most dominant framework: SmartThings[2] and IoTivity[3]. We analyze the frameworks with respect to access control models and the basic units used for binding between the subject and the object, which is summarized in Table 1.

2.1 SmartThings

Overview. SmartThings is a commercial IoT framework that integrates heterogeneous IoT ecosystems. It supports around 170 IoT devices and communication protocols (e.g., Zigbee and Z-Wave). A simple form of the SmartThings architecture consists of *SmartThings hub*, *SmartApps*, and *Device handlers*.

- SmartThings hub: acts as a gateway for connected IoT devices by connecting devices directly to a home network router. The hub is compatible with diverse communication protocols such as Zigbee, Z-Wave, and IP-accessible devices.
- SmartApp: provides the interface that allows users to operate the functionalities of connected IoT devices. A user can download and use it on smartphones, called SmartThings Mobile.
- Device handler: represents the virtual wrapper of physical devices.

SmartThings supports a web-based programming environment where app developers and device vendors can implement SmartApps and Device handlers.

Capability. A capability in SmartThings is the basic unit of authorization. It consists of two elements, namely, a set of *attributes* and *commands*. *Attributes* represent the properties of a device. *Commands* are ways that a user can control the device. For example, a *door control* capability has a *door status* attribute and two commands, *open()* and *close()*. A SmartApp has to declare a capability to connect with a device. Then, the system scans for the Device handlers that support the requested capability and asks the user to select

[2]https://www.smartthings.com/
[3]https://www.iotivity.org/

Table 1: Summary of access control mechanisms in IoT frameworks

Framework	Access Control (AC)	Connection Unit	Binding Units	
			Subject	Object
SmartThings	Account-based AC	Capability	SmartApp	Device handler
IoTivity	Device-based AC	Resource	Client device	Resource

a device from the scanned devices for binding. In this model, we consider a capability as the basic unit of connection.

Access Control. SmartThings provides a hierarchical framework for its security. *Accounts* (i.e., SmartThings users) are at the top of the framework. Under *accounts*, there are *locations* such as an office or a home. In general, SmartThings hubs are located in these *locations*. Under *location*, there are *groups* that represent physical spaces such as rooms. Finally at the bottom, there are *devices* that belong to a certain *group*. Once a user logs into a SmartApp with his account and grants the location permission on the host device, the application automatically gains access to a specified device through a SmartThings hub, which is bound to a *location*.

Most of the SmartApps contain the capability lists defined in their code. Once a SmartApp is installed via SmartThings Mobile, it asks a user to select one among the devices (Device handler) that contain the requested capability, and the selected device would be bound to the SmartApp.

2.2 IoTivity

Overview. IoTivity is an open-source IoT framework that enables seamless device-to-device connectivity to address the emerging needs of the IoT. It follows the Open Interconnect Consortium (OIC) standard specifications[4] and is available on various platforms [32]. The IoTivity architecture contains *servers*, *clients*, and *resource hosting devices*.

- Server: represents an IoT device or a hub device that aggregates the data of connected IoT devices. A server provides various functionalities of IoT devices to clients.
- Client: represents a user or a user device that attempts to access IoT devices (servers).
- Resource hosting device: helps clients to discover the address of servers and monitors server status. In general, this role is taken by gateway devices (e.g., routers for Wi-Fi communication).

IoTivity developers implement client and server applications with IoTivity API. A server application called a resource runs on an IoT device and handles requests from client applications on external devices.

Resource. The unit of connection and control is a *resource* in IoTivity. A resource consists of three elements: *identity*, *property*, and *attribute*. *Identity* is a uniform resource identifier that consists of each device's address and path. *Property*

_____
[4]https://openconnectivity.org/resources/specifications

includes each device's resource type or name defined by a server, and its interface type, (e.g., the Internet and Bluetooth). *Attribute* is a key-value data of functionalities (e.g., temperature, humidity, and an air circulation mode).

Access control. To determine whether a client has the right to access a server's resource, a server maintains security information such as an access control list (ACL). Each access control entry (ACE) in an ACL consists of *subject ID*, *resource*, and *permission*. *Subject ID* is the identity of a client device. *Resource* is the resource type of the server. *Permission* is a type of the client's privilege (e.g., read only, write only, or both read and write) to access the server's resource.

When the server receives a request from the client, the policy engine in the server conducts the following procedure. First, it looks up ACL with the subject ID in the request. Next, it searches the ACE that matches with the resource in the request, and checks whether the matching subject (client) has the permission. Finally, it either grants or denies access to the client.

2.3 Problems in Frameworks

We discuss the problems in two frameworks.

SmartThings. Fernandes *et al.* [13] analyzed the design of SmartThings and found several security flaws related to over-privilege and sensitive data (event) leakage. Furthermore, we investigate other design flaws of SmartThings. We concentrate on three problems among the identified security defects.

- SmartApp can access all capabilities of the implemented by Device handler of the selected devices, not only the requested capability.
- SmartApp can monitor any event data published by the Device handler.
- With the location permission on the host device, SmartApp gains access to location-bounded devices through the SmartThings hub.

IoTivity. We investigate the design of IoTivity access control and find three security flaws.

- Resource, the unit of connection and control, has a number of attributes, and IoTivity cannot grant different access policies to each attribute.
- All attributes data of the resource are stored in the same process or file system.
- Subject ID in the ACL maps to a client device, not an application. Thus, IoTivity cannot grant different access policies to each application in the client device.

3 DESIGN FLAWS AND GOALS

3.1 Design Flaws

We organize a number of security flaws in IoT frameworks and focus on the design flaws that cause the over-privileged application and the availability problems in SmartThings and IoTivity.

3.1.1 Coarse-grained Access Control.
The two IoT platforms implement the following access control models: an account-based access control and a device-based access control, which result in account-to-device and device-to-device authentication respectively. These models make an access control decision by checking whether a subject (an account or a host device) who sends a request has the privilege to access the corresponding device (a thing). Thus, we call this security model as a device-centric approach.

In the device-centric approach, the basic unit of control and usage is a device. Fig. 2 shows a conventional device-centric access control model in which a user has an IoT device providing three functionalities and aims to use it via a client application or device. The user can either allow or disallow an application to access the IoT device depending on their functionalities. Note that the device-centric access control takes an all-or-nothing approach; therefore, the user cannot specify which functionalities the client can use.

The device-centric access control is suitable for devices that have a single functionality. In the past, most IoT devices (e.g., sensors) have a single functionality; therefore, they did not require any fine-grained access control mechanisms in terms of the functionality. However, given the prevalence of devices with multiple functionalities (e.g., smartwatches), the coarse granularity of the device-centric access control introduces security problems. For example, in Fig. 2, a user wants to use the fn_c functionality. If the user binds the $Client$ with $Thing_c$, which has a single functionality, fn_c, no over-privileged problem will occur. However, if the $Client$ connects to $Thing_a$ with multiple functionalities, the $Client$ will be granted access to all functionalities defined in $Thing_a$, which include not only fn_c but also other functionalities fn_a and fn_b that do not correspond to the user's original intention. Furthermore, the device-centric access control disallows an application to access a device to protect privacy-sensitive functionalities, resulting in utility degradation. For example, if a user disallows an application to access one of the privacy sensitive functionalities, then the application will be restricted from accessing all of the functionalities declared in the application including the privacy-insensitive functionalities (e.g., clock, temperature, and humidity). Given that IoT devices deal with both public and private information simultaneously, this becomes a serious problem.

3.1.2 Lack of Resource Isolation.
An IoT device conceptually separates functionalities to provide only the requested access to the subject. Nevertheless, some concerns remain regarding availability, because most IoT frameworks and devices hardly support any resource isolation techniques. For example, a malicious application can exhaustively request a certain functionality to an IoT device (a type of DoS attack). These requests can exhaust the resource (e.g., CPU, memory, and storage) of the devices by running a computation-intensive process or abusing a log system. Moreover, because of developers' inexperience in mobile and IoT fields, recently released applications exhibit disruptive behaviors such as checking the status of the device too frequently and causing the devices' processor keep spinning [18]. Considering that the IoT hubs or devices do not have sophisticated request handling mechanisms, these malicious attempts can eventually damage the availability by freezing or shutting down a device [25].

3.2 Threat Models and Design Goals

3.2.1 Threat Models.
By exploiting the problems derived from the design flaws in the existing IoT frameworks, we consider two types of attacks, called *misusing the functionality* and *reducing the functionality*, can be performed against IoT devices. Note that we target application-level attacks on the IoT frameworks; therefore, other types of attacks including network and hardware attacks are out of the scope of this paper.

First, over-privileged applications can abuse the functionalities of IoT devices. An attacker attempts to access unauthorized functionalities of the IoT devices using a malicious or compromised application. For example, we assume a smart doorlock that has 1) battery status monitoring, 2) door status monitoring (open or closed), and 3) door locking and unlocking functionalities (Fig. 1a). A user wants to check a smart doorlock's battery status through an application; therefore, he/she grants the application the privilege to access the smart doorlock (e.g., the SmartApp declares a battery capability for SmartThings, and the client is registered to the ACL of the smartLock resource for IoTivity). Unfortunately, the application is malicious and has a backdoor to exploit other functionalities of the attached doorlock. While showing the battery status information to a user to fulfill the original objective, the application can check the lock status of the door and even stealthily unlock the door when it is locked.

Second, an attacker can freeze or cease the IoT devices. We revisit the smart doorlock case (Fig. 1b) to illustrate this attack scenario. The user runs two applications on his smartphone; $App1$ requests a functionality to monitor battery status. $App2$ asks functionalities to (un)lock the doorlock. However, if $App2$ repeatedly requests the smart doorlock device to lock and unlock, $App1$ would have no way to monitor the battery status.

3.2.2 Design Goals.
To solve the problems derived from the design limitations in the existing IoT frameworks, we aim to provide a novel access control mechanism that encompasses multiple functionalities of IoT devices with the following design goals.

- *The principle of least privilege*: The access control mechanism has to be able to grant privileges to a subject as least as it requests to an object.

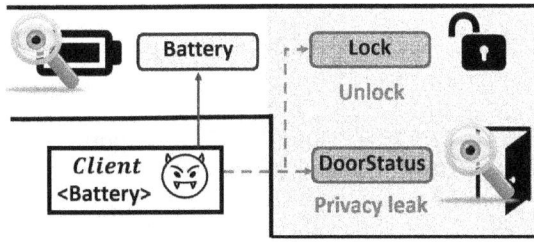

(a) Challenges in device security because of application backdoors that abuse unauthorized functionalities

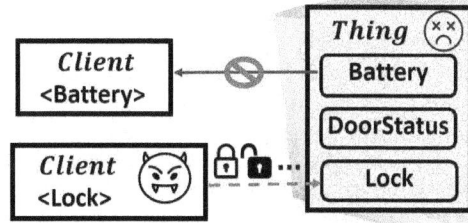

(b) Challenges in device availability because of lack of functionality separation

Figure 1: Attack scenarios induced by design flaws of existing IoT frameworks

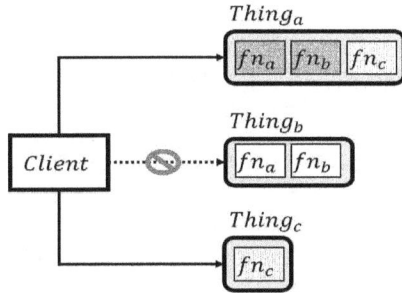

Figure 2: Device-centric access control in IoT frameworks (*Client*: client application or device, fn: functionality, and *Thing*: device)

Figure 3: Overview of FACT. (ACL: Access Control Lists, App: Application)

- *Availability*: The access control mechanism has to guarantee the availability of an IoT device even when it suffers from a subject's disruptive requests.

4 FACT

In this section, we propose FACT, a fine-grained functionality centric access control system for IoT frameworks. FACT is deployed on IoT devices, hubs, and clouds to achieve the goals defined in Section 3.2.2. It allows IoT frameworks to grant a subject *the least privilege* by providing only the requested functionalities. Furthermore, FACT isolates the functionalities from each other so that any disruption in one functionality would not affect the *availability* of the other functionalities.

4.1 Overview

Components. FACT mainly consists of six components (Fig. 3).

- **Functionality Request Handler (FRH):** A component to securely connect the application with authorized functionalities by interacting with Policy Manager and Functionality Manager shown below.
- **Policy Manager:** A component to manage the functionality permission information of each application.
- **Functionality Manager:** A component to manage the overall functionalities of currently registered IoT devices.

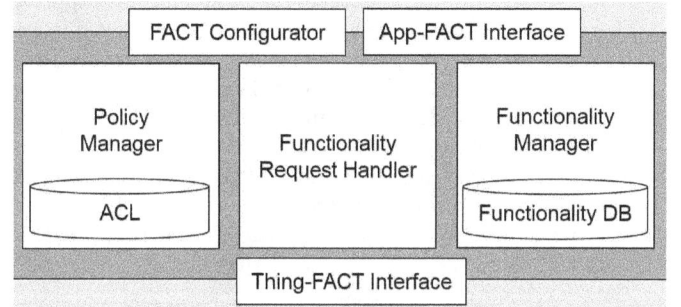

- **Application-FACT Interface (AFI):** An interface between applications and FACT to register applications and demanded functionalities.
- **Thing-FACT Interface (TFI):** An interface between IoT devices and FACT to manage IoT devices and process-requested functionalities.
- **FACT Configurator:** An administration application to manage the overall settings of FACT.

Procedure. The overall procedures of FACT are as follows. First, an IoT device is registered to FACT through the Functionality Manager. The Functionality Manager identifies the functionalities that the attached IoT devices provide and initiates a server for each functionality. Next, the user registers his application to FACT through the Policy Manager, which checks the functionalities requested by the application. Then, it asks the user to select a device with the requested functionalities he/she prefers to use with the application. Once the user selects a device, the Policy Manager asks the user to permit the applications to use the requested functionalities in the selected device. Finally, the application sends a request to the FRH. To check if the request is valid, the FRH searches for the applications' permission stored in the ACL of the Policy Manager. If the request is valid, the FRH communicates with the Functionality Manager to approve the actions corresponding to the request.

4.2 Functionality

FACT uses a *functionality* as a minimal object unit that represents an independent service entity. Functionalities are comprised of two types: *sensing* and *actuating*. A *sensing* functionality has only one method that receives sensor's data or status information. An *actuating* functionality can have multiple methods (e.g., lock and unlock in a smart doorlock device). To provide a fine-grained access control, FACT grants a client application different policies on different functionalities. For example, recall the smart doorlock, which has three functionalities, i.e., *battery*, *door status*, and *lock*. FACT can authorize client applications only to read lock's status, while prohibiting access to other functionalities.

4.2.1 Requesting Functionalities. To simplify the application registration process and reduce the developer's burden, we propose the FACT policy language (FPL). An application developer has to write all the required methods corresponding to the desired functionalities in FPL form and include it in the application's description. When a user or a system wants to register a client application to FACT, it finds things that support the requested functionalities.

Grammar. FACT adopts the Backus-Naur Form (BNF) notation [23] for context-free grammar that effectively expresses the clients' requested methods.

We define the syntax of FPL as shown below:

$$\langle policy\ rule \rangle ::= \varnothing\ |\ \langle\ functionality\ list \rangle$$

$$\langle functionality\ list \rangle ::= \langle functionality \rangle\ |$$
$$\langle functionality \rangle\ `,'\ \langle functionality\ list \rangle$$
$$\langle functionality \rangle ::= \langle sensing \rangle\ |\ \langle actuating \rangle$$

As mentioned previously, FACT considers two types of functionalities, namely, *sensing* and *actuating*. A *sensing*-type functionality represents an action to detect any occurrence of events or change of status. An *actuating*-type functionality represents an action that causes the device to move its component or change its status. To reflect these characteristics, each functionality can have different methods according to its type as follows:

$$\langle sensing \rangle ::= \langle sensing\ name \rangle\ `<'\langle sensing\ method \rangle`>'$$
$$\langle sensing\ name \rangle ::= string$$
$$\langle sensing\ method \rangle ::= `getStatus'$$

A *sensing* functionality has only one method which is receiving its sensor's status data. Note that functionality is a minimal object unit such that a sensor functionality cannot cover more than one sensor's data.

$$\langle actuating \rangle ::= \langle actuating\ name \rangle\ `<'\langle actuating\ methods \rangle`>'$$
$$\langle actuating\ name \rangle ::= string$$
$$\langle actuating\ methods \rangle ::= `all'\ |\ \langle method\ list \rangle$$
$$\langle method\ list \rangle ::= \varnothing\ |\ `getStatus'\ |\ `setStatus'\ |$$
$$\langle method\ name \rangle`,'\ \langle method\ list \rangle$$

$$\langle method\ name \rangle ::= string$$

An *actuating* functionality has multiple methods (a set of operations). It may contain vendor-defined methods, for an action which cannot be controlled through simply setting the status of the actuator. The FPL supports the vendor-defined methods by allowing a method type as a string (line 6). Furthermore, an application developer can conveniently declare device's own methods for the *actuating* functionality by adding 'all'. With this command, the developer does not need to register all methods of the target functionality (line 3).

4.2.2 Examples. In our previous example, the smartLock device has three functionalities, namely *battery*, *doorStatus*, and *(un)lock*. In FACT, the functions to obtain battery and door status information (*battery*, *doorStatus*) are *sensing* functionalities, while the actions to lock and unlock the door (*(un)lock*) are *actuating* functionalities.
Sensing. 1) battery - method: getStatus (battery remaining percentage), 2) doorStatus - method: getStatus (whether door is open or closed)
Actuating. 1) lock - method: setStatus (lock and unlock)

For a battery monitoring application, it needs to know the battery status only.

```
1   description{
2       battery<getStatus>
3   }
```

With this description, FACT can show a user the list of devices that have battery functionality that retrieves battery status. Then, the user selects one of the devices from the list to register the application to FACT. After registration, the application can access only the battery status of the selected device.

For an auto-lock application, the application locks a door when the door is closed and unlocked. To perform this job, the application requires a set of functionalities including the retrieval of the door and lock statuses as well as to lock the door.

```
1   description{
2       doorStatus<getStatus>,
3       lock<getStatus, setStatus>
4   }
```

In the case of an administration application, it requires all methods of functionalities.

```
1   description{
2       battery<getStatus>,
3       doorStatus<all>,
4       lock<all>
5   }
```

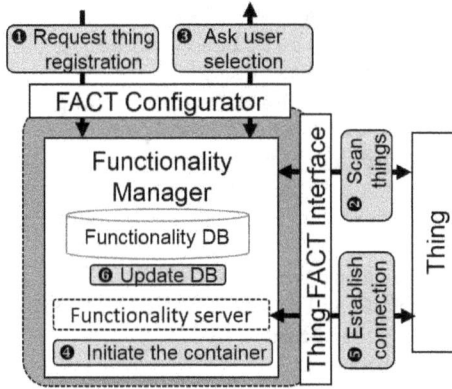

Figure 4: The procedures of how an IoT device and its functionalities are registered to FACT

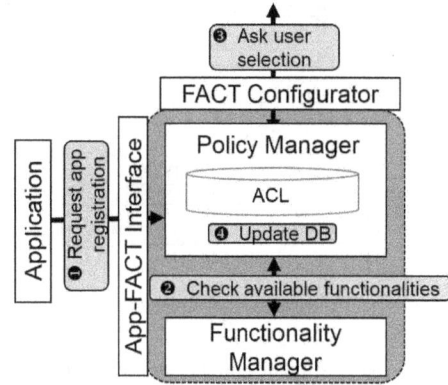

Figure 5: The procedure of how an application and its functionality demands are registered to FACT

Table 2: Functionality DB (Func ID: Functionality ID)

Thing ID	Func ID	State
smartLock	lock	Active
smartLock	battery	Active
smartBulb	switch	dormant
smartBulb	lightColor	dormant
temperatureSensor	temperature	Active
humiditySensor	humidity	Active

Table 3: Access control lists

App ID	Func ID	Methods
lockapp	lock	SetStatus
lockapp	battery	GetStatus
bulbapp	switch	SetStatus
bulbapp	lightColor	SetStatus
airConapp	temperature	getStatus
airConapp	humidity	getStatus

4.3 Management of Functionalities

4.3.1 Functionality Isolation.
To isolate each functionality from others, FACT applies *Linux Containers (LXC)* [16], one of virtualization techniques. LXC makes programs portable and isolated by packaging them in containers. It solves some problems such as dependency conflicts and platform differences, but we focus on its security benefits that isolate a container from a host and other containers. LXC virtualizes at the operating system level, whereas hypervisor-based techniques virtualize at the hardware level. Thus, LXC requires less computing and memory overheads than other hardware-level virtualization [11]. Therefore, LXC is a suitable isolating technique for the IoT frameworks, which fits for low-computing power devices. FACT creates some containers according to the number of functionalities. Given that FACT makes one functionality server run on each container, the container sandboxes its contained functionality from the other functionalities.

4.3.2 Managing Thing Functionalities.
We explain how the Functionality Manager enables a user to register and update functionality information of his/her IoT devices (Fig. 4).

❶ The thing registration process is initiated periodically. If the process is initiated by a user, it skips ❷-❸ which are device discovery processes, and goes to ❹.

❷ In the case of periodical registration, the Functionality Manager scans nearby IoT devices via TFI to discover new devices.

❸ The Functionality Manager asks a user's consent to register the discovered devices.

❹ If the user approves, the Functionality Manager creates some containers according to the number of functionalities and sets the default amount of resources (e.g., CPU, memory, and storage) to the containers automatically if the user does not assign specific values to them.

❺ Functionality servers establish a connection with the selected device. These servers can interact with external things via TFI.

❻ After the establishment, the Functionality Manager updates the *functionality DB* that stores the provided thing ID, functionality ID, and connection states as shown in Table 2.

In the case when the firmware is updated, an IoT device may obtain new functionalities. To handle the added functionalities, the Functionality Manager needs to update its DB. The update procedure is the same as the registration process except that it only deals with the new functionalities. Thus, we do not explain its details.

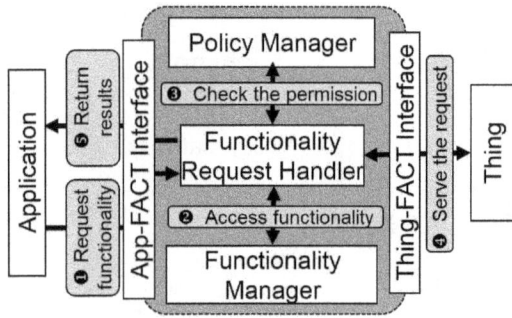

Figure 6: The procedure of how an application's functionality request is checked and delivered to an selected device

Some low-power IoT devices may not provide detailed information and malfunctioning devices may provide misinformation. Therefore, to obtain the complete and exact information of IoT devices, the Functionality Manager needs to interact with the external trusted server.

4.3.3 Managing Application Functionalities. The Policy Manager registers a newly installed application that is aware of FACT as shown in Fig. 5.

❶ The application contacts the Policy Manager via AFI to register itself with a list of functionalities it demands.

❷ The list can contain functionalities a user's IoT devices do not support, i.e., *not-available functionalities*. To exclude them from the list, the Policy Manager asks the Functionality Manager about the currently available functionalities.

❸ The Policy Manager displays the filtered list to the user and lets the user selectively grant permissions to the application.

❹ The Policy Manager updates the ACL according to the user's decision. The DB records the application ID, functionality ID, and the requested methods of the functionality as shown in Table 3.

The Policy Manager updates its DB when an application is updated, or a user wants to change the permission settings. The update procedure is the same as the registration procedure except that it only deals with new or changed functionality information. Therefore, we omit the detailed explanation on updating application information.

4.3.4 Processing Functionality Requests. We explicate the process of how FRH securely delivers an application's functionality request to the selected IoT device as shown in Fig. 6.

❶ A client application sends a functionality request to the FRH through AFI.

❷ The FRH connects to a container that includes the server deals with the requested functionality.

❸ The FRH asks the Policy Manager whether a user has permitted the application to access the requested functionality.

```
1   Response requesthandler(request){
2     switch (request.func.method){
3       case "getStatus":
4         if (!aclCheck(request.AppID,
              getStatus))
5           break;
6
7         return server.getStatus();
8
9       case "SetStatus":
10        if (!aclCheck(request.AppID,
              setStatus))
11          break;
12
13        return server.setStatus(request.
              setValue);
14
15      case default:
16        if (!aclCheck(request.AppID,
              request.func.method))
17          break;
18
19        return server.action(request.func.
              method);
20    }
21    return error("Access Denied");
22  }
23
24  bool aclCheck(AppID, method){
25    return pairMatch(server.id, AppID,
          method);
26  }
```

Listing 1: Request handling process

❹ If the application has a privilege to access the requested functionality, the FRH conveys the functionality request to the device through TFI. Otherwise, the FRH discards the request.

❺ The device returns the result to the application.

Listing 1 shows a request handling process after the FRH has accessed the requested functionality server. The FRH determines whether the requested method is *getStatus*, *setStatus*, or vendor-defined. Afterward, the FRH checks the permission through the ACL of the Policy Manager. These procedures are described in Lines 4, 10, and 16 of Listing 1. If the ACL has no matching ACE with the application's request, then the FRH returns an error message to the application (Line 21). If the request is legitimate, the FRH interacts with the things via the functionality server.

5 IMPLEMENTATION AND EVALUATION

In this section, we elaborate on how we implemented a prototype of FACT described in Section 4 and evaluate its security effectiveness and performance overhead.

5.1 Implementation Details

We implemented a prototype of FACT on Raspbian Jessie[5] with IoTivity version 1.2.1. We developed two IoT devices, one for a server and the other for a client device. For the server, we used RaspberryPi 3 connected to an ultrasonic sensor, a temperature sensor, an infrared light motion sensor, and a Phillips Hue smartbulb, which has switch and color change functionalities. The sample server applications that we have built were running on the device. The total components of the server consisted of 472 Source Lines of Code (SLoC). The SLoC associated with the functionality registration and method checks were 75 and 95 respectively. The server stored the ACLs in Samsung 32GB EVO Class 10 Micro SDHC Card (MB-MP32DA/AM). For the client, we built applications on another RaspberryPi 3 device. The total components of the client applications consisted of 196 SLoC. The SLoC related to the functionality discovery and functionality requests were 110 and 86 respectively.

To separate each functionality from the other functionalities, we adopt Docker[6] [24] to apply container techniques for functionality isolation. Using Docker, FACT can insulate each functionality server in each container and regulate the amount of resources for the container.

5.2 Security Evaluation

In our security evaluation scenario, a device owner wants to permit a client application to access the ultrasonic sensor, the temperature sensor, and the smartbulb's switch functionality, whereas disallow access to the infrared light motion sensor and the smartbulb's color change functionality. The owner has recorded corresponding permission rules in the ACLs according to above scenario (Table 4). We tested whether FACT can protect the IoT device from unpermitted functionality access. Furthermore, we conduct application-level DoS attacks on IoT devices, which apply FACT.

Over-privileged access prevention. The executed application on the device attempted to discover the resource and access the ultrasonic, temperature sensors, and the smartbulb's switch functionality, as well as the restricted infrared light motion sensor and the smartbulb's color change functionality. Without FACT, the IoT device could not distinguish the unpermitted functionality access from the permitted access. Even though the application only had access to the ultrasonic or temperature functionalities, the application was able to access all functionalities when the device owner granted the applications the privilege to access the IoT device. With FACT, the IoT device successfully differentiated access to each functionality. When the application attempted to access the device functionalities, the device checked the ACL to prevent access to unpermitted functionalities. As a result, the IoT device only granted access to the ultrasonic and temperature functionalities, and access to the infrared light motion functionality was successfully thwarted.

---

[5]https://www.raspberrypi.org/
[6]https://www.docker.com/

Table 4: Functionality permission rules in the scenario

App ID	Func ID	Methods
lockapp	ultrasonic	GetStatus
airConapp	temperature	GetStatus
airConapp	infrared light motion	✗
bulbapp	switch	SetStatus
bulbapp	changeColor	✗

Table 5: Effectiveness of FACT preventing attacks

Attack type	Attack description	Effectiveness
Misusing	Over-privileged application	✓
Reducing	Resource exhaustion	✓
	Packet flooding	✗

Availability. An application with a permission still can cause problems by generating excessive access to the functionality either by programming mistakes or with malicious intention. We conduct storage exhaustion attacks on the temperature functionality server by exploiting the sensor data log system. Without FACT, it disrupts the device's other functionalities because the device's resources are exhausted by the attacks. With FACT, the functionality isolation allows the device to confine how much resources of the device each functionality can consume (e.g., CPU, memory, and storage), and thus prevent the misbehaving functionality from disturbing other functionalities. Therefore, our fine-grained access control guarantees the availability of functionalities.

Furthermore, we conduct the UDP flood attack on a functionality, which is one of the popular DoS attacks. FACT is not able to protect an IoT device against the attack. However, this type of attack is out of scope because it is related to a network layer, not an application. Several researchers investigate the defending mechanisms against flooding-based DoS attack [1, 3, 12, 34]. Thus, when these mechanisms are combined with our system and applied to the IoT environments, the security and the availability of IoT devices can be more robust and reliable.

5.3 Performance Evaluation

FACT handles multiple functionality servers and uses Docker to apply container techniques for functionality isolation. We measured the performance overheads caused by the management of multiple functionalities in FACT.

We varied the supported functionalities of a device from 1 to 30 and checked the latency and memory overhead 10 times each in two cases: 'without Docker' and 'with Docker' cases. We considered the 'without Docker' scenario because currently some operating systems (e.g., Windows 7 and 8) do not support container techniques yet. Nevertheless, FACT without Docker can be applied on such OSes and still prevent over-privileged applications. In the 'Without Docker' case, we executed a server process per functionality to keep the

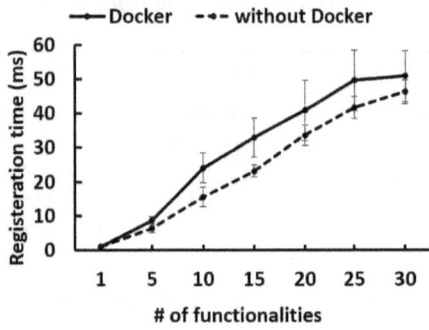

Figure 7: Registration time according to the number of functionalities

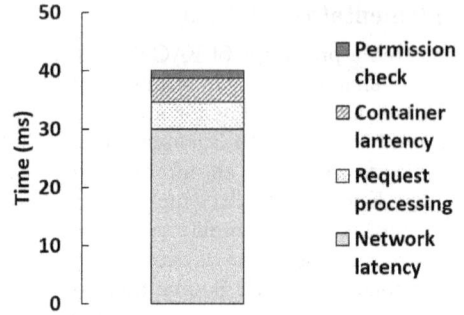

Figure 9: Breakdown of the overall communication latency with 1,000 permission rules in ACL

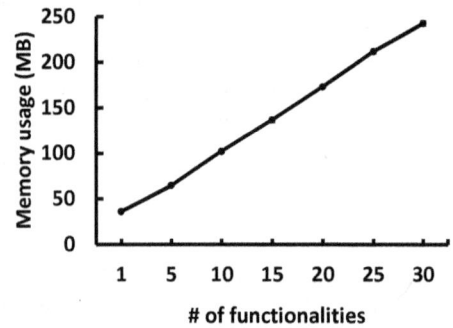

Figure 8: Discovery time according to the number of functionalities

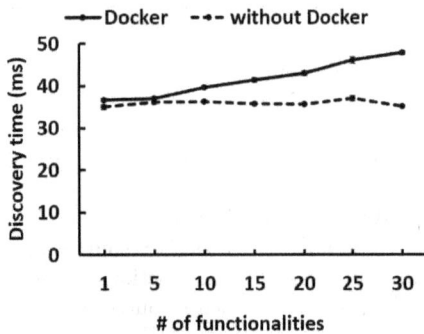

Figure 10: Memory usage according to the number of functionalities with Docker

functionality-centric access control without containers. In the 'With Docker' case, we made a container per functionality and executed a server in each container to separate the resources from the other functionality containers.

Latency Overheads. We measured the amount of time it took to register a thing, discover functionalities of the thing, and access a functionality. The thing registration time increased as the number of functionalities increased in both cases (Fig. 7) due to multiple updates in the functionality DB. Furthermore, Docker brings about 8 ms latency overhead because a registration request goes through via Docker bridges.

The functionality discovery time is constant (about 35 ms) in the 'without Docker' case. In contrast, the discovery time depends on the number of managed functionalities in the 'With Docker' case (Fig. 8). It should be note that as the number of containers that a hub device contains increases, the communication overhead between in and out of containers also increases.

We also measured the request processing latency when a client requires a functionality. The request processing latency is 4.59 ms in the 'without Docker' case and 8.64 ms in the 'with Docker' case. However, the latency difference between

the two cases has a low impact because the network latency is the dominant latency (over 85%) among the overall latency (Fig. 9).

Note that our experiments were performed in a small area (about 1 m^2). The network latency will increase in case of distant scenarios, and the percentage of the overhead becomes trivial compared to the entire latency in real situations.

Memory Overhead. Fig. 10 shows the memory usage with the increased number of functionalities in the 'with Docker' case. The Docker system spent 28 MB of memory and it spent an additional 8 MB of memory per container when the number of functionalities increases. We argue that the memory overhead of FACT is within acceptable limits for the hub devices, because personal PCs, smartphones, and even SmartThings hubs (contains 512 MB RAM) have enough memory to afford the additional memory usages.

When we executed a simple server application in the host and the container, the average memory usages of the server application in the host and in the container case were 310 KB and 344 KB, respectively. The container affects the additional memory usage of the server application about 30 KB, which is negligible for IoT hubs or clouds.

6 DISCUSSION

In this section, we discuss heterogeneous communication channels, operating system dependency, and the hub necessity.

Heterogeneous communication channels. Despite conducting our evaluation on Wi-Fi for communication, FACT can adapt to other communication channels such as Bluetooth, because most IoT frameworks serve APIs that cover heterogeneous communication channels. We only need to modify the communication APIs or parameters (e.g., interface types) associated with the communication channels.

Operating system dependency. The isolation technique of FACT relies on Docker, which is LXC-based, such that the operating system of the server devices should be a Linux-based system (e.g., CentOS, Raspbian, or Ubuntu) to work without any problems. However, Docker starts to support MacOS and Windows. Recent Windows (e.g., 64-bit Windows 10 Pro) can use Docker, and we expect that its coverage would expand in the near future.

Hub necessity. We show that FACT applies to hub-based IoT frameworks only. However, we can adopt FACT to device-to-device (distributed) environments if a thing that serves functionalities has abilities to make containers and run server processes. We expect that multiple functionality devices (e.g., smart watch) have sufficient computing power and memory to satisfy those abilities. Thus, the devices could adopt FACT.

7 RELATED WORKS

In this section, we explain some studies related to FACT: IoT security and over-privileged applications.

IoT security. Some researchers have proposed new IoT systems that consider security. HomeOS [9] is an operating system for a smart home, using a new type of abstraction to provide extensibility and management. It considers all devices in a home as peripherals. BOSS [6] is an operating system for a smart building with many IoT devices. It focuses on how to manage the relationship between components including sensors, location, and time. SIFT [22] is a safety-centric programming platform to build safe IoT environments. It especially focuses on how to manage a large number of safety rules while avoiding conflicts between the rules.

Given that smartphones are usually considered as the hub of IoT systems, some researchers have enhanced smartphones' security systems to secure the IoT systems. Dabinder [26] was the first study that considered the security problem of Android when managing external IoT devices. It has found that malicious applications can access any IoT devices by just obtaining a communication permission in the Android system. SEACAT [7] provided an effective solution to the problem by enhancing the Security-Enhanced Android (SEAndroid) [31] to distinguish external resources when defining and enforcing access control lists. Busold et al. [2] proposed context-aware service mobility frameworks that enable users to securely distribute the functionality of the application to mutually untrusted smart devices on Android. Levy et al. [21] proposed Beetle, a new hardware interface that allows many-to-many

secure connections between peripheral Bluetooth devices and applications .

Furthermore, as the IoT becomes a reality, some studies have analyzed the security defects of IoT devices and frameworks, and how to protect them securely. Grant et al. [17] examined the security of commercially-available smartlocks. Ronen et al. [30] proposed extending the functionality attack in the case of smart lights. Fernandes et al. [13] analyzed the security design flaws of SmartThings. They have shown that SmartThings applications, called SmartApps, support capability-based device scanning, but allow to access the whole capabilities of each scanned device because of coarse-grained access control.FlowFence [14] is a system that requires consumers of sensitive data to declare their intended data flow patterns using Quarantined Module. ContexIoT [20] is a context-based permission system for IoT platforms that provides contextual integrity by supporting context identification for sensitive actions.

The current approaches of IoT frameworks continue to be problematic because they do not consider each functionality of IoT devices. Therefore, many IoT frameworks cannot satisfy the principle of least privilege for IoT devices with multiple functionalities. To the best of our knowledge, FACT is the first functionality-centric approach that prevents applications from abusing any disallowed functionalities of IoT devices.

Over-privileged applications. Many researchers have considered security problems due to over-privileged applications. For example, researchers have discovered that many over-privileged applications exist on application markets [4, 10]. Moreover, they can abuse other components, such as advertisement libraries [15, 29, 35] and other benign applications for privilege escalation [5]. Furthermore, Tuncay et al. [33] raised the problems that originated in coarse-grained access control of in-app embedded browsers. Note that the explained studies have considered over-privilege problems within the Android system. To the best of our knowledge, FACT is the first approach to solving a new over-privileged problem regarding device functionalities.

8 CONCLUSION

Given that recent IoT devices are likely to provide multiple functionalities and interact with third-party applications, a new security mechanism to protect sensitive functionalities effectively from malicious applications is crucial. In this paper, we proposed a functionality-centric access control mechanism for IoT frameworks, called FACT. In FACT, a user can grant an application access to each functionality of IoT devices to fulfill the principle of least privilege in terms of device functionalities. Furthermore, FACT guarantees the availability of IoT devices by isolating each functionality of the device using LXCs from the other functionalities. The novel functionality-centric access control system proves that it can effectively guarantee the security and the availability for IoT frameworks. We implemented a prototype of FACT on IoTivity and showed that it satisfied our design goal with minimal overhead.

ACKNOWLEDGMENTS

We would like to thank the anonymous reviewers for their invaluable comments and suggestions. This work was supported by Samsung Research Funding Center of Samsung Electronics under Project Number SRFC-TB1403-04.

REFERENCES

[1] Alexander Afanasyev, Priya Mahadevan, Ilya Moiseenko, Ersin Uzun, and Lixia Zhang. 2013. Interest flooding attack and countermeasures in Named Data Networking. In *IFIP Networking Conference, 2013*. IEEE, 1–9.

[2] Christoph Busold, Stephan Heuser, Jon Rios, Ahmad-Reza Sadeghi, and N Asokan. 2015. Smart and Secure Cross-Device Apps for the Internet of Advanced Things. In *International Conference on Financial Cryptography and Data Security*. Springer, 272–290.

[3] Rocky KC Chang. 2002. Defending against flooding-based distributed denial-of-service attacks: a tutorial. *IEEE communications magazine* 40, 10 (2002), 42–51.

[4] Pern Hui Chia, Yusuke Yamamoto, and N. Asokan. 2012. Is This App Safe?: A Large Scale Study on Application Permissions and Risk Signals. In *International Conference on World Wide Web (WWW)*.

[5] Lucas Davi, Alexandra Dmitrienko, Ahmad-Reza Sadeghi, and Marcel Winandy. 2011. Privilege Escalation Attacks on Android. In *International Conference on Information Security (ISC)*.

[6] Stephen Dawson-Haggerty, Andrew Krioukov, Jay Taneja, Sagar Karandikar, Gabe Fierro, Nikita Kitaev, and David Culler. 2013. BOSS: Building Operating System Services. In *USENIX Symposium on Networked Systems Design and Implementation (NSDI)*.

[7] Soteris Demetriou, Xiaoyong Zhou, Muhammad Naveed, Yeonjoon Lee, Kan Yuan, XiaoFeng Wang, and Carl A. Gunter. 2015. What's in Your Dongle and Bank Account? Mandatory and Discretionary Protection of Android External Resources. In *Network and Distributed System Security Symposium (NDSS)*.

[8] Nitesh Dhanjani. 2015. *Abusing the Internet of Things: Blackouts, Freakouts, and Stakeouts*. O'Reilly Media, Inc.

[9] Colin Dixon, Ratul Mahajan, Sharad Agarwal, AJ Brush, Bongshin Lee, Stefan Saroiu, and Paramvir Bahl. 2012. An operating system for the home. In *USENIX Symposium on Networked Systems Design and Implementation (NSDI)*.

[10] Adrienne Porter Felt, Erika Chin, Steve Hanna, Dawn Song, and David Wagner. 2011. Android Permissions Demystified. In *ACM Conference on Computer and Communications Security (CCS)*.

[11] Wes Felter, Alexandre Ferreira, Ram Rajamony, and Juan Rubio. 2015. An updated performance comparison of virtual machines and linux containers. In *Performance Analysis of Systems and Software (ISPASS), 2015 IEEE International Symposium on*. IEEE, 171–172.

[12] Paul Ferguson. 2000. Network ingress filtering: Defeating denial of service attacks which employ IP source address spoofing. (2000).

[13] Earlence Fernandes, Jaeyeon Jung, and Atul Prakash. 2016. Security analysis of emerging smart home applications. In *Security and Privacy (S & P), 2016 IEEE Symposium on*. IEEE, 636–654.

[14] Earlence Fernandes, Justin Paupore, Amir Rahmati, Daniel Simionato, Mauro Conti, and Atul Prakash. 2016. FlowFence: Practical Data Protection for Emerging IoT Application Frameworks. In *USENIX Security Symposium*.

[15] Michael C. Grace, Wu Zhou, Xuxian Jiang, and Ahmad-Reza Sadeghi. 2012. Unsafe Exposure Analysis of Mobile In-app Advertisements. In *ACM Conference on Security and Privacy in Wireless and Mobile Networks (WiSec)*.

[16] Matt Helsley. 2009. LXC: Linux container tools. *IBM devloperWorks Technical Library* (2009), 11.

[17] Grant Ho, Derek Leung, Pratyush Mishra, Ashkan Hosseini, Dawn Song, and David Wagner. 2016. Smart locks: Lessons for securing commodity internet of things devices. In *Proceedings of the 11th ACM on Asia Conference on Computer and Communications Security*. ACM, 461–472.

[18] Peng Huang, Tianyin Xu, Xinxin Jin, and Yuanyuan Zhou. 2016. DefDroid: Towards a More Defensive Mobile OS Against Disruptive App Behavior. In *Proceedings of the 14th Annual International Conference on Mobile Systems, Applications, and Services (MobiSys '16)*. ACM, New York, NY, USA, 221–234. DOI:http://dx.doi.org/10.1145/2906388.2906419

[19] International Data Corporation (IDC). 2014. IDC Market in a Minute: Internet of Things. http://www.idc.com/downloads/idc_market_in_a_minute_iot_infographic.pdf. (2014).

[20] Yunhan Jack Jia, Qi Alfred Chen, Shiqi Wang, Amir Rahmati, Earlence Fernandes, Z Morley Mao, Atul Prakash, and Shanghai JiaoTong Unviersity. 2017. ContexIoT: Towards Providing Contextual Integrity to Appified IoT Platforms. In *NDSS*.

[21] Amit A Levy, James Hong, Laurynas Riliskis, Philip Levis, and Keith Winstein. 2016. Beetle: Flexible communication for bluetooth low energy. In *Proceedings of the 14th Annual International Conference on Mobile Systems, Applications, and Services*. ACM, 111–122.

[22] Chieh-Jan Mike Liang, Börje F. Karlsson, Nicholas D. Lane, Feng Zhao, Junbei Zhang, Zheyi Pan, Zhao Li, and Yong Yu. 2015. SIFT: Building an Internet of Safe Things. In *International Conference on Information Processing in Sensor Networks (IPSN)*.

[23] Daniel D McCracken and Edwin D Reilly. 2003. Backus-naur form (bnf). (2003).

[24] Dirk Merkel. 2014. Docker: lightweight linux containers for consistent development and deployment. *Linux Journal* 2014, 239 (2014), 2.

[25] S. Misra, M. Maheswaran, and S. Hashmi. 2016. *Security Challenges and Approaches in Internet of Things*. Springer International Publishing. https://books.google.co.kr/books?id=-Rz4DAAAQBAJ

[26] Muhammad Naveed, Xiaoyong Zhou, Soteris Demetriou, XiaoFeng Wang, and Carl A. Gunter. 2014. Inside Job: Understanding and Mitigating the Threat of External Device Mis-Bonding on Android. In *Network and Distributed System Security Symposium (NDSS)*.

[27] Colin Neagle. 2014. A guide to the confusing Internet of Things standards world. http://www.networkworld.com/article/2456421/internet-of-things/a-guide-to-the-confusing-internet-of-things-standards-world.html. (2014).

[28] Internet of Things Architecture (IoT-A). 2015. Requirements. http://www.meet-iot.eu/iot-a-requirements.html. (2015).

[29] Paul Pearce, Adrienne Porter Felt, Gabriel Nunez, and David Wagner. 2012. AdDroid: Privilege Separation for Applications and Advertisers in Android. In *ACM Symposium on Information, Computer and Communications Security (ASIACCS)*.

[30] Eyal Ronen and Adi Shamir. 2016. Extended functionality attacks on IoT devices: The case of smart lights. In *Security and Privacy (EuroS&P), 2016 IEEE European Symposium on*. IEEE, 3–12.

[31] Stephen Smalley and Robert Craig. 2013. Security Enhanced (SE) Android: Bringing Flexible MAC to Android. In *Network and Distributed System Security Symposium (NDSS)*.

[32] Ashok Subash. 2015. IoTivity – Connecting Things in IoT. In *TIZEN Development Summit*.

[33] Guliz Seray Tuncay, Soteris Demetriou, and Carl A Gunter. 2016. Draco: A System for Uniform and Fine-grained Access Control for Web Code on Android. In *Proceedings of the 2016 ACM SIGSAC Conference on Computer and Communications Security*. ACM, 104–115.

[34] Abraham Yaar, Adrian Perrig, and Dawn Song. 2004. SIFF: A stateless internet flow filter to mitigate DDoS flooding attacks. In *Security and Privacy, 2004. Proceedings. 2004 IEEE Symposium on*. IEEE, 130–143.

[35] Xiao Zhang, Amit Ahlawat, and Wenliang Du. 2013. AFrame: Isolating Advertisements from Mobile Applications in Android. In *Annual Computer Security Applications Conference (ACSAC)*.

An Enforcement Model for Preventing Inference Attacks in Social Computing Platforms

Seyed Hossein Ahmadinejad
Nulli
shan@nulli.com

Philip W. L. Fong
University of Calgary
pwlfong@ucalgary.ca

ABSTRACT

Social Network Systems (SNSs) allow third-party extensions to access user profiles by providing an Application Programming Interface (API). It has been demonstrated in the literature that this API can be exploited by malicious extensions to infer users' sensitive information from the information that is accessible through the API. To prevent this type of privacy violation, we propose a view-based protection model, in which a sanitizing transformation, called a view, is applied to the user profile when it is queried by a third-party extension. We demonstrate empirically that such a protection mechanism effectively reduces the statistical correlation between sensitive and accessible information. We also propose an optimization in which the materialization of views is performed lazily: rather than sanitizing the entire profile during a query, only the parts of the profile that are visible to the query are transformed. We demonstrate empirically that this optimization offers visible performance advantage, and propose a programming language-independent, probabilistic automata model for encoding such transformations.

CCS CONCEPTS

• **Security and privacy** → **Social network security and privacy**;

KEYWORDS

Social network systems, Facebook applications, privacy, sanitizing transformations, view-based protection, statistical correlation, optimization, tree transducers

ACM Reference format:
Seyed Hossein Ahmadinejad and Philip W. L. Fong. 2017. An Enforcement Model for Preventing Inference Attacks in Social Computing Platforms. In *Proceedings of SACMAT'17, Indianapolis, IN, USA, June 21-23, 2017,* 12 pages.
https://doi.org/http://dx.doi.org/10.1145/3078861.3078867

1 INTRODUCTION

Privacy is a serious concern in information systems that store sensitive, personal information. This concern has elevated in recent years by the pervasive adoption of SNSs. Users willingly and often indiscriminately upload personal information to their social profiles. It has been shown that the information in social profiles can be exploited for malicious purposes [2]. For example, consider the commonplace mechanism of asking security questions during an authentication session. "Who is your youngest sibling?" "Who is your favorite author?" When the primary authentication mechanism fails to verify an identity claim, these security questions become a fallback, and access will be granted to an account (e.g., bank, email, etc) if the security questions are correctly answered. The answers to security questions can often be gathered from a user's social profile. This means the social profile of a user contains information that, if properly harvested, helps a malicious party to launch an identity theft attack [3, 4].

There are at least two approaches by which the aforementioned identity theft attack can be launched. The first is by crawling the publicly accessible region of a social network, and collecting publicly available information of user profiles. Intelligent data mining techniques can be deployed to the resulting dataset for harvesting answers to typical security questions [6, 7, 12–15, 19, 20]. A second approach is to hide information harvesting logic in third-party extensions to SNS platforms. The present work targets this latter approach.

In 2006, Facebook extended its business model to provide further functionalities for its users in the form of applications, games, etc. Facebook recognized that its core business is constructing and maintaining the social graph of users rather than developing an endless array of social applications. The company therefore turned Facebook into an extensible platform. A platform API was released, allowing third-party developers to augment the feature set of Facebook through the development of software extensions called Facebook applications. This API allows Facebook applications to access user information in profiles. Intended for protecting user privacy, a permission-based access control model is imposed. A Facebook application can only access a profile attribute if the user grants the corresponding permission to the application.

This protection model, however, is ineffective in protecting user privacy against malicious applications. Suppose a user considers her birthday to be sensitive, and denies an untrusted application of the permission to access this attribute. The user also recognizes that the application needs access to its timeline, so that permission is granted. Now the application can use the platform API to scan through the timeline of the user, identifying a day when birthday greetings ("Happy birthday!") are sent to the user, and inferring that that day is likely the birthday of the user. The privacy preference of the user is therefore violated. Previous work has termed this the *SNS API Inference Attack*, and has demonstrated that such attacks can be launched through the Facebook API with alarming accuracy [2–4]. As some of the Facebook applications have millions of active users, even a modest success rate would translate to a large number of victims. Besides, Facebook applications may be granted permissions to access profile attributes that are not even visible through a public crawling of the social network, thus there are more channels for information leakage. Lastly, Facebook applications run on third-party servers, meaning that Facebook does not have the means to verify if the third-party applications are benign.

1.1 View-based Protection

The discussion above shows that controlling access is insufficient for preventing SNS API inference attacks. The reason is that there exists statistical correlation between sensitive information (which the user attempts to hide) and accessible information (which the user allows access). A malicious third-party application can exploit this correlation to infer sensitive information from the information that is legitimately accessible under the access control model. The key to protection is thus the breaking of correlation rather than simply denying access to sensitive information.

We advocate in this work a ***view-based protection model***. Under this model, when a third-party application A queries the profile P of user u through the API, the query Q is not evaluated against P itself. Instead, P first undergoes a sanitizing transformation T, before Q is evaluated against the sanitized profile $T(P)$. The transformation T is called a ***view***, which is specified by the user and/or the platform. T is thus an enforcement-layer privacy policy. A view may eliminate certain attributes (access control), or probabilistically transform the profile with the aim of perturbing the statistical correlation between sensitive and accessible information. In other words, view-based protection subsumes access control.

One of the contributions of this paper is to report first empirical evidence that view-based protection, implemented via query-time sanitizing transformations, can effectively reduce the success rate of SNS API inference attacks.

The mathematical formulation of privacy and utility goals, the proof method for establishing that a given view satisfies the two goals, as well as the mathematical trade-off between privacy and utility, are the topics of a related work [5], and are outside the scope of this paper.

1.2 The Challenge of View Materialization

How shall one implement view-based protection in an efficient manner? There are at least two possible approaches:

1. A naive approach is to compute $T(P)$ every time P is queried. The problem is that P can be large (imagine everything in one's timeline, photo albums, etc.), thereby causing even the most innocent query Q to be penalized in performance.
2. Another approach is to have the SNS store both P and $T(P)$. The problem is that $T(P)$ will have to be recomputed every time P is updated (which happens frequently). Not only that, T is specific to the user u and the application A, meaning that the SNS needs to store a $T(P)$ for every application A that user u subscribes to — a space inefficient option.

We propose a middle way in this work. The computation of $T(P)$ is called the ***materialization*** of view T. We argue that materialization should be performed in a lazy manner, at the time of query. To see this, the query Q may not access all components of profile P. Instead of eagerly applying T to the entire profile P, we apply T

to the parts of P that are visible to query Q. A simple query that involves only a small fragment of profile P will therefore incur only a meager amount of materialization, thereby preventing the performance penalty of Approach 1 above. As T is computed at the time of query, there is no need to maintain multiple materialized views, thereby preventing the view maintenance problem of Approach 2.

1.3 Contributions

This paper has three contributions:

1. **Empirical evidence for effectiveness of view-based protection.** We offer first evidence that view-based protection can effectively protect the privacy of sensitive information in user profiles (§3). Specifically, we implemented view-based protection mechanisms, based on handcrafted sanitizing transformations, against the 8 sample inference algorithms of Ahmadinejad *et al.* [3, 4], and demonstrated that the implemented views effectively reduce the correlation between accessible and sensitive information, thereby significantly lowering the accuracy of the inference algorithms.

2. **Empirical evidence for the advantage of eschewing view materialization.** We empirically demonstrate the performance advantage for avoiding the eager materialization of views (§4). Specifically, we implemented the aforementioned view-based protection mechanisms in Haskell, a programming language equipped with lazy evaluation. The latter feature was employed to simulate the effect of lazy materialization of views. Empirical data suggests that a view-based protection mechanism shall materialize views lazily.

3. **Language-independent enforcement mechanism with lazy materialization of views.** We propose a programming language-independent enforcement mechanism that materializes a view in a lazy manner (§6). Specifically, we encode a sanitizing transformation (aka a view) using a Probabilistic Multi Bottom-Up Tree Transducer (PMBUTT). As we model a user profile as a tree (e.g., an XML document), a tree transducer is an automata-based model for specifying a sanitization transformation of user profiles. The particular model that we propose, PMBUTT, is an extension of tree transducer models in existing literature. While supporting probabilistic sanitization (important for implementing, say, noise addition), PMBUTT has the theoretical property of closure under composition: there exists an algorithm for composing two sanitizing transformations to obtain a transformation that is also a PMBUTT. Composeability has two practical applications. First, it allows a policy engineer to build a complex view out of simpler views. Secondly, and more importantly, composeability is the key to lazy materialization of views. It turns out that an access query against a view can also be encoded as a PMBUTT. Suppose the query is specified as a PMBUTT Q, and the view is specified as a PMBUTT T. Then evaluating the query Q against a profile P protected by view T is equivalent to computing $Q \circ T(P)$. The composition PMBUTT $Q \circ T$ does not apply the sanitization of T to the entire tree P, but only the parts of P that query Q examines. This is precisely the idea of lazy materialization of views.

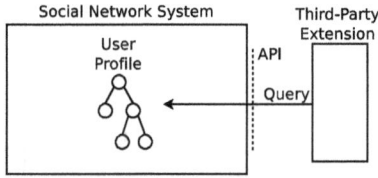

Figure 1: Original Design of Facebook Applications

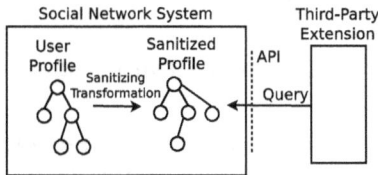

Figure 2: View-based Protection

2 SYSTEM OVERVIEW

2.1 Facebook Applications

An SNS such as Facebook maintains a social profile for each user (Fig. 1). A user may subscribe to third-party extensions (aka Facebook applications). These third-party extensions deliver their functionalities by querying personal information of the user through the SNS platform API. The queries are evaluated against the profile of the user.

A permission-based access control model determines if query evaluation is allowed or not, based on what permissions the owner of the profile has granted to the application. In other words, users declare their privacy preferences through the granting of permissions. As we have explained, access control is insufficient for preventing malicious third-party extensions from inferring sensitive information, simply because it fails to break the statistical correlation between sensitive and accessible information.

2.2 Query-time Profile Sanitization

In view-based protection, queries issued by a third-party application is evaluated against a sanitized version of the user profile (Fig. 2). The sanitized profile is constructed by a probabilistic transformation that is called a **view**. A view may (a) remove certain sensitive information, or (b) probabilistically transform the profile in such a way that any correlation between sensitive and accessible information is reduced or eliminated.

Since user profiles are semi-structured data, we model a user profile as a tree-shaped data structure (e.g., XML document). A view is therefore a probabilistic tree transformer.

The exact formulation of the view depends on the privacy preference of the user (what to hide) as well as the utility need of the application (what to release). These topics are discussed in details in a related work [5].

The view is materialized (i.e., applied to the user profile) when a query is issued by the application. To reduce computation overhead, view materialization is performed in a lazy manner: only the parts of the profile relevant to the query is transformed. See §4 and §5 respectively for a prototype and an automata model (PMBUTT)

Algorithm	Description
author	Infer the user's favorite author to be someone who authored the majority of books in the user's list of favorite books.
genre	Infer the user's favorite movie genre to be a genre that accounts for the majority of the movies in the user's list of favorite movies.
birthday	Infer the user's birthday to be a day when he/she received a considerable number of birthday wishes on his/her wall.
sibling	Infer the user's youngest sibling to be the youngest friend who listed the user in his/her profile as a sibling.
partner	Infer the user's partner to be a friend who is tagged in the the majority of the user's photos.
hometown	Infer the user's hometown to be a town where the user's primary school is located.
oldestF	Infer the user's oldest friend to be a friend who went to the same primary school as the user did.

Table 1: Sample inference algorithms

for lazy materialization. With lazy materialization, the SNS does not need to maintain a sanitized version of the profile for each application that the user subscribes to. Only a PMBUTT is stored for each user-application pair. *The size of the PMBUTT remains constant even as the user profile grows in size.* This is a major benefit of our approach.

3 EFFECTIVENESS OF VIEW-BASED PROTECTION

We began our investigation by an experiment conducted to demonstrate the effectiveness of view-based protection in reducing the success rate of SNS API inference algorithms.

3.1 Inference Algorithms and Dataset

In the study reported in [4], 8 sample inference algorithms are executed on the profiles of 424 users. In our experiment, we evaluate the success rate of these same inference algorithms against *profiles that are sanitized by probabilistic tree transformations*, and compare the result with what was reported in [4]. The intention is to demonstrate the effectiveness of query-time sanitization against inference algorithms. We, however, excluded one of those 8 algorithms because it had a very low success rate. Table 1 briefly summarizes the 7 sample inference algorithms that we have adopted from [4].

Since we did not have access to the user profiles collected in [4],[1] we generated a synthetic set of profiles. We generated the same number of profiles, which was 424, as [4] reported. The synthetic profiles are generated in such a way that preserve the success rates of the 7 sample inference algorithms. The following example illustrate how this is done for the inference algorithm author.

---

[1]To protect the privacy of the participants, the experiments of [4] were set up in such a way that the profile data is not stored.

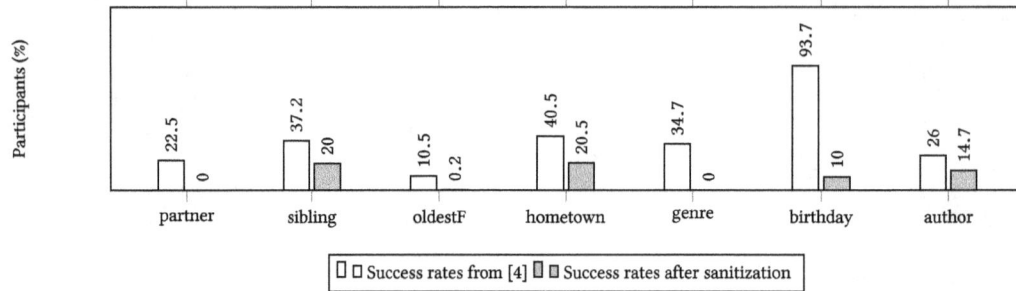

Figure 3: Comparing the success rate of inference algorithms before and after sanitizing profiles

Example 3.1 (Generating Profile Data for author*).* One of the inference algorithms of [4] is author (Table 1), which infers the user's favorite author to be the peron who has authored the majority of the books on the user's list of favorite books.

To generate a profile against which author will succeed in inferring the user's favorite author to be *Mark Twain*, all it takes is to add enough number of books written by *Mark Twain* into the list of favorite books in the user profile. On the contrary, to generate a profile against which author will fail, we simply create an empty list of favorite books.

The success rate of author was evaluated to 28.3% when it was allowed to make only one guess [4]. Using the method described in the previous paragraph, we thus generated 120 (= 0.283 × 424) profiles such that author would succeed, and 304 (= 424 − 120) profiles such that author would fail.

A similar approach is adopted for replicating the profile distribution for the other inference algorithms.

Once the synthetic dataset of profiles was generated, we implemented the inference algorithms described in [4] and ran them against the profiles. The success rates of algorithms were almost the same as the ones reported in [4], which shows that our simulation process was accurate enough.

3.2 Sanitizing Transformations

To demonstrate the effects of query-time sanitization, we design sanitizing transformations (aka views) that could eliminate the statistical correlation exploited by the inference algorithms reported in [4]. The user profiles are represented as trees, and the sanitizing transformations are programmed as probabilistic tree transformations. Here is an example.

Example 3.2. To counter the inference of the author algorithm, we transform user profiles by taking the following steps:

1. Suppose author a is the author who wrote the highest number of books in the user's list of favorite books. Let m be the number of favorite books written by author a.
2. With equal probabilities (0.5 and 0.5), randomly set n to be either $m + 1$ or $m - 1$,
3. Randomly select an author b who does not have any book in the favorite book list.
4. Insert n different book titles written by author b into the list of favorite books.

The effect is that, with probability 0.5, a will cease to be the dominating author in the favorite book list. Note that the transformation is probabilistic. The probabilistic behaviour is important. is important. Even when an attacker who knows how the sanitizing transformation work, it would still be confused because there is an equal chance that the dominating author in the favorite book list may or may not be the favorite author. Had we simply set $n = m + 1$, an attacker who knows how the sanitizing transformation works will conclude that the second dominating author in the favorite book list is the favorite author.

A sanitizing transformation algorithm was designed for each of the 7 sample inference algorithms. Due to space limitation, we refer the reader to §6.4 of [1] for details of the other 6 probabilistic tree transformations.

3.3 Results

Fig. 3 compares the success rate of the sample inference algorithms before and after transforming user profiles. The numbers in Fig. 3 show that sanitizing user profiles by probabilistic tree transformations can significantly reduce the success rate of the inference algorithms.

4 ADVANTAGE OF ESCHEWING VIEW MATERIALIZATION

While view-based protection is shown above to be an effective mitigation mechanism against SNS API inference attacks, a social networking platform will have to deal with the very practical issue of deciding when to materialize a view. We have argued in §1.2 that both the naive approach (sanitizing the entire profile when it is queried) and the stored-view approach (storing the sanitized profile) are inadequate. We claimed in §1.2 that performing lazy materialization at query time offers performance advantage against the naive approach, and prevents the frequent updates and storage overhead of the stored-view approach. In this section, we report an experiment conducted to demonstrate the performance advantage of lazy materialization of views.

4.1 Design

As an exploratory experiment, we are not tied to any particular programming language. We therefore take advantage of the *lazy evaluation* feature in the Haskell programming language, which is a purely functional language with mature implementations and

An Enforcement Model for Preventing Inference Attacks

extensive libraries, including those for tree/XML transformation. With lazy evaluation in Haskell, an expression is only evaluated if its value is absolutely needed for subsequent computation. Recall that, lazy materialization of views entails the application of a sanitizing transformation only to the parts of the tree that are relevant to the answering of a query. In this experiment, we model both the view $T(P)$ and the query $Q(P)$ as Haskel functions that take a tree P as argument. The querying of the sanitized tree is therefore the functional composition $Q(T(P))$. Haskell lazy evaluation will attempt to defer the application of T to the branches of P until Q actually asks for them. This is a convenient implementation of lazy view materialization. (In §6, we will examine a language-independent implementation of lazy view materialization via probabilistic tree transducers.)

Suppose *trans* is a sanitizing transformation. For now, assume *trans* involves noise addition designed for countering the author inference algorithm. Suppose further that *none* is a trivial query that returns a constant. That is, *none* is a transformation that suppresses the entire input profile.

To assess the effect of lazy view materialization, we evaluate $none(trans(t))$ for every profile t in the synthetic dataset of the previous section. Specifically, we do so in two different experimental configurations. In Configuration 1, we evaluate the expression in the regular Haskell runtime environment, allowing the full effect of lazy evaluation to be felt. Since the transformation *none* does not actually consume the return value of $trans(t)$, it is expected that lazy evaluation will optimize away the overhead of computing $trans(t)$. In Configuration 2, the Haskell runtime environment is forced to strictly evaluate $trans(t)$ first, which results in t', and then evaluate $none(t')$. Note that in Configuration 2, lazy evaluation is not completely turned off. Rather, eager evaluation is only enforced for the specific computation of $none(trans(t))$.

Haskell profiling tools are employed to compare the performance of evaluating the expression in the two configurations. The following metrics are used to compare the performance of view materialization in the two configurations:

1. allocated bytes in the heap,
2. copied bytes during garbage collection,
3. elapsed time to complete the evaluation, and
4. time spent for garbage collection.

4.2 Results

Table 2 compares the two configurations. Lazy evaluation (Configuration 1), which avoids materializing $trans(t)$, produced a significant improvement in performance. In Configuration 2, 82.5% of the total time of the computation were spent on garbage collection compared to only 0.4% in the first configuration. In Configuration 2, the Haskell runtime environment actually evaluated $trans(t)$, and that is why it needed to perform a lot of garbage collection afterwards. The above experiment was repeated by changing the transformation performed by *trans* to other sanitizing transformations that were designed for the remaining 7 sample inference algorithms in the previous section. We observed that the value of the performance metrics remain the same in Configuration 1, whereas they change in the second configuration. In other words, in Configuration 1, it does not matter for the Haskell runtime what transformation

		Configurations	
Metrics		Config. 1	Config. 2
Bytes allocated in the heap		219 KB	95572 KB
Bytes copied during GC		3 KB	15645 KB
Elapsed time		0.07 S	1.01 S
Time for GC		0.4%	82.6%

Table 2: Performance metrics for the Haskell compiler

is used in *trans* because that transformation does not need to be evaluated at all.

4.3 Discussion

The above experiment shows that avoiding view materialization as much as possible can make view-based protection much more efficient than otherwise. In the above experiment, we used Haskell as our programming language simply because of the convenience of built-in lazy evaluation. This may not always be acceptable in an industrial software development project. For instance, Haskell may not be the developer's preferred programming language. In addition, the behaviour of lazy evaluation may not appear predictable for programmers who do not possess deep knowledge of the Haskell programming model. What is needed, therefore, is a programming language-independent enforcement model that supports lazy materialization of views. Such an enforcement model is a main contribution of this work, a topic to which we now turn.

5 TREE TRANSDUCERS

Since we model user profiles as trees, the computation model that is to be proposed must be capable of transforming trees. In the literature, tree transducers have been proposed for exactly this purpose. We therefore adopt the same notion in order to propose the required computation model. This section is both an introduction to tree transducers as well as a requirement analysis for the kind of tree transducers needed by lazy view materialization.

5.1 Representation of Trees

User profiles are represented as trees, which are in turn represented by terms formed by function symbols.

Definition 5.1 (Ranked alphabet). A ranked alphabet is a pair (Σ, rk) where Σ is a finite set of function symbols, and $rk : \Sigma \to \mathbb{N}$ maps a function symbol to its arity.

We write Σ^n for the set of function symbols in Σ with rank n. We also write σ^k to highlight that $\sigma \in \Sigma^k$.

Example 5.2. One of the 8 sample inference algorithms in [4] aims at inferring a user's birthday by (a) scanning the user's wall in his/her profile, and (b) identifying the day in which a large number of birthday greetings ("Happy birthday") were posted.

The user's wall can be modeled using the ranked alphabet $\Sigma = \{en^3, bg^0, nbg^0, ts_1^0, ts_2^0, nil^0\}$. The function symbol *en* denotes an entry on the wall. It has three input arguments: (i) the timestamp of the entry, corresponding to constant symbols ts_1 or ts_2, (ii) the message of the entry which could be either a birthday greeting (denoted by constant symbol *bg*) or a message that does not correspond to a birthday greeting (denoted by constant symbol *nbg*), and (iii) the next entry on the wall, which could be either the constant *nil* (terminating the list of entries), or another *en* function.

For instance, $en(ts_1, bg, en(ts_2, nbg, nil))$ represents a wall with two entries. The first entry is a birthday greeting posted at time ts_1. The second entry, posted at time ts_2, is not a birthday greeting (*nbg*).

A tree transducer transforms a tree formed by a ranked alphabet to a sanitized tree of the same alphabet.

5.2 Requirement Analysis

Different types of tree transducers have been proposed in the literature. To identify which kind of tree transducers fits the requirements of view-based protection model, we need to first determine the properties we seek in a tree transducer based on the needs of the view-based protection model. The two main features we need are (a) closure under composition, and (b) high expressive power.

The first property, closure under composition, is required due to the fact that it is usually infeasible to create a single transducer that can completely handle a transformation task. A transformation is typically formed by composing two or more primitive transformations. Consequently, if we model two transformations as tree transducers of a particular class, we want their composition to belong to the same class of tree transducers. More importantly, we will model a profile query also as a tree transformation (i.e., transforming a profile tree to a query answer). By composing a sanitizing transformation T with a query Q, the composed transformation $Q \circ T$ will materialize only the part of T that is relevant to answering Q. Closure under composition is therefore the main vehicle by which lazy materialization is achieved.

The second property, high expressive power, requires the tree transducer to be expressive enough so that it can express commonly used sanitizing transformations, such as suppression, generalization, noise addition, and sampling. Most of the existing classes of tree transducers can perform simple types of transformations (e.g., replacing a subtree with another subtree). However, there are three specific properties that are rarely found simultaneously in existing tree transducer models, namely, look-ahead, differential copying and probabilistic behaviour. We informally define them in the following.

Look-ahead. A tree transducer with the look-ahead feature can look at deeper (one or more levels lower) nodes in a tree while parsing the nodes at upper parts of the tree. Consider the task of protecting the user's birth date in Example 5.2. To protect the user's birth date, we want to replace the timestamp of all the birthday greeting entries with ϵ (a constant symbol representing no information). For such a transformation, we need the look-ahead property. In other words, when the state machine arrives at a state where input is a wall entry, e.g., $en(ts_1, bg, en(ts_2, nbg, nil))$, it needs to be able to look at the function symbol in the second input argument, and if that function symbol is *bg*, then the machine replaces the first argument (the timestamp ts_1) with ϵ. Without look-ahead, the state machine only sees the *en* function symbol, and not its children nodes, thereby failing to respond accordingly.

Differential Copying. Random sampling is a classical sanitizing transformation. Rather than publishing the entire data set, a sanitized sample of it is published. In that way, statistics are preserved without disclosing the entire data set. In the birth date example in Example 5.2, one can sanitize the wall by first removing the timestamps, and then releasing a sample subset of the wall entries.

Our experience with encoding random sampling with tree transducers allows us to discover that we require a tree transducer model that supports a feature that we call *differential copying*.

Example 5.3 (Differential copying). Suppose there is an input tree $\sigma(t)$ where $\sigma \in \Sigma^1$ and $t \in \mathcal{T}_\Sigma$ is a branch of the input tree. We want to transform $\sigma(t)$ to $\sigma'(t, t')$ where t' is a transformation of t. This requires the tree transducer to copy t from the input tree to both children of σ', but the two children are treated differently: the one on the left (t) is preserved as is, but the one on the right is further transformed (t').

In short, the feature that we desire in a tree transducer is the ability to make copies of an input subtree, and to continue transformation of these copies in different states.

Probabilistic behaviour. To break statistical correlations, transformations may need to sanitize profiles in a probabilistic manner. To see this, recall the random mutation of the favorite book list in Example 3.2. In general, sanitizing strategies such as noise addition and random sampling require probabilistic transformations.

5.3 Top-down & Bottom-up Tree Transducers

Top-down and bottom-up tree transducers are the two main categories of tree transducers. Intuitively, a top-down tree transducer is like a Deterministic Finite Automaton (DFA), with the difference that the input is a tree. At the beginning, there is one read-head associated with the root of the input tree. Once the root is parsed, a different read-head will be associated to every child of the root node. In other words, the transducer spawns concurrent threads of execution to scan children of the root node. This process continues from the root to the bottom of the tree. Note that a DFA always has one read-head (one thread of execution) whereas a top-down tree transducer could have multiple read-heads concurrently.

Bottom-up tree transducers are different from top-down tree transducers in the sense that they parse the input tree from the bottom (leaves) to the top (root).

To facilitate comparison with our proposed transducer model in §6, we list below the definition of top-down and bottom-up tree transducers:

Definition 5.4 (Terms and variables). Let Σ be a ranked alphabet and $X = \{x_1, \dots, x_n\}$ be a set of constant symbols (aka variables). The set $\mathcal{T}_\Sigma(X)$ of terms formed by function symbols in Σ and variables in X is defined as follows:

a) $\Sigma^0 \cup X \subseteq \mathcal{T}_\Sigma(X)$.

b) If $t_0, \dots, t_{n-1} \in \mathcal{T}_\Sigma(X)$, and $\sigma \in \Sigma^n$, then $\sigma(t_0, \dots, t_{n-1}) \in \mathcal{T}_\Sigma(X)$.

When $X = \varnothing$, we abbreviate $\mathcal{T}_\Sigma(X)$ to $\mathcal{T}_\Sigma$. Given $t \in \mathcal{T}_\Sigma(X)$, we write $var(t)$ to denote the set of variables (i.e., members of X) appearing in t.

Definition 5.5 (Terms with roots taken from a given alphabet). Suppose Σ_1 and Σ_2 are two ranked alphabets. For a set $\Gamma \subseteq \Sigma_1$, and

$H \subseteq \mathcal{T}_{\Sigma_2}(X)$, $\Gamma(H)$ is defined to be $\{\gamma(t_1, \ldots, t_k) \mid \exists k \geq 0, \gamma \in \Gamma^k, t_1, \ldots, t_k \in H\}$. That is, $\Gamma(H)$ consists of terms formed by applying a function symbol from Γ to terms from H.

Definition 5.6 (Tree transducer). Let $M = (Q, \Sigma, q_0, R)$ be a tuple where

a) Q, the set of states, is a finite, ranked alphabet containing only unary function symbols (i.e., arity is 1),

b) Σ is a ranked alphabet of input and output symbols,

c) $F \subseteq Q$ is the set of designated states, and

d) R is a finite set of transition rules.

Then M is:

- a top-down tree transducer if transition rules in R are of the form $q(\sigma(x_1, \ldots, x_k)) \to r$ for some $q \in Q$, $\sigma \in \Sigma^k$, and $r \in \mathcal{T}_\Sigma(Q(X))$ such that $var(r) \subseteq \{x_1, \ldots, x_k\}$, or

- a bottom-up tree transducer if the transition rules in R are of either the form $\sigma(q_1(x_1), \ldots, q_k(x_k)) \to q(t)$ with $k \geq 1$, $\sigma \in \Sigma^k$, $q_1, \ldots q_k \in Q$, $t \in \mathcal{T}_\Sigma(X)$, and $var(t) \subseteq \{x_1, \ldots, x_k\}$, or the form $\sigma \to q(t)$ where $q \in Q$, $\sigma \in \Sigma^0$, and $t \in \mathcal{T}_\Sigma$.

Despite the rich expressive power of the top-down and bottom-up tree transducers, they do not satisfy the requirements of view-based protection. Top-down tree transducers suffer from the lack of look-ahead. Bottom-up tree transducers has the look-ahead feature, because they transform the input tree from the bottom to the top. Moreover, total deterministic bottom-up tree transducers are closed under composition, and every deterministic bottom-up tree transducer can be converted to an equivalent total deterministic bottom-up tree transducer. Deterministic transition in such a tree transducer model also eases the extension of the model to a probabilistic one. This stands in stark contrast to non-deterministic tree transducers.

The bottom-up tree transducer, however, has its own weaknesses. More specifically, while top-down tree transducers support differential copying, bottom-up tree transducers do not. In short, these two classes of tree transducers are incomparable in expressiveness [10], and none of the them support both look-ahead and differential copying.

5.4 Multi Bottom-up Tree Transducers

The weakness of bottom-up tree transducers is addressed in the **Multi Bottom-up Tree Transducer (MBUTT)**, which is a generalization of bottom-up tree transducer proposed by Maletti [11, 17]. More specifically, an MBUTT allows outputting a sequence of trees in each transition rule. This extension is signified by the word "multi". According to Definition 5.6, the right-hand side of every transition rule in a bottom-up tree transducer belongs to $Q(\mathcal{T}_\Sigma(X))$, while all states in Q are unary. As a result, only one tree from $\mathcal{T}_\Sigma(X)$ can be output in a transition rule. On the contrary, in the MBUTT, a sequence of trees might be output in a transition rule. This has been made feasible by allowing states to be of ranks larger than one. This means, in Example 5.3, an MBUTT can be designed so that when it parses t, it keeps one copy of t and one copy of its transformed form t'. When the MBUTT reaches the root σ, it has already transformed t to t' while it has preserved the original copy of t.

Below is the formal definition of MBUTTs.

Definition 5.7 (Linear and normalized terms). A term t is **linear** in $V \subseteq X$ if every variable $x \in V$ appears at most once in t. A term t is **normalized** if (a) $var(t) = \{x_1, \ldots, x_m\}$ for some $m \in \mathbb{N}$, (b) each variable appears exactly once, and (c) the variables appear in exactly the order $x_1, \ldots, x_m$.

Definition 5.8 (Multi bottom-up tree transducer [17]). A MBUTT is a tuple (Q, Σ, F, R) where

a) Q, the set of states, is a uniquely-ranked alphabet, disjoint with $\Sigma \cup X$,

b) Σ is a ranked alphabet of input and output symbols, disjoint with X,

c) $F \subseteq Q^1$ is the set of final states, and

d) R is a finite set of transition rules of the form $l \to r$ where $l \in \Sigma(Q(X))$ is normalized and linear in X, $r \in Q(\mathcal{T}_\Sigma(X))$, and $var(r) \subseteq var(l)$.

An MBUTT is **deterministic** (respectively, **total deterministic**) if for every $l \in \Sigma(Q(X))$, there exists at most one (respectively, exactly one) r such that $l \to r \in R$.

The semantics of MBUTT, specified by way of term rewriting, is detailed in [17]. It has been proved in the same work that every deterministic MBUTT can be converted to an equivalent total deterministic MBUTT. A composition construction has been given to show how two MBUTTs can be composed to create another MBUTT. It is proved in [17] that given two total deterministic MBUTTs, their composition is also a total deterministic MBUTT.

As explained in the previous section, the MBUTT has almost all the requirements we need including closure under composition (if it is total deterministic), look-ahead and differential copying. The only required feature that is missing is probabilistic behaviour. Therefore, the original definition of the MBUTT needs to be extended so that it allows the transducer to behave probabilistically.

6 PMBUTT

In this section we propose a new type of tree transducers, called the **Probabilistic Multi Bottom-up Tree Transducer (PMBUTT)**, which is obtained by extending MBUTT to incorporate probabilistic behaviour. We advocate the use of PMBUTT as a programming language-independent implementation of view materialization.

6.1 Syntax

The PMBUTT is defined by adding probabilistic behaviour to the MBUTT (Def. 5.8). In other words, a left-hand side may probabilistically transitions to multiple right-hand sides. The transition probabilities must add up to 1 for the same left-hand side. Deterministic behaviour can be simulated by assigning the maximum transition probability, which is 1, to a transition.

Definition 6.1 (Probabilistic multi bottom-up tree transducers). A PMBUTT is a tuple (Q, Σ, F, R) where

a) Q, the set of states, is a uniquely-ranked alphabet, disjoint with $\Sigma \cup X$.

b) Σ is a ranked alphabet of input and output symbols, disjoint with X.

c) $F \subseteq Q^1$ is a set of final states.

d) R is a finite set of probabilistic transition rules of the form $l \xrightarrow{p} r$ where $l \in \Sigma(Q(X))$ is normalized and linear in X, $r \in Q(\mathcal{T}_\Sigma(X))$, $var(r) \subseteq var(l)$, and $p \in [0,1]$.

e) For every rule $l \xrightarrow{p} r \in R$, $peer(l \xrightarrow{p} r)$ is defined to be $\{l \xrightarrow{p'} r' \mid l \xrightarrow{p'} r' \in R\}$. Then for every rule $u \in R$, the following must hold

$$\sum_{l \xrightarrow{p} r \,\in\, peer(u)} p = 1$$

In the above definition, $peer(u)$ (for some $u \in R$) contains all transition rules in R that share the same left-hand side with u. Therefore, item (e) enforces that transitions from the same left-hand side sum up to 1. Note that all transition rules in the PMBUTT consumes exactly one input symbol.

A PMBUTT M is total if for every $l \in \Sigma(Q(X))$, there exists at least one r such that $l \xrightarrow{p} r \in R$.

6.2 Semantics

The rewrite semantics for the PMBUTT $M = (Q, \Sigma, F, R)$ is defined by Definition 6.2.

Definition 6.2. Let $t, t' \in \mathcal{T}_\Sigma(Q(\mathcal{T}_\Sigma))$, and $l \xrightarrow{p} r \in R$. We write $t \Rightarrow_{M,p}^{l \xrightarrow{p} r} t'$ if $p > 0$ and there exists $w \in \mathcal{P}os(t)$ and $\theta : X \to \mathcal{T}_\Sigma$ such that $t|_w = l\theta$ and $t' = t[r\theta]_w$, and we write $t \Rightarrow_{M,p} t'$ if there exists $l \xrightarrow{p} r \in R$ such that $t \Rightarrow_{M,p}^{l \xrightarrow{p} r} t'$. Moreover, we write $t \leadsto_{M,p}^{s} t'$ if there exists a finite sequence of transition rules $s : l_1 \xrightarrow{p_1} r_1, l_2 \xrightarrow{p_2} r_2, \ldots, l_n \xrightarrow{p_n} r_n$ in R such that $t \Rightarrow_{M,p_1}^{l_1 \xrightarrow{p_1} r_1} t_1 \Rightarrow_{M,p_2}^{l_2 \xrightarrow{p_2} r_2} t_2 \ldots \Rightarrow_{M,p_n}^{l_n \xrightarrow{p_n} r_n} t'$, and $p = p_1 \times p_2 \times \ldots \times p_n$. If there are exactly $k \geq 1$ distinct sequences $s_1, \ldots, s_k$ of transition rules such that $t \leadsto_{M,p_i}^{s_i} t'$ for two fixed t and t', then we write $t \Rightarrow_{M,p}^{*} t'$ where $p = \sum_{i=1}^{k} p_i$. If all such sequences $s_1, \ldots, s_k$ are of length n, we write $t \Rightarrow_{M,p}^{n} t'$. The tree transformation computed by M is $\tau_M = \{(t, t'|_1, p) \in \mathcal{T}_\Sigma \times \mathcal{T}_\Sigma \times [0,1] \mid t \in \mathcal{T}_\Sigma, t' \in F(\mathcal{T}_\Sigma), t \Rightarrow_{M,p}^{*} t'\}$.

Note that given a tree $t \in \mathcal{T}_\Sigma$, the first rules that we have to apply are the ones that do not have any state in their left-hand side. Moreover, it is possible that a term t be transformed to t' by taking two different sequences of probabilistic transition rules. That is why that associated probability to $t \Rightarrow_{M,p}^{*} t'$ is the summation of all probabilities p_i for which there is a distinct sequence of transitions s_i such that $t \leadsto_{M,p_i}^{s_i} t'$.

Computation of M for a given input tree is always terminating because all transition rules are input consuming. Therefore, after finite number of transitions, there will be a point that either all input symbols are consumed or there is no more applicable transition rules. Note that τ_M is always a finite set for the same reason.

Example 6.3. Consider a user profile with a list of favorite books. Each book has a title and an author. For the sake of simplicity, we consider only the author of each book. Suppose also that there are only two names that could appear as the author of a book, a

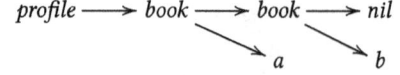

Figure 4: A sample user profile

and b. Such a profile could be modelled using an alphabet $\Sigma = \{profile^1, book^2, a^0, b^0, nil^0\}$ where $profile$ is a function symbol that appears only at the root of the profile. Fig. 4 shows a sample user profile created from Σ. Given such a profile, one can infer the user's favorite author by counting the number of times every author appeared in the user's list of favorite books. To counter that, we want to randomly inject books into that list. The PMBUTT $M = (\{q_0, q_1, q_2, q_f\}, \Sigma, \{q_f\}, R)$ can produce such a transformation with the following rules in R:

1) $\quad a \xrightarrow{1} q_1(a)$ $\qquad$ 2) $\quad b \xrightarrow{1} q_1(b)$

3) $\quad nil \xrightarrow{1} q_0(nil)$

4) $\quad book(q_1(x_1), q_0(x_2)) \xrightarrow{0.5} q_0(book(x_1, x_2))$

5) $\quad book(q_1(x_1), q_0(x_2)) \xrightarrow{0.125} q_0(book(x_1, book(a, x_2)))$

6) $\quad book(q_1(x_1), q_0(x_2)) \xrightarrow{0.125} q_0(book(x_1, book(b, x_2)))$

7) $\quad book(q_1(x_1), q_0(x_2)) \xrightarrow{0.125} q_0(book(a, book(x_1, x_2)))$

8) $\quad book(q_1(x_1), q_0(x_2)) \xrightarrow{0.125} q_0(book(b, book(x_1, x_2)))$

9) $\quad profile(q_0(x_1)) \xrightarrow{1} q_f(profile(x_1))$

When the PMBUTT parses a book in the list of books, with probability 0.5 it outputs the book as it is. Otherwise, it injects noise: with equal probabilities it randomly injects a book written by a or b before or after the current item in the list of books. The size of the list is at most doubled.

Example 6.4. The computation of the PMBUTT M, described in Example 6.3, is demonstrated on the input tree $profile(book(a, book(b, nil)))$. Note that r_i denotes rule i from Example 6.3.

$$profile(book(a, book(b, nil)))$$
$$\Rightarrow_{M,1}^{r_3} \quad profile(book(a, book(b, q_0(nil))))$$
$$\Rightarrow_{M,1}^{r_2} \quad profile(book(a, book(q_1(b), q_0(nil))))$$
$$\Rightarrow_{M,1}^{r_1} \quad profile(book(q_1(a), book(q_1(b), q_0(nil))))$$
$$\Rightarrow_{M,0.125}^{r_8} \quad profile(book(q_1(a), q_0(book(b, book(b, nil)))))$$
$$\Rightarrow_{M,0.125}^{r_5} \quad profile(q_0(book(a, book(a, book(b, book(b, nil))))))$$
$$\Rightarrow_{M,1}^{r_9} \quad q_f(profile(book(a, book(a, book(b, book(b, nil))))))$$

As a result, the following holds:

$$profile(book(a, book(b, nil))) \Rightarrow_{M,0.015625}^{*}$$
$$q_f(profile(book(a, book(a, book(b, book(b, nil))))))$$

6.3 Composition construction

The composition of two PMBUTTs M and N are denoted by $M; N$, in which the input tree is first processed by M and then the result will go through N. In this work, the composition construction proposed by Maletti in [17] is extended to compose two PMBUTTss. The main idea is similar to other composition constructions proposed for combining state machines, e.g., combining two DFAs to compute another DFA that accepts only sequences that are accepted by both of the automata. In these constructions, the set of states for the composed machine is the cross-product of the state sets of the two input machines. Moreover, this approach simulates the second state machine on the right-hand side of the transition rules of the first machine. We follow the same approach for creating the set of states in $M; N$. However, the difference is that a state from M may output more than one tree. That is why a state in a PMBUTT may have an arity larger than one. As a result, when we take the cross-product of the state sets from M and N to create the set of states in $M; N$, we should take this into consideration: i.e., output trees of a state in M arrives at multiple states in N. As a result, the states in $M; N$ will be of the form $q\langle h_1, \ldots, h_k \rangle$ where q is a state of rank k in M and $h_1, \ldots, h_k$ are states in N. The arity of a state $q\langle h_1, \ldots, h_k \rangle$ in $M; N$ will be the summation of the arities of h_1 to h_k.

Let $M = (Q, \Sigma, F_M, R_M)$ and $N = (H, \Sigma, F_N, R_N)$ where Q, H, and Σ are disjoint. A uniquely-ranked alphabet is defined as follows:

$$Q\langle H \rangle = \{ q\langle h_1, \ldots, h_n \rangle \mid q^n \in Q, h_1, \ldots, h_n \in H \}$$

where $rk(q\langle h_1, \ldots, h_n \rangle) = \sum_{i=1}^{n} rk(h_i)$ for every $q^n \in Q$ and $h_1, \ldots, h_n \in H$.

Now that we know how to create the set of states in $M; N$ from the set of states in M and N, we move on to show how the transition rules are created for the composed machine. Let $q\langle h_1, \ldots, h_n \rangle$ be a state in $M; N$ of rank k. This means we expect the term $q\langle h_1, \ldots, h_n \rangle (u_1, \ldots, u_k)$ to appear in the transition rules of $M; N$ where $u_i \in \mathcal{T}_\Sigma(X)$ for $1 \le i \le k$. Intuitively, this term is actually computed by $q(h_1(u_1, \ldots, u_{rk(h_1)}), \ldots, h_n(u_{k-rk(h_n)+1}, \ldots, u_k))$. As a result, a mapping needs to be defined to describe the equality between these two terms. Let $U = \mathcal{T}_\Sigma(X)$.

The mapping $\varphi : \mathcal{T}_\Sigma(Q\langle H \rangle(U)) \to \mathcal{T}_\Sigma(Q(H(U)))$ is defined such that for every $q\langle h_1, \ldots, h_n \rangle \in Q\langle H \rangle^k$, $u_1, \ldots, u_k \in U$, $\sigma \in \Sigma^k$, and $t_1, \ldots, t_k \in \mathcal{T}_\Sigma(Q\langle H \rangle(U))$:

$$\varphi(q\langle h_1, \ldots, h_n \rangle (u_1, \ldots, u_k)) = q(h_1(u_1, \ldots, u_{rk(h_1)}), \ldots,$$
$$h_n(u_{k-rk(h_n)+1}, \ldots, u_k))$$
$$\varphi(\sigma(t_1, \ldots, t_k)) = \sigma(\varphi(t_1), \ldots, \varphi(t_k))$$

So far, it has been shown that given $M = (Q, \Sigma, F_M, R_M)$ and $N = (H, \Sigma, F_N, R_N)$, $Q\langle H \rangle$ will be the set of states in $M; N$. This implies that transitions in $M; N$ will be of the form $l \xrightarrow{p} r$ where $l \in \Sigma(Q\langle H \rangle(X))$, $r \in Q\langle H \rangle(\mathcal{T}_\Sigma(X))$, and $p \in [0, 1]$. $l \xrightarrow{p} r$ appears in the transition rules of $M; N$, if there exist a u such that l is transformed to u by M, and then u is transformed to r by N. In other words, $l \Rightarrow_{M, p_1} u$ and $u \Rightarrow_{N, p_2} r$ where $p = p_1.p_2$. To make the syntax right, and simplify this requirement, we have to use the mapping φ and require $\varphi(l) (\Rightarrow_{M, p_1}; \Rightarrow_{N, p_2}) \varphi(r)$ to hold in order for $l \xrightarrow{p_1.p_2} r$ to appear in the transition rules in $M; N$. However, this requirement is not completely correct. The reason is that u may contain multiple symbols from Σ that must be all consumed by N. This is clarified via an example. Let $a, b, c \in \Sigma^1$, $q \in Q^1$, and $h \in H^1$.

Moreover, assume:

$$1) \qquad a(q(x_1)) \xrightarrow{1} q(b(c(x_1))) \in R_M$$

$$2) \qquad c(h(x_1)) \xrightarrow{1} h(c(x_1)) \in R_N$$

$$3) \qquad b(h(x_1)) \xrightarrow{1} h(b(x_1)) \in R_N$$

Now, given a left-hand side $l = a(q\langle h \rangle(x_1))$, we want to find a right-hand side r and a probability p such that $l \xrightarrow{p} r$ appears in $R_{M; N}$. Remember the requirement was that $\varphi(l) (\Rightarrow_{M, p_1}; \Rightarrow_{N, p_2}) \varphi(r)$ holds. We follow the below steps to find r:

$$\varphi(a(q\langle h \rangle(x_1))) = a(q(h(x_1)))$$
$$a(q(h(x_1))) \Rightarrow_{M, 1} q(b(c(h(x_1)))) \text{ via rule 1}$$
$$q(b(c(h(x_1)))) \Rightarrow_{N, 1} q(b(h(c(x_1)))) \text{ via rule 2}$$

$\varphi(r)$ equals $q(b(h(c(x_1))))$, which means $r = \varphi^{-1}(q(b(h(c(x_1)))))$. However, r cannot be computed because $q(b(h(c(x_1))))$ does not belong to the co-domain of the mapping φ which is $\mathcal{T}_\Sigma(Q(H(\mathcal{T}_\Sigma(X))))$. The reason is that in the right-hand side of the rule 1, there are more than one output symbol that must be consumed by N. Therefore, we need to continue applying transition rules from the second machine, N, to consume the other symbol too. This means the below step must be further followed:

$$q(b(h(c(x_1)))) \Rightarrow_{N, 1} q(h(b(c(x_1)))) \text{ via rule 3}$$

Now r is computed by $\varphi^{-1}(q(h(b(c(x_1)))))$ which equals $q\langle h \rangle(b(c(x_1)))$. As a result, $a(q\langle h \rangle(x_1)) \xrightarrow{p} q\langle h \rangle(b(c(x_1)))$ is inserted in $R_{M; N}$ where $p = 1 \times 1 \times 1 = 1$ because the associated probabilities to the three rules involved are all 1.

It is concluded that the requirement must be revised to $\varphi(l) (\Rightarrow_{M, p_1}^{*}; \Rightarrow_{N, p_2}^{*}) \varphi(r)$ in order for $l \xrightarrow{p_1.p_2} r$ to appear in the transition rules of $M; N$. Last but not least, since there might be different paths from $\varphi(l)$ to $\varphi(r)$ for two fixed l and r, we have to take all those paths into consideration and add up their probabilities.

Now, the composition algorithm is defined as follows:

THEOREM 6.5. *Let $M = (Q, \Sigma, F_M, R_M)$ and $N = (H, \Sigma, F_N, R_N)$ be two PMBUTTs s.t. Q, H and Σ are mutually disjoint. The composition of M and N is the PMBUTT*

$$M; N = (Q\langle H \rangle, \Sigma, F_M \langle F_N \rangle, R)$$

s.t. for every $l \in \Sigma(Q\langle H \rangle(X))$ and $r \in Q\langle H \rangle(\mathcal{T}_\Sigma(X))$, if there are exactly $k \ge 1$ rules $u_1, \ldots, u_k$ in R_M such that $\varphi(l) (\Rightarrow_{M, p_i^M}^{u_i}; \Rightarrow_{N, p_i^N}^{*}) \varphi(r)$, then $l \xrightarrow{p} r \in R$ where

$$p = \sum_{i=1}^{k} p_i^M \times p_i^N.$$

Therefore, any two PMBUTTss can be composed. A proof of this theorem is given in §5.4.4 (Theorem 5.4.6) of [1].

Example 6.6. This example goes through the details of composing two transformations M and N where the input profile is similar to the profile used in Example 6.3. M, which is a simpler version of the PMBUTT introduced in Example 6.3, randomly (with probability 0.5) injects a book authored by author a before every book in the list of favorite books in the user profile. Then, N transforms the output of M by generalizing the author of every book to the value ab which shows the author is either a or b. Note that the goal is only to exemplify how the composition algorithm works and actual effectiveness of the transformations performed by M and N is not the concern of this example.

The set of transition rules for $M = (Q_M, \Sigma, \{q_f\}, R_M)$ with $Q_M = \{q_0, q_1, q_f\}$ is defined as follows:

$$a \xrightarrow{1} q_1(a) \qquad b \xrightarrow{1} q_1(b) \qquad nil \xrightarrow{1} q_0(nil)$$

$$book(q_1(x_1), q_0(x_2)) \xrightarrow{0.5} q_0(book(x_1, x_2))$$

$$book(q_1(x_1), q_0(x_2)) \xrightarrow{0.5} q_0(book(a, book(x_1, x_2)))$$

$$profile(q_0(x_1)) \xrightarrow{1} q_f(profile(x_1))$$

The set of transition rules for $N = (Q_N, \Sigma, \{h_f\}, R_N)$ with $Q_N = \{h_0, h_1, h_f\}$ is defined as follows:

$$a \xrightarrow{1} h_1(ab) \qquad b \xrightarrow{1} h_1(ab) \qquad nil \xrightarrow{1} h_0(nil)$$

$$book(h_1(x_1), h_0(x_2)) \xrightarrow{1} h_0(book(x_1, x_2))$$

$$profile(h_0(x_1)) \xrightarrow{1} h_f(profile(x_1))$$

The first step to compose M and N is to convert them to total PMBUTTs using the technique describe in the proof of Lemma 5.4.9 in [1]. We skip this step as it is uninspiring. Now following the algorithm of Theorem 6.5 to obtain $M; N$ results in a PMBUTT with the following states:

$$\{ q_0\langle h_0 \rangle^1, q_0\langle h_1 \rangle^1, q_0\langle h_f \rangle^1, q_1\langle h_0 \rangle^1, q_1\langle h_1 \rangle^1, q_1\langle h_f \rangle^1,$$

$$q_f\langle h_0 \rangle^1, q_f\langle h_1 \rangle^1, q_f\langle h_f \rangle^1 \}$$

Some of the relevant transition rules of $M; N$ are as follows:

$$a \xrightarrow{1} q_1\langle h_1 \rangle(ab) \qquad b \xrightarrow{1} q_1\langle h_1 \rangle(ab) \qquad nil \xrightarrow{1} q_0\langle h_0 \rangle(nil)$$

$$book(q_1\langle h_1 \rangle(x_1), q_0\langle h_0 \rangle(x_2)) \xrightarrow{0.5} q_0\langle h_0 \rangle(book(x_1, x_2))$$

$$book(q_1\langle h_1 \rangle(x_1), q_0\langle h_0 \rangle(x_2)) \xrightarrow{0.5} q_0\langle h_0 \rangle(book(ab,$$
$$book(x_1, x2)))$$

$$profile(q_0\langle h_0 \rangle(x_1)) \xrightarrow{1} q_f\langle h_f \rangle profile(x_1)$$

As can be seen in the above transition rules, $M; N$ transforms a's and b's to ab and it may inject new book items with ab as the value of the author.

6.4 Evaluation

In the following, we assess the proposed model of view materialization. More specifically, the expressiveness of PMBUTT is evaluated in §6.4.1. Then the complexity of the composition construction is studied in §6.4.2.

6.4.1 Expressiveness. To assess the expressive power of PMBUTT, we demonstrate that it can capture classical sanitizing transformations from the literature, namely, suppression, generalization, noise addition, and random sampling.

Example 6.7 (Suppression). Suppression can easily be described by a PMBUTT. All it takes is to replace a branch with the constant symbol ϵ. For instance, consider the PMBUTT N from Example

6.6. We can simply suppress the author of every book with the following rule:

$$book(h_1(x_1), h_0(x_2)) \xrightarrow{1} h_0(book(\epsilon, x_2))$$

Example 6.8 (Generalization). The PMBUTT N from Example 6.6 performs generalization.

Example 6.9 (Sampling). Sampling requires probabilistic behaviour. Suppose we want to devise a transformation for the type of profiles used in Example 6.6, to sample from the list of books in the user profile. The following set of transitions can achieve this effect:

$$a \xrightarrow{1} h_1(a) \qquad b \xrightarrow{1} h_1(b) \qquad nil \xrightarrow{1} h_0(nil)$$

$$book(h_1(x_1), h_0(x_2)) \xrightarrow{0.5} h_0(book(x_1, x_2))$$

$$book(h_1(x_1), h_0(x_2)) \xrightarrow{0.5} h_0(x_2)$$

$$profile(h_0(x_1)) \xrightarrow{1} h_f(profile(x_1))$$

Example 6.10 (Noise addition). The PMBUTT M in Example 6.3 implements noise addition.

Note that the PMBUTT cannot model noise addition when the number of injected branches is selected randomly. The reason is that for such a transformation, we need to have a cycle with at least one transition that does not consume any input. However, the definition of PMBUTT does not allow epsilon rules: i.e., rules that do not consume any input. A PMBUTT can be defined to randomly inject up to m noisy branches, though the machine may get very large. However, if m is not pre-defined, then an arbitrary number is randomly selected at runtime, and such a transformation cannot be expressed in PMBUTT. In general, any transformation that requires epsilon rules is not expressible in PMBUTT.

The reader is referred to [1, §5.4.5.2] for examples of how PMBUTT can be used for specifying two other classical sanitizing transformations: noise multiplication and permutation.

6.4.2 Complexity of the Composition Construction. This section analyzes the complexity of the composition construction described in §6.3.

Given $t \in \mathcal{T}_\Sigma(X)$ and $V \subseteq \Sigma \cup X$, we write $|t|_V$ to denote the number of time symbols from V appear in term t. For example $|t|_{\Sigma \cup X}$ is the size of t.

We now attend to the complexity of the composition construction as described in Theorem 6.5. Suppose PMBUTTs $M = (Q_M, \Sigma, F_M, R_M)$ and $N = (Q_N, \Sigma, F_N, R_N)$ are composed to $M; N$. Three parameters are defined as follows:

$$c_1 = \max_{l \xrightarrow{p} r \in R_M} |l|_X \qquad c_2 = \max_{l \xrightarrow{p} r \in R_M} |r|_\Sigma$$

$$c_3 = \max_{u \in R_N} |peer(u)|$$

Parameter c_1 is the maximum number of variables that appear in the left-hand sides of the transition rules in R_M. Assume there is a transition rule in R_M as follows:

$$f(q_1(x_1, x_2), q_2(x_3)) \xrightarrow{p} q_1(g(m(x_1), x_2), m(x_3)) \qquad (1)$$

where $f^2, m^1, g^2 \in \Sigma$ and $q_1^2, q_2^1 \in Q_N$. Since there are three variables in the left-hand side of the above rule, when we compose M and N, three states from Q_N are needed to combine the above rule with rules from Q_N. For instance, if $Q_N = \{h_1^1, h_2^2\}$, then corresponding to the above rule, the following terms will appear in the left-hand side of the rules in $M; N$:

1) $f(q_1\langle h_1, h_1\rangle(x_1, x_2), q_2\langle h_1\rangle(x_3))$ (2)

2) $f(q_1\langle h_1, h_1\rangle(x_1, x_2), q_2\langle h_2\rangle(x_3, x_4))$

3) $f(q_1\langle h_1, h_2\rangle(x_1, x_2, x_3), q_2\langle h_1\rangle(x_4))$

⋮

8) $f(q_1\langle h_2, h_2\rangle(x_1, x_2, x_3, x_4), q_2\langle h_2\rangle(x_5, x_6))$

In the above example, since Q_N contains two states, and there are three variables in the left-hand side of the rule denoted by (1), there will be 8 ($= 2^3$) corresponding left-hand sides in the transition rules of $M; N$. We can generalize this figure to $|R_M|.|Q_N|^{c_1}$. Once we applied a transition rule from M on one of such left-hand sides, the result term could go through different probabilistic execution paths in N. For example, assume we apply the rule (1) from R_M on the $\varphi(l)$ where l is a candidate left-hand side denoted by (2). This means:

$$\varphi(f(q_1\langle h_1, h_1\rangle(x_1, x_2), q_2\langle h_1\rangle(x_3)))$$
$$= f(q_1(h_1(x_1), h_1(x_2)), q_2(h_1(x_3)))$$
$$\Rightarrow_{M,p} q_1(g(m(h_1(x_1)), h_1(x_2), m(h_1(x_3))))$$

Now we keep applying rules from R_N on the resulted right-hand side to consume all the symbols. In the above example, there are three symbols that must be consumed. c_2 is the upper bound on the number of symbols in the resulted right-hand-sides. If N is probabilistic, every one of those symbols may be consumed through applying a different transition. c_3 is the upper bound on the number of transitions in R_N that share the same left-hand side. As a result, $c_2^{c_3}$ possible right-hand sides might be resulted for every left-hand side. In total, there will be $\mathcal{O}(|R_M|.|Q_N|^{c_1}.c_2^{c_3})$ rules in $R_{M;N}$. Overall, the complexity of composing two PMBUTTs is $\mathcal{O}(|R_M|.|Q_N|^{c_1}.c_2^{c_3})$.

Although the complexity of the composition construction is exponential. Composition is performed only when a user subscribes to an application, and not during query time. Consequently, the system only needs to perform this costly computation once, and then store a constant number of PMBUTTs for each user-application pair

7   RELATED WORK

Inference Attacks against Social Network Datasets. Inference attacks were studied in the context of statistical databases [18]. To prevent inference attacks in statistical databases, a typical approach is to disallow some access queries. For instance, queries that retrieve too small or too large number of records will not be allowed.

In the context of social computing platforms, the dominant focus has been on inference attacks against social network datasets, i.e., a dataset of user profiles, no matter how the profiles have been collected. Zheleva and Getoor [20] discuss how friendship links and group affiliations can result in information disclosure. Two sources of information are used to infer the value of a sensitive attribute in a private user profile: (a) values of the same attribute public user profiles that participate in a friendship relation with the private profile, and (b) values of the same attribute in public user profiles that belong to the same social groups as the private profile does. They conducted an experiment to leverage these two sources of information for making inferences. A similar approach is adopted by Becker and Chen in [6]. Labitzke *et al.* [14] demonstrate empirically that some attributes such as location and age are strongly correlated among friends. By contrast, there are some attributes that are rarely made available to public and correlate little. Note that their experiment uses a dataset of profiles with publicly available attributes. Similar results were reported in [7].

There are also some works that use supervised machine learning methods for launching inference attacks against user profiles. [12, 13, 15, 19] employ Naive Bayesian Network classifiers to infer users' private information.

Extending the work of Ahmadinejad *et al.*, this work is unique in that the attacker does not have access to a full social network dataset, but instead performs inference attacks covertly via the extension API of an SNS [2–5]. A mathematical framework for specifying and establishing the privacy and utility goals of view-based protection is formulated by Ahmadinejad *et al.* [5]. They also formally articulate the trade-off between privacy and utility when a view is imposed on user profiles.

Protection Mechanisms for Social Network Systems. Previously proposed protection mechanisms for enhancing the privacy of user profiles have focused on either encrypting the content of user profiles, or providing a finer-grained authorization mechanism. These techniques do not prevent SNS API inference attacks in particular. For instance, Lucas *et al.* [16] proposed an architecture for social networks where the SNS has access to only encrypted user information. A Javascript client-side Facebook application, called *FlyByNight* plays the role of an information broker that encrypts every information before being uploaded to the SNS.

Egele *et al.* [8, 9] embed a fine-grained access control system, PoX (proxy on the client side), in a client-side Facebook application (i.e., no change to Facebook). Every request to access a user profile is sent to PoX where users can impose fine-grained access control on their data. If access is granted, the request is forwarded to Facebook.

As we argued in this paper, access control cannot break the statistical correlation between sensitive and accessible data, and inference attacks cannot be eliminated by authorization mechanisms only. Our proposed view-based protection model sanitizes the user profile using a probabilistic tree transformation, before the sanitized profile is queried by potentially malicious SNS extensions.

8   CONCLUSION

In this work, we first demonstrated that carefully sanitizing user profiles can significantly reduce the chance of malicious third-party extensions inferring users' private information. More specifically, we evaluated the reduction in success rate of the Ahmadinejad *et al.*'s inference algorithms [4] when view-based sanitization is performed. The benefit of probabilistic profile transformation is highly pronounced in our results. The performance of lazy view materialization is then evaluated. We made use of Haskell's lazy evaluation to demonstrate that when view materialization is performed in a lazy manner, significant performance gain can be observed. Lastly, we proposed a programming language-independent, probabilistic tree transducer model, PMBUTT, for materializing views. An important feature of the model is that it is closed under composition. We also showed via examples that the proposed tree transducer model is expressive enough for capturing classical sanitizing transformations such as suppression, generalization, noise addition and random sampling.

ACKNOWLEDGMENTS

This work is supported in part by a Discovery Grant from the Natural Sciences and Engineering Research Council of Canada (RGPIN-2014-06611) and a Canada Research Chair (950-229712).

REFERENCES

[1] Seyed Hossein Ahmadinejad. 2016. *A View-Based Protection Model to Prevent Inference Attacks by Third-Party Extensions to Social Computing Platforms.* Ph.D. Dissertation. University of Calgary.

[2] Seyed Hossein Ahmadinejad, Mohd Anwar, and Philip W. L. Fong. 2011. Inference attacks by third-party extensions to social network systems. In *Proceedings of 2011 IEEE International Conference on Pervasive Computing and Communications Workshops (PERCOM Workshops'2011).* Seattle, USA, 282–287.

[3] Seyed Hossein Ahmadinejad and Philip W. L. Fong. 2013. On the feasibility of inference attacks by third-party extensions to social network systems. In *Proceedings of the 8th ACM Symposium on Information, Computer and Communications Security (ASIACCS'13).* Hangzhou, China, 161–166.

[4] Seyed Hossein Ahmadinejad and Philip W. L. Fong. 2014. Unintended disclosure of information: Inference attacks by third-party extensions to Social Network Systems. *Computers and Security* 44 (2014), 75–91.

[5] Seyed Hossein Ahmadinejad, Philip W. L. Fong, and Rei Safavi-Naini. 2016. Privacy and Utility of Inference Control Mechanisms for Social Computing Applications. In *Proceedings of the 11th ACM Asia Conference on Computer and Communication Security (ASIACCS'2016).* Xi'an, China, 829–840.

[6] Justin Becker and Hao Chen. 2009. Measuring privacy risk in online social networks. In *Proceedings of the Web 2.0 Security and Privacy Workshop (W2SP'09).* Oakland, CA, USA, 8.

[7] Ratan Dey, Cong Tang, Keith Ross, and Nitesh Saxena. 2012. Estimating age privacy leakage in online social networks. In *Proceedings of the 2012 IEEE INFOCOM.* Orlando, Florida, USA, 2836–2840.

[8] Manuel Egele, Andreas Moser, Christopher Kruegel, and Engin Kirda. 2011. PoX: Protecting users from malicious Facebook applications. In *Proceedings of the IEEE International Conference on Pervasive Computing and Communications Workshops (PERCOM Workshops'2011).* Seattle, WA, USA, 288–294.

[9] Manuel Egele, Andreas Moser, Christopher Kruegel, and Engin Kirda. 2012. PoX: Protecting Users from Malicious Facebook Applications. *Computer Communications* 35, 12 (July 2012), 1507–1515.

[10] Joost Engelfriet. 1975. Bottom-up and Top-down Tree Transformations – A Comparison. *Mathematical Systems Theory* 9, 2 (June 1975), 198–231.

[11] Joost Engelfriet, Eric Lilin, and Andreas Maletti. 2009. Extended multi bottom-up tree transducers: Composition and decomposition. *Acta Informatica* 46, 8 (Dec. 2009), 561–590.

[12] Jianming He, Wesley W. Chu, and Zhenyu (Victor) Liu. 2006. Inferring privacy information from social networks. In *Proceedings of the 4th IEEE International Conference on Intelligence and Security Informatics (ISI'06).* San Diego, CA, USA, 154–165.

[13] R. Heatherly, M. Kantarcioglu, and B. Thuraisingham. 2009. *Preventing private information inference attacks on social networks.* Technical Report. Computer Science Department, University of Texas at Dallas.

[14] Sebastian Labitzke, Florian Werling, Jens Mittag, and Hannes Hartenstein. 2013. Do Online Social Network Friends Still Threaten My Privacy?. In *Proceedings of the Third ACM Conference on Data and Application Security and Privacy (CODASPY'13).* San Antonio, Texas, USA, 13–24.

[15] Jack Lindamood, Raymond Heatherly, Murat Kantarcioglu, and Bhavani Thuraisingham. 2009. Inferring private information using social network data. In *Proceedings of the 18th International Conference on World Wide Web (WWW'09).* Madrid, Spain, 1145–1146.

[16] Matthew M Lucas and Nikita Borisov. 2008. FlyByNight: Mitigating the privacy risks of social networking. In *Proceedings of the 7th ACM Workshop on Privacy in the Electronic Society (WPES'08).* Alexandria, VA, USA, 1–8.

[17] Andreas Maletti. 2008. Compositions of extended top-down tree transducers. *Information and Computation* 206, 9–10 (2008), 1187–1196.

[18] Dorothy Elizabeth Robling Denning. 1982. Inference Controls. In *Cryptography and Data Security.* Addison-Wesley, 331–390.

[19] Wanhong Xu, Xi Zhou, and Lei Li. 2008. Inferring privacy information via social relations. In *Proceedings of the 24th IEEE International Conference on Data Engineering Workshop (ICDEW'08).* Cancun, Mexico, 525–530.

[20] Elena Zheleva and Lise Getoor. 2009. To join or not to join: the illusion of privacy in social networks with mixed public and private user profiles. In *Proceedings of the 18th International Conference on World Wide Web (WWW'09).* Madrid, Spain, 531–540.

Secure Pick Up: Implicit Authentication When You Start Using the Smartphone

Wei-Han Lee
Princeton University
weihanl@princeton.edu

Xiaochen Liu
University of Southern California
liu851@usc.edu

Yilin Shen
Samsung Research America
yilin.shen@samsung.com

Hongxia Jin
Samsung Research America
hongxia.jin@samsung.com

Ruby B. Lee
Princeton University
rblee@princeton.edu

ABSTRACT

We propose Secure Pick Up (SPU), a convenient, lightweight, in-device, non-intrusive and automatic-learning system for smartphone user authentication. Operating in the background, our system implicitly observes users' phone pick-up movements, the way they bend their arms when they pick up a smartphone to interact with the device, to authenticate the users.

Our SPU outperforms the state-of-the-art implicit authentication mechanisms in three main aspects: 1) SPU automatically learns the user's behavioral pattern without requiring a large amount of training data (especially those of other users) as previous methods did, making it more deployable. Towards this end, we propose a weighted multi-dimensional Dynamic Time Warping (DTW) algorithm to effectively quantify similarities between users' pick-up movements; 2) SPU does not rely on a remote server for providing further computational power, making SPU efficient and usable even without network access; and 3) our system can adaptively update a user's authentication model to accommodate user's behavioral drift over time with negligible overhead.

Through extensive experiments on real world datasets, we demonstrate that SPU can achieve authentication accuracy up to 96.3% with a very low latency of 2.4 milliseconds. It reduces the number of times a user has to do explicit authentication by 32.9%, while effectively defending against various attacks.

KEYWORDS

Authentication; Security; Privacy; Machine Learning; Smartphone; Dynamic Time Warping; Mobile System

ACM Reference format:
Wei-Han Lee, Xiaochen Liu, Yilin Shen, Hongxia Jin, and Ruby B. Lee. 2017. Secure Pick Up: Implicit Authentication When You Start Using the Smartphone. In *Proceedings of SACMAT'17, Indianapolis, IN, USA, June 21-23, 2017,* 12 pages.
https://doi.org/http://dx.doi.org/10.1145/3078861.3078870

1 INTRODUCTION

Mobile devices such as smartphones and tablets are rapidly becoming our means for entering the Internet and online social networks. They also store sensitive and personal information, such as email addresses or bank account information of users. The hardware of today's mobile devices is quite capable with multi-core gigahertz processors, and gigabytes of memory and solid-state storage. Their relatively low cost, ease of use and 'always on' connectivity provide a suitable platform for many day-to-day tasks involving financial transactions and sensitive data, making mobile devices attractive attack targets (e.g., see attacks against the Apple iOS and Google Android platforms in [24]).

Passwords are currently one of the most common forms for user authentication in mobile devices. However, they suffer from several weaknesses. Passwords are vulnerable to guessing attacks [2, 14, 22, 39, 40] or password reuse [7]. The usability issue is also a serious factor, since users do not like to have to enter, and reenter, passwords [32, 35]. A recent study in [5] shows that 64% of users do not use passwords or PINs as an authentication mechanism on their smartphones.

Recently, more and more smartphones are equipped with fingerprint scanners, making authentication through fingerprints quite popular. However, such mechanisms also suffer from several weaknesses. It is possible to trick the scanner by using a gelatin print mold over a real finger. In addition, the response time for the fingerprint scanner to unlock the smartphone is often more than one second [27], degrading the usability of fingerprint-based authentication.

Other biometric-based authentication mechanisms (e.g., via face and keystroke dynamics) are also unreliable and vulnerable to forgery attacks [36, 37]. For instance, an attacker can obtain a photo of the targeted user (e.g., via Facebook) and present it in front of the camera to spoof face recognition on smartphones. Furthermore, these authentication mechanisms require frequent user participation, hindering their deployment in real world scenarios. Hence, it is important to design secure and convenient authentication methods for smartphone users, the topic of this paper.

Behavior-based authentication mechanisms are recently proposed to implement convenient and implicit authentication which does not require frequent user participation and can reduce the user's efforts (e.g., the number of times) needed to unlock their smartphones. Behavior-based authentication is increasingly gaining popularity since mobile devices are often equipped with sensors such as accelerometer, gyroscope, magnetometer, camera, microphone, GPS and so on. Implicit authentication relies on a distinguishable behavioral pattern of the user, which is accomplished by building the users' profiles [4, 6, 9, 10, 15–20, 26, 29, 32, 38, 43]. If a newly-detected user behavior is consistent with the behavior profile stored in the smartphone, the device will have high confidence that no explicit authentication action is required. Otherwise, if the newly-detected behavior deviates significantly from the stored behavior profile, alternative explicit authentication mechanisms should be triggered, such as requiring the user to enter a password, PIN or checking his/her fingerprint.

Existing behavior-based authentication systems exploit machine learning techniques to achieve good security performance [4, 10, 18, 19, 38, 43]. However, these systems have several limitations for real world user authentication: 1) they need a large amount of training data (including other users' data) to learn an authentication classifier, which may violate users' privacy and thus hinder users' motivation to utilize these systems; 2) their training process is usually computationally complicated, which requires additional computational services, e.g., cloud computing, thus requiring users to trust the remote server and always have network connection; 3) their system updating process for capturing the user's behavioral drift over time is also quite complex.

Other behavior-based authentication mechanisms exploit specific contexts of users' behavior, e.g., how do users walk [26], and how do users answer a phone call [6], for authentication. However, their corresponding experiments require users to follow restricted patterns for authentication, e.g., walk straight ahead at the same speed [26] or answer a call when the phone is on a table in front of a user [6]. These constraints are unrealistic for extracting effective behavior patterns of users, making these systems impractical for real world authentication.

To address these issues, we propose a lightweight, in-device, non-intrusive and automatic-learning authentication system, called Secure Pick Up (SPU), which can be broadly deployed in real world mobile devices. Our system aims to utilize a simple and general behavioral pattern of smartphone users, the way people bend their arms when they pick up a phone to interact with the device, to implicitly authenticate the users. For a smartphone that installs our SPU application, the device starts extracting a user's pick-up pattern from his/her arm movements when picking up a phone, and then the system determines whether the current user is legitimate or not. If the user's current behavior conforms to the established behavior profile stored in the smartphone, the user passes the authentication and can have access to the smartphone. If the user's current behavior deviates from the established behavior profile, the device would present explicit authentication challenges, e.g., input of a password, PIN or fingerprint. If these backup explicit authentication mechanisms pass, the user is allowed access to the smartphone and the user's profile stored in the smartphone is updated consequently; otherwise, the user is denied access. This paper aims to answer the question of whether we could build and deploy such a model in a practical, convenient and secure manner on today's mobile devices. Our key contributions include:

- We design a behavior-based implicit authentication system, SPU, by exploiting users' behavioral patterns recorded by smartphone

sensors when they bend their arms to pick up a phone. SPU can automatically learn a user's behavioral pattern in an accurate, efficient and stealthy manner. Furthermore, SPU does not require a large amount of training data of other users as previous work did, making our system easier to deploy in real world applications.

- Our system (including the profile updating process) can be implemented efficiently and entirely on personal smartphones. It does not require any additional computational services, e.g., cloud computing. To the best of our knowledge, it is the first using only a device's resources for implicit authentication, making SPU efficient and usable even without network access. For instance, our system can adaptively update the user's authentication model over time with rather low overhead, consuming negligible power of 2%.

- We propose an effective Dynamic Time Warping (DTW) algorithm to quantify similarities between users' pick-up patterns. More specifically, we modify the traditional DTW algorithm and propose a weighted multi-dimensional DTW technique to accommodate the multiple dimensions of sensor data in our setting, and to further improve authentication performance. Extensive experimental results verify the effectiveness of our method which can achieve high accuracy up to 96.3% in 2.4 milliseconds. Furthermore, we demonstrate that SPU can reduce a user's efforts by 32.9% to unlock his/her smartphone providing a more user-friendly experience and encouraging more users to protect access to their devices.

- Finally, our system is robust to various types of attackers, including the serious ones that observe victims' behaviors many times. For instance, our SPU can achieve 0% false acceptance rate (FAR) and 18% false rejection rate (FRR) for authenticating smartphone users under the worst case mimicry attacks (educated attacks).

2 SYSTEM DESIGN

The main objective of our SPU system is to increase the convenience for smartphone users by reducing their efforts (e.g., the number of times) to unlock the smartphone while guaranteeing their security through preventing unauthorized access to the smartphone. We now describe the threat model, design goals, key ideas and system architecture for SPU.

2.1 Threat Model

Compared to personal computers, smartphones are more easily lost or stolen, giving attackers more opportunity to obtain the sensitive data stored in the smartphones. We assume that the attackers have physical access to the smartphone and can even monitor and mimic the user's pick-up behavior. Therefore, they can launch mimicry attacks, to impersonate the legitimate user's behavior. Specifically, we consider three different levels of attacks as follows.

- Random Attack (RA): With no prior knowledge of the user's pick-up behavior, a RA attacker randomly picks up the smartphone and wishes to pass the authentication system. This is equivalent to a brute force attack against text-based password schemes.
- Context-Aware Attack (CAA): In a context-aware attack, an adversary knows the place where the user picks up his/her smartphone, but has not observed how the user does it.

- Educated Attack (EA): In an educated attack, an adversary has observed how and where the user picks up his/her smartphone.

In our SPU system, we consider a single-user model, which is in line with current smartphone usage scenarios. For multi-user models, our system can be generalized in a straightforward manner to incorporate multiple profiles (e.g., family members, guests) for progressive authentication as discussed in [21, 25]. Furthermore, we assume the availability of low-cost sensors in mobile devices for detecting a user's presence and behavior. Indeed, the sensors used in our implementation are the accelerometer and gyroscope, which are widely available in today's mobile devices. As more sensors become pervasive, they can easily be folded into our system.

2.2 Design Goals

Our system is designed to increase the convenience of smartphone users while guaranteeing their security, through implicitly authenticating the users in an unobtrusive manner. Furthermore, the whole authentication process should be implemented stealthily and efficiently. Overall, our design goals for the SPU system are:

- Accurate: the authentication system should not incorrectly authenticate a user.
- Rapid Enrollment and Updating: creating new user accounts or updating pick-up profiles for existing users should be quick.
- Rapid Authentication: the response time for the authentication system must be short, for the system to be usable in reality.
- Implicit: the authentication system should neither interrupt user-smartphone interactions nor need explicit user participation during the authentication process.
- Unobtrusive: the authentication system should be completely unobtrusive and should not invade the user's privacy; the user should be comfortable when using our system.
- Light-weight: the authentication system should not require intensive computations.
- Device only: the authentication system should work efficiently and entirely on mobile devices only even without network access. It should not depend on auxiliary training data of other users or additional computational capabilities, e.g., cloud computing.

2.3 Key Ideas

Our SPU system is designed to achieve all the design goals in Section 2.2. To increase the convenience for users and detect unauthorized access to the smartphone as soon as possible, it is required that we authenticate the users when they start using the smartphone. Therefore, we consider using the users' arm movements when they pick up their smartphones as a distinguishable behavior to authenticate the users. Our key idea stems from the observation that users' behavioral patterns are different from person to person when they start using their smartphones, from the time they pick up the phone to the time they press the *home* button or *power* button. More specifically, we extract the 'pick-up signal' from the user's arm movements measured by sensors (accelerometer and gyroscope) embedded in the smartphone.

To extract users' pick-up movements, we first define a particular user action and call it a 'trigger-action'. Here, we utilize the 'wake up' signal of a smartphone such as pressing the *home* button or

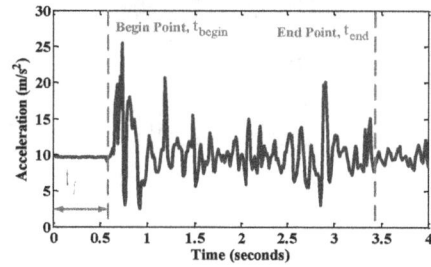

Figure 1: A real world instance of a user's pick-up movement. When a *wake up* signal is detected (*home* button or *power* button is pressed in the sleep mode) corresponding to the end point t_{end}, we backtrack the sensor measurements to find the begin point t_{begin} after detecting a flat signal lasting a period of t_f.

power button in the sleep mode, as the trigger action [1]. Whenever a trigger-action is performed, we extract the pick-up signal from the measurements of the accelerometer and gyroscope (described below). That is to say, our system authenticates the user only when the smartphone is triggered to wake up from the sleep mode. Note that there is no necessity to authenticate the user when the smartphone is locked.

Figure 1 shows a real world instance for the extracted signal stream that describes a user's pick-up movements from measurements collected by the *accelerometer*. When our system detects the *home* button signal or *power* button signal during the *sleep* mode, we record the time as the end of the pick-up signal t_{end}, and back-track the accelerometer measurements to construct the pick-up signal. If we detect a flat signal lasting for a time period of t_f, we consider the end time of the flat signal as the beginning of the pick-up signal t_{begin} as shown in Figure 1.

In order to backtrack the pick-up signal, we need to record the entire time-series measurements of the accelerometer and gyroscope, while the smartphone is in the *sleep* mode. In Section 6, we will show that this sensor measurement process is efficient, only costing an additional 2% in power consumption of the smartphone.

Note that we only consider authenticating pick-up movements from a stable state in our SPU system. We will show in Section 5.2 that this type of pick-up movement (from a stable state) constitutes the most important pick-up characteristic of users.

After extracting the pick-up signal, we propose a weighted multi-dimensional Dynamic Time Warping algorithm to effectively quantify similarities between users' pick up movements for authentication (detailed process will be discussed in Section 4.2.2). More specifically, we modify the traditional DTW algorithm to accommodate the multi-dimensional sensor data in our setting, to further improve authentication performance.

We will show the distinguishable properties of users' pick-up patterns in Section 5. We will show that the pick-up signals are still distinguishable even under impersonation attacks in Section 5.3.

---

[1] In our experiments, we used the *home* button or *power* button as the 'trigger-action'. Our method can be easily integrated with new trigger-actions, e.g., the automatic wake-up feature in the iphone 7.

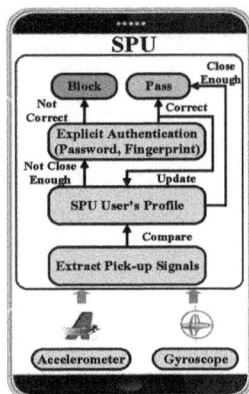

Figure 2: The flowchart of our SPU system.

Furthermore, our SPU system can significantly reduce users' efforts to unlock their smartphones as will be discussed in Section 5.4.

Unlike previous work, our SPU does not require a large amount of training data for learning a complex authentication classifier, and any additional computational capability of cloud servers, therefore more users would be motivated to use our system. In addition, our system can be easily combined with the state-of-the-art re-authentication systems [15, 16, 19, 38] to further improve the security of the smartphone.

2.4 System Architecture

Our system is designed for today's smartphones which are equipped with rich sensing capabilities. It could also be generally applied to tablets and other types of wearable devices such as smartwatches. Figure 2 shows the flowchart of our SPU system. System operation is in four phases:

Enrollment: When a user first enrolls in our SPU system, he/she is asked to pick up his/her smartphone in the same way as in his/her normal life. Our system then establishes the user's pick-up profile by extracting the pick-up signal and storing it in the smartphone.

Extracting pick-up signals: Our system keeps monitoring and recording the measurements of the accelerometer and gyroscope when the smartphone is in the sleep mode until it is picked up. We extract the pick-up signals from these sensor measurements in the enrollment phase and afterwards (detailed process discussed in Section 2.3).

Authentication: After extracting the pick-up signal, we compare the new incoming measurements (signal) with the user's pick-up profile stored in the smartphone by utilizing our proposed weighted multi-dimensional DTW technique (will be discussed in Section 4.2.2).

Post-Authentication: If the pick-up signal is authenticated as coming from the legitimate user, this testing passes and the current user can access the information and resources in the smartphone. Otherwise, the smartphone would request an explicit authentication, e.g., password, PIN or fingerprint, from the current user. We emphasize, however, that the desired response to such situations is a matter of policy. Furthermore, the stored user's profile will be

updated to accommodate the user's behavioral drift if the correct explicit authentication is provided. Otherwise, no access to the smartphone is allowed.

3 DATA COLLECTION

3.1 Sensor Selection

There are various built-in sensors in today's smartphones, from which we aim to choose a small set of sensors that can accurately represent a user's pick-up behavioral pattern. In this paper, we consider the following two sensors that are commonly embeded in current smartphones: the accelerometer and the gyroscope [11].

These two sensors represent different levels of information about the user's behavior, and are often called a 6-axis motion detector. The accelerometer records larger motion patterns of users such as how they move their arms or walk [26], while the gyroscope records fine-grained motions of users such as how they hold the smartphone [42]. Furthermore, these sensors do not require the user's permission when requested by mobile applications [12], making them useful for background monitoring as in our implicit authentication systems.

3.2 Dataset Collection

We utilize the open-source Android system as our implementation platform. We develop an Android application to implement SPU on Andriod smartphones. Note that our methods are not limited to this platform and can be easily applied to other platforms such as the Apple iOS platform on an iPhone.

In our experiments, each data sample is a time-series measurement collected by the accelerometer and gyroscope, which captures the user's behavioral pattern when picking up the smartphone. In our user study, we consider three experimental scenarios and describe the detailed settings for each experiment as follows. All the participants were shown the app that is installed in their phones. All of the participants volunteered to participate in our experiments. There is no security breach on users' data in smartphones since we collect data and do the authentication attempts offline.

The first experiment was conducted under a lab setting, aiming to provide fundamental intuition for our SPU system. We collected sensor data from 24 users whose detailed demographics are described in Section 5.1. We asked each user to pick up the smartphone in 6 different places while sitting or standing [2]. For each scenario, we collected 10 samples of the pick-up movement for each user, under the 12 situations (6 places × 2 user states). Therefore, we collected 2,880 (i.e., 24 × 12 × 10) pick-up samples in total. We will describe the detailed analysis for the first experiment in Section 5.1.

The second experiment was conducted under a more realistic setting which is designed to verify the effectiveness of our SPU system in real world applications. The same 24 users were invited to install our application on their own smartphones and use them freely in their normal lives for a week. From the collected data, we extracted 3,115 pick-up movement samples for these users. We will analyze the overall authentication performance of our system in real world scenarios in Section 5.2.

---

[2] 2 places are at a user's right hand side, another 2 places are in front of the user, and another 2 places are at a user's left hand side. In each of these three directions, one place is close while the other place is far.

Our third experiment was designed to analyze the security performance of SPU in defending against multiple attacks (e.g., impersonation attacks) as discussed in Section 2.1. In this experiment, we randomly select 6 out of the 24 users as victims and randomly select 12 out of the other 18 users (different from the victims) as adversaries. The experimental setting is the same as the first experiment. The only difference is that the adversaries are trying to mimic the victims under different levels of prior knowledge. Specifically, these adversaries perform the three attacks in Section 2.1 respectively, and the detailed attack processes are described as follows:

- Random Attack (RA): The random attacker tries to use the victim's smartphone without knowing any information about the victim. In total, we collected $12 \times 6 \times 10 = 720$ samples[3] of the pick-up signals under the random attack.
- Context-Aware Attack (CAA): We provided a context-aware attacker who is informed of the place where the victim picked up the smartphone. Note that these attackers have not observed how the victim picked up the smartphone. We also collected 720 pick-up samples under the context-aware attack.
- Educated Attack (EA): The victim user's behavior was recorded by a VCR and is clearly visible to the attacker. The attacker was asked to watch the video and mimic the victim's behavior to the best of his/her ability. In total, we also collected 720 pick-up samples under the educated attack.

We will discuss the security analysis for the third experiment in Section 5.3.

4 SPU AUTHENTICATION ALGORITHMS

We now describe the design of our authentication algorithm which aims to achieve the design goals in Section 2.2.

Previous implicit authentication algorithms exploit machine learning techniques to achieve good authentication performance [4, 10, 18, 19, 26, 38, 43]. However, we identify characteristics that the smartphone implicit authentication exhibits that are not well aligned with the requirements of machine-learning techniques. These include: 1) lack of training data especially those of other users; 2) fundamental limitations in computation capabilities for the training process and the updating process.

To overcome these challenges, we aim to design an implicit, lightweight and in-device authentication algorithm by matching the new incoming pick-up signal with the pick-up profile stored in the smartphone, instead of the complicated machine learning techniques of previous methods. Furthermore, the time duration of a pick-up movement varies across time and across users, and typically is within the range of 0.5 to 4 seconds. Therefore, our matching process should also automatically cope with time deformations and different speeds associated with time-dependent sensor data.

Towards these goals, we consider using the dynamic time warping technique [23] to carefully measure the distance between two time-series sensor data which may vary in time or speed. In DTW, the sequences are warped in a nonlinear fashion to match each other. It has been successfully applied to compare different speech patterns in automatic speech recognition and other applications in the data mining community. Furthermore, we propose an effective

weighted multi-dimensional DTW to accommodate our setting where the collected sensor data are of multiple dimensions, thus taking the different distinguishing power of each sensor dimension into consideration.

4.1 Data Pre-processing

Our system keeps monitoring and collecting the measurements of the accelerometer and gyroscope in the background, while the smartphone is in *sleep* mode. When the *wake up* signal (e.g., *home* button or *power* button is pressed in the sleep mode) is detected, our SPU records the time as the ending of the pick-up signal and back-tracks the collected data to find the beginning of the pick-up signal, as described earlier in Section 2.3.

4.2 DTW-based Authentication Algorithm

4.2.1 One-Dimensional DTW. DTW is a well-known technique to find the optimal alignment between two given (time-dependent) sequences $X := (x_1, x_2, \ldots, x_N)$ of length $N \in \mathbb{N}$ and $Y := (y_1, y_2, \ldots, y_M)$ of length $M \in \mathbb{N}$ under certain restrictions. While there is a surfeit of possible distance measures for time-series data, empirical evidence has shown that DTW is exceptionally difficult to beat. Ding et al. in [8] tested the most cited distance measures on 47 different datasets, and no method consistently outperforms DTW. Therefore, in our system, we utilize DTW to measure the distance between users' pick-up signals.

DTW calculates the distance of two sequences using dynamic programming [1]. It constructs an N-by-M matrix, where the (i, j)-th element is the minimum distance (called local distance) between the two sequences that end at points x_i and y_j respectively. An (N, M)-warping path $p = (p_1, p_2, \cdots, p_L)$ is a contiguous set of matrix elements which defines an alignment between two sequences X and Y by aligning the element x_{n_l} of X to the element y_{m_l} of Y. The boundary condition enforces that the first elements of X and Y as well as the last elements of X and Y are aligned to each other. The total distance $d_p(X, Y)$ of a warping path p between X and Y with respect to the local distance measure d is defined as $d_p(X, Y) = \sum_{l=1}^{L} d(x_{n_l}, y_{m_l})$. Therefore, the DTW for one dimensional time-series data can be computed as

$$DTW_1(X, Y) = \min d_p(X, Y) \qquad (1)$$

4.2.2 Multi-dimensional DTW. Different from the popular one-dimensional signal (such as speech signal), each pick-up signal in our setting is multi-dimensional (6 dimensions in total including 3 dimensions for accelerometer and 3 dimensions for gyroscope), which is a practical challenge for applying the DTW algorithm to our system. In order to address this challenge, we develop a weighted multi-dimensional DTW by carefully analyzing the distinguishing powers of different sensor dimensions.

Baseline Approach: We first consider an existing approach to process multi-dimensional signals [33] with DTW as the baseline approach. Consider two k-dimensional time-series signals $X := [X_1, X_2, \ldots, X_k]$ and $Y := [Y_1, Y_2, \ldots, Y_k]$, where X_i and Y_i are one dimensional time-series signals for each i. Assuming that each dimensional signal is independent of each other, the DTW algorithm

---

[3]In our experiments, we considered 12 attackers, 6 victims and 10 repeated iterations for each user's pick-up movement.

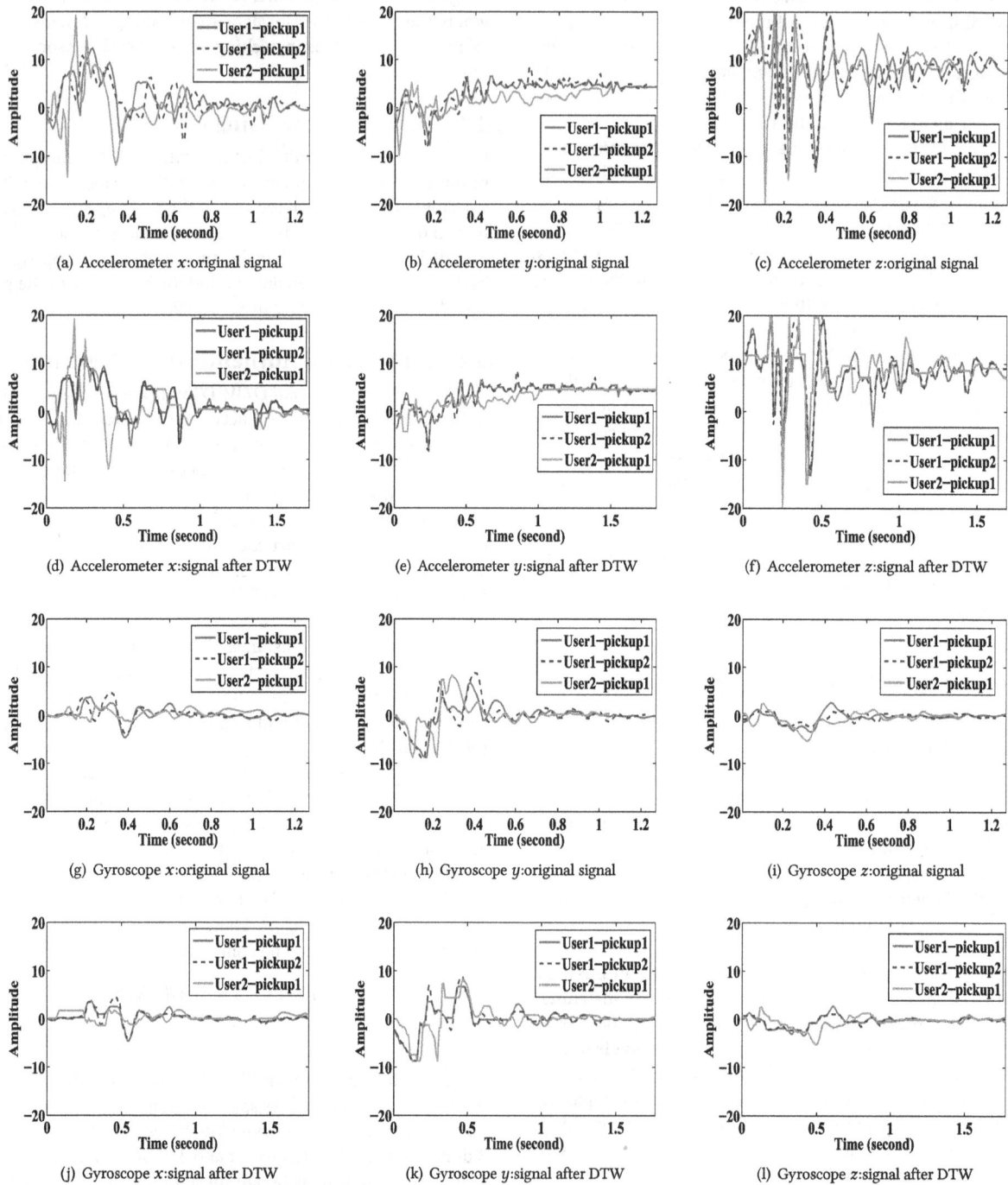

Figure 3: The visualization of pick-up signals extracted from the accelerometer and gyroscope on three different dimensions. We randomly select two pick-up signals from the same user (red solid and blue dashed dark lines) and a pick-up signal from another user (green light lines). We observe that the distance between two pick-up signals corresponding to the same user is smaller than that from a different user, which lays the foundation for our implicit authentication algorithm. We also observe that different dimensions of sensors may have different powers to distinguish users. For instance, the accelerometer is better than gyroscope in matching the same user's pick-up signals and differentiating different user's patterns, which demonstrates the necessity of our proposed weighted multi-dimensional DTW algorithm.

under the multiple dimensions setting can be computed as the average over each dimension where

$$DTW_k(X, Y) = \frac{1}{k} \sum_{i=1}^{k} DTW_1(X_i, Y_i) \qquad (2)$$

Weighted Multi-dimensional DTW: However, the above baseline approach considers each dimensional signal as contributing equally to the final matching performance, which is an unrealistic assumption. In real world scenarios as in our settings, different dimensions corresponding to different sensors may have varying degrees of influence on the matching performance, since they reflect different levels of a user's behavioral characteristics. Therefore, we propose our weighted multi-dimensional DTW for discriminating the distinguishing powers of different sensor dimensions as:

$$DTW_k(X, Y) = \sum_{i=1}^{k} w_i DTW_1(X_i, Y_i) \qquad (3)$$

where w_i is the weight for the i-th dimensional signal.

Figure 3 further demonstrates the various distinguishing power for each sensor dimension. We randomly select two pick-up signals corresponding to the same user and one pick-up signal corresponding to another user and compute the distance between these signals after implementing the one-dimensional DTW according to Eq. 1. From Figure 3, we observe that the distance between two pick-up signals corresponding to the same user is much smaller than that from a different user, which lays the basic foundation for our implicit authentication algorithm. We also observe that the accelerometer is more powerful than the gyroscope in matching the same user's pick-up signals and differentiating different users' pick-up signals, which demonstrates the empirical necessity of our proposed weighted DTW algorithm. The reason is that a user's pick-up movement is dominated by the translation which is relevant to the accelerometer, while the rotation relevant to the gyroscope is less significant.

We further analyze the weights for each dimension of accelerometer and gyroscope by varying their weights from 0.1 to 0.9 on the axis of x, y, z with summation equal to one. We observe that when each dimension corresponding to the same sensor is equally weighted, the overall authentication performance is the best (with highest authentication accuracy). In addition, we also vary the weights from 0.1 to 0.9 on the accelerometer and the gyroscope with summation equal to one. We observe that the best performance (highest authentication accuracy) is achieved when the ratio between the weight of the accelerometer and that of the gyroscope is 0.6 to 0.4. Our observations further demonstrate that the accelerometer is more informative than the gyroscope in improving the authentication performance.

In summary, our SPU system realizes implicit, lightweight and in-device authentication for smartphone users, which consists of sensor data collection, pick-up signal extraction and weighted multi-dimensional DTW processing. If the distance (computed by our multi-dimensional DTW) between two time-series signals is close enough (less than a threshold θ), the user passes the authentication and can have access to the smartphone. The detailed process for selecting a proper distance threshold θ will be described in Section 5.2.1.

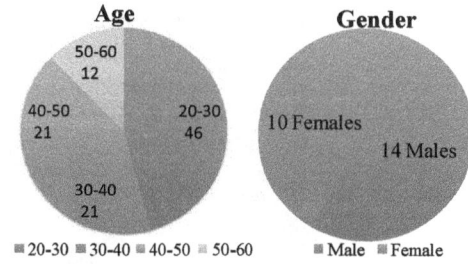

Figure 4: The demographics of users in our experiments.

4.3 System Updating

The updating process in previous authentication mechanisms usually involves retraining the authentication classifiers, which is computationally complicated and typically requires additional computing power such as the use of cloud computing. In comparison, we develop an efficient and lightweight updating process to accommodate the user's pick-up behavioral drift over time.

Our system would automatically update the user's profile in the device whenever the user fails the implicit authentication but successfully passes the subsequent explicit authentication. Our updating process is implemented by averaging the currently stored pick-up profile and the newly-detected pick-up signal. The key challenge for this updating process is that the previous profile and the newly-detected instance may not be of the same length. To solve this problem, we utilize our multi-dimensional DTW algorithm to first scale the two signals to the same length and then average them to obtain the updated user's profile for future authentication. We will show the effectiveness of our system updating process in Section 5.2.

5 EXPERIMENTS

To verify the effectiveness of our SPU system, we carefully analyze our collected data (as discussed in Section 3.2) and evaluate the authentication performance of SPU under different experimental scenarios and different system parameters. More specifically, the objectives for our experimental analysis are: 1) to provide empirical confirmation of our system that people's arm movements while they pick up the smartphone can be utilized as a distinguishable behavioral pattern for authentication, as will be discussed in Section 5.1; 2) to investigate the overall authentication performance of SPU under real world usage scenarios, as will be discussed in Section 5.2; 3) to understand the influence of different system parameters on our system, as will be discussed in Section 5.2.1; 4) to verify the effectiveness of our system updating process (recall Section 4.3), as will be discussed in Section 5.2.2; 5) to demonstrate the robustness of our system in defending against various impersonation attacks, as will be discussed in Section 5.3; 6) to verify the necessity of combining the accelerometer and gyroscope in our system, as will be discussed in Section 5.4.

5.1 Fundamental Intuition for Our System

Our first experiment was conducted under a lab setting (as described in Section 3.2), aiming to demonstrate the fundamental intuition

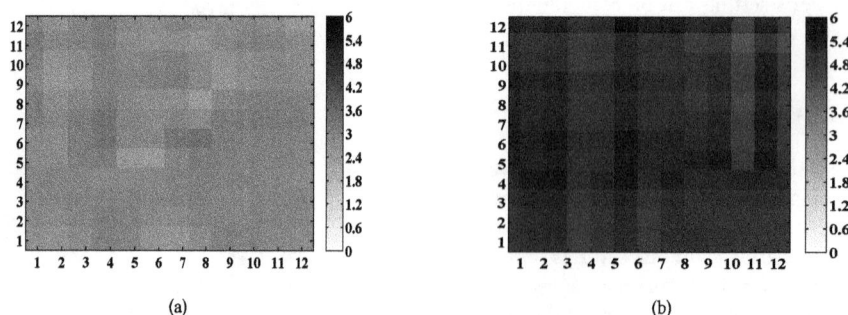

Figure 5: The heat map of applying weighted multi-dimensional DTW to our dataset. The average DTW distances between different pick-up signals in 12 contexts is collected for all 24 users from (a) the same user, and (b) different users. We can see that the DTW distances from the same user are much lower than that from different users, thus verifying the fundamental intuitions of our proposed algorithm.

and empirical confirmation for our SPU system. In this experiment, we asked each of the 24 users to pick up his/her smartphone in 6 different places while sitting or standing and repeat each movement for 10 iterations. Figure 4 shows the demographics of the 24 users in our experiments. The average age of the participants is 34.3 years old while the median is 31 years old. There are 14 males and 10 females.

After extracting the pick-up signals according to Section 2.3, we measure the distance between any two pick-up instances by exploiting the weighted multi-dimensional DTW technique as described in Section 4.2.2. In our algorithm, the weights for the accelerometer signal and the gyroscope signal are selected as 0.6 and 0.4 respectively, and each of the 3 dimensions of the same sensor is weighted equally (recall analysis in Section 4.2.2).

Figure 5(a) shows the average DTW distances of any two instances of pick-up signals corresponding to the same user. Both the x-axis and y-axis represent the 12 different pick-up scenarios (6 different places and 2 user states, i.e., sitting or standing). Lighter squares represent smaller DTW distances. In Figure 5(a), we observe the smallest DTW distances along the diagonal squares since they represent the distances between two pick-up signals corresponding to the same place and user state. By comparing the diagonal squares and the non-diagonal squares in Figure 5(a), we know the DTW distances across different pick-up scenarios do not vary drastically, demonstrating the robustness of our system under different context scenarios.

Figure 5(b) shows the average DTW distances of any two instances of pick-up signals corresponding to different users. From Figure 5, we observe that the DTW distances between pick-up signals corresponding to the same user are much lower than that between different users, which lays the fundamental intuition for our system that utilizes users' pick-up movements as distinguishable behavioral patterns for authentication.

5.2 Realistic Usage Scenario

Our second experiment was conducted under a more realistic setting, where the same 24 users (shown in Figure 4) were invited to

install our SPU application on their own smartphones and use them freely in their normal lives for a week (7 days)[4].

From the collected data, we extracted 3,115 pick-up signals according to Section 2.3. That is to say, we can detect 18.54 (i.e., 3115/7/24) pick-up samples for each user per day (with standard deviation 10.54). We also recorded the number of times users unlock their smartphones, which is 8,736 in a week. Therefore, the average number of times each user unlocks his/her smartphone is 52 (i.e., 8736/7/24) per day (with standard deviation 27.31).

Note that our system does not detect all the movements when the users try to unlock their smartphones, since we only extract pick-up signals starting from a stable state. In our experiment, we can detect 35.6% (i.e., 18.54/52, which correspond to the pick-up signals starting from a stable state) of users' pick-up movements when they try to unlock their smartphones. Therefore, we can save more than one third of the time that users need to unlock their smartphones explicitly. Furthermore, we also compute the DTW distance between other types of pick-up signals (e.g., picking up the smartphone from a bag or from a pocket) to investigate whether there are other pick-up patterns of users that can be utilized for authentication. Our observations show that the distance between other types of pick-up signals (not from a stable state) corresponding to the same user is very large, demonstrating that other types of pick-up signals can not be utilized as distinguishable patterns for user authentication. Therefore, the pick-up movements starting from a stable state which are extracted by our SPU system, constitute the most important pick-up characteristics of users. Our following experimental analysis are implemented on these detected pick-up movement samples.

5.2.1 Determining the Distance Threshold. A significant challenge in implementing our system is how to select a proper value for the distance threshold θ between the newly-detected pick-up signal and the stored pick-up profile of the user, which is an important system parameter to balance the trade-off between the usability of our system and the security of smartphone users. A smaller θ provides higher security, while a larger θ would result in better usability.

---

[4]We also let them use our application for another week for evaluating our system updating mechanism as discussed in Section 5.2.2.

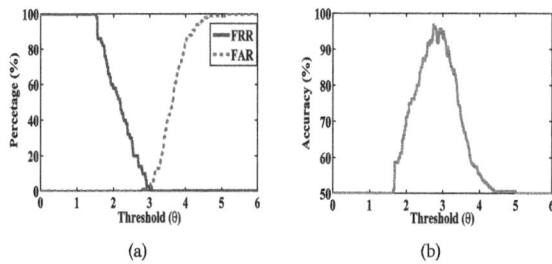

Figure 6: (a) FAR, FRR and (b) accuracy, varying with different distance threshold θ. We observe that when $\theta = 3.1$, the FRR is 0% and FAR is less than 10%. When $\theta = 2.8$ the FRR is 7.6% and FAR is 0%, resulting in an authentication accuracy higher than 96.3%. Therefore, θ can tradeoff the usability of our system (lower FRR) and users' security (lower FAR)

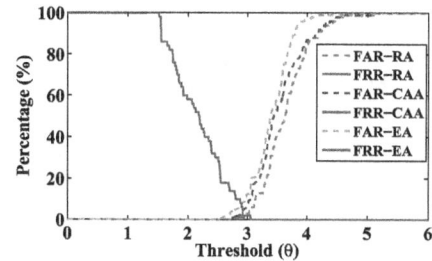

Figure 7: The FAR and FRR of SPU under various impersonation attacks.

Here, we utilize false acceptance rate (FAR) and false rejection rate (FRR) as metrics to quantify the authentication performance of our system. FAR is the fraction of other users' data that is misclassified as the legitimate user's. FRR is the fraction of the legitimate user's data that is misclassified as other users' data. For security protection, a large FAR is more harmful to the smartphone users than a large FRR. However, a large FRR would degrade the convenience of using our system. Therefore, we aim to investigate the influence of the distance threshold θ in balancing FAR and FRR, in order to choose a proper θ for our system.

Figure 6(a) shows the FAR and FRR with varying values of the distance threshold θ. We observe that FAR is less than 10% and FRR is 0% when $\theta = 3.1$. The FAR drops to 0% and FRR increases to 7.6% when $\theta = 2.8$. Therefore, θ is a trade-off between the usability of our system (lower FRR) and the security of smartphone users (lower FAR). In Figure 6(b), we observe that the authentication accuracy is higher than 96.3% when θ is around 2.8. Combining Figure 6(a) and Figure 6(b), we choose $\theta = 2.8$ in our experiments from now on and in our published system, aiming at minimizing FAR and maximizing the security of the smartphone users.

5.2.2 Incorporating the System Updating Process. In order to verify the effectiveness of our system updating process as described in Section 4.3, we let the same 24 users use their smartphones freely for another week. More specifically, we randomly divided the users into two groups. The 12 users in the first group installed our SPU application which incorporates the updating process, while the other group installed another version of SPU without the updating process. After careful analysis, we observed that the users in the first group needed to explicitly unlock their smartphones (at the same time, their pick-up profiles would be updated in the SPU system) 17 times per day on average. For the other group without system updating, the users needed to explicitly unlock their smartphones 35 times per day on average. We can see that incorporating the system updating process can further reduce 52% of times for users to unlock the smartphones. These observations show the effectiveness of our system updating process and the advantage of our system in increasing smartphone users' convenience.

5.3 Security Analysis

In our third experimental setting as described in Section 3.2, we aim to evaluate how robust our SPU system is in defending against various types of impersonation attackers (random attack, context-aware attack and educated attack).

For each of the three attacks, we computed FAR and FRR curves under different distance thresholds θ as shown in Figure 7, based on which we have the following observations: 1) SPU can effectively defend against random attacks. Here, 'random' attack indicates a brute force attack where the attacker picks up the smartphone randomly without knowing any information about the victim. 2) When the distance threshold $\theta = 2.5$, the FAR becomes 0% for all the three attacks and the corresponding FRR is 18%. Note that the FRR curve for the three attacks are the same since it evaluates the ratio that the victim is rejected by our system, which is irrelevant to the attacker's capability. 3) Furthermore, the user can defend against different levels of attacks by adjusting the distance threshold θ. These results suggest that our SPU system is more robust against random (brute force) attacks than other types of impersonation attacks (context-aware attacks and educated attacks) since these advanced attackers usually have access to partial information about the user's pick-up movements (recall Section 2.1 and Section 3.2).

In summary, SPU can defend against most realistic attacks robustly and effectively. Even with a strong attacker (i.e., an insider attacker), our system performs gracefully.

5.4 Further Experiments

We further demonstrate the necessity and advantages of combining the common sensors, acclerometer and gyroscope, in our SPU system. In Table 1, we observe that using the combination of accelerometer and gyroscope can achieve better performance than using each sensor individually, with the authentication accuracy up to 96.3%. Furthermore, our SPU can reduce the number of explicit authentications a user must do by 32.9% (i.e., $35.6\% \times (1 - 7.6\%)$) on average, where 35.6% is the ratio of detected pick-up signals (recall Section 5.2) and 7.6% is the FRR by using the combination of accelerometer and gyroscope.

Next, we went a step further to investigate whether our SPU system could benefit from more sensors than just the accelerometer and gyroscope. More specifically, we analyze the authentication performance of SPU when incorporating the measurements of a magnetometer and its combinations with the accelerometer and gyroscope. We consider the magnetometer since we can construct

Table 1: The authentication accuracy by using accelerometer and gyroscope with distance threshold $\theta = 2.8$.

	Accuracy	FAR	FRR
Accelerometer	90.9 %	6.4%	11.8%
Gyroscope	85.2 %	13.7%	15.2%
Acc+Gyr	96.3 %	0%	7.6%

Table 2: The authentication accuracy by using three motion sensors with distance threshold $\theta = 2.8$.

	Accuracy	FAR	FRR
Magnetometer	36.7%	54.4%	62.4%
Acc+Mag	67.2%	37.2%	48.7%
Gyr+Mag	54.8%	41.9%	57.1%
All three sensors	72.5%	27.6%	34.4%

the popular 9-axis motion detector of the smartphone by combining the 3-axis measurements of magnetometer with the 3-axis measurements of each of accelerometer and gyroscope. An interesting observation shown in Table 2 is that incorporating the magnetometer into our SPU system does not improve the overall authentication accuracy - in fact, it degrades the authentication accuracy! Using more sensors is not always better! The reason is that the magnetic field is rather sensitive to the direction of the smartphone, which makes it vary significantly when the same user picks up the smartphone in different directions - thus degrading the overall authentication performance.

These observations substantiate our choice of using only the accelerometer and gyroscope in our system.

6 OVERHEAD ANALYSIS

We now evaluate the system overhead of SPU on personal smartphones to demonstrate the applicability of our system in real world scenarios. In our source code, the DTW algorithm is implemented in the C language by using the Native Development Kit (NDK). We test our system on a Google Nexus5 with 2.3GHz, Krait 400 processor, 16GB internal storage and 2GB RAM, using Android 5.1.

6.1 Power Consumption

There are four different testing scenarios: 1) Phone is locked and SPU is off; 2) Phone is locked and SPU keeps running; 3) Phone is under use and SPU is off; 4) Phone is under use and SPU is running.

For cases 1) and 2), the test time is 12 hours each. We charge the smartphone battery to 100% and check the battery level after 12 hours. The average difference of battery charged level from 100% is reported in Table 3. For cases 3) and 4), *the phone under use* means that the user keeps unlocking and locking the phone. During the unlocked time, the user keeps typing notes. The period of unlocking and locking is two minutes and the test time in total is 60 minutes.

Table 3 shows the result of our power consumption test on battery usage. We find that in cases 1) and 2), the SPU-on mode consumes 1.8% more battery power than the SPU-off mode each hour. We believe the extra cost in battery consumption caused by SPU will not affect user experience in daily use. For cases 3) and 4), SPU consumes 2% more battery power performing 30 SPU implicit

Table 3: The power consumption under four different scenarios.

Scenario	Power Consumption
1) Phone locked, SPU off	1.1%
2) Phone locked, SPU on	2.9%
3) Phone unlocked periodically, SPU off	1.5%
4) Phone unlocked periodically, SPU on	3.5%

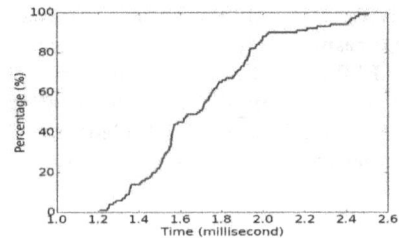

Figure 8: Cumulative distribution function of decision-making time in SPU. We can find that more than 90% of decision-making processes can be completed within 2 milliseconds and all the processes can be finished within 2.4 milliseconds.

authentications in one hour, which is also an acceptable cost for daily usage.

6.2 Response Time

Figure 8 shows the cumulative distribution function of decision-making time in SPU authentication. We find that more than 90% of the decision-making computations can be completed within 2 milliseconds and all can be finished within 2.4 milliseconds. This result shows that the latency caused by the SPU system for authentication is low enough to be user-friendly and reasonable for normal usage.

7 RELATED WORK

User authentication is one of the most important issues in smartphone security. Password-based authentication approaches are based on possession of secret information, such as passwords or PINs. Biometric-based approaches make use of distinct personal features, such as fingerprint or iris patterns. Behavior-based authentication identifies a user based on his/her behavioral pattern that is observed by the smartphone. Compared with the password-based and the biometric-based authentication, the behavior-based authentication is more convenient for smartphone users with good resilience to forgery attacks.

7.1 Password-based Authentication

The objective of most password-based authentication mechanisms, e.g., PIN or passwords, is to secure the phone from unwanted access. However, these methods require frequent participation of the user. This often leads to interruptions to the smartphone user, e.g. continuously prompting him/her with some challenges. As a result, many smartphone users tend to completely remove such authentication methods [35]. Our SPU system can overcome these weaknesses, which increases the convenience for smartphone users while guaranteeing their security, as shown in Section 5.

7.2 Biometric-based Authentication

Biometric-based authentications study static physical features of humans. Currently, there are many different physiological biometrics for authentication, such as face patterns, fingerprints [13], and iris patterns [28]. Biometric-based authentication systems involve an enrollment phase and an authentication phase. A user is enrolled by providing his/her biological data such as fingerprint or iris pattern. The system extracts these patterns from the provided data and stores the extracted patterns for future reference. During the authentication phase, the system compares the observed biological data against the stored data to authenticate a user.

However, biometric-based authentications also require frequent user participation, and hence is also an explicit authentication mechanism. For example, fingerprint authentication always requires the user to put his/her finger on the fingerprint scanner. On average, the response time is longer than 1 second [27], which is also much longer than the 2.4 milliseconds of our SPU system. Hence, unlike our implicit SPU authentication, these biometric-based approaches requiring user compliance are not as convenient as our SPU system.

7.3 Behavior-based Authentication

Another thread of authentication research measures the behavioral patterns of the user, where a user is identified based on his/her behavioral patterns, such as hand-writing pattern [10, 38], gait [26] and GPS location patterns [4].

With the increasing development of mobile sensing technology, collecting measurements through sensors built within the smartphone and other devices is now becoming not only possible, but quite easy through, for example, Android sensor APIs. Mobile sensing applications, such as the CMU MobiSens[41], run as services in the background and can constantly collect sensors' data from smartphones. Sensors can be either hard sensors (e.g., accelerometers) that are physically-sensing devices, or soft sensors that record information of a phone's running status (e.g., screen on/off). Therefore, sensor-based implicit authentication mechanisms have become very popular and applicable for behavior-based authentication.

In [4], an n-gram geo-based model is proposed for modeling a user's mobility pattern. They use the GPS sensor to detect abnormal activities (e.g., a phone being stolen) by analyzing a user's location history, and their algorithm can achieve 86.6% accuracy. However, the access to GPS require users' permissions, and cannot be done implicitly.

Nickel et al. [26] exploited a user's walking pattern to authenticate a smartphone user by using the k-NN algorithm. Conti et al. [6] utilized the user's movement of answering a phone call to authenticate a smartphone user. Shrestha et al.[34] utilized a tapping pattern to authenticate a user when the user does an NFC transaction. However, their experiments had strict restrictions on the users' behavior where the users have to walk or answer a phone call following a specific script (e.g., walk straight ahead at the same speed [26] or answer the phone which is on a table in front of a user [6]). These restrictions are impractical for a real use.

Users' behavior on a touch screen is one of the most popular research directions in behavior-based authentication [3, 10, 19, 31, 38]. Trojahn et al. [38] developed a mixture of a keystroke-based and a handwriting-based method to realize authentication by using the screen sensor. Their approach has achieved 11% FAR and 16% FRR. Frank et al. [10] studied the correlation between 22 analytic features from touchscreen traces and classified these features using k-NN and SVM. Li et al. [19] proposed another behavior-based authentication method where they exploited five basic movements (sliding up, down, right, left and tapping) and their related combinations, as the user's behavioral pattern features, to perform authentication. However, touch screen based authentications may suffer from a simple robotic attack [30].

SenSec [43] constantly collects data from the accelerometer, gyroscope and magnetometer, to construct gesture models while the user is using the device. SenSec has shown that it can achieve 75% accuracy in identifying owners and 71.3% accuracy in detecting the adversaries. Lee et al. [18] monitored the users' general behavioral patterns and utilized SVM techniques for user authentication. Their results show that the authentication accuracy can be higher than 90% by using a combination of sensors. However, these methods require a large amount of privacy sensitive training data from other users, and significant external computation power for learning the behavior models, unlike our in-device SPU authentication method.

In fact, almost all the existing behavior-based authentication mechanisms [4, 10, 18, 19, 26, 38, 43] heavily rely on a powerful remote server to share the tasks and take a relatively long time to complete the authentication process. In comparison, our SPU is a lightweight, in-device, non-intrusive and automatic-learning authentication system, which would increase the convenience for smartphone users while enhancing their security.

8 DISCUSSION AND FUTURE WORK

Our SPU system increases the convenience for smartphone users while enhancing their security. We will make SPU open source software, suitable for extensions with future research and experiments.

Future research can include more context-detection techniques to detect fine-grained pick-up patterns for users and embed it with SPU to further increase the convenience and security for smartphone users.

Users' pick-up patterns may vary when they are using other types of devices, e.g., tablets or smartwatches. It would be an interesting future direction to extend SPU to these mobile devices. Furthermore, the combination of multiple devices may possibly provide better authentication performance for the SPU system.

9 CONCLUSION

We proposed a novel system, Secure Pick Up (SPU), to implicitly authenticate smartphone users in a lightweight, in-device, non-intrusive and automatic-learning manner. Unlike previous work, SPU does not require a large amount of training data (especially those of other users) or any additional computational power from a remote server, which makes it more deployable and desirable for many users.

Our key insight is that the user's phone pick-up pattern is distinguishable from others, using smartphone sensor measurements. We propose a weighted multi-dimensional dynamic time warping algorithm to effectively measure the distance between pick-up signals in order to determine the legitimate user versus others.

Extensive experimental analysis shows that our system achieves authentication accuracy up to 96.3% with negligible system overhead (2% power consumption). Furthermore, our evaluation shows that SPU can reduce by 32.9% the number of explicit authentications a user must do, and can defend against various impersonation attacks effectively. Overall, SPU offers a novel feature in the design of today's smartphone authentication and provides users with more options in balancing the security and convenience of their devices.

REFERENCES

[1] Dimitri P Bertsekas. 1995. *Dynamic programming and optimal control*. Athena Scientific Belmont, MA.
[2] Joseph Bonneau. 2012. The science of guessing: analyzing an anonymized corpus of 70 million passwords. In *IEEE Symposium on Security and Privacy*.
[3] Daniel Buschek, Alexander De Luca, and Florian Alt. 2016. Evaluating the Influence of Targets and Hand Postures on Touch-based Behavioural Biometrics. In *Proceedings of the 2016 CHI Conference on Human Factors in Computing Systems*. ACM, 1349–1361.
[4] Senaka Buthpitiya, Ying Zhang, Anind K Dey, and Martin Griss. 2011. n-gram Geo-trace modeling. In *Pervasive Computing*.
[5] ConsumerReports. 2013. Keep your phone safe: How to protect yourself from wireless threats. *Consumer Reports, Tech.* (2013).
[6] Mauro Conti, Irina Zachia-Zlatea, and Bruno Crispo. 2011. Mind how you answer me!: transparently authenticating the user of a smartphone when answering or placing a call. In *ACM symposium on Information, computer and communications security*.
[7] Anupam Das, Joseph Bonneau, Matthew Caesar, Nikita Borisov, and XiaoFeng Wang. 2014. The tangled web of password reuse. In *Network and Distributed System Security Symposium*.
[8] Hui Ding, Goce Trajcevski, Peter Scheuermann, Xiaoyue Wang, and Eamonn Keogh. 2008. Querying and mining of time series data: experimental comparison of representations and distance measures. *VLDB Endowment* (2008).
[9] Nathan Eagle and Alex Sandy Pentland. 2009. Eigenbehaviors: Identifying structure in routine. *Behavioral Ecology and Sociobiology* (2009).
[10] Michael Frank, Ralf Biedert, En-Di Ma, Ivan Martinovic, and Dong Song. 2013. Touchalytics: On the applicability of touchscreen input as a behavioral biometric for continuous authentication. *Information Forensics and Security* (2013).
[11] Google. N/A. Android sensor manager. http://developer.android.com/guide/topics/sensors/sensors_overview.html. (N/A).
[12] Google. N/A. Android system permission. http://developer.android.com/guide/topics/security/permissions.html. (N/A).
[13] Lin Hong and Anil Jain. 1998. Integrating faces and fingerprints for personal identification. *Pattern Analysis and Machine Intelligence, IEEE Transactions on* (1998).
[14] Patrick Gage Kelley, Saranga Komanduri, Michelle L Mazurek, Richard Shay, Timothy Vidas, Lujo Bauer, Nicolas Christin, Lorrie Faith Cranor, and Julio Lopez. 2012. Guess again (and again and again): Measuring password strength by simulating password-cracking algorithms. In *IEEE Symposium on Security and Privacy*.
[15] Wei-Han Lee and Ruby Lee. 2016. Implicit Sensor-based Authentication of Smartphone Users with Smartwatch. In *International workshop on hardware and architectural support for security and privacy*.
[16] Wei-Han Lee and Ruby Lee. 2017. Implicit Smartphone User Authentication with Sensors and Contextual Machine Learning. In *International Conference on Dependable Systems and Networks*.
[17] Wei-Han Lee and Ruby B Lee. 2015. Implicit Authentication for Smartphone Security. In *Information Systems Security and Privacy*. Springer.
[18] Wei-Han Lee and Ruby B Lee. 2015. Multi-sensor authentication to improve smartphone security. In *International Conference on Information Systems Security and Privacy*.
[19] Lingjun Li, Xinxin Zhao, and Guoliang Xue. 2013. Unobservable Re-authentication for Smartphones. In *Network and Distributed System Security Symposium*.
[20] Chien-Cheng Lin, Deron Liang, Chin-Chun Chang, and Ching-Han Yang. 2012. A new non-intrusive authentication method based on the orientation sensor for smartphone users. In *Software Security and Reliability, IEEE International Conference on*.
[21] Yunxin Liu, Ahmad Rahmati, Yuanhe Huang, Hyukjae Jang, Lin Zhong, Yongguang Zhang, and Shensheng Zhang. 2009. xShare: supporting impromptu sharing of mobile phones. In *International conference on Mobile systems, applications, and services*.
[22] Jiaxin Ma, Weining Yang, Min Luo, and Ninghui Li. 2014. A study of probabilistic password models. In *IEEE Symposium on Security and Privacy*.
[23] Meinard Müller. 2007. Dynamic time warping. *Information retrieval for music and motion* (2007).
[24] Carey Nachenberg. 2011. A window into mobile device security: Examining the security approaches employed in Apple's iOS and Google's Android. *Symantec Security Response* (2011).
[25] Xudong Ni, Zhimin Yang, Xiaole Bai, Adam C Champion, and Dong Xuan. 2009. DiffUser: Differentiated user access control on smartphones. In *Mobile Adhoc and Sensor Systems, International Conference on*.
[26] Claudia Nickel, Tobias Wirtl, and Christoph Busch. 2012. Authentication of smartphone users based on the way they walk using k-NN algorithm. In *Intelligent Information Hiding and Multimedia Signal Processing*.
[27] PhoneArena. N/A. Fingerprint scanners comparison: Galaxy S6 vs iPhone 6 vs Note 4 vs Huawei Mate7 vs Meizu MX4 Pro. http://www.phonearena.com/news/Fingerprint-scanners-comparison-Galaxy-S6-vs\-iPhone-6-vs-Note-4-vs-Huawei-Mate7-vs-Meizu\-MX4-Pro_id71154. (N/A).
[28] Miao Qi, Yinghua Lu, Jinsong Li, Xiaolu Li, and Jun Kong. 2008. User-specific iris authentication based on feature selection. In *Computer Science and Software Engineering, International Conference on*.
[29] Oriana Riva, Chuan Qin, Karin Strauss, and Dimitrios Lymberopoulos. 2012. Progressive Authentication: Deciding When to Authenticate on Mobile Phones.. In *USENIX Security Symposium*.
[30] Abdul Serwadda and Vir V Phoha. 2013. When kids' toys breach mobile phone security. In *Proceedings of the 2013 ACM SIGSAC conference on Computer & communications security*. ACM.
[31] Michael Sherman, Gradeigh Clark, Yulong Yang, Shridatt Sugrim, Arttu Modig, Janne Lindqvist, Antti Oulasvirta, and Teemu Roos. 2014. User-generated free-form gestures for authentication: Security and memorability. In *Proceedings of the 12th annual international conference on Mobile systems, applications, and services*. ACM.
[32] Elaine Shi, Yuan Niu, Markus Jakobsson, and Richard Chow. 2011. Implicit authentication through learning user behavior. In *Information Security*. Springer.
[33] Mohammad Shokoohi-Yekta, Yanping Chen, Bilson Campana, Bing Hu, Jesin Zakaria, and Eamonn Keogh. 2015. Discovery of meaningful rules in time series. In *ACM SIGKDD International Conference on Knowledge Discovery and Data Mining*.
[34] Babins Shrestha, Manar Mohamed, Sandeep Tamrakar, and Nitesh Saxena. 2016. Theft-resilient mobile wallets: transparently authenticating NFC users with tapping gesture biometrics. In *Proceedings of the 32nd Annual Conference on Computer Security Applications*. ACM.
[35] Confident Technologies. N/A. Survey Shows Smartphone Users Choose Convenience Over Security. http://confidenttechnologies.com/news_events/survey-shows-smartphone-users-choose\-convenience-security. (N/A).
[36] Chee Meng Tey, Payas Gupta, and Debin Gao. 2013. I can be you: Questioning the use of keystroke dynamics as biometrics. Network and Distributed System Security Symposium.
[37] Shari Trewin, Cal Swart, Larry Koved, Jacquelyn Martino, Kapil Singh, and Shay Ben-David. 2012. Biometric authentication on a mobile device: a study of user effort, error and task disruption. In *Annual Computer Security Applications Conference*.
[38] Matthias Trojahn and Frank Ortmeier. 2013. Toward mobile authentication with keystroke dynamics on mobile phones and tablets. In *Advanced Information Networking and Applications Workshops, International Conference on*.
[39] Sebastian Uellenbeck, Markus Dürmuth, Christopher Wolf, and Thorsten Holz. 2013. Quantifying the security of graphical passwords: The case of android unlock patterns. In *ACM conference on Computer and communications security*.
[40] Matt Weir, Sudhir Aggarwal, Breno De Medeiros, and Bill Glodek. 2009. Password cracking using probabilistic context-free grammars. In *IEEE Symposium on Security and Privacy*.
[41] Pang Wu, Jiang Zhu, and Joy Ying Zhang. 2013. Mobisens: A versatile mobile sensing platform for real-world applications. *Mobile Networks and Applications* (2013).
[42] Zhi Xu, Kun Bai, and Sencun Zhu. 2012. Taplogger: Inferring user inputs on smartphone touchscreens using on-board motion sensors. In *ACM conference on Security and Privacy in Wireless and Mobile Networks*.
[43] Jiang Zhu, Pang Wu, Xiao Wang, and Joy Zhang. 2013. Sensec: Mobile security through passive sensing. In *Computing, Networking and Communications, International Conference on*.

Attribute Expressions, Policy Tables and Attribute-Based Access Control

Jason Crampton
Royal Holloway University of London
Egham Hill
Egham, Surrey TW20 0EX
jason.crampton@rhul.ac.uk

Conrad Williams
Royal Holloway University of London
Egham Hill
Egham, Surrey TW20 0EX
conrad.williams.2010@rhul.ac.uk

ABSTRACT

Attribute-based access control (ABAC) has attracted considerable interest in recent years, prompting the development of the standardized XML-based language XACML. ABAC policies written in languages like XACML have a tree-like structure, where leaf nodes are associated with authorization decisions and non-leaf nodes are associated with decision-combining algorithms. However, it may be difficult in XACML to construct a given policy due to the tree-structured nature of XACML and the way in which combining algorithms are defined. Furthermore, there is limited control over how requests are evaluated with respect to targets.

In this paper, we introduce the notion of an attribute expression, which generalizes the notion of a target, and show how attribute expressions are used to specify policies in tabular form. We demonstrate why representing policies in this manner is convenient, intuitive and flexible for policy authors, and provide a method for automatically compiling policy tables into machine-enforceable policies. Thus, we bridge the gap between a policy representation that is convenient for end-users and a policy that can be enforced by a PDP. We then describe various methods to reduce the size of policy tables.

In addition, we compare our language with XACML, highlighting various shortcomings of XACML and demonstrating how to express XACML policies in a tabular form. We then show how policy tables can be used as leaf nodes in a tree-structured language, providing a modular method for constructing enterprise-wide policies. Finally, we show how attribute expressions and policy tables can be used to make role-based access control and access control lists "attribute-aware".

KEYWORDS

Attribute-based access control; attribute expressions; AEPL; policy tables; XACML; PTACL

ACM Reference format:
Jason Crampton and Conrad Williams. 2017. Attribute Expressions, Policy Tables and Attribute-Based Access Control. In *Proceedings of SACMAT'17, June 21–23, 2017, Indianapolis, IN, USA, , 12 pages.*
DOI: http://dx.doi.org/10.1145/3078861.3078865

1 INTRODUCTION

Access control restricts the interactions that are possible between users (or programs operating under the control of users) and sensitive resources, and is an essential security service in any multi-user computing system. The most common means of implementing access control is to define an *authorization policy*, specifying which *requests* (that is, attempted user-resource interactions) are authorized and can thus be allowed. In a typical implementation, all requests are intercepted and evaluated with respect to the policy by trusted software components, often known as the *policy enforcement point* and *policy decision point*, respectively.

Thus, in general terms, an authorization policy is a function $P : Q \rightarrow D$, where Q is the set of requests and D is the set of authorization decisions. We assume 0 and 1 belong to D, representing the "deny" and "allow" decisions, respectively. Traditionally, Q was modeled as a set of triples of the form (s, o, a), where s is a subject, o is an object, and a is an action: a subject represents an authenticated entity, an object represents a protected resource, and an action is the means by which the subject wishes to interact with the object.

In recent years, we have seen the emergence of *attribute-based* access control, in part to cater for open, distributed computing environments where it is not necessarily possible to authenticate all entities directly. Instead, subjects and objects are associated with attributes, requests are collections of attributes associated with the subjects and objects, and these attributes determine whether a request is authorized or not. Thus we may imagine representing a policy as a table in which columns are indexed by attributes, rows represent the presence or otherwise of the respective attribute in a request, with the final column in the table indicating the authorization decision associated with a particular collection of attributes.

A simple example is shown in Figure 1, where 1 indicates the presence of the attribute in the request and 0 indicates the attribute is absent; the dash indicates that the presence or otherwise of a particular attribute is irrelevant to the decision. Thus the first row of the table indicates that the deny decision (0) should be returned if attributes a_1 and a_2 are present in a request. If no row exists for a particular combination, then we assume that the decision is $\perp$ ("not-applicable"); that is, the policy is "silent" for such a request and does not return a conclusive decision. Thus, for example, the decision is $\perp$ if attribute a_1 is not present in the request.

While it is certainly convenient and intuitive to represent authorization policies in tabular form, this representation is not compatible with many languages that have been developed for writing attribute-based authorization policies. XACML [11], PTaCL [6] and PBel [5], for example, are "tree-structured" languages, where policies are, essentially, terms in a logic-based formalism. These terms

a_1	a_2	a_3	d
1	1	–	0
1	0	1	1

Figure 1: A simple policy table

may be represented by trees, in which leaf nodes are attribute-decision pairs and interior nodes are attribute-operator pairs.[1]

Figure 2 illustrates the policy $((a_1, \mathrm{do}), ((a_2, 0), (a_3, 1)))$. In this case, the operator do represents the "deny-overrides" operator. A request is evaluated by first pruning the nodes that are not matched by the attributes in the request. Then the decisions in the remaining leaf nodes are combined using the policy combining operator(s). If, for example, all attributes are present in a request (so no pruning is performed), then the resulting decision is $0 \mathrm{\,do\,} 1 = 0$, corresponding to the first line in Figure 1.

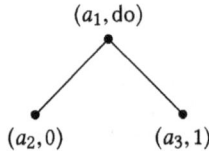

(a_1, do)

$(a_2, 0)$ $(a_3, 1)$

Figure 2: A simple tree-structured policy

In fact, the tree in Figure 2 represents an equivalent policy to the one tabulated in Figure 1, although this is not immediately apparent. It is this gap – between (i) how one is likely to conceive of a policy, and (ii) how one must construct the policy using existing languages for attribute-based access control – that provides the motivation for the work in this paper.

A further shortcoming of existing work on languages for attribute-based access control is the way in which requests and attributes are matched. Suppose we have an attribute name-value pair (n, v) and a request that contains multiple name-value pairs, including (n, v) and (n, v'), where $v' \neq v$. Then one might argue the request matches the attribute (since it contains (n, v)); on the other hand, one might argue it doesn't match the attribute (since it also contains (n, v')). XACML always assumes the former interpretation, which may be inappropriate if, for example, the policy author wishes to insist that the request contains exactly one name-value pair for the named attribute. Although PTaCL has a slightly more complex match semantics for requests and attributes, it ignores several possible match semantics that might be relevant in practice.

In this paper, we use prior work on canonical completeness to develop a new way of defining authorization policies using policy tables. In doing so, we support all possible match semantics for an attribute and request, thereby facilitating much greater control over policy specification. We then show how such tables can be automatically compiled into machine-enforceable policies. Thus, we are able to bridge the gap between a policy representation that is convenient for end-users and a policy that can be enforced

by a PDP. We also demonstrate that policy tables can be used as the leaf nodes in a tree-structured language, thereby facilitating the modular construction of enterprise-wide policies. Finally, we show how such policy tables can be used to enhance existing access control paradigms, such as access control lists and role-based access control, by making them "attribute-aware".

In summary, the main contributions of this paper are:

- the introduction of "attribute expressions" and match semantics for attribute based requests;
- the specification of a new policy authorization language AEPL, which represents policies as tables and provides a method for automatically converting policy tables into machine-enforceable policies;
- an overview of various policy compression methods which can be applied to AEPL policy tables;
- a method for converting tree-structured XACML policies into policy tables; and
- a demonstration of the various applications of AEPL, in enhancing existing paradigms such as access control lists and role-based access control.

In the following section we provide a brief introduction to canonical completeness for lattice-based logics, along with the specification of a 4-valued canonically complete logic [8], which we will use as the underlying logic for AEPL. In Section 3 we define the syntax and semantics of attribute expressions, along with a justification for why they are preferable to the use of traditional targets (found in XACML [11] and PTaCL [6]). Then, we specify the AEPL language, showing how policies are constructed as tables, and describe a method for automatically converting these tables into machine-enforceable policies. In Section 4, we investigate various methods for reducing the size of AEPL policy tables. We then discuss the limitations of targets in XACML, and demonstrate how an XACML policy can be converted into a policy table in Section 5. Section 6 discusses methods to build complex policies, enabling distributed specification and evaluation of policy tables, and ways to integrate policy tables with role-based access control and access control lists. We conclude the paper with a summary of our contributions and suggest ideas for future work.

2 BACKGROUND AND RELATED WORK

We focus our attention on 4-valued logics (and policy languages), where the set of decisions D is equal to $\{0, 1, \bot, \top\}$, corresponding to the authorization decisions "deny", "allow", "not-applicable" and "conflict", respectively [5, 10, 13]. In the context of decisions that arise from policy evaluation, we interpret 0 as a "deny" decision, 1 as "allow", $\bot$ as "not-applicable" and $\top$ as "conflict". We assume D is furnished with a partial ordering $\leqslant$ such that $(D, \leqslant)$ is a lattice, perhaps the most well-known logic of this kind being Belnap logic [4].

We begin with a brief introduction of Belnap logic in Section 2.1. Then, we summarize recent work by Crampton and Williams [8] in Section 2.2, which extends Jobe's [9] notions of canonical suitability, selection operators and canonical completeness to lattice-based logics, and their applications to attribute-based policy authorization languages.

---

[1]This is something of a simplification, but is a good approximation of how such policies are structured.

We conclude the related work section with a description of a lattice-based 4-valued canonically complete logic [8]. (For discussion on the use of a 4-valued decision set and lattice-based logics in access control the reader is the referred to the literature [5, 10, 13])

2.1 Belnap logic

Belnap logic [4] is one of the most well-known lattice-based logics, and has been used as the formal basis for authorization languages such as PBel [5], Rumpole [10] and BelLog [13]. It was developed with the intention of defining ways to handle inconsistent and incomplete information in a formal manner and uses the truth values $0, 1, \bot,$ and $\top$, representing "false", "true", "lack of information" and "too much information", respectively. In the remainder of this paper, we will denote the four valued decision set $\{\bot, 0, 1, \top\}$ by 4.

The set of truth values in Belnap's logic admits two orderings: a truth ordering $\leqslant_t$ and a knowledge ordering $\leqslant_k$. In the truth ordering $\leqslant_t$, 0 is the minimum element and 1 is the maximum element, while $\bot$ and $\top$ are incomparable indeterminate values. In the knowledge ordering $\leqslant_k$, $\bot$ is the minimum element, $\top$ is the maximum element while 0 and 1 are incomparable. Both $(4, \leqslant_t)$ and $(4, \leqslant_k)$ are lattices, forming the interlaced bilattice illustrated in Figure 3.

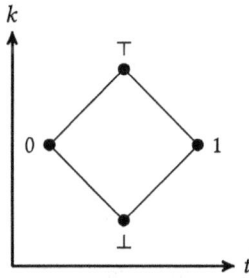

Figure 3: The 4 truth values in Belnap logic

We will assume the use of the knowledge ordering throughout this paper. The intuition is that $\bot$ ("not-applicable") represents no conclusive decision is possible because of lack of knowledge, while 0 and 1 are (incomparable) conclusive decisions, and $\top$ corresponds to too much knowledge because of conflicting conclusive decisions.

2.2 Canonical completeness

We now define canonical suitability, functional completeness, selection operators, normal form and canonical completeness for lattice-based logics [8].

Let $L = (V, \text{Ops})$ be a logic associated with a lattice $(V, \leqslant)$ of truth values and a set of logical operators Ops. We omit V and Ops when no ambiguity can occur. We write $\Phi(L)$ to denote the set of formulae that can be written in the logic L.

We say L is *canonically suitable* if and only if there exist formulae $\phi_{\max}$ and $\phi_{\min}$ of arity 2 in $\Phi(L)$ such that $\phi_{\max}(x, y)$ returns $\sup\{x, y\}$ and $\phi_{\min}(x, y)$ returns $\inf\{x, y\}$. If a logic is canonically suitable, we will write $\phi_{\max}(x, y)$ and $\phi_{\min}(x, y)$ using infix binary operators as $x \vee y$ and $x \wedge y$, respectively.

A function $f : V^n \to V$ is completely specified by a truth table containing n columns and m^n rows. However, not every truth table

can be represented by a formula in a given logic $L = (V, \text{Ops})$. L is said to be *functionally complete* if for every function $f : V^n \to V$, there is a formula $\phi \in \Phi(L)$ of arity n whose evaluation corresponds to the truth table. In this sense, XACML is not functionally complete [7], while PTaCL [6] and PBel [5] are.

Let $\underline{v}$ denote the minimum value in $(V, \leqslant)$. (Such a value must exist in a finite lattice.) We will write $\mathbf{a}$ to denote the tuple $(a_1, \ldots, a_n) \in V^n$ when no confusion can occur. Then, for $\mathbf{a} \in V^n$, the n-ary *selection operator* $S_{\mathbf{a}}^j$ is defined as follows:

$$S_{\mathbf{a}}^j(\mathbf{x}) = \begin{cases} j & \text{if } \mathbf{x} = \mathbf{a}, \\ \underline{v} & \text{otherwise.} \end{cases}$$

Note $S_{\mathbf{a}}^{\underline{v}}(x) = \underline{v}$ for all $\mathbf{a}, \mathbf{x} \in V^n$. Illustrative examples of unary and binary selection operators (for Belnap logic) are shown in Figure 4.

x	$S_0^0(x)$	$S_1^\top(x)$
$\bot$	$\bot$	$\bot$
0	0	$\bot$
1	$\bot$	$\top$
$\top$	$\bot$	$\bot$

		y			
$S_{(1,\top)}^0(x,y)$		$\bot$	0	1	$\top$
	$\bot$	$\bot$	$\bot$	$\bot$	$\bot$
	0	$\bot$	$\bot$	$\bot$	$\bot$
x	1	$\bot$	$\bot$	$\bot$	0
	$\top$	$\bot$	$\bot$	$\bot$	$\bot$

Figure 4: Examples of selection operators in Belnap Logic

Selection operators play a central role in the development of canonically complete logics because an arbitrary function $f : V^n \to V$ can be expressed in terms of selection operators. Consider, for example, the function

$$f(x, y) = \begin{cases} \top & \text{if } x = 0, y = 1, \\ 0 & \text{if } x = y = 0, \\ 1 & \text{if } x = 1, y = \bot, \\ \bot & \text{otherwise.} \end{cases}$$

Then it is easy to confirm that

$$f(x, y) \equiv S_{(0,1)}^\top(x, y) \vee S_{(0,0)}^0(x, y) \vee S_{(1,\bot)}^1(x, y).$$

Moreover, $S_{(a,b)}^c(x, y) \equiv S_a^c(x) \wedge S_b^c(y)$ for any $a, b, c, x, y \in V$. Thus,

$$f(x, y) \equiv (S_0^\top(x) \wedge S_1^\top(y)) \vee (S_0^0(x) \wedge S_0^0(y)) \vee (S_1^1(x) \wedge S_\bot^1(y))$$

In other words, we can express f as the "disjunction" ($\vee$) of "conjunctions" ($\wedge$) of unary selection operators.

More generally, given the truth table of function $f : V^n \to V$, we can write down an equivalent function in terms of selection operators. Specifically, let

$$A = \{\mathbf{a} \in V^n : f(\mathbf{a}) > \bot\};$$

then, for all $\mathbf{x} \in V^n$,

$$f(\mathbf{x}) = \bigvee_{\mathbf{a} \in A} S_{\mathbf{a}}^{f(\mathbf{x})}(\mathbf{x}).$$

Jobe established a number of results connecting the functional completeness of a logic with the unary selection operators, summarized in the following theorem.

THEOREM 2.1 (JOBE [9, THEOREMS 1, 2; LEMMA 1]). *A logic L is functionally complete if and only if each unary selection operator is equivalent to some formula in L.*

The *normal form* of formula ϕ in a canonically suitable logic is a formula ϕ' that has the same truth table as ϕ and has the following properties:

- the only binary operators it contains are $\vee$ and $\wedge$;
- no binary operator is included in the scope of a unary operator;
- no instance of $\vee$ occurs in the scope of the $\wedge$ operator.

A canonically suitable logic is *canonically complete* if every unary selection operator can be expressed in normal form. Crampton and Williams showed that there are considerable advantages to using a canonically complete logic as the basis for an authorization language [7]. In particular, it will often be easier to specify policies using a language based on a canonically complete logic and such policies can be compiled automatically into a normal form.

2.3 A 4-valued canonically complete logic

While Belnap logic is known to be functionally complete [3], Crampton and Williams [8] showed it is not canonically complete, essentially because only one unary operator (negation $\neg$) is defined. Crampton and Williams developed a new set of operators based on the knowledge ordering $(4, \leqslant_k)$, which produced a canonically complete 4-valued logic. For brevity, henceforth we denote the lattice $(4, \leqslant_k)$ by 4_k.

They defined two new unary operators $-$ and $\diamond$ whose truth tables are shown in Figure 5a: $-$ swaps the values of $\bot$ and $\top$; $\diamond$ permutes the values $\bot, 0, 1$ and $\top$. In addition, they reused the operator $\otimes$ which acts as the meet operation $(\wedge)$ for the lattice 4_k, whose truth table is shown in Figure 5b. We represent this logic using the notation $L(4_k, \{-, \diamond, \otimes\})$.

d	$-d$	$\diamond d$
$\bot$	$\top$	0
0	0	1
1	1	$\top$
$\top$	$\bot$	$\bot$

$\otimes$	$\bot$	0	1	$\top$
$\bot$	$\bot$	$\bot$	$\bot$	$\bot$
0	$\bot$	0	$\bot$	0
1	$\bot$	$\bot$	1	1
$\top$	$\bot$	0	1	$\top$

(a) $-$ and $\diamond$ 　　　　(b) $\otimes$

Figure 5: Canonically complete operators

Crampton and Williams [8] used the logic $L(4_k, \{-, \diamond, \otimes\})$ as a basis for the policy authorization language $\text{PTaCL}_4^{\lessgtr}$, highlighting the numerous advantages that can be gained in using a canonically complete logic as the underlying logic, opposed to other languages such as PBel [5] which use the canonically incomplete Belnap logic. Accordingly, we will use the logic $L(4_k, \{-, \diamond, \otimes\})$ as the underlying logic when we develop our new policy authorization language.

3 THE AEPL LANGUAGE

As we noted in the introduction, an authorization policy may be represented as a function $P : Q \to D$, where Q is the set of requests and D is the set of decisions. In other words, $P(q)$ represents the result of evaluating policy P for request q, thereby determining whether q is authorized by policy P.

In attribute-based access control, a *request* is assumed to be a set of name-value pairs, where a name is an attribute and a value is taken from some domain over which the binary relations $=, \neq, <, \leqslant, >$ and $\geqslant$ are defined. We assume it is possible to determine whether a pair of values belongs to a given relation efficiently. In particular, we assume henceforth that all attribute values are strings of bounded length defined over some alphabet Σ.

It is usually impossible to specify an attribute-based policy P by specifying a decision for every possible request, given the size of the domain of P. Thus, it is usual to specify P in terms of the relationship between a policy and the attribute name-value pairs that constitute a request. This relationship is typically expressed in terms of "targets", which are predicates specified in terms of attributes values and whose truth values are determined by comparing the attribute values specified in the target with those present in the request.

3.1 Attribute expressions

Our attribute-expression policy language, AEPL, is based on the idea of an *attribute expression*. Informally, the input to P is a tuple of logical values, and those values are determined by "matching" a request to a set of attribute expressions. More formally, we define an *attribute expression* to be a tuple $(n, v, \sim, \oplus)$, where n is an attribute name, v is an attribute value or regular expression, $\sim$ is an associative, commutative, binary relation, and $\oplus$ is a binary operator.

Given a binary relation R defined over some domain V, we write $\overline{R}$ to denote the complement of R: that is $(a, b) \in \overline{R}$ iff $(a, b) \notin R$. We will usually write R as an infix relation $\sim$ and $\overline{R}$ as $\nsim$. Typical examples of R and $\overline{R}$ include $=$ and $\neq$, $<$ and $\nless$ (that is, $\geqslant$).

In many cases, v will be an attribute value and $\sim$ will be a comparison operator, such as equality or greater-than. However, the use of regular expressions means that more complex attribute expressions may be defined. Given a regular expression e (defined over Σ), let $\mathcal{L}(e)$ denote the set of strings that match e. Then we define $\sim_e$ to be the set of pairs $\{(e, w) : w \in \mathcal{L}(e)\}$. Moreover, for any regular expression e, there exists a regular expression $\bar{e}$, the *complement* of e, such that $w \notin \mathcal{L}(e)$ if and only if $w \in \mathcal{L}(\bar{e})$.

In the interests of clarity of exposition, we will assume henceforth that $\sim$ is always $=$ (corresponding to exact string matching). Note that this does not affect the generality of our approach: we only require that it is efficient to determine whether a pair belongs to the relation $\sim$.

The operator $\oplus$ determines the result of evaluating a request in which some name-value pairs match the attribute expression and some don't. (This contrasts with the approach taken in XACML and PTaCL.) We discuss this in more detail in Section 3.2.

We define three binary operators in Figure 6: $\vee$ and $\wedge$ are defined on the set $\{0, 1, \bot\}$; and $!$ is defined on $\{0, 1, \bot, \top\}$. Since $\oplus$ is associative and commutative, the expression

$$(\ldots((x_1 \oplus x_2) \oplus x_3) \oplus \cdots \oplus x_{k-1}) \oplus x_k)$$

may be written without ambiguity as $\bigoplus_{i=1}^{k} x_i$.

$\wedge$	$\perp$	0	1
$\perp$	$\perp$	0	1
0	0	0	0
1	1	0	1

$\vee$	$\perp$	0	1
$\perp$	$\perp$	0	1
0	0	0	1
1	1	1	1

!	$\perp$	0	1	$\top$
$\perp$	$\perp$	0	1	$\top$
0	0	0	$\top$	$\top$
1	1	$\top$	1	$\top$
$\top$	$\top$	$\top$	$\top$	$\top$

Figure 6: Binary operators for attribute expressions

3.2 Evaluating requests

A *request* is a set of name-value pairs of the form (n, v). The *evaluation* of a request $q = \{(n_1, v_1), \ldots, (n_\ell, v_\ell)\}$ with respect to an attribute expression $\alpha = (n, v, \sim, \oplus)$ is denoted by $\mathrm{eval}(q, \alpha)$. Informally, $\mathrm{eval}(q, \alpha)$ is determined by combining the results of evaluating the elements of the request (n_i, v_i) using $\oplus$. More formally, we define:

$$\mathrm{eval}(\emptyset, (n, v, \sim, \oplus)) = \perp_m;$$

$$\mathrm{eval}(\{(n', v')\}, (n, v, \sim, \oplus)) = \begin{cases} 1_m & \text{if } n = n' \text{ and } v \sim v', \\ 0_m & \text{if } n = n' \text{ and } v \nsim v', \\ \perp_m & \text{otherwise.} \end{cases}$$

We say a name-value pair (n', v') *matches* an attribute expression α if $\mathrm{eval}(\{(n', v')\}, \alpha) = 1_m$; and we say (n', v') *does not match* α if $\mathrm{eval}(\{(n', v')\}, \alpha) = 0_m$. Throughout this section, we use the subscript m (for "match") to denote explicitly logical values that arise from the evaluation of attribute expressions (request matches). In Section 3.3, we use the subscript d to denote logical values that arise from policy evaluation (authorization decisions). When no ambiguity can occur we will omit the subscripts.

A request $q = \{(n_1, v_1), \ldots, (n_\ell, v_\ell)\}$ may contain two name-value pairs, one of which matches $\alpha = (n, v, \sim, \oplus)$ and one which doesn't. The choice of operator $\oplus$ determines how the results of the matches will be combined. Formally, we have

$$\mathrm{eval}(q, (n, v, \sim, \oplus)) = \bigoplus_{i=1}^{k} \mathrm{eval}(\{(n_i, v_i)\}, (n, v, \sim, \oplus)).$$

Thus, we have the following possibilities.

- $\mathrm{eval}(q, (n, v, \sim, \vee)) = 1_m$ if there exists i such that $\mathrm{eval}((n_i, v_i), (n, v, \sim, \vee)) = 1_m$; in other words, if the request contains at least one name-value pair that matches the attribute expression.
- $\mathrm{eval}(q, (n, v, \sim, \wedge)) = 0_m$ if there exists i such that $\mathrm{eval}((n_i, v_i), (n, v, \sim, \wedge)) = 0_m$; in other words, if the request contains at least one name-value pair that does not match the attribute expression.

- $\mathrm{eval}(q, (n, v, \sim, !)) = \top_m$, indicating conflict, if there exist i and j such that $\mathrm{eval}((n_i, v_i), (n, v, \sim, !)) = 0_m$ and $\mathrm{eval}((n_j, v_j), (n, v, \sim, !)) = 1_m$.

It is worth noting that neither XACML nor PTaCL provide this level of control over how a request is evaluated with respect to a target (the concept analogous to an attribute expression). Roughly speaking, target evaluation in both languages only returns 0_m or 1_m and (effectively) always assumes the use of $\vee$ when a request contains attribute values that both match and don't match a target.

3.3 AEPL policies

A *policy* in AEPL is a pair $P = (A(P), F(P))$, where

- $A(P) = \{\alpha_1, \ldots, \alpha_\ell\}$ is a set of attribute expressions,
- $D_i \subseteq \{\perp_m, 0_m, 1_m, \top_m\}$ is the range of values that $\mathrm{eval}(q, \alpha_i)$ can take, and
- $F : D_1 \times \cdots \times D_\ell \to \{\perp_d, 0_d, 1_d, \top_d\}$ is a function.

Then we define:

$$P(q) = F(\mathrm{eval}(q, \alpha_1), \ldots, \mathrm{eval}(q, \alpha_\ell)).$$

We will write A and F for $A(P)$ and $F(P)$, respectively, when P is clear from context. We will also write $\mathrm{eval}(q, A)$ for $\mathrm{eval}(q, \alpha_1), \ldots, \mathrm{eval}(q, \alpha_\ell)$ where no confusion can occur.

We may visualize F as a table having $\ell + 1$ columns. The first ℓ columns are indexed by the attribute expressions in A. The entries in the ith column are the possible values that $\mathrm{eval}(q, \alpha_i)$ can take. The final entry in the row with entries $d_1, \ldots, d_\ell$ is $F(d_1, \ldots, d_\ell)$. In other words, policies are defined in the form suggested in the introduction and illustrated in Figure 1. Thus we specify an AEPL policy in two steps: define the relevant attribute expressions; and then define the policy table. Note that a policy is defined directly in terms of the match relationships that exist between the elements of a request and the policy's attribute expressions.

In the remainder of the paper, we use an example of a simple policy containing two attribute expressions. Let $P_{\mathrm{ex}} = (A_{\mathrm{ex}}, F_{\mathrm{ex}})$ be a policy, where

$$A_{\mathrm{ex}} = \{\alpha_1, \alpha_2\} = \{(n_1, v_1, =, \wedge), (n_2, v_2, =, \wedge)\}$$

and F_{ex} is defined in Figure 7.

$x_1 = \mathrm{eval}(q, \alpha_1)$	$x_2 = \mathrm{eval}(q, \alpha_2)$	$P_{\mathrm{ex}}(x_1, x_2)$
$\perp_m$	$\perp_m$	$\perp_d$
$\perp_m$	0_m	$\perp_d$
$\perp_m$	1_m	1_d
0_m	$\perp_m$	0_d
0_m	0_m	0_d
0_m	1_m	0_d
1_m	$\perp_m$	1_d
1_m	0_m	0_d
1_m	1_m	1_d

Figure 7: Policy function defined as a table

The decisions in the final column of Figure 7 are determined by the policy author, for each combination of attribute expression matches. This allows for precise specification of how the policy P_{ex} should behave under each different attribute expression evaluation outcome and differs significantly from the evaluation of targets in XACML and PTaCL. We discuss this in more detail in Section 5.

3.4 Policies in normal form

Crampton and Williams [7] extended work by Jobe [9] to develop a method for converting arbitrary tables representing functions of the form $F : D^n \to D$, where D is the set of values in a multi-valued logic, into an equivalent logical formula using selection operators. We now show how this method can be applied to AEPL policies to generate standardized policy representations that can be evaluated automatically.

We write $\mathcal{D}$ to denote $D_1 \times \cdots \times D_\ell$. Given $(x_1, \ldots, x_\ell) \in \mathcal{D}$, we will write $\mathbf{x}$ where no ambiguity can occur. For each row in the table representing F, we may construct an equivalent logical formula comprising a "disjunction" of selection operators. Specifically, if $F(\mathbf{a}) = d$ for $\mathbf{a} \in \mathcal{D}$, then, we may write this as $S_{\mathbf{a}}^d(\mathbf{x})$. Let $\mathcal{D}^+ = \{\mathbf{x} \in \mathcal{D} : F(\mathbf{x}) \neq \bot\}$. Then

$$F(\mathbf{x}) = \bigvee_{\mathbf{a} \in \mathcal{D}^+} S_{\mathbf{a}}^d(\mathbf{x}) \qquad \text{and} \qquad S_{(a_1, \ldots, a_\ell)}^d(\mathbf{x}) \equiv \bigwedge_{i=1}^{\ell} S_{a_i}^d.$$

Hence F may be represented as a disjunction of conjunctions of unary selection operators [8].

Consider F_{ex}, and let $x_1 = \text{eval}(q, \alpha_1)$ and $x_2 = \text{eval}(q, \alpha_2)$. Then, we may express the policy $P_{ex}(q) = F_{ex}(x_1, x_2)$ as a disjunction of selection operators:

$$\begin{aligned}
F_{ex}(x_1, x_2) \equiv \; & S_{(\bot, \bot)}^{\bot}(x_1, x_2) \vee S_{(\bot, 0)}^{\bot}(x_1, x_2) \vee S_{(\bot, 1)}^{1}(x_1, x_2) \\
& \vee S_{(0, \bot)}^{0}(x_1, x_2) \vee S_{(0, 0)}^{0}(x_1, x_2) \vee S_{(0, 1)}^{0}(x_1, x_2) \\
& \vee S_{(1, \bot)}^{1}(x_1, x_2) \vee S_{(1, 0)}^{0}(x_1, x_2) \vee S_{(1, 1)}^{1}(x_1, x_2).
\end{aligned}$$

This, in turn, may be represented as a disjunction of conjunctions of unary selection operators (as described above).

Furthermore, Crampton and Williams have derived expressions for the unary selection operators in terms of the operators $\{-, \diamond, \otimes\}$ (see Appendix A). Hence, we can derive a formula in normal form for the policy $P_{ex} = (A_{ex}, F_{ex})$. Of course, one would not usually construct the normal form by hand, as we have done above. Indeed, Crampton and Williams [8] have developed an algorithm which takes an arbitrary policy expressed as a table as input, and outputs the equivalent normal form expressed in terms of the operators $\{-, \diamond, \otimes\}$.

3.5 AEPL policy trees

An AEPL *policy* is a pair (A, F). While this method of policy specification provides an intuitive and flexible method for defining policies, it will not scale to situations where many attribute expressions need to be specified and evaluated. In this case, it makes sense to use the policy-combining operators found in XACML and other tree-structured authorization languages to combine the results of evaluating multiple policies, each using a small number of attribute expressions. Thus, the set of attribute expressions in each policy will act in the same way as a target in a language like XACML.

In this section we revise the syntax and semantics for policy evaluation of the tree-structured ABAC language $\text{PTaCL}_4^{\leqslant}$ [8]. We use the operators $-, \diamond$ and $\otimes$ from $\text{PTaCL}_4^{\leqslant}$ (defined in Section 2.3) and demonstrate how policies of the form (A, F) can be used in tree-structured policies, and how we may replace targets with attribute expressions.

We define an *attribute expression based target*, or simply an *AE-target*, to be a pair (A, T), where $A = \{\alpha_1, \ldots, \alpha_\ell\}$ is a set of attribute expressions and $T \subseteq D_1 \times \cdots \times D_\ell$, where D_i is the set of values that $\text{eval}(q, \alpha_i)$ can take. If q is a request and T is an AE-target such that $\text{eval}(q, A) \in T$ then q is said to *match* T.

Given an AEPL policy $P = (A, F)$, then P, $\diamond P$ and $-P$ are AEPL policy trees, where

$$(\diamond P)(q) \stackrel{\text{def}}{=} \diamond(P(q)) \qquad \text{and} \qquad (-P)(q) \stackrel{\text{def}}{=} -(P(q)).$$

If P_1 and P_2 are AEPL policy trees and T is an AE-target, then $(T, P_1 \otimes P_2)$ is a AEPL policy tree, where

$$(T, P_1 \otimes P_2)(q) \stackrel{\text{def}}{=} \begin{cases} P_1(q) \otimes P_2(q) & \text{if } \text{eval}(q, A) \in T, \\ \bot & \text{otherwise.} \end{cases}$$

The ability to use AEPL policies (A, F) as leaf nodes (atomic policies) in AEPL policy trees provides us with a number of advantages (over $\text{PTaCL}_4^{\leqslant}$). We get the additional expressive power of policy specification for leaf nodes, together with the full power and functional completeness of $\text{PTaCL}_4^{\leqslant}$. By facilitating high-level operators in addition to specifying policies via a policy table and attribute expressions, we provide a hybrid means of constructing policies, which can be both bottom-up and top-down. This provides a great deal of flexibility and expressivity for policy authors. We can support low level policies specified by functions, and merge the policies using high-level policy operators. In addition, we have greater control of the applicability of policies due to the use of targets based on attribute expression (over "traditional" targets in $\text{PTaCL}_4^{\leqslant}$). We discuss $\text{PTaCL}_4^{\leqslant}$ targets and their limitations in more depth in Section 5.2.

4 POLICY COMPRESSION

While representing a policy P as a pair (A, F) is more concise and an easier task than specifying a decision for every possible request, the policy tables will be large when many attribute expressions are involved. To tackle this problem, we now investigate methods for policy compression, with the aim of reducing the size of these policy tables.

4.1 Removing redundancies

We begin with the following two remarks about methods for merging and omitting rows from policy tables.

REMARK 1. *Suppose $F(a, x_2) = d$ for all $x_2 \in D_2$, as illustrated in the policy table fragment below.*

x_1	x_2	$P(x_1, x_2)$
a	$\perp$	d
a	0	d
a	1	d
a	$\top$	d

Then it is easy to show that

$$S^d_{(a,\perp)}(x_1, x_2) \vee S^d_{(a,0)}(x_1, x_2) \vee S^d_{(a,1)}(x_1, x_2) \vee S^d_{(a,\top)}(x_1, x_2)$$

is equivalent to $S^d_a(x_1)$. (This equivalence is formally established in Table 14 in Appendix B.) And this may be represented in tabular form as a single row, shown below, where we use − to signify that x_2 can take any value.

x_1	x_2	$P(x_1, x_2)$
a	−	d

REMARK 2. *We may omit any rows from the policy table in which the final column contains the value $\perp$. Recall*

$$S^d_{\mathbf{a}}(\mathbf{x}) = \begin{cases} d & \text{if } \mathbf{x} = \mathbf{a}, \\ \perp & \text{otherwise.} \end{cases}$$

Moreover, $(\perp \vee x) = (x \vee \perp) = x$ for all $x \in \{0, 1, \perp, \top\}$. Thus

$$S^{d_1}_{\mathbf{a_1}}(\mathbf{x}) \vee S^{d_2}_{\mathbf{a_2}}(\mathbf{x}) \vee \ldots \vee S^{d_n}_{\mathbf{a_n}}(\mathbf{x}) = \perp,$$

except when $\mathbf{x} \in \{\mathbf{a_1}, \ldots, \mathbf{a_n}\}$.

Thus, we may assume the policy returns $\perp$ if the table does not contain an entry for a particular tuple $\mathbf{x}$. In this case, we say the policy is *not applicable* for any request q such that $\text{eval}(q, A) = \mathbf{x}$.

Returning to our example policy P_{ex}, we apply the results from the remarks above to reduce the size of the policy table which defines the function F_{ex}. First, note that

$$F_{ex}(0, \perp) = F_{ex}(0, 0) = F_{ex}(0, 1) = 0.$$

Thus, by Remark 1, we may merge these three rows into a single row, represented by $F_{ex}(0, -) = 0$. In addition, by Remark 2, we may omit the rows $F_{ex}(\perp, \perp)$ and $F_{ex}(\perp, 0)$ since they contain $\perp$ in the final column. Hence, we have the reduced policy table shown in Figure 8.

$x_1 = \text{eval}(q, \alpha_1)$	$x_2 = \text{eval}(q, \alpha_2)$	$P_{ex}(x_1, x_2)$
$\perp_m$	1_m	1
0_m	−	0
1_m	$\perp_m$	1
1_m	0_m	0
1_m	1_m	1

Figure 8: Reduced policy table

Expressing the policy $P_{ex}(q) = F_{ex}(x_1, x_2)$ as a disjunction of selection operators, we have

$$F_{ex}(x_1, x_2) \equiv S^1_{(\perp, 1)}(x_1, x_2) \vee S^0_0(x_1) \vee S^1_{(1, \perp)}(x_1, x_2) \vee$$
$$S^0_{(1, 0)}(x_1, x_2) \vee S^1_{(1, 1)}(x_1, x_2).$$

We may apply Remark 1 directly during policy specification. If, for example, a policy author decides during the construction of a policy table that if $x_1 = 0$ then the value of x_2 is irrelevant, the policy should return 0 (the case in our example). In other words, we can, if desired, directly encode a deny-overrides or allow-overrides in the policy table when certain attribute expressions are matched or not matched. And we can allow the policy author to use − as syntactic sugar for a "decision" in the policy table, thereby saving the policy author from entering multiple rows (as seen in Figure 7).

4.2 Policies as Boolean functions

We now demonstrate that it is possible to reduce certain policies to Boolean functions. Specifically, if $F(\mathbf{x}) \in \{0, 1\}$ for all $\mathbf{x} \in \mathcal{D}$, then we can eliminate the values $\perp$ and $\top$ from the policy table. In particular, we may replace an attribute expression $\alpha = (n, v, \sim, \oplus)$ with two simpler attribute expressions $\alpha_1 = (n, v, \sim)$ and $\alpha_2 = (n, v, \not\sim)$. We then encode the semantics of $\oplus$ directly in a policy table only containing 0s and 1s.

Consider the example in Table 9. There are four values in the decision set $D = \{\perp, 0, 1, \top\}$, and there are four unique combinations of 0 and 1, represented by the four rows in Table 9b. Each of these values arises because of matches or the absence of matches, thus allowing us to encode the semantics of $\oplus$ directly in a policy table only containing 0s and 1s.

$(n, v, \sim, !)$	F
$\perp$	0
0	0
1	1
$\top$	0

$(n, v, \sim)$	$(n, v, \not\sim)$	F
0	0	0
0	1	0
1	0	1
1	1	0

(a) Policy containing $\perp$ and $\top$ **(b) Policy using only 0 and 1**

Figure 9: Converting a simple policy into a Boolean function

There are a number of advantages in expressing an attribute expression $\alpha = (n, v, \sim, \oplus)$ as a combination of two attribute expressions $(n, v, \sim)$ and $(n, v, \not\sim)$ and encoding the semantics of $\oplus$ directly. In particular, the resulting policy table contains only binary values. Hence, we may employ existing techniques for Boolean function minimization [2].

5 COMPARISON WITH XACML AND PTACL

Having defined the AEPL policy authorization language, we now provide a brief summary of XACML and compare it with AEPL. We discuss the limitations of targets in XACML and PTaCL, before showing how XACML rules and policies may be represented in AEPL. We conclude by showing how an XACML policy set may be represented using a single AEPL policy.

5.1 XACML targets

An XACML *target*, like an attribute expression, is expressed in terms of attribute name-value pairs. It is used to determine whether a rule, a policy or a policy set is applicable to a request.

A target is defined in terms of AllOf and AnyOf elements. The AllOf element is used to group such pairs. Such an element is "matched" by a request if the request matches each of the name-value pairs. The AnyOf element is used to group AllOf elements. Such an element is matched if any one of the AllOf elements is matched. Evaluation of an XACML target returns one of two values ("matched" or "not-matched"), unlike the evaluation of an attribute expression.

Moreover, evaluation of an XACML target disregards whether a request contains a name-value pair that doesn't match a target if it also contains a name-value pair that does match. In other words, XACML provides less control over target evaluation than our approach for the evaluation of attribute expressions.

5.2 PTaCL targets

A PTaCL target is defined to be a tuple (n, v, f), where n is an attribute name, v is an attribute value and f is a binary predicate. The key difference between PTaCL targets and attribute expressions, comes in the choice of the binary operator $\oplus$ present in attribute expressions. Attribute expressions allow this operator to be selected from the set $\{\wedge, \vee, !\}$, dependent on the way in which conflicting attribute values should be handled. Targets in PTaCL implicitly assume that the operator $\vee$ is always used. This makes it impossible to distinguish scenarios where there are two name value pairs (n', v') and (n'', v'') such that $n = n', v = v'$ and $n = n'', v \neq v''$. Furthermore, PTaCL targets, much like XACML targets, are unable to return $\top$. Hence, our attribute expressions are more expressive, and provide greater control over their evaluation compared to the evaluation of targets in PTaCL.

5.3 XACML rules

An XACML rule is specified by a target t and a decision d (known as the "effect" of the rule in XACML), which may be either "allow" or "deny". The evaluation of a rule for a given request returns d if the request matches the target and "not-applicable" otherwise. Thus, an XACML rule may be encoded as a particularly simple policy table. Specifically:

- each AllOf element is encoded as a row in the table, in which the last entry is always d; and
- the AnyOf element is encoded by the different rows in the table.

Clearly, our policy tables can encode more general structures than XACML rules. Informally, a policy table would have to be encoded using two XACML rules, one for the rows for which the decision is 1 and one for the rows for which the decision is 0. Even so, such an encoding could not, for example, return $\top$. In other words, AEPL provides a richer framework than the target-decision paradigm for specifying the "leaf" policies in tree-structured languages such as XACML or PTaCL.

5.4 XACML policies

We now illustrate how attribute expressions can be used to encode an entire XACML policy set directly. Consider the tree-structured policy P illustrated in Figure 10, where dov and pov represent the XACML deny-overrides and permit-overrides combining algorithms respectively. This policy tree represents a XACML policy set (t_1, dov) which contains one policy (t_3, po) one rule $(t_2, 0)$; and the policy (t_3, pov) in turn contains two rules $(t_4, 1)$ and $(t_5, 0)^2$. We assume for simplicity that each target is a single name-attribute pair. In Section 6.1 we explain how we can extend our method of specifying a policy as a pair (A, F) to more complex scenarios.

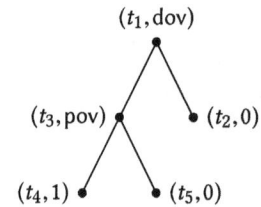

Figure 10: A simple tree-structured policy

Then we can represent this policy as the following policy table, which is created by considering every possible outcome of matching requests to targets. We write x_i to denote $\text{eval}(q, t_i)$, and $-$ to signify the value of $\text{eval}(q, t_i)$ is irrelevant.

x_1	x_2	x_3	x_4	x_5	$P(q)$
0	–	–	–	–	$\bot$
1	1	–	–	–	0
1	0	0	–	–	$\bot$
1	0	1	1	–	1
1	0	1	0	1	0
1	0	1	0	0	$\bot$

Hence, P may be represented by the pair (A, F), where $A = \{t_1, t_2, t_3, t_4, t_5\}$ and $F : \{0,1\}^5 \to \{\bot, 0, 1\}$ is defined in the table above. Then

$$F(x_1, \ldots, x_5) \equiv S^0_{(1,1)}(x_1, x_2) \vee S^1_{(1,0,1,1)}(x_1, x_2, x_3, x_4) \vee$$
$$S^0_{(1,0,1,0,1)}(x_1, x_2, x_3, x_4, x_5).$$

Note that we need not include the selection operators $S^\bot_0(x_1)$, $S^\bot_{(1,0,0)}(x_1, x_2, x_3)$ and $S^\bot_{(1,0,1,0,0)}(x_1, x_2, x_3, x_4, x_5)$ representing the first, third and sixth rows, since the policy evaluates to $\bot$ in these rows.

The representation of the policy tree in Figure 10 can be reduced to a simple policy table, which in turn is reduced into a formula comprising just three selection operators. By expressing this policy tree as a policy table, it is much easier for a policy author to understand how this policy will behave under each different result of target evaluation. Furthermore, we have a simple formula that can

---

^{2}This is a simplification in terms of the structure of XACML policy sets, policies and rules but approximate enough for the sake of exposition. For explicit definitions the reader is referred to the XACML standard [11].

be automatically converted into a machine-enforceable policy and evaluated by a PDP.

6 APPLICATIONS

We now demonstrate how complex policies can be built, enabling distributed policy specification and evaluation (much as in XACML and PTaCL). Furthermore, we explore how policy tables can be used to enhance existing access control paradigms, such as role-based access control and access control lists. Informally, in the first case, we show that a set of attribute expressions in an AEPL policy table (each of which evaluates to an element in $\{0, 1, \bot, \top\}$) may be replaced with a set of policies. And in the second case, we show that the policy decisions in an AEPL table can be replaced with a set of role identifiers or similar.

6.1 Complex policies as tables

By specifying policies as a pair (A, F), we implicitly restrict the depth of policies (or policy trees) to one. However, this may not be the way in which some policies are structured in the real world (indeed, most policy trees in XACML have depth greater than one). We now develop a method for constructing more complex policies from simple AEPL policies, using the structure of simple policies as a template. A complex policy $\mathcal{P}$ is a pair $(\{P_1, \ldots, P_\ell\}, F)$, where $P_i = (A_i, F_i)$ is a simple AEPL policy. We define

$$\mathcal{P}(q) = F(P_1(q), \ldots, P_\ell(q)).$$

Now, instead of the columns of the policy table representing the function F being indexed by attribute expressions, they are indexed by policies. Each row represents a possible combination of the values that may arise from the evaluation of the respective policies $P_1, \ldots, P_n$. Of course, each of these policies is itself defined by a set of attribute expressions and function (A_i, F_i), which will need to be specified and evaluated first. The policy $\mathcal{P}$, much like previous policies, can be automatically converted into a machine-enforceable form via the use of selection operators. Hence, we have developed a way in which to combine arbitrary policies into machine-enforceable form. This approach can be easily scaled, providing the means to construct policies of any desired depth (much in the same manner as XACML policies).

One of the main advantages in using this method for building up complex policies, is the distributed nature in which it can be applied. For instance, in a large organization, each department could construct their own complex policy, which can be converted into a tree. Each department's policy can then become a node in a bigger tree, and be combined with other policies through the use of another policy table. A simple example of this is shown in Figure 11, demonstrating how four individual policies P_1, P_2, P_3 and P_4 produced by each department can be combined in a policy table to create the overall organizations policy P_{org}.

This policy table can be specified by someone who understands the complete policy structure of the organization and can place adequate restrictions on the interactions of policies between departments. Constructing policies in this manner allows each department to design their own specific policy, without the need to worry about how their policy interacts with other department's policies. The

P_1	P_2	P_3	P_4	P_{org}
d_1	d_2	d_3	d_4	d_{org}
$\vdots$	$\vdots$	$\vdots$	$\vdots$	$\vdots$

Figure 11: Combining policies in another table

combination of policies is then moderated by a person who understands the organization wide policy strategy. We believe this both simplifies specification of complex corporate policies, and reduces the likely number of misconfigurations and errors.

In addition to the distributed nature in which policies can be specified using the approach, policy evaluation may also be distributed. In the real world it is common practice for multiple PDPs to be deployed, and this architecture may be leveraged by our method of specifying complex policies. For instance, imagine the scenario where a central PDP is in charge of evaluating the organization's policy P_{org}. This central PDP may then delegate the evaluation of policies $P_1, \ldots, P_4$ to other PDPs, and combine the resulting decisions that are reported back by each PDP. There are many reasons why distributing the evaluation of policies in this way could be advantageous: (i) the load on the central PDP is reduced, (ii) free or available PDPs are fully utilised, (iii) the evaluation time for policies is reduced, and (iv) in some instances requests may even be evaluated locally.

6.2 ABAC policies for RBAC

In role-based access control (RBAC) [12], we tend to assume that users are authorized for roles on the basis of identity. With the emergence of attribute-based access control, we have an alternative option: authorizing users on the basis of their attributes. Al-Kahtani and Sandhu [1] created a model for attribute-based user-role assignment, in which an enterprise defines a set of rules that are triggered to automatically assign roles to users. The motivation for a mechanism to do this, is to reduce the number of manual user-to-role assignments that are required, which can become troublesome in large environments such as utility companies and popular online websites [1].

We now demonstrate how we can automatically assign roles to users using policies in AEPL. Previously, authorization policies were represented by a function $P : Q \to D$, where Q is the set of requests and D is the set of decisions. Now, we represent a role assignment authorization policy by a function $P : Q \to R$, where Q is the set of requests and R is the set of roles. The function P is used to determine how users are assigned to roles based on their attributes. Consider the simple example for an attribute-role table which assigns roles based on the attribute "age" for the purpose of filtering age-restricted content, shown in Table 1 [1].

Let P be a policy which comprises of four attribute expressions $\alpha_1, \alpha_2, \alpha_3$ and α_4 where $\alpha_1 = (\mathrm{age}, 3, \geq)$, $\alpha_2 = (\mathrm{age}, 11, \geq)$, $\alpha_3 = (\mathrm{age}, 16, \geq)$ and $\alpha_4 = (\mathrm{age}, 18, \geq)^3$, with policy function F, defined in Figure 12.

---

[3] The choice of operator $\oplus$ is irrelevant in this example, since requests will not contain two pairs (n, v') and (n, v'') such that n is age and $v' \neq v''$, hence we omit it.

eval$(q,(age,3,\geq))$	eval$(q,(age,11,\geq))$	eval$(q,(age,16,\geq))$	eval$(q,(age,18,\geq))$	Role
1	0	0	0	Child
1	1	0	0	Juvenile
1	1	1	0	Adolescent
1	1	1	1	Adult

Figure 12: Policy table for attribute-based role assignment

Table 1: Age to role assignment

Age	Role
≥ 3	Child
≥ 11	Juvenile
≥ 16	Adolescent
≥ 18	Adult

Hence, we have represented the age-to-role assignment as a policy $P = (A, F)$, which may in turn be represented as a combination of selection operators and converted into a machine-enforceable policy. It is easy to imagine how this methodology could be extended and applied in a setting where it is useful to automatically assign roles to users on the basis of attributes rather than identity. Our approach is scalable, simple for policy authors to understand and can be applied with various other techniques discussed throughout this paper such as ways to compress policies and using policies as leaf nodes in tree-structured languages, to produce a machine-enforceable policy which assigns roles to users.

6.3 Access control lists

In an access control system using access control lists based on identifiers, a user is associated with one or more identifiers: a unique user identifier (UID) and zero or more group identifiers (GIDs). Each object is associated with an access control list (ACL). Each ACL may be modelled as a list of access control entries (ACEs), where an ACE comprises an identifier and a set of authorized actions. Finally, a request contains a UID and a set of GIDs, an object identifier (OID) and a requested action. The UID and GIDs in the request will be compared with those in the ACEs of the object's ACL and a decision will be reached based on the actions that are authorized by the ACEs and those that have been requested.

We may extend this idea of identity-based ACLs to attribute-based ACLs. Each ACE contains a group identifier, as before, which represents an attribute-based policy. Then, we represent a group membership policy as a function $P : Q \to G$, were Q is the set of requests and G is the set of group identifiers. The policy P specifies the attributes that a user must have to be regarded as a member of that group. We may represent this policy using a set of attribute expressions A and a function F defined as a policy table, in an identical manner to that illustrated in Section 6.2. Hence, we can use AEPL to support attribute-based access control in a ACL-based system.

7 CONCLUDING REMARKS

The development and specification of attribute-based access control languages such as XACML [11], PTaCL [6] and PBel [5] will continue to increase to meet the demand for open, distributed, interconnected and dynamic systems. While XACML is a standardized language, constructing some policies may be difficult (and may be impossible due to the functional incompleteness of XACML [7]), and there is little support or guidance provided for policy authors. This problem provides the primary motivation for this paper: the development of a convenient and intuitive method for authoring policies, which can be expressed in a form that may be easily evaluated by a PDP.

In this paper, we make important contributions to the development of ABAC authorization languages. First, we define attribute expressions, which provide greater control over how requests are evaluated, compared to XACML [11] and PTaCL [6]. Then, we specify policies as tables, in which the columns are indexed by attribute expressions. Defining policies in this manner is both simple and intuitive, and allows policy authors to specify how a policy will behave under each different evaluation of attribute expressions. In XACML and other tree-structured languages, it can be difficult to foresee how large policies will evaluate under different requests. This can often lead to policy misconfigurations and errors. In addition, we demonstrate how policy tables may be automatically compiled into machine-enforceable policies, and explore various methods for policy compression, thus reducing the size of policy tables.

Second, we compare XACML and PTaCL with AEPL, showing that AEPL provides more control over target evaluation than XACML and PTaCL. Furthermore, we show how an XACML policy can be converted into a policy table. By representing XACML policies in a tabular form, it becomes easier for a policy author to understand how policies will behave under each different result of target evaluation. Finally, we demonstrate the various applications of AEPL. We show how complex policies can be constructed as tables, thus enabling a distributed method for building and evaluating enterprise-wide policies. We also show how policy tables can be used in RBAC [12] and ACLs for role and group assignments respectively, making these paradigms "attribute-aware".

There is a considerable amount of future work which naturally proceeds from the work in this paper. We plan to develop policy authoring software that provides a graphical user interface for policy authors, allowing them to specify attribute expressions, and construct a table for the desired policy. This table will then be automatically converted into a machine-enforceable policy. Naturally, we hope to develop a modified XACML PDP that can evaluate attribute expressions and the machine-enforceable policies produced by policy authoring software at a PDP. There is also motivation to develop a tool which converts a policy expressed as a tree-structured policy into an equivalent policy table, much like the example in Section 5.4. This will help facilitate the smooth transition from XACML tree-structured policies to policies defined as tables. We would also like to investigate how arbitrary conditions (found in XACML) may be included in AEPL

We would also like to conduct a usability study to test the hypothesis that the construction of AEPL policy tables is easier and less error-prone than writing XACML policies. Our vision of this study requires the participants to construct a policy presented in natural language, first as a tree-structured XACML policy, and then as a policy table in AEPL. We may then compare various elements such as (i) the ease with which the testers could construct each policy, (ii) whether the XACML and AEPL policy are equivalent, (iii) the "correctness" of each policy (how close they are to the described policy in natural language), and (iv) other metrics such as the time taken to construct each policy.

REFERENCES

[1] Mohammad A. Al-Kahtani and Ravi S. Sandhu. 2002. A Model for Attribute-Based User-Role Assignment. In *18th Annual Computer Security Applications Conference (ACSAC 2002), 9-13 December 2002, Las Vegas, NV, USA*. IEEE Computer Society, 353–362. DOI : https://doi.org/10.1109/CSAC.2002.1176307

[2] Eric Allender, Lisa Hellerstein, Paul McCabe, Toniann Pitassi, and Michael E. Saks. 2006. Minimizing DNF Formulas and AC0 Circuits Given a Truth Table. In *21st Annual IEEE Conference on Computational Complexity (CCC 2006), 16-20 July 2006, Prague, Czech Republic*. IEEE Computer Society, 237–251. DOI : https://doi.org/10.1109/CCC.2006.27

[3] Ofer Arieli and Arnon Avron. 1998. The Value of the Four Values. *Artif. Intell.* 102, 1 (1998), 97–141. DOI : https://doi.org/10.1016/S0004-3702(98)00032-0

[4] Nuel D Belnap Jr. 1977. A useful four-valued logic. In *Modern uses of multiple-valued logic*. Springer, 5–37.

[5] Glenn Bruns and Michael Huth. 2011. Access control via Belnap logic: Intuitive, expressive, and analyzable policy composition. *ACM Trans. Inf. Syst. Secur.* 14, 1 (2011), 9. DOI : https://doi.org/10.1145/1952982.1952991

[6] Jason Crampton and Charles Morisset. 2012. PTaCL: A Language for Attribute-Based Access Control in Open Systems. In *Principles of Security and Trust - First International Conference, POST 2012, Proceedings*, Pierpaolo Degano and Joshua D. Guttman (Eds.). Lecture Notes in Computer Science, Vol. 7215. Springer, 390–409. DOI : https://doi.org/10.1007/978-3-642-28641-4_21

[7] Jason Crampton and Conrad Williams. 2016. On Completeness in Languages for Attribute-Based Access Control. In *Proceedings of the 21st ACM on Symposium on Access Control Models and Technologies, SACMAT 2016, Shanghai, China, June 5-8, 2016*, X. Sean Wang, Lujo Bauer, and Florian Kerschbaum (Eds.). ACM, 149–160. DOI : https://doi.org/10.1145/2914642.2914654

[8] Jason Crampton and Conrad Williams. 2017. Canonical Completeness in Lattice-Based Languages for Attribute-Based Access Control. *CoRR* abs/1702.04173 (2017). http://arxiv.org/abs/1702.04173 To appear in the Proceedings of CODASPY 2017; pre-print available at http://arxiv.org/abs/1702.04173.

[9] William H. Jobe. 1962. Functional Completeness and Canonical Forms in Many-Valued Logics. *J. Symb. Log.* 27, 4 (1962), 409–422. DOI : https://doi.org/10.2307/2964548

[10] Srdjan Marinovic, Naranker Dulay, and Morris Sloman. 2014. Rumpole: An Introspective Break-Glass Access Control Language. *ACM Trans. Inf. Syst. Secur.* 17, 1 (2014), 2:1–2:32.

[11] Erik Rissanen. 2012. eXtensible Access Control Markup Language (XACML) Version 3.0 OASIS Standard. (2012). http://docs.oasis-open.org/xacml/3.0/xacml-3.0-core-os-en.html.

[12] Ravi S. Sandhu, Edward J. Coyne, Hal L. Feinstein, and Charles E. Youman. 1996. Role-Based Access Control Models. *IEEE Computer* 29, 2 (1996), 38–47. DOI : https://doi.org/10.1109/2.485845

[13] Petar Tsankov, Srdjan Marinovic, Mohammad Torabi Dashti, and David A. Basin. 2014. Decentralized Composite Access Control. In *POST (Lecture Notes in Computer Science)*, Vol. 8414. Springer, 245–264.

A UNARY SELECTION OPERATOR ENCODINGS

Figure 13 shows the normal forms of the unary selection operators S_a^b. Note that $S_a^\perp(x) = \perp$ for all $a, x \in \{0, 1, \perp, \top\}$.

$S_a^\perp(x)$	$x \wedge (\diamond{-}x) \wedge (\diamond{-}\diamond{-}x)$
$S_\perp^0(x)$	$\diamond(x) \wedge (-\diamond{-}\diamond{-}x) \wedge (-\diamond{-}\diamond x)$
$S_0^0(x)$	$x \wedge (-x) \wedge (-\diamond{-}x)$
$S_1^0(x)$	$(\diamond{-}\diamond{-}x) \wedge (-\diamond{-}\diamond{-}x) \wedge (\diamond x)$
$S_\top^0(x)$	$(\diamond{-}x) \wedge (-\diamond{-}x) \wedge (\diamond\diamond{-}x)$
$S_\perp^1(x)$	$(\diamond{-}\diamond x) \wedge (-\diamond{-}\diamond x) \wedge (\diamond\diamond x)$
$S_0^1(x)$	$(\diamond x) \wedge (-\diamond x) \wedge (\diamond{-}x)$
$S_1^1(x)$	$x \wedge (-x) \wedge (\diamond\diamond{-}x)$
$S_\top^1(x)$	$(\diamond{-}\diamond{-}x) \wedge (-\diamond{-}\diamond{-}x) \wedge (\diamond\diamond{-}x)$
$S_\perp^\top(x)$	$(-\diamond{-}x) \wedge (-\diamond{-}\diamond{-}x) \wedge (-x)$
$S_0^\top(x)$	$(\diamond{-}\diamond{-}x) \wedge (\diamond{-}\diamond x) \wedge (\diamond\diamond x)$
$S_1^\top(x)$	$(\diamond x) \wedge (\diamond{-}x) \wedge (\diamond{-}\diamond\diamond{-}x)$
$S_\top^\top(x)$	$x \wedge (-\diamond x) \wedge (-\diamond{-}\diamond x)$

Figure 13: Normal forms for the unary selection operators

B EQUIVALENCE OF SELECTION OPERATORS

Figure 14 establishes the following equivalence of $S_a^d(x_1)$ and

$$S_{(a,\perp)}^d(x_1, x_2) \vee S_{(a,0)}^d(x_1, x_2) \vee S_{(a,1)}^d(x_1, x_2) \vee S_{(a,\top)}^d(x_1, x_2).$$

x_1	x_2	$S^d_{(a,\perp)}(x_1,x_2)$	$S^d_{(a,0)}(x_1,x_2)$	$S^d_{(a,1)}(x_1,x_2)$	$S^d_{(a,\top)}(x_1,x_2)$	$S^d_a(x_1)$
a	$\perp$	d	$\perp$	$\perp$	$\perp$	d
a	0	$\perp$	d	$\perp$	$\perp$	d
a	1	$\perp$	$\perp$	d	$\perp$	d
a	$\top$	$\perp$	$\perp$	$\perp$	d	d

Figure 14: Equivalence of selection operators

A Datalog Framework for Modeling Relationship-based Access Control Policies

Edelmira Pasarella
Universitat Politècnica de Catalunya
Computer Science Department
edelmira@cs.upc.edu

Jorge Lobo
Institució Catalana de Recerca i Estudis Avançats (ICREA)
Universitat Pompeu Fabra
jorge.lobo@upf.edu

ABSTRACT

Relationships like friendship to limit access to resources have been part of social network applications since their beginnings. Describing access control policies in terms of relationships is not particular to social networks and it arises naturally in many situations. Hence, we have recently seen several proposals formalizing different Relationship-based Access Control (ReBAC) models. In this paper, we introduce a class of Datalog programs suitable for modeling ReBAC and argue that this class of programs, that we called ReBAC Datalog policies, provides a very general framework to specify and implement ReBAC policies. To support our claim, we first formalize the merging of two recent proposals for modeling ReBAC, one based on hybrid logic and the other one based on path regular expressions. We present extensions to handle negative authorizations and temporal policies. We describe mechanism for policy analysis, and then discuss the feasibility of using Datalog-based systems as implementations.

CCS CONCEPTS

• **Security and privacy** → **Access control**;

KEYWORDS

Relationship-based Access Control; security and privacy policies; Datalog

ACM Reference format:
Edelmira Pasarella and Jorge Lobo. 2017. A Datalog Framework for Modeling Relationship-based Access Control Policies. In *Proceedings of SACMAT'17, Indianapolis, IN, USA, June 21-23, 2017,* 12 pages.
https://doi.org/http://dx.doi.org/10.1145/3078861.3078871

1 INTRODUCTION

Lately, there has been a growing interest within the access control community in the concept of Relationship-based Access Control (ReBAC). ReBAC has been used in social networks almost since their beginnings with the well-known friendship relationship of Facebook as its prototypical example. Technical awareness of the

concept was first reported in [15], and perhaps the first formalization in the context of social networks was reported in [5]. Describing access control policies in terms of relationships is not particular to social networks. For example, a doctor can look at your medical records if he or she is *your family doctor*, or you can read a paper in a repository if you are one of *its reviewers*. At the core of the model there is a graph in which nodes represent users and resources, and arcs are labeled with relationships. Policies are described through paths among nodes in the graph (e.g., a-friend-of-a-friend represents a path of three nodes and two arcs). Recently, several papers have proposed different formalizations for ReBAC [4, 7, 8, 13, 17]. In this paper we argue that Datalog provides a very general framework for ReBAC modeling. To support our claim we work with two of the most sophisticated proposals, one based on hybrid logic and the other one based on path regular expressions, and show how complementary features of the two approaches can be captured in Datalog. The hybrid logic proposal has been developed in a series of papers that started with a modal logic as a modeling language [14], then it evolved into a model based on hybrid logic [4, 13], and more recently, an implementation embedded in the open source medical records system OpenMRS has been reported in [25]. This provides some maturity to the project. The second proposal follows the more explicit approach of defining a path specification language over the relationship graph to write policies. Results for path based ReBAC are more dispersed since more emphasis has been given to describing other parts of the access control systems (see for example [6, 7, 17]) and less to the formal characterizations of the expressibility. The work we have chosen for path specification, [8], is one of the most recent proposals and it incorporates features of earlier works with a more precise description of its expressibility. We then show how working under the Datalog framework we can easily extend the model (in ways that it would not be obvious to do formally in hybrid logic), we can also do policy analysis and have efficient implementations. Our contributions in this paper are the following:

(1) We introduce a carefully selected subset of Datalog with equality constraints as a ReBAC policy specification language which ensures efficient implementations.

(2) We then extend the hybrid logic HL of [4] to be able to express the path expressions of [8] and show a sound and complete translation of the extended HL policies into ReBAC Datalog policies.

(3) We extend ReBAC Datalog policies to be able to express negative authorizations, all easily done formally because of Datalog.

(4) We show how we can also use Datalog itself to find policy gaps and policy conflicts, and briefly discuss how to implement conflict resolution strategies.

(5) We further extend the language to handle temporal policies.

(6) We present precise complexity and expressibility results of the basic ReBAC Datalog which together with item (2) characterize the complexity of the (extended) hybrid logic for ReBAC.

(7) We present evidence that policy evaluation can be done in the order of a few milliseconds using off-the-shelf Datalog engines with relationship graphs having hundred of thousands of arcs.

We end with some concluding remarks.

2 ReBAC DATALOG POLICIES

We are going to closely follow the terminology from the hybrid logic of [4] in our definitions, but first, we need to recall some basic notions of Datalog with constraints. For writing Datalog programs we need three disjoint (possibly infinite) sets C, Var and P of constant symbols, variables and predicate symbols. There is a positive integer associated to each predicate symbol called its airty. A *term* in Datalog is any variable or constant symbol. An *atom* is an expression of the form $p(t_1, \ldots, t_k)$, where p is a predicate symbol of arity k and t_1 through t_k are terms. A *literal* is any atom $p(t_1, \ldots, t_k)$ or its negation $\neg p(t_1, \ldots, t_k)$. A negated atom is called a *negative literal*; otherwise is called *positive*. If all the terms appearing in a literal/atom are constants the literal/atom is called *ground*. *Constraints* are expressions of the form $t_1 = t_2$ or $t_1 \neq t_2$ for any two terms t_1 and t_2. Variables will be denoted using capital letters. A Datalog rule is an expression of the form:

$$c_1, \ldots, c_k, L_1, \ldots, L_m \to A \qquad (1)$$

where the L_i are literals , A is an atom, the c_i are constraints, for $k, m \geq 0$. The expression $c_1, \ldots, c_k, L_1, \ldots, L_m$ is called the *body* of the rule, A the *head*, and the rule a *definition* of the predicate that appears in A. An informal reading of a Datalog rule is that if there is a ground instance of the rule (i.e., all variables in the rule are replaced with constants) for which the constraints in the rule are valid, and we already know that every ground literal in the body is true then we can infer that the ground instance of A in the head of rule is true. A Datalog program is a finite set of Datalog rules.

The intended meaning of a Datalog program is given by a set of ground atoms M and is defined in terms of another set of ground atoms I given as input to the program. The set M contains the (ground) atoms in I, which are assumed to be true, plus the set of ground atoms that can be inferred to be true using the rules and the input I. Ground atoms outside M are assumed to be false. More formally, given a set of Datalog rules D, we call the set of all constants mentioned in D the *active language* of D. We denote by $Gr(D)$ the set of Datalog rules obtained by replacing in all possible ways the variables in the rules with constants in the active language of D. Note that $Gr(D)$ will be empty if D does not mention any constant. Since ground atoms are also Datalog rules the same definitions of active language and $Gr(.)$ apply when we consider a Datalog program and an input. We will use for the interpretation of

constraints the unique name assumption [24] in which all constants are assumed to be different from each other. Given a set of ground atoms M, and an atom A, we write $M \models_{Datalog} A$ iff there exists a ground instance A′ of A such that A′ ∈ M. If A is ground and A ∉ M, we write $M \models_{Datalog} \neg A$.

Definition 2.1. Given a Datalog program D and an input I, a set of ground atoms M is a model of $I \cup D$ iff M is a minimal set (i.e., there is no a proper subset of M for which the following equation holds):

$M = \{A \mid c_1, \ldots, c_k, L_1, \ldots, L_m \to A \in Gr(I \cup D), \forall c_i : c_i$ is true, and $\forall L_i : M \models_{Datalog} L_i\}$.

In general, $I \cup D$ may have zero, one or more models. But as we will see later, policies will have a single model. In its most simplest form, a *query* to a Datalog program D with input I is to ask whether a ground atom A is true in every model of $I \cup D$. If this is the case we will write $I \cup D \models_{Datalog} A$; we write $I \cup D \models_{Datalog} \neg A$ if $\neg A$ is not true in any model of $I \cup D$. The definition can be extended to non-ground atoms if $I \cup D$ has a unique model $M: I \cup D \models_{Datalog} A$ iff $M \models_{Datalog} A$. We can also have a conjunction of literals $L_1, \ldots, L_m, m > 1$, as a query and we write $M \models_{Datalog} L'_1, \ldots, L'_m$ as an answer if and only if $L'_1, \ldots, L'_m$ are ground instances of the literals $L_1, \ldots, L_m$ where variables are consistently replaced across the literals and $\forall i\ M \models_{Datalog} L'_i$.

Protection states (see [4]) . The underlying principle behind ReBAC is that from the point of view of specifying access control policies it is sufficient to have an abstract representation of the state of the system to protect built upon three fundamental concepts: the set of objects that form part of the system (e.g., users, resources), a set of properties that can be associated to individual objects, and a set of binary relationships between these objects - a relationship graph where vertices are objects and edges are labeled with relationship names. Hence, a *protection state* in ReBAC Datalog will be described by a set of ground atoms where only two predicate symbols are used, a 3-ary predicate rel and a 2-ary predicate prop. The set of constants C, is partitioned into three disjoint sets, a set of nominal constants C_n representing names of objects, a set propositional constants C_p, representing properties, and a set of (binary) relationship names C_r. A ground atom of the form $rel(n_1, r_1, n_2)$ can be member of a protection state only if $n_1, n_2 \in C_n$ and $r_1 \in C_r$. A ground atom of the form $prop(n_1, p_1)$ can be member of a protection state only if $n_1 \in C_n$ and $p_1 \in C_p$. Intuitively speaking, C_n is the set of objects over which policies will be expressed. It contains the names of all the objects that can request access to resources, usually called *principals*, as well as the names of resources for which principals can request access to. C_r is the set of names of relationships that can be defined over these objects such as Alice is friend of Bob (rel(alice, friend, bob): a principal-to-principal relationship), Bob owns Printer1 (rel(bob, own, $printer_1$): a principal-to-resource relationship), or Alice is member of Department Alpha (rel(alice, member, alpha): here Alpha is an abstract entity which is used only to simplify policy specifications, e.g. all members of Alpha have access to Printer1). A propositional name in C_p is meant to represent a property that a collection of objects

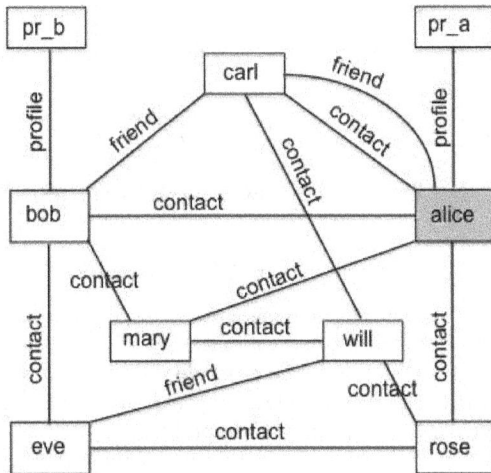

Figure 1: Partial view of the HHC protection state

may have, like being a medical doctor, prop(alice, doctor), or a patient, prop(bob, patient), or the property of being a Java program, prop(file.jar, java), or a video file, prop(file.avi, video).[1]

Policies. Policy defines a new relation between principals and resources that *grants* the principals access to the resources. In ReBAC Datalog policies this relationship is defined by checking properties of the objects typically reachable through the relationship graph either from the principal making the request or the resource that the principal wants to access as well as conditions over the paths used to reach these objects. This means that policies define new relations in terms of the relationships in the graph that represents the protection state under consideration.

Before we formally introduce policies let us examine a few examples based on the following scenario. Assume there is a head hunter company, HHC, that has a ReBAC system to manage the access privileges of its clients to profiles of its pool of candidates. To this end, HHC uses the LinkedIn and Facebook profiles of its candidates and clients. Fig. 1 depicts a partial view of the protection state held by HHC. In this graph principals are the nodes alice, bob, carl, eve, mary, rose and will and the nodes pr_b and pr_a are resources. Arcs are labeled with the relationship names profile (of), friend (of) and contact (of). HHC has a special group of candidates qualified as senior advisors depicted inside dark squares in the graph. The principal alice is in this group. Hence, the protection state will contain atoms like rel(bob, profile, pr_b), rel(carl, friend, alice), or prop(alice, senior_advisor), etc. HHC policies grant its clients (requesters) access to the professional profiles (resources) from its pool of candidates.

One of the simplest policies HHC could define is that any LinkedIn contact of the owner of a profile can access the profile. This policy can be expressed in Datalog as follows:

Policy1

$$rel(Res, profile, O), rel(Req, contact, O) \rightarrow grant(Req, Res)$$

Following this policy, if rel(pr_b, profile, bob) and rel(eve, contact, bob) are in the the protection state, eve is granted access to pr_b. It is easy to see that in the protection state depicted in Fig. 1, the access is granted, i.e., we are able to infer grant(eve, pr_b). Expressing this simple policy in Datalog allows us to highlight very basics features of the model. First, the protection state I will be defined independently from the set of policies D, and will be the input to the program to answer queries. Second, typically an access request comes with at least two parameters: *who/what* is making the request and *what* resource is being requested. This fact is captured in our formalization by granting to a requester (eve) access to a resource (pr_b), if the query grant(eve, pr_b) is true in $I \cup D$: $I \cup D \models_{Datalog}$ grant(eve, pr_b).

The initial motivation behind ReBAC came from social networks where policies are expressed in terms of the relationships between owners of resources and requesters independent of the resources (think of the friend relationship in Facebook and the access that having that relationship grants). Nevertheless, requesters ask for access to resources; the ownership relation is kept as a "tacit condition." Our policy makes explicit this "tacit condition" by reaching an owner of a resource through the relationship graph (e.g., rel(Res, profile, O)), and then, having identified the owner, checking conditions in the paths between the owner and the requester (e.g., rel(Req, contact, O))[2]. Now, let's assume HHC extends the access to any contact of a contact of the owner of the profile. This condition is modeled in Datalog by the rule below with the introduction of a new variable Z:

Policy2

$$rel(Res, profile, O), rel(Req, contact, Z),$$
$$rel(Z, contact, O) \rightarrow grant(Req, Res)$$

From this policy rule and the protection state depicted in Fig. 1 we have that $I \cup D \models_{Datalog}$ grant(will, pr_b). In this case, Z will be instantiated with mary. This policy alone grants access only to contacts that are at distance two of the owner of the profile. To keep access to direct contacts of the owner we need both policy rules. Several rules represent the disjunction of the rules, e.g., Policy1 or Policy2. Notice that neither carl nor rose has access to pr_b. To extend the chain to contacts at distance three we just need a new fresh variable, for instance, W and the rule will be:

$$rel(Res, profile, O), rel(Req, contact, Z),$$
$$rel(Z, contact, W), rel(W, contact, O) \rightarrow grant(Req, Res)$$

In general, fresh variables memorize intermediate nodes reached along the traversal of chains in the relationship graph to later be recalled in another part of the rule. Observe that evaluating the rule from left to right, in the sub-query rel(Req, contact, Z), the variable Req is bound since it occurs in the request and is "passed" to the program by a query such as grant(carl, pr_b). Then, if there exists an atom rel(carl, contact, o) in the protection state (like rel(carl, contact, will)), Z will get bound to o, and hence, bound in

---

[1]Other representations could be used (e.g., to better represent numerical attributes such as age), but they might never express relationships between objects. Our model just simplifies the presentation.

[2]For the sake of explanation, we describe as if the rule body is evaluated from left to right, but positive literals can be evaluated in any order. Datalog engines aim to find the order that produces the most efficient evaluation.

the sub-query rel(Z, contact, W) and so on. This way of traversing relationships in the protection state can be followed to limit the traversal of the graph during policy evaluation to be through objects related to Req or Res.

Next, assume HHC wants to grant access to senior advisors' profiles only when the requester has two different contacts in common with the advisor. This policy can be captured by the following rule: Policy3

$$\text{rel(Res, profile, O), prop(O, senior\_advisor),}$$
$$\text{rel(Req, contact, Z1), rel(Req, contact, Z2),}$$
$$\text{rel(O, contact, Z1), rel(O, contact, Z2),}$$
$$Z1 \neq Z2 \rightarrow \text{grant(Req, Res)}$$

This policy introduces two new features. One is an example of how properties over objects in the protection state are expressed - the second literal in the body of the rule. The second one is the use of inequalities to express some counting over relationships that will not be possible without constraints. From Policy3 and the protection state in Fig. 1, we get $I \cup D \models_{Datalog}$ grant(will, pr_a). To extend the policy to three or four contacts we merely need to add extra predicates to traverse the contact relation with new variables and then make sure that the variables get bound to different values by introducing more inequalities.

Suppose now that, to minimize conflicts of interest, HHC modifies Policy3, so that these two common contacts cannot both be personal friends of the senior advisor. The policy is modified as follows:
Policy4

$$\text{rel(X, friend, Z1), rel(X, friend, Z2)} \rightarrow \text{r(X, Z1, Z2)}$$

$$\text{rel(Res, profile, O), prop(O, senior\_advisor),}$$
$$\text{rel(Req, contact, Z1), rel(Req, contact, Z2),}$$
$$\text{rel(O, contact, Z1), rel(O, contact, Z2),}$$
$$Z1 \neq Z2, \neg r(O, Z1, Z2) \rightarrow \text{grant(Req, Res)}$$

The new feature in this policy is negation. The negative condition is defined in two steps. First, a new rule to describe the condition to be complemented is defined. Second, the negation of this condition is added to the policy rule. An important safety condition for the evaluation of negative sub-queries is that the values to check must be derived positively. This implies that all variable bindings in the negative conditions will be limited to values that are mentioned in the protection state (the active language). Hence. the negative sub-query $\neg r(O, Z1, Z2)$ must be evaluated after all its variables have been bound by other sub-queries in the rule. Considering Fig. 1, we can see that $I \cup D \models_{Datalog}$ grant(will, p_a) because $I \cup D \models_{Datalog} \neg r(\text{alice, carl, rose})$.

The last example introduces path traversals of unbounded length. HHC wants to grant access to a profile to any contact in the network of contacts of the candidate owning the profile. In this case, the condition over the network of contacts is that there must be a chain (of any length) with ending points the requester and the owner of the resource. This corresponds to checking whether for a requester u asking to get access to a resource r owned by o, the pair

(u, o) belongs the transitive closure of the contact relation. The formalization in Datalog is the following:
Policy5.

$$\text{rel(X, contact, Y)} \rightarrow \text{r(X, Y)}$$
$$\text{r(X, Y)} \rightarrow \text{r}_{tc}(X, Y)$$
$$\text{r(X, Z), r}_{tc}(Z, Y) \rightarrow \text{r}_{tc}(X, Y)$$

$$\text{rel(Req, contact, O), r}_{tc}(\text{Req, O}) \rightarrow \text{grant(Req, Res)}$$

The relation r_{tc} consists of all those pairs that appear in some path connecting u and o with all the arcs labeled contact. This relation is defined in Datalog as a recursive rule (i.e., a rule in which the predicate in the head of the rule also appears in the body). In Fig. 1, we have $I \cup D \models_{Datalog}$ grant(rose, pr_b).

In the rest of this section we formally define ReBAC Datalog policies. In particular, we define policies that cover all the features highlighted in Policy1–Policy5.

For writing policies, in addition to the predicates used in protection states, there are three more types of predicates in the language: a set of binary predicates called *derived relationship predicates*, $\{nr_1, \ldots, nr_s\}$, a corresponding set of binary predicates called *transitive closure relationship predicates* $\{tnr_1, \ldots, tnr_s\}$, and a set of predicates of different arities called *global property predicates* $\{g_1, \ldots, g_t\}$. We call nr_i the *basic predicate* of the transitive closure predicate tnr_i. We call *basic literal* any literal of the form rel(t_1, r, t_2), $\neg$rel(t_1, r, t_2), prop(t_1, p) and $\neg$prop(t_1, p), where $p \in C_p$, $r \in C_r$, and each t_i is either a variable or a constant in C_n. Similarly, we call derived relationship literals, transitive closure literals and global property literals to literals that use predicate symbols from the appropriate sets.

Definition 2.2. A ReBAC policy D, comprises two sets of Datalog rules:

(1) A non-empty ordered set $\hat{D} = \{r_1, \ldots, r_m\}$ such that the following conditions hold for every r_i:
  (a) Every variable that appears either in a negative literal or in a (positive or negative) global condition literal in the body of r_i, must also appear in the head or in a positive relationship, transitive closure or basic literal in the body of r_i.
  (b) If r_i defines a derived relationship predicate then every variable that appears in the head must also appear in either a derived relationship, transitive closure or basic positive literal in the body of r_i.
  (c) If a rule r_j defines either a derived relationship predicate or a global property predicate and the predicate appears in a literal in the body of r_i, then $j < i$.
  (d) Unless r_i defines grant, there is no other rule that defines the predicate defined by r_i.
  (e) The predicate grant does not appear in the body of r_i.
  (f) r_m defines the predicate grant.
(2) A set $\cup_{i=1}^{s} TR_i$, where there is a set TR_i for each derived relationship predicate nr_i containing the rules:

$$nr_i(X, Y) \rightarrow tnr_i(X, Y)$$
$$nr_i(X, Z), tnr_i(Z, Y) \rightarrow tnr_i(X, Y)$$

Condition (1a) is the safety condition for the evaluation of derived predicates discussed in the example (Policy4). Condition (1b) is also a safety condition. If variables appear in the head of a rule but not in the body then whenever a grounding of the rule body is true, it fixes the value of the variables in the head that appear in the body. The rest of the variables in the head can be bound to any constant independent of the active domain. Condition (1c) limits recursive definitions to the transitive closures. Condition (1d) limits disjunctive definitions to the predicate grant. Condition (1e) prevents grant to be defined recursively on itself and Condition (1f) makes sure the predicate grant is defined.

We recall that a Datalog program D is *hierarchical* if there exists an assignment of integers to the predicate symbols such that for every rule in D the integer assigned to the predicate in the head is larger than the integers assigned to the predicates in the body. D is called *stratified* if there is an assignment such that for every rule in D the integer assigned to the predicate in the head is larger than or equal to the integers assigned to the predicates appearing in positive literals in the body and larger than the integers assigned to predicates appearing in negative literals. It is easy to see that any ReBAC policy D is always stratified and if it does not use transitive closure relations, D can be limited to be just $\hat{D}$, and hence, D is hierarchical. It is a well-known property of stratified Datalog programs that they have a unique model [20]. Hence, for any protection state I and ReBAC policy D there is a unique *intended* model $M(D \cup I)$.

Definition 2.3. Given a ReBAC policy D and a protection state I, we say that a permission request (u, r), from a principal u to access a resource r is granted iff

$$D \cup I \models_{Datalog} \text{grant}(u, r)$$

Effective mechanisms to answer Datalog queries exist and a lot of effort has gone to optimize these methods since Datalog is the core mathematical foundation of the relational database model and the database query language SQL. More about the complexity and implementation of query answering procedures will be discussed later in the paper.

3 EHL REBAC POLICIES

The content of this section is mainly from Bruns et al. [4]. In [4] the authors introduced a hybrid logic HL for the specification of ReBAC policies. In this logic, from which we have borrowed the terminology for ReBAC Datalog, there are four disjoint sets of symbols, a set $\mathcal{N}$ of *nominal symbols*, an infinite set $\mathcal{V}$ of *variables*, a set $\mathcal{I}$ of *labels* and a set $\mathcal{P}$ of *propositional symbols*. We denote by n, X, i and p generic nominal symbols, variables, labels and propositional symbols respectively. Policies in HL represent properties involving a fixed number of arcs in a relationship graphs. Following [8], we extend the logic to also cover a subclass of properties that can refer to a finite but unbounded set of arcs described as simple regular expressions.

Definition 3.1. A formula in the extended hybrid logic EHL can be:

(1) any nominal symbol n, variable X or proposition p,

(2) any term of one of the following forms: $\neg\phi$, $\phi_1 \wedge \phi_2$, $@_n\phi$, $@_X\phi$, and $\downarrow X\phi$, $\pi\phi$, given that ϕ, ϕ_1 and ϕ_2 are hybrid formulas and π a path expression having one of the following forms:

  (a) ϵ representing the empty path

  (b) $\langle i \rangle$ or $\langle -i \rangle$

  (c) $\pi_1\pi_2$, for any two path expressions π_1, π_2

  (d) π^+, for any path expression π

The definition of HL formulas [4] considers only simple path expressions of the form (b) above. *Models* in EHL are triples $(S, \{R_i \subseteq S \times S | i \in \mathcal{I}\}, V)$, where S is a non-empty set of nodes, and $V : \mathcal{N} \cup \mathcal{P} \rightarrow 2^S$, a total function with $V(n)$ being a singleton set for any $n \in \mathcal{N}$. A *valuation* $g : \mathcal{V} \rightarrow S$, is a total function assigning variables to nodes. Let $g[X \mapsto s]$ denote the valuation that maps X to s and any $X' \neq X$ to $g(X')$. A nominal symbol n will denote the single object in $V(n)$. The pair $(S, \{R_i | i \in \mathcal{I}\})$ can be interpreted as a labeled graph in which its vertexes are the nodes in S and the labeled arcs between the vertexes are defined by the R_i relations.

Let us revisit the scenario of policies Policy1–Policy5 from the point of view of models in EHL. In Fig. 1, the set of nodes $S = \{alice, bob, carl, eve, mary, rose, will, pr\_a, pr\_b\}$ corresponds to the nominal symbols in $\mathcal{N}$, the relations are $profile = \{(pr\_b, bob), (pr\_a, alice)\}$, $contact = \{(alice, bob), (alice, carl), (bob, mary), (alice, mary), (alice, rose), (bob, eve), (eve, rose), (mary, will), (rose, will)\}$ and $friend = \{(alice, carl), (bob, carl), (eve, will)\}$. We assume that $V(alice) = \{alice\}$, $V(bob) = \{bob\}$, $V(pr\_b) = \{pr\_b\}$ and $senior\_advisor$ is a propositional symbol in $\mathcal{P}$. In this example, $V(senior\_advisor) = \{alice\}$, however, in general, for a propositional symbol p, $V(p)$ is not necessarily a singleton set. The pair $(S, profile \cup contact \cup friend)$ is called a social graph in [4]. Given an EHL model M, a node $s \in S$ and a valuation g, a satisfiability relation $\models$ over EHL formulas is defined inductively as follows:

Definition 3.2.   (1) $M, s, g \models X$ iff $g(X) = s$

  (2) $M, s, g \models n$ iff $V(n) = \{s\}$

  (3) $M, s, g \models p$ iff $s \in V(p)$

  (4) $M, s, g \models \neg\phi$ iff $M, s, g \not\models \phi$

  (5) $M, s, g \models \phi_1 \wedge \phi_2$ iff $M, s, g \models \phi_1$ and $M, s, g \models \phi_2$

  (6) $M, s, g \models \phi_1 \vee \phi_2$ iff $M, s, g \models \phi_1$ or $M, s, g \models \phi_2$

  (7) $M, s, g \models @_n\phi$ iff $M, s^*, g \models \phi$ and $V(n) = \{s^*\}$

  (8) $M, s, g \models @_X\phi$ iff $M, g(X), g \models \phi$

  (9) $M, s, g \models\downarrow X\phi$ iff $M, s, g[X \mapsto s] \models \phi$

 (10) $M, s, g \models \pi\phi$ iff $M, s', g \models \phi$ for some $(s, s') \in \mathcal{R}_\pi$, where $\mathcal{R}_\pi$ is inductively defined as follows:

  (a) $\mathcal{R}_\epsilon = \emptyset$

  (b) $\mathcal{R}_{\langle i \rangle} = R_i$

  (c) $\mathcal{R}_{\langle -i \rangle} = R_i^{-1}$

  (d) $\mathcal{R}_{\pi_1\pi_2} = \mathcal{R}_{\pi_1} \circ \mathcal{R}_{\pi_2}$, where $\circ$ denotes relation composition.

  (e) $\mathcal{R}_{\pi^+} = trans(\mathcal{R}_\pi)$, the transitive closure of $\mathcal{R}_\pi$.

Items 1-6, 10b and 10c are standard in modal logics. Items 7-9 are the hybrid operators. Informally speaking, $@_t$ jumps to the node named by t, i.e. $@_t\phi$ holds if ϕ holds at the node identified by t. In the case of Fig. 1, $@_{alice}senior\_advisor$ holds because after jumping to node $alice$, it holds that $alice \in V(senior\_advisor)$.

The term $\downarrow X$ binds the variable X to the current node, i.e., $M, s, g \models\downarrow X\phi$ holds if ϕ holds at s but with the valuation g now interpreting X as s (g is replaced with $g[X \mapsto s]$). In the case of Fig. 1, $@_{bob}\langle friend \rangle \downarrow X \phi$, jumps to node bob, then through the relation $friend$ arrives to node $carl$, therefore the variable X is bound to $carl$ and, thus, if X occurs in the sub-formula ϕ, it refers to $carl$. For another example, let us consider under Fig. 1 the formula $@_{bob}\langle contact \rangle \downarrow X_1 \langle contact \rangle \downarrow X_2 \langle contact \rangle \downarrow X_3 \phi$. The evaluation starts at the node bob and it holds if there exists a chain of contacts of length 3 and the sub-formula ϕ holds with variables $X_1, X2$ and X_3 bound to the nodes in the chain: *mary, will* and *rose* are examples of such nodes. The usual notions of free and bound variables in a formula are defined based on the bindings produced by $\downarrow$. Item 3.2.10e corresponds to the notion of closure for regular expressions.

As in ReBAC Datalog, policies are evaluated in the context of a concrete model M (corresponding to a *protection state*), and a request (u, r).

Definition 3.3. A *policy* is an EHL formula that may have at most *Res* and *Req* as free variables and is a Boolean combination of formulas of the form $@_{Res}\phi_1$ or $@_{Req}\phi_2$.

Definition 3.4. Given a policy ϕ, a permission request (u, r) is *granted* in a model M iff

$$M, s, g[Req \mapsto u, Res \mapsto r] \models \phi$$

for some $s \in S$ and valuation g.

Since *Res* and *Req* are the only variables that can occur free in ϕ, s and g are irrelevant for granting the permission. Thus, from the rest of the paper we will write $M, [X_1 \mapsto s_1, \ldots, X_m \mapsto s_m] \models \phi$, when the only free variables in ϕ are $X_1, \ldots, X_m$. In the presentation of the logic in [4], the owner of the resource and not the resource itself is used in the policies since M is presented as a "social graph", nodes are restricted to be principals, and policies are assumed to be associated to a particular resource for which the owner is known. However, the authors recognize that more general settings can be defined and refer to the general case described here as *heterogeneous* protection states. Having an action in the request is also common but we will discuss this later in the paper.

Some examples of EHL policies adapted from [4] are:

$$@_{Res}\langle -profile \rangle \langle contact \rangle Req \qquad (2)$$

that grants access to any contact of the owner of the resource.

$$@_{Res}\langle -profile \rangle \langle contact \rangle (Req \vee \langle contact \rangle Req) \qquad (3)$$

that grants access to a contact or a contact of a contact of the owner of the resource.

$$@_{Res}\langle -profile \rangle \langle contact \rangle (Req \wedge senior\_advisor) \qquad (4)$$

that grants access to a contact of the owner if he or she is a senior advisor.

$$@_{Res}\langle -profile \rangle \langle contact \rangle (Req \wedge \neg Bob) \qquad (5)$$

that grants access to a contact of the owner who can't be Bob.

$$@_{Res}\langle -profile \rangle (\langle friend \rangle Req \wedge \neg \langle friend \rangle \neg Req) \qquad (6)$$

that grants access to a friend of the owner if he or she is the only friend.

A salient feature of the original HL language (and thus, of EHL and ReBAC Datalog) is the ability to express graded modalities. Given a positive integer k, one can write $\langle i \rangle_k \phi$ as a shorthand for:

$$\downarrow X \langle i \rangle \downarrow Y_1 (\phi \wedge @_X \langle i \rangle \downarrow Y_2 (\neg Y_1 \wedge \phi \wedge$$
$$\cdots @_X \langle i \rangle \downarrow Y_k (\neg Y_1 \wedge \neg Y_{k-1} \wedge \phi) \ldots)$$

which informally says that the formula holds in a node s iff there are at least k R_i-successors of s at which ϕ holds. For example, a formula granting access to a requester that has at least three contacts in common with the profile's owner is:

$$@_{Res}\langle -profile \rangle \langle contact \rangle_3 (\langle contact \rangle Req) \qquad (7)$$

This essentially the same encoding of counting through inequalities done in Policy3.

The following policy is adapted from [8]:

$$@_{Res}\langle -profile \rangle (\langle member\_of \rangle \langle -supervise \rangle)^+ Req \qquad (8)$$

that grants permission to any supervisor in the management chain to access profiles owned by members of the groups under her management line.

4 FROM EHL TO ReBAC DATALOG

Given an EHL policy defined over sets $\mathcal{N}, \mathcal{V}, \mathcal{I}$ and $\mathcal{P}$, an EHL model $M = (S, \{R_i \subseteq S \times S | i \in \mathcal{I}\}, V)$, and a policy ϕ, we want to find an equivalent ReBAC Datalog policy $[\phi]$ and protection state $[M]$.

Without loss of generality, we assume that all bound variables in ϕ are named differently. We also assume that the model has been fixed. Hence, when we refer to S, R_i or V in any of the definitions we are referring to the nodes, relations and the function V of this model. The following equivalences of HL formulas are easy to verify:

(1) $@_{t_1} @_{t_2} \phi \equiv @_{t_2} \phi$;
(2) $\neg @_t \phi \equiv @_t \neg \phi$;
(3) $@_t (\phi_1 \vee \phi_2) \equiv (@_t \phi_1 \vee @_t \phi_2)$; and
(4) $\neg \downarrow X \phi \equiv \downarrow X \neg \phi$,

for any t, t_1 and t_2 nominal symbols or variables. Using these equivalences and De Morgan's laws we can normalize EHL formulas by pushing all negations to be in front of nominal symbols, variables, propositional symbols or non-empty path expressions, as well as removing multiple occurrences of @ in front of any formula. A formula is called *normal conjunctive* if it does not contain disjunctions, all the negations appear in front of nominal symbols, variables or non-empty path expressions and there are no redundant @-operators. A formula is in *disjunctive form* if it is a disjunction of normal conjunctive formulas. It easy to see that every formula has an equivalent formula in disjunctive form. For the rest of the presentation we assume that all EHL formulas are in disjunctive form. Let the sets $C = C_n \cup C_p \cup C_r$, Var, P of constant symbols, variables and predicate symbols be such that $\mathcal{N} \subseteq C_n, \mathcal{I} \subseteq C_r, \mathcal{P} \subseteq C_p$ and $\mathcal{V} \subseteq$ Var. Without loss of generality, we assume that for any nominal symbol n, $V(n) = \{n\}$.[3] In what follows, for the sake of readability, we will use italics in EHL formulas and continue using math serif font for Datalog. Intuitively, each normal conjunctive sub-formula occurring in a disjunctive formula representing a policy, can be seen as a partial definition of the policy. This intuition

---

[3]This is, the syntax of the constant in the language is the same as value in the model (Herbrand-like).

gives us insights about how to proceed in order to translate an EHL policy into a ReBAC program. Given an EHL formula ϕ, we define the program $[\phi]$ in three steps. Firstly, we provide a mechanism to translate each normal conjunctive sub-formula of ϕ into pairs where the first component is a set of literals and the second component is a set of ReBAC rules. Second, for each normal conjunctive formula in ϕ, we associate a definition of the binary predicate grant using each individual translation. Finally, we join all these grant definitions with the translation of the EHL model into a Datalog protection state to get the ReBAC policy and Input to evaluate queries. The next two definitions formalize these steps.

Definition 4.1. Given a variable $X \in \text{Var}$, for any conjunctive normal EHL formula ϕ, $[\phi]^X$ defines inductively a set B of constraints and literals, and a set R of Datalog rules in a pair (B, R) as follows:

(1) $[X']^X = (\{X' = X\}, \emptyset)$
(2) $[n]^X = (\{n = X\}, \emptyset)$
(3) $[p]^X = (\{\text{prop}(X, p)\}, \emptyset)$ iff $p \in \mathcal{P}$
(4) $[\neg\phi]^X = (\{X' \neq X\}, \emptyset)$, iff $\phi \equiv X'$;
    $[\neg\phi]^X = (\{n \neq X\}, \emptyset)$, iff $\phi \equiv n$ and $V(n) = \{n\}$;
    otherwise
    $[\neg\phi]^X = (\{\neg\bar{\phi}(\overline{V},X)\}, \{B \rightarrow \bar{\phi}(\overline{V},X)\} \cup R')$ iff $[\phi]^X = (B, R')$,
    $\overline{V}$ are the free variables appearing in ϕ, and $\bar{\phi}$ is a new global property predicate symbol of arity equal to the cardinality of $\overline{V}$ plus 1.
(5) $[\phi_1 \wedge \phi_2]^X = (B_1 \cup B_2, R_1 \cup R_2)$ iff $[\phi_1]^X = (B_1, R_1)$ and $[\phi_2]^X = (B_2, R_2)$
(6) $[@_n\phi]^X = (\{n = Y\} \cup B, R)$ iff $[\phi]^Y = (B, R)$, Y is a new fresh variable from Var
(7) $[@_{X'}\phi]^X = (B \cup \{X' = Z\}, R)$, Z is a new fresh variable from Var, and $[\phi]^Z = (B, R)$
(8) $[\downarrow X'\phi]^X = (\{X' = X\} \cup B, R)$ iff $[\phi]^X = (B, R)$
(9) For $[\pi\phi]^X$, when
    (a) $\pi \equiv \epsilon$, then $[\pi\phi]^X = [\phi]^X$
    (b) $\pi \equiv \langle i \rangle$, then $[\pi\phi]^X = (\{\text{rel}(X, i, Y)\} \cup B, R)$ if and only if $[\phi]^Y = (B, R)$ and Y is a new fresh variable from Var
    (c) $\pi \equiv \langle -i \rangle$, then $[\pi\phi]^X = (\{\text{rel}(Y, i, X)\} \cup B, R)$ if and only if $[\phi]^Y = (B, R)$ and Y is a new fresh variable from Var
    (d) $\pi \equiv \pi_1\pi_2$, then $[\pi\phi]^X = (B_{\pi_1 Y} \cup B_{\pi_2\phi}, R_{\pi_1 Y} \cup R_{\pi_2\phi})$, where
        $[\pi_1 Y]^X = (B_{\pi_1 Y}, R_{\pi_1 Y})$ and $[\pi_2\phi]^Y = (B_{\pi_2\phi}, R_{\pi_2\phi})$
    (e) $\pi \equiv \pi_1^+$, then
        $[\pi\phi]^X = (\{\text{pi}_+(X, Y)\} \cup B_\phi, R_\phi \cup R_{\pi_1 Y} \cup R_{tc})$ if and only if
        (i) $[\phi]^Y = (B_\phi, R_\phi)$, $[\pi_1 Y]^X = (B_{\pi_1 Y}, R_{\pi_1 Y})$ and Y is a new fresh variable from Var
        (ii) pi is a new derived relationship predicate symbol and pi_+ its corresponding transitive closure predicate, and

$$R_{tc} = \{B_{\pi_1 Y} \rightarrow \text{pi}(X, Y),$$
$$\text{pi}(X, Y) \rightarrow \text{pi}_+(X, Y),$$
$$\text{pi}(X, Z), \text{pi}_+(Z, Y) \rightarrow \text{pi}_+(X, Y)\}$$

Definition 4.2. For any EHL policy $\phi = \phi_1' \vee \cdots \vee \phi_m'$ in disjunctive form and an EHL model M. Let $\phi_i' = @_{X_i}\phi_i$ and $[\phi_i]^{X_i} = (B_i, R_i)$,

$i \in \{1, \ldots, m\}$. $[\phi]$ and $[M]$ define the following Datalog program and its input:

$$[\phi] = \cup_{i=1}^{m}(\{B_i \rightarrow \text{grant}(\text{Res}, \text{Req})\} \cup R_i)$$
$$[M] = \{\text{prop}(s, p) : p \in \mathcal{P}, s \in V(p)\} \cup \{\text{rel}(s, i, s') : (s, s') \in R_i\}$$

As we see, we are considering the $\vee$ operator separately and use Def. 4.1 and Def. 4.2 to get the translations for policies. Note that X_i is either Res or Req for every X_i in the definition. The next example illustrates several of the steps in the translation.

Example 4.3. Let us consider a very simple EHL path expression formula that grants access to a profile to any direct or indirect contact of the owner of the profile:

$$\phi = @_{Res}\langle -profile\rangle\langle contact\rangle^+ Req$$

This policy is already in disjunctive form with a single conjunctive formula, $\phi_1 = \langle -profile\rangle\langle contact\rangle^+ Req$ and $X_1 = \text{Res}$. Thus,

$$[\phi_1]^{Res} = [\overbrace{\langle -profile\rangle}^{\pi_1}\overbrace{\langle contact\rangle^+}^{\pi_2} Req]^{Res} = (B_{\phi_1}, R_{\phi_1})$$

$$(B_{\phi_1}, R_{\phi_1}) \overset{\text{Def. 4.1.9d}}{=} (B_{\pi_1 Y} \cup B_{\pi_2 Req}, R_{\pi_1 Y} \cup R_{\pi_2 Req}) \quad (9)$$

where $(B_{\pi_1 Y}, R_{\pi_1 Y}) = [\pi_1 Y]^{Res}$ and $(B_{\pi_2 Req}, R_{\pi_2 Req}) = [\pi_2 Req]^Y$

$$(B_{\pi_1 Y}, R_{\pi_1 Y}) \overset{\text{Def. 4.1.9c}}{=} (\{\text{rel}(Y_1, profile, Res), Y = Y_1\}, \emptyset) \quad (10)$$

since $[Y]^{Y_1} \overset{\text{Def. 4.1.1}}{=} (\{Y = Y_1\}, \emptyset)$

$$(B_{\pi_2 Req}, R_{\pi_2 Req}) \overset{\text{Def. 4.1.9e}}{=} (\{\text{pi}_+(Y, Y_2), Y_2 = Req\}, R_{\pi_2 Y_2} \cup R_{tc}) \quad (11)$$

since $[Req]^{Y_2} \overset{\text{Def. 4.1.1}}{=} (\{Y_2 = Req\}, \emptyset)$. Additionally,
$[\pi_2 Y_2]^Y \overset{\text{Def. 4.1.9b, Def. 4.1.1}}{=} (\{\text{rel}(Y, contact, Y_3), Y_3 = Y_2\}, \emptyset)$.
Hence

$$R_{tc} = \{\text{rel}(Y, contact, Y_3), Y_3 = Y_2 \rightarrow \text{pi}(Y, Y_2)$$
$$\text{pi}(Y, Y_2) \rightarrow \text{pi}_+(Y, Y_2)$$
$$\text{pi}(Y, Y_3), \text{pi}_+(Y_3, Y_2) \rightarrow \text{pi}_+(Y, Y_2)\} \quad (12)$$

and

$$(B_{\pi_2 Req}, R_{\pi_2 Req}) = (\{\text{pi}_+(Y, Y_2), Y_2 = Req\}, R_{tc}) \quad (13)$$

From (10), (12) and (13) we obtain that the pair (B_{ϕ_1}, R_{ϕ_1}) in (9) can be rewritten as

$$(\{\text{rel}(Y_1, profile, Res), Y = Y_1, \text{pi}_+(Y, Y_2), Y_2 = Req\},$$
$$\{\text{rel}(Y, contact, Y_3), Y_3 = Y_2 \rightarrow \text{pi}(Y, Y_2)$$
$$\text{pi}(Y, Y_2) \rightarrow \text{pi}_+(Y, Y_2)$$
$$\text{pi}(Y, Y_3), \text{pi}_+(Y_3, Y_2) \rightarrow \text{pi}_+(Y, Y_2)\})$$

and finally, rewriting the pair above we have that (B_{ϕ_1}, R_{ϕ_1}) equals to

$$(\{\text{rel}(Y, profile, Res), \text{pi}_+(Y, Req)\},$$
$$\{\text{rel}(Y, contact, Y_2), \rightarrow \text{pi}(Y, Y_2)$$
$$\text{pi}(Y, Y_2) \rightarrow \text{pi}_+(Y, Y_2)$$
$$\text{pi}(Y, Y_3), \text{pi}_+(Y_3, Y_2) \rightarrow \text{pi}_+(Y, Y_2)\})$$

Consequently, by Def.4.1 and Def.4.2 the ReBAC Datalog program associated to ϕ, $[\phi]$, is

$$\{rel(Y, profile, Res), pi_+(Y, Req) \rightarrow grant(Req, Res),$$
$$rel(Y, contact, Y_2), \rightarrow pi(Y, Y_2)$$
$$pi(Y, Y_2) \rightarrow pi_+(Y, Y_2)$$
$$pi(Y, Y_3), pi_+(Y_3, Y_2) \rightarrow pi_+(Y, Y_2)\}$$

Given a protection state, a policy and a permission request, the next theorem establishes the relationship between granting permissions in EHL and query answering in ReBAC Datalog programs.

THEOREM 4.4. *Given an* EHL *policy ϕ in disjunctive form, an* EHL *model M and a permission request (u, r)*

$$M, [Req \mapsto u, Res \mapsto r] \models \phi \ iff \ [M] \cup [\phi] \models_{Datalog} grant(u, r)$$

Proof sketch: the proof is based on the following lemma:

LEMMA 4.5. *Let ϕ be a normal conjunctive* EHL *formula, $M = (S, \{R_i \subseteq S \times S | i \in \mathcal{I}\}, V)$ a model, s a node in S and $g : \mathcal{V} \rightarrow S$ an assignment such that $M, s, g \models \phi$. Let $X \in Var$ be a fresh variable not appearing in ϕ. Then,*

$$[M] \cup \{X = s, B \rightarrow q(\overline{V}, X)\} \cup R \models_{Datalog} q(\overline{a}, X),$$

where $\overline{V}$ is the set of free variables in ϕ, $\overline{a}$ is the assignment of $\overline{V}$ in g, q is a fresh predicate and $[\phi]^X = (B, R)$

This lemma works over general normal conjunctive formulas without the restriction imposed in policies by EHL over free variables. Hence we are able to do an inductive proof based on the structure of ϕ. The case in which $\phi \equiv \pi^+ \phi'$ requires a second induction to cover the transitive closure.

5 FROM ReBAC DATALOG TO EHL

There are two types of ReBAC Datalog policies that cannot be expressed within EHL. An example of the first type of policies is the following:

$$rel(X, i, Y), prop(Y, p_1) \rightarrow r(X, Y)$$
$$r(X, Y) \rightarrow tr(X, Y)$$
$$r(X, Z), tr(Z, Y) \rightarrow tr(X, Y)$$
$$tr(Req, Res) \rightarrow grant(Req, Res)$$

In this policy, a property is checked on every object in the path between Res and Req. Such conditions cannot be imposed in a path expression. To limit the expressibility of ReBAC Datalog to path expressions and avoid this type of policies, we need *simple* definitions of derived relationships. We need to limit the literals that can appear in the body of a derived relationship definition to be either positive rel literals or transitive closure relationship literals – no negation and no basic or global property literals.

An example of the second type of policies is the following:

$$rel(X, i, Y) \rightarrow grant(Req, Res) \tag{14}$$

This says that access is granted if R_i in the protection state is not empty. To exclude this type of policies we need to limit the variables that appear in any ReBAC Datalog rule as follows:

Definition 5.1. For a Datalog rule of the form (1) we say that:

(1) A variable that appears in a literal L_k, $k \leq m$, is *seeded* iff it also appears either in A or in a literal L_j, $i < k$.
(2) A negative literal is *well-seeded* iff all its variables are seeded.
(3) A positive literal is well-seeded iff at least one of its variables is seeded.

The rule is *well-seeded* iff the literals in its body can be re-arrange so that all of them become well-seeded and the variables appearing in the constraints are seeded.

The rule in Eq.(14) is not well-seeded since neither of the variables, X or Y, appears in the head or in a predicate in the body together with another well-seeded variable (or constant). Now we have the following proposition.

PROPOSITION 5.2. *A ReBAC Datalog policy that only uses simple derived relationship definitions and all its rules are well-seeded can be translated to an* EHL *formula. Furthermore, if the policy does not use transitive closure relationships it can be translated into an* HL *formula.*

Proof sketch: the transformation starts from the grant rules and is more or less straightforward if it is done using a well-seeded order traversal of the literals in the rule by binding a variable with ↓ the first time the variable is encountered in the rule.

We skip the transformation due to space limitations. In addition, there is no equivalent EHL policies for most of the extensions discussed in the following section.

6 EXTENSIONS

Permissions are usually granted not to simply access a resource but to do something with it. For example, Alice may want access to a file to read and modify it. Hence the granularity of the permissions should be at the level of the operation. We can represent requests as a triple (u, r, a), where u is the principal requesting access to the resource r and a is the *action* the principal wants to apply to the resource. If the set of actions is part of S in the protection state, there could be an "implements" relations over resources and actions and we can allow three free variables in an EHL policy ϕ: Req, Res, A. A request (u, r, a) is granted under the policy ϕ iff

$$M, [Req \mapsto u, Res \mapsto r, A \mapsto a] \models \phi$$

and the grant Datalog rules will be of the form

$$B \rightarrow grant(Req, Res, A)$$

For example, the policy that let any friend of the owner of a resource Res to copy Res is written as follows:

$$rel(Res, implements, copy),$$
$$rel(O, owns, Res), rel(O, friend, Req) \rightarrow grant(Req, Res, copy)$$

Similar to permission granting rules, negative authorizations can be defined by a formula ϕ' such that access is denied when:

$$M, [Req \mapsto u, Res \mapsto r, A \mapsto a] \models \phi'$$

The Datalog rule of a negative authorization will be of the form

$$B \rightarrow deny(Req, Res, A)$$

Having negative authorizations introduces two problems. One is what to do if a request is neither granted nor denied. The second is what to do with conflicting decisions. The first issue of policy coverage is a semantic issue. We could have a meta-rule to cover the missing cases but this meta-rule may hide the gaps of what it could be an incomplete policy otherwise. In addition, if meta-rules are used one needs to re-examine the need of complicating the policy specification with negative and positive authorizations since one could, in principle, specify one type of policy and let the meta-rule cover the other type (like in *any request that is not granted is denied*). A more practical problem is to discover policy gaps. So far, we have used Datalog programs to answer ground queries (e.g., grant(u, r, a)). By typing the objects in a protection state and adding them as part of the input, we can also ask existentially quantified queries and do gap analysis with the rule:

prop(Req, principal), prop(Res, resource),

prop(A, action),

$\neg$grant(Req, Res, A), $\neg$deny(Req, Res, A) $\rightarrow$ gap(Req, Res, A)

and the query:

$$D \models_{Datalog} \exists Req \exists Res \exists A (gap(Req, Res, A))$$

For analysis, we are assuming that propositions exist in D typing the constants in the active domain.

There are three complexity characterizations for query evaluation in Datalog and logic programs. In one characterization, called data complexity, the complexity is characterized in terms of the input size (in our case, the protection state) while the Datalog program (in our case the ReBAC policies) and the query are fixed. If, on the other hand, the input is fixed and the program and the query size is what matters, the complexity of query evaluation is called program complexity. If both the program and the input are considered part of the problem size the characterization is called program+data complexity. Most of the time in database applications data complexity is considered sufficient since the size of the data represented by the input is much larger than the size of the program. We will show in the next section why this is also a reasonable assumption for ReBAC policies.

Efficient procedures (PTIME data complexity) exist not only to decide if the answer is yes or no, but also to obtain values for the existentially quantified variables in a query like the one to check for gaps.

Conflicts can be an indication of policy errors. However, including policy conflict resolution rules in the semantics of policy evaluation is a common practice since many times it facilitates policy specification. A typical policy conflict resolution rule is denies-override-allows. This can be easily incorporated into Datalog policies by rewriting each granting access rule as follows:

B, $\neg$deny(Req, Res, A) $\rightarrow$ grant(Req, Res, A)

There are many conflict resolution strategies that can be borrowed from other Datalog models – the interested reader can find in [18] an extensive study of authorizations overrides meta-policies and how to express them in terms of logic programs.

History-based Policies. It is common to find examples of access control policies that depend on the occurrence of past events. In the context of ReBAC, motivated by access control policies found in community-based collaborations, Fong et al [13] has extended

HL with linear past temporal operators. Two examples from [13] are:

- A user who has been reported for using inappropriate language twice is suspended for further editing.
- A user who has already created two distinct objects that have since remained untouched by any member of the community (including herself) is not allowed to further create new objects.

Handling history-based policies in the context of Datalog has been discussed in [22]. This is achieved by adding a time argument to all the predicates and allowing a limited class of time constraints over time variables. To illustrate how it works we will encode the second example above:

$$T_1 \le T, T_2 \le T,$$
$$rel(U, own, O_1, T_1), rel(U, own, O_2, T_2),$$
$$\neg twoEd(O_1, O_2, T), O_1 \ne O_2 \rightarrow deny(U, O, create, T)$$
$$T_1 \le T, T_2 \le T, rel(O_1, edited, U_1, T_1),$$
$$rel(O_2, edited, U_2, T2) \rightarrow twoEd(O_1, O_2, T)$$

The intuition behind the rules is that the T_i variables will be instantiated with time values, and events like creation of objects, or modifications of objects will be incorporated into the protection state (these events can be captured each time a request to execute these operations is granted/denied) and the state will evolve over time. Hence, given two objects o_1 and o_2, and a fixed time t, twoEd(o_1, o_2, t) will hold if there are time points t_1 and t_2 before (or equals to) t for which rel(u, edited, o_1, t_1) and rel(u, edited, o_2, t_2) are part of the corresponding states.

A *time constraint C* is any expression of the form $T_1 \oplus T_2 \pm c$, where T_1 and T_2 are different time variables, c is a non-negative real number and $\oplus$ is one of $\{=, \le, <\}$. These binary relations are interpreted under the standard order of time. Several constraints can appear in a rule but all the time variables in the constraints must also appear either in the head of the rule or in a literal in the body. In addition, if T is the time variable appearing in the head, and $C_1, \ldots, C_n$ all the constraints appearing in the body, then for any variable T_i that appears in the constraints, it must be the case that $C_1, \ldots, C_n \models_{Datalog} T_i \le T$. This ensures that policy evaluations do not depend on "future" states. In the non-temporal case, policies were evaluated in a protection state. In the case of temporal policies, all the ground atoms belonging to the same temporal protection state will be extended with an extra-argument which will be a time constant - the same constant in all the atoms. Note that there is no way to specify absolute values for the T_i's in the rules, all times are relative to T which is also a variable. Similar to [13], policy compliance is defined in terms of traces. A trace $\mathcal{T}$, is a (possibly infinite) sequence of temporal states $\langle S_0, S_1, \ldots \rangle$, such that constants t_i, t_j associated to the atoms in states S_i, S_j are such that $t_i \le t_j$ if $i \le j$. Intuitively, $\mathcal{T}$ represents the history of the protection state evolution over time. How the evolution happens over time is not relevant for our discussion. Given a set of temporal policy rules P and a trace $\mathcal{T}$, a permission request (req, res, a) is granted at time t iff

$$P \cup \mathcal{T} \models_{Datalog} grant(req, res, a, t)$$

The crucial point here is that conditions in any rule refer to properties that must be true either at the same state where the head of the rule is true or in an earlier state, and when a permission is requested it is assumed that the request is to grant the permission at the current time, i.e., the time when the request is made. The results in [22] also show how effective monitors that only keep the historical data required to evaluate the rules can be implemented instead of having copies of multiple states. Each update step executed by the monitor takes time proportional to the size of the update made to the protection state. This is in contrast to the results in [13] in which the steps take time proportional to the size of the state. The same monitors from [22] can be used for historical ReBAC if the only time variable that can appear in the rules representing path expressions is the variable that appears in the head (and thus there are not temporal constraints in the recursive rules). In other words path expressions refers to paths in a single protection state.

7 DATALOG AS AN IMPLEMENTATION

In contrast to policy analysis where time is not so much an issue, the complexity of access control decisions must consider the effect of the policy, i.e., the Datalog rules. Program complexity in Datalog is EXPTIME-complete [11]. In terms of ReBAC Datalog that would mean that fixing a protection state, there is a policy that takes exponential time to evaluate with respect to the size of the the policy itself + the fixed size of the protection state. This result applies even if the Datalog rules are well-seeded and no transitive closure relationships are used. Therefore, the result also applies to HL policies. The hardness part of the EXPTIME complexity proof depends on the fact that there are no limitations in the arity of the predicate relations that can define the Datalog program - the standard proof uses an encoding of a deterministic Turing machine that halts in less than 2^{n^k} steps and uses predicates of arity in the order of $O(n)$. These are very large programs. In ReBAC Datalog policies, all predicates of arity > 3 appear in global condition literals. If we assume a constant k exists that limits the maximal arity of any predicate the complexity reduces to NP. The intractability persists because of the inequalities. Inequalities permit to encode the Hamiltonian path problem [23]. The encoding of the problem for a path of length n uses n different variables in the inequalities of a single rule. Again, this is a very large program. If we can also assume that the number of different variables that appear in the inequalities of a single rule does not exceed a constant k we obtain tractability. Furthermore, the result is tight.

PROPOSITION 7.1. *ReBAC Datalog programs with all predicates with arity $\leq k$ and rules with constraints that used $\leq k$ variables is program+data complete for* P.

This follows directly from the facts that (1) Datalog programs that are limited to use $\leq k$ variables per rule is data+program complete for P [28], and (2) that using the result that Stratified Datalog with negation is data complete for P and program complete for EXPTIME [1] together with the same techniques from [28], one can show that stratified Datalog programs with negation that are limited to use $\leq k$ variables per rule are also data+program complete for P. These proofs rest on the fact that any intermediate result needed to evaluate the rules is no more than polynomially larger than the input size. In ReBAC Datalog programs, the size of any derived relation is a polynomial function on the size of the protection state. More precisely, if the number of constants in the protection state is m, the size of a derived relation can be bound to $O(m^k)$, assuming k to be the maximal predicate arity. Take, for example, grant(X, Y). The maximum number of different values that X or Y can take is m. Hence, the number of ground atoms is bound by m^2. The number of relations defined by policies (i.e., the number of different predicate names appearing in the head of at least one rule is limited by the number l of program rules, therefore, an evaluation of the ReBAC program can be done in $O(lm^{k^2})$. The square is added as an upper bound of rule evaluation in case there are recursive rules. In practice, this number is much smaller, and for a given request grant(u, r, a), l will be determined by how well we can index the rules based on u, r, and a, to pull out the subset of rules that apply to the specific request. One could use the principal matching rules concept from [8] or the user-to-user relationship-based access control model of [7] to organize policies and create an indexing.

There is a syntactic characteristic of the program rules that is used to ensure that intermediate results are kept small: we have already observed how the propagation of information through variable bindings happens in the rules. Take, for example, the rule:

$$rel(Res, profile, O), rel(Req, contact, Z),$$
$$rel(Z, contact, O) \rightarrow grant(Req, Res)$$

In terms of database operations, the evaluation of the rule requires two joins. We know that at the moment of evaluation, values for the variables Req and Res will be fixed. Therefore, the evaluation of rel(Res, profile, O) will produce a single value for O. The expected number of values for Z returned by the evaluation of rel(Req, contact, Z) can be estimated by the typical values of contact list sizes given that Req is fixed. Similarly, the expected number of values for Z in the evaluation rel(Z, contact, O) can be estimated. This is called the selectivity of the evaluation, the smaller the expected number of values, the higher the selectivity. Given that the selection operations in databases can be done much faster than the joins, modern database systems do query planning before query evaluation to find the right order to evaluate the joins. If, for example, the order is first to do the join rel(Req, contact, Z), rel(Z, contact, O), before doing the second join with rel(Res, profile, O) a projection over O is done in the relation obtained from the join rel(Req, contact, Z), rel(Z, contact, O) and the joint relation can be discarded before doing the (semi) join with rel(Res, profile, O). In this case there can never be a relation with more than m^2 tuples during the computation. In contrast, creating the (Res, O, Req, Z) joint table could in principal generate a relation with m^4 tuples. This dependency of shared variables is known as a Sideway Information Passing (SIP) optimization and it is fundamental for the Magic Sets optimization technique applied to recursive Datalog rules. Given that the evaluation of an access control decision in the Datalog program is always answering a ground query this optimization will be very effective, essentially transforming the query answering into a goal oriented procedure. This means that the search space will be very likely limited to nodes in the graph that are reachable from the constants passed as arguments in the query which, in many cases, will be much smaller than m. Furthermore, SIPs are useful for implementing and maintaining view materialization - this is a pre-computation of rule evaluations that generalizes the concept of catching suggested in [9].

There are several Datalog systems available to test implementations. Nevertheless, we are not presenting experimental evaluations since [21] already reports an evaluation and comparison of a few systems that includes experiments with rule sets with exactly the characteristics of ReBAC Datalog policies. Instead what we will do is to present the relevant results and put them in context with the experimental evaluation of a Java implementation of a subset of EHL policy evaluator reported in [25].

Since the publication of [21] there have been several new releases of the systems and the results of the experiments have been updated twice using the newer versions. The discussion below is based on the 2011 report [12]. The machine where all the experiments were conducted was a dual core 3GHz Dell Optiplex 755 with 4 gigabytes of main memory. It was running Ubuntu 7.10 with kernel 2.6.22. Although the experiments were ran using four different Datalog systems and no a single one outperformed the others in all the evaluations, we will only report the results obtained using Ontobroker [21] since it is the system that better performed in the majority of the tests. Ontobroker is also written in Java. We start reviewing the results of evaluating the following set of rules:

$$b1(X, Z), b2(Z, Y) \rightarrow a(X, Y)$$
$$c1(X, Z), c2(Z, Y) \rightarrow b1(X, Y)$$
$$c3(X, Z), c4(Z, Y) \rightarrow b2(X, Y)$$
$$d1(X, Z), d2(Z, Y) \rightarrow c1(X, Y)$$

The base relations that would correspond to the protection state were $c2, c3, c4, d1$ and $d2$, representing atoms of the form $rel(X, c2, Y)$, $rel(X, c3, Y)$, $rel(X, c4, Y)$, $rel(X, d1, Y)$, $rel(X, d2, Y)$. We will discuss the results for experiments that were conducted using $50K$ and $250K$ randomly generated arcs from a fixed set of 1000 nodes. For the query $a(X, Y)$, in which both variables were free, with $50K$ arcs the time to evaluate the query was 8.807sec. With $250K$ the evaluation took 59.259sec. At first glance, these times do not look encouraging. Nevertheless, if in the query we bind the first argument (e.g., $a(1, Y)$) the time to answer the query with $50K$ arcs reduces to 7msec. With $250K$ arcs the time reduces to 21msec. Tests with the second argument bound (e.g., $a(x, 2)$) resulted in similar performance of $50K$ arcs, but only 5msec for $250K$. This difference is explained by the fact that Ontobroker does query analysis and builds a cost model to decide what optimizations to use including the order to do the joint operators, the algorithm to use for the execution of each of the join operations as well as selectivity analysis. This improvement of at least three orders of magnitude shows the effect of limiting the search to reachable objects. For ReBAC, we can take the best of the times since queries $grant(u, r)$, will have both arguments bound.

It is difficult to make a direct comparison to the results reported in [25] for several reasons. One is that the number of arcs used in[25] is 2 orders of magnitude larger ($30000K$) than for the experiments in [12]. Furthermore, in [25] the arcs were not randomly generated, and the machine was more powerful: it had 8 cores of faster CPUs and 4 times more memory. They report having averages of 37msec for the policies most similar to the program above. These 37msec are an average over policy evaluations that could require the executions

of no joints at all and up to a maximum of three joints. This is in contrast to the query a(.) that has four joins. Evaluations with larger data sets can be done but it is worth noting that database sizes do not correlate directly with time to execute queries - not only the second argument bound query evaluation ran faster for the $250K$ set than the $50K$, but the time that took to run queries of the form $b2(X, Y)$ and $b1(X, Y)$ with one of the arguments bound using the $50K$ set and the $250K$ set took about the same time in each case, less than 4msec for b1 and less than 20msec for b2.

[12] also reports experiments over the evaluation of transitive closure rules:

$$par(X, Y) \rightarrow tc(X, Y)$$
$$par(X, Z), tc(Z, Y) \rightarrow tc(X, Y)$$

The results here are also remarkable. The largest input size consisted of 2000 nodes and 1M par arcs randomly generated. Two types of input were generated, for graphs with and without cycles. For queries with no bindings ($tc(X, Y)$) the times for evaluation were 87.3sec for data with no cycles and 200.9sec for data with cycles. Binding the first argument made very little difference, 86.5sec and 197.17sec respectively. But if the second argument was bound the results were 25msec for no cycles and 16msec for data with cycles. This demonstrates the effects of the Magic set optimization that re-writes the programs to take advantage of the bound arguments and the SIP derived from the rules syntax.

[25] does not have implementation for path expressions. The observation to make is that despite of the fact that the system in [25] was specially developed for EHL its performance is not particularly better than using an off-the-shelf Datalog system that also includes regular path evaluations, giving evidence of the excellent performance of Datalog systems contrary to the belief that they are not suitable for high throughput access control implementations.

A final observation about implementations: there is a result in parallel complexity that may explain some of the experimental results for the transitive closure above. A Datalog program is called linear if and only if each rule has at most one occurrence of the predicate in the head appearing in the body. Recall that a decision problem is in the NC complexity class if it can be solved in polylogarithmic time on a parallel computer with a polynomial number of processors. It is known that the data complexity of linear Datalog is in NC [26] and amenable to parallelization. Note that except for negation, ReBAC programs are linear. Among the optimization considered by Ontobroker is the use multiple cores and threading to parallelize query evaluation.

8 FINAL REMARKS

Research on access control policy languages has been extensive and logic programming has been a popular modeling choice [2, 3, 16, 18, 19]. But writing correct policies and developing correct and intuitive implementations of policy management systems are not easy tasks [10]. The attention ReBAC has received in the access control research community comes from the fact that it provides an expressive yet tractable model to intuitively capture the meaning of the "subjective" policies people may have in mind. The goal of this paper has been to show the benefits of using Datalog as a developing framework. Modeling ReBAC in Datalog is natural since Datalog is a good language to describe and talk about properties of graphs which is the essence of ReBAC. From a practical point of view there are two good reasons for choosing Datalog: Datalog specifications are easier to implement, and implementation techniques have been around for many years. These are complemented by extensive results in computational complexity which we were able to use almost directly to establish the expressibility and complexity results of ReBAC Datalog policies (and by Propositions 5.2 & 7.1, the complexity of HL and EHL policy evaluation). This does not mean that Datalog must be the syntax the policy author uses to write policies. ReBAC Datalog can be thought as target compilation language of a more user-friendly language for authoring.

There is a striking similarity between the definitions of properties and relationships in HL and the definitions of concepts and roles in Description Logics (DL). This has been our motivation for the "meta-relation" rel, as in rel(O, friend, R), instead of friend(O, R). This is a typical domain-independent representation of DL roles in Datalog. Since hash indexes can be built in relation columns, accessing the related items of a particular object can be done very efficiently. There is a lot of research in the DL community to develop fast deduction algorithms for very large data sets (see, for example, [27]). Developing a ReBAC model based on one of the tractable DLs is an avenue of research worth exploring. But what is more important to note is that many advances for high throughput Datalog systems have been driven by the interest of the Semantic Web community of using Datalog-like languages for Ontology reasoning. Even if a specialized ReBAC policy evaluator is developed all the experience gained developing high throughput Datalog systems cannot be ignored and will be of tremendous impact.

ACKNOWLEDGMENTS

Edelmira Pasarella was partially supported by the Spanish Ministry for Economy and Competitiveness (MINECO) and the European Union (FEDER funds) under Grant Ref.: TIN2013-46181-C2-1-R COMMAS. Jorge Lobo was partially supported by the Secretaria d'Universitats i Recerca de la Generalitat de Catalunya, the Maria de Maeztu Units of Excellence Programme and the Spanish Ministry for Economy and Competitiveness (MINECO) under Grant Ref.: TIN2016-81032-P.

REFERENCES

[1] Krzysztof R Apt and Howard A Blair. 1990. Arithmetic classification of perfect models of stratified programs. *Fundamenta Informaticae* 13, 1 (1990), 1–17.
[2] Steve Barker. 2002. Protecting deductive databases from unauthorized retrieval and update requests. *Data & Knowledge Engineering* 43, 3 (2002), 293–315.
[3] Moritz Y Becker, Cédric Fournet, and Andrew D Gordon. 2010. SecPAL: Design and semantics of a decentralized authorization language. *Journal of Computer Security* 18, 4 (2010), 619–665.
[4] Glenn Bruns, Philip WL Fong, Ida Siahaan, and Michael Huth. 2012. Relationship-based access control: its expression and enforcement through hybrid logic. In *Proceedings of the second ACM conference on Data and Application Security and Privacy.* ACM, 117–124.
[5] Barbara Carminati, Elena Ferrari, and Andrea Perego. 2009. Enforcing access control in web-based social networks. *ACM Transactions on Information and System Security (TISSEC)* 13, 1 (2009), 6.
[6] Yuan Cheng, Jaehong Park, and Ravi Sandhu. 2012. Relationship-based access control for online social networks: Beyond user-to-user relationships. In *Privacy, Security, Risk and Trust (PASSAT), 2012 International Conference on and 2012 International Confernece on Social Computing (SocialCom).* IEEE, 646–655.
[7] Yuan Cheng, Jaehong Park, and Ravi S. Sandhu. 2016. An Access Control Model for Online Social Networks Using User-to-User Relationships. *IEEE Trans. Dependable Sec. Comput.* 13, 4 (2016), 424–436. https://doi.org/10.1109/TDSC.2015.

2406705
[8] Jason Crampton and James Sellwood. 2014. Path conditions and principal matching: a new approach to access control. In *Proceedings of the 19th ACM symposium on Access control models and technologies.* ACM, 187–198.
[9] Jason Crampton and James Sellwood. 2015. Relationships, Paths and Principal Matching: A New Approach to Access Control. *arXiv preprint arXiv:1505.07945* (2015).
[10] Lorrie Faith Cranor and Simson Garfinkel. 2005. *Security and usability: designing secure systems that people can use.* " O'Reilly Media, Inc.".
[11] Evgeny Dantsin, Thomas Eiter, Georg Gottlob, and Andrei Voronkov. 2001. Complexity and expressive power of logic programming. *ACM Computing Surveys (CSUR)* 33, 3 (2001), 374–425.
[12] Paul Fodor, Senlin Liang, and Michael Kifer. 2011. OpenRuleBench: Report 2011. (2011).
[13] Philip WL Fong, Pooya Mehregan, and Ram Krishnan. 2013. Relational abstraction in community-based secure collaboration. In *Proceedings of the 2013 ACM SIGSAC conference on Computer & communications security.* ACM, 585–598.
[14] Philip WL Fong and Ida Siahaan. 2011. Relationship-based access control policies and their policy languages. In *Proceedings of the 16th ACM symposium on Access control models and technologies.* ACM, 51–60.
[15] Carrie Gates. 2007. Access control requirements for web 2.0 security and privacy. *IEEE Web* 2, 0 (2007).
[16] Yuri Gurevich and Itay Neeman. 2008. DKAL: Distributed-knowledge authorization language. In *Computer Security Foundations Symposium, 2008. CSF'08. IEEE 21st.* IEEE, 149–162.
[17] Hongxin Hu, Gail-Joon Ahn, and Jan Jorgensen. 2013. Multiparty access control for online social networks: model and mechanisms. *Knowledge and Data Engineering, IEEE Transactions on* 25, 7 (2013), 1614–1627.
[18] Sushil Jajodia, Pierangela Samarati, Maria Luisa Sapino, and VS Subrahmanian. 2001. Flexible support for multiple access control policies. *ACM Transactions on Database Systems (TODS)* 26, 2 (2001), 214–260.
[19] Lalana Kagal, Tim Finin, and Anupam Joshi. 2003. A Policy Based Approach to Security for the Semantic Web. *The Semantic Web-ISWC 2003* (2003), 402–418.
[20] Phokion G Kolaitis. 1991. The expressive power of stratified logic programs. *Information and Computation* 90, 1 (1991), 50–66.
[21] Senlin Liang, Paul Fodor, Hui Wan, and Michael Kifer. 2009. OpenRuleBench: an analysis of the performance of rule engines. In *Proceedings of the 18th international conference on World wide web.* ACM, 601–610.
[22] Jorge Lobo, Jiefei Ma, Alessandra Russo, Emil Lupu, Seraphin Calo, and Morris Sloman. 2011. Refinement of history-based policies. In *Logic programming, knowledge representation, and nonmonotonic reasoning.* Springer, 280–299.
[23] Christos H Papadimitriou and Mihalis Yannakakis. 1997. On the complexity of database queries. In *Proceedings of the sixteenth ACM SIGACT-SIGMOD-SIGART symposium on Principles of database systems.* ACM, 12–19.
[24] Raymond Reiter. 1984. Towards a logical reconstruction of relational database theory. In *On conceptual modelling.* Springer, 191–238.
[25] Syed Zain R Rizvi, Philip WL Fong, Jason Crampton, and James Sellwood. 2015. Relationship-based access control for an open-source medical records system. In *Proceedings of the 20th ACM Symposium on Access Control Models and Technologies.* ACM, 113–124.
[26] Jeffrey D Ullman and Allen Van Gelder. 1988. Parallel complexity of logical query programs. *Algorithmica* 3, 1-4 (1988), 5–42.
[27] Jacopo Urbani, Ceriel Jacobs, and Markus Krötzsch. 2016. Column-Oriented Datalog Materialization for Large Knowledge Graphs. In *Thirtieth AAAI Conference on Artificial Intelligence.* 258–264.
[28] Moshe Y Vardi. 1995. On the complexity of bounded-variable queries. In *Proceedings of the fourteenth ACM SIGACT-SIGMOD-SIGART symposium on Principles of database systems.* ACM, 266–276.

Towards a Top-down Policy Engineering Framework for Attribute-based Access Control

Masoud Narouei
INSPIRE Lab
University of North Texas
Denton, Texas
Masoudnarouei@my.unt.edu

Hamed Khanpour
Machine Learning Lab
University of North Texas
Denton, Texas
Hamedkhanpour@my.unt.edu

Hassan Takabi
INSPIRE Lab
University of North Texas
Denton, Texas
Hassan.Takabi@unt.edu

Natalie Parde
HiLT Lab
University of North Texas
Denton, Texas
Natalieparde@my.unt.edu

Rodney Nielsen
HiLT Lab
University of North Texas
Denton, Texas
Rodney.Nielsen@unt.edu

ABSTRACT

Attribute-based access control (ABAC) is a logical access control methodology where authorization to perform a set of operations is based on attributes of the user, the objects being accessed, the environment, and a number of other attribute sources that may be relevant to the current request. Once fully implemented within an enterprise, ABAC promotes information sharing while maintaining control of the information. However, the cost of developing ABAC policies can be a significant obstacle for organizations to migrate from traditional access control models to ABAC. Most organizations have high-level requirement specifications that define security policies and include a set of access control policies. Taking advantage of this rich source of information, we introduce a top-down policy engineering framework for ABAC that aims to automatically extract policies from unrestricted natural language documents and then, we present our methodology to extract policy related information using deep neural networks. We first create an annotated dataset comprised of 2660 sentences from real-world policy documents. We then train a deep recurrent neural network (RNN) to identify sentences containing access control policies (ACP) from irrelevant content. We applied the RNN to our new dataset as well as to five other, smaller datasets that have been employed in prior work on this task, and show that our model outperforms the state-of-the-art and leads to a performance improvement of 5.58% over the previously reported results.

CCS CONCEPTS

•Security and privacy → Security requirements; Access control;

SACMAT'17, June 21–23, 2017, Indianapolis, IN, USA
© 2017 ACM. ACM ISBN 978-1-4503-4702-0/17/06...$15.00.
DOI: http://dx.doi.org/10.1145/3078861.3078874

KEYWORDS

Access control policy; attribute-based access control; policy engineering; recurrent neural network; deep learning

ACM Reference format:
Masoud Narouei, Hamed Khanpour, Hassan Takabi, Natalie Parde, and Rodney Nielsen. 2017. Towards a Top-down Policy Engineering Framework for Attribute-based Access Control. In *Proceedings of SACMAT'17, June 21–23, 2017, Indianapolis, IN, USA, , 12 pages.*
DOI: http://dx.doi.org/10.1145/3078861.3078874

1 INTRODUCTION

Traditionally, access control has been based on the identity of a user requesting to perform an operation (e.g., write) on a resource (e.g., a database file), either directly, or via predetermined attribute types such as roles or groups assigned to that user. However, this approach has been shown to be hard to manage given the need to associate capabilities directly to users or their roles or groups (e.g. role explosion issue). It has also been noted that using identifiers such as roles and groups are often insufficient in the expression of real-world access control policies (ACPs). To overcome these shortcomings, there has been a growing demand from both government and industry for a more general and dynamic model of access control. This model, which grants or denies a request based on attributes of the user, the objects being accessed, the environment and a number of other attribute sources that may be relevant to the current request, is often referred to as attribute-based access control (ABAC). Previous literature has shown that ABAC is able to overcome the limitations of the dominant access control models (i.e, discretionary access control (DAC), mandatory access control (MAC, also known as lattice based access control or multilevel security), and role-based access control (RBAC)) while unifying their advantages [19].

Using ABAC, flexible enforcement of ACPs can be achieved solely based on the results of a boolean statement comparing different attributes. For example, *"user.type==student AND object.classification ==restricted"* grants permission only based on a subset of user and object attributes which already exist in the system and do not need to be manually entered by administration. As a result of this flexibility, ABAC has attracted interest across industry and government.

In fact, Gartner recently predicted that "by 2020, 70% of enterprises will use attribute-based access control ... as the dominant mechanism to protect critical assets" [11]. However, manual development of initial ABAC policies can be difficult, expensive, labor-intensive, and error prone [3, 16].

ABAC policy mining algorithms have been introduced to reduce the cost of ABAC policy development, by partially automating the process [50]. However, these approaches ignore an important source of policy information in organizations that could be very useful in the policy engineering process. Most organizations have high-level requirement specifications that determine who, under what circumstances, may access what information [16]. These documents define security policies and include a set of ACPs which describes allowable operations for the system. We refer to these documents (high-level requirement specifications) as natural language access control policies (NLACPs) which are defined as "statements governing management and access of enterprise objects. NLACPs are human expressions that can be translated to machine-enforceable access control policies" [16]. We propose to utilize this rich source of information in the process of developing ABAC policies. However, an issue in developing ABAC policies is that the information that needs to be encoded is typically buried within these NLACPs, and difficult to interpret. This requires processing natural language documents and extracting the related information from those documents.

In this paper, we take the first step towards our eventual goal of developing ABAC policies from unrestricted natural language documents (e.g., requirement documents, policy documents, etc.). We introduce a top-down policy engineering framework for ABAC that aims to automatically extract policies from NLACPs and then, we present our methodology to process unrestricted natural language documents and extract policy related information using deep neural networks.

NLACPs are often huge and consist of a lot of general descriptive sentences that lack any access control content. Manually processing these documents to extract policy related information and then using them to build an ABAC policy is a laborious and expensive process. Recent developments in deep learning has surprised many researchers due to high performances in many tasks such as Natural Language Processing (NLP) [41], even leading Manning (2016) to refer to the phenomenon as a neural network "tsunami". The most significant benefit of using deep neural networks is that they are not reliant on handcrafted features; instead, they manufacture features automatically from each word [46], sentence [26], or even long texts [38]. By taking aspirations from the previous reports in effectiveness of deep neural networks in domain-independent conversations [26], we propose a model based on a recurrent neural network, long short term memory (LSTM), that benefits from deep layers of networks and pre-trained word embeddings derived from Wikipedia articles. Word embeddings are semantic distributional representations of words that are used to solve the data sparsity problem [4]. This model will be used to distinguish ACP sentences from non-ACP content. Once the ACP sentences are identified, they can be analyzed in order to extract ABAC policy elements using different methods such as semantic role labeling [34].

The ACP domain suffers from a scarcity of publicly available data for researchers. To help alleviate this problem, we begin by creating a new dataset of real world policy information to serve the dual purpose of (1) making our evaluation of the proposed method more robust, and (2) providing the research community with more data, which will in turn allow other researchers interested in this same problem to evaluate their own work both more comprehensively and in direct comparison to ours.

The contributions of this paper are hence three-fold:

- We introduce a top-down policy engineering framework for ABAC.
- We take the first step towards developing the framework by proposing an automatic approach to identify access control policy sentences.
- We create a deep recurrent neural network that uses pre-trained word embeddings to identify sentences that contain access control policy content and show that the method is effective in doing so.

The rest of this paper is organized as follows: We begin with an overview of background information in section 2. This is followed by introduction of the proposed top-down policy engineering framework and its components in section 3. Section 4 presents the proposed ACP sentence identification and deep learning based approach in detail. The experiments and results are presented in section 5, followed by review of literature in section 6. Finally, the conclusion and future work wraps up the paper.

2 BACKGROUND

This section provides background information with regards to semantic role labeling and deep learning.

2.1 Semantic Role Labeling

Semantic role labeling (SRL), sometimes also called shallow semantic parsing, is a task in NLP for automatically identifying the semantic roles of each argument of each predicate (verb) in a sentence [12]. With the advent of resources such as FrameNet [9] and PropBank [36], SRL has experienced a flurry of activity in recent years [6]. SRL labels verb-argument structures using the notation defined by these resources, identifying who did what to whom where and when by assigning roles to constituents of the sentence representing entities related to a specific predicate. Answering these questions is the key step in automatic conversion of ACP sentences to ABAC elements (subject, operation, object). The following example represents the annotation of semantic roles using SRL:

$[A_0$ The system] $[V$ **retrieves**] $[A_1$ the student information] $[AM - LOC$ in the registration system].

Here, the roles for the predicate retrieves (retrieves.01, that is, the roleset of the predicate) are defined in the PropBank Frames scheme as:

- **Arg0-PAG**: *receiver (vnrole: 13.5.2-agent)*
- **Arg1-PPT**: *thing gotten (vnrole: 13.5.2-theme)*
- **Arg2-DIR**: *received from (vnrole: 13.5.2-source)*
- **Arg3-GOL**: *benefactive*

The Proposition Bank [36], generally referred to as PropBank, is a resource of sentences annotated with semantic roles. Since it is difficult to define a universal set of presentive roles, the semantic roles in PropBank are defined with respect to individual verb senses. Each sense, therefore, has a specific set of roles, which are given

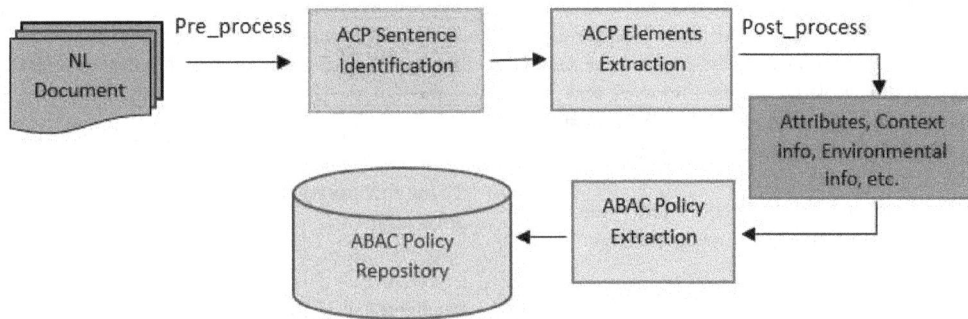

Figure 1: Overview of the Proposed Top-down Policy Engineering Framework

only numbers rather than names: Arg0, Arg1, Arg2, and so on. In general, Arg0 represents the PROTO-AGENT (subject), and Arg1, the PROTO-PATIENT (object or resource). The semantics of the other roles are less consistent, often being defined specifically for each verb. Nonetheless, there are some generalizations; the Arg2 is often the benefactive, instrument, attribute, or end state, the Arg3 the start point, benefactive, instrument, or attribute, and the Arg4 the end point [20]. PropBank has also a number of non-numbered arguments called ArgMs (ArgM-TMP, ArgM-LOC, Arg-DIR, etc.), which are relatively stable across predicates. Using these modifiers allow us to detect temporal or location of a specific ACP.

2.2 Deep Learning

Deep learning (also known as deep structured learning, hierarchical learning or deep machine learning) is a learning method that attempts to model high level abstractions in data using a deep network [8]. In a deep network, there are many layers between the input and output, allowing the algorithm to use multiple processing layers, composed of multiple linear and non-linear transformations. The first layer receives an input signal and then transforms it by a processing unit, like an artificial neuron, whose parameters are "learned" through training. Then it passes its transformed output to the next layer. Each successive layer uses the output from the previous layer as input. Deep learning has been used in both supervised or unsupervised settings and its applications include pattern analysis (unsupervised) and classification (supervised).

3 THE PROPOSED TOP-DOWN POLICY ENGINEERING FRAMEWORK

In order to extract ABAC policies from unrestricted natural language documents, we first need to process the documents and identify those sentences that carry ACP content. The ACPs describes who has access to what resource in what way. Once the ACP sentences are identified, our proposed framework will generate corresponding policy elements (e.g. subject, object, action). The framework also extract attributes, context information, environmental conditions, etc. Then, this information is used to generate machine readable and enforceable ABAC policies. An overall view

of the the proposed framework is shown in Figure 1. In the following sections, we describe each of these steps in detail.

3.1 ACP Sentence Identification

Often time NLACPs contain contents that describe functional requirements and are not necessary related to ACPs. Although these documents also contain ACPs, attempting to extract ACPs from the whole document is an error prone and tedious process. To correctly extract ACPs from NLACPs, it is very important to find out those sentences that have potentially ACP content and then perform further analysis only on those sentences to extract ACP elements. This step is one of the main contributions of this paper and discussed in more detail in Section 4 and Section 5.

3.2 ABAC Policy Elements Extraction

As we mentioned earlier, an issue prior to developing an ABAC policy is the information that needs to be encoded is typically buried within existing natural language (NL) artifacts, hence difficult to interpret. For example, consider the following ACP sentence for iTrust [31], "System displays only the applicable input entries to the UAP." This ACP sentence is not amenable for automated verification and enforcement, requiring manual effort in extracting the necessary elements (e,g., subject, object, action) from this sentence. To address this issue, various researchers have proposed approaches for automatically generating machine-enforceable ACPs from NL software documents in different formats such as eXtensible access control markup language (XACML) [49]. *ACRE* [40] used an iterative algorithm to discover patterns that represent ACP rules in sentences. They seeded this algorithm with frequently occurring nouns matching a subject-action-resource pattern throughout a document. The algorithm then searched for additional combinations of those nouns to discover additional patterns. The found instances were assumed to represent ACPs and the elements of the ACP were then extracted. In our previous work, we proposed SRL to automatically extract ACP elements from unrestricted NL documents, define roles, and build an RBAC model [34]. We did not attempt to identify ACP sentences, but instead used the already extracted sentences by [40] and left implementing the ACP sentence identification step for future work. By applying SRL on the ACP sentences to automatically identify predicate-argument structures, and a set of predefined rules on the extracted arguments, we were able to correctly identify ACPs with a precision of 75%, recall of 88%, and F_1 score of 80%. On average, our method bested *ACRE* with 2% increase in F_1. In this work, we extend that work and propose our methodology for ACP sentence identification alongside a new framework for ABAC policy engineering. Since our goal is to automate the process of generating ABAC policies, we adopt the same process as [34] and use the SRL arguments, extracted from analyzing each sentence, as our basic ABAC components.

3.3 Attribute Extraction

One of the main challenges in developing an ABAC policy is identifying attributes (e.g, subject attribute, object attributes and environment attributes). Most of the recent works assume that these attributes are provided as part of the data [50]; however, in real scenarios, especially while analyzing policy documents, no attributes are provided. To tackle this issue, we propose using SRL argument definitions as descriptors. In Propbank [36], in addition to the arguments for each predicate, a short definition is also provided for each argument. Considering the following roleset for *retrieve* in the sectence "The system retrieves the student information in the registration system":

- **Arg0-PAG**: *receiver (vnrole: 13.5.2-agent)*
- **Arg1-PPT**: *thing gotten (vnrole: 13.5.2-theme)*
- **Arg2-DIR**: *received from (vnrole: 13.5.2-source)*
- **Arg3-GOL**: *benefactive*

The argument A_0 has a short definition of *receiver*, and the argument A_1 has the definition of *thing gotten*, etc. Note that the definitions in the frame file for each role ("thing gotten", "received from") are informal glosses intended to be read by humans, rather than being formal definitions. However, these definitions are rather sufficient for our purpose. Hence, we consider *receiver* as the descriptor for A_0 and *thing gotten* as the descriptor for A_1. For our basic prototype, we only consider A_0 and A_1 and leave the rest of numbered attributes for future work. We use A_0's descriptor as subject attribute and A_1's as object attribute. Since some ACP predicates also include non-numbered arguments of *ArgM-TMP* and *ArgM-LOC*, we consider them as environment attributes. We consider *ArgM-TMP* as temporal attribute and *ArgM-LOC* as location attribute.

Following the above descriptions, we use the following function notation for the value assignment of attributes:

$$Definition(Argument) = Text$$

(1)

As an example, consider the following sentence:

[A_0 The system] [V **retrieves**] [A_1 the student information] [*ArgM-LOC* in the registration system].

Using the above function notation, the attributes would be represented as follows:

receiver(A_0)= "The system"
thing-gotten(A_1)= "the student information"
Location(*ArgM-LOC*)= "in the registration system"

We define *Sbj_Att* as the AND combination of subject attributes, *Obj_Att* as the AND combination of object attributes and *Env_Att* as the AND combination of environment attributes. In its most general form, an ABAC policy is a combination of individual attributes. We represent an ABAC policy using the following notation:

$$Policy : Action \leftarrow \{Sbj\_Att \wedge Obj\_Att \wedge Env\_Att\}$$

(2)

Using this notation, the above policy would be represented as the following:

retrieve ← {
receiver(A_0) = "The system" ∧
thing-gotten(A_1)= "the student information" ∧
Location(*ArgM-LOC*)= "in the registration system" }

This process is further depicted in Figure 2 using another ACP example.

4 THE PROPOSED ACCESS CONTROL POLICY SENTENCE IDENTIFICATION

In this section, we describe the ACP sentence identifier component which is the first step in top-down policy engineering process. The ACP sentence identification consists of a pre-process engine, and RNN sentence classifier as described below.

4.1 Pre-process Engine

Figure 3 presents part of a large policy document. It is obvious that there are many non-relevant contents such as titles, tables, etc. that need to be removed. As these formal documents are usually expressed in PDF format, the first step is to read each PDF document. For this purpose, we used Apache PDFBox[1] toolkit, which extracts texts and ignore the other contents such as tables. In order to parse the extracted text, we feed it into Stanford CoreNLP toolkit [30]. The tool will split the text by sentences boundaries where each sentence will be on a separate line and ended by a period. As many of the extracted sentences are not statements (e.g. titles), we introduce the following equation to filter out everything other than sentences.

$$Ratio(sent) = \frac{Capitals(sent)}{Tokens(sent)}$$

(3)

Where *Capitals* stand for the number of capital letters in the sentence (*sent*) and *Tokens* counts for the number of tokens in each sentences. If this ratio is less than 0.6, we consider the sentence for further processing. We used different ratios but 0.6 gave us the most accurate results. We also limited ourselves to sentences with more than 15 characters, which helped us remove more incomplete sentences. After this step, the following four sentences will be extracted from the document [2]:

- *The University respects its resident students' reasonable expectation of privacy in their rooms and makes every effort to ensure privacy in university residences.*
- *However, in order to protect and maintain the property of the university and the health and safety of the university's students, the university reserves the right to enter and/or search*

[1]https://pdfbox.apache.org/index.html
[2]http://policy.unt.edu/sites/default/files/07.022_AdministrativeEntrySearchesUniversity ResidenceHalls_201.pdf

The professor **enters** the student grades in the system only at a time interval 12:00-13:00 in a day.

Entity_entering   Place_or_thing_entered   Location   Temporal

Sbj_Att   Obj_Att   Env_Att

ABAC Policy: **enters** ◄——— {   ∧   ∧   }

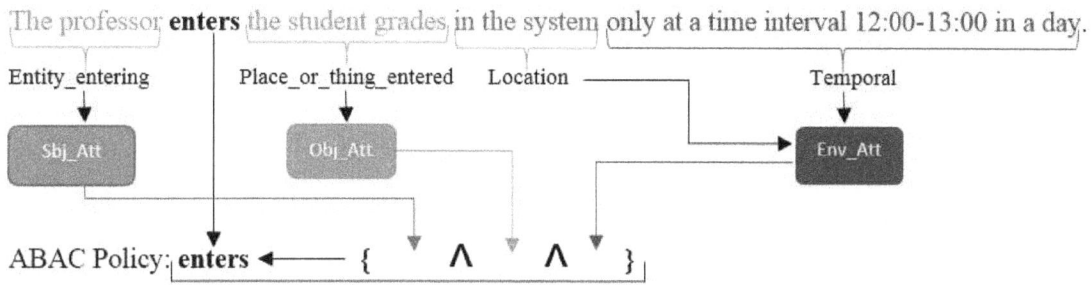

Figure 2: Attribute Extraction Scenario

Policies of the University of North Texas	
	Chapter 7
07.022 Administrative Entry and Searches of University Residence Halls	Student Affairs

Policy Statement. UNT respects its resident students' reasonable expectation of privacy in their rooms and makes every effort to ensure privacy in university residences. However, in order to protect and maintain the property of the university and the health and safety of the university's students, the university reserves the right to enter and/or search student residence hall rooms in the interest of preserving a safe and orderly living and learning environment.

Application of Policy. Resident students.

Procedures and Responsibilities.

1. Administrative room inspections

   a. Designated university officials are authorized to enter a residence hall room unaccompanied by a resident student to conduct room inspections under the following conditions:

      i. To perform reasonable custodial, maintenance, and repair services.

Figure 3: Part of a requirements document.

student residence hall rooms in the interest of preserving a safe and orderly living and learning environment.
- *Designated university officials are authorized to enter a residence hall room unaccompanied by a resident student to conduct room inspections under the following conditions.*
- *To perform reasonable custodial, maintenance, and repair services.*

Next, the extracted sentences will be fed to the deep neural network classifier in order to build the network and make predictions.

4.2 Recurrent Neural Network (RNN) Sentence Classifier

Recently, DNNs have been used with increasing frequency in a variety of text processing applications, from sentiment analysis [41] to conversational text processing for dialogue systems [22, 48]. Collobert *et al.* proposed an approach for generating word vectors based on contextual information gained from large amounts of unlabeled text, employing convolutional neural networks (CNNs) to develop an efficient application for part-of-speech tagging, chunking, named entity recognition, semantic role labeling, and syntactic

parsing, called *SENNA* [7]. They showed that their developed system outperformed almost all sophisticated traditional methods that perform these same NLP tasks, with the substantial added benefit of not needing to employ any handcrafted features, prior knowledge, or linguistic information. In this work, we will create a deep recurrent neural network (RNN) that uses pre-trained word embeddings in order to identify sentences that contain ACPs from large requirements documents.

Current approaches based on deep learning methods improved many state-of-the-art techniques in NLP, including dialogue act (DA) classification accuracy on open-domain conversations [26, 39]. Kalchbrenner and Blunsom used a mixture of CNN and RNN [21]. CNNs were used to extract local features from each utterance, and RNNs were used to create a general view of the whole dialogue. This work improved the state-of-the-art 42-tag DA classification on Switchboard [42] by 2.9% to reach 73.9% accuracy. Recently, Ji *et al.* presented a hybrid architecture that merges an RNN language model with a discourse structure that considers relations between two contiguous utterances as a latent variable [26]. This approach improved the result of the state-of-the-art method by about 3% (from 73.9 to 77) when applied on the Switchboard corpus.

4.2.1 Text Representation by Recurrent Neural Network. Figure 4 depicts a general view of an RNN that makes use of sequential information by building connections between current and previous inputs. This specificity is particularly meaningful when processing sequences of text in which each word is syntactically and semantically linked with previous words.

As can be seen in Figure 4, information from previous states is provided to the current state t by the previous hidden layer (h_{t-1}), which contributes to building h_t. We chose to use the RNN model to identify ACP sentences because it was designed to consider units in sequence to create a deterministic probability distribution over hidden layers, which enables the model to preserve much more information than its counterparts (e.g., HMM and CRF). Since in our task we need to discover specific relations among words in the sentence, our model needs to extract syntactic and semantic features that relate to one another sequentially. This makes RNNs the most appropriate choice since they are best able to contribute and remember the extracted features from each step.

The inputs of our model are word embeddings; each word from the sentence is represented as a vector, and each sentence is a vector

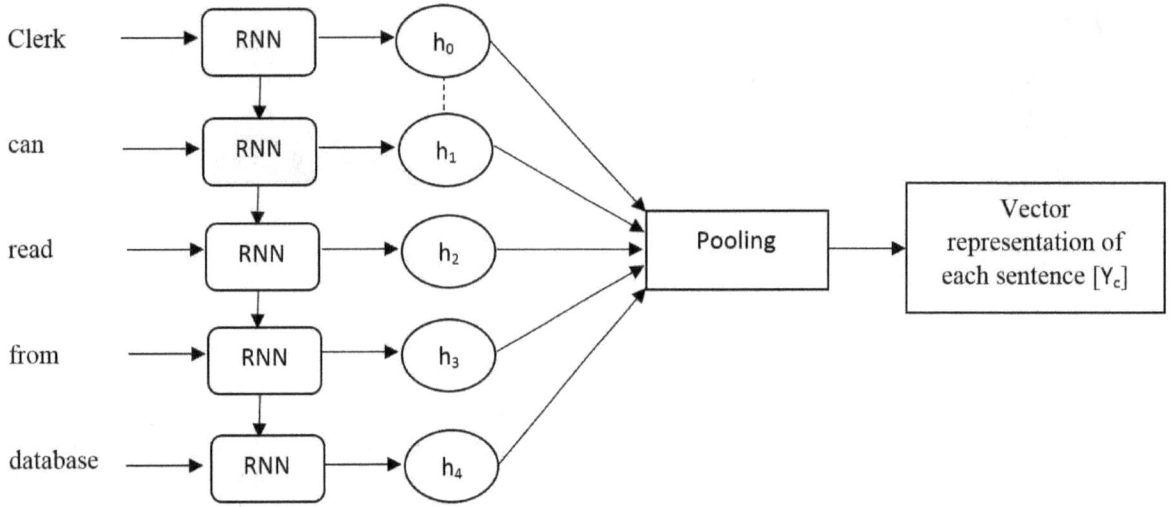

Figure 4: RNN structure for creating a vector-based representation of a sentence from its word.

of these word vectors, $< T_1, T_2, ..., T_{t-1}, T_t, ..., T_n >$. h_t is defined as follows:

$$h_t = \sigma\left(W^{hh}h_{t-1} + W^{hd}T_t\right) \quad (4)$$

where $W^{hh}\varepsilon R^{h\times h}$ and $W^{hd}\varepsilon R^{h\times d}$ are weight matrices, and σ refers to the logistic sigmoid function. Further, $y_t\varepsilon R^K$ is the class representation of each sentence, with K representing the number of classes for classification task (e.g., ACP and non-ACP). y_t is defined as follows:

$$y_t = softmax\left(W^{(S)}h_t\right) \quad (5)$$

In the pooling layer of our RNN (see Figure 4), our model takes all h vectors, $h_{1:n}$, and generates one output vector that carries the best features, namely those that are the best fit for the sentence. Performing this action can be done in one of three ways: mean-, max- or last-pooling. Mean-pooling measures the average of all h vectors, max-pooling takes the maximums from each h vector, and last-pooling takes the last h vector (i.e., h_t).

Although basic RNNs are theoretically able to carry the history of the network, they fail to maintain information over long distances in the text [5, 15]. Another problem with basic RNNs lies in the development of vanishing and exploding gradients, which lead the network to terminate prematurely [33, 37].

Long Short term memory (LSTM) networks are a variation of the RNN structure that are able to solve some of these issues. The LSTM structure is adjusted so that it holds long-distance relations as its default specificity. Using LSTMs results in a greater level of assurance that any useful features in the text will be captured and preserved. Since preserving trivial features, on the other hand, can be harmful to the classifier's result, a *forget gate layer* is designed in LSTMs to discard trivial low weight features from the cell state (see Eq. 7). Figure 5 shows the standard structure of an LSTM cell.

As can be seen in Figure 5, the LSTM cell at each time step t is defined by a set of vectors in R^d:

$$i_t = \sigma\left(W^{(i)}T_t + U^{(i)}h_{t-1} + b^{(i)}\right) \quad (6)$$

$$f_t = \sigma\left(W^{(f)}T_t + U^{(f)}h_{t-1} + b^{(f)}\right) \quad (7)$$

$$o_t = \sigma\left(W^{(o)}T_t + U^{(o)}h_{t-1} + b^{(o)}\right) \quad (8)$$

$$u_t = \tanh\left(W^{(u)}T_t + U^{(u)}h_{t-1} + b^{(u)}\right) \quad (9)$$

$$C_t = i_t \odot u_t + f_{(t)} \odot c_{t-1} \quad (10)$$

$$h_t = o_t \odot \tanh(c_t) \quad (11)$$

where i_t is the input gate, f_t is the forget gate, o_t is the output gate, c_t is the memory cell, h_t is the hidden state, and $\odot$ represents element-wise multiplication.

LSTMs have gates in each cell that control the types of signals that are allowed to pass through the whole chain. For instance, the forget gate f_t (Eq. 7) controls the amount with which the previous memory should be forgotten, the input gate (Eq. 6) controls the updating process, and the output gate controls the extent to which the internal memory state should be changed. The hidden layer h_t represents a gated, partial view of its cell state. LSTMs are able to view information over multiple time scales due to the fact that gating variables are assigned different values for each vector element [45].

By setting LSTM cells back to back, each cell is connected to one another via the hidden layer, h_t [13, 43]. This configuration of stacked LSTM cells is used to facilitate the identification of dependencies between tokens (T) across longer distances in the input chain of words.

In this study, stacked LSTMs with pre-trained word embeddings are used. We trained our word embeddings on Wikipedia using 300-dimensional vectors, setting our window and min-count parameters equal to 5 [32].

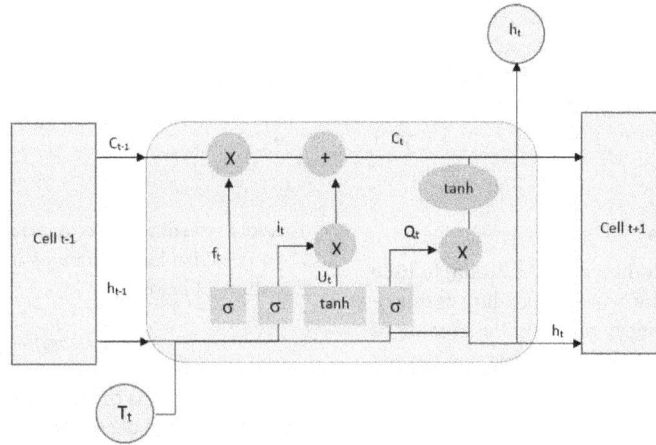

Figure 5: LSTM cell structure and parameters (http://colah.github.io).

5 EXPERIMENTS AND EVALUATION

5.1 Dataset

As mentioned earlier, the access policy domain suffers from a scarcity of publicly available data for researchers. To help alleviate this problem, we created a dataset to serve the dual purpose of (1) making our evaluation of the proposed method more robust, and (2) providing the research community with more data, which will in turn allow other researchers interested in this same problem to evaluate their own work both more comprehensively and in direct comparison to others.

We constructed our dataset from real-world policy documents from the authors' home institution. To do this, we gathered over 430 policy documents in PDF format from the University Policy Office[3], as well as policy documents from the university's Health Science Center[4]. The documents described security access authorizations for a wide variety of departments, including Human Resources, Information Technology, Risk Management Services, Faculty Affairs, Administration, Intellectual Property, Technology Transfer, and Equity Development, among others. Altogether, these documents were comprised of more than 21,000 sentences. Since manually labeling the sentences is a labor-intensive process, we limited our data to a randomly-selected subset of 2,660 sentences from the pool of sentences.

The sentences were annotated for the presence of ACP content by two Ph.D. students studying cybersecurity, who are familiar with ACPs and the contexts in which they occur. The first author of this paper adjudicated any discrepancies in the annotations after discussing them with both annotators. We computed Fleiss' kappa [10] on the annotations, finding $\kappa = 0.75$ between the two annotators. According to guidelines provided by Landis' and Koch's, scores between 0.41 and 0.60 indicate moderate agreement, scores between 0.61 and 0.80 indicate substantial agreement, and scores between 0.81 to 1.00 are considered almost perfect agreement [25].

The final annotated dataset is comprised of 1,460 ACP sentences and 1,200 non-ACP sentences. This dataset is available upon request.

---

[3] https://policy.unt.edu/
[4] https://app.unthsc.edu/policies

In addition to evaluating our approach on this new dataset, we also evaluated it on the same data that has been used in previous research in this area [40], to provide a direct comparison with the state-of-the-art. These prior datasets were manually labeled by Slankas *et al.* [40], and are described as follows:

- **iTrust for ACRE:** *iTrust* is an open source healthcare application for which 40 use-cases plus additional non-functional requirements are available. Two different versions of the *iTrust* data exist; this version, *iTrust for ACRE*, was extracted directly from the project's wiki [5] [31].
- **iTrust for Text2policy:** This second version of the *iTrust* data was taken from the documentations used by Xiao *et al.* [49].
- **IBM Course Management:** This dataset is comprised of eight use-cases from the IBM Course Registration System [17].
- **CyberChair:** This dataset is comprised of the *CyberChair* documents, which have been used in a variety of contexts across 475 different conferences and workshops [47].
- **Collected ACP Documents:** This dataset is comprised of a combined document of 142 sentences collected by Xiao *et al.* [49].

5.2 Evaluation Criteria

In order to evaluate results, we use recall, precision, and the F_1 measure. Precision is the fraction of ACP sentences that are relevant, while recall is the fraction of ACP sentences that are retrieved. To compute these values, the classifier's predictions are categorized into four categories. True positives (TP) are correct predictions. True negatives (TN) are sentences that we correctly predicted as non-ACP sentence. False positives (FP) are sentences that were mistakenly identified as an ACP sentence. Finally, false negatives (FN) are ACP sentences that we failed to correctly predict as an ACP sentence. Using these values, precision is calculated using $P = \frac{TP}{TP+FP}$ and recall using $R = \frac{TP}{TP+FN}$. To have an effective model, a high value for both precision and recall is required. Lower

---

[5] http://agile.csc.ncsu.edu/iTrust/wiki/doku.php

recall means the approach could more likely miss ACP sentences while a lower precision implies that the approach could more likely identify non-ACP sentences as ACP sentences. We define F_1 as the harmonic mean of precision and recall, giving an equal weight to both elements. F_1 measure is calculated using the $F_1 = 2 \times \frac{P \times R}{P+R}$ respectively.

5.3 Experimental settings

We used our new dataset, referred to herein as ACPData, to tune all necessary parameters such as the word embedding resource type, the word vectors' length, the decay rate, and the number of LSTM cells to be included in the network. We split the dataset into separate training, development, and test sets. The training process was stopped if the resultant F_1 value did not change for 20 consecutive epochs. We set one hyper-parameter value at a time and obtained the F_1 on the development set. We used the following parameter settings as our default settings and changed them one at a time to tune the performance on the development set. These settings are: *drop-out = 0.5, decay rate = 0.5, layer size = 2*, and Word2Vec (Wikipedia) with 300 dimensions.

5.4 Word Embedding Settings

We conducted experiments to determine the best word embedding settings (i.e., word embedding method, vector length, and resource type) for our data. We used pre-trained word vectors provided by Mikolov *et al.* [32] and Pennington *et al.* [38], which were trained on the Google News and Common Crawl datasets using the Word2Vec [32] and Glove [38] methods, respectively. We also generated 300-dimensional word vectors using the Word2Vec package [32], with Wikipedia as our resource. Table 1 shows the results obtained when applying different word-embedding parameters.

F_1 (%)	Resource	Dimension
83.0	Word2vec (Wikipedia)	75
83.5	Word2vec (Wikipedia)	150
84.91	Word2vec (Wikipedia)	300
86.0	Word2vec (GoogleNews)	75
86.6	**Word2vec (GoogleNews)**	**150**
86.3	Word2vec (GoogleNews)	300
83.5	Glove	75
85.1	Glove	150
82.7	Glove	300

Table 1: Comparison of F_1 using different word embedding parameters.

As can be seen in Table 1, our model achieved its best results on the development set using the word embeddings trained on Google News with 150 dimensions; thus, we use this setting in the remainder of our experiments.

5.5 Decay Rate

Equation 12 describes how the network's connection weights are adjusted, where E represents the error and W_{ij} represents the weight matrix between two nodes, i and j.

$$w_{ij} \leftarrow w_{ij} - \eta \frac{\partial E}{\partial w_{ij}}, \qquad (12)$$

To avoid overfitting, a regularization factor was added to Equation 12 to penalize large changes in w_{ij}, thus leading to the updated Equation 13 below.

$$w_{ij} \leftarrow w_{ij} - \eta \frac{\partial E}{\partial w_{ij}} - \eta \lambda w_{ij}. \qquad (13)$$

The term $-\eta \lambda w_{ij}$ is the regularization factor, with η as the learning rate, and λ as the decay factor that causes w_{ij} to decay in scale to its prior measure.

We tuned these parameters on our development set, comparing the resultant accuracies when using different decay rates (analysis shown in Table 2). As can be seen, the accuracy of the system peaks when λ is set to 0.7. Therefore, we set $\lambda = 0.7$ in our final experiments.

F_1 (%)	λ
84.59	0.1
84.63	0.2
84.68	0.3
84.76	0.4
84.91	0.5
85.17	0.6
85.53	0.7
84.42	0.8

Table 2: Decay factor λ vs. F_1.

5.6 Dropout

Dropout regularization is one of the most common methods for regularization among approaches that incorporate deep learning [14], and is designed to diminish the network's chances of overfitting. It works by "dropping out" some of the nodes in each training iteration, by randomly assigning a value of zero to their weights. The underlying goal in doing this is to encourage the nodes in the network to become less dependent on the other nodes to which they are connected. Dropout methods were originally introduced for feed-forward and convolutional neural networks, but recently have also been applied to the input embeddings layer of some recurrent networks, including LSTMs [2, 35, 51].

Bayer *et al.* showed that standard dropout does not work effectively with RNNs due to noise magnification in the recurrent process, which consequently results in malfunctions in the learning process [2] . Therefore, instead of using standard dropout, we apply the dropout technique proposed by Zaremba *et al.* [51] for regularizing RNNs, which is used by most studies that employ LSTM models [18, 27–29, 44]. Zaremba *et al.* [51] postulate that their approach reduces overfitting on a variety of tasks, including language modeling, speech recognition, image caption generation, and machine translation. We analyzed the performance of dropout probability measures ranging from 0.0 to 0.6 on our development set to learn the best dropout probability measure to apply in our final experiments.

As is shown in Table 3, we observed that by decreasing the dropout probability measure, our system's performace in terms of F_1 increased continuously. This led us to conclude that including dropout regularization has a negative impact on accuracy for this task; thus, we chose not to use any kind of dropout in our final model.

F_1 (%)	Dropout probability
84.11	0.6
84.91	0.5
84.53	0.4
84.87	0.3
84.00	0.2
84.12	0.1
84.14	0.0

Table 3: Dropout vs. F_1.

5.7 Number of Layers

After tuning the decay rate and dropout probability, we empirically determined the number of LSTM cells to include in our model. This measure influenced the extent to which the model was able to detect relevancy between two tokens within a text (e.g., a model with only one LSTM cell would have been unable to detect relevant tokens that were distant from one another, whereas a model with too many LSTM cells would have been prone to overfitting). Table 4 illustrates the impacts of including varying numbers of LSTM cells on our system's performance on the development set.

F_1 (%)	Depth
84.37	1
84.91	2
85.68	3
85.81	4
85.98	5
85.87	6
84.7	7
83.70	8
83.12	9
82.74	10

Table 4: Number of stacked LSTM cells vs. accuracy.

In addition to tuning the aforementioned parameters, we ran several experiments to learn the impacts of varying *L2-reg, pooling,*

activation, and SGD type, and ultimately set those values as $1e-5$, *last pooling, tanh,* and *ADAM* [23], respectively. These settings were consistent with previous findings in the literature, and we did not observe significant improvements by altering these values.

5.8 Experimental Results

The settings described in the previous section were tuned using our ACPData development set. After determining the optimal parameters for identifying access policy sentences using this set, we then applied the resulting settings when evaluating the overall performance of the system using all six of the datasets described earlier (ours plus five others).

Our dataset (ACPData) includes separate training and test sets. For the smaller, pre-existing datasets, we considered each as a separate fold of data, and trained on four of the datasets while testing on the fifth (i.e., *document-fold validation*). For instance, when evaluating our model on the *iTrust for Text2Policy* dataset, we combined the *IBM Course Management, CyberChair, iTrust for ACRE,* and *Collected ACP* datasets to create a single training set. This configuration allowed us to present a fair comparison between our model and the results presented in Slankas *et al.* [40] (referred to herein as *ACRE*), which were also produced using *document-fold validation* with these datasets. In addition to ensuring a fair comparison with prior work, analyzing the performance of our model on these datasets allowed us a more comprehensive evaluation of our model on many different ACP domains. We compared the results obtained from applying our model against the results obtained from applying a support vector machine (SVM) trained on a selection of n-gram features optimized for each dataset.

Table 5 presents the individual results for (1) our dataset, (2) each of the test folds used in the document-fold validation (results shown for each of these folds were obtained using our model, not *ACRE*), and (3) the overall document-fold validation results for both *ACRE* and our model. For each of the individual datasets, the results are presented for both our model and the baseline model. As can be seen, our model outperformed the SVM approach in all cases. Furthermore, it also led to a 5.58% improvement over *ACRE*. Worthy of note is the observation that our model consistently achieved higher precision than recall. This may have been a consequence of the training sets having originated from different domains (ranging from health care to conference management), which could have allowed the model to capture a variety of patterns while forgetting unrelated ones via the forget gate (a behavior that contrasts with that of traditional classifiers). Nevertheless, in comparison to *ACRE*, our model was able to extract more comprehensive features from the text, which enabled it to extract more access control sentences while not only maintaining its precision, but actually increasing it a small amount.

5.9 Discussion

In this section, we discuss threats to validity of the proposed approach and how they can be mitigated.

The threats to external validity include lack of representativeness of datasets, SRL tools domain dependence and long-term dependency problem in RNNs. The five datasets used in previous literature covered mostly limited grammars and many of their policies were

Corpus	Precision	Recall	F_1 (Our Model)	F_1 (SVM)
ACPData	89.12	88.91	89.00	70.86
iTrust for Text2Policy	77.19	72.46	74.75	64.10
iTrust for ACRE	92.10	76.20	83.40	81.50
IBM Course Management	86.62	82.24	84.37	80.53
CyberChair	76.25	70.19	73.09	64.59
Collected ACP	74.23	69.97	72.00	34.95

Corpus (Model)	Precision	Recall	F_1
Document-Fold Validation (ACRE)	81.00	65.00	72.00
Document-Fold Validation (Our Model)	**81.28**	**74.21**	**77.58**

Table 5: Individual dataset comparisons between our model, SVM, and a comparison between our model and the method proposed by [40] (ACRE) using leave-one-out cross validation at the dataset level.

of similar structure and form, not representing the diversity of policies in real-world. To reduce the threat, we evaluated our approach on policy documents from author's home institution. These documents covered a large variety of policies ranging from Human Resources, Information Technology, Risk Management Services, Faculty Affairs, Administration, Intellectual Property, Technology Transfer, and Equity Development, among others. To further reduce this threat, additional evaluation needs to be done to choose a more representative sample of dataset, instead of choosing sentences randomly. As another external threat, a current issue with SRL tools is that they are not consistent with specific target domains such as ACP domain. This is due to the fact that they were trained on publicly available corpora such as PropBank [36], which was taken from the Wall Street Journal. This means that the predicate-argument frames are usually specific to that domain, in this case, largely financial articles. One future direction would be to explore the idea of improving SRL tool's performance using domain-related knowledge.

As the last external threat, LSTMs are specifically designed to avoid the long-term dependency problem in RNNs. However, in many cases we have some important information from the past which are not equated appropriately. One possible solution to improve current structure of the network is to consider an external memory to preserve important data [1] for longer time.

The threats to internal validity include human factors for determining correct identification of ACP sentences from natural language documents. To reduce the human factor threats, the sentences were annotated for the presence of ACP content by two Ph.D. students studying cybersecurity, who are familiar with ACPs and the contexts in which they occur. The first author of this paper adjudicated any discrepancies in the annotations after discussing them with both annotators.

6 RELATED WORK

There are notably two previous reports on identifying ACP from non-ACP sentences. These two reports sought to identify sentences containing ACPs through the use of predefined patterns or existing machine learning approaches. Xiao *et al.* proposed *Text2Policy*,

which employs shallow parsing techniques with finite state transducers to match a sentence into one of four access control patterns [49]. An example pattern is the *Modal Verb in Main Verb* group, which positively identifies sentences as ACP sentences if the main verb contains a modal verb. If a pattern is successfully matched, *Text2Policy* uses the annotated portions of the sentence to extract the subject, action, and object from the sentence. Since *Text2Policy* is rule-based, it does not require a labeled training set. However, this comes at a great cost; it misses any ACP sentence that do not follow one of its four handcrafted patterns. It has been reported that only 34.4 % of identified ACP sentences follow one of *Text2Policy*'s patterns [40].

Slankas *et al.* proposed Access Control Rule Extraction (ACRE), a supervised learning approach that uses an ensemble of classifiers (composed of k-nearest neighbors (k-NN), naïve bayes, and support vector machine classifiers) to determine whether a sentence expresses an Access Control Rule or not [40]. To determine which classifier(s) to use, they defined a threshold value of 0.6 based on the k-NN classifier's computed distance between an instance and its neighbors, and the number of words in the sentence. If the computed distance for a test instance fell below the threshold, they returned the k-NN classifier's prediction. Otherwise, the output label returned was the result of a majority vote among the three classifiers.

Other similar approaches reported high performances in classifying user reviews. Kong *et al.* presented AUTOREB, a system that automatically identifies the security and privacy-related behaviors in Android apps by analyzing user reviews [24]. AUTOREB employed state-of-the-art machine learning techniques to infer the relations between users' reviews and four categories of security-related behaviors, namely spam, financial issues, over-privileged permissions, and data leakage. To do so, they adopted a keyword-based approach. The keywords were manually selected in an iterative fashion. The initial set of keywords included "security" and "privacy," and then new key words were selected from those that had a high co-occurrence with the current set of key words. This process was iterated until no more key words were selected. The system achieved an average accuracy of 94.05% in inferring the security behaviors from user reviews. However, one issue with their system was in determining the thresholds for feature learning and classification. Determination of these thresholds generally required both domain knowledge and cross validation.

7 CONCLUSION AND FUTURE WORK

ABAC is a promising alternative to traditional models of access control (i.e., DAC, MAC and RBAC) that is drawing attention in both recent academic literature and industry. However, the cost of developing ABAC policies can be a significant obstacle for organizations to migrate from traditional access control models to ABAC. In this paper, we introduced a top-down policy engineering framework and presented our methodology to extract ABAC policies from organizations' natural language documents. We empirically determined the optimal parameters for, and subsequently applied, a deep recurrent neural network to the task of identifying sentences containing access policy content in unstructured natural language documents. Moreover, we created an annotated dataset comprised of 2660 sentences from real-world policy documents. We applied our model to this new dataset as well as to five other, smaller datasets that have been employed in prior work, and showed that our model outperformed the SVM model results and led to a performance improvement of 5.58% over the state-of-the-art. Our results provided evidence that RNNs are well-suited to the task of access control policy identification, and that they are able to automatically generate more valuable features than those that were handcrafted in prior reports. We also presented the basic idea of our prototype for extracting ABAC policies from ACP sentences. Future works include a comprehensive presentation of our framework for extracting ABAC policies in order to support features required for real-world use of ABAC systems.

REFERENCES
[1] Dzmitry Bahdanau, Kyunghyun Cho, and Yoshua Bengio. 2014. Neural machine translation by jointly learning to align and translate. *arXiv preprint arXiv:1409.0473* (2014).
[2] Justin Bayer, Christian Osendorfer, Daniela Korhammer, Nutan Chen, Sebastian Urban, and Patrick van der Smagt. 2013. On fast dropout and its applicability to recurrent networks. *arXiv preprint arXiv:1311.0701* (2013).
[3] Matthias Beckerle and Leonardo A Martucci. 2013. Formal definitions for usable access control rule sets from goals to metrics. In *Proceedings of the Ninth Symposium on Usable Privacy and Security*. ACM, 2.
[4] Yoshua Bengio, Réjean Ducharme, Pascal Vincent, and Christian Jauvin. 2003. A neural probabilistic language model. *journal of machine learning research* 3, Feb (2003), 1137–1155.
[5] Yoshua Bengio, Patrice Simard, and Paolo Frasconi. 1994. Learning long-term dependencies with gradient descent is difficult. *IEEE transactions on neural networks* 5, 2 (1994), 157–166.
[6] Steven Bethard, Zhiyong Lu, James H Martin, and Lawrence Hunter. 2008. Semantic role labeling for protein transport predicates. *BMC bioinformatics* 9, 1 (2008), 277.
[7] Ronan Collobert, Jason Weston, Léon Bottou, Michael Karlen, Koray Kavukcuoglu, and Pavel Kuksa. 2011. Natural language processing (almost) from scratch. *The Journal of Machine Learning Research* 12 (2011), 2493–2537.
[8] Li Deng, Dong Yu, and others. 2014. Deep learning: methods and applications. *Foundations and Trends® in Signal Processing* 7, 3–4 (2014), 197–387.
[9] Charles J Fillmore, Charles Wooters, and Collin F Baker. 2001. *Building a large lexical databank which provides deep semantics*. Citeseer.
[10] Joseph L Fleiss. 1971. Measuring nominal scale agreement among many raters. *Psychological bulletin* 76, 5 (1971), 378.
[11] Gartner. 2014. Market Trends: Cloud-Based Security Services Market, Worldwide. (2014). https://www.gartner.com/doc/2607617
[12] Daniel Gildea and Daniel Jurafsky. 2002. Automatic labeling of semantic roles. *Computational linguistics* 28, 3 (2002), 245–288.
[13] Alex Graves, Navdeep Jaitly, and Abdel-rahman Mohamed. 2013. Hybrid speech recognition with deep bidirectional LSTM. In *Automatic Speech Recognition and Understanding (ASRU), 2013 IEEE Workshop on*. IEEE, 273–278.

[14] Geoffrey E. Hinton, Nitish Srivastava, Alex Krizhevsky, Ilya Sutskever, and Ruslan Salakhutdinov. 2012. Improving neural networks by preventing co-adaptation of feature detectors. *CoRR* abs/1207.0580 (2012).
[15] Sepp Hochreiter. 1991. Untersuchungen zu dynamischen neuronalen Netzen. *Diploma, Technische Universität München* (1991), 91.
[16] Vincent C Hu, David Ferraiolo, Rick Kuhn, Arthur R Friedman, Alan J Lang, Margaret M Cogdell, Adam Schnitzer, Kenneth Sandlin, Robert Miller, Karen Scarfone, and others. 2013. Guide to attribute based access control (ABAC) definition and considerations (draft). *NIST special publication* 800, 162 (2013).
[17] IBM. 2004. Course Registration Requirements. (2004).
[18] Aaron Jaech, Larry Heck, and Mari Ostendorf. 2016. Domain Adaptation of Recurrent Neural Networks for Natural Language Understanding. *arXiv preprint arXiv:1604.00117* (2016).
[19] Xin Jin, Ram Krishnan, and Ravi Sandhu. 2012. A unified attribute-based access control model covering DAC, MAC and RBAC. In *IFIP Annual Conference on Data and Applications Security and Privacy*. Springer, 41–55.
[20] Dan Jurafsky and James H Martin. 2014. *Speech and language processing*. Vol. 3.
[21] Nal Kalchbrenner and Phil Blunsom. 2013. Recurrent convolutional neural networks for discourse compositionality. *arXiv preprint arXiv:1306.3584* (2013).
[22] Hamed Khanpour, Nishitha Guntakandla, and Rodney Nielsen. 2016. Dialogue Act Classification in Domain-Independent Conversations Using a Deep Recurrent Neural Network.. In *COLING*.
[23] Diederik Kingma and Jimmy Ba. 2014. Adam: A method for stochastic optimization. *arXiv preprint arXiv:1412.6980* (2014).
[24] Deguang Kong, Lei Cen, and Hongxia Jin. 2015. Autoreb: Automatically understanding the review-to-behavior fidelity in android applications. In *Proceedings of the 22nd ACM SIGSAC Conference on Computer and Communications Security*. ACM, 530–541.
[25] J Richard Landis and Gary G Koch. 1977. The measurement of observer agreement for categorical data. *biometrics* (1977), 159–174.
[26] Ji Young Lee and Franck Dernoncourt. 2016. Sequential short-text classification with recurrent and convolutional neural networks. *arXiv preprint arXiv:1603.03827* (2016).
[27] Tao Lei, Regina Barzilay, and Tommi Jaakkola. 2015. Molding CNNs for text: non-linear, non-consecutive convolutions. *arXiv preprint arXiv:1508.04112* (2015).
[28] Tao Lei, Hrishikesh Joshi, Regina Barzilay, Tommi Jaakkola, Kateryna Tymoshenko, Alessandro Moschitti, and Lluís Màrquez. 2016. Semi-supervised Question Retrieval with Gated Convolutions. In *Proceedings of the 2016 Conference of the North American Chapter of the Association for Computational Linguistics: Human Language Technologies*. Association for Computational Linguistics, San Diego, California, 1279–1289. http://www.aclweb.org/anthology/N16-1153
[29] Liang Lu, Lingpeng Kong, Chris Dyer, Noah A Smith, and Steve Renals. 2016. Segmental Recurrent Neural Networks for End-to-end Speech Recognition. *arXiv preprint arXiv:1603.00223* (2016).
[30] Christopher D Manning, Mihai Surdeanu, John Bauer, Jenny Rose Finkel, Steven Bethard, and David McClosky. 2014. The stanford corenlp natural language processing toolkit. In *ACL (System Demonstrations)*. 55–60.
[31] Andrew Meneely, Ben Smith, and Laurie Williams. 2011. iTrust Electronic Health Care System: A Case Study. *Software and Systems Traceability* (2011).
[32] Tomas Mikolov, Kai Chen, Greg Corrado, and Jeffrey Dean. 2013. Efficient estimation of word representations in vector space. *arXiv preprint arXiv:1301.3781* (2013).
[33] Tomas Mikolov, Martin Karafiát, Lukas Burget, Jan Cernocký, and Sanjeev Khudanpur. 2010. Recurrent neural network based language model.. In *Interspeech*, Vol. 2. 3.
[34] Masoud Narouei and Hassan Takabi. 2015. Towards an Automatic Top-down Role Engineering Approach Using Natural Language Processing Techniques. In *Proceedings of the 20th ACM Symposium on Access Control Models and Technologies*. ACM, 157–160.
[35] Marius Pachitariu and Maneesh Sahani. 2013. Regularization and nonlinearities for neural language models: when are they needed? *arXiv preprint arXiv:1301.5650* (2013).
[36] Martha Palmer, Daniel Gildea, and Paul Kingsbury. 2005. The proposition bank: An annotated corpus of semantic roles. *Computational linguistics* 31, 1 (2005), 71–106.
[37] Razvan Pascanu, Tomas Mikolov, and Yoshua Bengio. 2013. On the difficulty of training recurrent neural networks. *ICML (3)* 28 (2013), 1310–1318.
[38] Jeffrey Pennington, Richard Socher, and Christopher D Manning. 2014. Glove: Global Vectors for Word Representation.. In *EMNLP*, Vol. 14. 1532–1543.
[39] Suman Ravuri and Andreas Stoicke. 2015. A comparative study of neural network models for lexical intent classification. In *Automatic Speech Recognition and Understanding (ASRU), 2015 IEEE Workshop on*. IEEE, 368–374.
[40] John Slankas, Xusheng Xiao, Laurie Williams, and Tao Xie. 2014. Relation extraction for inferring access control rules from natural language artifacts. In *Proceedings of the 30th Annual Computer Security Applications Conference*. ACM, 366–375.
[41] Richard Socher, Alex Perelygin, Jean Y Wu, Jason Chuang, Christopher D Manning, Andrew Y Ng, and Christopher Potts. 2013. Recursive deep models for

semantic compositionality over a sentiment treebank. In *Proceedings of the conference on empirical methods in natural language processing (EMNLP)*, Vol. 1631. Citeseer, 1642.

[42] Andreas Stolcke, Klaus Ries, Noah Coccaro, Elizabeth Shriberg, Rebecca Bates, Daniel Jurafsky, Paul Taylor, Rachel Martin, Carol Van Ess-Dykema, and Marie Meteer. 2000. Dialogue act modeling for automatic tagging and recognition of conversational speech. *Computational linguistics* 26, 3 (2000), 339–373.

[43] Ilya Sutskever, Oriol Vinyals, and Quoc V Le. 2014. Sequence to sequence learning with neural networks. In *Advances in neural information processing systems*. 3104–3112.

[44] Swabha Swayamdipta, Miguel Ballesteros, Chris Dyer, and Noah A Smith. 2016. Greedy, Joint Syntactic-Semantic Parsing with Stack LSTMs. *arXiv preprint arXiv:1606.08954* (2016).

[45] Kai Sheng Tai, Richard Socher, and Christopher D Manning. 2015. Improved semantic representations from tree-structured long short-term memory networks. *arXiv preprint arXiv:1503.00075* (2015).

[46] Joseph Turian, Lev Ratinov, and Yoshua Bengio. 2010. Word representations: a simple and general method for semi-supervised learning. In *Proceedings of the 48th annual meeting of the association for computational linguistics*. Association for Computational Linguistics, 384–394.

[47] Richard Van De Stadt. 2012. Cyberchair: A web-based groupware application to facilitate the paper reviewing process. *arXiv preprint arXiv:1206.1833* (2012).

[48] Tsung-Hsien Wen, Milica Gasic, Nikola Mrksic, Pei-Hao Su, David Vandyke, and Steve Young. 2015. Semantically conditioned lstm-based natural language generation for spoken dialogue systems. *arXiv preprint arXiv:1508.01745* (2015).

[49] Xusheng Xiao, Amit Paradkar, Suresh Thummalapenta, and Tao Xie. 2012. Automated extraction of security policies from natural-language software documents. In *Proceedings of the ACM SIGSOFT 20th International Symposium on the Foundations of Software Engineering*. ACM, 12.

[50] Zhongyuan Xu and Scott D Stoller. 2015. Mining attribute-based access control policies. *IEEE Transactions on Dependable and Secure Computing* 12, 5 (2015), 533–545.

[51] Wojciech Zaremba, Ilya Sutskever, and Oriol Vinyals. 2014. Recurrent neural network regularization. *arXiv preprint arXiv:1409.2329* (2014).

Poster: A Location-Privacy Approach for Continuous Queries

Doug Steiert
Department of Computer Science
Missouri University of Science and Technology
djsg38@mst.edu

Dan Lin
Department of Computer Science
Missouri University of Science and Technology
lindan@mst.edu

Quincy Conduff
Department of Computer Science
Missouri University of Science and Technology
qlcfz5@mst.edu

Wei Jiang
Department of Computer Science
Missouri University of Science and Technology
wjiang@mst.edu

ABSTRACT

With the prevalence of smartphones, mobile apps have become more and more popular. However, many mobile apps request location information of the user. If there is nothing in place for location privacy, these mobile app users are in great risk of being tracked by malicious parties. Although the location privacy problem has been studied extensively by resorting to a third-party location anonymizer, there is very little work that allows the users to fully control the disclosure of their data using their smartphones alone. In this paper, we propose a novel Android App called MoveWithMe which automatically generates mocking locations. Most importantly, these mocking locations are not random like those generated by original Android location mocking function. The proposed MoveWithMe app generates k traces of mocking locations and ensures that each trace looks like a trace of a real human and each trace is semantically different from the real user's trace.

ACM Reference format:
Doug Steiert, Dan Lin, Quincy Conduff, and Wei Jiang. 2017. Poster: A Location-Privacy Approach for Continuous Queries. In *Proceedings of SACMAT'17, Indianapolis, IN, USA, June 21-23, 2017,* 3 pages.
https://doi.org/http://dx.doi.org/10.1145/3078861.3084161

1 INTRODUCTION

Smartphones are a driving force in many actions that we do every day, and the number of smartphone owners has increased tremendously since their release. In correlation, the number of mobile phone applications have also exponentially risen alongside the growth of smartphone usage. A popular array of services that are combined with applications (apps) are known as Location Based Services (LBSs). While many users typically do not explicitly recognize these services being used, they are also unaware of the risks that are associated with them. In [1], Almuhimed et al. have conducted a field study on mobile app privacy and their findings show severe concerns on location privacy, e.g. someone's location has been shared 5,398 times with 10 apps within 14 days without being noticed by the user. Such loose control on location data by existing mobile apps has caused different types of privacy threats.

To mitigate risks to users' location-privacy, several strategies have been proposed. One typical approach is to add an access control mechanism to control the location disclosure to the selected service providers, such as the location privacy settings in iOS and Android systems. However, such access control does not prevent service providers which have been granted access permissions from tracking the users. In order to provide better privacy protection, some approaches [5] are proposed based on the spatial-temporal cloaking or k-anonymity. The basic idea is to let the user submit a bigger region instead of the exact location when requesting location-based services. Unfortunately, such strategies also have limitations. First, it trades-in the service quality since some types of services require accurate locations. For example, if a user would like to find nearby restaurants but tells the server his location at the city level, it would return all the restaurants in the city rather than just those near the user. There is a deeper issue in existing spatial-cloaking-based approaches, which is the lack of defense from attacks using aggregated information collected via continuous queries. For example, when someone uses an LBS constantly or frequently as he/she moves, the service provider may be able to narrow down possible places that the user visited and the user's moving direction.

In this research, we propose a novel location-privacy preservation app that is able to preserve smartphone users' location privacy. The main idea is to generate decoys that behave like real human movements and submit these decoys' locations to the service providers, along with the user's real locations. The goal is to prevent the service provider from profiling the real user. An overview of this approach is presented in Section 3.

2 RELATED WORK

Various approaches have been proposed to preserve location privacy, which can be classified into three main categories: (i) spatial-temporal cloaking based approaches; (ii) differential privacy based approaches; and (iii) encryption-based approaches.

The key idea of spatial-temporal cloaking is to generate a cloaking region that contains the user's real location and $k-1$ other users. In this way, the service provider would not be able to distinguish the k users in the same region and hence users achieve k-anonymity. The idea was first introduced by Gruteser et al. [7] and later has been extended by many [4, 14]. However, such approach suffers from the utility loss since users' queries would be based on the fuzzy locations and would no longer be accurate. To achieve 100% query accuracy while cloaking the user's locations, Lin et al. [13] propose to use geo-transformation that converts user's real locations into a set of fake locations by multiple agents in-between the user and the server. The main limitation of the approach is that it only supports LBSs that query on moving objects but not any static objects like restaurants. More recently, Zang and Bolot [21] propose to publish shorter trajectories at a coarse granularity to prevent correlation of information obtained from call detail records with the users' true locations. However, such published trajectories will have little data utility.

The differential privacy based approaches add noise to the users' real data so that the providers would not know the true user locations. Andres et al. apply Laplacian noise to location data in a discrete Cartesian plane in [2]. Users are able to adjust the level of desired privacy, which increases the amount of noise added to the location. However, the downfall to this work is that the area of interest may not fall into the area once noise is added. The authors in [16] look at using k-anonymity to try to traverse the adversary's malicious attempts. By using dummy-location selection based on the entropy of locations, the user is more likely to be hidden. However, the region in which this location selection is performed might not be big enough to hide the user, especially if the adversary has background knowledge. Also, the proposed approach does not support continuous location-based queries. Differential privacy is also used in [15], in which Ngo and Kim reduce the average size of cloaking regions generated by the Hilbert curve. Chen et al. propose LISA in [3], which does not rely on a trusted third party for anonymization. LISA's core algorithm is based on unobservability along with a Kalman filter to adjust noise to location data. The limitation of LISA is that injecting noise to a location multiple times may lead the location to converge back to its original value. To sum up, a common limitation in all the differential privacy based approaches is that they trade in the service quality since they are not able to provide exact query results.

The encryption-based approaches aim to fully preserve the location privacy by encrypting the location data and conducting queries directly on the encrypted data. One representative work is by Ghinita et al. [6] who propose a framework to support private nearest neighbor queries based on Private Information Retrieval. In [12], Li and Jung devise a privacy-preserving location query protocol in which the locations of users are shared based on a condition-matching system. Location data is encrypted using Pallier encryption to ensure data security. Yet, this work requires an anonymized network which is currently unavailable for smartphones. Guha et al. [8] introduce a privacy-preserving framework which provides a cloud-based matching service to return attributes and their values in an encrypted fashion. Puttaswamy et al. [18] attempt to preserve location privacy in geo-social applications. Their work relies on the exchanging of secrets in order to encrypt/decrypt using 128-bit AES. However, they are oblivious to man-in-the-middle attacks during the exchange, and an adversary may easily discover those key values. Combining oblivious transfer and private information retrieval, Paulet et al. [17] aim to enable efficient processing of location queries. However, all the prior encryption-based approaches are typically too costly to be applied in practice.

Although there have been extensive studies on location privacy, very few have been devoted into developing mobile apps for users to control their locations. For example, in [9], Hornyack et al. implement a system which returns a fixed location and phone number at all times. While this can ensure privacy for the user, that user will never be able to enjoy most utilities of LBSs. Shokri et al. [19] devise a collaborative approach that allows peer users to form MobiCrowd. When a user needs to contact an LBS, his/her request will not be directly sent to the server but be routed through the MobiCrowd. In this way, the service provider will not know who sent the query. However, such strategy falls short when there are not enough users nearby. Most recently, Fawaz et al. [5] conducted a detailed risk analysis of the use of mobile apps in terms of location privacy leak. They propose an app called LP-Doctor which allows users to adjust the amount of location information to be disclosed to various apps. Compared to existing works, our proposed MoveWithMe is unique in the following aspects. First, it is not constrained by people density and can be used at any time. Second, it ensures the service quality in that the user is able to obtain the same query result. Third, it introduces very little overhead as evaluated in our experiments.

3 OUR PROPOSED ALGORITHM

Our proposed app is called MoveWithMe since it automatically generates a number of decoys to move with the user and serve as distractions to the service providers. Figure 1 shows an example use case, whereby Fig. 1(a) depicts the real user (say Bob)'s trajectory and Fig. 1(b) and (c) depict two decoys' trajectories. Specifically, assume that Bob wants to access a location-based service app (e.g., Yelp) when he is at the golf course at Rolla in the morning. As soon as Bob opens Yelp, the MoveWithMe will be activated and immediately generate two decoys, Decoy I and Decoy II as shown in the figure. Decoy I is visiting a department store in Chesterfield while Decoy II is in a physics class in a university in Columbia. The number of decoys can be set according to the user's privacy needs. By intercepting the user's interaction with Yelp, MoveWithMe will send the three locations to Yelp, as well. As time passes, Bob accessed the location-based services, when he went to his research lab and then to the fast food restaurant and the gas station. Meanwhile, one of its decoys would have visited a bank, a movie theater and a hotel, and the other decoy would have visited a pizza place, a hospital and a park. Observe that these three traces are not only located in different cities, but also demonstrate different social behaviors. In this way, it would be challenging for the service provider to identify the real user's trajectory and profile the real user without additional knowledge.

At the first look, our approach may seem to resemble the traditional use of dummy trajectories. However, our algorithms to generate dummy trajectories are fundamentally different. Traditional dummy trajectories [11, 16, 20] are geographically close to the real trajectory, and adversaries may still be able to discover the real user movement pattern using some pattern mining technique as reported in [10]. In our system, we are generating decoys which are not only geographically, but also semantically different from the real user's trajectory. Last but not the least, unlike the previous dummy trajectory works which are mostly developed at a theoretical level and rely on a central server, our system is more practical.

Poster: A Location-Privacy Approach for Continuous Queries   SACMAT'17, June 21-23, 2017, Indianapolis, IN, USA

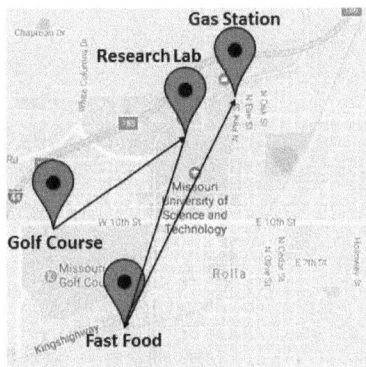

(a) Real User's Trajectory

(b) Decoy I's trajectory

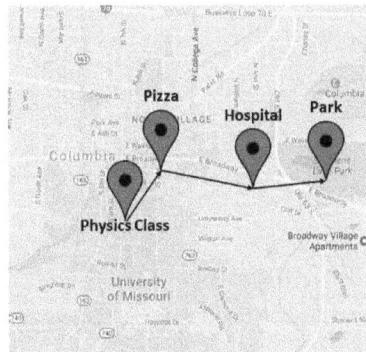

(c) Decoy II's trajectory

Figure 1: An Example of Decoy Generation in the MoveWithMe App

The proposed MoveWithMe system is designed as an Android app that is capable of providing the privacy preservation for users at the real time.

ACKNOWLEDGMENTS

This work is supported by the National Science Foundation under Grant No: DGE-1433659.

REFERENCES

[1] Hazim Almuhimedi, Florian Schaub, Norman Sadeh, Idris Adjerid, Alessandro Acquisti, Joshua Gluck, Lorrie Faith Cranor, and Yuvraj Agarwal. Your location has been shared 5,398 times!: A field study on mobile app privacy nudging. In *Proceedings of the 33rd Annual ACM Conference on Human Factors in Computing Systems*, pages 787–796. ACM, 2015.

[2] Miguel E. Andrés, Nicolás E. Bordenabe, Konstantinos Chatzikokolakis, and Catuscia Palamidessi. Geo-indistinguishability: Differential privacy for location-based systems. In *Proceedings of the 2013 ACM SIGSAC Conference on Computer & Communications Security*, CCS '13, pages 901–914, New York, NY, USA, 2013. ACM.

[3] Zhigang Chen, Xin Hu, Xiaoen Ju, and K. G. Shin. Lisa: Location information scrambler for privacy protection on smartphones. In *2013 IEEE Conference on Communications and Network Security (CNS)*, pages 296–304, Oct 2013.

[4] R. Cheng, Y. Zhang, E. Bertino, and S. Prabhakar. Preserving user location privacy in mobile data management infrastructures. In *Proc. Workshop on Privacy Enhancing Technologies*, 2006.

[5] Kassem Fawaz, Huan Feng, and Kang G. Shin. Anatomization and protection of mobile apps' location privacy threats. In *Proceedings of the 24th USENIX Conference on Security Symposium*, SEC'15, pages 753–768, Berkeley, CA, USA, 2015. USENIX Association.

[6] Gabriel Ghinita, Panos Kalnis, Ali Khoshgozaran, Cyrus Shahabi, and Kian-Lee Tan. Private queries in location based services: anonymizers are not necessary. In *Proceedings of the 2008 ACM SIGMOD international conference on Management of data*, pages 121–132. ACM, 2008.

[7] M. Gruteser and D. Grunwald. Anonymous usage of location-based services through spatial and temporal cloaking. In *Proc. MobiSys*, pages 31–42, 2003.

[8] Saikat Guha, Mudit Jain, and Venkata N. Padmanabhan. Koi: A location-privacy platform for smartphone apps. In *Proceedings of the 9th USENIX Conference on Networked Systems Design and Implementation*, NSDI'12, pages 14–14, Berkeley, CA, USA, 2012. USENIX Association.

[9] Peter Hornyack, Seungyeop Han, Jaeyeon Jung, Stuart Schechter, and David Wetherall. These aren't the droids you're looking for: Retrofitting android to protect data from imperious applications. In *Proceedings of the 18th ACM Conference on Computer and Communications Security*, CCS '11, pages 639–652, 2011.

[10] Po-Ruey Lei, Wen-Chih Peng, Ing-Jiunn Su, and Chien-Ping Chang. Dummy-based schemes for protecting movement trajectories. *Journal of Information Science and Engineering*, 28(2):335–350, 2012.

[11] Po-Ruey Lei, Wen-Chih Peng, Ing-Jiunn Su, Chien-Ping Chang, et al. Dummy-based schemes for protecting movement trajectories. *Journal of Information Science and Engineering*, 28(2):335–350, 2012.

[12] X. Y. Li and T. Jung. Search me if you can: Privacy-preserving location query service. In *2013 Proceedings IEEE INFOCOM*, pages 2760–2768, April 2013.

[13] Dan Lin, Elisa Bertino, Reynold Cheng, and Sunil Prabhakar. Location privacy in moving-object environments. *Transactions on Data Privacy*, 2(1):21–46, 2009.

[14] M. F. Mokbel, C. Y. Chow, and W. G. Aref. The new casper: Query processing for location services without compromising privacy. In *Proc. VLDB*, pages 763–774, 2006.

[15] H. Ngo and J. Kim. Location privacy via differential private perturbation of cloaking area. In *2015 IEEE 28th Computer Security Foundations Symposium*, pages 63–74, July 2015.

[16] B. Niu, Q. Li, X. Zhu, G. Cao, and H. Li. Achieving k-anonymity in privacy-aware location-based services. In *IEEE INFOCOM 2014 - IEEE Conference on Computer Communications*, pages 754–762, April 2014.

[17] Russell Paulet, Md. Golam Koasar, Xun Yi, and Elisa Bertino. Privacy-preserving and content-protecting location based queries. In *Proceedings of the 2012 IEEE 28th International Conference on Data Engineering*, ICDE '12, pages 44–53, Washington, DC, USA, 2012. IEEE Computer Society.

[18] Krishna P. N. Puttaswamy, Shiyuan Wang, Troy Steinbauer, Divyakant Agrawal, Amr El Abbadi, Christopher Kruegel, and Ben Y. Zhao. Preserving location privacy in geosocial applications. *IEEE Transactions on Mobile Computing*, 13(1):159–173, January 2014.

[19] R. Shokri, G. Theodorakopoulos, P. Papadimitratos, E. Kazemi, and J. P. Hubaux. Hiding in the mobile crowd: Locationprivacy through collaboration. *IEEE Transactions on Dependable and Secure Computing*, 11(3):266–279, May 2014.

[20] Tun-Hao You, Wen-Chih Peng, and Wang-Chien Lee. Protecting moving trajectories with dummies. In *8th International Conference on Mobile Data Management (MDM)*, pages 278–282, 2007.

[21] Hui Zang and Jean Bolot. Anonymization of location data does not work: A large-scale measurement study. In *Proceedings of the 17th Annual International Conference on Mobile Computing and Networking*, MobiCom '11, pages 145–156, New York, NY, USA, 2011. ACM.

Poster: Design of an Anomaly-based Threat Detection & Explication System

Robert Luh
Josef Ressel Center TARGET,
St. Pölten UAS, Austria
& De Montfort University Leicester
Leicester, UK

Sebastian Schrittwieser
Josef Ressel Center TARGET
St. Pölten UAS
St. Pölten, Austria

Stefan Marschalek
Josef Ressel Center TARGET
St. Pölten UAS
St. Pölten, Austria

Helge Janicke
De Montfort University Leicester
Leicester, UK

Edgar Weippl
SBA Research
Vienna, Austria

ABSTRACT

The poster corresponding to this summary depicts a proposition of a system able to explain anomalous behavior within a user session by considering anomalies identified through their deviation from a set of baseline process graphs. We adapt star structures, a bipartite representation used to approximate the edit distance between two graphs. Relevant processes are selected from a dictionary of benign and malicious traces generated through a sentiment-like bigram extraction and scoring system based on the log likelihood ratio test. We prototypically implemented smart anomaly explication through a number of competency questions derived and evaluated by a decision tree. The determined key factors are ultimately mapped to a dedicated APT attack stage ontology that considers actions, actors, as well as target assets.

CCS CONCEPTS

•Security and privacy → **Intrusion/anomaly detection and malware mitigation;** •Mathematics of computing → *Graph algorithms;*

KEYWORDS

Intrusion detection, malware, anomaly, behavioral analysis, knowledge generation, graph

ACM Reference format:
Robert Luh, Sebastian Schrittwieser, Stefan Marschalek, Helge Janicke, and Edgar Weippl. 2017. Poster: Design of an Anomaly-based Threat Detection
& Explication System. In *Proceedings of SACMAT'17, June 21–23, 2017, Indianapolis, IN, USA, , 2 pages.*
DOI: http://dx.doi.org/10.1145/3078861.3084162

The financial support by the Austrian Federal Ministry of Science, Research and Economy and the National Foundation for Research, Technology and Development is gratefully acknowledged.

1 INTRODUCTION

The system introduced on the corresponding poster to the original paper published at ICISSP 2017 [7] is designed to primarily combat advanced persistent threats (APTs) and the malicious software utilized by this class of cyber-attacks. APTs are highly targeted to one specific entity (organization, system, device) and usually cause significantly more damage than bulk attacks in terms of privacy breaches, or monetary damage. APTs increasingly affect less prominent targets; 60% of APTs target small and medium businesses in retail, finance, and healthcare sectors. Today's threat mitigation strategies such as signature-based detection systems are not effective against these attacks.

For threat definition and initial modeling we use an adapted version of the Cyber Kill Chain [2] combined with our own APT ontology [6]. This ontology models actors and assets, APT attack stages (from reconnaissance to actions on objective), individual attack actions and their semantic description, as well as events and anomalies that can be captured by various data providers.

2 SYSTEM DESIGN

Figure 1 depicts the proposed system and its components. There are six stages in the process of collecting, processing, and analyzing the potentially malicious behavioral data:

Data collection – Surveying several data providers [4], we designed a kernel driver able to capture various events in a Microsoft Windows environment: Process, thread, file, registry, image load operations, and network events are captured. This is complemented by a Netflow component.

Event linking – Events are linked by their process ID (PID) and thread ID (TID) as well as their timestamps, creating "smart traces" that consider process and thread context while retaining most of their internal chronology. Mimicry attacks are largely prevented.

Grammar inference – Sequitur is used to infer rules frequently seen in the trace [5]. This step includes lossless recursive compression and the application of a semantic labeling mechanism for inferred rules (i.e. compound events).

Sentiment mining – We use an approach akin to sentiment mining to identify relevant OS processes [9] to determine likely trace event pairs using the log likelihood ratio test. After learning a set of bigrams typically found in benign and malicious scenarios, we compile a dictionary and apply scoring to generate knowledge and

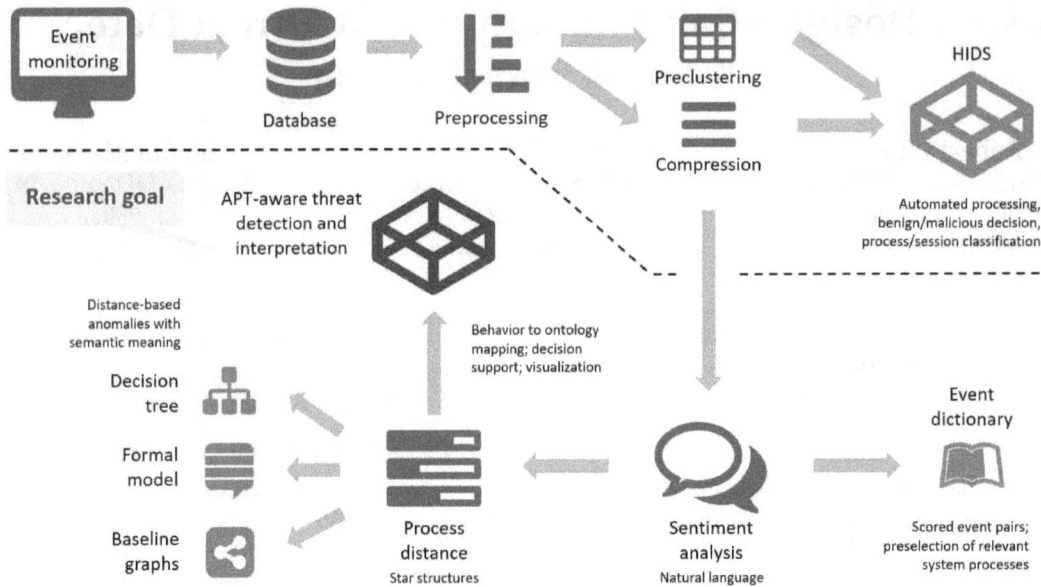

Figure 1: APT detection & explication system processing stages

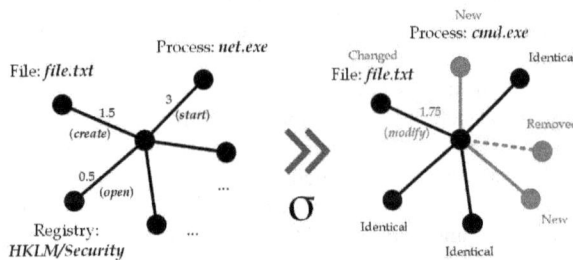

Figure 2: Transformation σ of baseline to target graph for example svchost.exe process [7]

ultimately determine which processes, event types and parameters contribute most to the good/bad decision.

Star construction – Events are broken down to star structures [1] $G = (U, V, E)$, where U and V are nodes and E is the respective edge. The edge label describes the basic operation. Both are used for minimal cost calculation based on bipartite graph matching using the Kuhn-Munkres algorithm [3]. For example: $G(svchost.exe, 1.5, file.txt)$ describes the creation of a file by OS process svchost.exe; edit operations σ are determined by type of event and type of operation E (create, modify, delete).

Anomaly detection & explication – Baseline templates for benign/known process behavior are created using Malheur heuristic clustering [8]. This automatically determines prototypes and value thresholds for anomaly detection. New traces are checked against these templates and the edit distance is calculated (see Figure 2).

Anomaly explication is two-pronged: Deviating events such as new processes, altered file operations, and the like are summarized in a human-readable report. These reports are then fed to a decision tree rooted in the six APT categories, sans weaponization [2].

3 CONCLUSION

The introduced star structure-based anomaly explication system is able to detect and interpret anomalous deviations in operating system process behavior. The returned output of detailed state changes as well as a tendency towards a specific APT stage or action is expressed through the mapping of semantic key factors to a dedicated attack ontology. The process was prototypically implemented and successfully tested using real-world process data captured on several company workstations. Please refer to [7] and the poster for additional information.

REFERENCES

[1] Xin Hu, Tzi-cker Chiueh, and Kang G Shin. 2009. Large-scale malware indexing using function-call graphs. In *16th conference on Computer and communications security*. ACM, 611–620.
[2] Eric M. Hutchins, Michael J. Cloppert, and Rohan M. Amin. 2011. Intelligence-driven computer network defense informed by analysis of adversary campaigns and intrusion kill chains. *Leading Issues in Information Warfare & Security Research* 1 (2011), 80.
[3] Harold W Kuhn. 1955. The Hungarian method for the assignment problem. *Naval research logistics quarterly* 2, 1-2 (1955), 83–97.
[4] Robert Luh, Stefan Marschalek, Manfred Kaiser, Helge Janicke, and Sebastian Schrittwieser. 2016. Semantics-aware detection of targeted attacks: a survey. *Journal of Computer Virology and Hacking Techniques* (2016), 1–39.
[5] Robert Luh, Gregor Schramm, Markus Wagner, and Sebastian Schrittwieser. 2017. Sequitur-based Inference and Analysis Framework for Malicious System Behavior. In *1st International Workshop on FORmal methods for Security Engineering, ICISSP*. https://doi.org/10.5220/0006250206320643
[6] Robert Luh, Sebastian Schrittwieser, and Stefan Marschalek. 2016. TAON: An ontology-based approach to mitigating targeted attacks. In *iiWAS 2016*. ACM.
[7] Robert Luh, Sebastian Schrittwieser, Stefan Marschalek, and Helge Janicke. 2017. Design of an Anomaly-based Threat Detection & Explication System. In *Proceedings of the 3rd International Conference on Information Systems Security and Privacy*. 397–402. https://doi.org/10.5220/0006205203970402
[8] Konrad Rieck, Philipp Trinius, Carsten Willems, and Thorsten Holz. 2011. *Automatic analysis of malware behavior using machine learning*. Journal of Computer Security.
[9] Sebastian Schrittwieser Robert Luh and Stefan Marschalek. 2017. LLR-based sentiment analysis for kernel event sequences. In *31st IEEE International Conference on Advanced Information Networking and Applications (AINA)*.

Poster: Constrained Policy Mining in Attribute Based Access Control

Mayank Gautam
IIT Kharagpur, India
gautamayank@gmail.com

Sadhana Jha
IIT Kharagpur, India
sadhanajha@iitkgp.ac.in

Shamik Sural
IIT Kharagpur, India
shamik@cse.iitkgp.ernet.in

Jaideep Vaidya
Rutgers University, USA
jsvaidya@business.rutgers.edu

Vijayalakshmi Atluri
Rutgers University, USA
atluri@rutgers.edu

ABSTRACT

In practical access control systems, it is important to enforce an upper bound on the time taken to respond to an access request. This response time is directly influenced by the size (often called the *weight*) of each of the underlying access control rules. We present a constrained policy mining algorithm which takes an access control matrix as input and generates a set of attribute based access control (ABAC) rules, such that the weight of each rule is not more than a specified value and the sum of weights of all the rules is minimized. Our initial experiments show encouraging results.

CCS CONCEPTS

• **Security and privacy** → **Access control**; *Authorization;*

KEYWORDS

ABAC, Policy mining, Constraint, Weight

ACM Reference format:
Mayank Gautam, Sadhana Jha, Shamik Sural, Jaideep Vaidya, and Vijayalakshmi Atluri. 2017. Poster: Constrained Policy Mining in Attribute
Based Access Control. In *Proceedings of SACMAT'17, June 21–23, 2017, Indianapolis, IN, USA, , 3 pages.*
DOI: http://dx.doi.org/10.1145/3078861.3084163

1 INTRODUCTION

Over the past few years, attribute based access control (ABAC) [5] has gained increasing importance due to its ability to unify most of the other access control models and its promise to facilitate ad-hoc and dynamic collaboration among multiple domains. Further, traditional access control models such as discretionary access control (DAC), which uses an access control matrix (ACM), and role-based access control (RBAC) [4], which uses the notion of roles, have been shown to be ineffective in handling fine grained access control,

thus generating an urgent need for existing organizations to migrate to ABAC.

The first step towards this is to create an appropriate set of ABAC rules (collectively called the ABAC policy of the organization). Each rule comprises a set of user, object and environmental attribute name-value pairs along with the name of an operation the rule permits. Granularity of access decision can be controlled by varying the number of attributes considered in such rules. However, adding more number of attributes affects the time needed to evaluate each rule when an access request is made. It also renders the ABAC policy unsuitable for automated security analysis. The organization, therefore, would like to limit the *weight* of each rule, which is a function of its size.

Keeping the above mentioned requirement in mind, we propose a constrained policy mining algorithm that takes an ACM as input and generates a minimal set of ABAC rules with a constraint on the maximum weight for each individual rule. Here, minimality is in terms of the total weight of all the rules. While there is some work reported in the literature on an unconstrained version of the problem [1], [6], and also on constrained versions of role mining in the context of RBAC [3], to the best of our knowledge, this is the first ever attempt towards formulating and solving ABAC policy mining under constraints.

2 ABAC POLICY SPECIFICATION

An ABAC system consists of a pre-defined set of user attributes ($\mathcal{U}_a$) and object attributes ($\mathcal{O}_a$). We leave aside environmental attributes for the sake of brevity. The proposed approach can be easily extended to include those as well. The possible set of values an attribute $a \in \{\mathcal{U}_a \cup \mathcal{O}_a\}$ can acquire is denoted as $V(a)$. $UAV(u, a) \in V(a)$ denotes the value of the attribute a for a given user u. OAV is defined similarly for objects.

The set of attribute name-value pairs associated with a user u and an object o are represented as $\mathcal{A}_u$ and $\mathcal{A}_o$, respectively. For instance, consider a user named *Tom* who is an adult and has premium membership in an online movie viewing application. This is represented as $\mathcal{A}_{Tom} = \{\text{ageGroup} = adult, \text{memberType} = premium\}$. An ABAC rule is of the form $\langle UC, OC, OP \rangle$, where UC, OC and OP respectively represent a set of user attribute name-value pairs, object attribute name-value pairs and the name of an operation. For instance, a rule of the form $\langle \{memberType = premium\}, \{release = recent\}, view \rangle$ conveys that any *premium* member can *view* movies released *recently*. . Each rule r is assigned a weight W, which can be defined in various ways. In this paper, we consider it to be the count of the total number of elements in r. For instance, for the rule given above, $W(r) = 3$. For a complete ABAC policy P comprised of a set of ABAC rules, the total weight, $TW(P)$ is the sum of the weights of the individual rules in P, i.e., $TW(P) = \sum_{r \in P} W(r)$.

3 CONSTRAINED ABAC POLICY MINING

The input for policy mining is an ACM, whose rows and columns represent users and objects, respectively. A cell (u, o) of the ACM stores the permission p that a user u has on an object o, and is denoted as (u, o, p).

3.1 Problem Definition

Definition 3.1. Constrained ABAC Policy Mining Problem (CAPM): Given an access control matrix UP, user attributes $\mathcal{U}_a$, object attributes $\mathcal{O}_a$, user attribute assignments UAV, object attribute assignments OAV and an integer value c, generate a set P of ABAC rules such that the following conditions are satisfied: (i) each entry in UP is covered by some rule $r \in P$ (ii) no user gets any extra permission, which is not present in UP through some rule $r \in P$ (iii) for each rule $r \in P$, $W(r) \leq c$, and (iv) $TW(P)$ is minimum.

3.2 Complexity Analysis of CAPM

To determine the complexity class of CAPM, we first define D_CAPM, the decision version of CAPM.

Definition 3.2. D_CAPM: Given $\mathcal{U}_a$, $\mathcal{O}_a$, UAV, OAV, UP and two integer values c and k, does there exist a set P of ABAC rules such that the rules in P together cover all $(u, o, p) \in UP$, and for each $r \in P$, $W(r) \leq c$ and $TW(P) \leq k$.

THEOREM 3.3. *D_CAPM is NP-complete*

PROOF. To prove D_CAPM is NP-complete, we show that D_CAPM is in NP and it is NP-hard.

D_CAPM is in NP: Suppose a certificate comprising $\mathcal{U}_a$, $\mathcal{O}_a$, UAV, OAV, UP along with a set P of ABAC rules and two integer values c and k are given and it is claimed that the rules in P together cover all $(u, o, p) \in UP$, for each rule $r \in P$, $W(r) \leq c$ and $TW(P) \leq k$. This claim can be easily verified by computing the weight of each rule in P, the total weight $TW(P)$ and searching a rule corresponding to each entry in the given UP. The above verification can be done in polynomial time. Thus, D_CAPM is in NP.

D_CAPM is NP-hard: We show that D_CAPM is NP-hard by reducing the decision version of unconstrained ABAC policy mining problem (D_APM), which is known to be NP-complete [6], to D_CAPM. D_APM can be stated as: Given a set of user attributes $\mathcal{U}'_a$, object attributes $\mathcal{O}'_a$, user attribute assignments UAV', object attribute assignments OAV' and an access control matrix UP', does there exist a set P' of ABAC rules such that the rules in P' together cover all $(u, o, p) \in UP'$. Given an instance $\langle \mathcal{U}'_a, \mathcal{O}'_a, UAV', OAV', UP' \rangle$ of D_APM, the steps for reducing it to a D_CAPM instance $\langle \mathcal{U}_a, \mathcal{O}_a, UAV, OAV, UP, c \rangle$ are as follows:
- set $\mathcal{U}_a = \mathcal{U}'_a$, $\mathcal{O}_a = \mathcal{O}'_a$, $UAV = UAV'$, $OAV = OAV'$
- set $UP = UP'$ and set c as a very large number

The above reduction can be done in polynomial time. Also, a *yes* (respectively *no*) answer to the constructed *D_CAPM* instance gives a *yes* (respectively *no*) answer to the *D_APM* instance. Hence, D_CAPM is NP-hard. Since, D_CAPM is NP-hard and is in NP, it is NP-complete. □

3.3 Solving CAPM using Constrained Weighted Set Cover Heuristic

Showing D_CAPM to be NP-complete in the last sub-section implies that one is not likely to find an efficient solution for CAPM. We, therefore, develop a heuristic solution for CAPM by mapping it to a variant of the well-known set cover problem. A constrained weighted set cover problem (CWSC) [2] can be defined as follows: Given a universal set U, a collection S of subsets of U, a function f that assigns a positive integer weight to each set $s \in S$, and an integer k, find a minimum weight sub collection M of S, such that for each set $m \in M$, $f(m) \leq k$ and $\cup_{m \in M} = U$.

To solve CAPM using the heuristics available for the CWSC problem, we map the CAPM problem to the CWSC problem as follows. Given an instance $\langle \mathcal{U}_a, \mathcal{O}_a, UAV, OAV, UP, c \rangle$ of CAPM, an instance $\langle U, S, f, k \rangle$ of CWSC can be generated as follows:
- Form U by performing the union of $\langle \mathcal{A}_u, \mathcal{A}_o, p \rangle$ for each $(u, o, p) \in$ UP.
- Set k equal to c, $f: S \rightarrow \{1...c\}$
- Form S by generating all possible combinations of the set $(\mathcal{U}_a \cup \mathcal{O}_a \cup OP)$, such that each generated set is constrained to have weight computed using the function f to be less than or equal to c.

If the total weight of the set of subsets obtained after solving the CWSC instance is t, then the total weight TW of the generated ABAC policy P would also be t. Since the range of the weight function is $\{1...c\}$, it is ensured that for each rule $r \in P$, $W(r) \leq c$. A minimum value of t ensures a minimum value of $TW(P)$.

An algorithm for solving CAPM (*Mine-ABAC-Policy*) is given in Algorithm 1. The set *UniversalUPOSet* consists of tuples of the form $\langle \mathcal{A}_u, \mathcal{A}_o, p \rangle$, where each tuple represents a $(u, o, p) \in$ UP. For each $\langle \mathcal{A}_u, \mathcal{A}_o, p \rangle \in$ *UniversalUPOSet*, *TotalAttrSet* stores the set of all attribute value pairs in $\mathcal{A}_u$, $\mathcal{A}_o$ and p. All possible ABAC rules having cardinality less than c are generated using the set of attributes present in the set *TotalAttrSet* and are stored in the set *AllPossibleRules*. From the generated set, rules that represent at least one entry in UP are selected and stored in *ValidRules*[i], where i represents the ith tuple in *UniversalUPOSet*. After retrieving the content of the *ValidRules* set for each $\langle \mathcal{A}_u, \mathcal{A}_o, p \rangle$ $\in$ *UniversalUPOSet*, a set of *EffectiveRules* is formed by combining the content of all the available *ValidRules*. For each rule $r_j \in$ *EffectiveRules*, *TuplesCoveredinUP*[r] stores the set of $(u, o, p) \in$ UP covered by r. The generated set

---

Algorithm 1: Mine-ABAC-Policy

Input: $UP, \mathcal{U}_a, \mathcal{O}_a, UAV, OAV, c$
Output: $Policy$
$i, EffectiveRules \leftarrow 0, ValidRules[i], RulesCoveredinUP,$
$UniversalUPOSet, UOP \leftarrow \phi$
for each $(u, o, p) \in UP$ **do**
$\quad| \ UniversalUPOSet \leftarrow UniversalUPOSet \cup \{\langle \mathcal{A}_u, \mathcal{A}_o, p \rangle\}$
end

for each $\langle \mathcal{A}_u, \mathcal{A}_o, p \rangle \in UniversalUPOSet$ **do**
$\quad| \ TotalAttrSet \leftarrow \mathcal{A}_u \cup \mathcal{A}_o \cup p$
$\quad| \ AllPossibleRules \leftarrow r| \ r \in 2^{\mathcal{A}_u \cup \mathcal{A}_o \cup p}$ and $|r| \leq c$
$\quad| \ ValidRules[i] \leftarrow r' | \ r' \in AllPossibleRules$ and r' covers at
$\quad| \ $ least one $(u, o, op) \in UP$
$\quad| \ $i++
end

for $j \leftarrow 0$ to i **do**
$\quad| \ EffectiveRules = EffectiveRules \cup ValidRules[j]$
end

for $j \leftarrow 0$ to $|EffectiveRules|$ **do**
$\quad| \ TuplesCoveredinUP[j] \leftarrow$ set of (u, o, p) covered by the
$\quad| \ $ jth rule in $EffectiveRules$
end

$UOP \leftarrow$ store each $(u, o, p) \in UP$
$TempRules \leftarrow GenMinSetCover(UOP, TuplesCoveredinUP)$
$Policy \leftarrow Merge\text{-}Rules(TempRules)$ **return** $Policy$

Algorithm 2: Merge-Rules

Input: $TempRules$
Output: $TempRules$ after merging
$Policy \leftarrow \phi$
for each $(r_1, r_2) \in TempRules$ **do**
$\quad|$ **if** $(|r_1 + r_2| \leq c$ and does not uncover any $(u, o, p) \in$
$\quad| \ UP)$ **then**
$\quad| \quad| \ r' \leftarrow uc(r_1) \cup uc(r_2) \cup oc(r_1) \cup oc(r_2) \cup op(r_1) \cup$
$\quad| \quad| \ op(r_2)$
$\quad| \quad| \ TempRules \leftarrow TempRules \setminus \{r_1, r_2\} \cup \{r'\}$
$\quad|$ **end**
end
return $TempRules$

---

of subsets along with the set UOP containing all (u, o, p) $\in UP$ is then passed to a function called $GenMinSetCover$, which returns the set $TempRules$ representing the minimal weighted set of rules covering all entries in UP.

For further reduction of the weight of the generated policy, we perform an additional merging step on the set of rules generated by $GenMinSetCover$. Merging of rules is done using the $Merge\text{-}Rules$ function given in Algorithm 2. It compares each pair of rules r_1 and r_2 in $TempRules$, checks for redundancy, and if $|W(r_1) + W(r_2)| \leq c$, merges r_1 and r_2 if merging does not introduce any new (u, o, p) which is not in UP. The set of rules generated after the merging operation forms the final ABAC policy.

4 EXPERIMENTAL RESULTS

We implemented our approach described in the last section and compared it with the policy mining algorithm presented in [6] using the data sets made available by them

Data set	W	TW ($|P|$)	Time (in secs)
Online-Video	4	21(6)	1.13
	4	19 (6)	0.09
Healthcare	4	117(33)	4.80
	4	88 (26)	2.50
University	8	243 (53)	9.10
	5	223 (49)	5.40
Project-Management	7	185 (40)	9.10
	5	182 (38)	19.90

Table 1: Comparative performance of the proposed approach with [6]

(http://www3.cs.stonybrook. edu/stoller). The experiments were run on an Intel Xeon E5-2697 v2 processor @ 2.70 GHz with 256 GB RAM.

Table 1 shows the maximum value of the weights W of the individual rules, total weight TW of the policy along with the number of rules $|P|$ within parenthesis, as well as the execution time for each approach. It may be noted that, each row of the table has two sub-rows, the first corresponds to [6] and the second is the value obtained by our approach. From the table, it can be seen that for most of the data sets, our approach outperforms the existing approach in terms of the total weight of the policies, number of rules as well as the execution time. Note that, while the existing approach does not explicitly try to impose any constraint on the weight of individual rules, the rules it generates are seen to have higher values of weights and hence, would not be valid if constraints are imposed. For most of the data sets, the proposed algorithm generates lightweight policies in lesser time, thus making it effective for mining ABAC policies under constraint.

5 CONCLUSION

This work presents a constrained policy mining algorithm for attribute based access control systems. Minimizing the total weight of all the rules in the mined policy while ensuring that no individual rule can have weight greater than a pre-specified constraint, helps to develop ABAC systems that are easy to enforce and are also amenable to efficient security analysis. Future work would involve enforcing other types of constraints and improving the efficiency of the approach.

REFERENCES

[1] Y. Benkaouz, M. Erradi, and B. Freisleben. Work in Progress: K-Nearest Neighbors Techniques for ABAC Policies Clustering. *ACM Intl. Workshop on ABAC*, 72–75.
[2] M. Cygan, L. Kowalik, and M. Wykurz. Exponential-time Approximation of Weighted Set Cover. *Inf. Proc. Let.* (2009), 957–961.
[3] P. Harika, M. Nagajyothi, J. C. John, S. Sural, J. Vaidya, and V. Atluri. Meeting cardinality Constraints in Role Mining. *IEEE Trans. Dep. and Sec. Com.* (2015), 71–84.
[4] R. S. Sandhu, J. E. Coyne, H. L. Feinstein, and C. E. Youman. Role-based Access Control Models. *IEEE Computer* (1996), 38–47.
[5] D. Servos and S. L. Osborn. Current Research and Open Problems in Attribute-Based Access Control. *ACM Comp. Sur.* (2017), 1–45.
[6] Z. Xu and S. D. Stoller. Mining attribute-based access control policies. *IEEE Trans. Dep. and Sec. Com.* 12, 5 (2015), 533–545.

POSTER: Access Control Model for the Hadoop Ecosystem

Maanak Gupta
Institute for Cyber Security
Dept. of Computer Science
UT San Antonio, One UTSA Circle
San Antonio, Texas 78249, USA
gmaanakg@yahoo.com

Farhan Patwa
Institute for Cyber Security
Dept. of Computer Science
UT San Antonio, One UTSA Circle
San Antonio, Texas 78249, USA
farhan.patwa@utsa.com

Ravi Sandhu
Institute for Cyber Security
Dept. of Computer Science
UT San Antonio, One UTSA Circle
San Antonio, Texas 78249, USA
ravi.sandhu@utsa.com

ABSTRACT

Apache Hadoop is an important framework for fault-tolerant and distributed storage and processing of Big Data. Hadoop core platform along with other open-source tools such as Apache Hive, Storm, HBase offer an ecosystem to enable users to fully harness Big Data potential. Apache Ranger and Apache Sentry provide access control capabilities to several ecosystem components by offering centralized policy administration and enforcement through plugins. In this work we discuss the access control model for Hadoop ecosystem (referred as HeAC) used by Apache Ranger (release 0.6) and Sentry (release 1.7.0) along with Hadoop 2.x native authorization capabilities. This multi-layer model provides several access enforcement points to restrict unauthorized users to cluster resources. We further outline some preliminary approaches to extend the HeAC model consistent with widely accepted access control models.

CCS CONCEPTS

•Security and privacy → Security requirements; Formal security models; Access control; Authorization;

KEYWORDS

Access Control; Hadoop Ecosystem; Big Data; Data Lake; Role Based; Attributes; Groups Hierarchy; Object Tags

ACM Reference format:
Maanak Gupta, Farhan Patwa, and Ravi Sandhu. 2017. POSTER: Access Control Model for the Hadoop Ecosystem. In *Proceedings of SACMAT'17, June 21–23, 2017, Indianapolis, IN, USA, , 3 pages.*
DOI: http://dx.doi.org/10.1145/3078861.3084164

1 INTRODUCTION

It is highly anticipated that Big Data will significantly impact and transform human society in 21st century. Enormous and varied data sets are generated and collected from smart home devices, genomes, pace makers, satellites, social blogs, etc., to garner valuable insights useful in business and commerce. Such Big Data requires distributed, scalable and robust system with fast computational capabilities, wherein Apache Hadoop [1] is a dominant open-source system. Hadoop 2.x core components (Hadoop Common, Hadoop Distributed File System (HDFS), MapReduce and

YARN) along with several Apache projects such as Hive, HBase, Storm, and Kafka, enable non-expert users to harness the potential hidden in the valuable data assets.

Hadoop data lake can jeopardize the confidentiality and integrity of data and cluster resources if they are not protected from nefarious actors. Distributed and massive scale of the platform results in broader attack surface making it vulnerable to security threats. For example, Hadoop service daemons such as HDFS NameNode, DataNode, and YARN ResourceManager, can be impersonated by malicious applications to communicate within the Hadoop cluster. Once these malicious services are registered, an attacker can easily access data blocks or modify other user applications running inside the cluster. An attacker can also execute denial of service attacks on the ecosystem by running highly intensive applications, exhausting cluster resources. Unencrypted RPC communication between DataNodes and across daemon services can also open transit data to attacks. These threats can be manifested from external or inside user of an enterprise.

The basic requirements in securing the Hadoop cluster include protecting machines, services and network. This can be done using network segmentation (physical or logical), firewalls, gateways, enabling SSL/TLS for secure communication between client-node and inter-nodes, intrusion detection and prevention systems, users or system validation, authorization rules etc. LDAP and Kerberos can be used for user and identity management to provide authentication. Users are authorized to access the service using ACLs (access control lists) via a single API gateway for all ecosystem services. Some strategies to secure data residing in HDFS are to use file or OS encryption, tokenization, data masking, ACLs, and POSIX file permissions. Data in motion can be secured by encrypted RPC or HTTP. Multi-tenant cluster also requires resources to be shared among several users. Hadoop 2.x includes YARN execution framework which schedules and manages cluster resources. YARN capacity (or fair) scheduler uses queues to allow authorized users to submit, modify or view applications in cluster using ACLs. Node labels are associated with different queues to restrict applications to run on specific compute nodes. Delegation and block access tokens are used to pass user authentication or authorization information among Hadoop components. Also, proper log auditing mechanisms are required to identify possible attacks.

In this paper we primarily focus on access control and describe the multi-layer authorization capabilities currently offered by Hadoop ecosystem specific to Apache Ranger [3], Apache Sentry [4] and Hadoop 2.x native access control features. The paper is organized as follows. Section 2 reviews some previous research work related to Hadoop and Big Data security. Section 3 presents the authorization model for Hadoop ecosystem (referred as HeAC) followed by some proposed fine grained HeAC extensions in Section 4. Section 5 summarizes our work.

2 RELATED WORK

Hu et al [10] proposed a generalized access control model for Big Data processing frameworks, which can be extended to Hadoop environment. The paper discusses trust chain among different entities to allow user access requests and to ingest data into the cluster. Security requirements and design in Hadoop system are discussed in several papers including [6, 16]. Fine-grained access policies for key-value pair in Big Data environment are proposed in [15]. Ulusoy et al [18] proposed fine grained access control for MapReduce systems. Colombo et al [5] presented a road map for achieving Big Data privacy. A multi-layer authorization framework for Hadoop ecosystem and several attribute based extensions to existing access control model are recently discussed in [7, 8].

3 ACCESS CONTROL MODEL

In the following subsection we summarize the authorization capabilities in Hadoop ecosystem provided by Hadoop 2.x, Apache Ranger and Sentry. We present the conceptual model for multi-layer access control model for Hadoop ecosystem (HeAC) in the next subsection.

3.1 Authorization in Hadoop Ecosystem

The first layer which acts as perimeter security, checks if a user is allowed to access ecosystem services and core Hadoop daemons inside the cluster before access to data and objects. This layer, called service-level authorization, provides ACLs to enforce authorization for access to HDFS NameNode, DataNode, YARN ResourceManager etc. Besides user to service interaction, cross-service communication (for example, between HDFS DataNode and NameNode) is also controlled by this layer. Apache Knox [2] offers a single point API gateway to control access to several Hadoop ecosystem services such as Apache Hive, HDFS, YARN ResourceManager etc., to authorized external users using ACLs.

Data level authorization involves extended ACLs and POSIX style permissions for files and directories in HDFS. Apache Ranger and Sentry also provide access control (using plugins) for several data and service objects across different services. For example, Apache HBase supports HBase Table column family supporting read and write operations, while Apache Storm has topology object with read and write operations. Attribute values (called Tags) can be associated with objects and are used to create Tag-based policies. The policy created on tags will then control access to all objects associated with the object tags.

In Hadoop 2.x, Apache YARN offers capacity (or fair) scheduler queues, which restrict cluster resources to authorized users. These queues are allotted set of resources which can be used only by users submitting applications to queues. Each queue has associated ACLs which determine the set of users allowed to submit or modify applications inside the cluster. Applications can be also protected from unauthorized modification using configuration files attached to each application. Cluster nodes can be assigned node labels which are associated with different capacity (or fair) scheduler

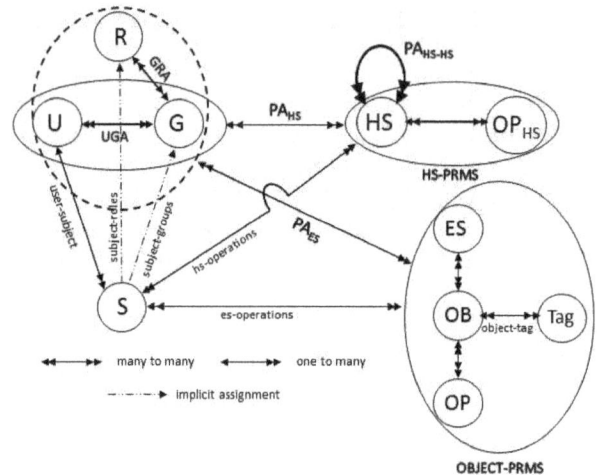

Figure 1: A Conceptual HeAC Model

queues to restrict users to run applications on set of nodes with particular node labels.

3.2 HeAC Model Components

In this subsection we discuss the components of HeAC model as shown in Figure 1. Users (U), Subjects (S) and Roles (R) are the conventional access control components [17]. Groups (G) are collections of users which have similar functional requirements. Apache Ranger allows object permissions to user and groups, whereas Apache Sentry assigns permissions to roles, which are assigned to groups and through groups to member users. Other components defined as sets in HeAC model are as follows.

- Ecosystem Services (ES): These are set of services such as HDFS, Apache Hive, Apache HBase, Apache Kafka etc., which are used by users and applications to access the ecosystem objects. Access to ecosystem service is required before the underlying objects are accessed.
- Objects (OB): Objects are resources secured from unauthorized users. Different services supports multiple objects with a many to many relation between them. For example, Apache Hive supports objects tables and databases whereas YARN has queue objects.
- Operations (OP): OP is the set of actions which can be performed on different objects by users. For example, Hive tables support select and create operations whereas YARN queue objects support submit-application and administer operations by authorized users.
- Object Tags (Tag): Tag is the set of attribute values which can be associated to objects. These values can define classification, content or any other attribute of objects. An object can be associated with multiple tags and vice-versa.
- Hadoop Service (HS): These are set of Hadoop 2.x daemon services used by users to submit jobs or to get status of submitted applications. Services such as HDFS NameNode, YARN ResourceManager also interact with each other for cluster resource or task updates. There are no objects associated with these services.

- Hadoop Operation (OP_{HS}): The set of operations which can be performed on Hadoop services. Most commonly such actions include access operation by user or by other Hadoop services.

As shown in Figure 1, there are two sets of permissions—Hadoop service permissions (HS-PRMS) and service object permissions (OBJECT-PRMS). HS-PRMS comprises operations on Hadoop services such as DataNode, NameNode, and can be assigned to both users and groups (reflected by PA_{HS}). On the other hand, OBJECT-PRMS comprises operations on objects in ecosystem services, and can be assigned to users, groups or roles as shown by PA_{ES}. Dotted circle encompassing U, G and R reflects PA_{ES} permission assignment. It should be noted that OBJECT-PRMS can be set on object or object tags associated with objects (shown by object-tag). Also, OBJECT-PRMS has ES service as a component, which specifies the need of service access before service objects are accessed. Interaction among different Hadoop services, for example, DataNode accessing NameNode or ApplicationMaster communication to ResourceManager, is reflected by self loop shown by PA_{HS-HS}. These permissions are generally set by Hadoop 2.x native service-level authorization ACLs.

With group membership, effective HS-PRMS of a user will be the union of direct HS-PRMS and permissions of member groups. For OBJECT-PRMS, a user will have direct permissions, permissions of member groups and the permissions of roles to which its member groups are assigned. Based on operations, a user may need both types of permissions. A subject S created by user will get all OBJECT-PRMS and HS-PRMS permissions of its creator user. It should be noted that we assume data is already ingested in the cluster and authorization model take effect when authenticated users try to access objects and services in the ecosystem.

4   PROPOSED HeAC EXTENSIONS

In this section, we outline strategies to reformulate HeAC model to more acceptable and generalized access models including roles and attributes, as follows.

- Role Based Model: A pure RBAC [17] can be implemented where permissions are assigned only to roles and user and groups are assigned to roles. This approach also presents a novel way to combine RBAC and object attributes (Tags) beyond NIST strategies.

NIST proposed strategies [14] for adding attributes to RBAC to achieve finer grained permissions can be also incorporated in HeAC. These extensions require introduction of attributes [9, 11, 12] for users, groups, services and objects. Users can also get attributes from group membership. Below we discuss NIST strategies for combining roles and attributes, and corresponding HeAC extensions.

- Dynamic Roles: This involves attributes of users and environment for user to role assignment. Policy rules are defined using policy language which includes attributes and corresponding roles. Similar permissions to roles assignment can be done based on object and service attributes present in the permission.
- Attribute Centric: This a pure attribute based approach where authorization policies comprising attributes are defined and access decision is made based on attributes of

ecosystem services or objects and users. Environment or contextual attributes can be added to access request to achieve finer grained permissions.

- Role Centric: In this approach, a user is assigned initial set of permissions through roles but these permissions are reduced based on attributes of entities. Filtering functions are defined using attributes based policies, which are checked to determine the final set of permissions of a user [13].

5   SUMMARY AND CONCLUSION

In this paper we present a conceptual Hadoop ecosystem access control model HeAC based on Hadoop native authorization capabilities and model used by Apache Ranger and Sentry. This model assigns different sets of permissions to users either directly or via groups and roles. The model also discusses the concept of object tags which are used for defining object permissions besides using objects. We proposed some extensions to HeAC model in line with conventional access models and NIST defined strategies. We further plan to introduce RBAC model for Hadoop Ecosystem and present trust models for data ingestion and processing.

ACKNOWLEDGMENTS

Sincere gratitude is extended to James Benson, Technology Research Analyst at Institute for Cyber Security, UTSA, for his useful comments. This research is partially supported by NSF Grants CNS-1111925, CNS-1423481, CNS-1538418, DoD ARL Grant W911NF-15-1-0518 and by The Texas Sustainable Energy Research Institute at University of Texas at San Antonio.

REFERENCES

[1] *Apache Hadoop.* http://hadoop.apache.org/.
[2] *Apache Knox.* http://knox.apache.org/.
[3] *Apache Ranger.* http://ranger.apache.org/.
[4] *Apache Sentry.* http://sentry.apache.org/.
[5] Pietro Colombo and Elena Ferrari. 2015. Privacy aware access control for Big Data: a research roadmap. *Big Data Research* 2, 4 (2015), 145–154.
[6] Devaraj Das, Owen O'Malley, Sanjay Radia, and Kan Zhang. 2011. Adding security to Apache Hadoop. *Hortonworks, IBM* (2011).
[7] Maanak Gupta, Farhan Patwa, James Benson, and Ravi Sandhu. 2017. Multi-Layer Authorization Framework for a Representative Hadoop Ecosystem Deployment. In *Proc. of ACM SACMAT (To appear)*. ACM, 8 Pages.
[8] Maanak Gupta, Farhan Patwa, and Ravi Sandhu. 2017. Object-Tagged RBAC Model for the Hadoop Ecosystem. In *Proc. of IFIP DBSec (To appear)*. Springer, 18 Pages.
[9] Maanak Gupta and Ravi Sandhu. 2016. The GURA$_G$ Administrative Model for User and Group Attribute Assignment. In *Proc. of NSS*. Springer, 318–332.
[10] Vincent C Hu, Tim Grance, David F Ferraiolo, and D Rick Kuhn. 2014. An access control scheme for Big Data processing. In *Proc. of IEEE CollaborateCom*. 1–7.
[11] Vincent C Hu, D Richard Kuhn, and David F Ferraiolo. 2015. Attribute-based access control. *Computer* 48, 2 (2015), 85–88.
[12] Xin Jin, Ram Krishnan, and Ravi Sandhu. 2012. A unified attribute-based access control model covering DAC, MAC and RBAC. In *Proc. of IFIP DBSec*. Springer, 41–55.
[13] Xin Jin, Ravi Sandhu, and Ram Krishnan. 2012. RABAC: role-centric attribute-based access control. In *Proc. of MMM-ACNS*. Springer, 84–96.
[14] D Richard Kuhn, Edward J Coyne, and Timothy R Weil. 2010. Adding attributes to role-based access control. *IEEE Computer* 43, 6 (2010), 79–81.
[15] Devdatta Kulkarni. 2013. A fine-grained access control model for key-value systems. In *Proc. of ACM CODASPY*. ACM, 161–164.
[16] Owen O'Malley, Kan Zhang, Sanjay Radia, Ram Marti, and Christopher Harrell. 2009. Hadoop security design. *Yahoo, Inc., Tech. Rep* (2009).
[17] Ravi S Sandhu, Edward J Coyne, Hal L Feinstein, and Charles E Youman. 1996. Role-based access control models. *IEEE Computer* 29, 2 (1996), 38–47.
[18] Huseyin Ulusoy, Murat Kantarcioglu, Erman Pattuk, and Kevin Hamlen. 2014. Vigiles: Fine-grained access control for MapReduce systems. In *Proc. of IEEE Congress on Big Data*. IEEE, 40–47.

Poster: On the Safety and Efficiency of Virtual Firewall Elasticity Control*

Hongda Li[†#], Juan Deng[†#], Hongxin Hu[†], Kuang-Ching Wang[†], Gail-Joon Ahn[‡], Ziming Zhao[‡]

and Wonkyu Han[‡]

[†]Clemson University   [‡]Arizona State University
{hongdal, jdeng, hongxih, kwang}@clemson.edu,   {gahn, zzhao30, iamhwk}@asu.edu

ABSTRACT

Firewalls have been typically used to enforce network access control. Network Functions Virtualization (NFV) envisions to implement firewall function as software instance (a.k.a virtual firewall). Virtual firewall provides great flexibility and elasticity, which are necessary to protect virtualized environments. In this poster, we propose an innovative virtual firewall controller, VFW Controller, which enables safe, efficient and cost-effective virtual firewall elasticity control. In addition, we implement the core components of VFW Controller on top of NFV and SDN environments. Our experimental results demonstrate that VFW Controller is efficient to provide safe elasticity control of virtual firewalls.

KEYWORDS

Virtual Firewall; Network Functions Visualization; Software-Define Networking; Elasticity Control

ACM Reference format:
Hongda Li[†#], Juan Deng[†#], Hongxin Hu[†], Kuang-Ching Wang[†], Gail-Joon Ahn[‡], Ziming Zhao[‡] and Wonkyu Han[‡] [†]Clemson University   [‡]Arizona State University {hongdal, jdeng, hongxih, kwang}@clemson.edu,   {gahn, zzhao30, iamhwk}@asu.edu . 2017. Poster: On the Safety and Efficiency of Virtual Firewall Elasticity Control. In Proceedings of SACMAT'17, Indianapolis, IN, USA, June 21-23, 2017, 3 pages.
https://doi.org/http://dx.doi.org/10.1145/3078861.3084166

1 INTRODUCTION

Firewalls have been widely used to enforce network access control. Traditional hardware-based firewalls are often placed at fixed network entry points and have a constant capacity with respect to the maximum amount of traffic they can handle per time unit. However, today's prevailing virtualized environments have fluid network perimeters and significantly variation of network traffic [1] [4]. Therefore, it is difficult to deploy hardware-based firewalls to protect virtualized environments. Two emerging network paradigms, Network Functions virtualization (NFV) and Software-Defined Networking (SDN) facilitate a new type of firewalls, *virtual firewall (VFW)*, which feature flexibility and elasticity and are well suited to protect virtualized environments. NFV implements firewall function as software instance that can be created or destroyed quickly to handle traffic volume variations, while SDN, recognized as complementary technology to NFV, seamlessly provides dynamic traffic steering support toward flexible, on-demand placement of virtual firewalls. Major commercial virtualized environments (e.g., VMware vCloud, Amazon AWS, VCE Vblock) have recently started to embrace virtual firewalls.

However, to fully take advantage of VFW benefits, our study reveals that there are great challenges to enable VFW elastic scaling. When VFW is overloaded, new instances are quickly created. Selective firewall rules and states are migrated to new instances and corresponding flow rules in SDN switches are updated to redistribute traffic. When multiple VFW instances are underloaded, some instances are destroyed, all firewall rules and states on them are migrated to remaining instances, and flow rules require update properly. The scaling of VFW must be *safe*, *efficient* and *optimal*. A *safe* scaling does not cause legal traffic to be dropped or illegal traffic to be allowed. An *efficient* scaling ensures that the latency overhead caused by scaling is bounded. An *optimal* scaling consumes minimum compute and network resources.

We identify four key challenges to achieve *safe*, *efficient* and *optimal* VFW scaling. First, semantic consistency of security policies must be preserved after scaling. Preserving semantic consistency of security policies after rounds of splits and mergences is non-trivial because firewall rules are often logically entangled with each other. Second, network flow rules in SDN switches must be correctly updated to redistribute traffic to corresponding instances. Third, a *safe* scaling also requires handling in-flight traffic during migration. Existing works [2] [3] buffer the in-flight traffic. However, in practice, buffer size is not unlimited and migration of different firewall rules incurs different amount of in-flight traffic. Therefore, care must be taken while selecting firewall rules to migrate to avoid buffer overflow. In addition, resources for VFW provision are neither unlimited nor free, thus it is important to optimize the resource usage during VFW scaling.

---

*A conference paper version of this poster appears in Proceedings of the 24th Network and Distributed System Security Symposium (NDSS), 2017.

#The first two authors contribute equally to the paper.

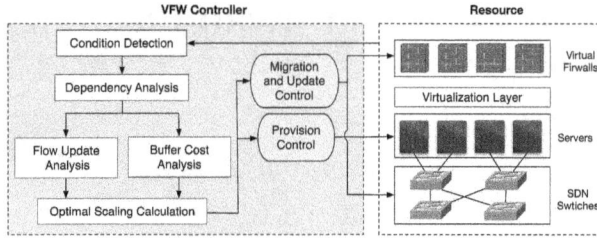

Figure 1: VFW Controller components and workflow.

In this poster, we propose a novel virtual firewall controller, VFW Controller to address above challenges and achieve *safe*, *efficient* and *optimal* VFW scaling. VFW Controller applies packet space analysis to identify intra-dependencies of firewall rules and group-based migration strategy to guarantee semantic consistency. To correctly update flow rules, inter-dependencies between firewall rules and flow rules are identified. To avoid buffer overflow, we model migration process and predict the amount of in-flight traffic during migration. Finally, VFW Controller adopts a three-step heuristic approach and integer linear programming to achieve optimal scaling. We implement VFW Controller on a real NFV and SDN platform and our experimental results show that our VFW Controller provides efficient VFW scaling control.

2 VFW CONTROLLER

The components and workflow of VFW Controller are shown in Figure 1. VFW Controller monitors each VFW instance and detects traffic overload and underload conditions. Once a condition is detected, VFW Controller first performs *Dependency Analysis*, *Flow Update Analysis* and *Buffer Cost Analysis*. Then the results are utilized by *Optimal Scaling Calculation*. Finally, *Provision Control* and *Migration and Update Control* interact with the compute and network resources and execute VFW scaling.

2.1 Dependency Analysis and Semantic Consistency

Definition 1 (Packet space). *Packet space of a rule r, denoted as $PS(r)$, is defined as a 5-dimensional hyperspace with dimensions being protocol, source IP, source port, destination IP, destination port.*

Definition 2 (Direct dependency). *Two rules r_i and r_j in a rule set $\mathbb{R}$ are directly dependent iff $PS(r_i) \cap PS(r_j) \neq \emptyset$, where $PS(r_i)$ is the packet space defined by r_i, and $PS(r_j)$ is the packet space defined by r_j.*

Definition 3 (Indirect dependency). *Two rules r_i and r_j in a rule set $\mathbb{R}$ are indirectly dependent iff $PS(r_i) \cap PS(r_j) = \emptyset$ and there exists a subset $R \subseteq \mathbb{R}\setminus\{r_i, r_j\}$ such that $PS(r_i) \cap PS(R) \neq \emptyset$ and $PS(r_j) \cap PS(R) \neq \emptyset$.*

Rules that have *direct* or *indirect dependencies* are put into one group. We identify the relation between a firewall rule group V and a flow rule group F is one of the following:

- Independency *iff $PS(V) \cap PS(F) = \emptyset$. We denote independency as $V \underline{ind} F$.*
- Congruence *iff $PS(V) = PS(F)$. We denote congruence as $V \underline{con} F$.*

- Superspace *iff $PS(V) \supset PS(F)$. We denote superspace as $V \underline{sup} F$.*
- Subspace *iff $PS(V) \subset PS(F)$. We denote subspace as $V \underline{sub} F$.*
- Intersection *iff $PS(V) \cap PS(F) \subset PS(V)$ and $PS(V) \cap PS(F) \subset PS(F)$. We denote intersection as $V \underline{int} F$.*

Definition 4 (Inter-dependency). *A firewall rule group V and a flow rule group F are inter-dependent if $PS(V) \cap PS(F) \neq \emptyset$.*

Group-Based Migration Strategy: *To guarantee semantic consistency, firewall rules in a group are migrated to the same destination virtual firewall instance in the same order as they are in the source virtual firewall instance. The destination instance can only start to process traffic matching rules in a group until all the rules and flow states associated with the group are ready on the destination instance.*

2.2 Flow Update Analysis

We identify two types of operations for flow update: CHANGE and INSERT. Let $V_i \in \mathbb{V} = \{V_1, ..., V_m\}$ be the firewall rule group to be migrated from a source VFW to a destination VFW instance and $\mathbb{F} = \{F_1, ..., F_n\}$ be the set of flow groups on the SDN switch (SW). To find the updates on $\mathbb{F}$, VFW Controller iterates through $\mathbb{F} = \{F_1, ..., F_n\}$ sequentially, and compares the inter-dependency relation between V_i and each $F_j \in \mathbb{F}$ to determine the updates.

- If $V_i \underline{ind} F_j$, no update is required.
- If $V_i \underline{con} F_j$ or $V_i \underline{sup} F_j$, only CHANGE operation is required. For every flow rule $f \in F_j$, the VFW Controller changes its forwarding action to redirect corresponding traffic to the new instance.
- If $V_i \underline{sub} F_j$ or $V_i \underline{int} F_j$, VFW Controller compares each pair of $PS(v)$ and $PS(f)$, where $v \in V_i$ and $f \in F_j$.
  (1) If $PS(v) \cap PS(f) = \emptyset$, f needs no update.
  (2) If $PS(v) \supseteq PS(f)$, CHANGE is performed to f to redirect the traffic defined by f to the new instance.
  (3) If $PS(v) \subset PS(f)$, INSERT operation is performed. A new flow rule f' is inserted right before f to redirect the traffic matching v to the new instance.
  (4) If $PS(v) \cap PS(f) \subset PS(v)$ and $PS(v) \cap PS(f) \subset PS(f)$, INSERT operation is performed. A new flow rule f' is inserted right before f. Each field of f' is the same as f, except that the protocol, source IP, source port, destination IP, destination port fields of f' are the intersection of the respective fields of v and f, and the forwarding action of f' forwards the traffic to the new instance.

2.3 Buffer Cost Analysis

We first model the process of migration and then predict the amount of in-flight traffic based on our model. Figure 2 shows the work flow of migration control. Then we define the parameters as follows:

- $t0$: is the time that VFW_1 starts to transfer the firewall rules and flow states specified in *fspace*;
- $t1$: is the time that SW finishes the update;
- $d1$: is the transmission delay between SW and VFW_1;
- $d2$: is the transmission delay between SW and VFW_2;
- $d3$: the transmission delay between VFW_1 and VFW_2;
- $b1$: is the average time that VFW_1 spends processing a packet;
- $b2$: is the average time that VFW_2 spends processing a packet.

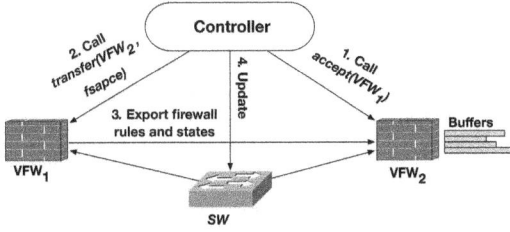

Figure 2: Workflow of migration control.

At *SW*, the traffic matching V_i that arrives before $t1$ is sent to VFW$_1$, and after $t1$ it is sent to VFW$_2$. Let Γ be a set comprising the matching traffic that arrives during $(t0 - d1, t1)$.

At **VFW$_1$**, the firewall rules and flow states defined in *fspace* are sent to VFW$_2$. Traffic in Γ starts to arrive after $t0$, and the last packet in Γ arrives before $t1 + d1$. VFW$_1$ processes all the traffic in Γ. VFW$_1$ finishes processing Γ before $t1 + d1 + b1$.

At **VFW$_2$**, traffic directly sent from *SW* starts to arrive after $t1 + d2$. The last packet in Γ arrives at VFW$_2$ before $t1 + d1 + b1 + d3$ and it is processed before $t1 + d1 + b1 + d3 + b2$. Therefore, traffic that is directly sent from *SW* and arrives at VFW$_2$ during $(t1 + d2, t1 + d1 + b1 + d3 + b2)$ is buffered.

Suppose there are k_i flows matching V_i and the rate of flow j is λ_j. Then we estimate the buffer cost of V_i as

$$\beta_i = (\sum_{j=1}^{k_i} \lambda_j) \times \{(t1 + d1 + b1 + d3 + b2) - (t1 + d2)\}$$

3 IMPLEMENTATION AND EVALUATION

We have implemented a prototype of VFW Controller on top of ClickOS, a Xen-based NFV platform. We used Floodlight and Open vSwitch to construct the SDN environments. We also implemented a stateful virtual firewall based on Click. In addition, we implemented 7 new Click elements to support our virtual firewall. Key functions of VFW Controller have been realized as individual modules. In particular, we have implemented a *Dependency Analysis* module based on Header Space Library (Hassel), a *Flow Updatea Analysis* module to find the correct flow updates, a *Buffer Cost Analysis* module to calculate buffer costs, and an *Optimal Scaling Calculation* module that realize the approaches for optimal scaling.

In the experiments, we setup three physical machines: *client*, *server* and *firewall*. The *client* sent traffic to the *server* via the *firewall* machine. Our VFW Controller was installed on *firewall* along with several VFW instances. We tested both TCP and UDP flows to see how quickly the VFW instances can scale when they were overloaded. Figure 3 shows that without scaling (black dashed), the throughput of *firewall* is around 1.3Gbps; with two parallel VFW instances (blue dashed), the throughput of *firewall* is around 2.8Gbps for UDP (Figure 3(a)) and 2.5Gbps for TCP (Figure 3(b)). We tested our VFW Controller by letting it control the VFW instance to scale when the instance was overloaded. We installed 400 firewall rules in a single VFW instance and 200 firewall rules in each of the paralleled VFW instances. For the VFW instance under test, we installed 400 firewall rules. It turns out that our VFW Controller can efficiently guide the overloaded VFW instance to scale out, in

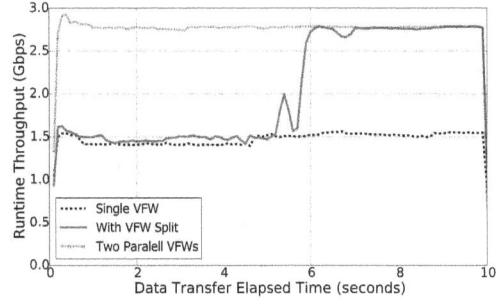

(a) Split with UDP flow overload.

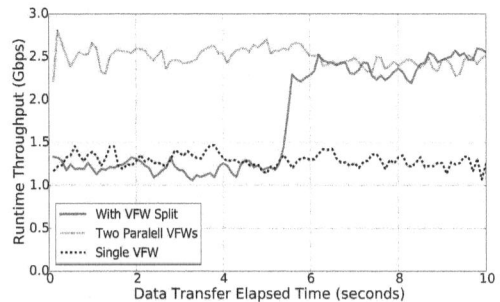

(b) Split with TCP flow overload.

Figure 3: VFW Controller for VFW elasticity.

less than 1 second in our experiments. After scaling, the throughput of *firewall* is equal to the throughput of two parallel VFW instances. In addition, this scaling preserved the TCP connection and UDP packet order.

4 CONCLUSIONS

In this poster, we have proposed VFW Controller, a virtual firewall controller, which enables *safe*, *efficient* and *optimal* virtual firewall scaling. Also, We have implemented the core components of VFW Controller on top of ClickOS. Our experiments showed that our VFW Controller is able to provide efficient and safe elasticity control of virtual firewalls.

ACKNOWLEDGMENTS

This work was partially supported by grants from National Science Foundation (NSF-ACI-1642143, NSF-ACI-1642031, NSF-IIS-1527421, and NSF-CNS-1537924).

REFERENCES

[1] Theophilus Benson, Aditya Akella, and David A Maltz. 2010. Network traffic characteristics of data centers in the wild. In *Proceedings of the 10th ACM SIGCOMM conference on Internet measurement*. ACM, 267–280.
[2] A. Gember-Jacobson and A. Akella. 2015. Improving the safety, scalability, and efficiency of network function state transfers. In *ACM SIGCOMM Workshop on Hot Topics in Middleboxes and Network Function Virtualization*.
[3] Aaron Gember-Jacobson, Raajay Viswanathan, Chaithan Prakash, Robert Grandl, Junaid Khalid, Sourav Das, and Aditya Akella. 2014. OpenNF: Enabling innovation in network function control. In *Proceedings of the 2014 ACM Conference on SIGCOMM*. 163–174.
[4] T. Benson and A. Anand and A. Akella and M. Zhang. 2009. Understanding data center traffic characteristics. In *Proceeding of SIGCOMM Workshop on Research on Enterprise Networking*. Barcelona, Spain.

Leveraging Hardware Isolation for Process Level Access Control & Authentication

Syed Kamran Haider[†]   Hamza Omar[†]   Ilia Lebedev[‡]   Srinivas Devadas[‡]   Marten van Dijk[†]

† University of Connecticut   ‡ Massachusetts Institute of Technology

[syed.haider,hamza.omar,marten.van_dijk]@uconn.edu

[ilebedev,devadas]@mit.edu

ABSTRACT

Critical resource sharing among multiple entities in a processing system is inevitable, which in turn calls for the presence of appropriate authentication and access control mechanisms. Generally speaking, these mechanisms are implemented via trusted software "policy checkers" that enforce certain high level application-specific "rules" to enforce a policy. Whether implemented as operating system modules or embedded inside the application ad hoc, these policy checkers expose additional attack surface in addition to the application logic. In order to protect application software from an adversary, modern secure processing platforms, such as Intel's Software Guard Extensions (SGX), employ principled *hardware isolation* to offer secure software containers or *enclaves* to execute trusted sensitive code with some integrity and privacy guarantees against a privileged software adversary. We extend this model further and propose using these hardware isolation mechanisms to shield the authentication and access control logic essential to policy checker software. While relying on the fundamental features of modern secure processors, our framework introduces productive software design guidelines which enable a guarded environment to execute sensitive policy checking code – hence enforcing application control flow integrity – and afford flexibility to the application designer to construct appropriate high-level policies to customize policy checker software.

CCS CONCEPTS

•**Security and privacy** → *Systems security; Software and application security;*

KEYWORDS

Hardware Isolation; Secure Processors; Program Authentication

ACM Reference format:
Syed Kamran Haider[†]   Hamza Omar[†]   Ilia Lebedev[‡]   Srinivas Devadas[‡] Marten van Dijk[†]. 2017. Leveraging Hardware Isolation for Process Level Access Control & Authentication. In *Proceedings of SACMAT'17, June 21–23, 2017, Indianapolis, IN, USA, , 9 pages.*
DOI: http://dx.doi.org/10.1145/3078861.3078882

1 INTRODUCTION

Technology plays a major role in shaping various different aspects of our lives in the modern digital world. We, as users, interact with hundreds of digital devices in our day-to-day lives such as mobile devices, electronic households, medical equipments, automobiles, media players and many more. One way or the other, these devices access certain resources that are shared among various entities, be it other users or internal management modules of the system. For instance, in a cloud setting, users share physical storage and computational resources to store their private data and perform arbitrary computations on this data. *Authentication* and *access control* mechanisms are vital components of such systems that verify a user's/task's identity and regulate its requests to access certain system resources respectively.

Authentication and access control are typically quite interrelated. In general, a user is granted or denied permission to access a certain resource by first authenticating its identity and then looking up an *access permissions list* corresponding to this particular user. Common authentication mechanisms include password based and public key based schemes [26]. Password based systems require an initial (secure) setup phase before the authentication phase, whereas public key based systems use a trusted certification authority. Other advanced mechanisms incorporate multiple authentication factors, e.g., by exploiting physiological biometrics (iris, fingerprints, hand, retinal), behavioral characteristics (voice, typing pattern) [11], and human psychology to understand and predict human behavior [21].

In modern applications, typically the authentication and access control mechanisms are implemented via trusted software "policy checker" modules that enforce certain high level application-specific "rules" to enforce a policy. Preventing any malicious manipulations to an application's control flow is crucial for the overall program integrity, as well as for any software based authentication/access control policies to be effective. Control flow manipulations in the untrusted (i.e., potentially buggy) parts of the application code are possible by exploiting any *memory safety violations*, e.g., through a buffer overflow vulnerability etc. Whereas parts of the application trusted to be bug-free, including the policy checker software, are not vulnerable to such attacks. Nevertheless, substantial amount of research has been done on the subject of detecting and protecting against software-level memory safety violations at instruction-by-instruction level fine granularity as well as checkpointing based coarse granularity. Among the various proposals are software only approaches [1, 3, 18–20] and partially or fully hardware-assisted approaches [5, 8, 24].

In spite of the policy checker software being trusted, a fundamental problem that still persists is that this software is vulnerable to *privileged software attacks*. For instance, a compromised operating system or hypervisor (that runs at a higher privilege level than the application – hence called a privileged software) having full control over the system resources can not only learn the application's sensitive information [25], but also tamper with its data and/or manipulate its control flow to bypass the policy checking software. State-of-the-art *secure processors*, such as Intel SGX [17] and Sanctum [6], offer hardware assisted secure containers or *enclaves* to run the sensitive application code (e.g., policy checker) in a protected environment. Although this paradigm protects the application against a bunch of privileged software attacks, yet it does not enforce the "correct" execution ordering of enclaves from the application's perspective. In other words, the application's control flow can still be manipulated at enclaves level granularity, resulting in crucial policy violations. For example, a compromised OS could completely bypass the policy checker enclave and allow the adversary an unauthorized access to the system resources.

In this paper, we introduce an application software design framework based on modern secure processors which, in a nutshell, uses an enclaved policy checker engine to manage the capabilities of the rest of the system. Given that the policy engine is a persistent trusted component, it offers a powerful security property: *trustworthy ordering* of enclaves' executions in the presence of compromised privileged software. In our approach, the application designer wraps the policy checker code into a separate *policy enclave* along with creating several other enclaves for sensitive parts of the application. The policy enclave, depending upon the application, administers corresponding rules for authentication and access control, as well as verifies the enclaves' execution flow at each step. While offering traditional isolation guarantees, the proposed approach ensures that the policy enclave is invoked upon all "sensitive" transitions of the program; particularly before each entry to a regular enclave. In addition to preventing the privileged software from circumventing the policy checks, our framework offers the application designer a global picture of the application execution state (through the policy enclave) which in turn provides the designer a much richer set of information to design policy checker software.

2 BACKGROUND

The attacks that can be performed on a computer system can broadly be classified into *physical attacks* and *software/remote attacks*. To launch physical attacks, the adversary having the physical access to the computer system might tamper with the system or exploit its physical implementation to perform an authorized operation or learning secret information. In contrast, remote adversaries can only launch software attacks which might involve executing potentially malicious software at the victim system and/or accessing the victim's confidential data. Generally, a remote adversary is more common than a physical adversary since usually the user either owns the system (e.g. a personal computer) or the computing infrastructure (e.g. a cloud server) is managed by trusted parties. With this model in mind, we only focus on the remote adversaries in this paper. Adversaries having physical access to the computer system are out of scope of this work.

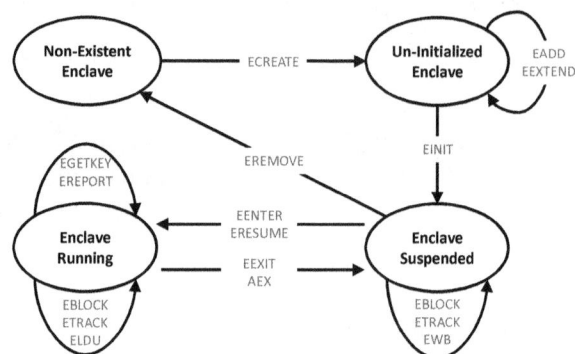

Figure 1: Life cycle of an enclave in Intel SGX.

2.1 Trusted Hardware

In the presence of physical adversaries, the privacy of user's sensitive data becomes a serious concern. To address this challenge, various *trusted-hardware* based secure processor architectures have been proposed in the literature [10, 13–17, 22, 23]. A trusted-hardware platform receives user's encrypted data, which is decrypted and computed upon inside the trusted boundary, and finally the encrypted results of the computation are sent to the user. The trusted-hardware is assumed to be *tamper-resistant*, i.e. an adversary cannot probe the processor chip to learn any information.

In addition to protecting against certain physical adversaries described above, secure processors also introduced the notion of *secure containers* based on two important properties, *Hardware Isolation* and *Attestation*. Secure containers also called *enclaves* can be used to defend against certain software adversaries. For example, the XOM architecture [13–15] uses isolated containers to execute sensitive code on the user's data without trusting the OS. Aegis [22, 23] makes use of a *trusted security kernel* to isolate each container from other software running on the computer system by configuring the page tables used for address translation. The security kernel is a subset of a typical OS kernel, and handles virtual memory management, processes, and hardware exceptions.

This leads us to give the reader a quick background of two state-of-the-art secure processor architectures: an industrial flagship architecture Intel SGX and an academic architecture Sanctum with a similar API. We will be using these systems as the underlying hardware for our proposed framework that fits both these architectures equally well.

2.2 Intel SGX

Intel's Software Guard Extentions (SGX) [17] follows Bastion's [4] approach of having the untrusted OS manage the page tables; and also adapts the ideas from Aegis and XOM to multi-core processors (having a shared, coherent last-level cache) by introducing the concept of *enclaves*. An enclave is a protected environment that contains the code and data of a security-sensitive computation. Each enclave's environment is isolated from the untrusted software outside the enclave, as well as from other enclaves. SGX maintains *isolation* by setting aside a memory region, called the *Processor*

Reserved Memory (PRM). The CPU protects the PRM from all non-enclave memory accesses, including kernel, hypervisor and system management mode accesses, and DMA accesses from peripherals. PRM holds an *Enclave Page Cache* (EPC) which contains information regarding enclave's code and data. An enclave is allowed to only access its own information stored in the EPC.

Intel SGX also provides the attestation capabilities for authentication purposes. Attestation allows an enclave to attest its execution environment to other enclaves on the same system platform *(Local Attestation)*, and also to the entities outside the platform *(Remote Attestation)*. Remote attestation is a method by which an SGX enabled processor authenticates its hardware and software configuration to a remote host. It is achieved with the help of a *Quoting Enclave*, a specially designed enclave that uses an attestation key to sign the execution "report" and allows the remote party to verify the signature using a public key.

Figure 1 shows how the enclaves in the SGX architecture are created, initialized, and loaded. It also explains how, with the use of specified instructions, an application designer can context switch between enclaves and/or non-enclave code. The following instructions (embedded as micro-code in the ISA), represented in Figure 1, explain the major transitions during a SGX enclave's life cycle.

- *ECREATE:* Creates a unique instance of an enclave.
- *EADD:* Adds pages and thread control structures into the enclave.
- *EEXTEND:* Generates a cryptographic hash of the content of the enclave.
- *EINIT:* Initializes the enclave and marks it ready to be used.
- *EENTER, ERESUME:* Enters the enclave or resumes after context switching/exiting.
- *EEXIT, AEX:* Exits the enclave synchronously, or asynchronously.
- *EREMOVE:* Refers to a tear-down of an enclave as it deallocates the page from the EPC permanently.
- *EREPORT:* Application enclave calls this instruction to generate a report structure for a desired target enclave for local attestation.
- *EGETKEY:* Used by the target enclave to retrieve the report key generated by the application enclave.

As complementary mechanisms, SGX also implements memory integrity verification and encryption of the memory.

2.3 Sanctum

Sanctum [6] follows SGX's API and offers the same promise of strong provable isolation of software running concurrently and sharing resources. It is built on top of an open source implementation of Rocket RISC-V core. Sanctum is a hardware software co-design that introduces a small *trusted software security monitor* that effectively extends the ISA as in SGX. Furthermore, Sanctum introduces nominal hardware extensions:

- *DMA Tranfer Filtering:* A protection circuitry to prevent peripherals accessing enclave's memory regions.
- *Cache Address Shifter:* An additional hardware to circularly shift the Physical Page Number to the right by a

certain amount of bits to map collections of cache sets to contiguous DRAM regions.
- *Page Walker Input:* A small circuit to select the appropriate page table base and forward either *EPTBR* (enclave page table base register) or *PTBR* (page table base register).

As discussed in section 2.2, SGX hardware ensures security via its high privileged microcode which extends to the Instruction Set Architecture (ISA). Updates to the microcode in SGX can only be made through Intel. In contrast, Sanctum uses an *open-sourced security monitor* implementation which is provided at the *machine level* (highest privilege level) in RISC-V. For updating the security monitor, Sanctum employs a *bootstrapping* mechanism which allows a user to write and update its own security monitor. All layers of Sanctum's trusted computing base (TCB) are open-sourced at www.github.com/pwnall/sanctum.

Unlike SGX, each Sanctum enclave is responsible for its own memory management with respect to page swapping between reserved enclave memory and the untrusted DRAM. The *security monitor* provides API calls to the OS and enclaves for DRAM region allocation and enclave management, and also guards sensitive registers, such as the page table base register. The life cycle of a Sanctum enclave is very similar to that of its SGX counterpart, as shown in Figure 1. Sanctum's software attestation process relies on *mailboxes*, a simplified version of SGX's crypto based local attestation mechanism (*EGETKEY* and *EREPORT*) that uses key-derivation and MAC algorithms. Enclave mailboxes are stored in metadata regions and isolated from other mailboxes, which cannot be accessed by any software/OS other than the *security monitor*. In Sanctum, an enclave (say A) can invoke a secure inter-enclave messaging service to send an *accept message* monitor call to specify the mailbox that will receive the message and the identity of the enclave (say B) that is expected to send the message. The sending enclave (B) performs a *send message* call that specifies the identity of the receiving enclave and a mailbox within that enclave. The security monitor delivers messages to mailboxes that expect them. It notifies the enclave (A) that it has received a message, which issues a *read message* call to the security monitor that moves the message from the mailbox into enclave's memory.

Unlike SGX, Sanctum protects against an important class of additional software attacks that infer private information through a program's cache access patterns. It employs the concept of cache partitioning based on page coloring. Sanctum shows that *isolation* of concurrent software modules (which relies on caching DRAM regions in distinct sets) provides strong security guarantees against a subtle software threat model at the cost of small performance overhead.

2.4 Promises vs. Limitations

As we discussed so far, modern secure processors offer strong isolated environments to securely execute sensitive code in the presence of strong software adversaries. Nonetheless, it is important to highlight *what secure processors do not promise!* In particular, SGX/Sanctum only guarantee that each *individual* enclave is securely and correctly executed, and this can be verified through the hash digest or so called *report* of the enclave. However, in an application with multiple enclaves having interdependencies, it

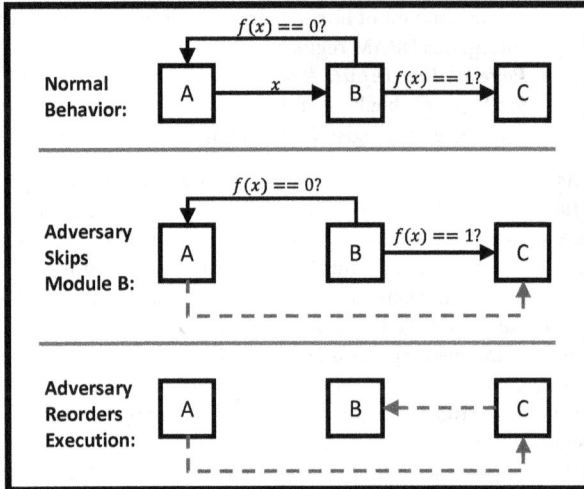

Figure 2: Possible control flow manipulations done by an adversary.

is the programmer's responsibility to not only verify (via enclave reports) that each enclave has executed the expected code on the expected/correct inputs, but also that the global order in which the enclaves are executed is consistent with the application design. The latter condition is equally important for the overall integrity and security of the application.

For instance, Figure 2 shows a toy example of a program with three enclaves A, B and C. Under the *normal behavior* of the program, enclave A provides some input credentials x to B which computes an authentication function f on x. If the authentication is successful, i.e. $f(x) = 1$, only then enclave C is allowed to execute (and then access some critical system resource). In case of authentication failure, i.e. $f(x) = 0$, the control is returned back to enclave A without executing C. Now, a strong adversary, who can alter the global ordering of enclaves' execution, can do the following: it can skip the authentication step performed by enclave B and directly execute C gaining an unauthorized access to the corresponding resource, or it can first execute C and then perform the (useless) authentication step as shown in Figure 2. Hence it is crucial to maintain the global execution ordering of the application modules. At least for now, it is out of scope for secure processors to enforce such invariants by themselves. Although these processors provide enclaves the capability of attesting themselves to other enclaves (local attestation) if requested by them, it is the programmer's job to actually ask for the attestation while switching between the modules/enclaves to ensure ordering consistency.

3 THREAT MODEL

We assume an insidious software adversary capable of subverting privileged system software (operating system or hypervisor), reconfiguring software-programmable devices (such as a DMA controller), and actively seeking to subvert a sensitive application executing on a modern "secure processor" system. The adversary is expected to attempt to mount a *privilege escalation* attack (in the context of sensitive software employing trusted and enclaved

authentication/access control mechanism) in order to achieve behavior that violates the application's policy.

Denial of service, however, is not in the scope of this work, as a privileged adversary controls resource allocation, and may easily deny resources to a victim application. Also not modeled is an adversary seeking to infer private information from direct or indirect side effects of the execution of the sensitive software.

The adversary is assumed to have full control of the OS/Hypervisor, and is able to arbitrarily orchestrate system resources, computation, and launch or destroy processes including enclaves at will. The secure processor is assumed to correctly implement the enclave primitive, consisting of a process with private memory with integrity and privacy guarantees (an adversary is unable to modify the text or data of an enclave, and is unable to tamper with the execution of an enclave other than to deny it service, destroy it, or falsify untrusted inputs).

In order to compromise the sensitive application, the attacker may directly manipulate the application's control flow (e.g., by exploiting a vulnerability in the application code), or via a privileged attack whereby malicious system software violates its own process abstraction, undermining the integrity of the program and/or its data.

The application is assumed to be designed in accordance with the principles outlined in this manuscript: a modular system whereby each module is responsible for some well-defined task, e.g., collecting clients' requests, policy checking, database access etc. Following the standard model of secure processors, we consider that the system is initially in a safe state, following a trusted bootstrapping process. It is assumed that the application code is provided by a trusted software vendor, and the various enclaved code is authenticated via the enclaves' measurement (signature) *SIGSTRUCT* through the vendor's verification key *VK*. The system is assumed to correctly implement enclave measurement, whereby the measurement of a sealed enclave is descriptive of its state. In the case of SGX, incorrect or extraneous pages loaded by an adversary via *EADD* alter the enclave's measurement created by *EEXTEND* and are detectable during attestation.

In order to minimize the trusted computing base, the application designer must not enclave the entire sensitive application, and instead employ several collaborative enclaves, as described in Section 4. The reason being security concerns – as large, buggy trusted code is not trustworthy – and performance considerations since enclave memory is limited and fragmented on systems such as SGX. In a system with multiple communicating enclaves the adversary is assumed capable of tampering with the order of enclave execution, mount replay attacks, and tamper with enclave communications (by dropping, reordering, or replaying messages, as enclaves are authenticated), as described in Section 2.4 (cf. Figure 2).

This work fully trusts enclave software modules and assumes that the modules are correctly implemented. This work does not guard against software vulnerabilities (buffer overflows and other examples where an application violates its own security) in critical enclaved modules.

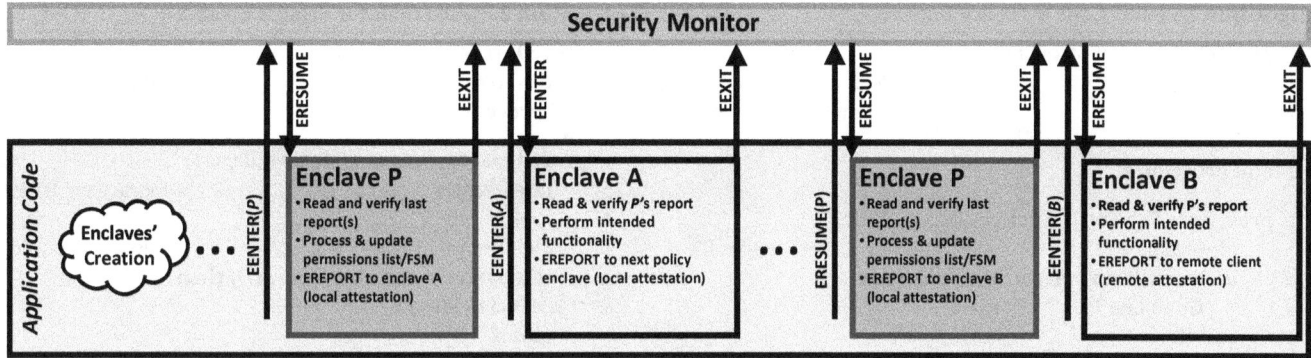

Figure 3: Application execution flow under the proposed framework on Sanctum architecture.

4 PROPOSED FRAMEWORK

Now that we have provided sufficient background regarding the functioning of secure processors and discussed our threat model, we move forward and present our proposed methodology through which these secure processors can be leveraged to offer concrete guarantees for authentication and access control schemes.

4.1 The Big Picture

4.1.1 Types of Application Enclaves. As mentioned earlier, the application designer is expected to design the application code in a modular fashion in order to perform different subtasks of the application. Since the application is designed to run on a secure processor, it is vital that all the *sensitive* modules of the application – such as authentication, access control, database accessing – are wrapped inside secure enclaves (also termed as "regular" enclaves in this paper). In our model, one specific responsibility of the programmer is to implement a centralized policy checker module for not only all the authentication and access control jobs, but also to enforce/verify the global execution ordering of various modules. This module must be wrapped inside a secure enclave, called *policy enclave*.

4.1.2 An Alternative Approach: Distributed FSM. In order to guarantee that the identity of a user/task requesting a certain resource is properly authenticated and proper access control checks are performed by the policy checker module, the policy enclave must be invoked accordingly. Moreover, since a compromised OS can control the order in which modules/enclaves are executed, it can completely bypass the policy enclave or execute it in an incorrect order to avoid the access control checks and hence perform an unauthorized access (cf. Figure 2). Since the secure processors in their current form do not enforce "correct" execution orderings of enclaves, this problem might not be detected through individual enclaves' reports. To counter this problem, the programmer may implement a "distributed" finite state machine (FSM) such that each subsequent enclave is provided with the report of the previous previous enclave in order to ensure the correct execution and enclave ordering. However, distributing the FSM implementation in this manner introduces much higher complexity for the programmer, and also makes it harder to reason about the security properties offered by such a scheme.

4.1.3 Proposed Approach: Centralized FSM. In order to address this issue and provide the programmer the flexibility of having a centralized ordering/policy checker FSM, we propose to design the application such that it always invokes the policy enclave before entering any regular enclave. The policy enclave is created at the start of the application, and being part of the application, it is created and initialized in the same fashion as the regular enclaves. A high level interaction between the policy enclave and the regular enclaves of the application is shown in Figure 3. Each time a regular enclave A is entered, the application calls the policy enclave P which is provided with a report of the last enclave executed. The policy enclave performs vital access control checks based on the available permission list, as well as verifies the provided report. A successful verification also ensures a correct enclave execution order (cf. Section 4.2 for details). Finally, P creates its own report and sends it to enclave A, which verifies it in a similar manner upon entry. Upon exit, enclave A sends its latest report to policy enclave for future use. This sequence continues until the application terminates with the execution of the final regular enclave B which attests itself to the remote client via remote attestation.

4.2 Implementation Details

Algorithm 1 and Algorithm 2 show detailed pseudo codes of the policy enclave and the regular enclave(s) under our framework respectively. Using these algorithms, any generic FSM can be mapped to our framework to keep track of the application's execution flow.

For an application with N unique regular enclaves, the policy enclave initializes two null initialized arrays Counters and Nonce each of size N through the SETUPPOLICYENCLAVE procedure which also resets its internal FSM. The application, after the initial setup, starts with calling its first regular enclave. After which, the RUNPOLICYENCLAVE is always called before running a regular enclave with an identifier *NextID* and is provided with the report *Report* of the previously executed regular enclave identified by *id*. *Report* also contains a monotonically increasing counter c and a random nonce r (cf. Algorithm 2), the purpose of which will be explained in Section 4.3. RUNPOLICYENCLAVE calls VERIFYREPORT that first verifies the consistency of c and r against the corresponding values stored in arrays Counters and Nonce for *id*, followed by updating the stored values upon successful verification. It then performs

---

Algorithm 1 Pseudo Code for Policy Enclave.

1: **procedure** SETUPPOLICYENCLAVE(N)
2:     Counters := $\{0\}^N$ ▷ Null initialized array.
3:     Nonce := $\{\perp\}^N$ ▷ Empty nonce array.
4:     FSM-RESET( )
5: **end procedure**

1: **procedure** RUNPOLICYENCLAVE($Report, NextID$)
2:     $id \leftarrow Report$ ▷ Extract sender ID.
3:     **if** VERIFYREPORT($Report$)$== false$ **then**
4:         Go to line 15.
5:     **end if**
6:     FSM-UPDATESTATE(id)
7:     $S \leftarrow$ FSM-GETNEXTSTATES()
8:     **if** ($NextID \in S$) **then**
9:         Nonce[$NextID$] $\leftarrow RandomNonce$
10:         $r :=$ Nonce[$NextID$]; $c :=$ Counters[$NextID$]
11:         $R := EREPORT(\cdot||r||c)$
12:         SENDREPORT($R, NextID$)
13:         **return**
14:     **end if**
15:     Raise Exception.
16:     **return**
17: **end procedure**

1: **procedure** VERIFYREPORT(R)
2:     $id \leftarrow R$ ▷ Extract sender ID.
3:     $r \leftarrow R$ ▷ Extract nonce.
4:     $c \leftarrow R$ ▷ Extract counter.
5:     **if** (Nonce[id] $\neq r \lor$ Counters[id] $\neq c$) **then**
6:         **return** $false$
7:     **else**
8:         Nonce[id] $\leftarrow RandomNonce$
9:         Counters[id] $+ +$
10:     **end if**
11:     Verify R via $EGETKEY$
12:     **if** Verification Unsuccessful **then**
13:         **return** $false$
14:     **else**
15:         **return** $true$
16:     **end if**
17: **end procedure**

Algorithm 2 Pseudo Code for Regular Enclaves.

1: **procedure** SETUPREGULARENCLAVE( )
2:     $Counter = 0$ ▷ Null initialized counter.
3: **end procedure**

1: **procedure** RUNREGULARENCLAVE($Report$)
2:     $id \leftarrow Report$ ▷ Extract sender ID.
3:     $r \leftarrow Report$ ▷ Extract nonce.
4:     $c \leftarrow Report$ ▷ Extract counter.
5:     **if** ($Counter \neq c \lor id \neq PolicyID$) **then**
6:         Go to line 17
7:     **end if**
8:     Verify $Report$ via $EGETKEY$
9:     **if** Verification Unsuccessful **then**
10:         Go to line 17
11:     **end if**
12:     Execute Application Functionality
13:     $Counter + +$
14:     $R := EREPORT(\cdot||r||c)$
15:     SENDREPORT($R, PolicyID$)
16:     **return**
17:     Raise Exception.
18:     **return**
19: **end procedure**

---

and after executing the intended application functionality of the enclave, a new report is created using the last nonce and counter values and sent to the policy enclave for future use. *Counter* is incremented to keep track of the execution count of the enclave.

4.3 Security of the Proposed Framework

4.3.1 Asynchronous Exits (AEX). So far we talked about enclaves voluntarily exiting, i.e., via the *EEXIT* instruction. However, the OS can swap out an enclave asynchronously whenever needed. Notice that the entry point to renter this enclave will only be available through the *ERESUME* instruction. If a compromised OS tries to execute some other enclave between *AEX* and *ERESUME*, it will fail the report verification step in RUNREGULARENCLAVE procedure since the policy enclave will not create a report for this enclave until the previously suspended enclave finishes its execution. This means that the system cannot proceed until the OS allows the suspended enclave (and the suspended enclave only) to run to completion, hence maintaining the sequential ordering of the program. The only other possibility is a denial of service attack which is out of scope of this work (cf. Section 3).

4.3.2 Preventing Replay Attacks. Since an adversary may try to replay/re-execute a regular enclave more than once with and/or without executing the policy enclave in between (i.e., to bypass the policy checker), we introduce a random nonce r in the report creation process which binds two back to back executions of a policy and regular enclave.

When a policy enclave grants permission to run a regular enclave *NextID*, it embeds a random nonce in its report sent to enclave *NextID* and stores it a local array. When the *NextID* enclave enters, it first expects a report from the policy enclave to be available, and

the standard full report verification according to the secure processor's provided mechanisms. The policy enclave's FSM is then updated and the set of next valid state transitions S is identified. If the requested transition (enclave *NextID*) is allowed, then a new report is created with updated nonce and counter values and sent to *NextID* enclave. Any failed verification during this process would raise an exception.

Each regular enclave maintains its execution count in a variable *Counter* initialized upon enclave creation by SETUPREGULAREN-CLAVE. RUNREGULARENCLAVE wrapper is called whenever the application wants to enter this enclave. It is also provided with a report *Report* of the policy enclave that was just executed, and this report is verified in a similar manner. Upon successful verification only executes if that is the case. When it finishes execution, it sends back a report to the policy enclave with the same random nonce embedded into it. Since the policy enclave expects the same random nonce, the verification succeeds.

The adversary can try the following cases:

(1) If it tries to illegitimately run a regular enclave more than once without calling the policy enclave in between, then upon the second run of the regular enclave, the report from the policy enclave will not be available since it was not run again. Same goes for multiple consecutive runs of the policy enclave.

(2) If it tries to run the combination of back to back executions of the policy and a regular enclave causing an execution flow that violates the normal behavior of the application, this would result in attempting an invalid transition in the FSM of the policy enclave. Consequently, an exception will be raised.

(3) If it tries to replay an instance of a regular enclave from an older run together with an instance of policy enclave from a newer run, with both the instances having same counter values, then the random nonce comes into the picture and causes the verification to fail.

4.3.3 Preventing Tear down of Enclaves. The compromised OS may tear down or destroy any enclave and recreate it to run from the start. In order to prevent this scenario, the policy enclave maintains a monotonically increasing counter for each regular enclave which is embedded in each report sent to the corresponding enclave. The regular enclave also maintains its execution count in an independent counter. Unless one of the two enclaves, namely the policy enclave and the regular enclave, is destroyed/reset, their *independent* counters remain consistent. As soon as one of these enclaves is destroyed/reset, the counters become inconsistent and this violation is detected. In the worst case, if the adversary resets *all* the enclaves at once, including the policy enclave, then this simply means running the whole application from start in a normal fashion.

Hence, by utilizing the isolation and attestation properties of modern secure processors, our framework allows an application programmer to design a simplified policy checker to not only perform standard authentication and access control tasks but also to verify the correct program control flow at a coarse module-level granularity. A centralized policy checker to enforce correct control flow is only made possible by the vital role played by the proposed wrappers and the design methodology for the secure enclaves.

5 APPLICATIONS AND DISCUSSION

In this section, we show and discuss a couple of applications of our proposed framework which, when combined with programmer's intelligence, can prove to be a strong authentication and access control framework. We discuss the vulnerabilities in a transaction processing system (TPS) and how such cases can be dealt with using the proposed framework. Furthermore, we extend our discussion from a TPS to a distributed system setting where multiple compute nodes communicate with each other and convey their execution states via the proposed scheme.

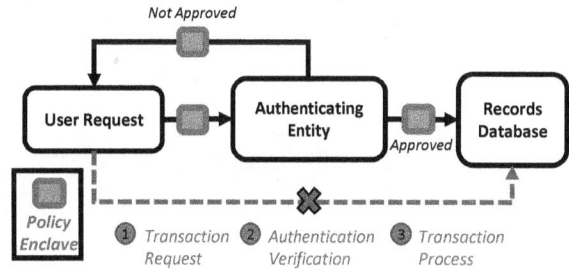

Figure 4: A Simple Transaction Processing System.

5.1 Transaction Processing System

Access control systems perform identity verification/authentication, access approval, and accountability of entities via login credentials such as passwords, personal identification numbers (PINs), biometric scans, and physical or electronic keys. In the past, authentication was almost synonymous with password systems, but today's authentication system must do more. One potential example that requires strong authentication and access control protocol can be a transaction process which should be authenticated, atomic and consistent.

Figure 4 shows a toy example of such a transaction processing system. Under normal conditions, the user inputs the request alongside its credentials to an *authenticating entity* which authenticates the user. Upon successful authentication, the user is granted permission to proceed with the request and execute a database query. The *database management system (DBMS)* processes the query and returns the corresponding result to the user.

Notice that the application flow in the transaction process is being managed by the underlying operating system. If the OS gets compromised, there can be multiple events where it can rattle the system (as shown in Figure 2) by either re-ordering the execution, or bypassing multiple steps to disrupt the process.

Our framework deals with such problematic scenarios as follows. When the user generates a request, the policy enclave verifies the *report* generated by the *user enclave*. Upon verification, the request is forwarded to the *authenticating enclave* to authenticate the user credentials. If the authentication does not succeed, the user is not granted permission to continue, and the request is terminated after the policy enclave updates its states for future requests. However, if the user authentication is successful then before accessing the database, first the policy enclave is invoked again which verifies that the last enclave executed was actually the authentication enclave. If the OS grants the user an unauthorized access to execute a database query without proper authentication (i.e., without authenticating its access permissions) then the above mentioned verification will fail and an exception will be raised. As the policy enclave enforces the correct execution order, there exists no such scenario where a compromised OS can re-order the enclave execution sequence, neither can it skip the execution of some enclaves. Hence, maintaining proper authentication and access control guarantees.

5.2 Smart Grid

Smart grid (SG) has emerged as the next generation of power grid due to its reliability, flexibility, and efficiency. In SG, the users are

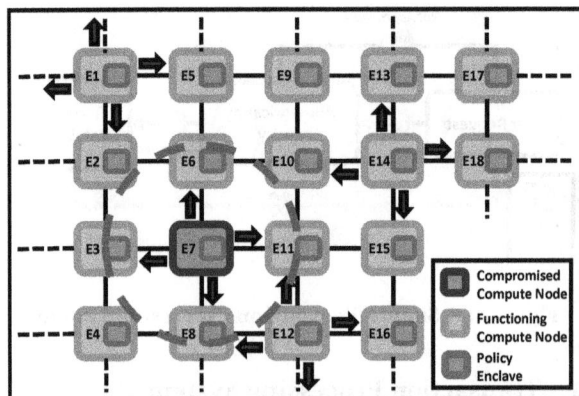

Figure 5: A distributed system with multiple compute nodes, each containing a policy checker. Logging mechanism of one node notifies the neighboring nodes about its status.

no longer passive players. Instead, they can undertake active roles to effectively minimize energy consumption by communicating back and forth with the provider. Smart grids follow the policy of *distributed systems* where work is divided among multiple compute nodes (devices). These devices communicate with each other to provide the final response to end users. Numerous machines including sensing devices, smart meters, and control systems are expected to be in between the provider and end users to facilitate this two-way communication system in SG.

In Section 5.1 we discussed how the proposed framework protects the transaction processing system via a stringent authentication and access control policy. Moving this discussion forward, consider a distributed system as shown in Figure 5. In such a system, the compute nodes communicate and interact with each other in order to achieve a common goal. If one of the nodes gets compromised, it might access some confidential information of other nodes in the system, and/or inject faulty messages into the network, consequently disrupting the whole process. In case of a smart grid, this unauthorized entity can send fabricated messages [12] to the neighborhood devices in the grid. If the messages cannot be filtered and processed, the control center might ultimately be misled and make incorrect decisions such as incorrect load balancing. Such scenarios can prove to be dreadful.

Consider that the policy enclave designed by the application developer has a "logging" functionality as well to report its system status to the neighboring nodes. Even with such a policy enclave, without enforcing the enclave execution ordering, the compromised OS might bypass the policy enclave preventing it from reporting its (compromised) status via the logging mechanism to the neighboring nodes.

On the other hand, under our framework with the correct execution ordering enforced, if the OS tries to inject new packets into the network, e.g., by executing a *network enclave*, this would require the policy enclave to be executed first (to maintain our framework's invariant). Therefore, at this point, either the the policy enclave must be executed first – which would result in reporting the compromised status log to the neighbors – or no "faulty" packets can be injected into the network. Communicating the log to the neighbors

would allow them to suspend/ignore their future communications with the compromised node until that node is recovered.

5.3 MapReduce

When processing distributed data sets of extreme size, MapReduce [7], as exemplified by *Apache Hadoop*, is a commonly used framework, as it offers a productive abstraction for large-scale multiprocessor data processing by hiding the complexity associated with fault tolerance, data movement, and work orchestration in a large computing environment.

The MapReduce framework is organized into three distinct operations: Map (a programmer-supplied program that emits key-value pairs), a Shuffle (whereby the mapped pairs are grouped by key), and Reduce (a programmer-supplied script that processes the values grouped by key). A canonical "big data" example of MapReduce is a word count application: Map processes chunks of text input and emits (*word*, 1) for each word in the input, and after Shuffle groups these pairs by key, Reduce counts the number of values associated with each key to obtain a word count.

Consider a software adversary that seeks to subvert the execution. While an enclaved system cannot defend against a privileged denial of service, an attacker may seek to bias the computation by suppressing or falsifying keys during a shuffle operation, or subverting the map or reduce nodes. The MapReduce controller (scheduler) is an unequivocally trusted component: the controller parcels out work to various nodes within a computing cluster, and orchestrates the communication streams (shuffle) between Map and Reduce nodes. Enclaving the controller is not alone sufficient to guard the MapReduce framework against a software adversary, however, as both the messages sent by the controller, and the mapper and reducer nodes must be authenticated and tied to trusted enclaved code. Even with individual nodes enclaved and therefore resistant to an adversary's attempts to tamper with the computation, MapReduce may be vulnerable to a capable adversary suppressing some key-value pairs during a shuffle operation, or performing replay attacks.

Consider the policy enclave implementing the functions of a MapReduce controller, parceling out shares of input data to (enclaved) mapper nodes, which 1). authenticate the controller's messages, and 2) produce a certificate attesting to the integrity of the result of the Map or Reduce operation. A software adversary is unable to defeat the integrity of the MapReduce controller (the policy enclave), and therefore cannot falsify the input partitioning or shuffle. Should an adversary tamper with Map or Reduce enclaves, they would either not run or not produce a certificate that authenticates their output, either being a failure, which the MapReduce framework is designed to tolerate.

A prudent system designer can extend this sketch to implement an augmented MapReduce, where the the mapper and reducer nodes enforce differential privacy [9], or aggregate secret datasets on behalf of multiple mutually distrusting entities. The system composed of enclaves orchestrated and authenticated by the policy enclave acting as a MapReduce controller offers a trusted, authenticated party that thwarts capable software adversaries and enforces high-level policies.

5.4 Discussion

Our framework opens up several other possibilities for richer application design. We discuss two of the possible improvements that can be made to the applications under this model.

Since the dynamic execution flow is guaranteed to be consistent with the application designer's intended control flow, one can extend the policy enclave to collect "behavioral" information about the regular enclaves running in the system. With some standard machine learning algorithms, the policy checker can be enhanced to incorporate multiple behavioral authentication factors resulting in dynamically adjusting to the program's behavior at run time. This can also be used to develop intelligent anomaly detection mechanisms. For instance, if a user/enclave starts reading unusually high amount of records from a database, this could potentially mean that this user is trying to replicate or clone the database and should be prevented from doing so.

The policy enclave can also be enriched by incorporating a logging mechanism for a distributed system setting. With our model, for example, the *stealthy logging* mechanism from [2] can potentially be simplified since the adversary (e.g., the compromised OS) cannot directly access the reserved memory of the policy enclave where the system's log is stored.

6 CONCLUSION

We have proposed a software application design methodology that leverages the software isolation container (enclave) primitive offered by modern secure processors to enforce correct flow of execution within a sensitive application. With no required changes to modern hardware, our methodology allows the application designer to securely perform authentication and access control. We provide a comprehensive discussion of security of the proposed scheme in the presence of a privileged software adversary. In addition to thwarting an adversary attempting to circumvent application policy checks, our framework offers the application designer a global view of application state via the policy checker enclave, which in turn enables high-level policies to be described and tailored for a given application.

ACKNOWLEDGMENTS

The work is partially supported by NSF grants CNS-1413920 and CNS-1413996 for MACS: A Modular Approach to Cloud Security.

REFERENCES

[1] Periklis Akritidis, Manuel Costa, Miguel Castro, and Steven Hand. Baggy Bounds Checking: An Efficient and Backwards-Compatible Defense against Out-of-Bounds Errors.. In *USENIX Security Symposium*.

[2] Kevin D Bowers, Catherine Hart, Ari Juels, and Nikos Triandopoulos. 2014. Pillarbox: Combating next-generation malware with fast forward-secure logging. In *International Workshop on Recent Advances in Intrusion Detection*. Springer, 46–67.

[3] Miguel Castro, Manuel Costa, and Tim Harris. Securing software by enforcing data-flow integrity. In *Proceedings of the 7th Symposium on Operating Systems Design and Implementation*.

[4] David Champagne and Ruby B Lee. 2010. Scalable architectural support for trusted software. In *High Performance Computer Architecture (HPCA), 2010 IEEE 16th International Symposium on*. IEEE, 1–12.

[5] Shimin Chen, Michael Kozuch, Theodoros Strigkos, Babak Falsafi, Phillip B Gibbons, Todd C Mowry, Vijaya Ramachandran, Olatunji Ruwase, Michael Ryan, and Evangelos Vlachos. Flexible hardware acceleration for instruction-grain program monitoring. *ACM SIGARCH Computer Architecture News* 36, 3 (2008).

[6] Victor Costan, Ilia Lebedev, and Srinivas Devadas. 2016. Sanctum: Minimal Hardware Extensions for Strong Software Isolation. In *25th USENIX Security Symposium (USENIX Security 16)*. USENIX Association, Austin, TX, 857–874. https://www.usenix.org/conference/usenixsecurity16/technical-sessions/presentation/costan

[7] Jeffrey Dean and Sanjay Ghemawat. 2008. MapReduce: Simplified Data Processing on Large Clusters. *Commun. ACM* 51, 1 (Jan. 2008), 107–113. https://doi.org/10.1145/1327452.1327492

[8] Joe Devietti, Colin Blundell, Milo MK Martin, and Steve Zdancewic. 2008. Hardbound: architectural support for spatial safety of the C programming language. In *ACM SIGARCH Computer Architecture News*, Vol. 36. ACM, 103–114.

[9] Cynthia Dwork. 2006. Differential Privacy. In *Automata, Languages and Programming, 33rd International Colloquium, ICALP 2006, Venice, Italy, July 10-14, 2006, Proceedings, Part II*. 1–12. https://doi.org/10.1007/11787006_1

[10] Christopher Fletcher, Marten van Dijk, and Srinivas Devadas. 2012. Secure Processor Architecture for Encrypted Computation on Untrusted Programs. In *Proceedings of the 7th ACM CCS Workshop on Scalable Trusted Computing; an extended version is located at http://csg.csail.mit.edu/pubs/memos/Memo508/memo508.pdf (Master's thesis)*. 3–8.

[11] Hugo Gamboa and Ana Fred. 2004. A behavioral biometric system based on human-computer interaction. In *Defense and Security*. International Society for Optics and Photonics, 381–392.

[12] H. Li, R. Lu, L. Zhou, B. Yang, and X. Shen. 2014. An Efficient Merkle-Tree-Based Authentication Scheme for Smart Grid. *IEEE Systems Journal* 8, 2 (June 2014), 655–663. https://doi.org/10.1109/JSYST.2013.2271537

[13] D. Lie, J. Mitchell, C. Thekkath, and M. Horwitz. 2003. Specifying and Verifying Hardware for Tamper-Resistant Software. In *Proceedings of the IEEE Symposium on Security and Privacy*.

[14] D. Lie, C. Thekkath, and M. Horowitz. 2003. Implementing an Untrusted Operating System on Trusted Hardware. In *Proceedings of the Nineteenth ACM Symposium on Operating Systems Principles*. 178–192.

[15] David Lie, Chandramohan Thekkath, Mark Mitchell, Patrick Lincoln, Dan Boneh, John Mitchell, and Mark Horowitz. 2000. Architectural Support for Copy and Tamper Resistant Software. In *Proceedings of the 9th Int'l Conference on Architectural Support for Programming Languages and Operating Systems (ASPLOS-IX)*. 168–177.

[16] Martin Maas, Eric Love, Emil Stefanov, Mohit Tiwari, Elaine Shi, Krste Asanovic, John Kubiatowicz, and Dawn Song. 2013. Phantom: Practical oblivious computation in a secure processor. In *Proceedings of the 2013 ACM SIGSAC conference on Computer & communications security*. ACM, 311–324.

[17] Frank McKeen, Ilya Alexandrovich, Alex Berenzon, Carlos V Rozas, Hisham Shafi, Vedvyas Shanbhogue, and Uday R Savagaonkar. 2013. Innovative instructions and software model for isolated execution.. In *HASP@ ISCA*. 10.

[18] Santosh Nagarakatte, Milo Martin, and Stephan A Zdancewic. 2012. Watchdog: Hardware for Safe and Secure Manual Memory Management and Full Memory Safety. In *Proceedings of the 39th International Symposium on Computer Architecture*.

[19] Santosh Nagarakatte, Jianzhou Zhao, Milo M.K. Martin, and Steve Zdancewic. SoftBound: Highly Compatible and Complete Spatial Memory Safety for C. In *Proceedings of the 2009 ACM SIGPLAN Conference on Programming Language Design and Implementation*.

[20] George C Necula, Jeremy Condit, Matthew Harren, Scott McPeak, and Westley Weimer. 2005. CCured: Type-safe retrofitting of legacy software. *ACM Transactions on Programming Languages and Systems (TOPLAS)* 27, 3 (2005), 477–526.

[21] Elaine Shi, Yuan Niu, Markus Jakobsson, and Richard Chow. 2010. Implicit authentication through learning user behavior. In *International Conference on Information Security*. Springer, 99–113.

[22] G. Edward Suh, Dwaine Clarke, Blaise Gassend, Marten van Dijk, and Srinivas Devadas. 2003. AEGIS: Architecture for Tamper-Evident and Tamper-Resistant Processing. In *Proceedings of the 17th ICS (MIT-CSAIL-CSG-Memo-474 is an updated version)*. ACM, New-York. http://csg.csail.mit.edu/pubs/memos/Memo-474/Memo-474.pdf(revisedone)

[23] G. Edward Suh, Charles W. O'Donnell, Ishan Sachdev, and Srinivas Devadas. 2005. Design and Implementation of the AEGIS Single-Chip Secure Processor Using Physical Random Functions. In *Proceedings of the 32nd ISCA'05*. ACM, New-York. http://csg.csail.mit.edu/pubs/memos/Memo-483/Memo-483.pdf

[24] Jonathan Woodruff, Robert NM Watson, David Chisnall, Simon W Moore, Jonathan Anderson, Brooks Davis, Ben Laurie, Peter G Neumann, Robert Norton, and Michael Roe. 2014. The CHERI capability model: Revisiting RISC in an age of risk. In *Computer Architecture (ISCA), 2014 ACM/IEEE 41st International Symposium on*. IEEE, 457–468.

[25] Yuanzhong Xu, Weidong Cui, and Marcus Peinado. Controlled-channel attacks: Deterministic side channels for untrusted operating systems. In *IEEE S&P'15*.

[26] Larry Zhu, Sam Hartman, and Karthik Jaganathan. 2005. The Kerberos Version 5 Generic Security Service Application Program Interface (GSS-API) Mechanism: Version 2. (2005).

A Framework for the Cryptographic Enforcement of Information Flow Policies

James Alderman
Information Security Group
Royal Holloway, University of London
Egham, Surrey TW20 0EX, UK
James.Alderman@rhul.ac.uk

Jason Crampton
Information Security Group
Royal Holloway, University of London
Egham, Surrey TW20 0EX, UK
Jason.Crampton@rhul.ac.uk

Naomi Farley
Information Security Group
Royal Holloway, University of London
Egham, Surrey TW20 0EX, UK
Naomi.Farley.2010@live.rhul.ac.uk

ABSTRACT

It is increasingly common to outsource data storage to untrusted, third party (e.g. cloud) servers. However, in such settings, low-level online reference monitors may not be appropriate for enforcing read access, and thus cryptographic enforcement schemes (CESs) may be required. Much of the research on cryptographic access control has focused on the use of specific primitives and, primarily, on how to generate appropriate keys and fails to model the access control system as a whole. Recent work in the context of role-based access control has shown a gap between theoretical policy specification and computationally secure implementations of access control policies, potentially leading to insecure implementations. Without a formal model, it is hard to (i) reason about the correctness and security of a CES, and (ii) show that the security properties of a particular cryptographic primitive are sufficient to guarantee security of the CES as a whole.

In this paper, we provide a rigorous definitional framework for a CES that enforces read-only information flow policies (which encompass many practical forms of access control, including role-based policies). This framework (i) provides a tool by which instantiations of CESs can be proven correct and secure, (ii) is independent of any particular cryptographic primitives used to instantiate a CES, and (iii) helps to identify the limitations of current primitives (e.g. key assignment schemes) as components of a CES.

KEYWORDS

Cryptographic Enforcement Scheme; Information Flow Policy; Access Control; Cryptography; Key Assignment Scheme; Attribute-based Encryption

ACM Reference format:
James Alderman, Jason Crampton, and Naomi Farley. 2017. A Framework for the Cryptographic Enforcement of Information Flow Policies. In *Proceedings of SACMAT'17, Indianapolis, IN, USA, June 21-23, 2017,* 12 pages.
https://doi.org/http://dx.doi.org/10.1145/3078861.3078868

James Alderman was supported by the European Comission through H2020-ICT-2014-1-644024 "CLARUS".

Naomi Farley was supported by the UK EPSRC through EP/K035584/1 "Centre for Doctoral Training in Cyber Security at Royal Holloway".

1 INTRODUCTION

Many multi-user systems require some form of access control which requires specifying and enforcing a policy that defines the actions each user is authorized to perform. Traditionally, enforcement has required trusted on-line monitors to evaluate access requests. However, this approach is not necessarily appropriate for systems where the policy enforcement mechanism is not controlled by a trusted party (e.g. the policy author), or if the mechanism is not always available. An alternative is to use cryptographic techniques.

A *Cryptographic Enforcement Scheme* (CES) to control *read access* to data objects must, at its most basic, provide a method to protect (encrypt) data and issue users the necessary cryptographic materials (keys) to access (decrypt) data that they are authorized to read. Furthermore, changes to the policy, such as extending or retracting the access rights of a user, or changing the security level of an object should be supported by the CES; such policy changes can have an effect on both the required cryptographic material, and on the security and correctness of the policy enforcement itself. Furthermore, as cryptographic material is vulnerable to compromise or leakage through exposure, a CES should provide a mechanism to refresh cryptographic material.

Whilst enforcement by a trusted monitor is *guaranteed* to permit only authorized requests, efficient cryptographic primitives are usually *computationally* secure (due to their probabilistic nature). Further, there may be real-world concerns to be addressed by an implementation that are not required in idealized, theoretical models. Thus, as observed by Ferrara *et al.* [12], there may exist a gap between the theoretical specification of an access control policy and a cryptographic implementation of an enforcement mechanism. Hence, one must carefully consider whether cryptographic primitives can achieve the correctness and security requirements to properly enforce an access control policy and, if multiple primitives are required, they can be safely combined. A vital part of such consideration is the establishment of rigorous definitions and security models for the required functionality of a CES.

To emphasize the gap between policy specification and cryptographic enforcement mechanisms, let us consider Key Assignment Schemes (KASs) [3] used to enforce an information flow policy (similar arguments can be made for other primitives such as functional encryption schemes). In general, KASs define how key material is generated, and derived, for a given access structure but do not define algorithms for encrypting objects, updating key material, or for carrying out changes to the policy. In fact, this additional functionality can have a significant effect on the cryptographic material supplied by the KAS — e.g. assigning a user additional access rights may require extra keys to be securely distributed to the user, whilst the removal of a user typically requires that all of their keys (at least) be updated, under the assumption that users may locally store their keys and could continue to decrypt objects for which they are no longer authorized. If such changes are not implemented carefully, the security and correctness of the KAS itself could be compromised, as well as that of the CES as a whole.

1.1 Related Work and Motivation

Many cryptographic enforcement mechanisms have been proposed, primarily to enforce *read* access to data objects via an encryption mechanism. Two particularly notable proposals are Key Assignment Schemes (KASs) [2, 9] and functional encryption schemes, especially *Attribute-based Encryption* (ABE) [6, 17]. Throughout this paper, we shall periodically refer to both KASs and ABE as example cryptographic mechanisms that may be used within the context of a CES.

In general, *write* access can be more difficult than read-access to cryptographically enforce and typically requires additional assumptions on the trustworthiness and capabilities of the storage provider, or additional trusted entities [10]. In particular, whilst one can often use cryptographic primitives that provide data origin authentication to *detect* data originating from an unauthorized writer [14, 22], it can be difficult to *prevent* unauthorized writes to the (externally controlled) file-system in the first place. Furthermore, to ensure correctness of the system following an unauthorized write, one must ensure the storage provider maintains the ability to 'roll-back' data objects or to otherwise ensure that legitimate writes are maintained. In this paper, like most related work, we focus our attention on read-only policies, with the observation that *detection* mechanisms should be a simple future extension to this work if required.

Key Assignment Schemes (KASs) [2, 9] are symmetric cryptographic primitives that can be used to enforce read-only information flow policies. Security notions for KASs [3] capture the requirements that no (collusion of) users may compute a key for which they are unauthorized (*key recovery*), and the stronger notion that no information is leaked about keys for which users are unauthorized (*key indistinguishability (KI)*).

While the above security notions capture the required security of generated keys (i.e keys do not reveal information about other keys), they do not capture the *distribution, use* and *update* of such keys. Furthermore, when considering the use of a KAS *within* a CES, it becomes clear that key recovery is not a suitable property and that key indistinguishability alone is not sufficient. Indeed, the security requirements of a KAS and CES are intrinsically different.

Key indistinguishability of a KAS states that a user who is not authorized to hold a *key* cannot learn anything about the key even having learned the keys of other unauthorized users. We argue that a secure CES requires that an unauthorized user attempting to access a particular *object* cannot learn anything about the *data* written to that object[1] even if it can learn the keys of other unauthorized users, see the entire file-system, know the data written to other objects, and force certain policy updates. In other words, security for KASs is defined in terms of decryption keys, whilst we

consider the more relevant property of access to objects which, as we will see, is not the same as prior security notions.

Clearly, without defining the required protection properties for objects, which keys are to be used, and how keys should be handled, it is not necessarily true that a lack of knowledge about a single key implies that nothing is learned about an object in a CES. Indeed, the logical combination of a KI-secure KAS and an IND-CPA secure encryption scheme [5] can be trivially insecure if, for example, the file-system leaks information about other keys defined by the KAS when writing objects. Whilst this simple example is very easy to avoid, other scenarios may be more subtle, especially when using multiple, complex cryptographic primitives with intricate security properties in a system, such as a CES, comprising many components, entities and feasible execution paths. Thus we believe that the requirements of a CES system *as a whole* must be considered rather than just a single component. At the very least, it must be clear what the security and correctness objectives of the system are in order to select suitable cryptographic components.

To this end, Ferrara *et al.* [12] emphasize the importance of providing a formal model for secure Cryptographic Role-based Access Control. They describe how cryptographic access-control schemes often only informally analyze the gap between policy specification and a proposed implementation. To illustrate this point, they describe how cryptographic guarantees are *probabilistic* whilst policies are *deterministic* (some party does/does not have access to some object). Gifford [15] previously presented a framework for cryptographic access control (including information flow), but could not, at the time, consider modern cryptographic security notions for computationally secure primitives, and presented separate models for symmetric and asymmetric primitives. In contrast, our framework provides formal cryptographic games to model correctness and security and is defined independently of particular cryptographic primitives. In concurrent work, Damgård *et al.* introduced the notion of *Access Control Encryption* [10] which aims to restrict write access within an encryption scheme. Whilst this work certainly appears to be in a promising direction, it requires an additional entity known as the *Sanitizer* to process all data sent over public channels.

1.2 Contributions

In order to ensure that a cryptographic mechanism adequately enforces an information flow policy, it is vital to have a rigorous and concrete framework to specify the functional, correctness and security requirements of a CES. The aim of this paper is to introduce such a framework, which is intended to be useful to designers and implementers of CESs, both to guarantee the adequacy of existing proposals and to identify areas that need further research.

Ferrara *et al.* [12] studied the setting of *role-based access control* (RBAC). In this paper, we consider CESs for read-only information flow policies. Crampton [8] showed that many access control policies of practical interest, such as attribute- and role-based policies, can be represented as information flow policies; therefore, our framework is widely applicable and can be viewed as a continuation of the work of Ferrara *et al.* to bridge the gap between the specification of access control models and the capabilities of cryptographic primitives. Indeed, as future work, Ferrara *et al.* [12]

---

[1] In the context of a CES where objects are stored on an externally controlled file-system, we cannot prevent physical access to an object but instead must protect the *data* written to an object from being learned by unauthorized entities.

suggested modeling general access control frameworks; one can view our work as a step towards this goal.

Whilst there is a wealth of work considering cryptographic access control requirements [1, 2, 9, 11, 14, 17–21], such works often focus on using particular cryptographic primitives or are tailored to a specific application. In contrast, we start from the specification of a general access control policy (information flow policies), from which we identify the requirements of a CES. We do not target any particular primitives and, instead, aim to provide a framework that can be instantiated by a range of cryptographic primitives, both symmetric and public key. We define several classifications of CESs based on their desired, generic, functionality. As a result, we hope to provide a framework within which one can analyze specific CES instantiations to ensure correctness and security.

We begin in Section 2 by introducing some notation and recalling basic concepts related to information flow policies. In Section 3, we introduce our model of CESs and classify the required functionality, before defining correctness and security in Section 4. In Section 5, we discuss some example schemes, highlighting their shortcomings in the context of our model. We conclude the paper with a summary of our contributions and some ideas for future work.

2 PRELIMINARIES

We write $a \leftarrow x$ to denote the assignment of x to variable a, whilst $a \xleftarrow{\$} X$ denotes a being assigned a value selected uniformly at random from the set X. We write $a \leftarrow B(c)$ to denote a polynomial time algorithm B being run on input c and the output being assigned to a, and write $a \xleftarrow{\$} B(c)$ if B is probabilistic polynomial time (PPT). We denote a security parameter by ρ and its unary representation by 1^ρ. A function f is *negligible* if, for every polynomial $p(\cdot)$, there exists an N such that for all integers $n > N$, $f(n) < \frac{1}{p(n)}$.

We use the symbol $\perp$ to denote (i) failure when output by an algorithm, and (ii) a null value when assigned to a variable. We denote the elements of a list or array A of n elements by $A[0], \ldots, A[n-1]$.

A *partially ordered set* or poset is a pair $(L, \leqslant)$, where $\leqslant$ is a binary, reflexive, anti-symmetric, transitive relation on L. For a poset $(L, \leqslant)$, we write $x < y$ if $x \leqslant y$ and $x \neq y$ and may write $x > y$ if $y < x$. The empty set is denoted $\emptyset$.

A *read-only information flow policy* is a tuple $P = ((L, \leqslant), U, O, \lambda)$, where (i) $(L, \leqslant)$ is a partially ordered set of *security labels*; (ii) U is the set of users; (iii) O is the set of data objects; and (iv) $\lambda : U \cup O \rightarrow L$ is a function mapping users and objects to security labels in L. We say $u \in U$ is *authorized* to read an object $o \in O$ if $\lambda(o) \leqslant \lambda(u)$.

For simplicity, and without loss of generality, we may choose U and O to be arbitrarily large and fixed, and assume that L has a top element $\sqcap$ and a bottom element $\sqcup$. For any object o that is "dormant" or "inactive", we set $\lambda(o)$ equal to $\sqcap$; and for any user u that is dormant, we set $\lambda(u)$ to be $\sqcup$. No user is assigned to $\sqcap$ and no object is assigned to $\sqcup$. In other words, inactive objects cannot be read by any user, and inactive users cannot read any object. Then, to model the addition of a user or object, we can instead activate a dormant user or object by changing the security label from $\sqcup$ or $\sqcap$, respectively; users and objects can similarly be removed by setting the security label to $\sqcup$ or $\sqcap$.

Traditionally, access control policies can be enforced by intercepting all attempts by users to interact with protected objects and determining whether the interaction is authorized. These functions are performed by what is known as a reference monitor (or, in more modern settings, the policy enforcement and policy decision points), a trusted software component that implements the logic of the authorization policy to evaluate a request from u to read o. Roughly speaking, the reference monitor instructs an unintelligent storage system to release an object to the user if the interaction is found to be authorized.

3 CRYPTOGRAPHIC ENFORCEMENT OF INFORMATION FLOW POLICIES

Recently, we have seen considerable interest in outsourcing the storage of data. In this case, the storage provider, not the data owner, controls access to the data. Moreover, the storage provider may have incentives to inspect the data it stores on behalf of its clients. Conversely, the data owner may not wish the storage provider to have read access to the data. Thus, informally, the data owner may wish to encrypt data before giving it to the storage provider, thus preventing the storage provider (and any entity to which the storage provider releases the data) from reading the data. In addition, the data owner will distribute appropriate keys to authorized users.

As mentioned, we focus on *read* access in this paper. We assume that the data owner (or a *manager* entity) is responsible for the protection of all objects and supplying the encrypted objects to the storage provider via an authenticated channel. (In practice, the manager could represent a set of authorized writers if required.) The storage provider simply stores all encrypted objects it is given and releases them on request to users. In other words, the storage system is essentially public and *all* users have access to *all* encrypted objects (but not all users have access to all decryption keys). We model the storage provider as an honest-but-curious adversary — it will store objects correctly and release them on request, but may try to learn information about the stored contents.

As mentioned in the introduction, we believe it is important, especially when considering complex cryptographic primitives, to have a rigorous framework for the requirements of a CES, both to aid the design of CESs and to identify areas for future work. In this section, we formulate the requirements of a read-only CES, building from the access control requirements of the policy with no particular instantiation or cryptographic primitives in mind. Indeed, our definitions of the algorithms that a CES must implement are intentionally general, in order to cater for different possible instantiations. In particular, our definitions may be instantiated using symmetric or asymmetric cryptographic primitives. Where appropriate, we shall, however, refer to example instantiations to illustrate certain concepts.

3.1 State Requirements

In a CES, data objects are encrypted using some kind of cryptographic primitive and access to an object is effected by decrypting. Thus, any CES needs to maintain a certain amount of cryptographic material, some of which will be public and some secret, held by different entities. We begin our development of a framework by considering the information, or state, that each entity within a CES must maintain, distinguishing between user, object and system states. We distinguish between an object (as created by the data

Notation	Meaning	Part of
$\text{st}_{\mathcal{M}}$	State of the manager/system	-
$\alpha(l)$	Secret material associated to label l	$\text{st}_{\mathcal{M}}$
ϕ	Private additional information held by the manager	$\text{st}_{\mathcal{M}}$
Π	Public information including the file-system FS	-
FS	Public file-system	Π
$\pi(l)$	Public material associated to label l	Π
ψ	Additional public information	Π
o	An object identifier	O
$d(o)$	Data written to o	o
$\overline{d(o)}$	Protected form of o	FS
u	A user identifier	U
st_u	State of user u	-

Table 1: Notation used for modeling states of entities

owner) and its state in the system (in a protected format with any necessary metadata). We will then, in Section 3.2, consider the algorithmic requirements to use, maintain and update these states, which will lead us to consider a classification of CESs according to their functional requirements. Table 1 summarizes the notation we shall introduce in the next section to describe states in a CES.

3.1.1 System. Clearly, within a CES, some cryptographic material must be generated. This is performed by the trusted system manager (or data owner), $\mathcal{M}$. The manager will also need to use some of the generated material to *protect* objects as they are written (recall that the manager performs all write operations in a read-only CES), to *refresh* existing material throughout the lifetime of the system, and to *grant access* to users (by distributing appropriate material). Therefore, the manager must store some or all of the material it generates for later use. We denote the *state*, containing all information currently held by the manager, by $\text{st}_{\mathcal{M}}$.

In information flow policies, access is determined in terms of security labels. Hence, a CES for such policies may require, for each label $l \in L$:

- some secret information, denoted $\alpha(l)$ (e.g. cryptographic material for performing encryption and decryption of objects that have security label l); and
- some public information, denoted $\pi(l)$ (e.g. public information to aid the derivation of $\alpha(l)$ in a KAS).

Each user u must be provided with a means to learn some or all of $\alpha(l)$ for all $l \leqslant \lambda(u)$. Similarly, each object o must be protected using some or all of $\alpha(\lambda(o))$.

The manager must store (or be able to efficiently regenerate) $\alpha(l)$ for each label such that it may be issued to users when relevant. $\mathcal{M}$ may also require additional material to perform his duties (beyond that associated purely to labels) e.g. additional system parameters. We denote such material, which is known only to $\mathcal{M}$, by ϕ. The *private state* of $\mathcal{M}$ is therefore:

$$\text{st}_{\mathcal{M}} = (\phi, \{\alpha(l)\}_{l \in L}).$$

The manager must also make certain information publicly available to users and the storage provider. We have already seen that some public information, $\pi(l)$, related to security labels may be required. In addition, the file-system, FS, containing all protected objects (i.e. the information that is outsourced to the storage provider) is assumed to be publicly available (as any entity can request any outsourced data directly from the storage provider) and therefore forms part of the public state of the system. Finally, we may define ψ to be any additional public information required by a particular instantiation. The *public state* of the system is therefore:

$$\Pi = (\psi, \{\pi(l)\}_{l \in L}, FS).$$

We refer to the state of the system as a whole as $\text{st}_{\mathcal{M}}$ and Π and note that, together, they model all information held in the system (we shall shortly introduce user states which will identify which components of the system state is held by which entities).

Example 3.1. Consider a CES instantiated using the ABE scheme of Goyal *et al.* [17], where each attribute corresponds to a security label. Then, for each label $l \in L$, the manager must define a secret exponent $\alpha(l) \in \mathbb{Z}_p$ and compute a public group element $\pi(l) = g^{\alpha(l)}$. Furthermore, the manager must store additional secret information $\phi \in \mathbb{Z}_p$ (the system-wide secret exponent). Finally, Π must additionally store the masking term $\psi = e(g, g)^{\phi}$.

3.1.2 Objects. Each object within a CES must be protected according to its security label. The protected object is written to a file-system maintained by an untrusted storage provider.

In non-cryptographic settings for information flow policies, objects can be abstractly modeled *entirely* by an identifier and their security label — a reference monitor is guaranteed to permit or deny access to objects based only on consideration of security labels. This is *not* the case in a CES: the enforcement mechanism (encryption) operates not only on the label but also on the *content* of an object o (the data) and the cryptographic material ($\alpha(\lambda(o))$ and $\pi(\lambda(o))$) associated to the label.

With these considerations in mind, we introduce the following notation to fully describe an object in O:

- o is a unique *identifier* which allows us to refer simply to an object and to apply the labeling function λ;
- $d(o)$ is the data written to the object o and to which we wish to control access; and
- $\overline{d(o)}$ denotes the protected form of o that is outsourced and to which all entities have access. We may assume that $\overline{d(o)}$ includes the label $\lambda(o)$.

Hence, we assume that the set of objects O is a set of pairs of the form $(o, d(o))$. Then the public data includes the file-system FS which contains a set of pairs of the form $(o, \overline{d(o)})$.[2] It may be helpful to think of o as a filename, $d(o)$ as the contents of a file and $\overline{d(o)}$ as the encrypted file. Clearly, one can refer to the entire object simply by referring to the filename, and writing to the file may change the content $d(o)$ without changing the filename.

---

[2]Note that in this work, we aim to protect only $d(o)$, and not any further meta-data of objects. In particular, the identifiers and security labels of objects are assumed to be public such that users can efficiently decide which objects to retrieve from the file-system and how to decrypt them.

3.1.3 Users. A user u is authorized to read an object o if $\lambda(u) \geqslant \lambda(o)$. Hence, u must be given information (derived from material contained in st_M) that enables u to decrypt objects. This information may simply be the decryption keys associated with labels $l \leqslant \lambda(u)$, or data that enables the derivation of those keys. For example, in many key assignment schemes [3], a user $u \in U$ is given a single secret $\sigma(\lambda(u))$ enabling the derivation of decryption keys associated to any $y \leqslant \lambda(u)$. We may assume that st_u contains the label $\lambda(u)$.

3.2 Functional Requirements

Having determined the minimal information that each entity must hold within a CES, we now look at the required algorithms. We shall see that one can model many different forms of CES depending on the required functionality, and this shall lead us to produce a classification of CESs.

A CES must support, at least, the following algorithms:

$$(st_M, \{msg_u\}_{u \in U}, \Pi) \xleftarrow{\$} \text{Setup}(1^\rho, P);$$
$$(d(o) \text{ or } \perp) \leftarrow \text{Read}(o, st_u, \Pi).$$

Setup is probabilistic and takes the policy $P = ((L, \leqslant), U, O, \lambda)$ and a security parameter 1^ρ as input. (Informally, ρ determines the strength of cryptographic keys.) It generates an initial system state (st_M and Π) enabling the remaining algorithms to run, and a set of messages that will be sent to users so that users can initialize their respective user states, st_u. The initial data $d(o)$ for all objects $o \in O$ is protected and written to the file-system (within Π).

We assume that msg_u is sent over a secure channel to the user $u \in U$. In effect, we assume that any messages sent by the manager to users are received as intended and without leaking any information to an adversary. (However, as we discuss in Section 4.2, we will allow an adversary to corrupt users, thereby allowing the adversary to learn user state.)

Read, run by a user u, is a deterministic algorithm which takes as input the identifier of an object to which access is being requested, the state of the user requesting access and the public information for the CES, which includes the file-system and, in particular, $\overline{d(o)}$. The algorithm uses the cryptographic material contained within st_u (and perhaps Π) to attempt to remove the protection mechanism applied to the data $d(o)$. It outputs $d(o)$ (the data last written to o) if $\lambda(u) \geqslant \lambda(o)$, and an error symbol $\perp$ otherwise.

The Setup and Read algorithms alone are sufficient to provide the basic functionality required to enforce an information flow policy cryptographically — that is, Setup generates cryptographic material and protects objects, whilst Read removes the protection if the user is authorized. However, we note that it may be necessary, more efficient or otherwise convenient to extend the number of algorithms used. We now discuss some of these alternatives.

3.2.1 Writeable. Although Setup writes the initial data $d(o)$ specified by the policy for each object in O, in many systems one may wish to update the data stored in objects over the course of the system lifetime. A *writeable* CES allows the manager to update objects and supports the following algorithm:

$$\Pi \xleftarrow{\$} \text{Write}(o, d(o)', st_M, \Pi)$$

This algorithm takes as input the object identifier o to be written to, the data $d(o)'$ to be written to object o, the state of the manager, and public information. It outputs updated public information, which includes $(o, \overline{d(o)'})$ in *FS*.

3.2.2 Refreshability. Over time, cryptographic material may need to be *refreshed* if material is compromised or lost, or following the removal of an authorized user. Computing advances or the threat of a long-running attack may also necessitate periodic key refreshing. Thus, many CESs should include a mechanism by which cryptographic material can be updated.

Whilst a trivial solution would be to update cryptographic material simply by re-running the Setup algorithm, this will update *all* keys within the system simultaneously. It is likely more efficient to provide a targeted Refresh algorithm (to be run by the manager):

$$(st_M, \{msg_u\}_{u \in U}, \Pi) \xleftarrow{\$} \text{Refresh}(l, st_M, \Pi).$$

Refresh takes a label $l \in L$, the state st_M of the manager and Π as input (which, together, contain the material $\alpha(l)$ and $\pi(l)$ associated to the target label), and outputs updated values of st_M and Π, along with a set of messages $\{msg_u\}_{u \in U}$, which may contain updated cryptographic material for authorized users.

We say that a CES is *refreshable* if it uses a Refresh algorithm, rather than Setup, to update cryptographic material on a per-label basis. Refreshes may also result in changes to the cryptographic material associated with other security labels; we denote this set of labels by L'. (In a CES instantiated using an iterative key assignment scheme [3], for example, $L' = \{l' \in L : l' \leqslant l\}$.) Following a refresh, therefore, we may need to update Π, st_u for some users (typically those where $\lambda(u) \in L'$) and $\overline{d(o)}$ for objects o where $\lambda(o) \in L'$.

3.2.3 Dynamic Policy. In some settings, it may be that the sets of objects and users never change (the policy is static). The Setup algorithm may assign the appropriate labels and cryptographic materials for all users and objects, and write all objects to the file-system. In some systems, however, a user or object's label may be changed to/from any label in L during the lifetime of the system (e.g. in the event that a user's role changes or an object becomes declassified). A basic solution to fulfilling this requirement is to re-run the Setup algorithm with a modified labelling function.

A more dynamic (and potentially more efficient) approach is to introduce randomized algorithms ChUsL and ChObL, for changing a user and object's label respectively:

$$(st_M, \{msg_u\}_{u \in U}, \Pi) \xleftarrow{\$} \text{ChUsL}(u, l', st_M, \Pi);$$
$$(st_M, \{msg_u\}_{u \in U}, \Pi) \xleftarrow{\$} \text{ChObL}(o, l', st_M, \Pi).$$

Both algorithms take the identifier of the user or object and the new label $l' \in L$ to be assigned, along with the manager state and public information, and result in updated manager states and public information along with update messages for each user that may update the user state st_u.

Note that, for example, ChUsL may affect the states of other users (or the secret information $\alpha(y)$ associated to labels $y \neq l'$) e.g. if the access rights of u are *decreased* then the cryptographic material for all labels that u is no longer authorized for may need to be changed; subsequently, objects protected using keys that have

CES Class	Algorithms	Run by
Basic	Setup	Manager
	Read	User
Writeable	Write	Manager
Refreshable	Refresh	Manager
Dynamic	ChUsL	Manager
	ChObL	Manager
Decentralized	UserUpdate	User

Table 2: Algorithms required in different classes of CES

been updated may require re-protecting. Typically, ChObL could be implemented by decrypting $\overline{d(o)}$, calling Refresh on $\lambda(o)$ and re-encrypting $d(o)$ using $\alpha(l')$.

Recall that we assume a large population of users, many of which may be assigned to $\sqcup$. The "creation" of a user may be modeled as the activation of a user that has been assigned to $\sqcup$, whilst user deletion can be modeled as the assignment of an existing user to $\sqcup$. We can create and delete objects in a similar fashion by assigning from and to the label $\sqcap$. We say a CES is *dynamic* if it supports ChUsL and ChObL.

3.2.4 Decentralized Updates.
Note that several algorithms (Setup, ChUsL and Refresh) are run by the manager and require resulting updates to a user's local state st_u. Certainly, since user states are subsets of the manager state, the manager could compute the updated st_u for all u that are affected, and distribute msg_u containing st_u. We call this a *centralized update* as it is performed entirely by the manager. However, this may place an unnecessarily onerous burden on the manager. In some instantiations, a more efficient solution (in terms of manager workload and bandwidth costs) may be to provide each user u with (a smaller amount of) data that enables u to derive st_u themselves. For example, each user could use some key derivation function to update their own user state using a counter value or nonce broadcast by the manager. Hence, we introduce a final algorithm UserUpdate, run by the user:

$$st_u \leftarrow \text{UserUpdate}(st_u, msg_u, \Pi).$$

3.2.5 Classes of CES.
We have seen that CESs in different settings may require different functionality. In Table 2, therefore, we classify CESs according to their required properties. We do not claim this classification to be exhaustive but believe that it captures many of the generic requirements of CESs. Each class of CES also includes the algorithms of those in the Basic class, and classes may be combined. Each algorithm may return $\perp$ to denote failure e.g. if the inputs are invalid.

To achieve a general definition satisfiable by *any* suitable cryptographic primitives, we have strived to define general, abstract input and output parameters for each algorithm that act as general 'containers', into which one can place the required cryptographic components of the particular primitives in use. Whilst our definitions may appear complicated, due to their generality, we believe that they give the simplest possible definition of a CES, since they show the required information flow between algorithms without relating parameters with their supposed format within a particular

instantiation (e.g. we do not specify that an input is a cryptographic key, but a more general parameter that may or may not contain one or more keys when instantiated by a particular construction). For example, looking at the Setup algorithm, we see that to initialize the system one must specify the policy to be enforced and the level of security required, and the algorithm simply generates some private information (state) for each entity (manager and users) and some public information accessible to all. We shall see concrete examples of how such a CES can be instantiated in Section 5.

3.2.6 System State Transition.
The evolution of a CES over time can be modeled as a series of state transitions, $S_t \xrightarrow{a} S_{t+1}$, where a is an algorithm run by the manager that results in a change to the policy.[3] In a CES for a static, refreshable policy, for example, the Setup and Refresh algorithms cause a transition to another state – Read does not change the state of the system and thus produces a trivial or null state transition.

We now attempt to specify the minimal sets of items within the system that must be updated in some way to ensure that the enforcement scheme reflects the updated system following a command. The specific forms of updates will be very dependent on the specific implementation. Some schemes may choose to update additional items (e.g. non-refreshable schemes may update *all* user states following an update). Here, we simply attempt to identify the *minimal* sets of items that are affected and that any implementation *must* deal with. For our purposes, we assume that all necessary updates are performed immediately i.e. we do not employ a lazy update mechanism.

Note that a transition from a state $S_t = (st_{\mathcal{M}}, \Pi)$ to another state $S_{t'} = (st'_{\mathcal{M}}, \Pi')$ *only* occurs if the associated conditions hold.

- Write($o, d(o)', st_{\mathcal{M}}, \Pi$): if $o \in O$, the manager protects $d(o)'$ (using cryptographic material related to o and $\lambda(o)$) and updates $\overline{d(o)} \in \Pi$.
- Refresh($l, st_{\mathcal{M}}, \Pi$): If $l \in L$, then let L' be the set of labels whose cryptographic material depends on that of l (e.g. in an iterative KAS [9], $L' = \{l' \in L : l' \leqslant l\}$). Then $\{\alpha(l), \pi(l) : l \in L'\}$ gets updated. All objects that are protected under cryptographic material that has been updated will need re-protecting under the refreshed material. Let O' be the set of such objects, then $\{\overline{d(o)} : o \in O'\}$ must be updated. In addition, a set of users, U', whose cryptographic material has been updated will also need to be issued material to update their user states.
- ChUsL($u, l', st_{\mathcal{M}}, \Pi$): If $l' \in L \setminus \sqcap$, $u \in U$ and $\lambda(u) \neq l'$, set $L' = \{l \in L : l \leqslant \lambda(u), l \not\leqslant l'\}$ (this is precisely the set of labels for which u is no longer authorized). Then we need to update the set $C = \{\alpha(l), \pi(l) : l \in L'\}$, and set $\lambda(u) \leftarrow l'$. For every object $o \in O$ protected using material in C, $\overline{d(o)}$ is updated. The smallest set of users whose state needs updating is the set of users $\{u' \in U : \lambda(u') \in L'\}$.
- ChObL($o, l', st_{\mathcal{M}}, \Pi$): Let $l = \lambda(o)$. If $l' \in L \setminus \sqcup$, $o \in O$ and $l \neq l'$, set $\lambda(o) \leftarrow l'$ and update $\overline{d(o)}$. κ_l and $\pi(l)$ should

---

[3]Since user states can be computed from the manager state and public information, they need not form part of the system state; therefore we do not consider UserUpdate as an algorithm that causes a system state transition.

be refreshed[4]. Such key refreshes are required to prevent the following scenario: suppose a user u locally stores $\overline{d(o)}$, where $\lambda(o) = l$, and u is not authorized for l. Suppose o is reassigned to label l', where $l' > l$, or $l' \parallel l$, and ChUsL is run such that $\lambda(u) = l$. Now, if κ_l has not been updated, then u can access the contents of his stored copy of $\overline{d(o)}$, although u is not authorized for o since $\lambda(o) \not\leqslant \lambda(u)$.

4 CORRECTNESS AND SECURITY

The security properties of a system employing cryptographic primitives are often defined using games. A game is "played" between a *challenger* and an *adversary*, $\mathcal{A}$, and seeks to model the actions of the adversary and its interactions with the system (represented by the challenger). A game typically comprises an interleaving of calls made by the challenger to algorithms provided by the system, and calls made by the adversary to "oracles". An adversary given oracle access is denoted $\mathcal{A}^O$, where the O denotes the set of oracles to which the adversary has access. We assume that all data sent amongst entities is done so via confidential and authenticated channels; the adversary is given access to publicly observable information, and oracles model his ability to act as the storage provider and to corrupt users to learn any confidential information available to attackers in a real system that take similar actions.

Informally, oracles allow the adversary to influence the system by triggering the execution of algorithms, without necessarily knowing all inputs to each algorithm. This mechanism allows the adversary, to some degree, to 'embed' information of its choosing into the system and to control its execution; the resulting knowledge of the system represents any prior knowledge an adversary may have about a real system. Furthermore, oracles model an adversary taking 'real-world' actions that result in an algorithm being run by the manager — for example, an adversary may take a course of action (e.g. placing an order with a company) which it suspects will cause some data to be written to the file-system, and it may have some guess about the contents of that data; in the cryptographic game, this is modeled by allowing the adversary to request data (its guess) to be written (via a Write oracle), even though the adversary does not have the capability (e.g. the necessary access rights or encryption keys) to write to the file-system in the real system. If an adversary can glean any *additional* information from seeing protected objects (where the adversary knows the contents) in the game, it may be able to determine such information about the contents of data objects in a real file-system.

Most oracles include a call to a system algorithm and take as input a subset of the inputs to that algorithm. We do not provide oracles for Setup or any user-run algorithms as the adversary can run these itself. An oracle may also perform some validation of the inputs to ensure that the adversary does not provide inputs that could permit a "trivial win". The only information the adversary may learn is that which is explicitly given to it as input and that which is output from oracles (together this should be chosen to reflect all possible leakage in the real system).

For the purposes of this framework, we make the assumption that all updates following a state transition occur immediately. In practice, one may need to lock files whilst updates are performed [14].

4.1 Correctness

Informally, an information flow policy is correctly enforced if all authorized requests are permitted — that is, if a user u can read any object o where $\lambda(o) \leqslant \lambda(u)$. When considering a cryptographic enforcement mechanism, we would like to consider a stronger notion of correctness whereby we ensure that it is not possible for the system to enter a state in which an authorized user performing a Read operation does not receive the correct data (the last data that should have been written to the object). To do so, we model the system as a game, given in Figure 1, played between a *scheduler* $\mathcal{A}$ which can observe and control the execution of the system and a challenger; by considering all such schedulers we consider all possible valid sequences of algorithms.

The aim of the experiment (from the scheduler's perspective) is to force the system into a state in which the output of reading an object $o^\star$ does not equal the data that should have been last written to this object. We must ensure that the protection mechanism can be applied to, and removed from, data correctly by authorized users, and that the algorithms specified in the CES do not interfere with this operation. Recall that the storage provider is modeled as an honest-but-curious adversary; we therefore need not consider integrity properties since the provider is trusted to accept data only from the manager and to store it (unmodified) in the file-system. In effect, we must ensure our specified algorithms conform to our expectation of a correct execution; we do not consider malicious storage providers that deviate from these algorithms in this work.

The experiment, given as $\text{Exp}_{CES,\mathcal{A}}^{\text{Correctness}}(1^\rho, P)$ in Figure 1, begins with the challenger setting up the system and initializing an array A, where $A[o]$ contains the data $d(o)$ for each object $o \in O$ defined in the policy; this array is used to store the data that (according to the policy and any subsequent write requests) should currently be stored by the storage provider. The challenger then gives $\mathcal{A}$ the public information and access to a set of oracles (also shown in Figure 1), which enables $\mathcal{A}$ to run CES algorithms on inputs of its choice. Most oracles simply check that the inputs are valid, update the policy or the array A as required, and then call the relevant CES algorithm. The CORRUPT oracle allows the scheduler to learn the user state for a queried user (i.e. everything that the user knows) which models compromised or colluding users. The challenger maintains a list Cr of users that have been corrupted.

Recall that some algorithms output a set of update messages for some users. Messages for users that the scheduler has corrupted are given to $\mathcal{A}$ (in this way, $\mathcal{A}$ learns any additional, leaked, information from the update messages and can choose to update the corrupted user state itself in a decentralized CES). The challenger runs the UserUpdate algorithm to update the state of all *non-corrupted* users so that they remain synchronized with the remainder of the system, and so any future corruptions will reveal a correctly updated user state.

After polynomially many queries to the oracles, the scheduler selects a challenge object identifier $o^\star \in O$ and a user $u^\star \in U$. The challenger then runs Read for $o^\star$ using the state of the user $u^\star$. If

---

[4] An efficient instantiation may add l to a refresh list and only update its key and public information when necessary (e.g. use lazy update mechanisms).

$$
\begin{array}{|lll|}
\hline
\end{array}
$$

$\mathbf{Exp}^{\mathrm{Correctness}}_{CES,\mathcal{A}}(1^\rho, P)$

$\mathsf{Cr} \leftarrow \emptyset$

foreach $o \in O$:
  $A[o] \leftarrow d(o)$

$(\mathsf{st}_{\mathcal{M}}, \{\mathsf{msg}_u\}_{u \in U}, \Pi) \xleftarrow{\$} \mathsf{Setup}(1^\rho, P)$

$(o^\star, u^\star) \xleftarrow{\$} \mathcal{A}^O(1^\rho, P, \Pi)$

if $(\lambda(u^\star) \geqslant \lambda(o^\star))$ **and** $(\mathsf{Read}(o^\star, st_{u^\star}, \Pi) \neq A[o^\star])$:
  return true

else : **return** false

Oracle $\mathrm{CORRUPTU}(u)$

if $u \notin U$: **return** $\perp$
$\mathsf{Cr} \leftarrow \mathsf{Cr} \cup \{u\}$
return st_u

Oracle $\mathrm{CHUSL}(u, l')$

if $(u \in U$ and $l' \in L \setminus \sqcap)$:
  $\lambda(u) \leftarrow l'$

$(\mathsf{st}_{\mathcal{M}}, \{\mathsf{msg}_u\}_{u \in U}, \Pi) \xleftarrow{\$} \mathsf{ChUsL}(u, l', \mathsf{st}_{\mathcal{M}}, \Pi)$

foreach $u \in U \setminus \mathsf{Cr}$:
  $st_u \leftarrow \mathsf{UserUpdate}(st_u, \mathsf{msg}_u, \Pi)$

return $(\{\mathsf{msg}_u\}_{u \in \mathsf{Cr}}, \Pi)$

Oracle $\mathrm{CHOBL}(o, l')$

if $(o \in O$ and $l' \in L \setminus \sqcup)$:
  $\lambda(o) \leftarrow l'$

$(\mathsf{st}_{\mathcal{M}}, \{\mathsf{msg}_u\}_{u \in U}, \Pi) \xleftarrow{\$} \mathsf{ChObL}(o, l', \mathsf{st}_{\mathcal{M}}, \Pi)$

foreach $u \in U \setminus \mathsf{Cr}$:
  $st_u \leftarrow \mathsf{UserUpdate}(st_u, \mathsf{msg}_u, \Pi)$

return $(\{\mathsf{msg}_u\}_{u \in \mathsf{Cr}}, \Pi)$

Oracle $\mathrm{WRITE}(o, d(o)')$

if $(o \in O)$:
  $A[o] \leftarrow d(o)'$

$\Pi \xleftarrow{\$} \mathsf{Write}(o, d(o)', \mathsf{st}_{\mathcal{M}}, \Pi)$
return Π

Oracle $\mathrm{REFRESH}(l)$

if $l \notin L$: **return** $\perp$

$(\mathsf{st}_{\mathcal{M}}, \{\mathsf{msg}_u\}_{u \in U}, \Pi) \xleftarrow{\$} \mathsf{Refresh}(l, \mathsf{st}_{\mathcal{M}}, \Pi)$

foreach $u \in U \setminus \mathsf{Cr}$:
  $st_u \leftarrow \mathsf{UserUpdate}(st_u, \mathsf{msg}_u, \Pi)$

return $(\{\mathsf{msg}_u\}_{u \in \mathsf{Cr}}, \Pi)$

Figure 1: Correctness of a CES

$u^\star$ is authorized for $o^\star$, and Read does not output $A[o^\star]$ (the data that *should* have been most recently written to $o^\star$), the scheduler wins — it has found a sequence of state transitions that results in an authorized user not gaining the correct data.

Definition 4.1. Let $P = ((L, \leqslant), \mathcal{U}, O, \lambda)$ be an information flow policy. A CES for P is *correct* if for all probabilistic polynomial-time schedulers $\mathcal{A}$, all valid policies P and all security parameters ρ:

$$\Pr\left[\mathsf{true} \leftarrow \mathbf{Exp}^{\mathrm{Correctness}}_{CES,\mathcal{A}}(1^\rho, P)\right] = 0$$

4.2 Security

Informally, a CES for a read-only information flow policy is *secure* if it denies all unauthorized read requests e.g. a user u cannot learn $d(o)$ if $\lambda(u) \not\geqslant \lambda(o)$. A stronger cryptographic notion of security may require that unauthorized users can learn *nothing* about the contents of objects for which they are unauthorized.[5] Unlike an enforcement mechanism based on a reference monitor, there are often no absolute guarantees of security in a CES because cryptographic primitives are probabilistic. Thus, security is defined in terms of the probability of an adversary learning something about an object that they are not authorized to read.

An ideal notion of security may be *semantic security* [16]. Unfortunately, it can be difficult to model exactly what is meant by an adversary learning 'no information' in arbitrary settings as one must account for any prior information the adversary may have about data in the file-system (e.g. the language). Instead, it is common to consider an indistinguishability game [5] in which the adversary can choose data to be written (a chosen plaintext attack).

In our indistinguishability game for a CES, the adversary chooses a challenge object (for which it is unauthorized) and two data values. The challenger chooses one of the data values at random and writes it to the chosen object. To win, the adversary, having observed the file-system, must state which data item was written. The adversary can clearly win 50% of the time by guessing; thus we model the

adversary's advantage in this game as the difference between the probability of identifying the encrypted data correctly and $\frac{1}{2}$. For a secure CES, we require this advantage to be close to 0.

This notion of indistinguishability implies (is stronger than) the notion that a user is not able to decrypt $\overline{d(o)}$ if $\lambda(u) \not\geqslant \lambda(o)$. Whilst the weaker notion requires only that the *entirety* of $d(o)$ is not revealed, our notion requires that *no* information about $d(o)$ may be leaked from an outsourced $\overline{d(o)}$ (even when the adversary may choose the data options to maximize its ability to distinguish the resulting protected data items). This ensures that the file-system reveals nothing about written data (except perhaps metadata such as file-size); if any additional information were to leak, an adversary could win this game by choosing two messages that can be distinguished by the leaked information.

Our notion of *security* of a CES for an information flow policy $P = ((L, \leqslant), \mathcal{U}, O, \lambda)$ is captured in $\mathbf{Exp}^{\mathrm{Ind}}_{CES,\mathcal{A}}(1^\rho, P)$ in Figure 2. The challenger C randomly chooses a bit $b \in \{0, 1\}$ and a challenge object identifier $o^\star$, and initializes an empty list Cr of corrupted users. C then initializes the system via Setup and then provides the adversary $\mathcal{A}$ with the public information and oracle access.

After polynomially many oracle queries, $\mathcal{A}$ chooses an object identifier $o^\star$ and two data items d_0 and d_1 (of equal length). C checks that no corrupted user is authorized for $o^\star$ (to prevent a trivial win for the adversary) and writes d_b to $o^\star$. The resulting public parameters, and oracle access, are given to the adversary who must correctly identify the data item written to the object.

Oracles may perform 'housekeeping' to ensure that inputs are valid and do not permit a trivial win by allowing $\mathcal{A}$ to:

(1) corrupt a user who is authorized for $o^\star$;
(2) change the challenge object's label such that a corrupted user is now authorized for $o^\star$;
(3) change a corrupted user's label such that the user is now authorized for $o^\star$.

Note that the set of oracles the adversary has access to depends on the class of CES. Recall that a non-refreshable CES may be (inefficiently) refreshed by recalling Setup with new policy inputs;

---

[5]Whilst a user u who was authorized for an object o may have learned the contents of $d(o)$ prior to the object's label being changed such that u is no longer authorized for o, the user should not be able to read any further writes to o.

$\mathbf{Exp}^{\mathrm{Ind}}_{CES,\mathcal{A}}(1^\rho, P)$	Oracle $\textsc{ChObL}(o, l')$	Oracle $\textsc{ChUsL}(u, l')$	Oracle $\textsc{Write}(o, d(o)')$
$b \xleftarrow{\$} \{0,1\}; o^* \leftarrow \perp; \mathrm{Cr} \leftarrow \emptyset$	**if** $o = o^*$:	**if** $(u \in Cr$ **and** $\lambda(o^*) \leqslant l')$: **return** $\perp$	$\Pi \xleftarrow{\$} \mathsf{Write}(o, d(o)', \mathrm{st}_\mathcal{M}, \Pi)$
$(\mathrm{st}_\mathcal{M}, \{\mathrm{msg}_u\}_{u \in U}, \Pi) \xleftarrow{\$} \mathsf{Setup}(1^\rho, P)$	**foreach** $u \in \mathrm{Cr}$:	**if** $(u \in U$ **and** $l' \in L \setminus \sqcap)$:	**return** Π
$(o^*, d_0, d_1) \xleftarrow{\$} \mathcal{A}^\mathcal{O}(1^\rho, P, \Pi)$	**if** $l' \leqslant \lambda(u)$: **return** $\perp$	$\lambda(u) \leftarrow l'$	
if $|d_0| \neq |d_1|$: **return** false	**if** $(o \in O$ **and** $l' \in L \setminus \sqcup)$:	$(\mathrm{st}_\mathcal{M}, \{\mathrm{msg}_u\}_{u \in U}, \Pi) \xleftarrow{\$} \mathsf{ChUsL}(u, l', \mathrm{st}_\mathcal{M}, \Pi)$	Oracle $\textsc{CorruptU}(u)$
foreach $u \in \mathrm{Cr}$:	$\lambda(o) \leftarrow l'$	**foreach** $u \in U \setminus \mathrm{Cr}$:	**if** $u \notin U$: **return** $\perp$
if $\lambda(o^*) \leqslant \lambda(u)$:	$(\mathrm{st}_\mathcal{M}, \{\mathrm{msg}_u\}_{u \in U}, \Pi) \xleftarrow{\$} \mathsf{ChObL}(o, l', \mathrm{st}_\mathcal{M}, \Pi)$	$\mathrm{st}_u \leftarrow \mathsf{UserUpdate}(\mathrm{msg}_u, \mathrm{st}_u)$	**if** $\lambda(u) \geqslant \lambda(o^*)$:
return false	**foreach** $u \in U \setminus \mathrm{Cr}$:	**return** $(\Pi, \{\mathrm{msg}_u\}_{u \in \mathrm{Cr}})$	**return** $\perp$
$\Pi \xleftarrow{\$} \mathsf{Write}(o^*, d_b, \mathrm{st}_\mathcal{M}, \Pi)$	$\mathrm{st}_u \leftarrow \mathsf{UserUpdate}(\mathrm{msg}_u, \mathrm{st}_u)$		$\mathrm{Cr} \leftarrow \mathrm{Cr} \cup \{u\}$
$b' \xleftarrow{\$} \mathcal{A}^\mathcal{O}(1^\rho, P, \Pi)$	**return** $(\Pi, \{msg_u\}_{u \in \mathrm{Cr}})$	Oracle $\textsc{Refresh}(l)$	**return** st_u
if $b = b'$: **return** true		$(\mathrm{st}_\mathcal{M}, \{\mathrm{msg}_u\}_{u \in U}, \Pi) \xleftarrow{\$} \mathsf{Refresh}(l, \mathrm{st}_\mathcal{M}, \Pi)$	
else return false		**foreach** $u \in U \setminus \mathrm{Cr}$:	
		$\mathrm{st}_u \leftarrow \mathsf{UserUpdate}(\mathrm{msg}_u, \mathrm{st}_u)$	
		return $(\Pi, \{msg_u\}_{u \in \mathrm{Cr}})$	

Figure 2: Security of a CES

we therefore provide a Refresh oracle so that the adversary can influence the manager to call Setup. A non-refreshable CES will replace the call to Refresh within the Refresh oracle with a call to Setup with the current policy as input. In our model, we do not permit the poset to change over time, and hence the only input to the Refresh oracle is the label to be refreshed; the adversary may not specify the new policy as this may include an alternative poset (permitted policy changes can be effected through other oracles).

Whenever the policy is to be updated, the challenger updates the policy correctly and calls the relevant algorithm. Thus, the challenger's view of the policy is always correct, enabling the checks for trivial wins to be performed correctly.

Definition 4.2. A CES for an information flow policy is *secure* if for all probabilistic polynomial-time adversaries $\mathcal{A}$, all valid policies P and all security parameters ρ:

$$\left| \Pr\left[\text{true} \leftarrow \mathbf{Exp}^{\mathrm{Ind}}_{CES,\mathcal{A}}(1^\rho, P) \right] - \frac{1}{2} \right| \leqslant f(\rho)$$

where f is a negligible function.

One may observe that a *secure* CES, in accordance with Definition 4.2, must employ some form of *forward-security* (e.g. one should not be able to learn old versions of label keys). This prevents users locally storing ciphertexts for objects that used to be assigned to a security label l, obtaining authorization for l, and being able to derive the old key for l to enable successful decryption of such ciphertexts.

5 EXAMPLE INSTANTIATIONS

A Key Assignment Scheme (KAS) [3] is defined by:

- $(\{\kappa_x, \sigma_x\}_{x \in L}, Pub) \xleftarrow{\$} \mathsf{KAS.Setup}(1^\rho, (L, \leqslant))$ takes a security parameter and a poset and outputs a key κ_x and secret σ_x for each label $x \in L$, along with some public derivation information Pub; and
- κ_x or $\perp \leftarrow \mathsf{KAS.Derive}(x, y, \sigma_y, Pub)$ takes labels $x, y \in L$, the secret for y and Pub, and outputs the key for label x if and only if $x \leqslant y$, else it outputs $\perp$.

Each user is given a secret associated to their security label and can derive all keys for which they are authorized. Figure 3 gives

$(\mathrm{st}_\mathcal{M}, \{\mathrm{msg}_u\}_{u \in U}, \Pi) \xleftarrow{\$} \mathsf{Setup}(1^\rho, P)$	$d(o) \leftarrow \mathsf{Read}(o, \mathrm{st}_u, \Pi)$
Parse P as $((L, \leqslant), U, O, \lambda)$	**if** $o \notin O$: **return** $\perp$
$(\{\kappa_x, \sigma_x\}_{x \in L}, Pub) \xleftarrow{\$} \mathsf{KAS.Setup}(1^\rho, (L, \leqslant))$	$\kappa_{\lambda(o)} \leftarrow \mathsf{KAS.Derive}(\lambda(o), \lambda(u), \sigma_{\lambda(u)}, Pub)$
foreach $x \in L$:	**if** $\kappa_{\lambda(o)} \neq \perp$:
$\alpha(x) \leftarrow \{\kappa_x, \sigma_x\}$	Parse $\overline{d(o)}$ as $(c_o, o, \lambda(o))$
$\phi \leftarrow P$	**return** $\mathsf{SE.Decrypt}_{\kappa_{\lambda(o)}}(c_o)$
$\mathrm{st}_\mathcal{M} \leftarrow (\phi, \{\alpha(x) : x \in L\})$	**return** $\perp$
foreach $u \in U$:	
$\mathrm{st}_u \leftarrow (\sigma_{\lambda(u)}, \lambda(u))$	$\Pi \xleftarrow{\$} \mathsf{Write}(o, d(o)', \mathrm{st}_\mathcal{M}, \Pi)$
foreach $o \in O$:	**if** $o \notin O$: **return** $\perp$
$\overline{d(o)} \xleftarrow{\$} (\mathsf{SE.Encrypt}_{\kappa_{\lambda(o)}}(d(o)), o, \lambda(o))$	$\overline{d(o)} \xleftarrow{\$} (\mathsf{SE.Encrypt}_{\kappa_{\lambda(o)}}(d(o)'), o, \lambda(o))$
$FS \leftarrow \left\{ \overline{d(o)} : o \in O \right\}$	$FS \leftarrow \left\{ \overline{d(o)} : o \in O \right\}$
$\psi \leftarrow (Pub, (L, \leqslant))$	$\Pi \leftarrow (\psi, FS)$
$\Pi \leftarrow (\psi, FS)$	**return** Π
return $(\mathrm{st}_\mathcal{M}, \{\mathrm{st}_u\}_{u \in U}, \Pi)$	

Figure 3: A Writeable, Centralized CES using a KAS

an example CES instantiation using a KAS (KAS) and a symmetric encryption scheme (SE) where the key space for KAS and SE is the same. The manager state includes all generated keys and secrets; each user state includes the secret assigned to the user's security label, and Π includes the public information output by the KAS.

THEOREM 5.1. *Let KAS be secure in the sense of key indistinguishability and let SE be IND-CPA secure. Then the instantiation in Figure 3 is a secure static, writeable, centralized, non-refreshable CES.*

The proof of Theorem 5.1 can be found in Appendix A. It is interesting to note that, although KASs are often proposed as symmetric cryptographic enforcement mechanisms for information flow policies, the natural pairing of a KI-secure KAS and an IND-CPA secure encryption scheme yields a rather basic CES according to our classifications. Indeed, it appears that constructing a richer class of CES using current KASs as a black box (i.e. using the defined algorithms without using the particular details of a specific instantiation) would be challenging. Current KASs specify only two algorithms and the Setup algorithm generates and outputs *all* public and secret information for the entire system; there is no alternative method by which to generate subsets of this information.

Thus allowing for dynamic or refreshable CESs will be problematic — there is no mechanism by which a single key can be generated or replaced for example. Whilst some KAS constructions do allow for some aspects to be altered [4], this mechanism is scheme dependent and does not form part of the definition or, crucially, the security model. Future work on KASs should aim to meet the requirements of our proposed framework if they are to ensure utility as a component of a CES; in particular, a KAS used to instantiate a more complex CES will require algorithms to update and refresh components, and the KI security notion will need to be adapted to accommodate changes to cryptographic material over time.

Our second example uses a large-universe key-policy attribute-based encryption (KP-ABE) [17] scheme:

- $(MK, PP) \stackrel{\$}{\leftarrow} \mathrm{Setup}(1^p)$ takes a security parameter and outputs a master secret and public parameters;
- $C \stackrel{\$}{\leftarrow} \mathrm{Encrypt}(m, \gamma, PP)$ takes a message m, a set of attributes γ and PP, and outputs a ciphertext;
- $k_{\mathbb{A}} \leftarrow \mathrm{KeyGen}(\mathbb{A}, MK, PP)$ takes as input an access structure (policy) $\mathbb{A}$, the master secret key and public parameters, and outputs a key for the policy; and
- $(m \text{ or } \bot) \leftarrow \mathrm{Decrypt}(C, k_{\mathbb{A}}, PP)$ takes a ciphertext C encrypting m using an attribute set γ, a key $k_{\mathbb{A}}$ for a policy $\mathbb{A}$ and PP. It outputs the encrypted message m if $\gamma \in \mathbb{A}$ (the policy is satisfied) or $\bot$ otherwise.

Then, Figure 4 gives an instantiation of a dynamic, centralized, refreshable, writeable CES. Each security label is associated with an attribute, objects are encrypted using the singleton attribute set $\{\lambda(o)\}$ and user decryption keys are generated using the disjunctive policy $\bigvee_{l \leqslant \lambda(u)} l$; hence users can decrypt any object where $\lambda(o) \leqslant \lambda(u)$ as required. Whilst more efficient instantiations are likely possible (e.g. using revocable KP-ABE [24]), we have aimed here to use a simple, standard KP-ABE scheme. We use a large-universe construction (where any string can be an attribute) to enable 'versions' of attributes to disable out-of-date keys (a counter is appended to each attribute and is updated whenever a user loses access to an object assigned that attribute).

Again, by considering cryptographic primitives within our framework, it becomes apparent that some existing proposals for enforcement mechanisms for access control are not entirely sufficient. For example, whilst there are many works considering revocation within ABE [24, 25], it seems more difficult to reduce access rights rather than remove the user completely without assigning an entirely new user identifier.

6 CONCLUSION

We have developed a rigorous definitional framework for the cryptographic enforcement of information flow policies. Our framework has been developed 'bottom up' from the requirements of the access control policy, rather than targeting a particular cryptographic primitive or application scenario. We have provided several example classes of CES and discussed the algorithmic requirements of each, and provided a formal notion of correctness and security. Finally we have provided two instantiations, based on very different primitives, to exemplify the utility of our framework. Further work should develop the definitions for key assignment schemes to

meet the requirements of our framework for richer classes of CES. One could also expand our framework to consider other policies, including write-access, and security goals such as hiding the labels of users and objects.

REFERENCES

[1] Martín Abadi and Bogdan Warinschi. 2008. Security analysis of cryptographically controlled access to XML documents. *Journal of the ACM (JACM)* 55, 2 (2008), 6.
[2] Selim G. Akl and Peter D. Taylor. 1983. Cryptographic Solution to a Problem of Access Control in a Hierarchy. *ACM Trans. Comput. Syst.* 1, 3 (1983), 239–248.
[3] Mikhail J. Atallah, Marina Blanton, Nelly Fazio, and Keith B. Frikken. 2009. Dynamic and Efficient Key Management for Access Hierarchies. *ACM Trans. Inf. Syst. Secur.* 12, 3 (2009).
[4] Mikhail J. Atallah, Marina Blanton, and Keith B. Frikken. 2007. Efficient techniques for realizing geo-spatial access control. In *ASIACCS*, Feng Bao and Steven Miller (Eds.). ACM, 82–92.
[5] Mihir Bellare, Anand Desai, E. Jokipii, and Phillip Rogaway. 1997. A Concrete Security Treatment of Symmetric Encryption. In *38th Annual Symposium on Foundations of Computer Science, FOCS '97, Miami Beach, Florida, USA, October 19-22, 1997.* IEEE Computer Society, 394–403. https://doi.org/10.1109/SFCS.1997.646128
[6] John Bethencourt, Amit Sahai, and Brent Waters. 2007. Ciphertext-Policy Attribute-Based Encryption. In *IEEE Symposium on Security and Privacy.* IEEE Computer Society, 321–334.
[7] Arcangelo Castiglione, Alfredo De Santis, and Barbara Masucci. 2016. Key Indistinguishability versus Strong Key Indistinguishability for Hierarchical Key Assignment Schemes. *IEEE Trans. Dependable Sec. Comput.* 13, 4 (2016), 451–460. https://doi.org/10.1109/TDSC.2015.2413415
[8] Jason Crampton. 2010. Cryptographic Enforcement of Role-Based Access Control. In *Formal Aspects in Security and Trust (Lecture Notes in Computer Science)*, Vol. 6561. Springer, 191–205.
[9] Jason Crampton, Keith M. Martin, and Peter R. Wild. 2006. On Key Assignment for Hierarchical Access Control. In *CSFW.* IEEE Computer Society, 98–111.
[10] Ivan Damgård, Helene Haagh, and Claudio Orlandi. 2016. Access control encryption: Enforcing information flow with cryptography. In *Theory of Cryptography Conference.* Springer, 547–576.
[11] Sabrina De Capitani Di Vimercati, Sara Foresti, Sushil Jajodia, Stefano Paraboschi, and Pierangela Samarati. 2007. Over-encryption: management of access control evolution on outsourced data. In *Proceedings of the 33rd international conference on Very Large Data Bases.* VLDB endowment, 123–134.
[12] Anna Lisa Ferrara, Georg Fuchsbauer, and Bogdan Warinschi. 2013. Cryptographically Enforced RBAC. In *CSF.* IEEE, 115–129.
[13] Eduarda S. V. Freire, Kenneth G. Paterson, and Bertram Poettering. 2013. Simple, Efficient and Strongly KI-Secure Hierarchical Key Assignment Schemes. In *CT-RSA (Lecture Notes in Computer Science)*, Vol. 7779. Springer, 101–114.
[14] William C Garrison, Adam Shull, Steven Myers, and Adam J Lee. 2016. On the practicality of cryptographically enforcing dynamic access control policies in the cloud. In *Security and Privacy (SP), 2016 IEEE Symposium on.* IEEE, 819–838.
[15] David K Gifford. 1982. Cryptographic sealing for information secrecy and authentication. *Commun. ACM* 25, 4 (1982), 274–286.
[16] Shafi Goldwasser and Silvio Micali. 1984. Probabilistic encryption. *Journal of computer and system sciences* 28, 2 (1984), 270–299.
[17] Vipul Goyal, Omkant Pandey, Amit Sahai, and Brent Waters. 2006. Attribute-based encryption for fine-grained access control of encrypted data. In *ACM Conference on Computer and Communications Security.* ACM, 89–98.
[18] Ehud Gudes. 1980. The design of a cryptography based secure file system. *IEEE Transactions on Software Engineering* 5 (1980), 411–420.
[19] Shai Halevi, Paul A Karger, and Dalit Naor. 2005. Enforcing Confinement in Distributed Storage and a Cryptographic Model for Access Control. *IACR Cryptology ePrint Archive* 2005 (2005), 169.
[20] Anthony Harrington and Christian Jensen. 2003. Cryptographic access control in a distributed file system. In *Proceedings of the Eighth ACM Symposium on Access Control Models and Technologies.* ACM, 158–165.
[21] Bin Liu and Bogdan Warinschi. 2016. Universally Composable Cryptographic Role-Based Access Control. Cryptology ePrint Archive, Report 2016/902. (2016). http://eprint.iacr.org/2016/902.
[22] Hemanta K. Maji, Manoj Prabhakaran, and Mike Rosulek. 2011. Attribute-Based Signatures. In *CT-RSA (Lecture Notes in Computer Science)*, Aggelos Kiayias (Ed.), Vol. 6558. Springer, 376–392.
[23] Matthew G. Parker (Ed.). 2009. *Cryptography and Coding, 12th IMA International Conference, Cryptography and Coding 2009, Cirencester, UK, December 15-17, 2009. Proceedings.* Lecture Notes in Computer Science, Vol. 5921. Springer.
[24] Nuttapong Attrapadung and Hideki Imai. 2009. Attribute-Based Encryption Supporting Direct/Indirect Revocation Modes, See [23], 278–300.

$(\mathrm{st}_{\mathcal{M}}, \{\mathrm{msg}_u\}_{u \in U}, \Pi) \xleftarrow{\$} \mathsf{Setup}(1^\rho, P)$

Parse $P = ((L, \leqslant), U, O, \lambda)$

$(\mathrm{MK}, \mathrm{PP}) \xleftarrow{\$} \mathsf{ABE.Setup}(1^\rho)$

for $l \in L$:
$\quad A[l] \leftarrow 0$

$k_M \xleftarrow{\$} \mathsf{ABE.KeyGen}((\bigvee_{l \in L} l \| A[l]), \mathrm{MK}, \mathrm{PP})$

$\phi \leftarrow (A, k_M, P, \mathrm{MK})$

$\mathrm{st}_{\mathcal{M}} \leftarrow \phi$

foreach $u \in U$:
$\quad k_u \xleftarrow{\$} \mathsf{ABE.KeyGen}((\bigvee_{l \leqslant \lambda(u)} l \| A[l]), \mathrm{MK}, \mathrm{PP})$
$\quad \mathrm{st}_u \leftarrow (k_u, \lambda(u))$

foreach $o \in O$:
$\quad c_o \xleftarrow{\$} \mathsf{ABE.Encrypt}(d(o), \{\lambda(o) \| A[\lambda(o)]\}, \mathrm{PP})$
$\quad \overline{d(o)} \leftarrow (c_o, o, \lambda(o))$

$FS \leftarrow \{\overline{d(o)} : o \in O\}$

$\psi \leftarrow (\mathrm{PP}, (L, \leqslant))$

$\Pi \leftarrow (\psi, FS)$

return $(\mathrm{st}_{\mathcal{M}}, \{\mathrm{st}_u\}_{u \in U}, \Pi)$

$d(o) \leftarrow \mathsf{Read}(o, \mathrm{st}_u, \Pi)$

if $o \in O$:
$\quad$ Parse $\overline{d(o)} = (c_o, o, \lambda(o))$
$\quad$ Parse $\mathrm{st}_u = (k_u, \lambda(u))$
$\quad$ return $\mathsf{ABE.Decrypt}(c_o, k_u, \mathrm{PP})$

return $\perp$

$(\mathrm{st}_{\mathcal{M}}, \{\mathrm{msg}_u\}_{u \in U}, \Pi) \xleftarrow{\$} \mathsf{Refresh}(l, \mathrm{st}_{\mathcal{M}}, \Pi)$

if $l \in L$:
$\quad A[l] = A[l] + 1$
$\quad k'_M \xleftarrow{\$} \mathsf{ABE.KeyGen}((\bigvee_{l \in L} l \| A[l]), \mathrm{MK}, \mathrm{PP})$
$\quad$ foreach $u \in \{u \in U : l \leqslant \lambda(u)\}$:
$\qquad \mathrm{st}_u \xleftarrow{\$} (\mathsf{ABE.KeyGen}((\bigvee_{l' \leqslant \lambda(u)} l' \| A[l']), \mathrm{MK}, \mathrm{PP}), \lambda(u))$
$\quad$ foreach $o \in \{o \in O : \lambda(o) = l\}$:
$\qquad$ Parse $\overline{d(o)} = (c_o, o, \lambda(o))$
$\qquad d \leftarrow \mathsf{ABE.Decrypt}(c_o, k_M, \mathrm{PP})$
$\qquad \overline{d(o)} \xleftarrow{\$} (\mathsf{ABE.Encrypt}(d, \{\lambda(o) \| A[\lambda(o)]\}, \mathrm{PP}), o, \lambda(o))$
$\quad \phi \leftarrow (A, k'_M, P, \mathrm{MK})$
$\quad \mathrm{st}_{\mathcal{M}} \leftarrow \phi$
$\quad FS \leftarrow \{\overline{d(o)} : o \in O\}$
$\quad \Pi \leftarrow (\psi, FS)$
$\quad$ return $(\mathrm{st}_{\mathcal{M}}, \{\mathrm{st}_u\}_{u \in U}, \Pi)$

return $(\mathrm{st}_{\mathcal{M}}, \emptyset, \Pi)$

$(\mathrm{st}_{\mathcal{M}}, \{\mathrm{msg}_u\}_{u \in U}, \Pi) \xleftarrow{\$} \mathsf{ChObL}(o, l', \mathrm{st}_{\mathcal{M}}, \Pi)$

if $o \in O$ and $l' \in L \setminus \sqcup$:
$\quad l \leftarrow \lambda(o)$
$\quad$ Parse $\overline{d(o)} = (c_o, o, \lambda(o))$
$\quad d \leftarrow \mathsf{ABE.Decrypt}(c_o, k_M, \mathrm{PP})$
$\quad \overline{d(o)} \xleftarrow{\$} \mathsf{ABE.Encrypt}(d, \{l' \| A[l']\}, \mathrm{PP}), o, l')$
$\quad FS \leftarrow \{\overline{d(o)} : o \in O\}$
$\quad \lambda(o) \leftarrow l'$
$\quad \Pi \leftarrow (\psi, FS)$
$\quad$ return $\mathsf{Refresh}(l, \mathrm{st}_{\mathcal{M}}, \Pi)$

return $(\mathrm{st}_{\mathcal{M}}, \emptyset, \Pi)$

$(\mathrm{st}_{\mathcal{M}}, \{\mathrm{msg}_u\}_{u \in U}, \Pi) \xleftarrow{\$} \mathsf{ChUsL}(u, l', \mathrm{st}_{\mathcal{M}}, \Pi)$

if $u \in U$ and $l' \in L \setminus \sqcap$:
$\quad X \leftarrow \{l \in L : l \leqslant \lambda(u), l \not\leqslant l'\}$
$\quad$ foreach $x \in X$:
$\qquad A[x] = A[x] + 1$
$\qquad$ foreach $o \in \{o \in O : \lambda(o) = x\}$:
$\qquad\quad$ Parse $\overline{d(o)} = (c_o, o, \lambda(o))$
$\qquad\quad d \leftarrow \mathsf{ABE.Decrypt}(c_o, k_M, \mathrm{PP})$
$\qquad\quad \overline{d(o)} \xleftarrow{\$} (\mathsf{ABE.Encrypt}(d, \{\lambda(o) \| A[\lambda(o)]\}, \mathrm{PP}), o, \lambda(o))$
$\quad$ if $X \neq \emptyset$:
$\qquad k_M \xleftarrow{\$} \mathsf{ABE.KeyGen}((\bigvee_{l \in L} l \| A[l]), \mathrm{MK}, \mathrm{PP})$
$\qquad \phi \leftarrow (A, k_M, P, \mathrm{MK})$
$\qquad \mathrm{st}_{\mathcal{M}} \leftarrow \phi$
$\qquad FS \leftarrow \{\overline{d(o)} : o \in O\}$
$\qquad \Pi \leftarrow (\psi, FS)$
$\qquad$ foreach $u' \in \{u' \in U \setminus u : \exists x \in X, x \leqslant \lambda(u')\}$:
$\qquad\quad \mathrm{st}_{u'} \xleftarrow{\$} (\mathsf{ABE.KeyGen}((\bigvee_{x \leqslant \lambda(u')} x \| A[x]), \mathrm{MK}, \mathrm{PP}), \lambda(u'))$
$\quad \lambda(u) \leftarrow l'$
$\quad \mathrm{st}_u \xleftarrow{\$} (\mathsf{ABE.KeyGen}((\bigvee_{x \leqslant l'} x \| A[x]), \mathrm{MK}, \mathrm{PP}), l')$
$\quad$ return $(\mathrm{st}_{\mathcal{M}}, \{\mathrm{st}_u\}_{u \in U}, \Pi)$

return $(\mathrm{st}_{\mathcal{M}}, \emptyset, \Pi)$

$\Pi \xleftarrow{\$} \mathsf{Write}(o, d(o)', \mathrm{st}_{\mathcal{M}}, \Pi)$

if $o \in O$:
$\quad \overline{d(o)} \xleftarrow{\$} (\mathsf{ABE.Encrypt}(d(o)', \{\lambda(o) \| A[\lambda(o)]\}, \mathrm{PP}), o, \lambda(o))$
$\quad FS \leftarrow \{\overline{d(o)} : o \in O\}$
$\quad \Pi \leftarrow (\psi, FS)$
return Π

Figure 4: Construction of a Dynamic, Centralized, Refreshable, Writeable CES using Attribute-based Encryption

---

$\mathbf{Exp}_{\mathcal{A}, (L, \leqslant)}^{\mathrm{S-KI-ST}}(1^\rho)$

$l^\star \xleftarrow{\$} \mathcal{A}(1^\rho, (L, \leqslant))$

$((\sigma_l, \kappa_l)_{l \in L}, Pub) \xleftarrow{\$} \mathsf{Setup}(1^\rho, (L, \leqslant))$

$b \xleftarrow{\$} \{0, 1\}$; if $b = 1$ then $\kappa^\star \leftarrow \kappa_{l^\star}$, else $\kappa^\star \xleftarrow{\$} K$

$b' \xleftarrow{\$} \mathcal{A}(Pub, Corrupt, Keys, \kappa^\star)$

return $b' = b$

Figure 5: Static Strong Key Indistinguishability of a KAS

[25] Jun-lei Qian and Xiao-lei Dong. 2011. Fully secure revocable attribute-based encryption. *Journal of Shanghai Jiaotong University (Science)* 16 (2011), 490–496.

A SECURITY PROOF OF THEOREM 1

A symmetric-key encryption scheme [5] comprises:

- $SK \xleftarrow{\$} \mathsf{KeyGen}(1^\rho)$ takes a security parameter and outputs a secret key.
- $c \xleftarrow{\$} \mathsf{Encrypt}_{SK}(m)$ takes as input a secret key SK and a message m and outputs a ciphertext c.
- $(m$ or $\perp) \leftarrow \mathsf{Decrypt}_{SK}(c)$ takes a key and a ciphertext, and outputs a message m or a failure symbol $\perp$.

A KAS is *Strongly Key Indistinguishable* (SKI) [13] if for all PPT adversaries $\mathcal{A}$ and posets $(L, \leqslant)$:

$$2 \left| \Pr\left[\mathbf{Exp}_{\mathcal{A}, (L, \leqslant)}^{\mathrm{S-KI-ST}}(1^\rho) = b \right] - \frac{1}{2} \right| \leqslant f(\rho),$$

where f is a negligible function, $\mathbf{Exp}_{\mathcal{A}, (L, \leqslant)}^{\mathrm{S-KI-ST}}(1^\rho)$ is given in Figure 5 where K is the key space, $Corrupt = \{\sigma_l : l \in L, l < l^\star\}$ and $Keys = \{\kappa_l : l \in L, l \neq l^\star\}$.

PROOF. We first define a modified game, **Game 1**, which is the same as that defined in Definition 4.2 (which we call **Game 0**) except that the key used to encrypt the challenge object $o^\star$ is chosen randomly rather than derived within the KAS. We show that an adversary cannot distinguish **Game 1** from **Game 0** with non-negligible advantage. Therefore, we may run the adversary against **Game 1**, and with all but negligible probability, the adversary will run correctly.

Having transitioned to **Game 1**, we are in a position where the challenge encryption is generated using a random key; therefore we can reduce security to IND-CPA of the symmetric encryption scheme. We show that if an adversary $\mathcal{A}_{CES}$ can break the security of our CES, then we can construct an adversary $\mathcal{A}_{IND}$ that, using $\mathcal{A}_{CES}$ as a subroutine, can break the IND-CPA security of the symmetric encryption scheme. Since the encryption scheme is assumed to be secure, such an adversary should not exist; therefore a successful adversary against the CES cannot exist.

Although Theorem 5.1 requires a Key Indistinguishable (KI) KAS, we instead use the Strong KI (SKI) [13] property instead which is polynomially equivalent [7] but provides the adversary with *all* keys (except the challenge key) to model key leakage. We find SKI more convenient for proving interactive reductions as all keys are immediately available.

We first show that **Game 1** is indistinguishable from **Game 0**. Suppose, for contradiction, that $\mathcal{A}_{CES}$ is an adversary that can distinguish these games. Let C_{KI} be a challenger for the SKI game. We construct an adversary $\mathcal{A}_{KI}$ which uses $\mathcal{A}_{CES}$ to break the SKI security of the KAS.

$\mathcal{A}_{KI}$ must simulate either **Game 0** or **Game 1** for $\mathcal{A}_{CES}$. It forms a policy P, using $(L, \leqslant)$ from its game with C_{KI}, and its choice of U, O and λ. Note that $\mathcal{A}_{KI}$ is given a single challenge key for a single security label and that, in this static CES, all keys are replaced whenever Refresh is called. Thus, to correctly embed the SKI challenge into **Game 0** or **Game 1** before $\mathcal{A}_{CES}$ decides its challenge parameters, $\mathcal{A}_{KI}$ must guess the challenge label that $\mathcal{A}_{CES}$ will choose *and* which version of that key will be challenged (i.e. how many times Refresh will be called before the challenge). Let r be a counter, initially 0, denoting the number of calls $\mathcal{A}_{CES}$ makes to Refresh. Thus, $\mathcal{A}_{KI}$ makes a guess $c \xleftarrow{\$} L$ for the challenge label and guesses $i \xleftarrow{\$} \{0, 1, \ldots, q\}$, for $q = poly(\rho)$, for the value of r when the challenge parameters are chosen.

$\mathcal{A}_{KI}$ sends c to C_{KI} as its SKI challenge label. C_{KI} runs $(\{\sigma_l, \kappa_l\}_{l \in L}, Pub) \xleftarrow{\$} $ KAS.Setup$(1^\rho, (L, \leqslant))$, and chooses a random bit $b \xleftarrow{\$} \{0, 1\}$; if $b = 0$, $\kappa^\star = \kappa_c$, else $\kappa^\star$ is chosen randomly from the key space. C_{KI} sends the KAS public information, the set of all keys except for the challenge key, the set of all secrets for labels $l' \leqslant c$, and the challenge key $\kappa^\star$ to $\mathcal{A}_{KI}$. $\mathcal{A}_{KI}$ initializes $Cr = \emptyset$ and $o^\star = \perp$.

Now, if $i \neq 0$, then $\mathcal{A}_{KI}$ does not embed the challenger's outputs in the initial CES setup. Instead, it runs Setup as in Figure 3, running KAS.Setup itself. Else, when $i = 0$, $\mathcal{A}_{KI}$ sets $st_\mathcal{M}$ to include $\{\{\sigma_{l'} : l' < c, l' \in L\}, \{\kappa_l : l \in L \setminus \{c\}\}\}$ and Π to include Pub. For each user, if $\lambda(u) < c$, $\mathcal{A}_{KI}$ defines $st_u = \{\sigma_{\lambda_u}, \lambda_u\}$, and $st_u = \{\cdot, \lambda_u\}$ otherwise.

$\mathcal{A}_{CES}$ is given Π and a set of oracles O as in Figure 2. If $\mathcal{A}_{CES}$ calls CorruptU on a user $u \in U$ where $\lambda(u) > c$, then $\mathcal{A}_{KI}$ loses the game (c would now be an invalid challenge and so the initial guess of c was wrong). Similarly, $\mathcal{A}_{KI}$ loses if $\mathcal{A}_{CES}$ chooses $o^\star$ such that $\lambda(o^\star) \neq c$. Whenever the Refresh oracle is called, r is increased by 1.

When $r = i$, $\mathcal{A}_{KI}$ runs Refresh but instead of running KAS.Setup, it uses the key material received from C_{KI}, and re-initializes the state of the manager, users, and objects as described above in Setup where $i = 0$. $\mathcal{A}_{KI}$ loses the game if r exceeds i and $\mathcal{A}_{CES}$ has not yet chosen a challenge object.

Eventually, $\mathcal{A}_{CES}$ guesses that it was playing **Game** b'. $\mathcal{A}_{KI}$ forwards b' to C_{KI} as its guess of whether the key for the challenge label was real ($b = 0$) or random ($b = 1$). $\mathcal{A}_{KI}$ wins with non-negligible probability $\frac{\text{Adv}(\mathcal{A}_{CES})}{q|L|}$ where $q = poly(\rho)$ is the number

of calls to the refresh oracle. Since the KAS is assumed SKI-secure, such a distinguisher $\mathcal{A}_{CES}$ with non-negligible advantage cannot exist. We can therefore hop from **Game 0** to **Game 1**.

We now show that if an adversary $\mathcal{A}_{CES}$ playing **Game 1** can identify the message written to a challenge object with non-negligible probability, then an adversary $\mathcal{A}_{IND}$ can use $\mathcal{A}_{CES}$ to win the IND-CPA game against a challenger C_{IND}.

C_{IND} randomly selects a key k from the key space, selects a random bit $b \xleftarrow{\$} \{0, 1\}$, and gives $\mathcal{A}_{IND}$ access to an encryption oracle $\eta_{k,b}$, which takes two messages m_0, m_1 of the same length and always outputs the encryption of m_b under key k. (We use the LoR IND-CPA game instead of Find-then-Guess [5] as it allows multiple challenges; thus we need only guess the challenge label and not the object itself.)

$\mathcal{A}_{IND}$ runs line 1 of the CES experiment and guesses the security label c of the challenge object $o^\star$ that $\mathcal{A}_{CES}$ will choose. All encryptions using the key κ_c will be replaced by encryptions under k. When an object o with label c is to be written, the adversary calls the encryption oracle $\eta_{k,b}$ on inputs $(d(o)', d(o)')$ to obtain an encryption under k. $\mathcal{A}_{IND}$ runs line 2 of the CES experiment and gives oracle access to $\mathcal{A}_{CES}$. If $\mathcal{A}_{CES}$ corrupts a user $u \in U$ such that $\lambda(u) \geqslant c$, the experiment fails (the guess of c was wrong). Eventually, $\mathcal{A}_{CES}$ chooses a challenge object $o^\star$ and two messages m_0, m_1. If $\lambda(o^\star) \neq c$, the experiment fails; else, $\mathcal{A}_{IND}$ calls $\eta_{k,b}(m_0, m_1)$, and writes the result to $\overline{d(o^\star)}$.

Eventually, $\mathcal{A}_{CES}$ sends b' to $\mathcal{A}_{IND}$ as its guess of b; $\mathcal{A}_{IND}$ forwards this to C_{IND}. If $\mathcal{A}_{CES}$ can correctly guess which data was written with non-negligible advantage Adv$(\mathcal{A}_{CES})$, then $\mathcal{A}_{IND}$ wins the IND-CPA game with non-negligible advantage $\frac{\text{Adv}(\mathcal{A}_{CES})}{|L|}$. This is a contradiction, since the encryption scheme is assumed IND-CPA secure.   □

Towards PII-based Multiparty Access Control for Photo Sharing in Online Social Networks

Nishant Vishwamitra[†], Yifang Li[†], Kevin Wang[†], Hongxin Hu[†], Kelly Caine[†] and Gail-Joon Ahn[‡]

[†]Clemson University   [‡]Arizona State University
{nvishwa, yifang2, kwang2, hongxih, caine}@clemson.edu, ahn@asu.edu

ABSTRACT

The privacy control models of current Online Social Networks (OSNs) are biased towards the content owners' policy settings. Additionally, those privacy policy settings are too coarse-grained to allow users to control access to individual portions of information that is related to them. Especially, in a shared photo in OSNs, there can exist multiple Personally Identifiable Information (PII) items belonging to a user appearing in the photo, which can compromise the privacy of the user if viewed by others. However, current OSNs do not provide users any means to control access to their individual PII items. As a result, there exists a gap between the level of control that current OSNs can provide to their users and the privacy expectations of the users. In this paper, we propose an approach to facilitate collaborative control of individual PII items for photo sharing over OSNs, where we shift our focus from *entire* photo level control to the control of individual PII items within shared photos. We formulate a PII-based multiparty access control model to fulfill the need for collaborative access control of PII items, along with a policy specification scheme and a policy enforcement mechanism. We also discuss a proof-of-concept prototype of our approach as part of an application in Facebook and provide system evaluation and usability study of our methodology.

KEYWORDS

Access control, privacy, PII, multiparty, online social networks

ACM Reference format:
Nishant Vishwamitra[†], Yifang Li[†], Kevin Wang[†], Hongxin Hu[†], Kelly Caine[†] and Gail-Joon Ahn[‡] [†]Clemson University   [‡]Arizona State University {nvishwa, yifang2, kwang2, hongxih, caine}@clemson.edu, ahn@asu.edu . 2017. Towards PII-based Multiparty Access Control for Photo Sharing in Online Social Networks. In *Proceedings of SACMAT'17, June 21–23, 2017, Indianapolis, IN, USA, ,* 12 pages.
https://doi.org/http://dx.doi.org/10.1145/3078861.3078875

1 INTRODUCTION

Online social networks (OSNs) have faced a tremendous growth in recent years and become a major aspect of the Internet for socializing and sharing information among hundreds of millions of users. Facebook, for example, claims that it has 1.86 billion current active users [28]. OSNs like Facebook allow sharing information such as photos, videos and text messages, which can possibly contain sensitive and private information. Especially in sharing of visual data, such as photos, users are likely to share private information with an unknown audience, due to limited control over sharing such visual data [18]. To protect such sensitive information, access control has received considerable attention as a central feature of OSNs [2].

A vast majority of current Internet users are also OSN users [1], which implies that more users are shifting to OSNs for information exchange. As a result, users themselves have emerged as the largest contributers of content towards OSNs. A critical implication of this is that users are now faced with the additional responsibility of managing the online content that is associated with them. A large part of the shared information on Facebook consists of photos [27]. Facebook allows users to share photos with other users, but the responsibility of managing the audience of the photo lies with the uploader of the photo [10]. Furthermore, in a group photo setting, also known as *multiparty* photo, users appearing in the photo have no control over who can view their personal information in the photo. Existing OSNs do not provide effective mechanisms to sufficiently address how users appearing in a multiparty photo can control the visibility of their individual private information.

Although it may appear that the main focus of a multiparty photo is user *faces* [12], there are numerous other private information of a user that can also appear in a multiparty photo. These private information points of a user are called as Personally Identifiable Information (PII) of the user. In the context of OSNs, PII can be defined as *"information which can be used to distinguish or trace an individual's identity either alone or when combined with other public information that is linkable to a specific individual"* [14]. There are a large number of PII items that can be leaked in a multiparty photo. For example, a user who has a very unique tattoo on her/his *body* can be used to identify the user in a photo. Similarly, a user who has a unique *belonging*, such as a uniquely colored vehicle, may be identified using the *belonging* in the multiparty photo. As research in the field of PII have pointed out [13, 14, 21, 26], there are numerous such PII items that can link a user with her/his identity in a multiparty photo.

Current OSNs, such as Facebook, do not provide any mechanisms for collaborative control of PII items in multiparty photos. In fact, Facebook does not provide any means of collaborative control of shared visual information. Facebook privacy policy allows the uploader of the photo to completely control photo sharing. Facebook has traditionally supported three levels of photo sharing: Public, Friends and Only Me. Recently, in an attempt to increase the granularity of photo sharing, Facebook has introduced *smart lists* [22]. Using these smart lists, an uploader can specify a subset of users from her/his friends list for sharing a photo, such as close friends and colleagues. However, numerous studies have shown that users struggle to adopt this feature for managing their friends and customizing their privacy settings [4, 7, 25], because of a non-trivial process [17, 30]. As a result, significant privacy violations and mismatched user expectations in OSNs have been identified [19, 20, 32].

The need of collaborative management for data sharing, especially photo sharing, in OSNs has been addressed by some recent research [5, 9, 11, 15, 29, 31]. However, all those solutions can only enable a collaborative control based on the *entire* photo level and lacks the support for the control of individual PII items in the shared photos. Face/Off [12] adopts a simple access control model to enable users to collaboratively control their *faces* in a shared photo in OSNs. When a viewer who does not have access to view the face of a user views a photo of the user, Face/Off uses the technique of *blurring* to hide the portion of the user's face in the photo, so that it is not visible to the unauthorized viewers. A main issue with this solution is that it does not enable specifying fine-grained access control policies for other crucial PII items, such as *body* and *belonging*, of a user. In addition, the nature of PII items differ substantially. For example, several PII items can be shared amongst multiple users, such as *location* information of a multiparty photo. A certain user may not wish to share the location of the photo, whereas another user might want to share the same location information with all her/his friends. Hence, this gives rise to additional *conflicts* in collaborative control of individual PII items in a multiparty photo. Therefore, it is essential to develop a more effective and flexible access control mechanism for multiparty photo sharing in OSNs, accommodating the special authorization requirements coming from multiple associated users for managing their individual PII items collaboratively.

In this paper, we propose an approach to enable collaborative management of shared visual data such as photos in OSNs, by enabling *fine-grained, PII-level* control. A PII-based Multiparty Access Control (PMAC) model is formulated to accommodate the core requirements of PII-level multiparty authorization in photo sharing in OSNs. We also provide a PII-based multiparty policy specification scheme and a policy evaluation mechanism. Since policy conflicts are inevitable in multiparty authorization enforcement, a conflict resolution method unique to PII-level privacy control is further introduced to deal with policy conflicts via balancing the need for privacy protection and information sharing. In addition, we provide a prototype implementation of our approach in the context of Facebook. Our experimental results based on comprehensive system evaluation and usability study demonstrate the feasibility and practicality of our solution.

The rest of the paper is organized as follows. In Section 2, we overview Facebook privacy management mechanism and evaluate the importance of PII level control in photo sharing in OSNs. We articulate our proposed PMAC model, including multiparty authorization specification and multiparty policy evaluation in Section 3. The details about prototype implementation and experimental results are described in Section 4. We overview the related work in Section 5. Section 6 concludes this paper and discusses our future directions.

2 PRELIMINARIES
2.1 Facebook's Privacy Model
Facebook allows its users to manage the privacy settings of their uploaded content, such as photos, videos, posts and comments. Currently, Facebook allows 4 levels of granularity for photo sharing: *Public, Friends, Only Me* and *Custom* [3]. The *Public* level allows all users of Facebook to access the shared content. The *Friends* level allows all users present in the user's friends list to access the shared content. In this level, a user can also specify if shared content should also be made available to *friends of friends* of the users tagged in the shared content. The *Custom* level allows users to specifically allow or deny a certain group of users to access the shared content. The default sharing setting is the *Public* level, i.e, if a user does not change her/his sharing settings, the shared content is accessible to everyone.

Users are provided with an option to create and maintain special lists, such as *Colleagues, Close friends* and *Family*, which offer more granular control of content sharing. Users can add/remove their friends to/from special lists. Users can manage trust levels by maintaining different privacy settings for different lists. The visibility of such lists is private, unless explicitly changed by users.

However, Facebook does not provide content stakeholders with any control over visibility of the shared content, allowing the content owner to be the sole controller of the shared content. In addition, Facebook does not provide any control over the visibility of context factors or mutual friends.

2.2 Importance of PII Privacy Control in Online Photo Sharing
Personally Identifiable Information (PII) can be defined as *any information about an individual maintained by an agency, including (1) any information that can be used to distinguish or trace an individual's identity, such as name, social security number, date and place of birth, or biometric records; and (2) any other information that is linked or likable to an individual, such as medical, educational, financial, and employment information* [21]. In addition to conventional PII items, there are several PII items that can be potentially used to identify a person, such as a person's location, belongings, certain distinguishing characteristics of their bodies and affiliations [14, 21]. Thus, the privacy leakage due to PII is a crucial privacy issue in OSNs [14]. Especially, due to large-scale photo sharing supported by OSNs, there is an immense compromise of user privacy in terms of users' PII items, since a problem of *linking* arises as a result, where a user in a photo can be associated with their identities by their PII items. However, current OSNs such as Facebook are not equipped with privacy models having PII level granularity.

Table 1: Example of PII Items and Leaked Private Information.

PII	Leaked Private Information
Face/Body	Gender
	Sexual orientation
	Relationship status
Affiliation	Groups affiliated to
	Job/Occupation
	School information
Belonging	Official documents
	Relationship status
	Religion
	Interests
	Favorite music
	Favorite books
Location	Physical address
	Hometown

Table 1 gives examples about the kind of private information that is leaked when PII items are viewed by unauthorized users [16, 21]. These examples of PII items are especially relevant to photo sharing in OSNs. For example, let's assume that an OSN user uses the Face/Off solution [12] to blur her/his face from unknown users in all her/his shared photos. Let's assume this user has a unique tattoo on her/his hand that many users who are not her/his friends know about. Even though this user uses face blurring to hide her/his identity from unknown users, the unknown users may guess her/him in the photo through her/his tattoo. As a second example, assume that an OSN user works at a firm, which does not allow its employees to disclose their association with the firm to anyone outside the firm. Let's assume that this user is photographed at a party, wearing her/his firm's uniform, with the firm logo clearly seen on the front of her/his shirt. In this case, there are two possibilities. First, even if the user chooses to blur her/his face, people who met her/him at the same party may recognize her/him by her/his firm logo. In addition, her/his firm might come to know of her/his violation of the firm's policy of non disclosure.

Besides, in a multiparty photo, an individual's privacy can be compromised by the presence of mutual friends of the individual and the viewer [12]. For example, assume Bob and Jane are photographed together. Suppose Bob does not want to be seen with Jane by users who are not his friends, hence he uploads a photo where his face is not clearly visible. But, since Jane's friends know that Bob and Jane are friends, they conclude that the other person in the photo with Jane is Bob. Since not all friends of Jane and Bob are friends with each other, users who are not Bob's friends end up viewing the photo and learning about Bob in the photo. Hence, a privacy policy related to mutual friends in a photo must be enforced as well.

3 PII-BASED MULTIPARTY ACCESS CONTROL FOR OSNS

To enable collaborative control of individual PII items for photo sharing in OSNs, we formalize the PMAC model (Section 3.1), along with a policy scheme (Section 3.2) and a policy evaluation mechanism (Section 3.3) for the specification and enforcement of PMAC policies in OSNs.

3.1 PMAC Model

An OSN system, such as Facebook, typically contains a set of users, a set of user profiles, a set of user visual data, and a set of user relationships (called friends lists in Facebook). *User profile* indicates who a user is in the OSN, including identity and personal information, such as name, birthday and interests. *User visual data* represents visual information, such photos and videos, that the user has in the OSN, created through various activities in the OSN. *User relationship* shows who a user knows in the OSN, representing user connections with friends, mutual friends, family, coworkers, colleagues, and so on.

Existing OSNs including Facebook do not provide effective mechanism to support collaborative privacy control of PII items over shared visual data. Several access control schemes [6, 9, 10, 33, 36] have been introduced that propose collaborative access control in OSNs. Unfortunately, these schemes only allow coarse-grained control of the whole visual data and do not offer any solutions for fine-grained control of PII items. An effective access control mechanism should allow fine-grained, collaborative control of individual PII items associated with a user.

One exception to the above schemes is the Face/Off model [12]. This model enables collaborative control of a user's *face* in multiparty photos. However, several previous work [14, 16, 21] have discussed the importance of PII items in compromising privacy of an individual. In a multiparty photo, there are numerous PII items apart from *face*, that can compromise the privacy of an OSN user as well. In addition, PII items may be co-owned by several users, hence we also need a robust mechanism to address potential conflicts caused by the collaborative control of PII items. A flexible access control mechanism in a multi-user environment like OSNs should allow multiple controllers, who are associated with the shared visual data, to specify access control policies that can control individual PII items. As we have discussed in Section 2.2, in addition to the *owner* of content, *stakeholder* (the tagged user associated with the content) need to govern the access of the shared data as well due to possibly different privacy concerns. Additionally, every controller must be allowed to govern access control to their PII items to minimize the compromise of privacy.

In the context of OSNs that allow photo sharing, we have identified three kinds of PII items that can be associated with a user:

- **Unique PII.** A user's unique PII items uniquely identify the user in an OSN. For example, a user's face, body and belongings are unique PII items;
- **Shareable PII.** A user's shareable PII items can be linked to the user's identity and are shared with other users in an OSN. For example, a user's location is a shareable PII, as other users present in a photo share the location information in a photo; and
- **Relational PII.** The PII items that can be indirectly used to identify a user, based on the user's relationships with other users in an OSN are relational PII items. For example, *mutual friendship* in Facebook is a relational PII, because

in a multiparty photo, a viewer can guess the identity of a friend's friend in the photo, by the knowledge of the friend's identity.

Next, we formally define *Unique PII* and *Sharable PII* for PMAC model (see Figure 1) as follows:

DEFINITION 1. *(Unique PII). Let d be a visual data in the social network. Let u be a user identified in d. Unique PII (UP) of u constitutes the portion of the visual data that uniquely identifies u and it is owned by u. In PMAC model, a user's face, body and belonging are Unique PII items.*

DEFINITION 2. *(Shareable PII). Let d be a visual data in the social network. Let u be a user identified in d. Shareable PII (SP) of u constitutes the portion of the visual data that is collaboratively owned by u and a set of m users $\{u_1, \ldots, u_m\}$, $m \geq 1$. In PMAC model, a user's affiliation and location are Shareable PII items.*

Three types of controllers are identified in PMAC model. We define these types of controllers as follows:

DEFINITION 3. *(Visual Data Owner). Let d be a visual data item in the space of user $u \in U$ in the social network. The user u is called the Visual Data Owner of d.*

DEFINITION 4. *(PII Item Owner). Let d be a visual data item in the social network. Let $p \in I$ be a PII item identified in d, where I is a set of PII items in a set of Unique PII items, UP. Let u be a user who is linked to p. The user u is called the PII Item Owner of p.*

DEFINITION 5. *(PII Item Stakeholder). Let d be a visual data item in the social network. Let $p \in I$ be a PII item identified in d, where I is a set of PII items in a set of Shareable PII items, SP. Let T be the set of users who can be linked to p. A user u is called the PII Item Stakeholder of p, if $u \in T$.*

Different PII items tend to have different levels of importance for different user privacy concerns. Users tend to distinguish visibility of their PII items from various friends groups and also assign them different priorities called *sensitivity levels*. For example, a user may want to share her/his face with only her/his close friends. Therefore, her/his face has a *high* sensitivity level. In addition, the same user would not want her/his colleagues to learn about her/his personal belongings. Facebook introduced the concept of "smart lists" to enable sharing different content with different online social relationships. Using these smart lists, users can classify their friends into separate groups with different sharing settings, such as close friends, colleagues, and school. However, Facebook does not provide fine-grained sharing of PII items with separate smart lists, forcing users to share *entire* visual data with different friends lists. Of course, users in OSNs would assign different degrees of sensitivity to different PII items, and a PII item's sensitivity level can be leveraged to determine who are authorized to access the PII item. Several existing approaches [9, 10] have discussed how *sensitivity levels* can be utilized in OSNs. The concept of sensitivity level is also applicable to our PII-based collaborative sharing scenario. Therefore, in our model, we make the assumption that users can explicitly specify how sensitive their PII items are to their respective privacy concerns by assigning each PII item a sensitivity level when they specify their policy.

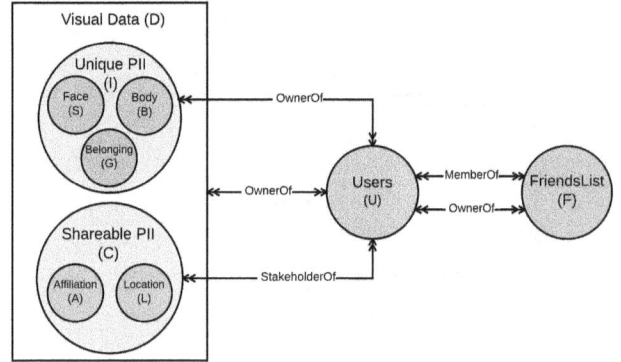

Figure 1: PMAC Model: Components and Relations.

Figure 1 represents the core components and relationships of our PMAC model. Note that in our model, a *user* can be the *owner* of her/his face, body and belonging, which is constituted by *PII item owner*, but a *stakeholder* of other types of *PII items*, such as *affiliation* and *location*, constituted by *PII item stakeholder*. Users are *owners* of their friends lists and can be *members* of other users' friends lists. A user can be a *viewer* of a visual data item, but a user who uploads a visual data item is the *owner* of the visual data item. We now formally define our model as follows:

- $U = \{u_1, \ldots, u_n\}$ is a set of users of the OSN. Each user has a unique identifier;
- $F = \{f_1, \ldots, f_m\}$ is a set of friends lists created by users in the OSN. Each friends list is identified by a unique identifier;
- $D = \{d_1, \ldots, d_p\}$ is a set of visual data items in the OSN. Each visual data item is identified by a unique identifier;
- $S = \{s_1, \ldots, s_l\}$ is a set of user faces in the OSN. Each user face is a *<u: sl: face-id>* tuple, $s_i = < u_i : sl_i : sid_i >$, where u_i is a face owner identifier, sl_i is a sensitivity level identifier and sid_i is a face identifier;
- $B = \{b_1, \ldots, b_t\}$ is a set of user body in the OSN. Each user body is a *<u: sl: body-id>* tuple, $b_i = < u_i : sl_i : bid_i >$, where u_i is a body owner identifier, sl_i is a sensitivity level identifier and bid_i is a body identifier;
- $A = \{a_1, \ldots, a_o\}$ is a set of user affiliations in the OSN. Each user affiliation is a *<u: sl: affiliation-id>* tuple, $a_i = < u_i : sl_i : aid_i >$, where u_i is an affiliation stakeholder identifier, sl_i is a sensitivity level identifier and aid_i is an affiliation identifier;
- $G = \{g_1, \ldots, g_s\}$ is a set of user belongings in the OSN. Each user belonging is a *<u: sl: belonging-id>* tuple, $g_i = < u_i : sl_i : gid_i >$, where u_i is a belonging owner identifier, sl_i is a sensitivity level identifier and gid_i is a belonging identifier;
- $L = \{l_1, \ldots, l_w\}$ is a set of user locations in the OSN. Each user location is a *<u: sl: location-id>* tuple, $l_i = < u_i : sl_i : lid_i >$, where u_i is a location stakeholder identifier, sl_i is a sensitivity level identifier and lid_i is a location identifier;
- $UF = \{uf_1, \ldots, uf_r\}$ is a collection of user friends lists, where $uf_i = \{uf_{i1}, \ldots, uf_{is}\}$ is a set of friends lists created by a user $i \in U$, where $uf_{ij} \in F$;

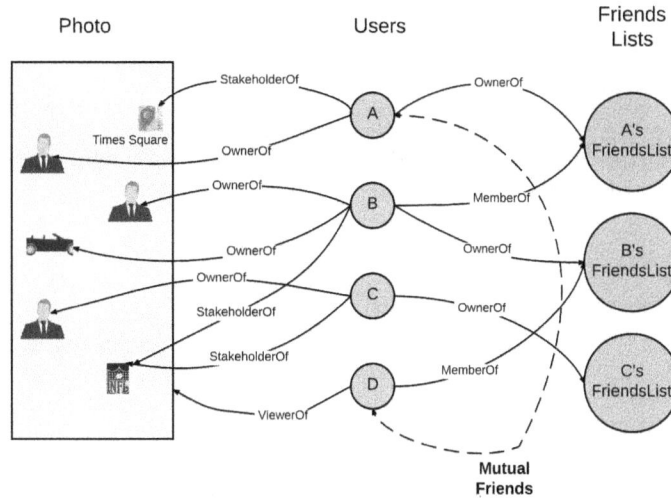

Figure 2: An Example of PII-based Multiparty Social Network.

- $CT = \{VO, PO, PS, VW, MB\}$ is a set of controller types, indicating *VisualDataOwnerOf*, *PIIItemOwnerOf*, *PIIItem-StakeholderOf*, *ViewerOf* and *MemberOf*, respectively;

- $CD = \{CD_{ct_1}, \ldots, CD_{ct_x}\}$ is a collection of binary user-to-PII item relations, where $CD_{ct_i} \subseteq U \times D$ specifies a set of $< user, visual\ data\ item >$ pairs with a controller type $ct_i \in CT$;

- $SL = \{sl_1, \ldots, sl_y\}$ is a set of supported sensitivity levels, which are assumed to be in the closed interval [0,1] in our model;

- $FU \subseteq F \times U$ is a set of 2-tuples $< FriendsList, user >$ representing user-to-friends list ownership relations;

- $controllers : D \xrightarrow{CT} 2^U$, a function mapping a visual data item $d \in D$, to a set of users who are the controllers of the visual data item with the controller type $ct \in CT$:
  $controllers(d : D, ct : CT) = \{u \in U \mid (u, d) \in CD_{ct}\}$;

- $visual\_data\_items : U \xrightarrow{CT} 2^D$, a function mapping each user $u \in U$ to a set of visual data items, where the user is a controller of the visual data items with the controller type $ct \in CT$:
  $visualDataItems(u : U, ct : CT) = \{d \in D \mid (u, d) \in CD_{ct}\}$;

- $user\_own\_friends\_lists : U \to 2^F$, a function mapping each user $u \in U$ to a set of friends lists created by this user:
  $user\_own\_friends\_lists(u : U) = \{f \in F \mid (\exists uf_u \in UF)[f \in uf_u]\}$;

- $friends\_list\_contain\_users : F \to 2^U$, a function mapping each friends list $f \in F$ to a set of users who are the members of this friends lists:
  $friends\_list\_contain\_users(f : F) = \{u \in U \mid (c, u) \in FU\}$;

- $user\_belong\_friends\_lists : U \to 2^F$, a function mapping each user $u \in U$ to a set of friends lists to which this user belongs:

  $user\_belong\_friends\_lists(u : U) = \{f \in F \mid (f, u) \in FU\}$;

- $UPS \subseteq U \times P \times S$ is a set of 3-tuples $< User, PIIItem, SensitivityLevel >$ representing user assigned sensitivity levels to PII items of the user;

- $sensitivity\_level : U, p \to SL$, a function returning the sensitivity level of a user-to-PII-item relation:
  $sensitivity\_level(u : U, p : (S \cup B \cup A \cup G \cup L)) = \{sl \in SL \mid (u, p, sl) \in UPS\}$;

- $all\_friends\_users : U \to 2^U$, a function mapping a user $u \in U$ to a set of users who are the members of the user's friends list:
  $all\_friends\_users(u : U) = \{u' \in U \mid (\exists f \in user\_own\_friends\_lists(u))[u' \in friends\_list\_contain\_users(F)]\}$; and

- $mutual\_friends\_list : F \to 2^U$, a function mapping a pair of users $< u, u' >$, $\{u, u'\} \in U$ to a set of users who belong to friends lists of both u and u'.
  $mutual\_friends\_list(u : U, u' : U) = \{all\_friends\_users(u) \cap all\_friends\_users(u')\}$.

Figure 2 depicts an example of PII-based multiparty OSN representation. It contains four individuals, Alice (*A*), Bob (*B*), Carol (*C*) and Dave (*D*), along with their relations with visual data items and friends lists. Note that a user may be related to more than one friends list, thus forming complex relationships. For example, in Figure 2, Bob is a *memberOf* Alice's friends list and also the *ownerOf* his own friends list. Dave is a *memberOf* Bob's friends list. Hence Alice and Dave are mutual friends, through Bob. This example depicts that a collaborative visual data item has multiple controllers. Since the photo depicts Alice, Bob and Carol, all three of them are controllers of the photo. The controller types are depicted in the example. In addition, a visual data item can have multiple *stakeholders*. For example, Bob and Carol are both stakeholders of the "NFL" logo. In our model, each user has complete ownership of her/his face, body and belongings, as shown by the *ownerOf* relationship in Figure 2.

3.2 PMAC Policy Specification

To achieve authorization requirements with respect to the multiparty privacy concerns owing to multiple PII items, it is essential for access control policies to be in place to regulate access over individual PII items contained in a shared visual data associated with multiple controllers. Our policy specification scheme is constructed based on the proposed PMAC model. In our model, each controller of a shared visual data can specify one or more rules, as her/his policy governs who can view the PII items associated with them, contained in the shared visual data.

Viewer Specification: Viewers are a set of users who are granted/denied access to the visual data item. We formally define the viewer specification as follows:

DEFINITION 6. *(Viewer Specification). The viewer specification of a user $u \in U$ is defined as a set, $\{a_1, \ldots, a_n\}$, where each element is a user friends list $uf_u \in UF$, a set of users, $\{u_1, \ldots, u_m\}$, where $u_i \in U$, or everyone (*).*

For example, Alice can specify her colleagues, a particular set of users from her friends list, as viewer specification in her rule.

PII Item Specification: In OSNs, users can share their visual data, such as photos, with others. To facilitate effective policy conflict resolution for multiparty access control (Section 3.3.1), we introduce *sensitivity levels* for PII item specification, which are assigned by the controllers to the shared PII items. A user's judgment of the sensitivity level of the PII item is not binary (private/public), but multi-dimensional with varying degrees of sensitivity. Formally, the PII item specification is defined as follows:

DEFINITION 7. *(PII Item Specification). Let $dt \in D$ be a data item. Let P be the set of PII items of a user $u \in U$ in dt. Let sl be a sensitivity level, which is a rational number in the range [0,1], assigned to PII items in P. The PII item specification is defined as a tuple $< p, sl >$, where p is a PII item .*

Access Control Policy: To summarize the above-mentioned policy elements, we give the definition of PMAC access control rule as follows:

DEFINITION 8. *(PMAC Rule). A PMAC rule is a 5-tuple $R = <$ controller, viewer, shared visual data, PII items, effect $>$, where*

- *controller $\in U$ is a user who can regulate the access of data;*
- *viewer is a set of users to whom the authorization is granted/ denied, representing with an access specification defined in Definition 6.*
- *shared visual data is a specific photo or all photos (*) where in the user is identified.*
- *PII items is a set of PII items that the user wants to regulate access to, representing with an PII item specification defined in Definition 7.*
- *effect is a tuple defined as $< p, share/blur >$ where p represents a PII item associated with the controller and share/blur represents the authorization effect of the rule regarding p.*

Suppose a controller can leverage five sensitivity levels: 0.00 (*none*), 0.25 (*low*), 0.50 (*medium*), 0.75 (*high*), and 1.00 (*highest*) for the shared visual data, the following is an example rule:

Example 3.1. Alice denies users who are in her "Colleagues" friends list, from viewing her face, body and location in all photos that she is tagged in, where Alice considers her location with a high sensitivity level:
$r_1 = (Alice, \{< Colleagues >\}, *, \{< face : 1 >, < body : 1 >, < location : 0.75 >\}, \{< face : blur >, < body : blur >, < location : blur >\}).$

We apply this rule to the example social network shown in Figure 2. Let us assume Bob is a colleague of Alice. Bob satisfies this rule, since he is in "Colleagues" friends list of Alice. Let us assume Bob comes across a photo, "party.jpg", taken at a popular downtown bar near Times Square, "Times Square Bar" depicting Alice. As an effect of this rule, Alice's face, body and location ("Times Square Bar") would be blurred out, so that they are not visible to Bob.

Furthermore, a PII item stakeholder may define more than one rule in her/his policy for a shared visual data. In this case, users who satisfy *any* rule in the policy are considered as authorized users for the resource. The following is another example rule:

Example 3.2. In addition to the rule defined in Example 3.1, let's consider another authorization requirement from *Alice*, where she wants to disclose all her PII items in all photos to users in her "Close Friends" list:
$r_2 = (Alice, \{< CloseFriends >\}, *, \{*\}, \{* : share\}).$

Example 3.3. There are cases where relational PII items, such as mutual friends, can leak the privacy of a stakeholders, as shown in Example 3.1. Let's consider an authorization requirement from *Alice* where, in addition to Example 3.1, she wants to deny one of her colleagues, *Dave*, to view their mutual friends' faces:
$r_3 = (Alice, Dave, *, \{< face : 1 >, < body : 1 >, < location : 0.75 >, < mutual\_friends\_list(Alice, Dave).face : 0.75 >\}, \{< face : blur >, < body : blur >, < location : blur >, < mutual\_friends\_list(Alice, Dave).face : blur >\}).$

When we apply this rule to the example social network (Figure 2), Dave will not be able to see Bob's face, in addition to Alice's specified PII items.

3.3 PMAC Policy Evaluation

In our PMAC model, we adopt two steps to evaluate a viewer request over multiparty access control policies as shown in Figure 3. In the first step, we first perform some pre-evaluation procedures that involve the detection of controllers and *PII items* in the photo. Then, the privacy policies of the controllers are retrieved, following their detection. In PMAC model, a controller can leverage a positive rule to define a set of viewers to whom the controller's *PII items* are visible, or/and a negative policy to exclude some specific viewers from whom the *PII items* should be blurred. A *PII item owner* has complete ownership of the *unique PII items* that they own. As a result, only the *PII item owner's* policy is used for determining the effect on *unique PII items*. However, in case of *shareable* and *relational PII items*, several co-owners, known as *PII item stakeholders* can have different privacy policies associated with them, based on different privacy needs and concerns.

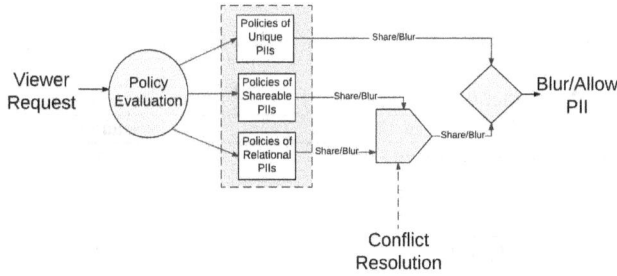

Figure 3: PMAC Policy Evaluation Process.

In the second step, decisions from all controllers corresponding to each *PII item* in the photo pertaining to the viewer request are first aggregated. Since those controllers may generate different decisions (share and blur) with respect to the *shareable PII items* and *relational PII items* for the viewer request, conflicts may occur. Conflict resolution is used in our PMAC policy evaluation process in this step. We will address our approach for resolving such conflicts in detail subsequently, where we use a strategy called *privacy adjustment*. As can be seen in Figure 3, policies concerning *unique PIIs* are directly used to determine the effect, whereas policies concerning *shareable PIIs* and *Relational PIIs* are first aggregated to perform conflict resolution, followed by the effect decision.

3.3.1 Conflict Resolution in PII-based Multiparty Access Control.
Due to collaborative control of photo sharing in PMAC model, we have two main areas of conflicts as follows:

- **Relational PII Conflict.** Mutual friends are users who are common friends of two users in the OSN. There may exit a conflict between a mutual friend's own policy for her/his PII items and a user's policy applied to the mutual friend's PII items. For example, assume Bob and Jack are friends and John is a friend of Jack but not a friend of Bob. Bob wants his friend Jack's face to be blurred to all users who are not his friend. But, Jack as a mutual friend of Bob and John wants all his friends to view his face. Thus, there is a conflict about whether or not to blur Jack's face, when John is the viewer.
- **Shareable PII Conflict.** As shown in Figure 2, there can exist multiple stakeholders for a single PII item. Stakeholder conflict occurs when the privacy concerns of the collaborating stakeholders for the same PII items do not match. For example, assume Jack and Bob both work for the *same* company. While Jack wants to share his affiliation with the company with all his friends, Bob does not want anyone except his close friends to learn about his affiliation with his company. Jack and Bob are photographed together with the company logo in the background. The stakeholder conflict arises for viewers who are in both Jack's and Bob's target viewers list: whether to blur the company logo according to Bob's policy or to show the company logo according to Jack's policy.

The process of privacy conflict resolution makes a decision to allow or deny the viewer access to view *conflicted* PII items. In

general, allowing a viewer to view a conflicted PII items may cause *privacy leakage*, but denying a viewer access to the conflicted PII items may result in *sharing loss*. Our privacy conflict resolution approach employs a *privacy adjustment* mechanism that ensures that there is minimum privacy leakage for users who want to blur PII items, but at the same time allow users to share PII items. We employ this mechanism differently to ensure optimum conflict resolution for *Relational PII Conflict* and *Shareable PII Conflict*.

Relational PII Conflict Resolution Through Privacy Adjustment. We consider a multiparty photo containing a user and a mutual friend of the user. Let v be a viewer of the photo who is a friend of the mutual friend but not a friend of the user. Table 2 depicts the conflicting PII items and resolution strategy for the user and the mutual friend. In the last scenario, conflict occurs because the user wishes to blur her/his own face and blur the mutual friend's face from v, but the mutual friend wishes to share her/his face and body with v. In this case, we use *privacy adjustment* to resolve this conflict, defined as follows.

- **Policy Restrictiveness**: The restrictiveness of a policy p defined by a user i is the level of restriction imposed by p on the visibility of PII items of i, denoted by R_i. For example, a user's policy that is set to blur *both* face *and* body has higher *policy restrictivenss* than a user's policy that is set to only blur her/his face. In PMAC model, the restrictiveness of a policy is computed by summing the pre-defined weights (w) of PII items in PMAC model. These weights are defined based on the degree of identification for a user that the PII item provides. For example, a user's face can reveal the identity of the user much more effectively, when compared to the location information of the user. The computation of policy restrictiveness in shown in Equation 1.

$$R_i = \sum_{j \in PIIs_{User}(i)} w_j \qquad (1)$$

Where the function $PIIs_{User}(i)$ returns a set of PII items associated with the user i.

- **Privacy Adjustment**: Automatically adjust the privacy policy of a user in case of a conflict by increasing the *policy restrictiveness* of the user, so that a higher level of privacy is achieved by restricting visibility of additional PII items of the user. For example, let's assume Bob is a user who has set his policy to blur his own face and blur his mutual friend's face, when John is the viewer. Let's say Jack is a mutual friend of Bob and John. Conflict occurs if Jack has set his policy to share his face with all his friends. In this case, *Privacy Adjustment* mechanism increases the *policy restrictiveness* of Bob's policy by blurring both his body and face, but allows Jack to share his face with his friends.

The ability to control individual PII items in PMAC model enables us to use *privacy adjustment* to resolve conflicts. For example, in the third scenario depicted in Table 2, since the mutual friend is the owner of her/his own face and body, we allow the mutual friend to share her/his face and body with v. At the same time, since this decision compromises privacy of the user, we use *privacy adjustment* to automatically blur the user's *body*, in addition to

Table 2: Example of Relational PII Conflict Between Mutual Friend (MF) and User

MF's Own Policy		User's Policy				Conflict?	MF Conflict Resolution	User Conflict Resolution
Face	Body	Own Face	Own Body	MF Face	MF Body			
Blur	Blur	Blur	Blur	Blur	Blur	No	Blur Face and Body	Blur Face and Body
Share	Share	Blur	Blur	Share	Share	No	Share Face and Body	Blur Face and Body
Share	**Share**	**Blur**	**Share**	**Blur**	**Share**	**Yes**	**Share Face and Body**	**Blur Face and Body**

the face of the user so that there is a minimum compromise in the user's privacy. This ensures an optimum trade off between date sharing and privacy protection.

We use *privacy adjustment* for conflict resolution in case of multiple mutual friends and users in a multiparty photo. Since the PMAC model emphasizes the importance of privacy of individuals in multiparty photo sharing, it does not allow the majority decision to override the privacy concerns of users. Therefore, in case of conflict, PMAC model uses *privacy adjustment* to address the privacy concern of users by making the policy of users more restrictive.

We summarize the conflict resolution decision of mutual friend i and user j as follows.

$$Decision = \begin{cases} \text{Share} + Privacy\ Adjustment & \text{if } R_i < R_j \\ \text{Blur} & \text{if } R_i \geq R_j \end{cases} \quad (2)$$

Where R_i and R_j are the *policy restrictiveness* of the mutual friend and the user, respectively, for at least *minimum* R_j for user, which is to blur face.

Shareable PII Conflict Resolution Through Sharing Risk Measurement and Privacy Adjustment: Our basic premise for conflict resolution in case of stakeholder conflict is the following: a) a PII item conflicting stakeholder policies must be shared if the *majority* of stakeholder policies are in favor of sharing the PII item; and b) PMAC must use the *privacy adjustment* for the stakeholder policies, which are in favor of blurring the PII item. In order to facilitate effective conflict resolution for shareable PII conflicts, we define sensitivity of shared PII item and aggregate decision value as follows:

- **Sensitivity of shared PII item**: PII item sensitivity defines stakeholder's perception about the confidentiality of the PII item being shared. The sensitivity level of the shared PII item defined by a stakeholder j is denoted as sl_j. This factor depends on the stakeholder themselves, since certain PII items are more confidential for some stakeholders than some others; and

- **Aggregate decision value**: A *sharing risk based* scheme is used by PMAC to compute an aggregated decision value, in favor of sharing a PII item and in favor of blurring the PII item. The total number of stakeholders in favor of sharing a PII item k, is denoted by $N_{sh}(k)$ and the total number of stakeholders in favor of blurring the PII item k is denoted by $N_{Bl}(k)$.

In order to measure the aggregate value in favor of sharing and in favor of blurring a PII item k, denoted by $AV_{total}^{Sh}(k)$ and $AV_{total}^{Bl}(k)$, we can use following equations.

$$AV_{total}^{Sh}(k) = \sum_{i \in stakeholders_{Sh}(k)} sl_i \times N_{sh}(k) \quad (3)$$

and

$$AV_{total}^{Bl}(k) = \sum_{j \in stakeholders_{Bl}(k)} sl_j \times N_{bl}(k) \quad (4)$$

Where functions $stakeholders_{Sh}(k)$ and $stakeholders_{Bl}(k)$ return the number of stakeholders of k who wish to share and blur k, respectively.

Then, following equation can be utilized to make the decisions (sharing or blurring a PII item for a viewer request) for the stakeholder conflict resolution.

$$Decision = \begin{cases} \text{Share} + Privacy\ Adjustment & \text{if } AV_{total}^{Bl}(k) < AV_{total}^{Sh}(k) \\ \text{Blur} & \text{if } AV_{total}^{Bl}(k) > AV_{total}^{Sh}(k) \end{cases} \quad (5)$$

4 IMPLEMENTATION AND EVALUATION

4.1 System Implementation

We implemented a proof-of-concept Facebook application called *AppX*. *AppX* is a third-party Facebook application written in PHP and MySQL and hosted on Apache servers. The user interface also contains jQuery. External APIs were used extensively. Using Facebook's Graph API, the users' Facebook profile can be accessed to authenticate the user and import the friends list to the database. *AppX* is a social media application that implements the PMAC mechanism. The current implementation is restricted to photo sharing, but the system can be generalized to other forms of visual media sharing. We use Face++ for face recognition and Google Vision for logo and text detection and Microsoft Computer Vision for description tags. For object and body recognition, py-faster-rcnn was used with the VGG16 trainval on the Palmetto server, a high performance computing cluster with 12 GBs of RAM, 8 CPU cores, and a K40 GPU. A RESTful API was created for py-faster-rcnn using the Flask library in Python.

When first accessed, the user is asked to grant *AppX* Facebook permissions to view basic profile information (see Figure 4). After the user is authenticated, *AppX* will then download the user's profile picture and import the user's Facebook friends into the database. The profile picture is used for face detection. If *AppX* cannot detect a single face in the picture, it will ask the user to upload a portrait. After this, *AppX* presents the user the settings page. The settings page allows the user to access all of the PMAC policies. After initialization, the user is presented the picture feed, where they will see all of the picture uploaded to *AppX* by the user and the user's friends, similar to Facebook's home page. The user can change the settings or upload a picture.

When a picture is uploaded, it is saved locally on the server and processed on the fly when they are viewed. When the photo is viewed, it is first processed and edited in accordance to the PMAC policy before being shown to the user. Each face in the picture is recognized and their PMAC policies are loaded from the database and applied. Any face, body, or item in the photo may be blurred if permission is not allowed.

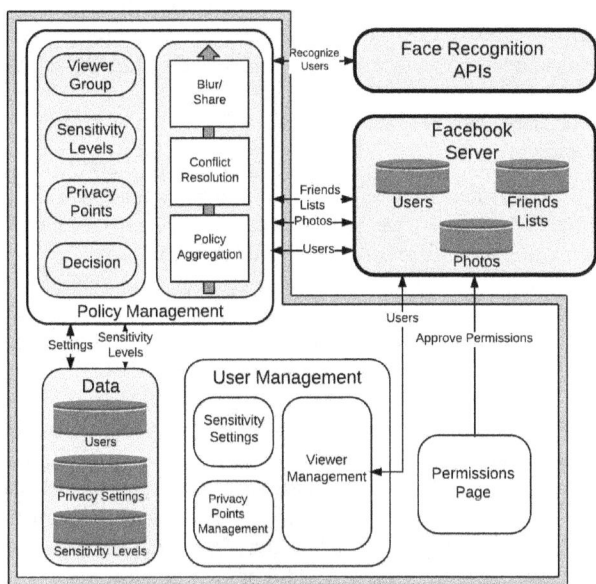

Figure 4: System Architecture of *AppX*.

The principal components of *AppX* are depicted in Figure 4. Since the sensitivity of PII items is specific to every user's privacy concerns, the *User Management* component provides options to adjust it. We have various PII items, such as location, belongings and affiliation. A user can add or remove the PII items that they are concerned about using the *User Management* component. In addition, due to the evolving nature of social media, *AppX* provides support for adding more PII items according to the PMAC model policy updates. Updates in the *policy settings* reflect in the *Data* component. As a result, *AppX* updates policy levels in the *Policy Management* component.

4.2 System Evaluation

4.2.1 Performance Evaluation. A single photo was used as a background image, and 1 to 10 people were added to the picture by substituting arguments to the API. Each person is box 72x153 pixes, and is 20 pixels apart from each other in a line. The processing and database time for the PMAC system were recorded. As more people are detected in the picture, more PMAC policies have to be retrieved and processed. Each person has a PMAC policy with only body blurring enabled. Each person's PMAC policy is then enforced. To prevent the test runs from interfering with each other, caching was turned off. The database calls increase linearly as the number of people increase because the database calls were made separately in sequential order for each person. Figure 5 depicts the performance of *AppX* as a plot of number of people in a photo against average time in milliseconds.

As depicted in figure 5, there is a slight and proportional increase in the processing time and the database time as the number of PII items in the photo increases. This is an expected observation, as there are more computations involved as the PII items in a photo

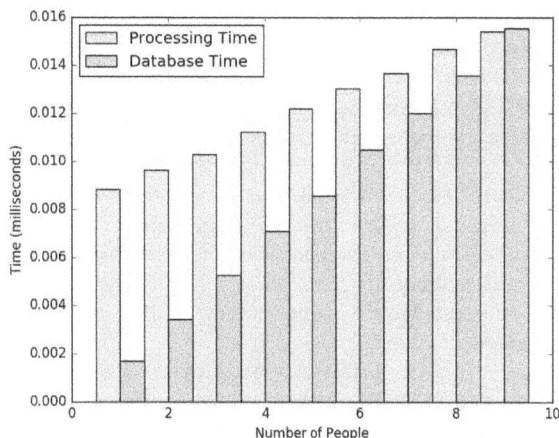

Figure 5: Performance Evaluation of *AppX*.

increases. For the maximum case, we only observed a difference of around 0.006 milliseconds. Hence, PMAC could only add little overhead to the current Facebook photo control mechanism.

4.2.2 Effectiveness Evaluation. To evaluate the effectiveness of our approach, we compared the privacy of a shared photo from the perspective of PII privacy for Facebook solution, Face/Off solution [12] and our PMAC solution for 30 randomly selected photos from Facebook. The metric we used for evaluation is the total Privacy of all controllers and all PII items in a photo, based on the assumption that a viewer is not authorized to see PII items of any of the controllers present in a photo.

The Facebook solution does not allow users to control viewer access to PII items. The Face/Off solution allows users to control access to their face only. Our model allows users to control access to their *unique*, *shareable* and *relational* PII items. In order to evaluate the impact of each type of PII in a photo, we used certain factors derived from [21] that are relevant to the context of online photo sharing. These factors are listed below:

- **Identifiability**: *Identifiability* of a PII item is a measure of how easily the PII item can be used to identify a user.
- **Quantity of PII**: *Quantity of PII* is the total number of PII items in a photo.
- **Data Field Sensitivity**: Some PII items, such as face of a user, are more sensitive than other PII items like location. The *data field sensitivity* of a PII item is a measure of the sensitivity of the PII item.
- **Context of Use**: *Context of use* reflects the purpose for which a PII item can be used for. For example, the location of a user can be used to learn about the whereabouts of the user.

In our evaluation, we allocated *identifiability*, *quantity of PII*, *data field sensitivity* and *context of use* scores for each PII item that we have considered in our model, in order to capture the impact of the privacy of these PII items for the 30 randomly selected Facebook photos. We then used the computed scores of each type of PII items to evaluate the effectiveness of all 30 cases of our randomly selected Facebook photos. In our effectiveness evaluation, a user's unique PII items were allocated with the highest score, as they are most crucial to the user and uniquely identify a user. This is followed by the shareable PII items and relational PII items.

We evaluated the outcomes of 30 cases for Facebook, Face/Off and our PMAC solutions, as depicted in Figure 6. The Facebook privacy policy is owner centric. That is, the owner decides the privacy of the complete photo and hence there is no collaborative control. In addition, the Facebook solution is not *fine-grained* and hence, users cannot control their PII items. Since our evaluation is PII privacy centric, the Facebook solution does not address any of the above mentioned factors. Hence, in all 30 cases Facebook solution is evaluated as the lowest privacy solution for PII items among all three solutions.

The Face/Off solution enables multiparty access control and users can control who can see their faces in a shared photo. From a PII privacy perspective, a user's privacy can be compromised by several other PII items. For example, a popular celebrity having a unique tattoo on her/his body can be easily identified by the tattoo on her/his body, even though her/his face is blurred. In addition to this, shareable PII items can be responsible for privacy compromise of more than one user in a shared photo, with the additional overhead of conflict resolution in a collaborative environment. We can also see from the example in Figure 2 that relational PII items also play an important role in privacy compromise is shared photos. Therefore, the Face/Off solution has been scored for only protecting the privacy of the face of a user in the 30 cases. The results are depicted in Figure 6. Obviously, the Face/Off solution is better than the Facebook solution in every case.

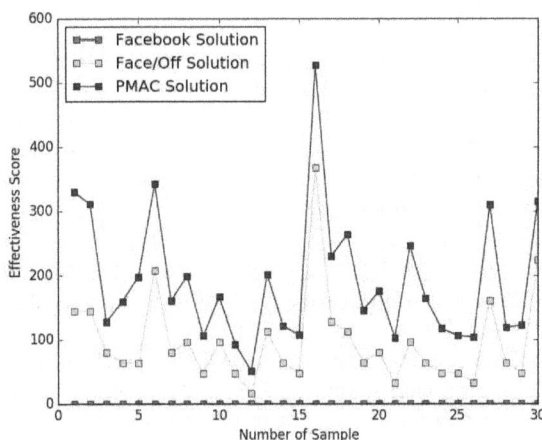

Figure 6: Effectiveness Evaluation of Facebook, Face/Off and PMAC Solutions.

As depicted in Figure 6, our solution performs the highest among all three solutions. This is because, from a PII privacy perspective, our solution provides the highest control to users over who can have viewer access to individual PII items. This observation is confirmed in all 30 cases of our experiment.

However, it can be observed that in some cases, such as the cases 3 and 12 the Face/Off solution comes close to our solution in terms of PII privacy protection, but in some cases such as the cases

1 and 27, there is a comparatively larger difference in effectiveness. This is due to the fact that the cases 3 and 12 had very few observed PII items, apart from face. Therefore, since both Face/Off and our solution are effectiveness in protection of face PII, the effectiveness is close. However, in the cases 1 and 27, a large number of PII items in addition to face are present. Since the Face/Off solution provides no control for these PII items, there is a large difference in the effectiveness between the Face/Off solution and our PMAC solution.

4.2.3 Preliminary Study of Privacy Filter. To determine the potential of our system, we conducted a preliminary survey for identifying the likability and adoption willingness of the privacy filter, *blurring*, used in our system. We conducted an online survey with 30 participants, and measured the users' likability towards as is (no filter) and body blurring filter with the question "I like the privacy filter" which derived the interface preference scale [23]. We also measured their general adoption willingness using the question "I want online social networks (Facebook etc.) to adopt the privacy filters so that I can be obscured in certain photos my friends upload (group photo etc.)". Both response scales are 7-point likert scale from 1 "Strongly disagree" to 7 "Strongly agree". Thirty participants were recruited from MTurk. Nineteen of them are female, ten are male, and one participant selected "I prefer not to answer".

We created two identical group photos with four people as foreground and a campus scene as background. In one photo, we applied body blurring filter on one target person. First, the participants saw one photo, and rated their likeability from 1 to 7; then they were shown another photo and rated the likeability. Afterwards, they rated their adoption willingness of this type of privacy filters.

The result shows the mean of likability of as is condition is 5.33 (Somewhat agree); and for body blurring filter, it is 4.1 (neither disagree nor agree). Seventy seven percent of the participants like the original photo without any filter (as is condition), while 53% like the body blurring filter. We expected this result as people may be preferential towards original photo as compared to the photo with body blurring privacy filter. However, the neutral mean of the body blurring filter also indicates that our privacy filter does not seriously degrade user experience.

The mean of general adoption willingness is 4.7 (somewhat agree). Sixty percent of the participants have a positive attitude (rating from 5-7), suggesting the majority of the participants may be willing to use the blurring filter.

4.2.4 Survey (User Study) of PMAC Model. We conducted a survey ("user study") to evaluate users' naive perceptions about the policy settings as implemented in a Facebook application (*AppX*). First, we presented users with an *AppX* policy setting user interface. Next, we presented five scenarios focused on privacy of each of the *PII items* supported by our model. All scenarios had sample photos so that participants can understand the privacy concerns in the scenarios. Figure 7 illustrates five scenarios in *AppX*. Next, we asked them questions about their perceptions of the app and the settings it enables. We used two criteria for evaluation: *adoption willingness* and *control*. *Adoption willingness* is a measure of a user's willingness to adopt a particular feature in current OSNs. It can also help us identify if users perceive a feature as useful. *Control* is a measure of the user's perceived control of their private information.

Table 3: Adoption Willingness and Perceived Privacy Control for PMAC Model. Response scales are 7-point likert scale from 1 "Strongly disagree" to 7 "Strongly agree".

Metric	PII items														
	Body			Mutual Friend			Affiliation			Belonging			Location		
	Mean	SEM	% PR	Mean	SEM	% PR	Mean	SEM	% PR	Mean	SEM	% PR	Mean	SEM	% PR
Adoption Willingness	4.32	0.16	90.32	3.87	0.20	70.97	4.17	0.19	90.00	3.96	0.18	78.57	4.14	0.17	85.72
Control	4.52	0.14	90.32	4.23	0.16	83.87	4.14	0.17	82.76	4.00	0.18	78.58	4.32	0.16	85.71

We measured users' *adoption willingness* of *AppX* by asking "If Facebook implemented this feature in its privacy policy, I would use it". We measured *control* by asking "I believe that I can better control the visibility of my *PII* to only users that I want to share it with in *AppX* when compared to Facebook", where *PII* was each of body, mutual friend, affiliation, belonging and location. We asked these two questions for each of the five *PII items*. Both response scales are 5-point likert scale from 1 "Strongly disagree" to 5 "Strongly agree".

We conducted the online survey using the Qualtrics platform. There were a total of thirty nine participants, with 40.74% of participants in the age group of 18-24 years, 48.15% in the age group of 25-34 years and 11.11% in the age group of 35-44 years. The participants consisted of students as well as working professionals. Among the participants, a majority (96.30%) claimed to use Facebook and 85.19% of the participants claimed to use Instagram and Google+.

Figure 7: Illustration of PII Scenarios in *AppX*: (a) Body, (b) Mutual Friends, (c) Affiliation, (d) Object, and (e) Location.

Table 3 depicts the results from the survey, where we record mean, standard error mean (SEM) and percentage positive response (PR). The means for all the scenarios for *adoption willingness* are above 3, which indicates that naive users, without having used the system, may be willing to consider using *AppX*. The means for *control* are above three for all scenarios, indicating that users may perceive that *AppX* provides them some control over the five *PIIs* in photos. Participants rated their potential willingness to adopt *body* privacy the highest as compared to the other *PII* items. One possible reason is that participants may consider their body as the most sensitive *PII item* in the photos shared in OSNs. However, it could be that they simply find body blurring the least offensive in terms of visual affect to the photos. A similar speculation can be applied around the degree of perceived control of *body* in a multiparty photo.

We see that the lowest mean of *adoption willingness* among all the *PII items* is *mutual friends*, although it is above three (indicating a positive perception). We speculate that the comparatively low score for *mutual friends* could be attributed to the lack of familiarity of the people in the photo. The mutual friends PII is based on relationship between the viewer and the people in the photo. Since participants were not related to the people in the photo, we could argue that

they might not recognize or appreciate the importance of mutual friends privacy presented in this scenario.

5 RELATED WORK

The need of collaborative management for data sharing, especially photo sharing, in OSNs has been addressed by some recent research [5, 9–11, 15, 29, 31]. For example, Hu et al. [10] formulated a MultiParty Access Control (MPAC) model to capture the essence of multiparty authorization requirements. They also investigated a collaborative data sharing mechanism to support the specification and enforcement of multiple privacy concerns, along with a conflict detection and resolution mechanism. In addition, they proposed an approach with the support of both theoretical and empirical analyses on privacy control in OSNs through analyzing the strategic behaviors of rational users using a game-theoretic model [11]. However, all those work can only facilitate collaborative control for an *entire* photo and lacks the support for the control of *individual PII items* in a shared photo.

The importance of PII items for privacy control has been discussed in several prior work [13, 14, 26]. For example, the ReCon system [26] discusses PII privacy in mobile networks and provides machine learning solutions to reveal leakage of PII items and also provides tools to control such a kind of privacy leakage. Recently, Face/Off solution [12] was proposed to model and express access control policies to control the view of users' faces in shared photos in OSNs. Face/Off adopts a face blurring technique to hide a user's identity in multiparty photos. In addition, extensive user studies conducted in [12] provide us with valuable inferences about user opinions regarding more fine-grained privacy control for user faces in shared photos in OSNs. However, Face/Off solution cannot support the specification of fine-grained access control policies for other important PII items, such as body, affiliation, and belonging in shared photos in OSNs. Besides, an access control scheme for the control of individual parts of a shared object in OSNs is provided by the CooPeD system [8]. The CooPeD system presents a model for the co-management of decomposable parts in shared objects in OSNs. However, the CooPeD model does not provide a solution to address the issue of the same shared parts belonging to multiple users. In ideal scenarios, there may exist many shared parts in an image that could be co-owned by multiple users. In contrast, our PMAC model can address such an issue and also use its conflict resolution and privacy adjustment mechanisms to effectively resolve PII-based privacy conflicts.

A solution for the video privacy protection in OSNs was provided by the BEPS system [24]. BEPS can detect and separate *intentionally captured persons* (ICP) from *non-intentionally captured persons* (non-ICPs), following which the non-ICPs are removed from the image using in-painting techniques. However, this work fails to recognize the importance of PIIs with respect to the privacy and identification of subjects in shared videos. Although a non-ICP subject could be removed from a video, the non-ICP subject's PIIs can still cause privacy compromise of the subject. In our approach, in addition to blocking access to directly identifiable parts such as face and body of a subject, we further offer an access control mechanism that allows users to control visibility of their other PIIs.

6   CONCLUSION AND FUTURE WORK

In this paper, we have proposed a new mechanism for collaboratively controlling PII items in multiparty photos in OSNs. A PII-based multiparty access control model has been formulated, along with a policy specification and corresponding policy evaluation mechanism. In addition, our conflict resolution strategy leverages the flexible control of individual PIIs for effective conflict resolution. We have also described a proof-of-concept implementation of our solution called *AppX*, and provided system evaluation and usability study of our approach.

As part of our future work, we plan to conduct more comprehensive user studies to evaluate the user needs with respect to PII privacy in multiparty photo sharing in OSNs. In addition, we would extend our work in multiparty policy specifications to use machine learning techniques so that intuitive policy models that need minimal user interaction can be formulated.

ACKNOWLEDGMENT

This work was partially supported by grants from National Science Foundation (NSF-IIS-1527421, NSF-IIS-1527268, and NSF-CNS-1537924).

REFERENCES

[1] 2011. The State of Social Media 2011: Social is the new normal. (2011). http://www.briansolis.com/2011/10/state-of-social-media-2011/.
[2] 2017. Facebook Privacy Policy. (2017). http://www.facebook.com/policy.php/.
[3] 2017. Facebook Sharing Settings. (2017). www.facebook.com/help/459934584025324/.
[4] F. Adu-Oppong, C.K. Gardiner, A. Kapadia, and P.P. Tsang. 2008. Social circles: Tackling privacy in social networks. In *Symposium on Usable Privacy and Security (SOUPS)*. Citeseer.
[5] A. Besmer and H. Richter Lipford. 2010. Moving beyond untagging: Photo privacy in a tagged world. In *Proceedings of the 28th international conference on Human factors in computing systems*. ACM, 1563–1572.
[6] J.Y. Choi, W. De Neve, K.N. Plataniotis, Y.M. Ro, S. Lee, H. Sohn, H. Yoo, WD Neve, CS Kim, YM Ro, and others. 2010. Collaborative Face Recognition for Improved Face Annotation in Personal Photo Collections Shared on Online Social Networks. *IEEE Transactions on Multimedia* (2010), 1–14.
[7] L. Fang and K. LeFevre. 2010. Privacy wizards for social networking sites. In *Proceedings of the 19th international conference on World wide web*. ACM, 351–360.
[8] Lorena González-Manzano, Ana I González-Tablas, José M de Fuentes, and Arturo Ribagorda. 2014. Cooped: Co-owned personal data management. *Computers & Security* 47 (2014), 41–65.
[9] Hongxin Hu, Gail-Joon Ahn, and Jan Jorgensen. 2011. Detecting and Resolving Privacy Conflicts for Collaborative Data Sharing in Online Social Networks. In *Proceedings of the 27th Annual Computer Security Applications Conference (ACSAC'11)*. ACM.
[10] Hongxin Hu, Gail-Joon Ahn, and Jan Jorgensen. 2013. Multiparty access control for online social networks: model and mechanisms. *IEEE Transactions on Knowledge and Data Engineering* 25, 7 (2013), 1614–1627.
[11] Hongxin Hu, Gail-Joon Ahn, Ziming Zhao, and Dejun Yang. 2014. Game theoretic analysis of multiparty access control in online social networks. In *Proceedings of the 19th ACM symposium on Access control models and technologies*. ACM, 93–102.
[12] Panagiotis Ilia, Iasonas Polakis, Elias Athanasopoulos, Federico Maggi, and Sotiris Ioannidis. 2015. Face/off: Preventing privacy leakage from photos in social networks. In *Proceedings of the 22nd ACM SIGSAC Conference on Computer and Communications Security*. ACM, 781–792.
[13] B. Krishnamurthy and C.E. Wills. 2010. On the leakage of personally identifiable information via online social networks. *ACM SIGCOMM Computer Communication Review* 40, 1 (2010), 112–117.
[14] Balachander Krishnamurthy and Craig E Wills. 2009. On the leakage of personally identifiable information via online social networks. In *Proceedings of the 2nd ACM workshop on Online social networks*. ACM, 7–12.
[15] A. Lampinen, V. Lehtinen, A. Lehmuskallio, and S. Tamminen. 2011. We're in it together: interpersonal management of disclosure in social network services. In *Proceedings of the 2011 annual conference on Human factors in computing systems*. ACM, 3217–3226.
[16] Yair Levy and Michelle M Ramim. 2016. Towards an Evaluation of Cyber Risks and Identity Information Sharing Practices in e-Learning, Social Networking, and Mobile Texting Apps. (2016).
[17] H.R. Lipford, A. Besmer, and J. Watson. 2008. Understanding privacy settings in facebook with an audience view. In *Proceedings of the 1st Conference on Usability, Psychology, and Security*. USENIX Association Berkeley, CA, USA, 1–8.
[18] Eden Litt and Eszter Hargittai. 2014. Smile, snap, and share? A nuanced approach to privacy and online photo-sharing. *Poetics* 42 (2014), 1–21.
[19] Y. Liu, K.P. Gummadi, B. Krishnamurthy, and A. Mislove. 2011. Analyzing Facebook Privacy Settings: User Expectations vs. Reality. In *Proceedings of the 2011 annual conference on Internet measurement (IMC'11)*. ACM.
[20] M. Madejski, M. Johnson, and S.M. Bellovin. 2011. The Failure of Online Social Network Privacy Settings. Technical Report CUCS-010-11, Columbia University, NY, USA. (2011).
[21] Erika McCallister, Timothy Grance, and Karen A Scarfone. 2010. Sp 800-122. guide to protecting the confidentiality of personally identifiable information (pii). (2010).
[22] Mainack Mondal, Yabing Liu, Bimal Viswanath, Krishna P Gummadi, and Alan Mislove. 2014. Understanding and specifying social access control lists. In *Symposium on Usable Privacy and Security (SOUPS)*. 11.
[23] Kyle B Murray and Gerald Häubl. 2010. Freedom of choice, ease of use, and the formation of interface preferences. (2010).
[24] Yuta Nakashima, Noboru Babaguchi, and FAN Jianping. 2016. Privacy Protection for Social Video via Background Estimation and CRF-Based Videographer's Intention Modeling. *IEICE Transactions on Information and Systems* 99, 4 (2016), 1221–1233.
[25] F.K. Ozenc and S.D. Farnham. 2011. Life "Modes" in Social Media. In *Proceedings of the 2011 annual conference on Human factors in computing systems*. ACM, 561–570.
[26] Jingjing Ren, Ashwin Rao, Martina Lindorfer, Arnaud Legout, and David Choffnes. 2016. Recon: Revealing and controlling pii leaks in mobile network traffic. In *Proceedings of the 14th Annual International Conference on Mobile Systems, Applications, and Services*. ACM, 361–374.
[27] Cooper Smith. 2013. Facebook users are uploading 350 million new photos each day. *Business insider* 18 (2013).
[28] Craig Smith. 2016. By the Numbers: 200+ Amazing Facebook Statistics. (2016).
[29] A.C. Squicciarini, M. Shehab, and F. Paci. 2009. Collective privacy management in social networks. In *Proceedings of the 18th international conference on World wide web*. ACM, 521–530.
[30] K. Strater and H.R. Lipford. 2008. Strategies and struggles with privacy in an online social networking community. In *Proceedings of the 22nd British HCI Group Annual Conference on People and Computers: Culture, Creativity, Interaction-Volume 1*. British Computer Society, 111–119.
[31] K. Thomas, C. Grier, and D. Nicol. 2010. unFriendly: Multi-party Privacy Risks in Social Networks. In *Privacy Enhancing Technologies*. Springer, 236–252.
[32] Y. Wang, S. Komanduri, P. Leon, G. Norcie, A. Acquisti, and L. Cranor. 2011. I regretted the minute I pressed share": A qualitative study of regrets on Facebook. In *Symposium on Usable Privacy and Security*.
[33] R. Wishart, D. Corapi, S. Marinovic, and M. Sloman. 2010. Collaborative Privacy Policy Authoring in a Social Networking Context. In *2010 IEEE International Symposium on Policies for Distributed Systems and Networks*. IEEE, 1–8.
[34] Li Yifang, Vishwamitra Nishant, Knijnenburg Bart, Hu Hongxin, and Caine Kelly. (2017). Blur vs. Block: Investigating the Effectiveness of Privacy-Enhancing Obfuscation for Images. In *The First International Workshop on The Bright and Dark Sides of Computer Vision: Challenges and Opportunities for Privacy and Security (CV-COPS 2017)*.
[35] Li Yifang, Vishwamitra Nishant, Hu Hongxin, Knijnenburg Bart, and Caine Kelly. 2017. Effectiveness and Users' Experience of Face Blurring as a Privacy Protection for Sharing Photos via Online Social Networks. In *Proceedings of the Human Factors and Ergonomics Society Annual Meeting*, Vol. 61. SAGE Publications.
[36] Y. Zhu, Z. Hu, H. Wang, H. Hu, and G.J. Ahn. 2010. A Collaborative Framework for Privacy Protection in Online Social Networks. In *Proceedings of the 6th International Conference on Collaborative Computing (CollaborateCom)*.

Verifiable Assume-Guarantee Privacy Specifications for Actor Component Architectures

Claiborne Johnson
University of Texas at San Antonio
imm589@my.utsa.edu

Thomas MacGahan
Accenture Federal Services
thomas.macgahan@gmail.com

John Heaps
University of Texas at San Antonio
john.heaps@utsa.edu

Kevin Baldor
University of Texas at San Antonio
kevin.baldor@utsa.edu

Jeffery von Ronne*
University of Texas at San Antonio
vonronne@acm.org

Jianwei Niu
University of Texas at San Antonio
jianwei.niu@utsa.edu

ABSTRACT

Many organizations process personal information in the course of normal operations. Improper disclosure of this information can be damaging, so organizations must obey privacy laws and regulations that impose restrictions on its release or risk penalties. Since electronic management of personal information must be held in strict compliance with the law, software systems designed for such purposes must have some guarantee of compliance. To support this, we develop a general methodology for designing and implementing verifiable information systems. This paper develops the design of the History Aware Programming Language into a framework for creating systems that can be mechanically checked against privacy specifications. We apply this framework to create and verify a prototypical Electronic Medical Record System (EMRS) expressed as a set of actor components and first-order linear temporal logic specifications in assume-guarantee form. We then show that the implementation of the EMRS provably enforces a formalized Health Insurance Portability and Accountability Act (HIPAA) policy using a combination of model checking and static analysis techniques.

CCS CONCEPTS

• **Social and professional topics** → **Privacy policies**; • **Theory of computation** → *Modal and temporal logics*; • **Applied computing** → *Health care information systems*;

KEYWORDS

privacy policy; first-order linear temporal logic; safety and liveness properties; assume-guarantee specifications; static analysis

ACM Reference format:
Claiborne Johnson, Thomas MacGahan, John Heaps, Kevin Baldor, Jeffery von Ronne, and Jianwei Niu. 2017. Verifiable Assume-Guarantee Privacy Specifications for Actor Component Architectures. In *Proceedings of SACMAT'17, June 21-23, 2017, Indianapolis, IN, USA, , 12 pages.*
DOI: http://dx.doi.org/10.1145/3078861.3078873

*Now at Google, Inc.

1 INTRODUCTION

Our society is becoming increasingly dependent on computer information systems for the proper management of private data. Medical records, financial data, and personal information collected from Internet users are just a few examples. Organizations are required to keep and share such information in a manner that conforms to specific privacy policies, which are mandated by custom, sound business practice, good citizenship, contract, and often by law. Examples of privacy policies that carry the force of law include those resulting from the Health Insurance Portability and Accountability Act (HIPAA) [16], the Gramm-Leach-Bliley Act (GLBA) [2], and the Children's Online Privacy Protection Act (COPPA) [1]. In addition to legal regulations, organizations typically have their own business rules that add further privacy requirements.

Privacy policies differ from access control policies in many ways and privacy policy design has to consider them. First, privacy policies govern access and transmission rights concerning data *about* some individual end users (the *subject*). The subject typically has certain rights to control how data about her is collected, stored, used, and shared. However, this control is not absolute, so the subject cannot be considered to be the "owner" of the data in the sense the term is used in access control literature. Second, privacy policies need to indicate the purposes of collection and sharing of data whereas access control policies largely ignore the purposes. For instance, if personal information is shared or used for some class of purposes, it may become obligatory to notify the subjects that this has occurred. Third, while for the most part, access control policies specify safety requirements, privacy policies can also express liveness requirements. Intuitively, *safety* properties say that some bad thing never happens and *liveness* properties say that some good thing eventually happens [4, 20, 28]. For instance, "in the future the service provider must send the subject a notification about certain usage of data" is a liveness property.

Several frameworks have been proposed for specifying and analyzing privacy policies, including the Enterprise Privacy Authorization Language (EPAL) [5], Contextual Integrity (CI) [6], Privacy APIs [25], Ponder [11], and work by Breaux and Anton [8]. To date, most of the work in this area has concentrated on frameworks for expressing privacy policies [5, 6, 11], answering queries requesting rulings as to whether transmitting a certain piece of information is permitted [5, 11], methodologies for converting regulations expressed in legal language into formal system requirements [8], or analyzing privacy policies to determine whether they satisfy various properties [25]. In contrast, we have found a lack of enforcement frameworks comprising techniques and tools that support the development and verification of information systems that adhere to privacy policies.

There has been a great deal of work in enforcement of access control policies, particularly in the area of runtime monitors [14, 21, 27]. Runtime monitoring addresses a problem that resembles ours in some respects. The classic approach [27] enforces safety properties, but is unworkable in reactive systems; when a software system attempts to perform an illegal action, execution is terminated. More recent work gets around this problem by introducing edit automata [7, 22], which enable execution to proceed by either suppressing the illegal action, or performing other actions prior to the requested one so as to make the desired action permissible. However, all monitoring-based approaches share a common characteristic: they separate security concerns from basic functionality. This is very suitable for many applications, such as adding security features to legacy code. However, separating policy enforcement from basic functionality is counter productive in privacy policy enforcement for information systems. The user of an information system plays a central role in the system's operation. When a user attempts to transmit information that would cause a privacy violation, providing an explanation is a central part of the system's functionality. For instance, in the context of electronic medical records, an administrative assistant may request the system to transmit portions of a patient's record for which prior consent by the patient is required. If consent has not been obtained, the administrative assistant needs this to be explained, enabling him to request consent from the patient. Such an explanation is best managed as a part of the system's basic functionality, rather than as a separate wrapper. Our prior work on the History Aware Programming Language (HAPL) [29] has outlined a language design with features for providing privacy management without need for a separate component, such as a monitor, to intervene by modifying the system's behavior during runtime.

In this paper, we aim to develop our HAPL design into a full framework with a working prototype of an Electronic Medical Record System (EMRS) that can be statically checked against formal privacy policy specifications for HIPAA. In order to bridge the gap between policy specifications and our implementation, we develop formal system specifications in assume-guarantee form [18]. Static analysis techniques are applied to verify that the implementation matches this specification, while a model checker is used on small specification sets reflecting the formal specifications to ensure that the system's formal specification enforces HIPAA.

Organization. Section 2 introduces background information used in this paper. We overview our framework in Section 3. Section 4 details the decomposition and specification of the EMRS into an actor component architecture. In Section 5, we cover the slicing and small model reduction processes we employ to simplify our specifications into a machine-verifiable form. The evaluation of these specifications are summarized in Section 6. Section 7 discusses the static analysis performed on the EMRS which enforces the behavior described in the specifications. Section 8 concludes and surveys future work.

2 BACKGROUND

This section summarizes prior work that we use or build on, including temporal logic, a privacy policy specification language that formalizes HIPAA, the actor model of concurrent computation, and the assume-guarantee format of specifying an open system.

2.1 Temporal Logic

Temporal logic [26] characterizes the behavior of reactive systems in terms of traces, which are sequences of states and/or events. The policy specification language discussed in subsection 2.2 uses a many-sorted, first-order linear temporal logic (FOTL) [12]. Linear temporal logic (LTL) is a variant of temporal logic that deals with a relative ordering of events, such that events are not described with a discrete time variable, but only as how they temporally relate to other events. A brief summary of FOTL follows.

FOTL generalizes propositional LTL as first-order logic generalizes propositional logic. FOTL formulas include non-temporal formulas made up of a base of atomic formulas, with possible variables, logical connectives, and quantifiers. FOTL formulas may also contain unary and binary temporal operators, which operate on the appropriate number of FOTL sub-formulas. We use just a small subset of the standard temporal operators available, which are as follows. *Future Operators.* Henceforth: $\Box\ \phi$ declares that formula ϕ holds in all future states in the trace. Eventually: $\Diamond\ \phi$ declares that formula ϕ holds in some future state in the trace. *Past Operators.* Historically: $\boxminus\ \phi$ declares that formula ϕ held in all preceding states in the trace. Once: $\Diamondminus\ \phi$ declares that formula ϕ held in some preceding state in the trace. Since: $\phi_1\ \mathcal{S}\ \phi_2$ declares that ϕ_2 held at some preceding state, and since then ϕ_1 has held in every state.

2.2 Privacy Policy Specification

The privacy policy specification language we have developed [9] decomposes policy formulas into norms by restricting temporal logic formulas to a form similar to that done in the work of Barth et al. on Contextual Integrity [6]. A positive norm allows a message transmission *if* the condition associated with it holds, while a negative norm allows a message transmission *only if* its condition holds. An action is thus allowed by the policy if it satisfies at least one of the positive norms and all the negative norms. A notable difference from Contextual Integrity is that our specification language [9] is limited to a restricted subset of FOTL that makes our privacy policies enforceable.

We use this language to formalize the restrictions and requirements of HIPAA as a set of these communication norms. Of note, the disclosure of Personal Health Information (PHI) is represented by the sending of a message from a principal (i.e., person) that knows information about a subject to another principal that does not. Additionally, principals hold certain roles (e.g., psychiatrist, patient) and messages are sent for specific purposes (e.g., treatment, billing).

A communication action is denoted by $send(p, q, m)$, in which p is the sending principal, q is the receiving principal, and m is the message being sent. Each message contains a set of principal attribute pairs. The predicate $contains(m, q, t)$ holds if message m contains attribute t of subject principal q, such that the recipient of message m would learn the attribute t about q. Roles can be bound to principals via the *inrole* predicate, where *inrole(p, r)* holds if *(p, r)* ∈ *roleAssignment*. Similarly, *for-purpose(m, u)* enforces that message *m* is sent for purpose *u*.

2.3 The Actor Model and Assume-Guarantee Specification

In the actor model [3, 15], a software system is considered to be a collection of concurrently operating actors that communicate through asynchronous message passing. Each actor has a mailbox through which it receives messages, and an actor may only act in response to these messages. Based on its state/behavior, an actor reacts to the messages it receives one at a time—but not necessarily in the order they arrive—by performing some action. The synchronous actions an actor takes in response to the receipt of an asynchronous message can involve sending a finite number of messages to other actors it knows about, creating a finite number of new actors, or changing its state/behavior so that it will take different actions in response to future messages.

Bengt Johnsson et al. established the use of LTL as sets of assume-guarantee specifications for formally specifying behavior of an open system [18]. In short, the way in which a system interacts with its environment can be specified through assumptions on the behavior of its environment and guarantees on the behavior the system can/will exhibit if the assumptions on its environment hold true. Safety assumptions and safety guarantees describe that bad things cannot happen, by stating conditions that must hold on the information the system receives from its environment and the information the system sends to its environment, respectively. Liveness guarantees describe that good things must eventually happen, by stating conditions that force the system to eventually communicate information to its environment. Assume-guarantee specifications are well-suited for formally specifying the behavior of an actor system by describing under what conditions actors can send or receive certain types of messages.

3 FRAMEWORK

We have developed a framework for implementing actor systems that meet assume-guarantee specifications described above and that can present a compliant system to an end-user (e.g., an auditor) of that system [23]. Broadly, the framework shown in figure 1 takes in formal privacy regulations and organizational policies that are manually refined into assume-guarantee specifications of the information system. This framework is based on and implements our HAPL language [29]. This language can be used to define applications with attendant web-based user interfaces that comply with specification. This compliance is guaranteed by a static analysis phase requiring that the HAPL implementation honors the specification. Failing that, the static analysis phase will return with error contexts explaining the failure. Finally, we evaluate the framework by implementing a functioning EMRS prototype that complies with a representative subset of HIPAA requirements.

3.1 Language and Actor System Generation

HAPL is a general purpose, actor-based, imperative programming language that incorporates history queries. HAPL is split into a user interface specification [24] (which is beyond the scope of this paper),

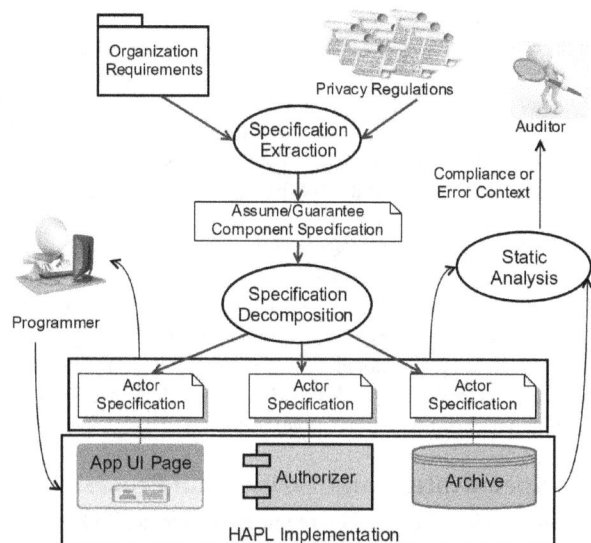

Figure 1: Framework Function

actor behavior specification, static analysis and interpretation. The language, loosely modeled on Scala syntax, allows for defining actors and the principals they represent, as well the role in which actors represent principals. In HAPL, actors are considered to be acting in a particular role for a particular principal whenever they send or receive a message. This assumption simplifies our approach to our assume-guarantee specification and decomposition described in section 4.

HAPL includes a variety of structures for expressing computation, but a subset was implemented due to scope constraints. These structures include: if-statements, assignments, print statements, identifiers in complex expressions, declaration with initialization, tuple definitions, tuple lookups, conses with tails and heads, a *new* command, actor definitions and LTL history queries as shown in figure 2. Example actor definitions can be seen in appendix B.

```
str = "hello" //variable assignment
print( "Here's a message: " + message )
status = "the status is " + ok
var havePatientPrincipal: Bool  = false
phi newPatientRecord: String   = ""
psi newPsychRecord: String     = ""
var names: List[String] = list()
names = "name" :: names
record.get(2) //tuples with lookups
dirElt = tuple( id, principal, name )
var dir: Directory = new Directory( sys)
actor Directory
    [x; inrole(sys,HealthCareProvider)]
    ( sys: Principal ) representing sys
if( newRcrd != "" ) { //code
ltlquery(once receive
    <from PatientActor as P[Patient]>
    (authRelease) with prnc where prnc = subj)
```

Figure 2: Language Features

As per the actor paradigm, computation in HAPL is done through creation of and communication between actors. We constrain HAPL actors to synchronous control only of private data, and communication with other actors only by sending asynchronous messages.

In HAPL, actor behavior must only be triggered in response to messages and, while executing in response to a message, it may only modify local data, create other actors, and send messages to other actors [15, 29]. Through messages, we allow composition of an actor system which is exposed through a web interface. We demonstrate this language by prototyping an EMRS with a number of use cases that are illustrative of the type of specifications needed to specify HIPAA.

We further implement a special control structure, *ltlquery*, which behaves like an if statement. The first block will execute if the LTL expression is true, the second branch otherwise. A representation of the history of messages that an actor has received is kept at each actor which is used to decide the truth of an *ltlquery* condition. This allows us to set up guards to verify that certain messages have been received prior to, for example, releasing PHI.

3.2 Specification and Verification Process
In order to verify the behavior of our EMRS written in HAPL, we first design and detail specifications in section 4. The EMRS is decomposed into a set of communicating actors (figure 1) whose behavior is specified as a set of FOTL formulas in assume-guarantee form. Some of these base level actors are additionally composed into a mid-level component to encapsulate the system's internal communication, and we provide a proven composition theorem for showing the validity of this refinement.

Once we have our EMRS specifications in place, we would like to verify that the system behaves correctly by showing that it is HIPAA-compliant. From our prior work [9], we have a set of FOTL formulas that describe norms of communication in terms of when PHI can be disclosed according to HIPAA. Thus, we can verify HIPAA-compliance of our specifications by showing that any disclosure by our system entails a valid disclosure described in the policy norms.

The natural next step would be to use a theorem prover such as Coq[1] to prove the correctness of this entailment. However we were unable to find an appropriate LTL package that can cleanly implement our sets of FOTL formulas. We turn to using a model checker instead, but model checkers cannot handle first-order formulas due to unbounded state, so in section 5 we take intermediate steps to simplify our input. To reduce computational complexity, we first slice the set of policy norms to remove specification of optional behavior that our system does not perform. We then create small model theorems to reduce both sets of FOTL formulas to larger sets of simpler, behaviorally-equivalent propositional LTL formulas. Lastly, the entailment of the resulting sets are mechanically verified with a model checker in section 6.

3.3 Static Analysis Overview
We use static analysis to bind HAPL code to the constraints detailed in our assume-guarantee specifications. By making statements about type-correctness in assignment, message parameters, message handlers, and send message *inroles*, as well as verifying that certain properties hold in the abstract syntax tree, such as verification that a specific *ltlquery* guards the release of records in

the archive, we are able to verify compliance with certain assume-guarantee specifications. The static analysis phase therefore reports non-compliance and fails compilation so that an actor system is not generated where it cannot be proved that the code matches appropriate assume-guarantee specifications. Section 7 goes over this process in more detail.

3.4 Use Cases and HAPL EMRS Prototype
To demonstrate the language and evaluate our framework, we build a EMRS prototype with simple implementations of five use cases specified to comply with HIPAA. These are intended to be a representative subset of the release scenarios described in HIPAA. In particular, this includes cases involving releases that are required, releases that are permitted without consent, and releases that are permitted only with authorization.

While it is possible to fulfill the privacy requirements of HIPAA by rejecting all release requests except for those made by the patient for their own records[2] [16], we designed the following five use cases in order to demonstrate a responsive non-trivial EMRS.

(1) **Record contains no PHI**: If a message contains no PHI, then that information may be released without authorization.
(2) **Patient requests own PHI**: HIPAA has a liveness requirement that any patient request for their own PHI records must eventually be fulfilled. Thus any request by a patient role for their own records must be honored by the EMRS.
(3) **Originating doctor requests patient's psychotherapy note PHI**: A doctor who is acting as a physician for a patient may obtain that patient's psychotherapy notes without the consent of any principal if that physician is also the author of that PHI.
(4) **Doctor requests patient's non-psychotherapy PHI**: A doctor who is acting as the physician for a patient may obtain that patient's PHI without any principal's consent, so the prototype will honor requests by a doctor for patient data.
(5) **Third party requests patient PHI**: Third parties may request patient PHI for marketing purposes. These requests may be honored if it is determined that the patient that is the subject of this PHI has authorized release of it for this purpose.

As part of the framework, HAPL source is compiled into a web application that is run by the Lift framework[3] to generate a web-based UI that interacts with these actors via page definitions controlling the specific actors handling the application logic of a user interface. An example of the web interface for a physician is shown in figure 3. In this example interface, the physician is able to set PHI for a patient (including psychotherapy note PHI) or retrieve a patient's records. Our EMRS prototype implements a representative subset of use cases in HIPAA involving requests for release of records that may contain PHI or even more strongly protected psychotherapy note PHI by various interested parties. This resulting functional

---
[1]https://coq.inria.fr/

[2]Under HIPAA, a covered entity is also required to notify the Secretary of HHS under certain circumstances, but we make a concession for the simplicity of the EMRS and ignore this obligation.
[3]Liftweb: https://www.liftweb.net/

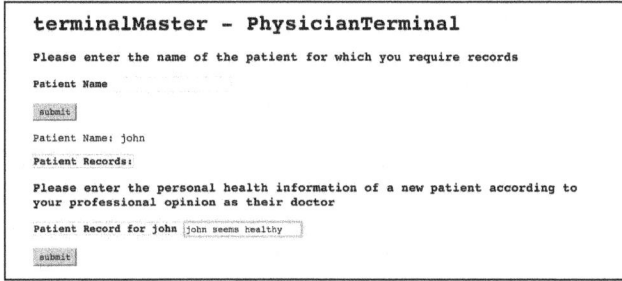

Figure 3: Example Physician Interface Page

prototype represents an evaluation of the framework. The implementation may be open-sourced following review.

4 DECOMPOSITION AND SPECIFICATION

As described in section 3.2, we detail the design of our EMRS by decomposing the system into an actor component specification of FOTL formulas in assume-guarantee form [17]. This is a top-down procedure, but for ease of understanding, we present the details bottom-up. We also describe what is required to verify the consistency of different levels of decomposition, and provide a methodology. Verification of this specification against the EMRS is discussed in section 7.

4.1 System Decomposition

As a first step towards creating specifications for the HAPL EMRS, we conceptualized a decomposition of the system into a set of actors, each of which has a set of responsibilities that it upholds by communicating with the other actors.

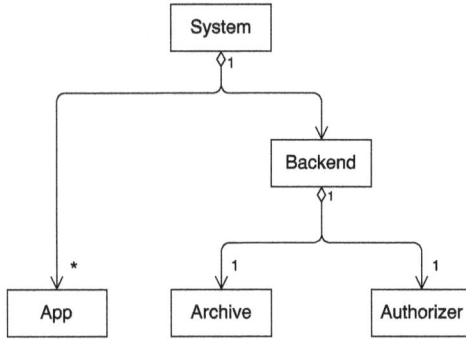

Figure 4: EMRS Decomposition

As shown in figure 4, we decompose the HAPL EMRS into three actor types: the App, the Archive, and the Authorizer.

There are many App actors which act on behalf of human principals and provide them an interface to access the EMRS. Through this interface, a principal may request that the EMRS release medical records to them and receive the corresponding reply. An App also allows patient principals to grant authorization for their records to be released to another principal by sending a message to the Authorizer, or reject an incoming request from the Authorizer for such

an authorization. Additionally, an App allows doctor principals to add records to the EMRS by sending them to the Archive.

The Archive and Authorizer are both singleton actors which act on behalf of the organization whose combined behavior can be composed into a component referred to as the Backend. The role of the Archive is to store and retrieve records about patients as requested, and the Authorizer keeps track of information necessary to make policy decisions for the EMRS and makes those decisions for the Archive when requested. When an App sends messages which request some action on a record to be performed, the Archive forwards the necessary information to the Authorizer. The Authorizer then attempts to make the policy decision according to the actor specification and previous system actions. If the policy decision cannot be concretely made from the system history, the Authorizer sends an authorization request message to the App belonging to the subject of the record. After receiving the final decision back from the App if necessary, the Authorizer returns the appropriate response message to the Archive, and the Archive sends the corresponding final reply to the App which made the original request.

4.2 Actor Specification

Actor specifications are the foundation on which higher-level specifications (which have a similar structure) are established. Each actor type has an assume-guarantee specification that prescribes how instances of that actor type may interact with its environment (i.e., the messages it may or must send to other actors).

The language we use for actor specifications shown in figure 5 is built on top of the language we developed to specify policies [9], as prior described in subsection 2.2, and uses a similar meta-variable syntax. The same temporal restrictions apply, most notably that future sub-formulas are only described in β', such that $\Diamond$ can be applied only to positive, non-temporal formulas ($\Diamond \mu'$). Likewise, we also do not include the $\ominus$ operator in our past temporal operators available in ψ'. We also specify our formulas as local due to the additional restriction that actors are only aware of actions in which they participate. Note that $R(\vec{x})$ is used to refer to an expression matching the syntax of metavariable R with $\vec{x}$ as the only free variables.

$$
\begin{aligned}
\text{(Local Atomic) } \gamma' ::= \quad & R(\vec{x}) \,|\, true \\
\text{(Local Non-temporal) } \mu' ::= \quad & \gamma' |\mu' \wedge \mu'|\mu' \vee \mu'|\exists \vec{x} : \tau.\mu'| \\
& \forall \vec{x} : \tau.(\mu_1'(\vec{x}) \to \mu_2'(\vec{x})) \\
\text{(Local Pure Past) } \psi' ::= \quad & \mu'|\psi' \wedge \psi'|\psi' \, \mathcal{S} \, \psi'|\exists \vec{x} : \tau.\psi'| \\
& \neg \psi'|\forall \vec{x} : \tau.(\mu_1'(\vec{x}) \to \mu_2'(\vec{x})) \\
\text{(Local Obligation) } \beta' ::= \quad & \Diamond \mu'|\beta' \wedge \beta' \\
\text{(Local Mixed) } \chi' ::= \quad & \beta'|\psi'|\psi' \to \beta'|\chi' \wedge \chi'| \\
& \forall \vec{x} : \tau.\chi'(\vec{x})
\end{aligned}
$$

Figure 5: FOTL Actor Formula Syntax.

Given our actor formula syntax, our actor specifications take the form:

$$
\left(\Box \bigwedge_{\psi' \in A\text{-Assum}} \psi' \right) \to \left(\Box \bigwedge_{\psi' \in A\text{-Safety}} \psi' \wedge \bigwedge_{\chi' \in A\text{-Liveness}} \chi' \right)
$$

in which, for the given actor, A-Assum is a set of safety assumption clauses, A-Safety is the set of safety guarantee clauses and A-Liveness is the set of liveness guarantee clauses. Safety assumption clauses $\psi' \in$ A-Assum are restricted to take the form[4]:

$$\forall a : A.\forall m : M.\mathrm{receive}(self, a, m) \rightarrow \psi'(a, m)$$

safety guarantee clauses $\psi' \in$ A-Safety are restricted to take the form:

$$\forall a : A.\forall m : M.\mathrm{send}(self, a, m) \rightarrow \psi'(a, m)$$

and liveness guarantee clauses $\chi' \in$ A-Liveness are restricted to take the form:

$$\forall \vec{x}.\psi'(\vec{x}) \rightarrow \Diamond \exists a : A.\exists m : M.\mu'(a, m, \vec{x}) \wedge \mathrm{send}(self, a, m)$$

Here we assume that $\forall \vec{x}$ includes specification of appropriate sorts. The requirements on the syntactic forms of safety assumption and safety guarantee clauses (an implication with a receive by *self* or a send by *self*, respectively, as antecedent) serve to syntactically isolate a specific action, so that the clause as a whole describes under what circumstances that action is permitted. Furthermore, this restriction serves to ensure that the safety clause is incrementally verifiable, and moreover, that violations of the safety clause can be associated with a specific send action. Similarly, liveness clauses are restricted to take the form of an implication which has an antecedent that contains a local pure past formula, whereas the consequent is restricted to requiring the actor to send some action in the future as constrained by a local non-temporal formula.

To show how these clauses are used for our EMRS, we provide some examples. One Archive safety assumption states that it will only receive an authorization or rejection to release a record if it once sent out the corresponding request. In contrast, a safety guarantee for the Archive says that it may only send a message that releases a record if it once received an authorization to release that record. A liveness guarantee for the Authorizer states that if it receives a request to authorize release of a patient's PHI, and the request for the PHI originated from the subject of that PHI, it is obligated to eventually authorize that request.

4.3 Component Specification

Specifications for components are similarly structured, with clauses on communication taking place between actors internal and external to the component.

Figures 6 and 7 show a safety guarantee for the EMRS Backend component [17] that stores and releases records and an associated negative policy norm [9] that it enforces. This norm in the context of the policy specifications states that a communication of psychotherapy notes from the covered entity to another entity implies that the individual that the psychotherapy notes are about gave authorization for the communication. The safety guarantee maps on top of the norm, with the local component actor *self*, which acts on behalf of covered-entity *p1*, sending a message containing a record to the requesting actor *a*, which acts on behalf of recipient *p2*. As such, the safety guarantee enforces that a release of a record containing psychotherapy notes can only take place if the component prior received a message from the individual which granted

---

[4] *self* is a metavariable referring to the local actor which is used to restrict specification to local communication.

authorization. Note that for flexibility, the safety guarantee also allows communication to take place if this is not a true disclosure, either because there is not PHI involved or it is communicated to an individual that has access by definition.

We skip formal specification of the fully composed system, as there is not any external communication to describe due to the scope of our EMRS prototype. However, the decomposition and verification techniques we describe between components and their comprising actors follow similarly for higher-level components which decompose into subcomponents.

4.4 Verification of Component Specification

In principle, a component's specifications are shown to be correctly implemented by showing that they are entailed by the composition of specifications of the subcomponents or actors that make up the component. Without loss of generality, we will focus on a component composed directly of actors and assume that there is only one assumption, guarantee, and liveness clause per component/actor. These clauses should be of the syntactic form described above for actors and of an analogous form for components.

The following theorem establishes sufficient conditions (ASSUMPTION CONSISTENCY, SAFETY REFINEMENT, and LIVENESS REFINEMENT) for showing that the specification of the actors that make up a component (SAFETY VALID and LIVENESS VALID) are a correct refinement of the specification of the component (COMPONENT SPEC).

THEOREM 4.1 (COMPONENT REFINEMENT). *Given, a component C made up of actors $\mathcal{A}$, an assumption about operation causality $\chi_{\therefore}^A$, a specification of C (consisting of an assumption ψ_C^A, a safety guarantee ψ_C^S, and a liveness guarantee χ_C'), a specification of each actor $i \in \mathcal{A}$ (consisting of an assumption $\psi_i'^A$, a safety clause $\psi_i'^S$, liveness clause χ_i'), and a universe Σ of infinite traces of interleaved send or receive operations, then the component specification is valid, that is, for any trace $\sigma \in \Sigma$ for which $\sigma \models \chi_{\therefore}^A$,*

$$\sigma \models \psi_C^A \rightarrow \psi_C^S \wedge \chi_C' \qquad \text{(COMPONENT SPEC)}$$

if every individual actor specification is valid, i.e., for any trace $\sigma \in \Sigma$ for which $\sigma \models \chi_{\therefore}^A$,

$$\sigma \models \bigwedge_i \left(\Box \psi_i'^A \rightarrow \Box \psi_i'^S \right) \qquad \text{(SAFETY VALID)}$$

$$\sigma \models \bigwedge_i \left(\Box \psi_i'^A \rightarrow \Box \chi_i' \right) \qquad \text{(LIVENESS VALID)}$$

and for any trace $\sigma \in \Sigma$, for which $\sigma \models \Box \psi_C^A \wedge \chi_{\therefore}^A$,

$$\sigma \models \bigwedge_i \Box \psi_i'^S \rightarrow \bigwedge_i \Box \psi_i'^A \qquad \text{(ASSUMPTION CONSISTENCY)}$$

$$\sigma \models \bigwedge_i \Box \psi_i'^S \rightarrow \Box \psi_C^S \qquad \text{(SAFETY REFINEMENT)}$$

$$\sigma \models \bigwedge_i \Box \psi_i'^S \rightarrow \Box \chi_C' \qquad \text{(LIVENESS REFINEMENT)}$$

PROOF. Suppose an arbitrary σ for which $\sigma \models \psi_C^A \wedge \chi_{\therefore}^A$. It must be the case that

$$\sigma \models \Box \bigwedge_i \left(\psi_i'^A \rightarrow \psi_i'^S \right), \qquad (1)$$

$$\forall a : A. \forall m : M.(\text{send}(self, a, m) \rightarrow \forall subject : P. \forall record : E. \forall requester : P. \forall role : R. \forall id : I.(\text{releaseRecord}(m, subject, record) \rightarrow$$

$$\exists m' : M. \diamondsuit (\text{receive}(self, a, m') \wedge \text{requestReadRecord}(m', subject, id) \wedge \text{recordId}(record, id) \wedge \text{recordSubject}(record, subject)$$

$$\wedge \text{ messageSender}(m', requester) \wedge \text{messageSenderRole}(m', role) \wedge (\neg\text{containsPHI}(record) \vee (requester = subject)$$

$$\vee (role = \text{``HealthCareProvider''} \wedge (\neg\text{containsPsychNotes}(record, subject) \vee \text{recordOriginator}(record, requester)))$$

$$\vee (\exists a' : A. \exists m'' : M. \diamondsuit(\text{receive}(self, a', m'') \wedge \text{grantAuthorization}(m'', requester, role, id) \wedge \text{messageSender}(m'', subject)))))))$$

Figure 6: Example Safety Guarantee

$$\S164.508(a)(2) \equiv \text{inrole}(p1, coveredentity) \wedge \text{inrole}(q, individual) \wedge \text{in}(t, psychnotes) \rightarrow obtainedAuthorization(p1, p2, q, t, u)$$

Figure 7: Example Policy Norm

because otherwise there would be some i, some prefix σ' of σ and the infinite extension σ'' of σ' by stuttering for which $\sigma', |\sigma'| \models \psi_i'^A$, $\sigma', |\sigma'| \not\models \psi_i'^S$, and $\sigma'' \not\models \Box \psi_i'^A \rightarrow \Box \psi_i'^S$, contradicting SAFETY VALID. Similarly, from ASSUMPTION CONSISTENCY, it must be that

$$\sigma \models \Box \left(\bigwedge_i \psi_i'^S \rightarrow \bigwedge_i \psi_i'^A \right). \qquad (2)$$

Now, note that (as in the logic of Jonsson and Yih-Kuen [18]) in our FOTL, for any pure past FOTL formula ψ, $\sigma \models \Box\psi$ if and only if $\sigma \models \Box\boxminus\psi$. From this, and the mutual exclusivity of send and receive operations, we can rewrite the equations 1 and 2 (using $\ominus$ for "weak yesterday")[5] as:

$$\sigma \models \Box\boxminus \bigwedge_i \left(\ominus\psi_i'^A \rightarrow \psi_i'^S \right) \qquad (3)$$

$$\sigma \models \Box\boxminus \bigwedge_i \ominus\psi_i'^S \rightarrow \bigwedge_i \psi_i'^A \qquad (4)$$

Now we can derive,

$$\sigma \models \Box\boxminus \left(\bigwedge_i \psi_i'^A \wedge \bigwedge_j \psi_j'^S \right) \qquad (5)$$

by induction on the prefixes of σ and using equations 3 and 4. This can be rewritten as

$$\sigma \models \Box \bigwedge_i \psi_i'^A \wedge \bigwedge_j \psi_j'^S \qquad (6)$$

using the equivalence of $\Box\psi$ and $\Box\boxminus\psi$. Finally, by modus ponens and equations 6, SAFETY REFINEMENT, LIVENESS VALID, and LIVENESS REFINEMENT, we have $\sigma \models \psi_C^S \wedge \chi_C'$. $\qquad\square$

In applying this theorem, the causality assumption should specify that no message is received without first being sent and every message that is sent will eventually be received:

$$\chi_{..}^A \equiv \begin{array}{c} (\forall a_1. \forall a_2. \forall m. \text{receive}(a_2, a_1, m) \rightarrow \diamondsuit \text{send}(a_1, a_2, m)) \\ \wedge \\ (\forall a_1. \forall a_2. \forall m. \text{send}(a_1, a_2, m) \rightarrow \diamondsuit \text{receive}(a_2, a_1, m)) \end{array} \qquad (7)$$

Due to the small scale of the actor component set in our EMRS specifications, we leave the formal proof of the composition of the

Archive and Authorizer into the Backend as future work. In lieu of this, we provide an example on how our composition is applied, by showing the composition of the following three safety guarantees for our EMRS actors. For brevity, we replace the FOTL with an English approximation:

(1) sg_1 on *Archive* a_1: outgoing *requestAuthorizeRelease* (m_2 to *Authorizer* a_2) follows incoming *requestReadRecord* (m_1 from *App* a_3) since confirm add was sent (to some *App*)

(2) sg_2 on *Authorizer* a_2: outgoing *authorizeRelease* (m_3 to *Archive* a_1) follows incoming *requestAuthorizeRelease* (m_2 from *Archive* a_1) and authorization subclause holds

(3) sg_3 on *Archive* a_1: outgoing *releaseRecord* (m_4 to *App* a_3) follows incoming *authorizeRelease* (m_3 from *Authorizer* a_2)

We compose these guarantees together by removing all internally communicated messages but keeping any restrictions placed on their communication. From this, we obtain sg_4 on *Backend* c: outgoing *releaseRecord* (m_4 to *App* a_3) follows incoming *requestReadRecord* (m_1 from *App* a_3) since *confirmAdd* was sent (to some *App*) and authorization subclause holds. Note that this is the safety guarantee displayed in figure 6, though the since clause that sanity checks that the record exists has been trimmed for brevity.

5 SLICING AND REDUCTION

As discussed in section 3.2, our FOTL specifications are too computationally complex to be analyzed with model checking. A small model theorem states that we can use finite sets of elements from infinite carriers to reduce a language to a propositional form that represents a target behavior [13]. In this section, we detail a preliminary slicing procedure, followed by the creation of small model theorems which we use to reduce our slices of the EMRS specifications and policy specifications to propositional input for model checking in section 6.

5.1 Component and Policy Slicing

Before creating our small model theorems, we first want to simplify our input sets by slicing out the portions relevant to our models from the full sets of formulas. For our EMRS specifications, we only need the specifications which map to the disclosures in the entailment we are trying to prove. The entailment we want to show is that any record release case described in the EMRS specifications entails a corresponding PHI release case in the policy norms. Notably, our specifications do not describe any behavior external

---

[5]The $\ominus$ oeprator is not part of our specification language, but $\ominus\psi$ is used here with its standard LTL semantics to use the prior rather than current operation in evaluating the antecedant.

to the system at the top level and the App is simply a UI that delivers messages between the user and the rest of the EMRS. Thus we keep only the safety and liveness guarantee specifications for the Backend component that specify when the system can or must release records.

As the policy specifications are very large, we must perform a more involved slice. Specifically, we remove many exceptions to requirements for PHI transmissions as well as some enabling release cases which are not applicable to our EMRS prototype. We additionally remove some restrictions on PHI transmission to family members or related equivalents, however these releases then fall to a more general negative norm which is stricter. These removals are sound as the resulting set of policy norms are at least as strict as before about releasing PHI. We make one concession on soundness by removing a liveness requirement which requires transmission to a secretary for investigation, as our EMRS prototype currently does not model this obligation.

5.2 Component Slice Reduction

We create the small model theorem in theorem 5.1 for our component slice. More details on the resulting set of finite carriers and the restrictions we place on combinations can be found in appendix A.

THEOREM 5.1 (EMRS SMALL MODEL THEOREM). *The EMRS specifications allow the release of a record for infinite carriers of sorts $I, \mathcal{E}, \mathcal{P}, \mathcal{R}, \mathcal{A}, \mathcal{M}$ if and only if the EMRS specifications allow the release of a record for finite carriers $\hat{I}, \hat{\mathcal{E}}, \hat{\mathcal{P}}, \hat{\mathcal{R}}, \hat{\mathcal{A}}, \hat{\mathcal{M}}$ in which $|\hat{I}| = 3, |\hat{\mathcal{E}}| = 2, |\hat{\mathcal{P}}| = 5, |\hat{\mathcal{R}}| = 3, |\hat{\mathcal{A}}| = 5,$ and $|\hat{\mathcal{M}}| = 7.$*

We consider two types of records, one that contains normal PHI and one that contains psychotherapy note PHI. We do not represent a record containing no PHI, as its release is irrelevant to HIPAA. We match each of these records to a corresponding id. We also add an id that refers to no existing record to model the behavior where a nonexistent record is requested. This does not map to any specified behavior in HIPAA but provides completeness for the specifications which explicitly handle this case. This covers all distinct types of PHI that would affect release behavior as specified by HIPAA.

We consider three types of roles, which are doctor, patient, and third party which cover all distinguishing role behavior in the EMRS specifications. We then match these roles to the principals that act in them. One third party principal is sufficient, but we split doctors and patients into two principals each due to distinguishing behavior for record originators and subjects, respectively. This covers all behaviorally distinct principals in the specifications. Equivalently, we could have had multiple instances for each record instead. We also match these principals to the actors, with each principal getting their own actor. As actors are a wrapper used by the system to communicate with the principals they act on behalf of, one for each principal is sufficient. As we are only concerned with communication coming in and going out of the EMRS for release behavior, we do not need to model actors for the system itself.

We model a different message instance for each message type used in the Backend specification guarantees, which map simply into each place they are used, as every specification always uses a predicate to match the type of message being discussed. One instance of each message is sufficient to cover specification behavior,

as they are just wrappers for describing the type of communication taking place.

5.3 Policy Slice Reduction

Before we attempt to develop a small model theorem for our policy slice, we impose a restriction proposed in [9], which aids in the concreteness of the model by forcing each send event to be for a single message containing a single attribute sent for a single purpose to a single principal. To this end, we remove the *contains* and *for-purpose* predicates from the policy and move those bindings into the *send* predicate, such that its new signature is $\mathcal{P} \times \mathcal{P} \times \mathcal{P} \times \mathcal{T} \times \mathcal{U}$, and then remove the message sort ($\mathcal{M}$) entirely. This enforces our restriction by forcing all specification of message contents into the new send predicate $send(p1, p2, q, t, u)$, whose signature must obey it. We have the resulting small model theorem for our policy slice in theorem 5.2.

THEOREM 5.2 (POLICY SLICE SMALL MODEL THEOREM). *The sliced policy allows the release of PHI for infinite carriers of sorts $\mathcal{T}, \mathcal{U}, \mathcal{P}$ if and only if the sliced policy allows the release of PHI for finite carriers $\hat{\mathcal{T}}, \hat{\mathcal{U}}, \hat{\mathcal{P}}$ in which $|\hat{\mathcal{T}}| = 3, |\hat{\mathcal{U}}| = 6, |\hat{\mathcal{P}}| = 6.$*

Three types of attributes exist in the policy slice, which include PHI, psychotherapy notes (PSN), and directory information (dii). For the carrier of attributes $\mathcal{T}$ in our policy slice, PSN,PHI,dii $\in \mathcal{T}$, PSN $\in$ PHI, and dii $\notin$ (PHI $\cup$ PSN). We divide these sets into three distinct attributes such that t1 $\in$ (PHI \ PSN), t2 $\in$ (PHI $\cap$ PSN), and t3 $\in \mathcal{T}$ \ (PHI $\cup$ PSN). These three distinct attributes can simulate all possible attributes in the policy slice. The purposes found in our policy slice include access, treatment, payment, health-care-operations, and marketing. We additionally add other-purpose to capture purposes other than those explicitly labeled for the sake of completeness. These six distinct purposes capture all possible purposes present in the policy slice. For the carrier of principals $\mathcal{P}$ in our policy slice, covered-entity,patient,provider,work-force-member $\in \mathcal{P}$, provider $\in$ work-force-member, work-force-member $\in$ covered-entity. We initially model one principal for each of these roles, and one additional principal with no roles. One principal for each role is sound as long as the policy does not differentiate between two principals in a role. This is not true of principals in the patient role, which can be checked if they are the same principal that is the subject of PHI. Thus, we split patient into two distinct principals, one of which is the subject of all PHI and the other which is the subject of none. We additionally divide the subset roles to be distinct from their supersets, as done before with attributes. Our model thus contains six principals: p1 $\in$ (covered-entity \ (work-force-member $\cup$ provider)), p2 $\in$ (covered-entity $\cap$ (work-force-member \ provider)), p3 $\in$ (covered-entity $\cap$ (work-force-member $\cap$ provider)), p4,p5 $\in$ patient, p6 $\in$ ($\mathcal{T}$ \ covered-entity $\cup$ patient $\cup$ provider $\cup$ work-force-member).

6 EVALUATION OF EMRS SPECIFICATION

After using small model theorems to reduce the first-order nature of the privacy policy and EMRS specifications to a finite set of elements, we are able to apply model checking techniques to evaluate whether the assume-guarantee specifications entail the privacy policy in the EMRS prototype. Automation of the proof process provides a level of confidence in the validity of the EMRS prototype that is essentially too tedious, or even infeasible, to achieve by manual means.

6.1 Proof Using Model Checking

We use model checking to verify that the EMRS specifications imply all negative norms and at least one positive norm of the privacy policy before any disclosure of PHI. We selected the symbolic model checker NuSMV [10] to perform the checking because the size of the specification formulas can be large, causing the state space of the model to be large. Additionally, NuSMV supports both past and future temporal logic operators, which are used in both the formal policy norms and EMRS specifications.

NuSMV is a symbolic model checking tool for verifying a model of a finite-state system against properties specified in temporal logic. The model is specified by states and state transitions. A state is an assignment of all variables within the system. A state transition defines an allowable change in variable assignments in response to an event or condition.

NuSMV supports only variables of finite-range. We use two types of terms for our model: environmental variables and derived variables (macros). An environmental variable is one not directly controlled by the system, but that affects the system's behavior (e.g., an actor requesting authorization to read a record). In this project, macros are used to define terms from the FOTL that have become constants after the application of the small model theorem.

We use our small model to identify the finite elements sufficient to encode the terms of the FOTL EMRS and policy specifications in NuSMV. NuSMV then symbolically determines if the formulas are verified, and if a violation is found, a counterexample is generated.

6.2 NuSMV Encoding

We wish to show that the EMRS satisfies the privacy policy. To do this, the EMRS specifications must entail all of the negative norms and at least one positive norm of the privacy policy for each disclosure of PHI. To show this, we encode EMRS entailment formulas, in LTL form, in NuSMV using the small model and FOTL reductions from section 5.

Environmental variables were defined as booleans since the EMRS specification and policy norm variables could be true or false at any given time. For example, the message *requestReadRecord(requestReadRecord, Subject, PHI)* contains a request to read a record containing PHI about a particular subject. Any actor can send this request at any time. So, at any moment the request is either true (it occurred) or false (it did not occur). These variables are encoded as environmental for two reasons. The first is that these variables (like the request to read a record just mentioned) are not controlled by the EMRS, and are instead generated by actors from outside the EMRS. The second is that we wish to explore all possible combinations and occurrences of events of the privacy policy norms and EMRS specifications. That is, we wish to be certain that the EMRS satisfies the privacy policy under all possible scenarios.

While most terms from the policy specification are encoded as boolean environmental variables, there are some that have been encoded as macros with values *TRUE* or *FALSE*. This was a consequence of the reduction and transformation of the FOTL formulas and variables to propositional LTL. For example, *in(t, phi)* checks if record *t* includes any PHI. When reduced and transformed to propositional form, three distinct values took the place of *t*: *in(psychotherapy-notes, phi)*, *in(phi, phi)*, and *in(dii, phi)*. Each of these checks if a record that contains psychotherapy notes contains PHI, if a record that contains PHI contains PHI, and if a record that is directory information contains PHI, respectfully. Because all variables were encoded as booleans, each of these propositional variables must evaluate to true or false: psychotherapy notes are PHI by definition so *in(psychotherapy-notes, PHI)* must always evaluate to true, *in(phi, phi)* is vacuously always true, and directory information contains no PHI so *in(dii, phi)* must always be false. Because they are always true or always false at any given state, they have been encoded as macros.

6.3 Results

Model checking uncovered some subtle errors in our own preliminary specifications. Additionally, verification of the specifications found some violations for some of the formulas. The violations were due to a temporal logic statement involving subjects granting authorization to certain actors. Since all variables were listed as environmental, there were times when a previous state had granted authorization to release a record, but in a following state that authorization was changed to false. In the system, an authorization only needs to be granted once for the record to be released at any later time. This conflict arose as a result of the encoding process – specifically the use of unconstrained booleans to model external inputs into the system. This caused certain release cases to evaluate to false when they were, in fact, true. A separate pre-condition was encoded in order to overcome this scenario, stating simply that if authorization was granted once in a previous state for a record release that record release should still be authorized for the current state.

No other violations or conflicts were detected by NuSMV. All entered formulas were satisfied by the EMRS. This means that the EMRS specifications implied at least one positive and all negative norms, thereby showing that EMRS entailed the privacy policy. NuSMV was tested on both Windows 7 and Linux environments, 64-bit OS, with 8GB of memory. NuSMV completed in an average of 2.3 seconds.

7 STATIC ANALYSIS

Beyond basic syntax and type checking, HAPL's static analysis is intended to ensure that the implementations of the actors meet the assume-guarantee conditions upon which the model checking relies. The current implementation is rudimentary, but the ultimate approach is to employ an iterative data-flow analysis to compute, for each location in an action method, information about the histories that reach that location.

This information takes the form of three-valued truth assignments over sub-formulas of the *formulas of interest*: the assume-guarantee formulas for, and temporal queries within, the given action method. Each sub-formula that is assigned *true* is satisfied by every reaching history; each that is assigned *false* is not satisfied by any reaching history. Finally, if the formula is neither known to be satisfied by all reaching histories nor is it known to be satisfied by no reaching history, then the formula is assigned *unknown*.

Each iteration of the data-flow analysis computation simulates the effect that executing the program has on the truth value of the *formulas of interest*. Consider the code of figure 8 that describes the steps taken by the Authorizer in determining whether the *sender* should be allowed access to the PHI of *subject*. In short, it authorizes the release of the PHI only if the patient has previously authorized its release.

```
1   // declarations and lookup method omitted
2   actor Authorizer [ auth ; inrole( sys , CareProvider ) ]( dir :
        Directory , sys : Principal) representing sys {
3     on requestAuthRelease []( sender : Actor , requestingPrinc :
          Principal , subject : Principal , record : Tuple[Int , Principal ,
          Principal , String] ) {
4       originator = record.get(3)
5       data = record.get(4)
6       if( (!isPHI( data )) || (( requestingPrinc == originator) || (
            requestingPrinc == subject)) ) {
7         send<sender>(authRelease(this , sys , record))
8       } else {
9         ltlquery (once receive<from PatientTerminal as P[Patient]> (
            authOwnRecordFor) with owner, releaseTo where owner = subject
            and requestingPrinc = releaseTo ) {
10          send<sender>(authRelease(this , sys , record))
11        } else {
12          requests = tuple(sender , subject , record)
13          send<dir>(lookupPrinc(this , subject))
14      }}}
15      on authOwnRecordFor []( owner : Principal , releaseTo : Principal )
          {
16        foreach req in (requests) {
17          subjectPrinc = (req.get(3)).get(3)
18          if( subjectPrinc == owner ) {
19            requestor = req.get(1)
20            subjectRecord = req.get(3)
21            ltlquery( once receive<from Patient as P[Patient]> (
              requestAuthorizeRelease) with subject where subject = owner )
              {
22              send<requestor>(authRelease(this , sys , subjectRecord))
23            } else {
24              print("preemptive auth by: "+owner)
25      }}}}}
```

Figure 8: Authorizer Fragment

From line 2 of the assumptions we learn that *sys* is a *CareProvider* and that information is known to be true at each statement within the method. The static analysis also adds that the condition statement of the *ltlquery* on line 9 is *true* to any statement within its *then* branch of the (in this case only the *send* statement of line 10) and that it is *false* to any statement on its *else* branch. In this case, the static analysis determines that the actor will authorize the sending of medical records for a patient if that same patient has authorized its release in the past.

This analysis is essentially a generalization of a three-value version of the approach of Krukow *et al.* [19], which propagates information from sub-formulas to formulas. Since the query-conditional statements and assumption clauses contain *formulas of interest* directly, it is possible for those statements to 'learn' new facts that must be propagated to the sub-formulas.

The current implementation falls short of this general analysis, but still ensures that the assume-guarantee specifications are met by requiring that conditionals in the code precisely match those

of the specifications. That is, it can not infer from a pair of nested query-conditionals that their conjunction is satisfied. Yet, it still provides a guarantee that the runtime code will never violate the specifications upon which its correctness has been evaluated by the model checking step. It is also less general in that a number of HIPAA-specific terms are hard-coded into the implementation for the sake of expedience.

8 CONCLUSION

In this paper we have presented a methodology for designing and implementing verifiable information systems. We have developed the design of HAPL into a full framework and created an EMRS prototype in an actor component architecture. We additionally develop assume-guarantee specifications for this architecture which we statically verify enforce the HIPAA privacy policy. Though this is a proof of concept, we believe that this direction of building information systems with verifiable privacy policy compliance is promising. To conclude, we inventory some areas of future work we have left to explore.

Our prototype EMRS currently supports a limited number of use cases designed to be representative of several key points in HIPAA, but a full system would need to be further developed. Another use case that would be desirable to support includes releasing records to a delegate, such that an individual who has been granted delegation privileges for a subject should be treated the same as the subject. Additionally, a full system should provide a path for a subject to revoke authorization, and an appropriate use case would check that a previously authorized record is not released after the authorization is revoked. There also exist many additional permitted release cases an EMRS can implement, such that the EMRS can release records in these cases without requiring authorization from the subject.

We provide a theorem with an accompanying proof that can be leveraged towards this end, however we do not formally verify that the component specification for our EMRS is entailed by the specification of its comprising actors. As our refinement is very simple, we instead focused our efforts on proving entailment of the system specification to the policy specifications. A full system with a larger actor component architecture would require a stronger assurance that the component refinement step is performed correctly, especially as the system changes.

In its current form, the static analysis is limited in two ways that reduce its general applicability: first, it requires a perfect match between the assume-guarantee specification and the formulas in the query conditional, and second, it is hardcoded to use HIPAA roles and messages. Ideally, the first issue would be addressed by implementing the more general algorithm described in section 7. Barring that, at least some common cases, like conjoining the formulas of nested query-conditionals and allowing commutations such as $A \wedge B = B \wedge A$, should be supported. Parameterizing the static analysis with respect to roles and messages will enable the framework to be used for other specifications.

ACKNOWLEDGEMENT

The authors are supported in part by NSF award CNS-0964710 and by the NSA Grant on Science of Security.

REFERENCES

[1] 1999. Federal Trade Commission, How to comply with the children's online privacy protection rule. (1999). DOI:https://doi.org/bcp/conline/pubs/buspubs/coppa.htm Public Law.

[2] 1999. Senate Banking Committee, Gramm-Leach-Bliley Act. (1999). Public Law 106-102.

[3] Gul A. Agha, Ian A. Mason, Scott F. Smith, and Carolyn L. Talcott. 1997. A foundation for actor computation. *Journal of Functional Programming* 7, 01 (1997), 1–72. DOI:https://doi.org/10.1017/S095679689700261X arXiv:http://journals.cambridge.org/article_S095679689700261X

[4] Bowen Alpern and Fred B. Schneider. 1987. Recognizing safety and liveness. *Distributed Computing* 2 (1987), 117–126. Issue 3. http://dx.doi.org/10.1007/BF01782772

[5] Paul Ashley, Satoshi Hada, GÅijnter Karjoth, Calvin Powers, and Matthias Schunter. 2003. Enterprise Privacy Authorization Language (EPAL 1.2). (November 2003). W3C Member Submission.

[6] Adam Barth, Anupam Datta, John C. Mitchell, and Helen Nissenbaum. 2006. Privacy and Contextual Integrity: Framework and Applications. In *IEEE Symposium on Security and Privacy*. IEEE Computer Society, Washington, DC, USA, 184–198. DOI:https://doi.org/10.1109/SP.2006.32

[7] Lujo Bauer, Jarred Ligatti, and David Walker. 2002. More Enforceable Security Policies. In *Foundations of Computer Security*.

[8] Travis Breaux and Annie Antón. 2008. Analyzing Regulatory Rules for Privacy and Security Requirements. *IEEE Trans. Softw. Eng.* 34, 1 (2008), 5–20.

[9] Omar Chowdhury, Andreas Gampe, Jianwei Niu, Jeffery von Ronne, Jared Bennatt, Anupam Datta, Limin Jia, and William H Winsborough. 2013. Privacy promises that can be kept: A policy analysis method with application to the HIPAA privacy rule. In *Proceedings of the 18th ACM symposium on Access control models and technologies*. ACM, 3–14.

[10] A. Cimatti, E. Clarke, F. Giunchiglia, and M. Roveri. 2000. NuSMV: A New Symbolic Model Checker. *International Journal of Software Tools for Technology Transfer* 2 (2000), 410–425.

[11] Nicodemos Damianou, Naranker Dulay, Emil Lupu, and Morris Sloman. 2001. The Ponder Policy Specification Language. In *POLICY*. Springer-Verlag, London, UK, 18–38.

[12] E. Allen Emerson. 1990. Temporal and modal logic. In *Handbook of theoretical computer science*, Jan van Leeuwen (Ed.). MIT Press, Cambridge, MA, USA, 995–1072. http://portal.acm.org/citation.cfm?id=114891.114907

[13] E. Allen Emerson and Kedar S. Namjoshi. 1995. Reasoning about rings. In *POPL '95*.

[14] Klaus Havelund and Grigore Roşu. 2004. Efficient monitoring of safety properties. *Int. J. Softw. Tools Technol. Transf.* 6 (2004), 158–173. Issue 2. DOI:https://doi.org/10.1007/s10009-003-0117-6

[15] Carl Hewitt. 1977. Viewing control structures as patterns of passing messages. *Artificial Intelligence* 8, 3 (1977), 323 – 364. DOI:https://doi.org/DOI:10.1016/0004-3702(77)90033-9

[16] HIPAA 1996. Health Insurance Portability and Accountability Act (HIPAA). (1996). (42 U.S.C. §300gg, 29 U.S.C §1181 *et seq.*, and 42 U.S.C §1320d *et seq.*; 45 CFR Parts 144, 146, 160 162, and 164).

[17] Claiborne Johnson. 2016. *An Actor-Based Framework for Verifiable Privacy Policy Enforcement: Assume-Guarantee Specification of an Actor-Component Architecture.* Master's thesis. University of Texas at San Antonio.

[18] Bengt Jonsson and Tsay Yih-Kuen. 1996. Assumption/guarantee specifications in linear-time temporal logic. *Theoretical Computer Science* 167, 1-2 (1996), 47 – 72. DOI:https://doi.org/10.1016/0304-3975(96)00069-2

[19] Karl Krukow, Mogens Nielsen, and Vladimiro Sassone. 2008. A Logical Framework for History-based Access Control and Reputation Systems. *J. Comput. Secur.* 16, 1 (Jan. 2008), 63–101. http://dl.acm.org/citation.cfm?id=1370684.1370686

[20] L. Lamport. 1977. Proving the Correctness of Multiprocess Programs. *IEEE Transactions on Software Engineering* 3, 2 (1977), 125–143.

[21] Martin Leucker and Christian Schallhart. 2009. A brief account of runtime verification. *Journal of Logic and Algebraic Programming* 78, 5 (2009), 293–303. DOI:https://doi.org/DOI:10.1016/j.jlap.2008.08.004 The 1st Workshop on Formal Languages and Analysis of Contract-Oriented Software (FLACOS'07).

[22] Jay Ligatti, Lujo Bauer, and David Walker. 2009. Run-Time Enforcement of Nonsafety Policies. *ACM Trans. Inf. Syst. Secur.* 12, Article 19 (January 2009), 41 pages. Issue 3. DOI:https://doi.org/10.1145/1455526.1455532

[23] Thomas MacGahan. 2016. *Towards Verifiable Privacy Policy Compliance of an Actor-Based Electronic Medical Records System: An extension to the HAPL language focused on exposing a user interface.* Master's thesis. University of Texas at San Antonio.

[24] Thomas MacGahan, Claiborne Johnson, Armando Rodriguez, Jeffery von Ronne, and Jianwei Niu. 2017. Provable Enforcement of HIPAA-Compliant Release of Medical Records Using the History Aware Programming Language. *In Proceedings of 22nd ACM Symposium on Access Control Models and Technologies*, 10.

[25] Michael J. May, Carl A. Gunter, and Insup Lee. 2006. Privacy APIs: Access Control Techniques to Analyze and Verify Legal Privacy Policies. In *CSFW*. IEEE Computer Society, Washington, DC, USA, 85–97. DOI:https://doi.org/10.1109/CSFW.2006.24

[26] A. Pnueli. 1977. The Temporal Logic of Programs. In *Proceedings of the 18th IEEE Symposium on Foundations of Computer Science*, Vol. 526. 46–67.

[27] Fred B. Schneider. 2000. Enforceable security policies. *ACM Transactions on Information and System Security* 3 (2000), 2000.

[28] A. Prasad Sistla. 1994. Safety, liveness and fairness in temporal logic. *Formal Aspects of Computing* 6 (1994), 495–511. Issue 5. http://dx.doi.org/10.1007/BF01211865 10.1007/BF01211865.

[29] Jeffery von Ronne. 2012. Leveraging actors for privacy compliance. In *Proceedings of the 2nd edition on Programming systems, languages and applications based on actors, agents, and decentralized control abstractions*. ACM, 133–136.

A REDUCED EMRS CARRIERS

Table 1: Reduced EMRS Carriers

Finite Carrier	Instances
$\hat{I}$ (id)	idPHI, idPsychPHI, idNotExists
$\hat{\mathcal{E}}$ (record)	PHIRec, PsychPHIRec
$\hat{\mathcal{P}}$ (principal)	subject, nonSubject, originator, nonOriginator, thirdParty
$\hat{\mathcal{R}}$ (role)	doctor, thirdParty, patient
$\hat{\mathcal{A}}$ (actor)	subjectApp, nonSubjectApp, originatorApp, nonOriginatorApp, thirdPartyApp
$\hat{\mathcal{M}}$ (message)	requestReadRecord, releaseRecord, rejectReadRequest, requestGrantAuth, grantAuthorization, rejectGrantAuthorizationRequest, confirmAdd

The finite carriers resulting from theorem 5.1 can be found in table 1. Although the sets of instances in our carriers would seem to create an overly large combination, instances are combined strictly along valid bindings. For example, we do not combine the *doctor* instance of $\hat{\mathcal{R}}$ with the *subject* instance of $\hat{\mathcal{P}}$, nor do we combine the *idPsychPHI* instance of $\hat{I}$ with the *PHIRec* instance of $\hat{\mathcal{E}}$, as these do not create logical pairings in the system. Additionally, we do not need to combine with all instances of $\hat{I}$ and $\hat{\mathcal{M}}$ for every specification. We only need to use the *idNotExists* element from $\hat{I}$ when discussing an id received in a *requestReadRecord* message, as it has no corresponding record and will be precluded from progressing into following system messages that require a record to be identified. We also only need to combine with instances of $\hat{\mathcal{M}}$ when they are matched to their predicate in the specifications, with multiple instances of $\hat{\mathcal{M}}$ only necessary when an instance can be matched to one of multiple message predicates, which occurs only in a couple specifications.

B HAPL LANGUAGE EXAMPLES

This appendix includes examples of a couple actor definitions in HAPL, as well as some supporting role and message definitions:

```
role CareProvider
role Patient
role Marketing
role Doctor
message requestAuth[ x ; inrole( sys , CareProvider ) ]( sender:
    Authorizer , sys: Principal )
message decideAuth[]( sender: Actor , requestor: Principal ,
    subjectRecord: Tuple[Int , Principal , Principal , String] )
message authRelease[ x ; inrole( authingPrinc , CareProvider ) ](
    sender: Actor , authingPrinc: Principal , record: Tuple[Int ,
    Principal , Principal , String] )
message authOwnRecordFor[ x ; inrole( owner , Patient ) ]( owner:
    Principal , releaseTo: Principal )
message requestAuthRelease[ x ; inrole( sendingPrinc , CareProvider
    ), inrole( subject , Patient ) ]( sender: Actor , sendingPrinc
    : Principal , subject: Principal , record: Tuple[Int , Principal ,
    Principal , String] )
message registerLogin[]( landingActor: Actor , loggedInPrinc:
    Principal , nameOfPrinc: String )
message lookupPrinc[]( sender: Actor , nameOfPrinc: String )
message foundPrinc[]( owner: Principal , ownersActor: Actor )
message princNotFound[]()
```

Figure 9: Message and Role Definitions

```
//actor for binding names to principals
actor Directory [ x ; inrole( sys , CareProvider ) ]( sys:
    Principal ) representing sys {
 var dirList: List[Tuple[Int , Actor , Principal , String]] = list ()
 var idCounter: Int = 0 ; var found: Bool = false
 //Receive notification of a login
 on registerLogin[]( landingActor: Actor , princ: Principal , name:
    String ) {
   found = false
   print( "Directory received notification of a login by " + name
     )
   foreach record in (dirList) {
     if( (record.get(3)) == princ ) {
       found = true
       print( "Found record " + record )
   }}
   if( !found ) { //then first login
     dirList = tuple(idCounter , landingActor , princ , name ) ::
     dirList
     idCounter = idCounter + 1
 }}
 on lookupPrinc[]( sender: Actor , nameOfPrinc: String ) {
   found = false
   foreach record in (dirList) {
     if( (record.get(4))  == nameOfPrinc ) {
       send<sender >(foundPrinc(record.get(3) , record.get(2)))
       found = true
   }}
   if( !found ) { send<sender >( princNotFound() ) }
}}
```

Figure 10: Directory Definition

```
actor Authorizer [ auth ; inrole( sys , CareProvider ) ]( dir:
    Directory , sys: Principal) representing sys {
 var requests: List[Tuple[Actor , Principal , Tuple[Int , Principal ,
    Principal , String]]] = list ()
 var requestor: Actor ; var requestingPrinc: Principal
 var originator: Principal ; var subjectPrinc: Principal
 var subjectRecord: Tuple[Int , Principal , Principal , String]
 var data: String
 on requestAuthRelease[]( sender: Actor , requestingPrinc:
    Principal , subject: Principal , record: Tuple[Int , Principal ,
    Principal , String] ) {
  originator = record.get(3)
  data = record.get(4)
  if( (!isPHI( data )) || ((requestingPrinc == originator) || (
  requestingPrinc == subject)) ) {
    send<sender >(authRelease(this , sys , record))
  } else {
    ltlquery(once receive <from PatientTerminal as P[Patient]> (
    authOwnRecordFor) with owner , releaseTo where owner = subject
    and requestingPrinc = releaseTo ) {
      send<sender >(authRelease(this , sys , record))
    } else {
      requests = tuple(sender , subject , record)
      send<dir >(lookupPrinc(this , subject))
}}}
 on foundPrinc[]( owner: Principal , ownersActor: Actor ) {
   foreach req in ( requests ) {
     if( ((req.get(3)).get(3)) == owner ) {
       requestingPrinc = req.get(2)
       subjectRecord = req.get(3)
       send<ownersActor >(decideAuth( this , requestingPrinc ,
    subjectRecord ))
}}}
 on authOwnRecordFor[]( owner: Principal , releaseTo: Principal )
   {
   foreach req in (requests) {
     subjectPrinc = (req.get(3)).get(3)
     if( subjectPrinc == owner ) {
       requestor = req.get(1)
       subjectRecord = req.get(3)
       ltlquery( once receive <from Patient as P[Patient]> (
    requestAuthorizeRelease) with subject where subject = owner )
       {
         send<requestor >(authRelease(this , sys , subjectRecord))
       } else {
         print("preemptive auth by: "+owner)
}}}}}
```

Figure 11: Authorizer Definition

Authorization Enforcement Detection

Ehood Porat
Jerusalem College of Technology
Jerusalem, Israel
ehoodp41@gmail.com

Shmuel Tikochinski
Jerusalem College of Technology
Jerusalem, Israel
molli68@gmail.com

Ariel Stulman
Jerusalem College of Technology
Jerusalem, Israel
stulman@jct.ac.il

ABSTRACT

One of the many aspects of website security is the question of authorization breach. It is an attack in which un-authorized entities are allowed access to restricted space. As the complexity of website code increases, the human capability of handling authorization rules and semantics decreases accordingly. In this project, we demonstrate an automated authorization enforcement detection (AED) tool which allows website administrators to check if they have authorization vulnerabilities on their sites.

CCS Concepts

• **Security and privacy** → **security services**; *Authentication, Access control, Authorization*

KEYWORDS

Authorization; Cookies; CSRF-TOKEN;

ACM Reference format:

E. Porat, S. Tikochinski, and A. Stulman. 2017. Authorization Enforcement Detection. In Proceedings of 22nd ACM Symposium on Access Control Models and Technologies, Indianapolis, Indiana USA, July 20177 (SACMAT'17), 4 pages.
DOI: 10.1145/3078861.3084172

1 INTRODUCTION

The human mind can handle a lot of data, but is limited at some point. The increase in website code complexity causes the human tester to fail miserably. Our project's goal is to provide automated detection of authorization vulnerabilities; in effect, provide authorization enforcement in websites. We want to provide administrators or their representatives (white-hat pen-

SACMAT'17, June 21-23, 2017, Indianapolis, IN, USA
© 2017 Copyright is held by the owner/author(s). Publication rights licensed to ACM.
ACM 978-1-4503-4702-0/17/06...$15.00
http://dx.doi.org/10.1145/3078861.3084172

testers, etc.) with the knowledge of if and how an attacker can bypass authorization access control. According to the 2016 annual statistical report published by White Hat Security [1] the likelihood that a website will have an *insufficient authorization* based vulnerability is greater than 10%. Even in well maintained sites such as YouTube and Facebook, such authorization breaches exist [2, 3].

The motivation is clear, but is better understood with an (real) example. Creating even the simplest WordPress site using the templates provided, will contain an order of 760 calls to the function "current_user_can" in its source code. This implies that the developer conjured approximately 760 cases which require authorization checks. With such a huge number of cases, can one be sure others weren't missed? Is it even possible to hand check for this kind of vulnerability with the specific environment each of these calls was made from? Many operations are implicitly assumed authoritatively safe as the user isn't supposed to get access to what triggers them. Is this a fair assumption or the product of necessity? An automated process is clearly required.

2 BACKGROUND

2.1 Cookies

Cookies are used by web servers to differentiate between users, and allow for user tailored operations (e.g. pre-saved preferences). Typically, these cookies are provided to the client (browser) by the server as a response to some previous identification mechanism (e.g. the login process). By re-submitting these cookies a client is uniquely identified, providing the server with the mechanism by which it can also deduce whether the user has already been authenticated. Granting access to services or performing other restricted operations is based on this deduction.

2.2 CSRF

Cross-Site Request Forgery (CSRF) is an attack that forces an end user to execute unwanted actions on a web application in which they're currently authenticated [4]. Thus, perceived as emanating from an authenticated user, the request will have the privileges of the victim, and is allowed to perform undesired operations (usually *state-changing* requests) on the victim's behalf. [1] places the likelihood of such a vulnerability at over 20%.

The basic mechanism coaxes the user to access some unwanted site, and exploits the browser's mechanism of automatically including all session cookies associated with the site. As both a legitimate request and a forged one originate from the victim, the site has no way of distinguishing between them.

2.3 CSRF Tokens

Synchronizer tokens were specifically introduced to thwart cross-site request forgery (CSRF) attacks [5]. For any state changing request, the server expects to receive a one-time, *random* token, which provides a security mechanism for preventing CSRF attacks. The CSRF token was passed to the client at a prior stage (either as a hidden form field, in a response body containing JSON or others techniques). The server expects the token be returned, rejecting a request if the CSRF token fails validation.

Approximately 35% of vulnerable sites use this technique to remediate their problem [1]. Hence, any automated tool must be able to cope with these tokens in-order to accurately assess a vulnerability's presence.

3 AED

The proposed tool, Authorization Enforcement Detection (AED)[1], allows for an ADMIN to casually surf the website. Behind the scenes, every request made is intercepted by the AED Proxy and then forwarded to the web server. When a response containing a cookie is detected, the corresponding request and response are saved for future analysis. Other request/response pairs are discarded for AED efficiency. We call this the *recording phase*. When the ADMIN stops recording, the analysis phase begins.

3.1 The Analysis

The analysis is composed of two parts. The first is gathering information for sending a proper request, containing valid tokens, with modified cookies. We will refer to this part as *round one*. The actual sending of modified requests and analysis of the response will be referred to as *round two*. Both rounds use a dictionary (hash-table), the format of which is detailed in Tables 1 and 2 for rounds one and two, respectively.

TABLE 1.   **RESPONSE Dictionary**

key	value	purpose

res-id[a]	Another dictionary	{
		 Token-1 → [],
		 Token-2 → []
		 }

Token-1	Array of tokens	Tokens found in the original response.
Token-2	Array of tokens	Tokens found in the response to copy request made in round one.

[a] *The identifier of the RESPONSE. All RESPONSEs in the dictionary contain a token*

---

[1] Tool can be found at https://github.com/ehood/aed

TABLE 2.   **REQUEST Dictionary**

Key	Value	Purpose
Req-id[b]	Array of dictionaries	{[{Token-Index → value, Res-id→ value}]}
Res-id	Identifier of the Response	To identify the response from which the token came from.
Token-index	Number	The index of the token in the above response.

[b] *The identifier of the REQUEST*

3.1.1 Round one. Every recorded request (those that contained cookies in the corresponding response) is replicated. This is done for two reasons: The first is to allow for flagging false positives which can occur due to one-time operations (e.g. file delete); operations which will invariably return different results the second time they are executed. As CSRF-token protection is prevalent, AED must be able to cope with supporting sites as well. Hence replication allows for capturing CSRF-tokens needed for the proper execution of future requests.

The check is achieved by iterating over the response tokens (Table 1), looking for a match in subsequent requests. This proves that the request uses a token. This information is stored in the request dictionary (Table 2), accordingly. As clients must be provided with valid CSRF-tokens before they can re-submit them, AED checks for requests with such embedded tokens. Our core assumption is that a token invariably would have been contained in some preceding response (usually the one directly preceding its use). Before sending the *copy* request, we will replace the expected token (stored in Table 1 token-1) with the corresponding token (stored in the token-2 array).

For extracting tokens from the response, however, a simple difference comparison does not suffice. Although one can safely assume that different responses to the same request will be identical except for the random unique tokens, common ending characters shared between the sequences will crop the tokens early, thwarting the difference comparison technique. Examination of poplar CSRF-token implementations, however, allows for flagging certain characters as the start and end of the token values. These are used in Algorithm 1, *StartChars* and *EndChars* for common starting and ending characters, to extract the tokens from the responses.

Algorithm 1 Find Tokens in responses

```
1:  procedure FINDTOKENS(response1, response2)
2:      i ← 0
3:      while i < length[response1] ⋀ i < length[response2] do
4:          if response1[i] ≠ response2[i] then
5:              j ← k ← i
6:              while i < length[response1] ⋀ response1[i] ∉ EndChars do
7:                  i ← i + 1
8:              end while
9:              while k < length[response2] ⋀ response2[k] ∉ EndChars do
10:                 k ← k + 1
11:             end while
12:             while j ≥ 0 ⋀ response1[j] ∉ StartChars do
13:                 j ← j − 1
14:             end while
15:             if i ≠ k then
16:                 token1 ← token1 + response1[j : i]
17:                 token2 ← token2 + response2[j : k]
18:             end if
19:             response1 ← response1[: i]
20:             response2 ← response2[: k]
21:             i ← 0
22:         else
23:             i ← i + 1
24:         end if
25:     end while
26:     return token1, token2                                    ▷
27: end procedure
```

Algorithm 2 Get new Token for request

```
1:  procedure GETNEWTOKEN(requestId)
2:      for item ∈ requestDictionary[requestId]
3:          if item ∈ requestDictionary[res_id] then
4:              t ← GetNewToken(item[res_id])
5:              response ← sendRequestWithNewTokens(item[res_id], t)
6:              responseOriginal ← GetOriginalResponse(item[res_id])
7:              t1, t2 ← FindTokens(response, responseOriginal)
8:              token ← t2[item[token_index]]
9:              tokens ← tokens + token              ▷ Tokens is an array
10:         else
11:             response ← sendRequest(item[res_id])
12:             responseOriginal ← GetOriginalResponse(item[res_id])
13:             t1, t2 ← FindTokens(response, responseOriginal)
14:             token ← t2[item[token_index]]
15:             tokens ← tokens + token              ▷ Tokens is an array
16:         end if
17:     end for
18:     return tokens
19: end procedure
```

Algorithm 1 explained: The algorithm loops through the two responses until one terminates. As long as the charcters match, the search index is incremented (lines 22-23). Upon encountring a character discrepancy (line 4), the start of a CSRF-token is suspected. Hence, the end of the token is searched for with the help of *EndChars* (lines 6-8 for the first response, and 9-11 for the second). As tokens might begin with the same sequence (e.g. *AODF11dk* for the first and *AODF05po* for the second), we must reverse search (lines 12-14) to find where the real token begins (with the help of *StartChars*). The tokens are then extracted for storage.

3.1.2 Round two. For every request/response pair recorded in *round one*, we check if the request requires a token for it to be accepted. As the request dictionary was updated in *round one* to contain all requests that have tokens, all pairs not in the dictionary do not require a token. The algorithm used for acquiring an additional token in shown in Algorithm 2.

Algorithm 2 explained: For each item of *requestDictionary*, we check if the response that contained the token is dependent on requests that required tokens themselves in order to operate correctly. Since the ID of a request and its corresponding response is the same, checking the *requestDictionary* at the index of the response containing a token is analogous to checking if the request uses a token. When a token is not required, a simple request is made and the token in the response is extracted and stored in the *tokens* array (lines 11-15). When a token is required, we recursively run the current function on the new request, and assign the extracted token to a temporary variable, *t*. A request is generated containing the new acquired token (stored in *t*), and the returned tokens are extracted from the response (lined 3-9).

After acquiring new tokens, we re-send the requests with modified cookies; expecting response "strings" to differ as un-authenticated (hence, un-authorized) cookies have been submitted. Similar results are treated as authorization breaches.

The actual analysis is done with ssdeep [6], a program for computing fuzzy hashing. This enables us to compute the *similarity* of "strings". If we find a matches with similarities being greater than 95%, it is tagged as a *breach*. If the similarity score is only greater than 80% but less than 95%, it is flagged *suspicious*. Below these thresholds the request is marked as safe.

4 SIMILAR TOOL

The only tool that remotely resembles our work is *Autorize*, a Burp add-on [7]. The solutions, however, differ. Besides dealing with CSRF-token enabled sites which *Autorize* cannot cope with, AED preforms a deeper analysis than simply comparing response codes and length. This is a very important distinction, as similar pages with minute differences (e.g. different embedded name tags) will not be detected by *Autorize* as the page length varies. The analysis performed by AED, will detect these variations.

5 FUTURE IMPROVEMENTS

AED's performance can be further improved by enabling the user to interact with the tool (e.g. enter a valid CSRF-Token), allowing for specific tweaks that might not be caught with the automated deduction mechanism. This will reduce false negatives. In addition, filters can be added to remove specific requests the user doesn't want inspected. Currently, longer session degrades the tool's performance, as many inconsequential paths are automatically inspected; hence, manual or automatic filtering would lighten the tool's load, further improving its performance.

6 DEMONSTRATION SCENARIO

We will present a template bases WordPress site, which, as mentioned in the section 1, contains multiple calls to the "current_user_can" function for authorization checking of the current user. An authorization vulnerability will be deliberately inserted to a page the user was not supposed to have accessed. We then show that by omitting even one call to the aforementioned function, the entire site can be manipulated at will.

The demonstration will include not only simple pages, but also pages that are "protected" with CSRF-tokens. We will detect, duplicate and extract the tokens needed for AED to properly find the vulnerability.

REFERENCES

[1]   "Web applications security statistics report", White Hat Security, 2016. Online: https://info.whitehatsec.com/rs/675-YBI-674/images/WH-2016-Stats-Report-FINAL.pdf

[2]   Swati Khandelwal, "How hackers could delete any YouTube video with just one click", The Hacker News. April 1, 2015. Online: http://thehackernews.com/2015/04/hack-delete-youtube-video.html

[3]   Swati Khandelwal, " Facebook Vulnerability Allows Hacker to Delete Any Photo Album", The Hacker News. Feb. 12, 2015. Online: http://thehackernews.com/2015/02/hacking-facebook-photo-album.html

[4]   Cross-Site   Request   Forgery   (CSRF).   OWASP.   Online: https://www.owasp.org/index.php?title=Cross-Site_Request_Forgery_(CSRF)&oldid=227768

[5]   Wichers, D., Petefish, P., Sheridan, E., Cross-Site Request Forgery (CSRF) Prevention   Cheat   Sheet.   OWASP.   Online: https://www.owasp.org/index.php/Cross-Site_Request_Forgery_(CSRF)_Prevention_Cheat_Sheet

[6]   SSDEEP.   Online: http://dfrws.org/sites/default/files/session-files/paper-identifying_almost_identical_files_using_context_triggered_piecewise_hashing.pdf

[7]   Tawily,   B.,   and   Dotta,   F.,   Autorize.   Online: https://github.com/Quitten/Autorize/blob/master/Autorize.py

[8]   Video   of   the   tool: https://www.dropbox.com/s/7up6h46g2zew4pu/AED.mp4?dl=0

Multi-Layer Authorization Framework for a Representative Hadoop Ecosystem Deployment

Maanak Gupta, Farhan Patwa, James Benson and Ravi Sandhu

Institute for Cyber Security and Department of Computer Science

University of Texas at San Antonio, One UTSA Circle, San Antonio, TX, 78249, USA

gmaanakg@yahoo.com, {farhan.patwa,james.benson,ravi.sandhu}@utsa.edu

ABSTRACT

Apache Hadoop is a predominant software framework to store and process vast amount of data, produced in varied formats. Data stored in Hadoop multi-tenant data lake often includes sensitive data such as social security numbers, intelligence sources and medical particulars, which should only be accessed by legitimate users. Apache Ranger and Apache Sentry are important authorization systems providing fine-grained access control across several Hadoop ecosystem services. In this paper, we provide a comprehensive explanation for the authorization framework offered by Hadoop ecosystem, incorporating core Hadoop 2.x native access control features and capabilities offered by Apache Ranger, with prime focus on data services including Apache Hive and Hadoop 2.x core services. A multi-layer authorization system is discussed and demonstrated, reflecting access control for services, data, applications and infrastructure resources inside a representative Hadoop ecosystem instance. A concrete use case is discussed to underline the application of aforementioned access control points. We use Hortonworks Hadoop distribution HDP 2.5 to exhibit this multi-layer access control framework.

CCS CONCEPTS

•Security and privacy → Security requirements; Access control; Authorization;

KEYWORDS

Access Control; Hadoop Ecosystem; Big Data; Data Lake; Role Based; Attributes; Object Tags

ACM Reference format:
Maanak Gupta, Farhan Patwa, James Benson and Ravi Sandhu. 2017. Multi-Layer Authorization Framework for a
Representative Hadoop Ecosystem Deployment. In *Proceedings of SACMAT'17, June 21–23, 2017, Indianapolis, IN, USA,* , 8 pages.
DOI: http://dx.doi.org/10.1145/3078861.3084173

1 INTRODUCTION

In past several years, enterprises have grown their reliance on Big Data for critical financial and strategic decisions. An estimate in IDC's Digital Universe study, predicts world's data size to reach 44 zettabytes by 2020 [10]. Multi-format Big Data is collected from diverse sources including sensors, tennis rackets, web browsing, social media, power meters etc., to improve organization's operational efficiency, revenue and to offer personalised customer experience. Leveraging full potential and gaining valuable insights of such massive data sets require enormous infrastructure for storage and computation in real time manner.

Apache Hadoop [3] offers a distributed, scalable and cost-efficient open-source framework for storing and analysing structured, unstructured and semi-structured data in variety of formats. Resilient storage and rich analytical capabilities provided by Hadoop and its ecosystem components (Apache HBase, Apache Hive etc.) makes it a prime choice as a Big Data processing system in government and industry. Such wide acceptability of Hadoop ecosystem comes with the responsibility to make it secure against cyber attacks.

The Multi-tenant Hadoop Data lake stores sensitive information including credit card numbers, medical records and social security numbers (SSNs), requiring the cluster to be protected against cyber threats. Unauthorized access to data assets can have serious impact on its confidentiality and integrity. An inside user can masquerade by running malicious code to impersonate Hadoop core services including HDFS NameNode, DataNode or YARN ResourceManager. A nefarious user can also modify, view or delete other users' applications. It is also possible to execute denial of resources attack, where a malicious user can submit lengthy jobs which consume all the cluster resources preventing other users from submitting new jobs. The challenges to mitigate these threats include distributed and partitioned file system and computing, scale of Hadoop cluster, multi-tenant environment and multi-level access of same data elements to different users. Correspondingly, Hadoop ecosystem has deployed several security measures including authentication, authorization, data encryption and network security.

Access Control [13][20] mechanisms are vital in restricting users and applications access to authorized resources. Apache Hadoop deploys a multi-layer authorization framework using Access Control Lists (ACLs) to authorize users to access data, infrastructure resources and services in Hadoop cluster. Apache Ranger [5] and Apache Sentry [6] are two widely deployed systems to enforce fine grainer authorization across several Hadoop ecosystem services. Both systems offer a centralized administration console to store and manage security policies for multiple ecosystem components. They provide plugins which are hooked to ecosystem services to decide and enforce access control, based on the policies pulled from central policy server. Sentry supports role-based authorization model, whereas Ranger assigns permissions to users and groups.

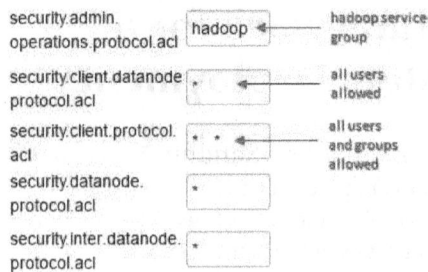

Figure 1: Hadoop Daemons Access Configuration

In this paper we present a unified explanation for authorization mechanisms in Hadoop ecosystem primarily focusing on data access via Apache Hive. We demonstrate the capabilities using multiple Apache projects as a part of Hortonworks Hadoop distribution HDP (Hortonworks Data Platform) 2.5 sandbox [14]. For our purpose we assume data is already ingested in the cluster.

The paper is organized as follows. Section 2 discusses and demonstrates individual access control points offered in Hadoop ecosystem. A complete multi-layer authorization architecture is presented in Section 3. We discuss a concrete use case in Section 4. Section 5 reviews related work, followed by conclusions in Section 6.

2 HADOOP ECOSYSTEM ACCESS CONTROL MECHANISMS

Hadoop ecosystem deploys Defense in Depth approach to enforce access control security mechanisms across the cluster. A user is allowed to access data services and Hadoop daemons in the cluster through service level authorization layer. Data stored in HDFS (Hadoop Distributed File System) is secured by POSIX-style file and directory permissions or extended ACLs. Cluster resources are segregated through YARN capacity (or fair) scheduler queues which restrict applications to use limited resources and also prevent application modifications from unauthorized users. Apache Ranger further offers data masking, filtering and dynamic contextual information to achieve finer-grained authorization. This section discusses and demonstrates these access control mechanisms using Hortonworks HDP 2.5.

2.1 Hadoop and Data Services Access

Once a user is authenticated, the first layer of access control mechanisms is provided by service layer authorization. This layer controls access to ecosystem services (Apache Hive, HDFS, Apache HBase) inside Hadoop cluster, much before data underlying the services is accessed. It also checks if a user is allowed to access Hadoop daemons such as HDFS NameNode, YARN ResourceManager, and ApplicationMaster, to submit applications or to query status. Several Hadoop core services also need communication with each other for task updates or cluster resource status, which is also controlled by this layer. This cross-service authorization prevents rogue processes from impersonating as Hadoop daemons and gaining control to data and resources.

By default, service level authorization is disabled in Hadoop. It is enabled in `core-site.xml` configuration file by setting property `hadoop.security.authorization = true` in

Figure 2: WebHDFS Access via Apache Knox

all the nodes of Hadoop cluster. The ACLs for various Hadoop services (daemons) are set in `hadoop-policy.xml` file. An example Hadoop service access control property is `security.client.datanode.protocol.acl`. This property lists the set of users which can access HDFS DataNode, required for data block recovery. An example of cross Hadoop services ACL property is `security.resourcetracker.protocol.acl`, which is used when YARN ResourceManager and NodeManager communicate with each other for resource monitoring. The recommended value for this ACL is 'yarn' service user. It should be noted that all Hadoop services run under a service user Unix account, and the ACLs for cross service should include permissions for the service users. Using Apache Ambari [1], these properties can be changed under HDFS configuration. Figure 1 shows sample Hadoop services ACL properties. These ACLs include allowed users and groups information, with a special value * including all users or groups. Similar ACLs can also be specified for blocked services or users. Note that some ACLs, for example, `security.job.task.protocol.acl` used by Map and Reduce tasks to communicate with YARN Node-Manager, may give permissions to all users (*) as the identity of applications running these tasks cannot be enumerated in advance.

Apache Knox [4] offers an API gateway to provide access to several Hadoop ecosystem services (WebHDFS, Hive etc.) to external users. It provides a single access point to Hadoop REST services by intercepting user access requests and enforcing policies to allow or deny users to access services. Internal ports to ecosystem services are not accessible to end users. Apache Knox validates permissions of users to access cluster services much before data or other resource access decisions are made, thereby preventing unauthorized access at early stage of user request lifecycle. As shown in Figure 2 (a) (Apache Ranger logs), a user guest trying to access HDFS NameNode service via Knox by issuing a list files curl command `curl -iku guest:guest-password -X GET 'https://10.x.x.255:8443/gateway/default/webhdfs/v1/ ?op=LISTSTATUS'` is denied access as the user is not allowed to access HDFS service inside the cluster protected by Apache Knox gateway. Once the policy is set in Apache Ranger (for Knox

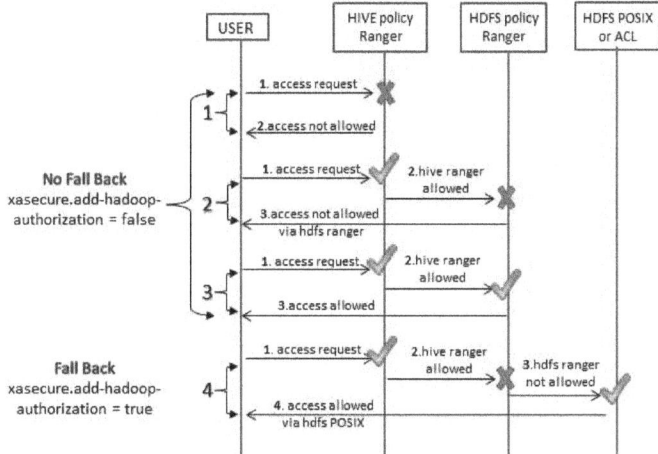

Figure 3: Hive and HDFS Access Configurations

Figure 4: Policy Creation using Grant Command

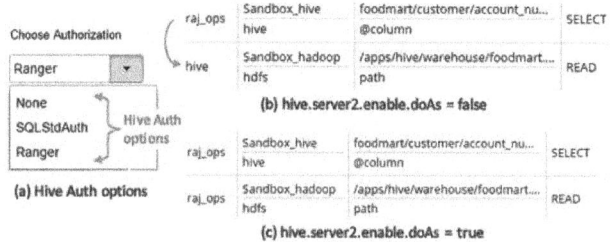

Figure 5: Authorization Options and Impersonation

service) to allow access to WebHDFS service to guest user (Figure 2 (b)), the user will be allowed access to HDFS NameNode. Similar policies can be set for other ecosystem services such as Apache Hive, HBase, YARN ResourceManager or Ambari, to allow external users to access cluster. Hence, the perimeter security offered by Apache Knox enables secure access to several ecosystem services from users outside the cluster. It should be noted that Apache Knox gateway can protect multiple clusters and offer single endpoint to all services across clusters.

2.2 Data Objects Access

The backbone of Hadoop ecosystem is fault-tolerant and distributed file system for storing data, called Hadoop Distributed File System (HDFS). With YARN architecture, same data can be read directly from HDFS or through several data engines (or services) such as Apache Hive or Apache Pig, to perform operations on supported data model. Data layer authorization (using Apache Ranger plugins) ensures access to HDFS directly or via different data engines, to authorized users and applications. HDFS supports both POSIX style permissions (read, write and execute) on files and directories, and extended Access Control Lists. ACLs authorization is disabled by default in HDFS which can be enabled by setting dfs.namenode.acls.enabled = true in configuration file hdfs-site.xml for HDFS NameNode. ACLs can be set on files and directories using setfacl. To check ACLs on a particular file getfacl command is used. For example, to add ACL permission read on file marketing for members in group execs and to get the list of permissions on file marketing, following commands are issued:

```
hdfs dfs -setfacl -m group:execs:r-- /marketing
hdfs dfs -getfacl /marketing
  group:execs:r--
```

Apache Ranger plugin can be enabled for HDFS service via Ranger configuration in Apache Ambari, which will manage and enforce security policies on HDFS files and directories [15]. Security administrator has option to configure layers of authorization controls to check access to HDFS by setting property xasecure.add-hadoop-authorization in ranger-hdfs-security.xml under Ranger configuration in Ambari. When the property is set to true, authorization engine will check HDFS ACLs if Ranger policy is not defined or denies access, whereas property set to false will make decision based only on Ranger policies without checking HDFS ACLs.

When a user attempts to access data through data services such as Apache Hive, access policies for both data service and HDFS are checked. As shown in Figure 3, when a user tries to access table using Apache Hive, Hive Ranger policies are first checked followed by HDFS Ranger policies for the corresponding data files. When the value of xasecure.add-hadoop-authorization is set to false, only HDFS Ranger policies are checked. If Hive Ranger policy allows access and HDFS Ranger denies, the user is not allowed to operate on the data. Both Hive and HDFS permissions must allow access to data. If xasecure.add-hadoop-authorization = true and HDFS Ranger policy does not allow access, HDFS POSIX permissions are further checked to make decision. Apache Ranger audit logs will reflect the policies (HDFS or Ranger ACLs) used to make access decision. Therefore, a user may need to have access authorization at multiple data service levels to perform operations on data items. Security administrator can set policies in Apache Ranger using UI, REST API or SQL grant/revoke commands. Ranger UI offers drop-down menu for several ecosystem services where administrator can select resources, users and actions along with contextual or policy conditions. SQL grant command issued by administrator (using command line tools such as beeline) will be intercepted by Apache Ranger plugin and will create corresponding policies. As shown in Figure 4, admin user raj_ops issuing command grant select, update on table foodmart.customer to user holger_gov; will generate policy in Ranger allowing user holger_gov for select and update action on table foodmart.customer.

Most of the services in Hadoop ecosystem have in-built authorization mechanisms, besides the centralized access control framework provided by Hadoop core, Apache Ranger and Apache Sentry. For example, Apache Hive has storage-based authorization, SQL standard based authorization and default-mode authorization models. Storage-based authorization uses the file system permissions

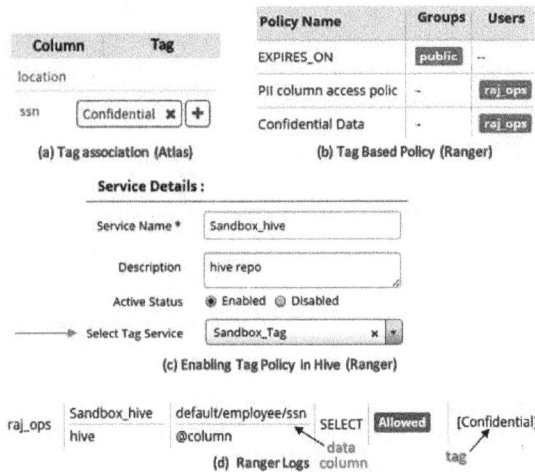

Figure 6: Tag Based Policy in Apache Ranger

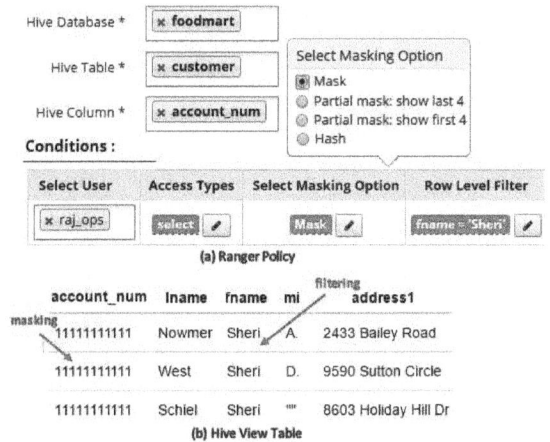

Figure 7: Data Masking and Row Filtering

to be applied for metastore and is primarily used when Hive acts as a table storage layer. This mode only provides authorization at table, database or partition level. SQL standards based authorization provides a fine-grained control to columns, rows or views by using grant/revoke commands, and uses HiveServer2 to enforce controls. Both these modes can be used simultaneously depending on the requirements and use case. In our demonstration, we use Ranger as the authorization provider for all the services in Hortonworks HDP 2.5. As shown in Figure 5(a), Apache Ambari provides dropdown in Hive configuration to select the authorization model which will automatically change the required configuration properties in `hive-site.xml` and `hiveserver2-site.xml`.

As Hadoop data storage layer is managed by HDFS, it is possible that user might be required to access data only via certain data engines such as Apache Hive or Pig, and not directly in HDFS. For example, business analyst users may get access to data using HiveQL via Apache Hive query but may not be allowed to access corresponding data files at HDFS level through MapReduce jobs (as HiveQL query changes to MapReduce job). In such requirements, the end user issuing HiveQL command is changed to 'hive' service user (user running Apache Hive service) for underlying HDFS level data access. Another use-case may need users to have data access at both Apache Hive and HDFS level. Such user impersonation is managed by changing `hive.server2.enable.doAs` property in Ambari Hive configuration, which changes the user running jobs at HDFS level. As shown in Apache Ranger audit logs (Figures 5(b) and (c)), with `hive.server2.enable.doAs` set to false, raj_ops is end user running HiveQL command which changes to 'hive' service user when accessing HDFS data through corresponding MapReduce job. For `hive.server2.enable.doAs = true`, end user raj_ops is accessing data at both Hive level and HDFS [16].

Besides resource-based policies (set on tables, files or queues) offered in Ranger, resource tags (attribute values) can be used to create tag-based policies. Apache Atlas [2] is used to associate attribute values with resources in ecosystem based on content, expiration time or sensitivity of resources. This metadata information (tag) can be used to create tag policy using tag service in Ranger.

This tag service is then attached to several data services to use tag-based policies. Once attached, all the resources associated with a particular tag will be secured by corresponding tag-based policy. As shown in Figure 6, confidential tag is created and assigned to column ssn in Apache Atlas, and a tag-based policy on confidential tag is created under tag service in Ranger. Once the policy is set, Apache Hive (or other service) is configured to support tag-based policy by selecting tag service in Hive configuration under Ranger. With this change, Apache Hive will support both resource and tag-based policy. When user raj_ops tries to access object ssn, Ranger audit logs will reflect the tag policy used along with the tag name. In this way, instead of creating separate policies across each data service for same resource, single tag policy can be used for all services. Tags can also have attributes such as expiration time which will reject access to associated object after certain time or date.

Apache Ranger can also set policies to perform column masking and row filtering on data items in Hive for certain users. Column masking helps to conceal data columns having sensitive information from users and applications by replacing data with random characters. Several masking options including complete mask, partial mask, hash mask, and date mask, are available. With row filtering, some rows are hidden from users based on the where clause and conditions set in policies. In Figure 7, column masking and row filtering are demonstrated together. Here, for raj_ops user, masking has been done on account_num column in table customer. Also row filtering has been applied where only rows with fname=Sheri are to be displayed. With these policies, the resultant access when raj_ops issues `select * from customer` command is shown in Figure 7(b). It can be seen that account_num is masked and only rows with fname=Sheri are displayed as a result for user raj_ops.

2.3 Context Enricher and Policy Conditions

Some authorization use-cases may require finer grained access to resources not only based on the subjects and objects, but also on certain environmental or contextual information. For example, it may be required to give access to a user when the user is at a specific location, between a particular time frame or from a designated IP address. Apache Ranger provides context enricher and condition

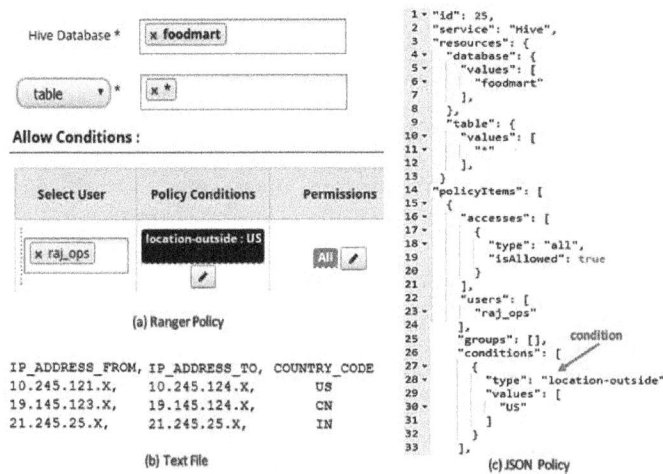

Figure 8: Geo Location Based Ranger Policies

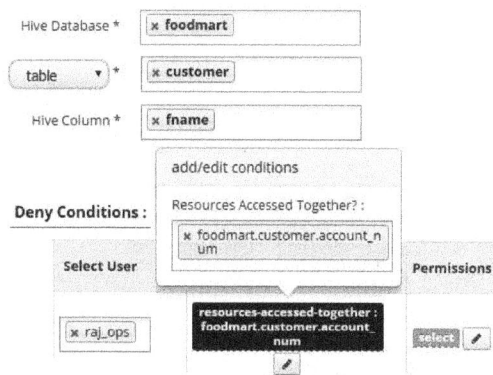

Figure 9: Prohibiting Data Combination

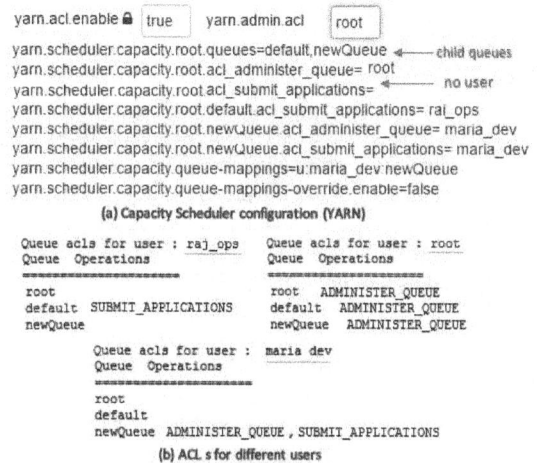

Figure 10: YARN Queues Sample Configuration

evaluators to realize dynamic policies, which change the access results based on contextual information. Context enricher is a java class which is used to enhance user access request by adding extra information such as location or user's IP address, based on mapping stored in a separate text file. Condition evaluators are used to add the access under certain conditions in Ranger policies [9]. To enable context enricher and condition evaluation, service definitions of each Hadoop ecosystem service should be enhanced with enricher and evaluation information. As shown in Figure 8(a), a Ranger policy is created to allow all actions to user raj_ops on all tables in database foodmart when its requesting location is outside US. When raj_ops tries to access table in foodmart database, Ranger Hive plugin will intercept this request and based on raj_ops ip address and the text file (which maps IP address to location and shown in Figure 8(b)), context enricher will add location information of raj_ops to the access request [18]. When Ranger plugin evaluates this request based on the policy (shown in Figure 8(c)) cached from central server, it will check the subjects, objects and operations involved and also if policy condition is satisfied. If the policy condition is not satisfied it will deny the access request even if other parameters are satisfied. Deny conditions can also be specified in Ranger by setting enableDenyAndExceptionsInPolicies = true in definitions of ecosystem services. Therefore, a policy can be formulated where a user can be denied access to resources based on specific user locations. Similarly, fine-grained access policies involving attributes can be defined using context enricher and condition evaluator hooks in Ranger. Role-based access control can be implemented using these hooks where a text file can have the current user to roles mapping and the policy condition can require the user to have a certain role to perform actions on resources. In such case, when a user requests access, context enricher will add roles of user to the request and evaluator will check against roles in policy condition to allow or deny access.

Privacy policies may require certain data-sets combinations not revealed to specific users. For example, SSN should not be shown together with name and address to sales users. Such a requirement can be encapsulated using prohibition policies, which can be defined using policy conditions and helps prevent certain data sets combination to be accessed together. Apache Ranger includes RangerHiveResourcesAccessedTogetherCondition condition evaluator which can check if the particular data sets can be accessed together. As shown in Figure 9, a deny condition can be set in a policy which prevents user raj_ops from performing a select operation on fname and account_num column together in customer table in foodmart database.

Note that the data-level access controls discussed in subsection 2.2 and 2.3, take effect only after the user is allowed to access Hive service through service-level authorization.

2.4 Cluster Resource and Application Access

Multi-tenant Hadoop cluster requires optimized sharing of resources among several tenants. In Hadoop 2.x, YARN capacity (or fair) scheduler defines queues with resource limits so that users submitting application in one of the queues can access a fraction of total cluster resources. YARN queues further prevent rogue users from submitting application to Hadoop cluster and prevent users from killing or modifying other user applications. Capacity (or fair) scheduler queues have ACLs associated with them which determine

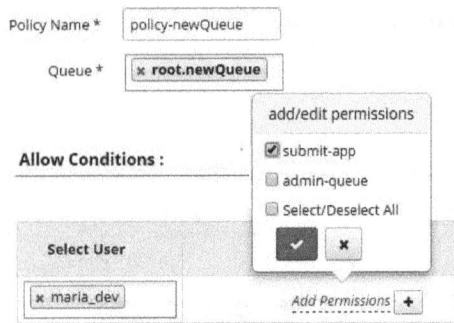

Figure 11: YARN Queues Authorization in Ranger

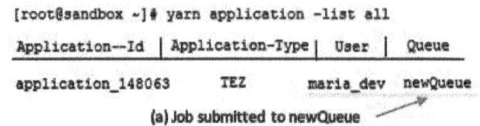

Figure 12: Queue and Job Access Control

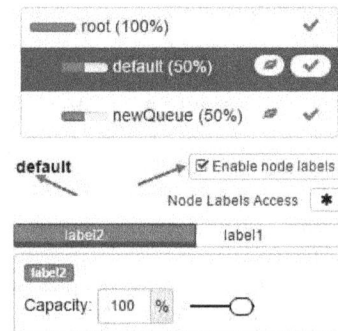

Figure 13: Node Labels and YARN Queues

the set of users who can submit applications or who can administer submitted application. By default, owner of application and queue administrator can modify or view applications submitted to a queue. These queues are hierarchial in nature where the resources allocated to the parent queue are distributed among child queues. ACLs defined at parent level are descended downwards to child queues, while applications are always submitted at leaf queue levels. YARN ACLs can be defined in YARN capacity scheduler configuration in Apache Ambari. Apache Ranger also provides plugin to enforce access control on YARN queues.

As shown in Figure 10(a), YARN ACLs are enabled by setting `yarn.acl.enable = true` under resource manager configuration in Apache Ambari. Also root is set as admin for YARN cluster via `yarn.admin.acl` property. As shown, YARN capacity scheduler configuration has two new child queues created (default and newQueue) under root parent queue. We have set root user as the administrator of root queue. The hierarchial nature of queues will descend the administrative privileges of root user to all the child queues, thereby making user root as administrator for both default and newQueue also. None of the users should be allowed to submit application to root queue (leave blank) as that will allow them to submit in all child queues also. It should be noted that two ACLs, one for administration and other for submit application operation, should be set for each YARN queue. User raj_ops is now set to submit application only to default queue, while maria_dev can administer and submit applications in newQueue child queue. With this capacity scheduler configuration, when each user issues `mapred queue -showacls` command to see the list of queues along with permissions, it can be seen in Figure 10(b) that root is admin for all three queues while raj_ops can only submit to default queue and maria_dev has administrator and submit application permissions on newQueue. Similar access control requirements can be achieved using Apache Ranger via YARN service plugin. As shown in Figure 11, a policy is set where user maria_dev is allowed to submit application in newQueue under root parent queue.

With aforementioned configurations, when user maria_dev tries to access data by issuing a HiveQL command `select min(customer.account_num) from foodmart.customer` using Hive service, its corresponding MapReduce (or Tez) job will be submitted to newQueue child queue (Figure 12(a)). If user raj_ops tries to kill or view the details of the job submitted by maria_dev, raj_ops is not allowed as the user is neither the admin nor the owner of job (shown by Ranger audit logs in Figure 12(b)). ACLs can also be included in the configuration files of application submitted, to restrict access to the application. For MapReduce job, ACLs are first enabled by setting `mapreduce.cluster.acls.enabled = true`. The list of users or groups which can modify or view job is set using `mapreduce.job.acl-modify-job` and `mapreduce.job.acl-view-job` properties respectively.

Cluster nodes can be assigned node labels for restricting node access to certain users and applications. By associating labels, sub-clusters can be created so that user applications can be executed on certain set of nodes, specific to application requirements. These node labels are associated with YARN capacity scheduler queues such that all the users submitting jobs to a particular queue will run their jobs only on nodes with labels that were assigned to the queue. These node labels can be enabled in YARN configuration using Ambari. Once enabled, administrator can issue command to create new labels. For example `sudo -u yarn yarn rmadmin -addToClusterNodeLabels "label1(exclusive=true),label2(exclusive=false)"` will add two labels label1 and label2, which can be verified using `yarn cluster --list-node-labels`. Here "exclusive=true" means only the applications running in the queue associated with the label can use the node. Therefore, if resources are free in that node, these cannot be used by applications in other queues. Once label is created it is associated with node-managers using `yarn rmadmin -replaceLabelsOnNode "<node-address>=label2"`. Node labels and associated nodes can be checked in YARN ResourceManager web interface (port 8088) under node labels tab.

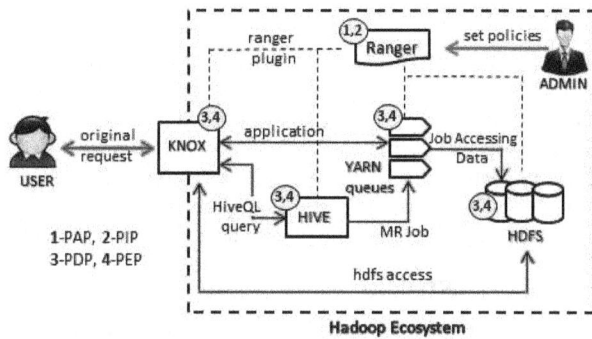

Figure 14: Hadoop Ecosystem Authorization Architecture

After labels are assigned to nodes, queues should be associated with node labels via YARN Queue Manager in Ambari (shown in Figure 13). Here with root as parent queue, and newQueue and default as children, we have assigned node-label label2 to default queue. The capacity specifies percentage of node resources (associated with label) that can be accessed by applications in default queue. As shown in Figure 13, applications in default queue can access all resources of the node which has label label2. YARN capacity scheduler configuration will automatically set `"yarn.scheduler.capacity.root.default.accessible-node-labels=label2"` property. With this configuration, it follows that raj_ops which was previously allowed to submit application in default queue, will run all its applications on node with label label2.

3 MULTI-LAYER AUTHORIZATION ARCHITECTURE

In this section we present a unified authorization architecture in a Hadoop ecosystem. This multi-layer architecture outlines how the individual access control points demonstrated in previous section fit into ecosystem to offer 'Defense in Depth' approach to protect cluster resources. Figure 14 shows several layers of access control decision and enforcement points to authorized access to resources in services such as Apache Hive and HDFS. Apache Ranger provides a centralized Policy Administration and Policy Information Point (1-PAP, 2-PIP) whereas its plugins appended with individual services, periodically cache policies from policy server and provide Policy Decision and Enforcement Points (3-PDP, 4-PEP). The architecture portrays how several Apache projects work in a coherent manner to realize multi-layer authorization in a Hadoop ecosystem.

An authenticated user is first examined by the perimeter security layer offered by Apache Knox, which checks if the user is allowed to access services inside the ecosystem. This external user interacts with all ecosystem services via single access point REST API provided by Apache Knox. When a user issues a request, it is intercepted by Apache Ranger plugin attached to Apache Knox, which checks its policies to decide and enforce access to services inside the ecosystem. If a user wants to submit an application or to check application status, the user should be allowed to access YARN ResourceManager through Apache Knox. If a user issued HiveQL using a client, the user should be allowed access to Apache Hive (HiveServer2) when trying to access HDFS files directly, access to

WebHDFS service (REST access to HDFS) should be allowed. This is the first layer which a user must pass through, much before access to data is checked, which helps to restrict users at an early stage.

Once admitted through perimeter layer, if user requires data access at HDFS layer, permissions for files and directories are checked using HDFS Ranger plugin. If a user issues HiveQL command, two layers of data services are checked: one at Apache Hive level and other for the corresponding data files at HDFS level. Both can be done using Apache Ranger plugin attached with each of these services. If a user is submitting a YARN application, the user should be authorized to access YARN queues to submit the application. This is done after YARN ResourceManager access is allowed through Apache Knox. YARN queue policies are enforced either through YARN capacity scheduler configuration or through Ranger plugin. This will prevent unknown users from submitting jobs in the cluster. User's access to YARN queues is also required when HiveQL command is issued, since the command results in a MapReduce or Tez job, which is also submitted to YARN queues. Since these jobs will access data in HDFS, owners of the jobs should have permissions on HDFS files also. Further, data masking or policy conditions can be applied at individual services to get fine-grained access control.

Based on the architecture, it can be understood that several authorization check points come into play to protect unauthorized access to cluster resources. We have not discussed cross-service access between Hadoop core daemons since this does not involve the user directly, and is mainly enforced using core Hadoop service ACLs and not through Ranger plugin. Moreover these daemon processes always run in background and their communication is essential for the proper functioning of Hadoop ecosystem.

4 USE CASE

In this section we present real world use cases to demonstrate the application and configuration of multiple access control mechanisms offered in a Hadoop ecosystem. We assume users are authenticated by some external mechanism and data ingestion is already done.

Suppose an Internet of Things (IoT) provider gathers data from devices assembled in smart homes. The data generated from smart devices is continuously stored in Hadoop Data Lake, which is analysed by the provider to offer better customer experience. As there are multiple IoT providers using the same Hadoop lake for storing and processing their data, security and privacy requirements are extremely critical. Let us say that the provider has two different functional users Alice and Bob, Alice belonging to sales and Bob to data-analyst group. Both users access data in the same Hadoop cluster with different operational and data permissions. Alice can only access data using Apache Hive ecosystem service via beeline client, with no access directly to HDFS data whereas Bob, as a data-analyst, can run YARN applications inside the cluster and may also require access to HDFS data directly. This service level security requirement is achieved by creating Knox policy using Ranger, which will allow Alice to access Hive service from outside the cluster. Another policy will allow Bob to access WebHDFS service and YARN ResourceManager via Knox gateway as discussed in Subsection 2.1.

Based on Hadoop cluster resources and service level agreement, cluster administrator is required to assign set of resources to users from IoT enterprise. The administrator has to ensure that only authorized users are allowed to submit YARN applications and access data. To accomplish this, cluster administrator creates a queue-IoT with a set of resources and allows both Alice and Bob to submit application in queue-IoT using Apache Ranger. Further, node labels (nLabel1, nLabel2, nLabel3) are assigned to three worker nodes and queue-IoT is associated with these three labels using YARN Queue manager in Ambari. Now, whenever Alice issues a HiveQL command or Bob runs a YARN application inside the cluster, it will only pass through queue-IoT and will run on three nodes with set labels. This configuration will also ensure that only Alice and Bob are allowed to submit jobs from IoT enterprise and they are both assigned a set of resources using capacity scheduler configuration and node labels. Further no user is allowed to kill or modify jobs submitted by Alice and Bob. Complete configuration to achieve this use case is discussed in Subsection 2.4.

Data generated from IoT devices is stored in HDFS files. User Bob is allowed to access all data files from IoT enterprise stored under data-IoT directory. Alice is only allowed select operation on address and temperature column on table table-thermostat-texas created from file file-thermostat-texas in directory data-IoT. Further, only zipcode part of the address should be visible to Alice. It is also required to give data access to Alice only when Alice belongs to Marketing project, since it is possible Alice might be shifted to other department in the organization. To allow Bob to have all permissions on data-IoT directory, either HDFS POSIX or ACLs can be used or Apache Ranger plugin can set policy to allow all operations on data-IoT directory. This will ensure that all applications run by Bob can access all files in data-IoT directory. For user Alice, Apache Hive policies are set to allow select operation on column address and temperature in table table-thermostat-texas. For displaying only zip-code field from address, data masking is done on the remaining part. Since the requirement denies direct access of user Alice at HDFS level, hive.server2.enable.doAs is set to false, which will only allow hive service user to access HDFS files and not Alice end user. Here two layers of data access are checked: for Hive service, access is checked for Alice and for HDFS, access is checked for Hive service user. Therefore policy for Hive service user should be also set in Apache Ranger. Alice's current project membership is required to allow access to table table-thermostat-texas. This is ensured by use of context enricher and condition evaluators. The enricher will use a text file with the current user and project mapping. Security administrator will create a policy including marketing as the policy condition. Whenever Alice will try to access table table-thermostat-texas, context enricher will add Alice's current project to the access request using the text file, which will be checked against policy condition by the evaluator to allow or deny access. Security administrator can also use tags to create policy. In this case, Apache Atlas will be used to create a tag tag-IoT and will be associated with columns address and temperature. A policy will be created on tag-IoT under Tag service in Ranger, which will enforce access to columns address and temperature. Subsection 2.2 and 2.3 discuss additional details about these configurations.

These use-case requirements clearly illustrate how a layered authorization framework (involving service, data and resource access) is applied and configured to restrict unauthorized resources access.

5 RELATED WORK

Several books, reports and papers have been published [8, 11, 12, 19, 21–23] to discuss security aspects of Hadoop ecosystem and Big Data. Hortonworks HDP (Hortonworks Data Platform) [14] uses Apache Ranger as authorization framework. Cloudera [7] CDH (Cloudera Distribution including Apache Hadoop) offers Apache Sentry [6] as central access control component. MapR Converged Data Platform [17] offers Hadoop with data placement control.

6 CONCLUSION

In this paper we discuss and demonstrate authorization capabilities provided by a representative Hadoop ecosystem deployment. The multi-layer authorization framework offered by Apache Hadoop and Apache Ranger covering services, data, cluster resources and application access is presented. This document can be read as a reference guide to understand access control capabilities and how they are achieved in Hadoop ecosystem using Apache Ranger. We have also discussed real world use-cases which exhibit the application of individual access control points in a coherent manner, including extensions enabled by context enrichers.

ACKNOWLEDGMENTS
This work is partially supported by NSF grants CNS-1111925, CNS-1423481, CNS-1538418, DoD ARL Grant W911NF-15-1-0518 and The Texas Sustainable Energy Research Institute at UTSA.

REFERENCES
[1] Apache Ambari. https://ambari.apache.org/.
[2] Apache Atlas. http://atlas.apache.org/.
[3] Apache Hadoop. http://hadoop.apache.org/.
[4] Apache Knox. https://knox.apache.org/.
[5] Apache Ranger. http://ranger.apache.org/.
[6] Apache Sentry. http://sentry.apache.org/.
[7] Cloudera. Cloudera Distribution Hadoop. https://www.cloudera.com/.
[8] Devaraj Das, Owen O'Malley, Sanjay Radia, and Kan Zhang. 2011. Adding Security to Apache Hadoop. Hortonworks, IBM (2011).
[9] Balaji Ganeshan and Alok Nath. 2015. Dynamic Policy Hooks in Ranger. https://cwiki.apache.org/confluence/display/RANGER/Dynamic+Policy+Hooks+in+Ranger+-+Configure+and+Use. (2015).
[10] John Gantz et al. 2012. Digital universe in 2020: Big data, bigger digital shadows, and biggest growth in the far east. IDC iView: IDC Analyze the future (2012).
[11] Maanak Gupta, Farhan Patwa, and Ravi Sandhu. 2017. Object-Tagged RBAC Model for the Hadoop Ecosystem. In Proc. of IFIP DBSec (To appear). Springer, 18 Pages.
[12] Maanak Gupta, Farhan Patwa, and Ravi Sandhu. 2017. POSTER: Access Control Model for the Hadoop Ecosystem. In Proc. of ACM SACMAT (To appear). ACM, 3 Pages.
[13] Maanak Gupta and Ravi Sandhu. 2016. The GURA_G Administrative Model for User and Group Attribute Assignment. In Proc. of NSS. Springer, 318–332.
[14] Hortonworks. Hortonworks Data Platform. https://hortonworks.com/.
[15] Robert Hryniewicz. 2016. Best Practices in HDFS Autorization with Apache Ranger. https://hortonworks.com/blog/best-practices-in-hdfs-authorization-with-apache-ranger/. (2016).
[16] Robert Hryniewicz. 2016. Best Practices in Hive Autorization with Apache Ranger. https://hortonworks.com/blog/best-practices-for-hive-authorization-using-apache-ranger-in-hdp-2-2/. (2016).
[17] MapR. Converged Data Platform. https://mapr.com/.
[18] Madhan Neethiraj. 2016. Geo-location based policies. https://cwiki.apache.org/confluence/display/RANGER/Geo-location+based+policies. (2016).
[19] Owen O'Malley, Kan Zhang, Sanjay Radia, Ram Marti, and Christopher Harrell. 2009. Hadoop Security Design. Yahoo, Inc., Tech. Rep (2009).
[20] Ravi S Sandhu, Edward J Coyne, Hal L Feinstein, and Charles E Youman. 1996. Role-based access control models. IEEE Computer 29, 2 (1996), 38–47.
[21] Ben Spivey and Joey Echeverria. 2015. Hadoop Security. Protecting your Platform. " O'Reilly Media, Inc.".
[22] Tom White. 2012. Hadoop: The Definitive Guide. " O'Reilly Media, Inc.".
[23] Chandhu Yalla et al. 2016. Big Data: Intel IT's Secure Hadoop Platform. (2016).

Provable Enforcement of HIPAA-Compliant Release of Medical Records Using the History Aware Programming Language

Thomas MacGahan
Accenture Federal Services
thomas.macgahan@gmail.com

Claiborne Johnson
University of Texas at San Antonio
imm589@my.utsa.edu

Armando Rodriguez
University of Texas at San Antonio
armando.rodriguez@utsa.edu

Jeffery von Ronne*
University of Texas at San Antonio
vonronne@acm.org

Jianwei Niu
University of Texas at San Antonio
jianwei.niu@utsa.edu

ABSTRACT

Dependence on reliable information systems to safeguard personally identifiable information implies a need for privacy policies which guide the release and management of such information, whose mismanaged disclosure can be damaging to both the subject and the organization that releases it. Enforcing such policies requires attention to detail and care, and thus any aid that a compiler can render may be of value. We present a demonstration of compiler enforcement of privacy policy by implementation of the History Aware Programming Language (HAPL) framework. This framework allows expression of arbitrary HAPL code for actors in an actor system to be used to back a web application. This code is then checked for compliance with privacy policies described in assume-guarantee form before being assembled into a functioning application. The framework is demonstrated by implementing five use cases based on scenarios described in the Health Insurance Portability and Accountability Act (HIPAA), and the performance of the framework is tested.

CCS CONCEPTS

•Social and professional topics → Privacy policies; •Software and its engineering → *Domain specific languages;* •Applied computing → *Health care information systems;*

KEYWORDS

privacy policy; domain specific language; static analysis; scala; web application

ACM Reference format:
Thomas MacGahan, Claiborne Johnson, Armando Rodriguez, Jeffery von Ronne, and Jianwei Niu. 2017. Provable Enforcement of HIPAA-Compliant Release of Medical Records Using the History Aware Programming Language. In *Proceedings of SACMAT'17, June 21–23, 2017, Indianapolis, IN, USA, , 8 pages.*
DOI: http://dx.doi.org/10.1145/3078861.3084176

*Now at Google, Inc.

1 INTRODUCTION

Society is increasingly dependent on computer information systems for management of private data. Examples of such applications include medical, banking, and identification systems. Organizations are required to keep and share such information in a manner that conforms to specific privacy policies as mandated by custom, sound business practice, good citizenship, contract, and often by law. Privacy policies such as those decsribed in the Health Insurance Portability and Accountability Act (HIPAA) [5], the Gramm-Leach-Bliley Act (GLBA) [2], and the Children's Online Privacy Protection Act (COPPA) [1], all carry the force of law. In addition to legal regulations, organizations typically have their own business rules that add further privacy requirements. It is therefore desirable, where possible, to enforce compliance with such privacy policies.

We implement the HAPL design [10] as a full framework with a working prototype of an Electronic Medical Record System (EMRS) that can be statically checked against formal privacy policy specifications for HIPAA. We briefly descibe how policy specifications are prepared for use in the framework that take the form of formal assume-guarantee specifications [8].

The design of HAPL in our previous work [10] allows the specification of arbitrary programs and which supports a novel construct, the *ltlquery* for inspecting and asserting over the history of messages received by individual actors in these programs. The language also supports definition of actors and user interface elements for interacting with these actors. As designed, HAPL also contains constructs for defining roles (*inrole*). Static analysis techniques are then applied to this language to verify that the implementation matches assume-guarantee specifications. In this paper, we implement the language as part of a framework that can produce functioning web applications.

Any program that passes this static analysis phase will then be compiled into a functioning web application backed by an Akka actor system to service core functionality and by LiftWeb[1] to run a user interface and to mediate requests between the application layer and the backing actor system. Five use cases (see section 5) are implemented in the language which constitute a representative subset of HIPAA requirements. These use cases pass static analysis and are composed into a single functioning prototype EMRS web application.

Organization. Section 2 introduces foundational concepts and technologies that will be referred to in this paper. We describe the

[1]Liftweb: https://www.liftweb.net/

architecture of the HAPL framework in section 3. We outline the different components of the framework as implemented in section 4, and detail aspects of framework implementation in section 5. In section 6, we give examples of code and systems that make use of the HAPL framework, and go into some depth in discussion of some of our use cases. We conclude with section 7.

2 FOUNDATIONS

The technology of HAPL is strongly rooted in Scala and related technologies. Actors are essential to our assume-guarantee based approach to specification, and we make use of Scala's Akka library to generate and manipulate these actors. Further, LiftWeb is an actor-based web framework which we use to allow interaction with systems generated in HAPL. Specification is handled through assume-guarantee decomposition techniques. All of these together are required for our approach to the design and implementation of the HAPL language and its attendant framework.

Scala / LiftWeb. LiftWeb is an actor-oriented framework written in Scala for developing web applications. Comet actors supply dynamic behavior for statically served templates, which communicate with actors by passing messages. The LiftWeb library contains many functions for producing correct and compatible JavaScript, taking advantage of Scala's ability to present library functions in the style of an internal DSL. LiftWeb was selected because of HAPL's actor-based approach, and operates by way of forwarding events to programmer-defined handler. The programmer may then respond to those events in a variety of ways, including, if desired, updates to be pushed to the client. These updates may include HTML rewriting, and in this way it is possible to update a client's view of the webpage in response to events that occur on the server.

Actors. In the actor paradigm, computation is done through creation of and communication between actors. Actors are constrained to synchronous control only of private data, and to communicate with other actors only by sending asynchronous messages. Actor behavior must only be triggered in response to messages. An actor, while executing in response to a message, may only modify local data, create other actors, and send messages to other actors [4, 10]. For our specific purposes, we make use of the Akka library in Scala, which provides a convenient foundation for specification of their behavior. We use Akka to track actors that are created by our actor assembler, and to handle message passing between actors.

Assume-guarantee Decomposition. The HAPL EMRS is decomposed into a set of actor components described in first-order linear temporal logic (FOTL), each of which has distinct responsibilities that it upholds by communicating with the other actors. In short, the App actor provides an interface into the EMRS to human principals, the Archive actor manages stored records and fields requests for those records, and the Authorizer actor makes policy decisions on how the Archive should manage records when requested. Additionally, the Archive and Authorizer actors are decomposed from a higher-level component called the Backend which models their combined behavior [6].

In general, assume-guarantee specifications formally specify the behavior of an open system. The way a system interacts with its environment can be specified through assumptions about the

behavior of its environment and guarantees on the behavior the system can/will exhibit if the assumptions on its environment hold true. Safety assumptions and safety guarantees describe that bad things cannot happen, by stating conditions that must hold on the information the system receives from its environment and the information the system sends to its environment, respectively. Liveness guarantees describe that good things must eventually happen, by stating conditions that force the system to eventually communicate information to its environment. Assume-guarantee specifications are well-suited for formally specifying the behavior of an actor system by describing under what conditions actors can send or receive certain types of messages [8][7].

3 ARCHITECTURE

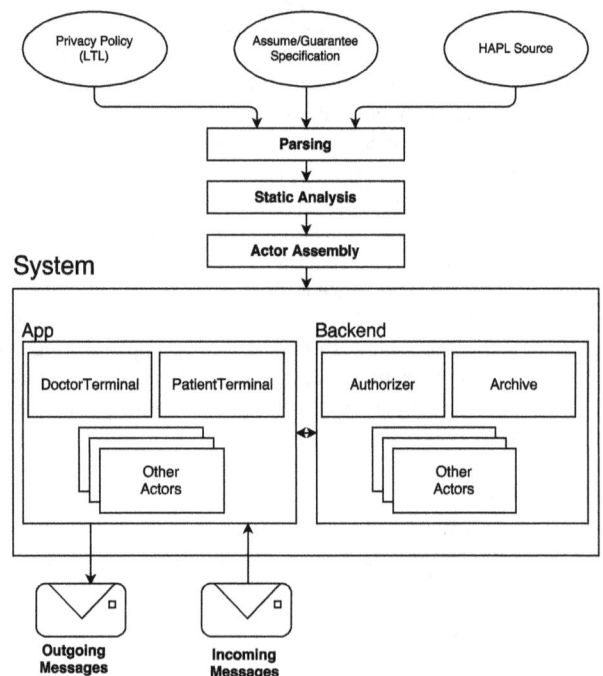

Figure 1: High-level architecture of HAPL

Figure 1 shows the high-level architecture of the HAPL framework. Broadly, a manually generated privacy policy expressed in linear temporal logic (LTL), an assume-guarantee specification, and HAPL source describing a program are inputs of the parsing and static analysis components of the framework [3, 6]. Here, the source is to be parsed, type-checked, and statically analyzed for compliance with the privacy policy and assume-guarantee specification.

This compliance is guaranteed by a static analysis phase requiring that the HAPL implementation honors the specification. Failing provability of compliance, the static analysis phase will return with errors explaining the failure.

The resulting vetted abstract syntax tree (AST) is then used to construct a runtime system in the form of a web application, described by its HAPL source. This AST is then fed to an Actor

Assembler, which produces the System. This System tracks instantiated actors through Akka. It also has an App component which is to respond to incoming messages and to reply with outgoing messages, as handled by the application's PageActor and PageInterpreter modules (see section 5). For the purposes of the present work, this App component serves the role of user interface, while incoming and outgoing messages represent user interactions mediated by the PageInterpreter service. Further, there is a Backend component, which handles bootstrapping of the EMRS as well as directory services, storage and authorization of records and their release.

3.1 Design Goals

The framework is designed with several use cases in mind and must fulfill certain requirements. Namely, the framework is required to:

Produce an actor system. The framework, given valid source, must result in an actor system that is capable of dynamically executing behavior specified by the HAPL system at runtime in response to messages. This must include the ability to instantiate new actors, send messages, and modify local actor state. Further, any system events that are of concern to the HAPL program must be properly captured and forwarded to the actor system as messages that can be responded to with behavior defined in HAPL.

Support history queries. The framework language must support methods for statically verifying compliance with assume-guarantee specifications. Since these assume-guarantees pre-suppose assertions on message histories, it is useful to expose the message history in the form of history queries. These history queries, if they are part of the language, can then be used in the static analysis phase to verify certain aspects of the assume-guarantee specification.

Support user interaction. The framework must support user interaction. In our design, this interaction takes place as part of a web application. The framework must therefore support the production of a web application that is specified by HAPL source. The framework must also ensure that the application is able to send and receive messages to and from the generated actor system. This must be done in such a way as to make possible meaningful user interaction with that actor system. Hence, it is necessary to ensure that the language is able to express user interface concerns.

Require provable compliance. The framework must ensure that a useful subset of programs are approved by a static analysis component. However, since the privacy policy we aim to enforce, HIPAA, is law, this is contingent on the constraint that no non-compliant programs are approved.

3.2 Design

The main components of the framework are the parser, the static analyser, the actor assembler, and the page interpreter. HAPL sources are fed into the parser, and if parsing passes then the resulting AST is given to the static analyser which decides acceptance of the program. This AST is used to assemble Akka actors at boot-time for the web application. The sections of the AST that describe the behavior of pages in the web application are kept in memory and

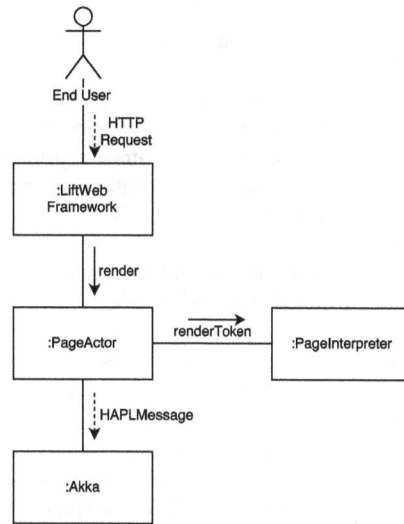

Figure 2: Map of Communications Between Runtime Entities

dynamically interpreted when requests for pages are received by the LiftWeb framework.

As can be seen in figure 2, these requests may result in control messages which need to be forwarded to the Akka actor system. At this stage, communications between actors are decided by the behaviors defined in HAPL sources. This behavior may result in updates that must be pushed to the user, and in this case, messages will be forwarded back to the page interpreter, which then will forward messages to the LiftWeb framework. The LiftWeb framework in turn has facilities for pushing updates to the end user.

4 FRAMEWORK

To implement this architecture, we have built a framework which we refer to collectively as HAPL. This framework contains the tools required to parse programs written in the HAPL language itself, statically analyse them for compliance, and assemble a web application for end-user interaction from these sources where compliance with our specification of HIPAA can be proven.

The HAPL framework supports a general purpose, actor-based programming language that incorporates history queries. HAPL is split into a user-interface specification, an actor behavior specification, a static analysis phase, an actor assembly phase, and a runtime ui interpretation system. In general, our framework is aimed at the implementation of five specific use cases.

4.1 Language and Parsing

The framework's language, loosely modeled on Scala syntax, allows for defining actors and the principals they represent, as well as in what role those actors represent these principals.

HAPL is an imperative language founded on the actor paradigm, which makes use of message passing as specified by our assume-guarantees. HAPL actors are considered to be acting in a particular role for a particular principal at the time they receive a message, and when they send a message [4, 10]. In our implementation, we require that every actor represent a specific principal in a particular role.

This includes a variety of structures for expressing computation, but a subset was implemented due to scope constraints. These structures include: if-statements, assignments, print statements, identifiers in complex expressions, declaration with initialization, tuple definitions, tuple lookups, conses with tails and heads, a *new* command, actor definitions and LTL history queries as shown in figure 10 and 11. Example actor definitions can be seen in section 6. Parsing is accomplished by use of the Scala parser combinators library[2].

We further implement a special control structure, *ltlquery*, which behaves like an if statement. The first block will execute if the LTL expression is true, the second branch otherwise. A representation of the history of messages that an actor has received is kept at each actor which is used to decide the truth of an *ltlquery* condition. This allows us to set up guards to verify that certain messages have been received prior to, for example, releasing PHI.

4.2 Static Analysis

In order to statically verify the behavior of our prototype as specified by their HAPL source code, we first design and detail specifications in section 2 for the EMRS that is implemented. The EMRS is decomposed into a set of communicating actors (figure 2) whose behavior is specified as a set of FOTL formulas in assume-guarantee form.

Once we have our EMRS specifications in place, we can verify that the system behaves correctly, and that it is HIPAA-compliant. We accomplish this by encoding our assume-guarantee specifications in our static analysis phase [9].

We use static analysis to bind HAPL code to the constraints detailed in our assume-guarantee specifications. By making statements about type-correctness in assignment, message parameters, message handlers, and send message *inroles*, as well as verifying that certain properties hold in the abstract syntax tree, such as verification that a specific *ltlquery* guards the release of records in the archive, we are able to verify compliance with certain assume-guarantee specifications. The static analysis phase therefore reports non-compliance and fails compilation so that an actor system is not generated where it cannot be proved that the code matches appropriate assume-guarantee specifications[7, 9].

4.3 Actor Assembly

In order to construct a functioning actor system, it is necessary to decide the behavior of each actor in accordance with the parsed program that describes it. In general, all dynamic actor behavior is triggered in response to a message. We can therefore view actors having a state, a routine for initializing that state implied by declarations with initialization, and a map of message names to the executable actions associated with those names. It is thus necessary to determine what variables are in scope for the actor, to produce an executable routine that correctly initializes that actor's state in the order expressed in the language, and then to produce some way of instructing the runtime to execute the action described in HAPL

---

[2]http://www.scala-lang.org/files/archive/api/2.11.4/scala-parser-combinators

code while making the state available for read and write during the execution of that action.

This process takes place at compile time, receiving the abstract syntax tree that results from parsing and producing a set of factories associated with each actor's name as described in its source. These factories will produce an actor with behavior described by its source upon invocation. Factories may be invoked as the result of actions that are executed at runtime. This method allows the servicing of *new* commands.

To bootstrap the actor system, the actor assembler invokes the factory corresponding to the name "Main," runs its initialization routine, and sends it the *execute* system signal (see section 4.5). At this point, the assembled system is now a functioning runtime.

To assemble the factories, a list of all actor definitions in the form of AST nodes is generated. A list of messages is then extracted from each actor definition node, and sent to a subsystem of the actor assembler that produces commands, where a command is here defined as a Scala function value that takes an actor's state and returns nothing, but which may have side effects. Each command is itself composed of commands, and in this way we can recursively descend through the AST representation of a message handler. Commands may include sends, state updates, foreach loops, or any of the various structures permitted by the grammar [9]. In general, wherever a state is read or written, this is accomplished by closing over the name of the identifier to be read or written, and that name is resolved to a value when the command is supplied with the appropriate state at execution time.

This method of using function values closed over the names of identifiers is useful for prototyping, although it comes with a performance penalty (see section 7).

4.4 Page Interpreter

The user-facing components are layered on top of LiftWeb, whose bootstrap sequence been modified to include an interpretation process. This interpretation process results in an AST which is stored in memory on the server until it becomes necessary to service a request.

A special Scala class, PageInterpreter, interprets the Scala native AST data structure on page request. With some pre-processing to separate out the pages, the PageInterpreter is notified of a page request, looks up the appropriate subtree of the AST corresponding to that request, and interprets that subtree to dynamically construct the page HTML in the process.

This HTML, once generated, is pushed to the client, which renders as can be seen in figure 3. It contains JavaScript that will send notifications to the LiftWeb framework whenever certain events are triggered. These events can be caught, and in response to form submission events in particular, the HAPL framework can be notified that user input has been entered. Handling these notifications is the responsibility of the PageActor described in section 5.

4.5 System Bindings

While implementing the actor assembler and attempting to integrate it with the page interpretation layer, it became clear that capturing certain system events and allowing the programmer to define behavior in response to those events was desirable. In order

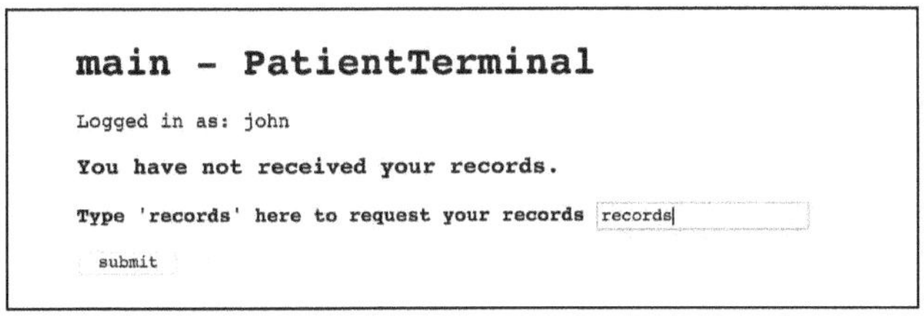

```
main – PatientTerminal

Logged in as: john

You have not received your records.

Type 'records' here to request your records  [records]

    submit
```

Figure 3: Patient interface

to honor the requirement that all actor behavior should be defined as actions in response to messages, we implemented special system-generated messages, which we call system signals, that are sent to specific actors when certain events are detected by the HAPL framework. Actors can choose to define behavior to capture those signals and react to them, or simply ignore them.

While there are other signals in the framework, one example is *execute*. This signal was added because of a need that became apparent in early testing of the actor assembler. We found that some bootstrapping mechanism, analogous to a main function or method as in C or Java, was necessary. The *execute* system signal satisfies this need by providing a place that is guaranteed to be called exactly once by the system when static analysis completes.

Another example of a system signal is *login*, which is sent to the Main actor whenever a new user logs in, which is useful for directory services. It could also be useful for preparing other forms of state required for each user that may not necessarily be appropriate in actors that are more tightly coupled to that user.

5 IMPLEMENTATION

To demonstrate the language and evaluate our framework, we built a prototype EMRS [9] with simple implementations of five use cases specified to comply with HIPAA. These are intended to be a representative subset of the release scenarios described in HIPAA. In particular, this includes cases involving releases of personal information that are required, releases that are permitted without authorization, and releases that are permitted only with authorization.

While it is possible to fulfill the privacy requirements of HIPAA by rejecting all release requests except for those made by the patient for their own records[3] [5], we designed the following five use cases in order to demonstrate a responsive non-trivial EMRS with respect to the release of personal health information (PHI) under HIPAA.

1. **Record contains no PHI**: If a message contains no PHI, then that information may be released without authorization.
2. **Patient requests own PHI**: HIPAA has a liveness requirement that any patient request for their own PHI records must eventually be fulfilled. Thus any request by a patient role for their own records must be honored by the EMRS.

3. **Originating doctor requests patient's psychotherapy note PHI**: A doctor who is acting as a physician for a patient may obtain that patient's psychotherapy notes without the consent of any principal if that physician is also the author of that PHI.
4. **Doctor requests patient's non-psychotherapy PHI**: A doctor who is acting as the physician for a patient may obtain that patient's PHI without any principal's consent, so the prototype will honor requests by a doctor for patient data. See section 6.
5. **Third party requests patient PHI**: Third parties may request patient PHI for marketing purposes. These requests may be honored if it is determined that the patient that is the subject of this PHI has authorized release of it for this purpose. See section 6.

As part of the framework, HAPL source is compiled into a runtime that is run by the LiftWeb framework to generate a web-based user interface. This interface interacts with actors via page definitions controlling the specific actors handling the application logic of a user interface. An example of the interface for a physician is shown in figure 5. In this example interface, the physician is able to set PHI for a patient (including psychotherapy note PHI) or retrieve a patient's records. Such a page can be generated from source like that found in figure 6.

Figure 6 describes an early form of the main page for presenting an interface to a patient in the system. The page header, identifiable from the *page* keyword, is declared to belong to Patient, is identified as the main page for that role, and describes an underlying actor called PatientTerminal.

In this example, the function of the page as described by its source is rather simple. Specifically, it will, when the PatientTerminal actor's local variable 'recordsReceived' evaluates to false, show a form with exactly one field that will be annotated with the phrase "Type 'records' to get your records". This field will be populated with the value of the variable 'request', and will store the contents of that field into the field 'result' when submit is pressed. The described actor, 'PatientTerminal' will then be sent an update message, notifying it that its local variables have been updated by the page, and it can then take action in an 'update' message block. Use of 'main' here as the page identifier denotes that this page definition is the main page for this role, and so is the page served to anyone authenticated to this role when no other page is specifically requested.

In any case, updates to the described actor's state may result in messages sent from this block which might, for example, request the patient's records from the Archive. In this way, we can see how a user request can be translated into a request to the Archive.

In the implementation of requests to the Archive, it is clearly necessary to have different principals and the actors that represent them occasionally communicate with each other. To facilitate this, we have implemented language elements (*send* and actor methods) that allow the definition, sending, and receipt of messages. Further, via *ltlquery* keywords, it is also possible to inspect, assert on, and reason about the history of messages seen by a specific actor.

We can see a representative summary of the interactions between actors defined in HAPL source, the HAPL framework, and the

---

[3]Under HIPAA, a covered entity is also required to notify the Secretary of HHS under some circumstances, but we make a concession for the simplicity of the prototype and ignore this obligation.

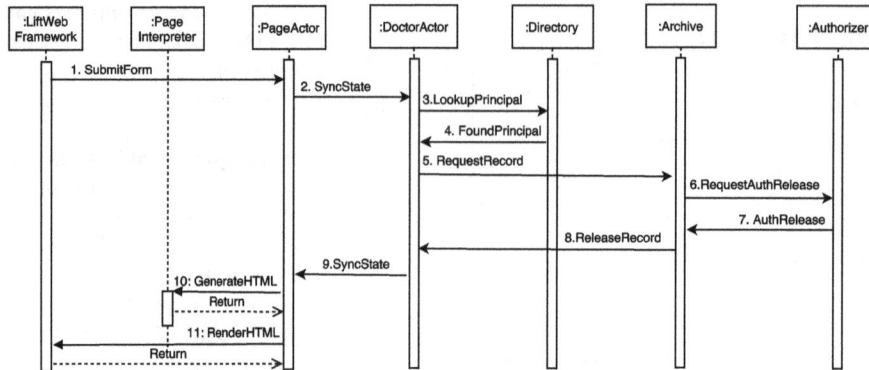

Figure 4: Lifecycle of a doctor requesting a patient's records

Figure 5: Physician interface

```
page Patient main describes PatientTerminal {
  show( "Logged in as: " + patient )
  if( !recordsReceived ) {
    form( "You have not received your records." ) {
      field( request, "Type 'records' to get your records",
      request )
  }}
  if( !authed ) {
    form( "You have not authorized the release of your records." )
      {
      field( request, "Type 'authorize' to authorize records
      release", request )
  }}
  show( status )
}
```

Figure 6: Page definition source

LiftWeb framework in figure 4. There, we can see that a user request begins with a message sent by LiftWeb to the HAPL framework, to be handled by PageActor. PageActor will then take the updated variables from the page, notify the actor described by the current page which in this case is DoctorActor. DoctorActor will then, by virtue of internal logic defined in its HAPL source, look up the appropriate principal and request their records from the Archive. This request will be validated by the Authorizer, and in the case that it is approved will result in the DoctorActor sending a notification back to the PageInterpreter, which in turn will generate HTML for the web application. Note that although the Authorizer may approve the doctor's request, in the event that the doctor is the

the originator of the record, permission from no principal will be required.

6 EMRS STRUCTURE AND FUNCTION

We now present a view of the function of the prototype EMRS in the context of how HAPL was used in its construction. There are five use cases, but we will focus here mainly on the implementation of the Backend. In particular, we will examine the Advertiser and the Authorizer the most detail.

6.1 Backend Overview

HAPL programs are in general bootstrapped from a main actor, given the name 'Main'. There, certain boot-strapping activities can be taken care of, such as ensuring that specific actors are instantiated and always available. Further, this Main actor is sent signals whenever certain system events are trapped. By this means, we are able to set up a directory and ensure that there is exactly one such directory. We can also, through the use of system signals, guarantee that the directory is notified whenever someone authenticates, and so serve its purpose of tracking all users that log in to the system, and which actors are associated with those users.

Also important to this process is that the Archive has a reference to the Authorizer as soon as it is instantiated. Thus it is necessary for the Main actor to create the Authorizer and Archive in sequence, and to retain and supply a reference to the Authorizer for the Archive's use. More generally, the Main actor can ensure that any Backend actors that need to be in communication with each other are able to do so.

Directory. The directory is necessary for verification purposes we test equality of principal-type values. While it is legal to hold a reference to a principal, there is no mechanism for creating one. Rather, principals are supplied to the actors described by the main pages for each role. It is the responsibility of that actor to make the rest of the system aware of the principal-type value it holds. Since it is necessary for some principals such as doctors to be aware of principals it does not know about a priori, such as patients, there needs to be some central repository of stored principal values.

The directory is this repository. It works by receiving notifications of login events forwarded to it by the main actor, and it stores each principal with its username in a list of username / principal-value tuples. When a request is made to the Directory requesting the principal value for a particular username, which is assumed to be communicated out of band, it will return the principal value so that records that are stored by principal may be retrieved.

This Directory service was not included in our initial design, but the expressivity of the HAPL language allowed us to solve this problem of principal binding within the language.

User-serving actors. Actor definitions have a signature with a *representing* keyword and a signature describing what types of value are required to create an instance of that definition. Within the actor, state variables may be declared, initializations defined, and message responses may be described.

The keyword *representing* denotes the principal value the actor is acting on behalf of. This has a number of practical effects including requiring the actor declaration to contain that principal value, and ensuring that the variable is in scope in the actor. Further, the keyword *inrole* is a type hint that requires both that some principal be described in the actor's signature, and that the principal so described is in the role supplied to the *inrole* as an argument. While all actors are required to be in some role, this is particularly important and intuitive for those actors that serve users directly, such as the PatientTerminal, the PhysicianTerminal and the Advertiser.

6.2 Advertiser

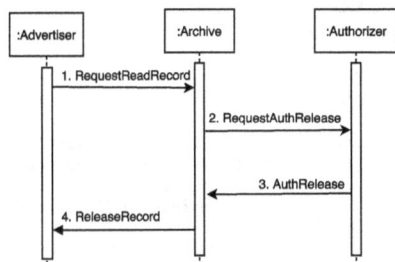

Figure 7: Advertiser requests patient records

In the AdvertisingHandler definition in figure 10, we can see these keywords at play as well. There, we see that AdvertisingHandler must represent a principal (advertiser) in the role of Marketing.

AdvertisingHandler is an example of a user-serving actor. It is a simple actor backing the Advertiser interface page, shown in figure 8 and defined in figure 9. This page definition will show a form with a single field, populated with the value of the request variable defined in the AdvertisingHandler definition in figure 9.

As we can see in figure 7, this request, once submitted, may be replied to by the Archive if the Authorizer (see section 6.3) is able to verify that permission for the release of those records is granted. If records are received, then the status will be updated, and this will result in a push that will ultimately update the user of the advertiser page.

6.3 Authorizer

The Authorizer, as its name suggests, is responsible for deciding whether or not to authorize the release of certain records. This

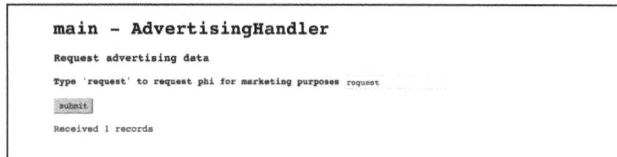

Figure 8: Advertiser interface

```
page Advertiser main describes AdvertisingHandler{
      form("Request advertising data") {
              field(request, "Type 'request' to request phi for
      marketing purposes", request)
      }
      show(status)
}
```

Figure 9: Advertiser Page Definition

```
actor AdvertisingHandler [ advertiser ; inrole( advertiser,
    Marketing ) ](advertiser: Principal) representing advertiser
    {
        var records: List[String] = list() ; var sentOnce: Bool =
    false
        var status: String = "" ; var received: Int = 0
        var request: String = "" ; var archive: Archive
        on notifyServices[](arch: Archive, dir: Directory, auth:
    Authorizer) {
                archive = arch
        }
        on update[]() {
                print( "vars updated!" )
                if( !sentOnce && request == "request" ) {
                        send<archive>(requestReadRecord(this,
    advertiser, 1))
                        send<archive>(requestReadRecord(this,
    advertiser, 2))
                        send<archive>(requestReadRecord(this,
    advertiser, 3))
                        send<archive>(requestReadRecord(this,
    advertiser, 4))
                        sentOnce = true
                        status = "Request sent"
        }}
        on releaseRecord[]( subject: Principal, content: String )
    {
                print( "Receveied a record: " + content )
                received = received + 1
                status = ("Received " + received) + " records"
                records = content :: records
                updateUI()
}}
```

Figure 10: Advertiser Definition

is accomplished by relying on several *ltlqueries*. Inuitively, the Authorizer definition seen in figure 11 requires that any release request must be preceded by a grant of permission to release those records. Other ways that the data could be released are that the requestor must either be the originator of the data, or if the data is not PHI. If these paths fail, then the Authorizer will locate the subject and ask that subject to decide whether or not to authorize the request for their PHI.

In figure 11 we see the *inrole* statement requiring that the principal system be in the role of HealthCareProvider. This principal is also the first argument in the actor's signature, and is the principal that the Authorizer will be representing. Through type-checking, we can guarantee that the principal represented by the actor is present at creation time, and will be in the role of HealthCare-Provider.

7 CONCLUSION

In this paper we have presented a framework which in conjunction with assume-guarantee decomposition [7] can implement verifiable information systems. We have developed the design of HAPL into a full framework and created an EMRS prototype in an actor component architecture which when assume-guarantee specifications are appropriately developed, allow it to statically verify and enforce the HIPAA privacy policy. Though this is a proof of concept, we believe that this approach to privacy policy enforcement shows promise.

While performance evaluations of HAPL code executing generally showed an order of magnitude slowdown over native Scala, we believe this to be largely due to executing closures within actors, instead of generating native or java bytecode. We therefore

expect that the most significant performance gains would be made by revising the generated runtime.

Our prototype EMRS currently supports a limited number of use cases designed to be representative of several key points in HIPAA, but a full system would need to be further developed. Another use case that would be desirable to support includes releasing records to a delegate, such that an individual who has been granted delegation privileges for a subject should be treated the same as the subject. Additionally, a full system should provide a path for a subject to revoke authorization, and an appropriate use case would check that a previously authorized record is not released after the authorization is revoked. There also exist many additional permitted release cases an EMRS can implement, such that the EMRS can release records in these cases without requiring authorization from the subject.

In its current form, the static analysis is limited in two ways that reduce its general applicability: first, it requires a perfect match between the assume-guarantee specification and the formulas in the query conditional, and second, it is hardcoded to use HIPAA roles and messages. Ideally, these issues would be addressed by implementing the more generalized approach described in our other published works [7].

ACKNOWLEDGEMENT

The authors are supported in part by NSF Award CNS-0964710, and by the NSA Grant on Science of Security.

REFERENCES
[1] 1999. Federal Trade Commission, How to comply with the children's online privacy protection rule. (1999). DOI:https://doi.org/bcp/conline/pubs/buspubs/coppa.htm Public Law.
[2] 1999. Senate Banking Committee, Gramm-Leach-Bliley Act. (1999). Public Law 106-102.
[3] Omar Chowdhury, Andreas Gampe, Jianwei Niu, Jeffery von Ronne, Jared Bennatt, Anupam Datta, Limin Jia, and William H Winsborough. 2013. Privacy promises that can be kept: A policy analysis method with application to the HIPAA privacy rule. In *Proceedings of the 18th ACM symposium on Access control models and technologies*. ACM, 3–14.
[4] Carl Hewitt. 1977. Viewing control structures as patterns of passing messages. *Artificial Intelligence* 8, 3 (1977), 323 – 364. DOI:https://doi.org/DOI:10.1016/0004-3702(77)90033-9
[5] HIPAA 1996. Health Insurance Portability and Accountability Act (HIPAA). (1996). (42 U.S.C. §300gg, 29 U.S.C §1181 et seq., and 42 U.S.C §1320d et seq.; 45 CFR Parts 144, 146, 160 162, and 164).
[6] Claiborne Johnson. 2016. *An Actor-Based Framework for Verifiable Privacy Policy Enforcement: Assume-Guarantee Specification of an Actor-Component Architecture.* Master's thesis. University of Texas at San Antonio.
[7] Claiborne Johnson, Thomas MacGahan, John Heaps, Kevin Baldor, Jeffery von Ronne, and Jianwei Niu. 2017. Verifiable Assume-Guarantee Privacy Specifications for Actor Component Architectures. *In proceedings of 22nd ACM Symposium on Access Control Models and Technologies* (2017), 12 pages.
[8] Bengt Jonsson and Tsay Yih-Kuen. 1996. Assumption/guarantee specifications in linear-time temporal logic. *Theoretical Computer Science* 167, 1-2 (1996), 47 – 72. DOI:https://doi.org/10.1016/0304-3975(96)00069-2
[9] Thomas MacGahan. 2016. *Towards Verifiable Privacy Policy Compliance of an Actor-Based Electronic Medical Records System: An extension to the HAPL language focused on exposing a user interface.* Master's thesis. University of Texas at San Antonio.
[10] Jeffery von Ronne. 2012. Leveraging actors for privacy compliance. In *Proceedings of the 2nd edition on Programming systems, languages and applications based on actors, agents, and decentralized control abstractions.* ACM, 133–136.

```
actor Authorizer [ auth ; inrole( sys, CareProvider ) ](dir:
    Directory, sys: Principal) representing sys {
  var requests: List[Tuple[Actor,Principal,Tuple[Int,Principal,
    Principal,String]]] = list()
  var requestor: Actor ; var requestingPrinc: Principal
  var originator: Principal ; var subjectPrinc: Principal
  var subjectRecord: Tuple[Int,Principal,Principal,String]
  var data: String
  on requestAuthRelease[]( sender: Actor, requestingPrinc:
    Principal, subject: Principal, record: Tuple[Int,Principal,
    Principal,String] ) {
    originator = record.get(3)
    data = record.get(4)
    if( (!isPHI( data )) || ((requestingPrinc == originator) || (
    requestingPrinc == subject)) ) {
    send<sender>(authRelease(this,sys,record))
    } else {
    ltlquery(once receive<from PatientTerminal as P[Patient]> (
    authOwnRecordFor) with owner, releaseTo where owner = subject
    and requestingPrinc = releaseTo ) {
      send<sender>(authRelease(this,sys,record))
    } else {
      requests = tuple(sender,subject,record)
      send<dir>(lookupPrinc(this,subject))
    }}}
  on foundPrinc[]( owner: Principal, ownersActor: Actor ) {
    foreach req in ( requests ) {
    if( ((req.get(3)).get(3)) == owner ) {
      requestingPrinc = req.get(2)
      subjectRecord = req.get(3)
      send<ownersActor>(decideAuth( this, requestingPrinc,
    subjectRecord ))
    }}}
  on authOwnRecordFor[]( owner: Principal, releaseTo: Principal )
    {
    foreach req in (requests) {
    subjectPrinc = (req.get(3)).get(3)
    if( subjectPrinc == owner ) {
      requestor = req.get(1)
      subjectRecord = req.get(3)
      ltlquery( once receive<from Patient as P[Patient]> (
    requestAuthorizeRelease) with subject where subject = owner )
    {
        send<requestor>(authRelease(this,sys,subjectRecord))
      } else {
        print("preemptive auth by: "+owner)
    }}}}}
```

Figure 11: Authorizer Definition

NTApps: A Network Traffic Analyzer of Android Applications

Rodney Rodriguez, Shaikh Mostafa, and Xiaoyin Wang
Department of Computer Science, University of Texas, San Antonio
One UTSA Circle, San Antonio, Texas, 78249
{rodney.rodriguez, shaikh.mostafa, xiaoyin.wang}@utsa.edu

ABSTRACT

Application-level network-traffic classification is important for many security-related tasks in network management. With the knowledge of which application certain network traffic belongs to, the network managers are able to allow/block certain applications in the network (whitelisting/blacklisting), or to locate known malicious applications in the network. To support application-level network-traffic classification, the network managers require a network-signature for each possible applications in the network, so that they can match these signatures with the network traffic at runtime to identify the ownership of the traffic. The traditional approaches to generating network-signatures for applications require either manual inspection of the application or accumulated annotated network traffic of the application. These approaches are not efficient enough nowadays, given the recent emergence of mobile application markets, where hundreds to thousands of mobile apps are added everyday. In this paper, we present a fully automatic tool called NTApps to generate network signatures for the mobile apps in android market. NTApps is based on string analysis, and generates network signatures by statically estimating the possible values of network API arguments.

ACM Reference format:
Rodney Rodriguez, Shaikh Mostafa, and Xiaoyin Wang. 2017. NTApps: A Network Traffic Analyzer of Android Applications. In *Proceedings of SACMAT'17, June 21–23, 2017, Indianapolis, IN, USA, , 8 pages.*
DOI: http://dx.doi.org/10.1145/3078861.3084175

1 INTRODUCTION

Application-level network-traffic classification is a preliminary requirement for many security-related network management tasks. For example, after classifying network traffic to applications, the network managers are able to enforce white list or black list of applications to block certain network-using applications. Furthermore, based on the classification results, the network managers are also able to check whether known malicious applications are used by some terminals in the network, and further locate which terminals are running the malicious application. Moreover, the network managers may also use the network-traffic classification tool to analyze logged network traffic history to discover suspicious human behaviors. The problem of automatically identifying the applications generating network traffic is called *application identification*. A *traffic classifier* is a tool for application identification. Payload-based classifiers inspect and compare the contents of payloads with a pre-existing signature database. Payload-based techniques have higher accuracy than other classifiers [33] and have been used as ground-truth in comparative studies of traffic classifiers [19].

To perform application-level network-traffic classification, the current practice in the industry is to generate a network signature for each application so that the network management system can match network traffic with these signatures to decide which applications the traffic may belong to. The signatures can be based on network-traffic features (throughput, intervals, etc.) [24] [13] or based on the content of the packets in the traffic [34] [15]. The traffic-feature-based signatures are often not precise enough, because different applications may share similar network-traffic features and network-traffic features may be affected by various environment factors (e.g., the network speed, number of terminals). By contrast, the content-based signatures are much more precise and robust, and therefore are especially suitable for security-related network-management tasks. Though initial payload techniques could not handle encrypted traffic, later work showed that encrypted traffic can be handled using distributions over payload contents [22]. Generating a signature database for payload-based classification is time consuming, requiring a large volume of network traces and manual effort for signature construction.

However, to generate content-based network signatures for all possible applications in the network is far more than trivial work. The existing approaches to generating these signatures fall into two categories. The first category of approaches[34] depend on manually inspecting the code or generated network traffic of an application, which is tedious and costly. The second category of approaches [21] [27] try to automatically extract network signatures of an application from a large amount of its network traffic, using data mining techniques. Although the extraction phase is automatic, the accumulation of network traffic usually takes non-trivial time.

Recently, the emergence of mobile application markets brings new challenges to the above existing approaches. Both Apple App Store[1] and Google Play Store[2] hold hundreds of thousand apps, and several hundred apps are added to the markets each day. The low efficiency of the existing approaches makes them difficult to keep up with the growing speed of the number of apps in the mobile application markets. Therefore, more efficient and automatic approaches are of eager requirement. In this paper, we propose a novel fully-automatic approach to generate network signatures for large numbers of android apps. The basic idea of our approach is

---

[1]http://store.apple.com/
[2]https://play.google.com/

to statically analyzes the byte code of an android app, and to use string analysis to estimate the possible contents of the packets sent to the network[3]. Our approach is based on the observation that, the content of the sent network packets are usually generated with one or more packet-generation APIs (which we refer as network APIs in the rest of this paper) by concatenating the arguments of these APIs. Therefore, we will be able to estimate the content of sent network packets, if we are able to estimate the possible values of the arguments of network APIs, and to modelling the network APIs on how they generate the contents of network packets. We use program analysis to avoid the time-consuming steps of data collection and manual signature construction. The modular nature of program analysis allows us to tune the precision of signatures generated by use of different abstractions. Though our framework is general, we follow the practice in the literature, by instantiating and evaluating our work on Android applications. In the literature, the word application is sometimes used for application layer protocols. In this paper, the words application and app always refer to smartphone applications.

In particular, our approach consists of the following five steps. First, for a given android app, we translate the Dalvik byte code in its apk file to Java byte code using our existing tool. Second, we locate in the Java byte code all the invocations of the network APIs that are in our pre-defined network API list[4]. Furthermore, for each network API invocation, we build an *API grammar summary* which presents how the API manipulates its arguments to generate a network packet. Third, we set each argument *arg* of these located network API invocations as the input of string analysis and perform string analysis on the byte code to generate a string-operation grammar that estimates the possible values of *arg*. Fourth, for each network API invocation, we combine its API grammar summary with the string-operation grammars of all of its arguments, to generate a *combined grammar* that is able to estimate the network-packet content generated by this network API invocation. Fifth, we extract network signatures as a set of constant-string sequences, from all the combined grammars of an app.

Our work builds upon insights about traffic generated by smartphones and the structure of smartphone applications. The first insight is that a significant portion of smartphone traffic is HTTP. A recent study found that between 92% to 97% of traffic generated by handheld devices is unencrypted HTTP [11]. In contrast, 72% to 81% of traffic generated by larger devices is HTTP. The same study also found that 82% of the HTTP traffic consumed by smartphones is related to non-browser applications, while only 10% of the HTTP traffic of larger devices is not browser related. Thus, traffic classification based on payloads is feasible, and will provide insight into the applications operating on a network.

Our second insight is that smartphone applications are downloaded and installed from a small number of application markets. Download and installation statistics available from application markets provide data about applications operating on a network. Studies have shown that the applications used on a network vary greatly depending on the time of day, week, and geographical location [49]. Collecting a representative sample of software run by users is possible and requires significantly less time and effort than collecting a representative sample of traffic generated by users.

The third insight is that smartphone applications use a small set of APIs to generate network traffic. A network signature for an application, or a class of applications is a summary of the data that is passed as an argument network APIs. Viewed this way, network signature generation can be reduced to a static analysis problem.

Static analysis has several advantages, which we describe briefly below and justify empirically in the paper. The main advantage is automation. Signatures need not be constructed manually or generated from network data, both of which are time consuming. The second advantage is flexibility in choosing the trade-off between precision and efficiency. The quality and efficiency of signature generation can be tuned by plugging abstractions of different precision into a static analyzer. Constant propagation with strings is extremely fast and produces coarse signatures. Inter-procedural analysis with context free grammars produces detailed signatures but is more expensive. From an implementation perspective, the lattice-based static analysis framework allows us to easily implement different signature generation techniques. Different types of signatures can be generated by changing a single component of the classification infrastructure, rather than changing the entire infrastructure.

The goal of our analysis is to summarise the data sent over a network. Like much existing work on smartphone applications, we focus on Android applications. Unlike existing static analyses for Android [8, 10], which focus on control rather than data-flow, we need to summarise the contents of payloads in an application. Designing such an analysis involves several challenges that have not been addressed by existing work.

The rest of this paper is organized as below. Section ?? presents the major challenge in our tool construction. Section 3 presents the overview and components of our tool architecture. Section 4 presents how our tool can be started and its input / output. Then we discuss some important issues in Section 5. Before we conclude in Section 7, we introduce a list of related research efforts in Section 6.

2 CHALLENGES OF TOOL CONSTRUCTION

The first significant challenge is the event-driven nature of Android applications. Program analysis is based on computing fixed points using control-flow or data-flow graphs. The flow of control in Android applications is largely determined by system callbacks, so there is no explicit flow of control to the entry point of methods. Event handlers must be considered by our analysis because the network is often accessed in response to user events. To discover which methods are called, the static analyzer must be aware of application lifecycles, listeners, and callbacks to event handlers.

The second challenge is to model APIs used to construct and manipulate payloads. Android applications extensively use `java.lang.string`, `java.lang.URL`, `java.lang.URLConnection`, `org.apache.http`, among other APIs to access and process data that is sent over the network. The analysis must precisely capture the semantics of such APIs.

The third challenge is inter-procedural analysis. Existing analyses of Android applications are either intra-procedural [8], or follow

---

[3]It should be noted that although the detailed design and implementation of our approach is for android apps, the basic idea of our approach may be applicable to other mobile apps or even PC applications
[4]Note that this list is generated manually only once and then used when generating network signatures for all android apps.

method calls in a limited way [10], or do not track data [12]. Data that is sent over the network is usually constructed and sanitized using several different methods in an application. In our experiments, we have found that inter-procedural analysis is sometimes required to even derive the hostnames an app interacts with. Up to 61% of applications in some data sets have been observed to use reflection [10]. Our analysis must also handle reflection to produce useful results. The problem we address is automatic generation of network signatures for Android applications.

3 TOOL STRUCTURE

As mentioned above, network signatures of mobile apps are very useful for packet inspection and network management. Figure 2 shows how our NTApps tool can be integrated with network management tools. Specifically, after NTApps generates signatures for various apps, the signatures as a tree or automaton can be fed into the packet classifier in the gateway of the network. NTApps is based on static analyzing the apk files of android apps. The overview of our approach is presented in Figure 1. From the figure, we can see that the input of our approach is an apk file and a pre-generated list of network API specifications. The output of our approach is a network signature, which is in the form a set of constant sequences which can be presented as a tree by combining common prefixes.

The NTApps tool includes five main components. The first component uses the our existing tool to convert the Dalvik code in the apk file to Java byte code. The second component is for network API handling. It locates all the network API invocations in the Java byte code, and will further build an API grammar summary for each the network API invocations according to the semantic of the API, based a list of pre-generated API grammar templates for network APIs in the android library. The third component uses the arguments of the located network API invocations as input, and apply string analysis to the Java byte code, so that this component is able to generate an context-free grammar for each argument. The fourth component of NTApps combines the API grammar summary *sum* of each network API invocation *inv*, with the context-free grammar generated by the string-analysis component for each argument of *inv*, and form a combined grammar of *inv*. The last component takes all the combined grammars as its input and extracts network signatures from the combined grammars. In the following sections, we do not introduce the first component because it is not the contribution of this papers.

3.1 Handling Network API Invocations

In this subsection, we introduce how we handle network API invocations. Our work includes two parts. The first part is building a list of network API specifications that are able to model the semantics of these APIs (modeling how they generate the network-packet contents by concatenating their arguments). We use *API grammar templates* to specify the semantics of each API, and then we can automatically generate API grammar summaries for the invocations of these APIs at runtime. An API grammar template of an API is a context-gree grammar with parameters. The parameters represent the parameters of the API, the start variable of the grammar template represents the generated network-packet content,

and the productions in the grammar helps to model the semantics of the API.

To generate the list of API grammar templates, we need to manually study the possible network libraries in android system. Since we focus on HTTP network traffic in this paper, we focus on the network APIs that may generate HTTP network-packet contents. In the android library, there are mainly three sources of network APIs: Java network libraries, Apache network libraries, and Android network libraries. It should be noted that, for each android app, android system requires all its required third-party libraries to be packaged within the app. This design decision is made to help separate apps at runtime for better security of the system. It also means that it is sufficient for us to collect the network APIs in the android library. Because the byte code of all the other third-party network libraries must be packaged within the apk, and can be directly analyzed.

3.2 Combining Network APIs

Combining network APIs are typically a group of API method in a packet-generation class (e.g. Uri.builder). An instance (object) of the class, after initiated, will call methods in this group for one or more times to acquire all the data to be put into a network packet. Therefore, to handling combining network APIs, we need to trace the lifetime of packet generation instances, and build an API grammar segment for the instance as a whole. Therefore, the API grammar templates for combining network APIs are special, because it must consider the current state of the packet-generation object.

3.3 Apply String Analysis

The third component of NTApps uses string analysis to estimate the possible values of all the network arguments in the located network API invocations. String analysis is a technique to estimate the possible values of a given string variable in the code. By analyzing the data flow of string variables and string concatenations, for a given string variable v, string analysis is able to generate a context-free grammar, whose language represents the possible values of v.

3.4 Grammar Combination

The component of grammar combination, for each network API invocation *inv*, combines the API grammar summary of *inv* with the grammar of each argument of *inv*. This process is straightforward. We just replace the arguments in the API grammar summary of *inv* with the start variables of the grammar of each argument.

3.5 Extracting Network Signatures

Finally, we need to extract the network signatures from a set of combined grammars generated from the grammar combination component. The most common form of network signatures is a set of constant-string sequences, and we also leverage this form. To generate signatures of constant string sequences, we enumerate all the limited deduction trees of the grammar (i.e., we deduce only once for recursive nonterminals). Therefore, for each deduction tree, we generate a sequence of constant strings by ignoring the terminals which are not constant strings.

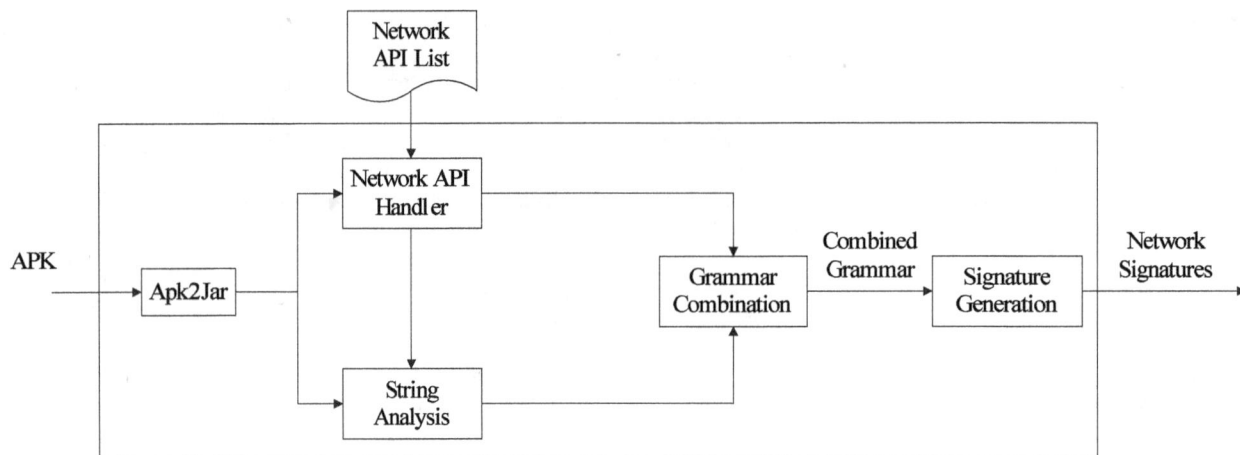

Figure 1: The overview of our approach

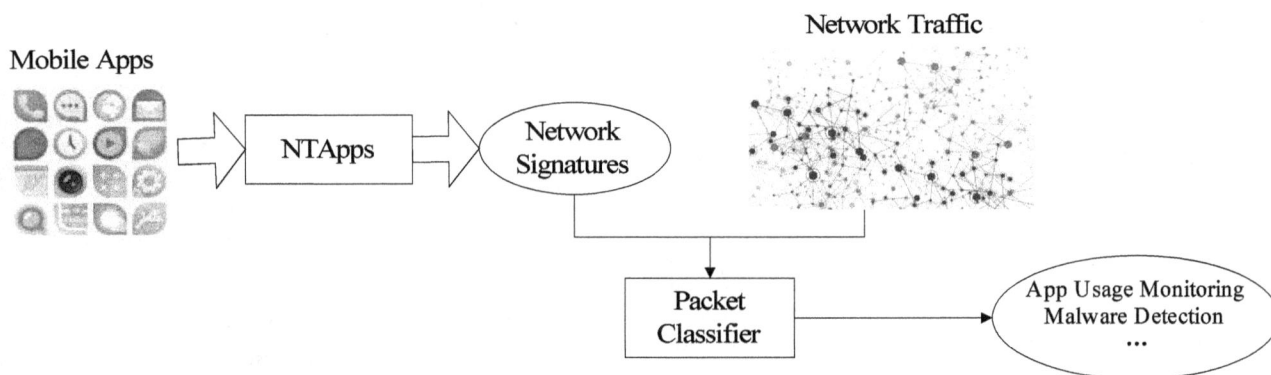

Figure 2: Usage Scenario of NTApps

Using the approach above, we can generate a set of constant-string sequences from each combined grammar. Then, we merged all these sets, and compared all these constant-string sequences to remove all the duplicate constant-string sequences. Finally, we try to extract the host name part in each constant-string sequence in the signature. It is important to extract the host name, because host names are stored separately as an item in the content of an HTTP packet, and host names are of great importance in matching network traffic. We automatically do this with the following heuristic. If the first constant string in the sequence contains both "http://" and a single '/', we extract the host name directly according to the syntax of URL. If we can find common host name postfixes (e.g., .com, .net), we extract all the constant strings after "http://" (if there is one), and before these postfixes, and then we further add these postfixes. Otherwise, we are not able to extract the host name from the constant-string sequence. If this happen, we will further check whether this constant-string sequence is trivial by checking whether there at least two constant strings in the sequence that contain letters. If not, we will remove these constant string sequences from the signature.

Figure 3: Input of NTApps

4 USAGE OF NTAPPS

NTApps provides a simple command line interface to allow the batch analysis of a large number of apps. As shown in Figure 3, for each app, NTApps requires just the path to the app and to the configuration file listing all the network API methods considered. Specifically, as shown in Figure 4, in the configuration file, for each API method, we specify its type (i.e., combining or simple). While a default configuration file is available with NTApps, the users have the flexibility to block certain network API methods or add more API methods in the future.

The output of NTApps is a plain text file with string constant sequences one per line, to support post-analysis filtering, signature checking, or abnormal detection. For more efficient examination in packet classifiers and users' convenience on manual inspection, we

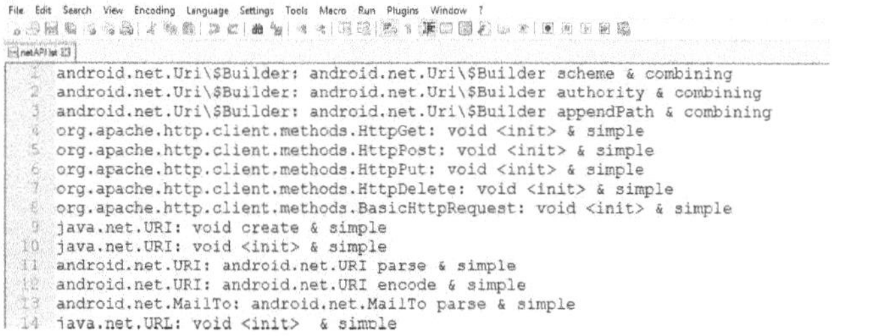

```
android.net.Uri\$Builder: android.net.Uri\$Builder scheme & combining
android.net.Uri\$Builder: android.net.Uri\$Builder authority & combining
android.net.Uri\$Builder: android.net.Uri\$Builder appendPath & combining
org.apache.http.client.methods.HttpGet: void <init> & simple
org.apache.http.client.methods.HttpPost: void <init> & simple
org.apache.http.client.methods.HttpPut: void <init> & simple
org.apache.http.client.methods.HttpDelete: void <init> & simple
org.apache.http.client.methods.BasicHttpRequest: void <init> & simple
java.net.URI: void create & simple
java.net.URI: void <init> & simple
android.net.URI: android.net.URI parse & simple
android.net.URI: android.net.URI encode & simple
android.net.MailTo: android.net.MailTo parse & simple
java.net.URL: void <init> & simple
```

Figure 4: Configuration File with A List of Network APIs

further combine the sequences to generate a tree of common prefixes, and output the tree as dot file format for easier visualization. Part of a sample output signature tree of the app Zedge is shown in Figure 5, and part of our output signature tree for the app Soliterinc is shown in Figure 6.

5 DISCUSSION

Our approach to generate network signature is based on pure static analysis and we generate content-based signatures. Therefore, we have the following main limitations.

First of all, for encrypted network traffic such as HTTPS, we can generate the explicit signature as well. But those signatures are useless because the real network traffics are encrypted and we will never match any of them. Actually, all content-based signatures can not handle encrypted network traffic well. However, according to our statistics, more than 70% apps with Internet access do not use HTTPS. Even for the apps that use HTTPS, they often use it only in the authentication phase of the session and use HTTP for rest of the user interaction. So the HTTP signature is sufficient to identify most of the application. Our method only handle the network traffics that send out by applications.

Second, for the incoming network traffic (i.e., responses from the server), we cannot generate the corresponding signatures without the server side code. However, our evaluation shows that it is sufficient to detect apps using only outcoming network traffic (i.e., HTTP Request Packet). Furthermore, for the blocking scenario, successfully identify the outcoming network traffic is enough because once the outcoming traffic are blocked, there will be no incoming traffic.

Third, our approach is not able to handle the payloads which dynamically loaded. Actually, it is impossible to handle them statically. However, we believe that it is possible to detect the existence of dynamically loaded payload, and guide some other dynamic approach to generate such payloads.

From our evaluation, we can see that, static network signature generation, and learning-based network signature generation both have their advantages and disadvantages. The static approach is able to automatically generate network signatures for most of the apps, and it is able to cover the whole code base of the app, so it is able to find some network behaviors that are very difficult to be revealed dynamically. However, the static approach may be not precise enough in some apps, may generate invalid signatures, and cannot handle dynamically loaded payloads. In this paper, we proposed measurements to measure the quality of signatures without using them. Therefore, it is possible to first apply static approach on all the apps (since it is cheaper), and then schedule the more expensive approaches according to the quality of the statically generated signatures. The better the quality of the statically generated signature of an app is, the later can we apply more expensive approaches on it.

6 RELATED WORKS

In this section, we discuss the related works of our papers. These research efforts mainly fall into three categories: network-traffic classification, android security, and static analysis.

Network-traffic classification. A recent technique NetworkProfiler [5] is able to extract signatures with details, but it requires exhaustive exploration of the mobile apps. Statistical-information based approaches [24] [13] [2] mainly use the statistical information or the contents of the network traffic (e.g., packet size, data transferring rate, packet intervals) to perform a protocol/domain classification of network traffic. These approaches are able to identify network traffic belonging to applications of certain domains, such as database applications, video players, etc. However, similar to port-based approaches, these approaches are also coarse-grain and cannot support application-level network-traffic classification.

Content-based approaches are able to support application-level network-traffic classification by matching the payload of network packets with pre-generated signatures of specific applications. One necessary and challenging step in these approaches is to generate signatures for large number of applications. Sen et al. [34] proposed to use content-based signatures to identify the P2P network traffic of different P2P applications. These signatures are constructed manually through careful reverse engineering the P2P applications. The other group of approaches try to extract content based network signatures of an application from a large amount of network traffic of the application. There have been many efforts in this part focusing on generating the network signatures of worms from their collected network traffic. These efforts (e.g., Autograph [20], EarlyBird [35], PolyGraph [15], Hamsa [21]) basically extract common byte flows in worms' network traffic and generate a content-based signature (in the form of a string or a regular expression) for a certain worm or a group of worms. More recently, Park et al. [27] proposed to use the Longest Common Subsequence (LCS) alogrithm to generate a fingerprint of an application from the packets' content in the application's network traffic. Recently, Perdisci et al. [28] proposed a clustering-based approach to generate a signature for a group of malware sharing similar network behavior. This approach generates signatures for various HTTP-based software (not limited to worms, but also include other software applications such as adware, spyware). Although the above network-traces based signature-generation approaches are fully automatic during the signature-extraction phase. All of these efforts require a large amount of annotated representative network traffic for the application under study. Therefore, they all need manual generation of network traffic or the accumulation of network traffic from a monitored network, both of which require a relatively long time and much cost. Compared with the above approaches, our approach leverages and adapts string analysis techniques to statically generate the content-based signatures of android apps

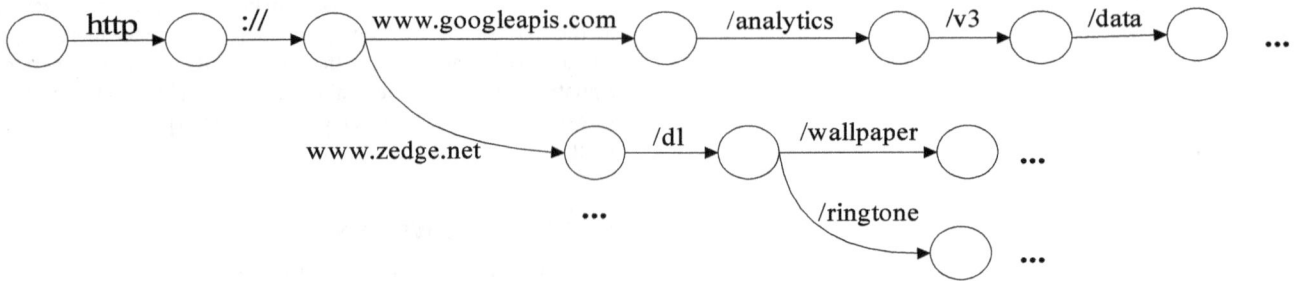

Figure 5: Output of our approach

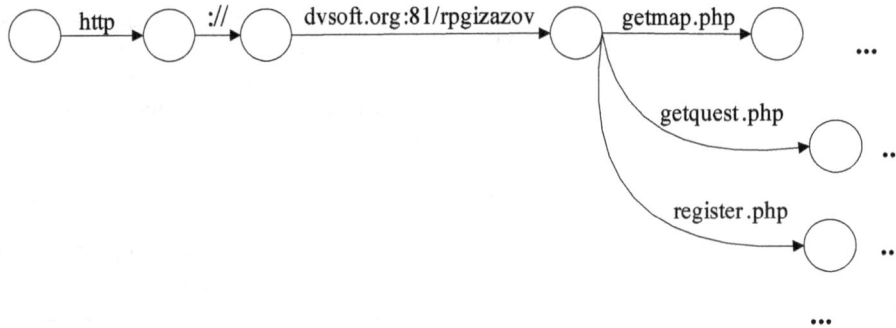

Figure 6: Another exemplar network signature

without requiring any annotated network traffic. This advantage is especially important for the signature generation of android apps because of the huge number of existing android apps and the rapid development of new android apps.

Signature generation of applications based on system level behavior (e.g., system calls) is another well studied area. Most of the approaches in this area execute the application under monitored environment and collect system event sequences as the behavior signature of the application [3] [30]. Therefore, usually, network accesses are recorded as simple system calls without considering the content sent to or received from the network. Recently, Bayer et al. [1] proposed an approach to cluster malware based on system behavior. Their approach take into account more detailed network traffic information but the considered information still only limited high-level information such as the names of downloaded files.

There are also research efforts focusing on identifying certain user-behaviors, such as browsing habits [17] or spam emails [48] [29]. These efforts usually also base their approach on a large set of network traces accumulated from real-world networks. Due to the different nature between users and apps, it is impossible and unnecessary for these efforts to provide any support for automatically generation of the network traces. So, our paper focuses on addressing a different challenge compared to these efforts.

Analysis of Mobile Applications. Our work is also related to the security analysis of mobile applications. This area is an emerging field in academic research, and some of the recent representative research efforts are presented as below. PiOS [6] is static analysis

framework for iOS, which is able to check the leaking of sensitive information by combining data flow analysis and slicing techniques. Stowaway [10] is a automatic tool that is able to determine whether an Android application requests more permissions than it actually requires. The tool is based on a pre-generated mapping from Android system APIs to Android permissions. Enck et al. [9] analyzed the permission system and the permission combinations of Android System to collect a list of dangerous permission patterns and developed Kirin, a service which identifies Android application requesting dangerous permission, so that the users can be warned when installing them. Later, Enck et al. [8] further proposed ded, a de-compiler for Android application, which is able to convert Dalvik Virtual Machine code to JVM code, and then decompile the JVM code using existing Java de-compilers. As for dynamic techniques, TaintDroid [7] dynamically monitors the information flow in Android applications by tracking the propagation of taints throughout the android system. Apex [26] and TISSA [50] are two recent advancements over the current Android permission system to provide more fine-grained permission control and dynamic permission adjustability. Rocky et al. [36] proposed a novel approach to automatically detect inconsistencies between application code and privacy policies. These works mainly focus on information leaking or permissions instead of network analysis, and none of these efforts are able to generate network signatures for android apps.

Static Program Analysis. In the field of static program analysis, the research efforts that are the most related to our work is code dependency analysis [38] [37], and especially string analysis. String analysis is a recent improvement over data-flow analysis [16]. Christensen et al. [4] first suggested string analysis, which is an approach for obtaining possible values of a string variable. Then, string analysis is widely used in various areas, especially for detecting and sanitizing SQL Injection vulnerabilities and Cross-Site-Scripting vulnerabilities. Halfond and Orso [14] used string analysis to detect and neutralize SQL injection attacks. Minamide [23] first applied string analysis on web applications. He also first suggested to simulate string operations in the extended CFG with FSTs, and implemented a string analyzer on PHP code to predict the possible values of dynamically generated web pages. Based on Minamide's work, Xie and Aiken [47] suggested a technique to detect SQL injection vulnerabilities in scripting languages. Later, Wassermann and Su first developed string-taint analysis [44] to more precisely detect the above two kinds of vulnerabilities [45]. After that, Wassermann and Su [46] further extended their work, and developed an approach to generating test cases for security vulnerabilities. Kieyzun et.al. [18] further improved their approach by considering strings that flow through the database. Wang et al. extended string analysis and developed generalized string-taint analysis [42] [41] [40], and dynamic string-taint analysis [43]. Sexena et al. [31] proposed an approach to sanitize the two kinds of vulnerabilities based on dynamic symbolic execution [32] [39] [25]. Compared to these approaches, we apply string analysis on statically generating network signatures, which is a totally different problem. We further proposed techniques to handle obfuscation and various network APIs.

7 CONCLUSIONS

In this paper, we propose a novel approach to statically generate network signatures for android apps. Our approach is based on string analysis, with adaptations to tolerate the loss of type information in the Java byte code converted from obfuscated Dalvik byte code.We further propose new techniques to handle complex network API invocations, and generating signatures from string-operation grammars. Furthermore, we introduce a formal presentation of the signature generation and matching problem, and propose the important properties of the generated network-signature set.

ACKNOWLEDGMENT

The research presented in the paper is supported in part by NSF grant CCF-1464425, and DHS grant DHS-14-ST-062-001.

REFERENCES

[1] U. Bayer, P. M. Comparetti, C. Hlauschek, C. Krügel, and E. Kirda. Scalable, behavior-based malware clustering. In NDSS, 2009.
[2] L. Bernaille, R. Teixeira, I. Akodkenou, A. Soule, and K. Salamatian. Traffic classification on the fly. SIGCOMM Comput. Commun. Rev., 36:23–26, April 2006.
[3] A. Bose, X. Hu, K. G. Shin, and T. Park. Behavioral detection of malware on mobile handsets. In Proceedings of the 6th international conference on Mobile systems, applications, and services, MobiSys '08, pages 225–238, New York, NY, USA, 2008. ACM.
[4] A. Christensen, A. Møller, and M. Schwartzbach. Precise analysis of string expressions. In Proc. SAS, pages 1–18, 2003.
[5] S. Dai, A. Tongaonkar, X. Wang, A. Nucci, and D. Song. Networkprofiler: Towards automatic fingerprinting of android apps. In INFOCOM, 2013.
[6] M. Egele, C. Kruegel, E. Kirda, and G. Vigna. Pios: Detecting privacy leaks in ios applications. In NDSS, 2011.
[7] W. Enck, P. Gilbert, B. gon Chun, L. P. Cox, J. Jung, P. McDaniel, and A. Sheth. Taintdroid: An information-flow tracking system for realtime privacy monitoring

on smartphones. In OSDI, pages 393–407, 2010.
[8] W. Enck, D. Octeau, P. McDaniel, and S. Chaudhuri. A study of android application security. In Proceedings of the 20th USENIX Security Symposium, 2011.
[9] W. Enck, M. Ongtang, and P. D. McDaniel. On lightweight mobile phone application certification. In ACM Conference on Computer and Communications Security, pages 235–245, 2009.
[10] A. P. Felt, E. Chin, S. Hanna, D. Song, and D. Wagner. Android permissions demystified. In Proceedings of the 18th ACM conference on Computer and communications security, CCS '11, pages 627–638, New York, NY, USA, 2011. ACM.
[11] A. Gember, A. Anand, and A. Akella. A comparative study of handheld and non-handheld traffic in campus Wi-Fi networks. In Passive and active measurement, PAM, pages 173–183, Berlin, Heidelberg, 2011. Springer-Verlag.
[12] M. Grace, Y. Zhou, Z. Wang, and X. Jiang. Systematic detection of capability leaks in stock Android smartphones. In Network and Distributed System Security Symposium, Feb. 2012.
[13] P. Haffner, S. Sen, O. Spatscheck, and D. Wang. Acas: automated construction of application signatures. In Proceedings of the 2005 ACM SIGCOMM workshop on Mining network data, MineNet '05, pages 197–202, New York, NY, USA, 2005. ACM.
[14] W. G. J. Halfond and A. Orso. Amnesia: Analysis and monitoring for neutralizing SQL-injection attacks. In Proc. ASE, pages 174–183, 2005.
[15] N. James, B. Karp, and D. Song. Polygraph: Automatically generating signatures for polymorphic worms. In Proceedings of the 2005 IEEE Symposium on Security and Privacy, pages 226–241, Washington, DC, USA, 2005. IEEE Computer Society.
[16] J. Kam and J. Ullman. Global data flow analysis and iterative algorithms. Journal of the ACM (JACM), 23(1):158–171, January 1976.
[17] R. Keralapura, A. Nucci, Z.-L. Zhang, and L. Gao. Profiling users in a 3g network using hourglass co-clustering. In Proceedings of the sixteenth annual international conference on Mobile computing and networking, MobiCom '10, pages 341–352, New York, NY, USA, 2010. ACM.
[18] A. Kieyzun, P. J. Guo, K. Jayaraman, and M. D. Ernst. Automatic creation of SQL injection and cross-site scripting attacks. In Proc. ICSE, pages 199–209, 2009.
[19] H. Kim, K. Claffy, M. Fomenkov, D. Barman, M. Faloutsos, and K. Lee. Internet traffic classification demystified: myths, caveats, and the best practices. In ACM CoNEXT Conference, CoNEXT, pages 11:1–11:12, New York, NY, USA, 2008.
[20] H.-A. Kim and B. Karp. Autograph: toward automated, distributed worm signature detection. In Proceedings of the 13th conference on USENIX Security Symposium - Volume 13, SSYM'04, pages 19–19, Berkeley, CA, USA, 2004. USENIX Association.
[21] Z. Li, M. Sanghi, Y. Chen, M.-Y. Kao, and B. Chavez. Hamsa: Fast signature generation for zero-day polymorphicworms with provable attack resilience. In Proceedings of the 2006 IEEE Symposium on Security and Privacy, pages 32–47, Washington, DC, USA, 2006. IEEE Computer Society.
[22] J. Ma, K. Levchenko, C. Kreibich, S. Savage, and G. M. Voelker. Unexpected means of protocol inference. In Conference on Internet measurement, IMC, pages 313–326, New York, NY, USA, 2006. ACM.
[23] Y. Minamide. Static approximation of dynamically generated web pages. In Proc. WWW, pages 432–441, 2005.
[24] A. W. Moore and D. Zuev. Internet traffic classification using bayesian analysis techniques. In Proceedings of the 2005 ACM SIGMETRICS international conference on Measurement and modeling of computer systems, SIGMETRICS '05, pages 50–60, New York, NY, USA, 2005. ACM.
[25] S. Mostafa and X. Wang. An empirical study on the usage of mocking frameworks in software testing. In Quality Software (QSIC), 2014 14th International Conference on, pages 127–132. IEEE, 2014.
[26] M. Nauman, S. Khan, and X. Zhang. Apex: extending android permission model and enforcement with user-defined runtime constraints. In Proceedings of the 5th ACM Symposium on Information, Computer and Communications Security, ASIACCS '10, pages 328–332, New York, NY, USA, 2010. ACM.
[27] B.-C. Park, Y. J. Won, M.-S. Kim, and J. W. Hong. Towards automated application signature generation for traffic identification. In NOMS, pages 160–167, 2008.
[28] R. Perdisci, W. Lee, and N. Feamster. Behavioral clustering of http-based malware and signature generation using malicious network traces. In Proceedings of the 7th USENIX conference on Networked systems design and implementation, NSDI'10, pages 26–26, Berkeley, CA, USA, 2010. USENIX Association.
[29] A. Ramachandran and N. Feamster. Understanding the network-level behavior of spammers. In Proceedings of the 2006 conference on Applications, technologies, architectures, and protocols for computer communications, SIGCOMM '06, pages 291–302, New York, NY, USA, 2006. ACM.
[30] K. Rieck, T. Holz, C. Willems, P. Düssel, and P. Laskov. Learning and classification of malware behavior. In DIMVA, pages 108–125, 2008.
[31] P. Saxena, D. Akhawe, S. Hanna, F. Mao, S. McCamant, and D. Song. A symbolic execution framework for javascript. In IEEE Symposium on Security and Privacy, pages 513–528, 2010.
[32] K. Sen, D. Marinov, and G. Agha. Cute: A concolic unit testing engine for c. In Proceedings of the 10th European Software Engineering Conference Held Jointly with 13th ACM SIGSOFT International Symposium on Foundations of Software Engineering, ESEC/FSE-13, pages 263–272, New York, NY, USA, 2005. ACM.

[33] S. Sen, O. Spatscheck, and D. Wang. Accurate, scalable in-network identification of p2p traffic using application signatures. In *Proceedings of the 13th international conference on World Wide Web*, WWW '04, pages 512–521, New York, NY, USA, 2004. ACM.

[34] S. Sen, O. Spatscheck, and D. Wang. Accurate, Scalable In-Network Identification of P2P Traffic Using Application Signatures. In *WWW2004*, May 2004.

[35] S. Singh, C. Estan, G. Varghese, and S. Savage. Automated worm fingerprinting. In *Proceedings of the 6th conference on Symposium on Opearting Systems Design & Implementation - Volume 6*, pages 4–4, Berkeley, CA, USA, 2004. USENIX Association.

[36] R. Slavin, X. Wang, M. B. Hosseini, J. Hester, R. Krishnan, J. Bhatia, T. D. Breaux, and J. Niu. Toward a framework for detecting privacy policy violations in android application code. In *Proceedings of the 38th International Conference on Software Engineering*, pages 25–36. ACM, 2016.

[37] H. Tang, X. Wang, L. Zhang, B. Xie, L. Zhang, and H. Mei. Summary-based context-sensitive data-dependence analysis in presence of callbacks. In *ACM SIGPLAN Notices*, volume 50, pages 83–95. ACM, 2015.

[38] X. Wang, D. Lo, J. Cheng, L. Zhang, H. Mei, and J. X. Yu. Matching dependence-related queries in the system dependence graph. In *Proceedings of the IEEE/ACM international conference on Automated software engineering*, pages 457–466. ACM, 2010.

[39] X. Wang, L. Zhang, and P. Tanofsky. Experience report: How is dynamic symbolic execution different from manual testing? a study on klee. In *Proceedings of the 2015 International Symposium on Software Testing and Analysis*, pages 199–210. ACM, 2015.

[40] X. Wang, L. Zhang, T. Xie, H. Mei, and J. Sun. Transtrl: An automatic need-to-translate string locator for software internationalization. In *Proceedings of the 31st International Conference on Software Engineering*, pages 555–558. IEEE Computer Society, 2009.

[41] X. Wang, L. Zhang, T. Xie, H. Mei, and J. Sun. Locating need-to-translate constant strings in web applications. In *Proceedings of the eighteenth ACM SIGSOFT international symposium on Foundations of software engineering*, pages 87–96. ACM, 2010.

[42] X. Wang, L. Zhang, T. Xie, H. Mei, and J. Sun. Locating need-to-externalize constant strings for software internationalization with generalized string-taint analysis. *IEEE Transactions on Software Engineering*, 39(4):516–536, 2013.

[43] X. Wang, L. Zhang, T. Xie, Y. Xiong, and H. Mei. Automating presentation changes in dynamic web applications via collaborative hybrid analysis. In *Proc. FSE*, 2012.

[44] G. Wassermann and Z. Su. Sound and precise analysis of web applications for injection vulnerabilities. In *Proc. PLDI*, pages 32–41, 2007.

[45] G. Wassermann and Z. Su. Static detection of cross-site scripting vulnerabilities. In *Proc. ICSE*, pages 171–180, 2008.

[46] G. Wassermann, D. Yu, A. Chander, D. Dhurjati, H. Inamura, and Z. Su. Dynamic test input generation for web applications. In *Proc. ISSTA*, pages 249–260, 2008.

[47] Y. Xie and A. Aiken. Static detection of security vulnerabilities in scripting languages. In *Proc. USENIX Security Symposium*, 2006.

[48] Y. Xie, F. Yu, K. Achan, R. Panigrahy, G. Hulten, and I. Osipkov. Spamming botnets: signatures and characteristics. In *Proceedings of the ACM SIGCOMM 2008 conference on Data communication*, SIGCOMM '08, pages 171–182, New York, NY, USA, 2008. ACM.

[49] Q. Xu, J. Erman, A. Gerber, Z. Mao, J. Pang, and S. Venkataraman. Identifying diverse usage behaviors of smartphone apps. In *SIGCOMM conference on Internet measurement conference*, IMC '11, pages 329–344, New York, NY, USA, 2011. ACM.

[50] Y. Zhou, X. Zhang, X. Jiang, and V. W. Freeh. Taming information-stealing smartphone applications (on android). In *Proceedings of the 4th international conference on Trust and trustworthy computing*, TRUST'11, pages 93–107, Berlin, Heidelberg, 2011. Springer-Verlag.

On the Satisfiability of Workflows with Release Points

Jason Crampton
Royal Holloway, University of London
Egham, United Kingdom
jason.crampton@rhul.ac.uk

Gregory Gutin
Royal Holloway, University of London
Egham, United Kingdom
g.gutin@rhul.ac.uk

Rémi Watrigant
Inria Sophia Antipolis
Sophia Antipolis, France
remi.watrigant@inria.fr

ABSTRACT

There has been a considerable amount of interest in recent years in the problem of workflow satisfiability, which asks whether the existence of constraints in a workflow specification means that it is impossible to allocate authorized users to each step in the workflow. Recent developments have seen the workflow satisfiability problem (WSP) studied in the context of workflow specifications in which the set of steps may vary from one instance of the workflow to another. This, in turn, means that some constraints may only apply to certain workflow instances. Inevitably, WSP becomes more complex for such workflow specifications. In this paper, we present the first fixed parameter algorithms to solve WSP for workflow specifications of this type. Moreover, we significantly extend the range of constraints that can be used in workflow specifications of this type.

KEYWORDS

workflow satisfiability, release points, workflow composition, xor-branching

ACM Reference format:
Jason Crampton, Gregory Gutin, and Rémi Watrigant. 2017. On the Satisfiability of Workflows with Release Points. In *Proceedings of SACMAT'17, June 21–23, 2017, Indianapolis, IN, USA, , 11 pages.*
DOI: http://dx.doi.org/10.1145/3078861.3078866

1   INTRODUCTION

Many businesses use computerized systems to manage their business processes. A common example of such a system is a workflow management system which is responsible for the co-ordination and execution of steps in a business process. A business process may be executed many times and by different users. However, the structure of the process is fixed and may be defined by a set of steps that must be performed in a particular sequence. In addition, we may wish to impose some form of access control on the execution of a business process, limiting which users may perform which steps. This control may take the form of an authorization policy, which defines which users are authorized to perform which steps, and authorization constraints, which limit the combinations of users that may perform certain sets of steps in the business process. A simple form of constraint could prohibit the same user from performing two (or more) particular security-sensitive steps.

The structure of a business process or workflow need not be linear. There may be subprocesses that can be performed in parallel, or there may be subprocesses that are mutually exclusive (and only one of the subprocesses is executed in a particular instance of the workflow). Thus, the steps executed in a workflow may vary from one instance to another. Moreover, there may be constraints that only apply when certain subprocesses are executed. Basin, Burri and Karjoth introduced a mechanism for modeling such constraints using *release points* [3]. Informally, release points allow a constraint to be "switched off" when some given points of an instance workflow are reached. In particular, when different release points are located in different mutually exclusive subprocesses, it is possible to encode conditional constraints.

Determining whether a workflow specification is satisfiable – in the sense that there exists an allocation of authorized users to steps such that all constraints are satisfied – is an important question. An algorithm for deciding the so-called *workflow satisfiability question* (WSP) is important from the point of view of static analysis of workflow specifications and for workflow management systems in which users select which steps to execute [10, Section 2.2]. However, most work on WSP has assumed that the set of steps is the same for all workflow instances. The exception is the work of Crampton and Gutin [10], who introduced a simple language for workflow composition, to model workflows with parallel and exclusive-or branching. However, their work does not consider the effect of release points on satisfiability. Conversely, the work of Basin *et al.* does not provide an exact algorithm for solving the enforcement process existence (EPE) problem, a problem essentially equivalent to WSP in the presence of release points. The heuristic algorithm developed by Basin *et al.* to solve the EPE problem produces good results "when the set of users is large and the static authorizations are equally distributed among them". It is unclear whether the requirement that static authorizations be equally distributed is likely to hold in practical settings.

In this paper, we extend the work of Crampton and Gutin [10], who introduced a simple language for composing workflows and solving WSP for workflows specified using this language, to incorporate release points. We then extend the definition of constraint satisfaction, relative to a particular execution of the steps in such a workflow, in the presence of release points. Finally, we develop fixed-parameter algorithms that solve WSP for workflows incorporating release points, thereby providing the first results in this area. Moreover, our notion of constraints with release points is a significant generalization of that used by Basin *et al.*

In the remainder of this section we introduce relevant notation, terminology and background material. In Section 2, we define the notion of a compositional workflow with release points, extending the notion of constraint satisfaction accordingly. In Section 3, we describe our method for solving WSP and provide an analysis of its complexity. We briefly discuss related work in Section 4. The paper concludes with a summary of our contributions and our ideas for future research in this area.

1.1 Notation and Terminology

A directed graph (*digraph* for short) is a pair $G = (V, E)$, where V is the set of vertices, and $E \subseteq V \times V$ is the set of edges. A directed acyclic graph (*DAG* for short) is a digraph which does not contain any directed cycle, *i.e.* no sequence $(u_0, u_1 \ldots, u_{k-1}, u_0)$ such that each pair of consecutive vertices belongs to E. For $u \in V$, we define the *in-neighborhood* of u to be the set $N^-(u) = \{t \in V | (t, u) \in E\}$; the *in-degree* of u is the size of its in-neighborhood. Similarly, the *out-neighborhood* of u is the set $N^+(u) = \{w \in V | (u, w) \in E\}$ and the *out-degree* of u is the size of its out-neighborhood. A vertex of in-degree 0 is called a *source*, while a vertex of out-degree 0 is called a *sink*. For $S \subseteq V$, we denote by $G[S]$ the *induced subgraph* $(S, E \cap (S \times S))$. By abuse of notation, we will sometimes write $G \setminus S$ as a shortcut for $G[V \setminus S]$. For more information about graphs and DAGs, we refer the reader to [2, 13].

Sometimes, it is convenient to represent a DAG with a partial order on its vertices. Indeed, we may write $u \leq v$ for $u, v \in V$ whenever $u = v$ or there exists a directed path from u to v. By extension, we may write $u < v$ if $u \leq v$ and $u \neq v$.

For any positive integer n, let $[n] = \{1, \ldots, n\}$. An ordered sequence $\sigma = (v_1, \ldots, v_q)$ of distinct vertices of V is called a *linear subextension* of G iff for every $i, j \in [q]$, $v_i \leq v_j$ implies $i \leq j$. If σ contains all vertices of V, then we say that σ is a *linear extension* of G.

Many decision problems take several parameters as input. It can be instructive to consider how the complexity of the problem may change if we assume one or more of those parameters is small relative to the others. The purpose of multivariate analysis of the complexity of a problem is to obtain efficient algorithms when the chosen parameters take small values in practice. We say that a decision problem is *fixed-parameter tractable* (FPT) if there exists an algorithm that decides if an instance is positive in $O(f(k)p(n))$ time for some computable function f and some polynomial p, where n denotes the size of an instance, and k is a parameter of the instance. Accordingly, we will call such an algorithm an *FPT algorithm*. For more details about parameterized complexity, we refer the reader to the monographs of Downey and Fellows [14] and Cygan *et al.* [12].

1.2 The workflow satisfiability problem

A *workflow specification* is defined by a directed acyclic graph $G = (S, E)$, where S is the set of steps to be executed, and $E \subseteq S \times S$ defines a partial ordering on the set of steps in the workflow, in the sense that $(s_1, s_2) \in E$ means that step s_1 must be executed before s_2 in every instance of the workflow. Note that the order is not required to be total, so the exact sequence of steps may vary from instance to instance. In addition, we are also given a set of users U and an *authorization policy* $A \subseteq S \times U$, where $(s, u) \in A$ means that user u is authorized to execute step s. A workflow specification $G = (S, E)$ together with an authorization policy is called a *workflow schema*. Throughout the paper, we will assume that for every step $s \in S$, there exists some user $u \in U$ such that $(s, u) \in A$.

A workflow *constraint* (T, Θ) limits the users that are allowed to perform a set of steps T in any execution of the workflow. In particular, Θ identifies authorized (partial) assignments of users to steps in T, i.e. Θ is a set of functions from T to U. A (partial) plan is a function $\pi : S' \to U$, where $S' \subseteq S$. A plan $\pi : S \to U$ represents an allocation of steps to users. The workflow satisfiability problem (WSP) is concerned with the existence or otherwise of a plan that is authorized and satisfies all constraints.

More formally, let $\pi : S' \to U$, where $S' \subseteq S$, be a plan. Given $T \subseteq S'$, we write $\pi|_T$ to denote the function π restricted to domain T; that is $\pi|_T : T \to U$ is defined by $\pi|_T(s) = \pi(s)$ for all $s \in T$. Then we say $\pi : S' \to U$ *satisfies* a workflow constraint (T, Θ) if $T \not\subseteq S'$ or $\pi|_T \in \Theta$.

In practice, we do not define a constraint by giving the family of functions Θ extensionally, as the size of such set might be exponential in the number of users and steps. Instead, we will assume that constraints have "compact" descriptions, in the sense that it takes polynomial time to test whether a given plan satisfies a constraint. This is a reasonable assumption, as all constraints of relevance in practice satisfy such a property. For instance, the two most well-known constraints are perhaps *binding-of-duty (BoD)* and *separation-of-duty (SoD)*. The *scope* of these constraints is binary: a plan π satisfies a BoD constraint $(\{s_1, s_2\}, =)$ iff $\pi(s_1) = \pi(s_2)$; and π satisfies an SoD constraint $(\{s_1, s_2\}, \neq)$ iff $\pi(s_1) \neq \pi(s_2)$. A natural generalization of these constraints are atmost and atleast constraints, in which the scope may be of arbitrary size, and the definition of such constraints includes an additional integer k. Given $T \subseteq S$, a plan satisfies atmost(T, k) (resp. atleast(T, k)) iff $|\pi(T)| \leq k$ (resp. $|\pi(T)| \geq k$).

User-independent constraints generalize all these forms of constraints [6]. Informally, such a constraint limits the execution of steps in a workflow, but is indifferent to the particular users that execute the steps. More formally, a constraint (T, Θ) is user-independent if whenever $\theta \in \Theta$ and $\psi : U \to U$ is a permutation then $\psi \circ \theta \in \Theta$ (where $\circ$ denotes function composition). A separation of duty constraint, on two steps for example, simply requires that two *different* users execute the steps, not that, say, Alice and Bob (in particular) must execute them. Similarly, a binding of duty constraint on two steps only requires that the *same* user executes the steps. More generally, atleast and atmost constraints are user-independent. It appears most constraints that are useful in practice are user-independent: all constraints defined in the ANSI-RBAC standard [1], for example, are user-independent.

A *constrained workflow authorization schema* is a tuple $(G = (S, E), U, A, C)$, where (G, U, A) is a workflow schema, and C is a set of constraints. We say that a plan $\pi : S \to U$ is *authorized* if $(s, \pi(s)) \in A$ for every $s \in S$, and we say that π is *valid* if it is authorized and if it satisfies all $c \in C$. We are now ready to introduce the WORKFLOW SATISFIABILITY PROBLEM, as defined by Wang and Li [25]:

WORKFLOW SATISFIABILITY PROBLEM (WSP)

    Input: A constrained workflow authorization schema
        $W = (G = (S, E), U, A, C)$
  Question: Is there a valid plan $\pi : S \to U$?

We present as a running example a simple purchase-order workflow [8] in Figure 1. We will extend this example in subsequent sections in order to illustrate the concepts introduced in this paper. In the first step of this workflow, the purchase order is created and approved (and then dispatched to the supplier). The supplier will submit an invoice for the goods ordered, which is processed by the create payment step. When the supplier delivers the goods, a goods received note (GRN) must be signed and countersigned. Only then may the payment be approved and sent to the supplier. Observe that this workflow specification contains parallel branches, in the sense that the processing of both s_3 and s_4 must occur before s_6, but the relative ordering of s_3 and s_4 is of no importance. We will extend this example to include mutually exclusive branches.

The workflow specification also includes constraints (each having binary scope), mainly in order to reduce the possibility of fraud. Such constraints may be depicted as an undirected, labeled graph, in which the vertices represent steps and edges denote constraints, as illustrated in Figure 1(b). One requirement, for example, is that the steps to create and approve a purchase order are executed by different users. We will extend the example to include constraints having release points.

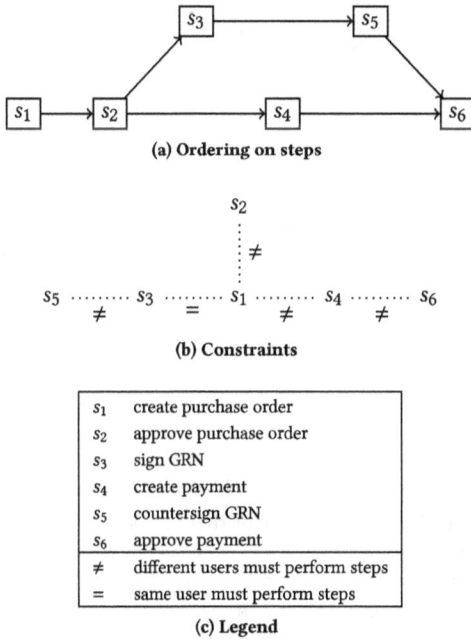

(a) Ordering on steps

(b) Constraints

s_1	create purchase order
s_2	approve purchase order
s_3	sign GRN
s_4	create payment
s_5	countersign GRN
s_6	approve payment
$\neq$	different users must perform steps
$=$	same user must perform steps

(c) Legend

Figure 1: A simple constrained workflow for purchase order processing

2 COMPOSITIONAL WORKFLOWS AND RELEASE POINTS

We now extend the definitions of workflow specification and workflow schema to a compositional variant. We also extend the constraints model to introduce release points.

2.1 Workflow composition

We now introduce a convenient way to represent situations where, at some points of a workflow execution, one would like to branch

into several subworkflows independently, a notion also known as *OR-forks* [23] or *exclusive gateways* [26]. To that end, we use the model defined by Crampton and Gutin [10] called *Workflow Composition*.

A *compositional workflow specification* is defined recursively using three operations: serial composition, parallel branching and xor branching. Like a "classical" workflow specification, it can be represented as a DAG $G = (V, E)$. However, in the case of a compositional workflow, not all vertices represent steps. In addition to the set of (classical) steps, V also contains R, the set of *release points*, and O, the set of *orchestration points*. Orchestration points will be introduced shortly. Release points limit actions of constraints by restricting their scopes and will be introduced in Section 2.3. We will sometimes directly define a compositional workflow specification as $G = (S \cup R \cup O, E)$.

The DAG of a compositional workflow always contains two special orchestration points: a source vertex α, called *input* and a sink vertex ω, called *output*. Moreover, an atomic compositional workflow (i.e. the base case for constructing such a workflow) is composed of a single step or release point v, and can be represented by the DAG $G = (\{\alpha, v, \omega\}, \{(\alpha, v), (v, \omega)\})$. Given two compositional workflows $G_1 = (V_1, E_1)$ and $G_2 = (V_2, E_2)$ with respective input and output vertices α_1, ω_1 and α_2, ω_2, respectively, we may construct new compositional workflows using serial composition, and parallel and xor branchings, denoted by $G_1; G_2$, $G_1 \parallel G_2$ and $G_1 \otimes G_2$, respectively. We assume that $V_1 \cap V_2 = \emptyset$.

For *serial composition*, all the steps in G_1 must be completed before the steps in G_2. Hence, the DAG of $G_1; G_2$ is formed by taking the union of V_1 and V_2, the union of E_1 and E_2, and the addition of a single edge from ω_1 to α_2. Thus, α_1 (resp. ω_2) is the input (resp. output) vertex of $G_1; G_2$.

For *parallel composition*, the execution of the steps in G_1 and G_2 may be interleaved. Hence, the DAG of $G_1 \parallel G_2$ is formed by taking the union of V_1 and V_2, the union of E_1 and E_2, the addition of new input and output vertices $\alpha_\parallel$ and $\omega_\parallel$, and the addition of edges $(\alpha_\parallel, \alpha_1), (\alpha_\parallel, \alpha_2), (\omega_1, \omega_\parallel)$ and $(\omega_2, \omega_\parallel)$. This form of composition is sometimes known as an *AND-fork* [23] or a *parallel gateway* [26].

In both serial and parallel compositions, all steps in G_1 and G_2 are executed. In *xor composition*, either the steps in G_1 are executed or the steps in G_2, but not both. In other words, xor composition represents non-deterministic choice in a workflow specification. The DAG $G_1 \otimes G_2$ is formed by taking the union of V_1 and V_2, the union of E_1 and E_2, the addition of new input and output vertices $\alpha_\otimes$ and $\omega_\otimes$, and the addition of edges $(\alpha_\otimes, \alpha_1), (\alpha_\otimes, \alpha_2), (\omega_1, \omega_\otimes)$ and $(\omega_2, \omega_\otimes)$. Given $G_1 \otimes G_2$, we will say that every pair of vertices $(v, v') \in V_1 \times V_2$ are *exclusive*. We say that a compositional workflow is *xor-free* if it can be constructed with only serial and parallel operations.

For the sake of readability, we will sometimes simplify the representation of a compositional workflow by replacing an orchestration point having a single in-neighbor u and a single out-neighbor v by the edge (u, v) (for instance, a path $(\alpha_1, s_1, \omega_1, \alpha_2, s_2, \omega_2)$ will be replaced by $(\alpha_1, s_1, s_2, \omega_2)$).

A compositional workflow specification $G = (V, E)$ together with an authorization policy $A \subseteq S \times U$ will be called a *compositional workflow schema*. An example of a compositional workflow

(a) Ordering on steps

(b) Constraints

s_1	create purchase order
s_2	approve purchase order
s_3	sign GRN
s_3'	sign GRN
s_4	create payment
s_5	countersign GRN
s_6	approve payment
$\neq$	different users must perform steps
$=$	same user must perform steps

(c) Legend

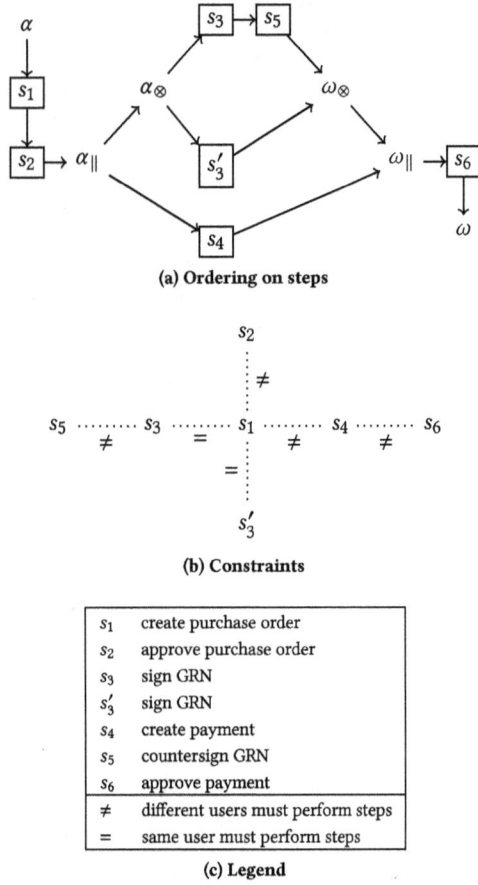

Figure 2: Example of a compositional workflow specification; vertices with no border represent orchestration points

specification is shown in Figure 2. It extends the example in Figure 1 by including orchestration steps and an xor branching. We model the fact that orders below a certain value will not require a countersignature on the GRN. Thus, one branch includes steps to sign and countersign the GRN (which is taken when the value of the order exceeds a certain value), while the other branch contains only the sign GRN step.

2.2 Execution sequences

In a compositional workflow having an xor branching, there exists more than one set of steps that could comprise a workflow instance. And in a compositional workflow having only parallel branching, two different workflow instances will contain the same steps but they may occur in different orders. Here, we introduce the idea of an *execution sequence*, which is an ordered sequence of steps and release points. An execution sequence may be empty. For execution sequences $\sigma = (a_1, \ldots, a_k)$ and $\sigma' = (b_1, \ldots, b_k)$, we define the following two sets of execution sequences:

$$\sigma + \sigma' = \{(a_1, \ldots, a_k, b_1, \ldots, b_\ell)\}$$
$$\sigma * \sigma' = \{(a_1) + \sigma'' : \sigma'' \in (a_2, \ldots, a_k) * (b_1, \ldots, b_\ell)\} \cup$$
$$\{(b_1) + \sigma'' : \sigma'' \in (a_1, \ldots, a_k) * (b_2, \ldots, b_\ell)\}$$
$$\sigma * () = () * \sigma = \sigma$$

In other words, $\sigma + \sigma'$ represents concatenation of σ and σ'; and $\sigma * \sigma'$ represents all possible interleavings of σ and σ' that preserve the ordering of elements in both σ and σ'. Given sets of execution sequences Σ and Σ', we write $\Sigma + \Sigma'$ to denote $\{\sigma + \sigma' : \sigma \in \Sigma, \sigma' \in \Sigma'\}$ and $\Sigma * \Sigma'$ to denote $\{\sigma * \sigma' : \sigma \in \Sigma, \sigma' \in \Sigma'\}$.

For a compositional workflow G, we write $\Sigma(G)$ to denote the set of execution sequences for G. Then:

- for workflow specification G comprising a single step or release point v, $\Sigma(G) = \{(v)\}$;
- $\Sigma(G_1; G_2) = \Sigma(G_1) + \Sigma(G_2)$;
- $\Sigma(G_1 \parallel G_2) = \Sigma(G_1) * \Sigma(G_2)$; and
- $\Sigma(G_1 \otimes G_2) = \Sigma(G_1) \cup \Sigma(G_2)$.

The possible execution sequences for the example in Figure 2 are:

- $(s_1, s_2, s_4, s_3, s_5, s_6)$
- $(s_1, s_2, s_3, s_4, s_5, s_6)$
- $(s_1, s_2, s_3, s_5, s_4, s_6)$
- $(s_1, s_2, s_4, s_3', s_6)$
- $(s_1, s_2, s_3', s_4, s_6)$

For an execution sequence σ, let σ_S and σ_R be the restriction of σ to the set of steps and release points, respectively. Similarly, let $S(\sigma)$ and $R(\sigma)$ be respectively the set of steps and release points contained in σ.[1]

Given an execution sequence $\sigma = (v_1, \ldots, v_n)$ of G and $i \in [n]$, we define $\text{left}_\sigma(v_i) = (v_1, \ldots, v_{i-1})$, $\text{right}_\sigma(v_i) = (v_{i+1}, \ldots, v_n)$. Also, if $1 \leq i < j \leq n$, then define $\text{btw}_\sigma(v_i, v_j) = (v_{i+1}, \ldots, v_{j-1})$. We will omit the σ subscript from left_σ, right_σ and btw_σ when it is obvious from context.

2.3 Constraints with release points

Suppose we have a requirement that two steps s_1 and s_2 be performed by the same user if a certain instance-specific condition holds; and they should be performed by different users otherwise. In other words, the constraint on the execution on s_1 and s_2 varies depending on the instance.

Release points can be used to encode such requirements by positioning different release points in different, mutually-exclusive branches of the workflow and specifying both constraints on the two steps. Then passing through one branch "switches off" the separation-of-duty constraint, while passing through the other branch switches off the binding-of-duty constraint. In this section, we introduce a formalism for modeling such constraints and their satisfaction.

Let $W = (S \cup R \cup O, E, U, A)$ be a compositional workflow schema. A *constraint with release points* has the form $c = (T, \Theta, P)$, where

---

[1]Hence, the difference between σ_S and $S(\sigma)$ (resp. σ_R and $R(\sigma)$) is that the former is an ordered sequence, while the latter is a set. In particular, it might be the case, for two ordered sequences σ, σ', that, say, $S(\sigma) = S(\sigma')$ while $\sigma_S \neq \sigma'_S$, in the case where σ and σ' are two different orderings of a same set of steps.

$T \subseteq S$ is the scope of the constraint, $P \subseteq R$ represents the release points of the constraints, and Θ is a family of functions with domain T and range U. For $Q \subseteq S$, we denote by $\Theta|_Q = \{f|_Q : f \in \Theta\}$ the restriction of the family Θ to Q.

Let σ be an execution sequence of W, and $\sigma_P = (r_1, \ldots, r_q)$ be the ordering of release points of P in σ. For every $i \in \{1, \ldots, q-1\}$, define

$$T_0 = T \cap S(\text{left}(r_1));$$
$$T_i = T \cap S(\text{btw}(r_i, r_{i+1})), \text{ for } i \in [q-1];$$
$$T_q = T \cap S(\text{right}(r_q)).$$

In other words, for $i \in [q-1]$, T_i is the set of steps of T occurring between r_i and r_{i+1} in σ.

Given a constraint $c = (T, \Theta, P)$ and an execution sequence σ, we define the *restriction* of c to T_i to be the constraint $c_i = (T_i, \Theta|_{T_i})$. (That is, a constraint with scope limited to T_i and having no release points.) We say that a plan $\pi : S(\sigma) \to U$ *satisfies* c iff for all $i \in \{0, \ldots, q\}$, $\pi|_{T_i}$ satisfies c_i, i.e. if $\pi|_{T_i} \in \Theta|_{T_i}$. Informally, a plan satisfies c iff its restriction to each subscope T_i, $i \in \{0, \ldots, q\}$, can be extended to a valid tuple (*i.e.* a tuple which belongs to Θ). We say σ *satisfies* c if there exists a plan $\pi : S(\sigma) \to U$ that satisfies c.

For constraints with a binary scope, such as classical binding-of-duty or separation-of-duty constraints, the addition of release points is a natural generalization. Indeed, a separation-of-duty constraint with two steps s_1, s_2 as scope and P as the set of release points will be satisfied (i) by any plan π if some $r \in P$ occurs between s_1 and s_2, or (ii) by any plan π such that $\pi(s_1) \neq \pi(s_2)$.

For constraints with a larger scope, the meaning of release points is less transparent. Consider, for example, the constraint atleast$(\{s_1, s_2, s_3, s_4\}, 3, \{r\})$, where r is the release point, and the following assignment:

$$\pi(s_1) = \pi(s_3) = u_1, \ \pi(s_2) = \pi(s_4) = u_2.$$

If r occurs before or after all steps in the scope of the constraint in the execution sequence, then this assignment violates the constraint, as only two different users are assigned to these steps. If, however, the execution sequence is (s_1, s_2, s_3, r, s_4), then the constraint is satisfied. Indeed, the restriction of this assignment to $\{s_1, s_2, s_3\}$ can be extended to a valid assignment (by assigning, say, u_3 to s_4). Similarly, the restriction of this assignment to $\{s_4\}$ can also be extended to a valid assignment (assigning, say, u_1 to s_1, u_3 to s_2, and any user to s_3).

We extend our running example by modifying the SoD constraint defined between s_1 and s_4 in order to illustrate how execution sequences and release points might affect the satisfiability of an instance. The resulting workflow specification is illustrated in Figure 3.) Specifically, the constraint released by r positioned between $\omega_\otimes$ and $\omega_\|$. The intuition is to prevent the same person from creating the purchase order and the payment, except when the GRN has been signed (and countersigned, if the upper branch of the xor branching is chosen). Hence, if the "create payment" is processed before the signature/countersignature of the GRN, then the user which has created the purchase order cannot create the payment. Otherwise, if the "create payment" is processed after the signature/countersignature of the GRN, then the SoD constraint is released. In the case where the authorization policy is such that only one user is authorized to execute steps s_1 and s_4, then some

execution sequences will be satisfiable, whereas some others will not be satisfiable.

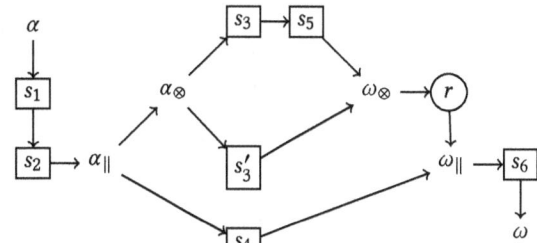

(a) Ordering on steps

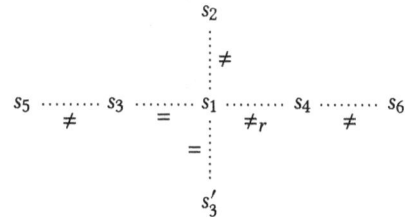

(b) Constraints

s_1	create purchase order
s_2	approve purchase order
s_3	sign GRN
s_3'	sign GRN
s_4	create payment
s_5	countersign GRN
s_6	approve payment
r	release point of the constraint blue ($s_1, s_4, \neq$)
$\neq$	different users must perform steps
$=$	same user must perform steps
$\neq_r$	same as $\neq$ but released by r

(c) Legend

Figure 3: A constrained compositional workflow specification with release points; vertices bordered by a rectangle (resp. circle) represent steps (resp. release points); vertices with no border are orchestration points.

Notice that our definitions of constraints with release points allow us to model the SoD and BoD constraints as defined by Basin *et al.* [3]. In their work, a SoD constraint is defined by two sets of steps T_1 and T_2 together with a set of release points P. Then, whenever a user u executes some step $s_1 \in T_1$, this constraint prohibits u from executing any step $s_2 \in T_2$ unless a release point is reached. One can observe that this constraint can be transformed into $|T_1| \cdot |T_2|$ binary SoD constraints with scope $(s_1, s_2) \in T_1 \times T_2$ and release points P. Basin *et al.* define a BoD constraint to be a set of steps T and a set of release points P. Once a user u has executed some step in T, u must execute the remaining steps in T unless a release point is reached. Again, we may transform this into an equivalent set of constraints with binary scope by specifying $\binom{|T|}{2}$ binary BoD constraints with scope $(s, s') \in T \times T$ (with $s \neq s'$) and release points P. Thus our definition of constraints with release points is considerably more general than existing ones.

A constrained compositional workflow schema (c.c.w.s. for short) is a tuple $(G = (S \cup R \cup O, E), U, A, C)$, where (G, U, A) is a compositional workflow schema, and C is a set of constraints with release points. We assume the scope of a constraint does not contain two exclusive steps. This is a reasonable assumption since two exclusive steps never occur in the same execution sequence. We say constraint $c = (T, \Theta, P)$ is user-independent (UI) iff for every $\theta \in \Theta$ and every permutation $\phi : U \to U$, we have $\phi \circ \theta \in \Theta$.

2.4 WSP with release points

Given a constrained c.c.w.s. $W = (S \cup R \cup O, E, U, A, C)$, we say that an execution sequence σ is *satisfied* if there exists an authorized plan $\pi : S(\sigma) \to U$ that satisfies all constraints in C. Observe that authorization does not depend on the ordering of steps or release points. We say that W is *strongly satisfiable* (resp. *weakly satisfiable*) iff every (resp. at least one) execution sequence of W is satisfiable. We are now able to define the following decision problem which is the main subject of this paper:

WSP with Release Points
  Input: A constrained compositional workflow schema
    $W = (S \cup R \cup O, E, U, A, C)$
  Question: Is W strongly satisfiable ?

There is a possibility that in practice weak rather than strong satisfiability is of interest. It is not hard to modify the algorithm described later in the paper to solve the weakly satisfiability version of WSP with Release Points. Clearly WSP with Release Points is a generalization of WSP (indeed, a WSP with Release Points with no xor branching and whose all constraints have no release point is equivalent to a WSP instance), and is thus NP-hard and $W[1]$-hard when parameterized by $k = |S|$ [25]. Moreover, it has been shown that if all considered constraints are user-independent, then WSP can be solved in time $O(2^{k \log_2 k} |W|^{O(1)})$, where k is the number of steps [18] ($|W|^{O(1)}$ means a polynomial in the size of the workflow instance), and that this is the best possible: WSP cannot be solved in time $O(c^{k \log_2 k} |W|^{O(1)})$ for any constant $c < 2$ [15] unless the Strong Exponential Time Hypothesis[2] is false, which is unlikely. This lower bound directly transfers to WSP with Release Points. Despite the seeming difficulty of the problem (since all execution sequences have to be considered), we will be able to show that WSP with Release Points is FPT parameterized by the number of vertices of the DAG (*i.e.* number of steps, release points and orchestration points) if only user-independent constraints are considered.

3 SOLVING THE COMPOSITIONAL WSP WITH RELEASE POINTS

Our aim is thus to provide an algorithm to solve the WSP with Release Points. Recall that the problem asks whether *every* execution sequence is satisfiable. Hence, a naive approach would be to enumerate all execution sequences, and test whether each of them is satisfiable. In the next section, we show that such an exhaustive

enumeration is wasteful. More precisely, we define an equivalence relation over execution sequences, and show that all execution sequences which belong to the same equivalence class behave the same with respect to satisfiability.

3.1 Execution arrangements

Let $\sim$ be the following relation over the set of all execution sequences of a workflow: $\sigma \sim \sigma'$ iff (i) $\sigma_R = \sigma'_R$ (ii) $S(\sigma) = S(\sigma')$ and (iii) for all $s \in S$, $R(\text{right}_\sigma(s)) = R(\text{right}_{\sigma'}(s))$. It is easy to see that $\sim$ defines an equivalence relation. Its equivalence classes are called *execution arrangements*. Informally, all execution sequences of an execution arrangement have the same set of steps and release points, their release points are in the same order, and every step occurs between the same pair of release points.

From this observation, it makes sense to define a "compact" representation of an execution arrangement. More precisely, we define an execution arrangement as an ordered sequence $(S_1, r_1, S_2, r_2, ..., r_{q-1}, S_q)$ which satisfies the following properties:

(1) $\{S_1, ..., S_q\}$ is a partition of S (we may have $S_i = \emptyset$ for some $i \in [q]$);
(2) $(r_1, ..., r_{q-1})$ is a linear subextension of G containing all release points;
(3) for all $(s_1, ..., s_q) \in S_1 \times \cdots \times S_q$, $(s_1, r_1, ..., r_{q-1}, s_q)$ is a linear subextension of G.

Notice the abuse of notation in the last property if $S_i = \emptyset$ for some $i \in [q]$. In this case, we simply omit such steps s_i in the sequence $(s_1, r_1, ..., r_{q-1}, s_q)$. For instance, if $S_2 = \emptyset$, then the sequence is actually $(s_1, r_1, r_2, s_3, ..., r_{q-1}, s_q)$.

The execution arrangements and the corresponding execution sequences for the example in Figure 3 are tabulated below.

Arrangement	Sequence
$\{s_1, s_2, s_3, s_5\}, r, \{s_4, s_6\}$	$(s_1, s_2, s_3, s_5, r, s_4, s_6)$
$\{s_1, s_2, s_3, s_4, s_5\}, r, \{s_6\}$	$(s_1, s_2, s_3, s_5, s_4, r, s_6)$
	$(s_1, s_2, s_3, s_4, s_5, r, s_6)$
	$(s_1, s_2, s_4, s_3, s_5, r, s_6)$
$\{s_1, s_2, s'_3\}, r, \{s_4, s_6\}$	$(s_1, s_2, s'_3, r, s_4, s_6)$
$\{s_1, s_2, s'_3, s_4\}, r, \{s_6\}$	$(s_1, s_2, s'_3, s_4, r, s_6)$
	$(s_1, s_2, s_4, s'_3, r, s_6)$

As we can see, even with one xor branching and one release point, the number of execution arrangements (4) is smaller than the number of execution sequences (7). Naturally, this difference increases with the number of xor branchings and release points.

The idea of defining this equivalence relation comes from the fact that the ordering of steps between two release points is of no importance for determining the satisfiability of a given execution sequence. We will exploit this property and prove that the satisfiability of two execution sequences of an execution arrangement are equivalent, *i.e.* one is satisfiable iff the other is. This is formalized by the following lemma.

Lemma 3.1. *Let $W = (G = (S \cup R \cup O, E), U, A, C)$ be a c.c.w.s.. Given two execution sequences σ, σ' of W with $\sigma \sim \sigma'$, σ is satisfiable if and only if σ' is.*

Proof. Let $c = (T, \Theta, R) \in C$. By definition of $\sim$, we have $\sigma_R = \sigma'_R = (r_1, ..., r_q)$. Now, let $i \in \{1, ..., q-1\}$, and denote by T_i the set

---

[2]The Strong Exponential Time Hypothesis [16] states that a CNF SAT formula on n variables cannot be solved in c^n time for any $c < 2$.

$T \cap S(\text{btw}_\sigma(r_i, r_{i+1}))$ and by T_i' the set $T \cap S(\text{btw}_{\sigma'}(r_i, r_{i+1}))$. Again by definition of $\sim$, it holds that $R(\text{right}_\sigma(s)) = R(\text{right}_{\sigma'}(s))$ for every $s \in S(\sigma)$, which implies $S(\text{btw}_\sigma(r_i, r_{i+1})) = S(\text{btw}_{\sigma'}(r_i, r_{i+1}))$, and thus $T_i = T_i'$. It proves that σ satisfies c iff σ' satisfies c. Finally, recall that authorization does not depend on the ordering of steps or release points. Hence, since $S(\sigma) = S(\sigma')$ by definition, an authorized plan for σ will also be an authorized plan for σ', and conversely. □

Lemma 3.1 states that in order to test the satisfiability of a c.c.w.s., it is sufficient to test the satisfiability of only one execution sequence per execution arrangement. Observe that the number of possible execution sequences can be as large as $(|S| + |R|)!$, even with no xor branching, while the number of execution arrangements is bounded above by $|R|! |R|^{|S|}$.

Thus, the main issue is now to enumerate all possible execution arrangements of an instance, and, for each of them, to test its satisfiability. The enumeration is itself a non-trivial question, not least because of the possible interleaving of several xor and parallel branchings. In particular, the presence of xor branchings implies that the set of steps and release points might be different depending on the executions. Hence, our approach can be decomposed into three subtasks:

(1) elimination of xor branchings;
(2) enumeration of all execution arrangements of a xor-free instance; and
(3) testing the satisfiability of an execution arrangement.

The next three subsections address these subtasks in turn. In Section 3.2, we develop a method for decomposing a problem instance into subproblems that do not contain any xor branching. Our algorithm will run in FPT time parameterized by the number of xor branchings of the instance, and polynomial space. In Section 3.3, we describe an algorithm to enumerate execution arrangements running in FPT time parameterized by the number of steps and release points, and using polynomial space. Finally, in Section 3.4, we show that each subproblem can be reduced to the classical WSP, allowing us to use any known method for solving this problem in order to terminate the algorithm.

Algorithm 1 summarizes the general procedure in an informal manner. In Section 3.5, we provide a theoretical analysis of our algorithm.

Algorithm 1 General algorithm

Input: $W = (S, R, O, E, U, A, C)$ a c.c.w.s.
1: **for all** xor-free subinstance W' **do**
2:    **for all** execution arrangement Σ of W' **do**
3:       **if** Σ is unsatisfiable **then**
4:          **return** UNSATISFIABLE INSTANCE
5:       **end if**
6:    **end for**
7: **end for**
8: **return** SATISFIABLE INSTANCE

3.2 Elimination of xor branchings

Recall that in an execution sequence σ of a compositional workflow specification containing a xor branching of two subworkflows $G_1 = (V_1, E_1)$ and $G_2 = (V_2, E_2)$, either $V_1 \subseteq V(\sigma)$ or $V_2 \subseteq V(\sigma)$. Such a branching is identified by its corresponding input and output vertices $\alpha_\otimes$ and $\omega_\otimes$, respectively. For such a pair $x = (\alpha_\otimes, \omega_\otimes)$, we construct the compositional workflow schemas G_1^x and G_2^x from G by removing all vertices from G_2 and G_1, respectively. Now, given a set X of pairs of *xor* input and output vertices, we define the set of *reduced compositional workflows* as follows:

- if $X = \{x\}$, then $red_X(G) = \{G_1^x, G_2^x\}$;
- otherwise, for an arbitrary $x \in X$ whose branches do not contain themselves another xor branching, $red_X(G) = red_{X \setminus \{x\}}(G_1^x) \cup red_{X \setminus \{x\}}(G_2^x)$.

Figure 4 illustrates these definitions applied to our running example. In the first workflow, steps s_3 and s_5 are removed, while in the second one, step s_3' is removed (then both are simplified using rules described in Section 2.1, allowing us to remove $\alpha_\otimes$ and $\omega_\otimes$).

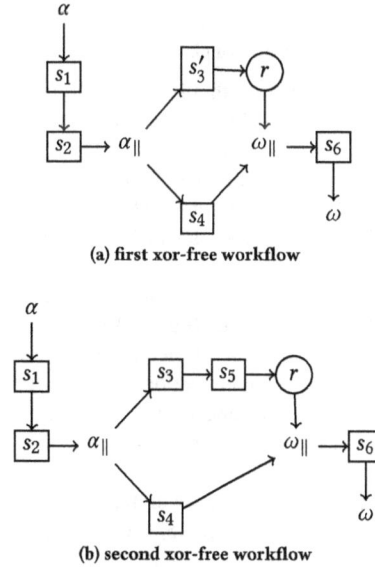

(a) first xor-free workflow

(b) second xor-free workflow

Figure 4: The two workflows obtained after removing the xor branching of Figure 3.

We denote by $\mathcal{B}$ be the set of all pairs of xor input and output vertices of a given c.c.w.s. $W = (G = (S \cup R \cup O, E), U, A, C)$. Informally, $red_{\mathcal{B}}(G)$ contains all possible compositional workflows obtained from G by removing, for every xor branching, one of the two branches. Hence, any $G' \in red_{\mathcal{B}}(G)$ is xor-free, and, in particular, does not contain two exclusive steps. For $G' = (V', E') \in red_{\mathcal{B}}(G)$, let $W[G']$ be the c.c.w.s. induced by G': $W[G'] = (G' = (S \cap V', R \cap V', O \cap V', E), U, A \cap (V' \times U), C)$ (as mentioned earlier, we may assume that constraints do not contain exclusive steps, hence there is no need for restricting the scopes of constraints). We now use this construction in the following result.

LEMMA 3.2. *Using the notation above, W is satisfiable if and only if $W[G']$ is satisfiable for every $G' \in red_{\mathcal{B}}(G)$.*

PROOF. Simply observe that every execution sequence of $W[G']$ is also an execution sequence of W, and, conversely, for every execution sequence σ of W, there exists $G' \in red_{\mathcal{B}}(G)$ such that σ is an execution sequence of $W[red_{\mathcal{B}}(G)]$. □

3.3 Enumeration of execution arrangements

Throughout this subsection, we will assume we are given a c.c.w.s. $W = (G = (S, R, O, E), U, A, C)$ which does not contain any xor branching. Our objective is to provide an algorithm enumerating all execution arrangements of W.

Since W is assumed to be xor-free, we know that all execution sequences (and thus all execution arrangements) that can be obtained from G have the same set of steps and release points, namely S and R, respectively.

Let us recall the properties satisfied by an execution arrangement $(S_1, r_1, S_2, r_2, ..., r_{q-1}, S_q)$:

(1) $\{S_1, ..., S_q\}$ is a partition of S (we may have $S_i = \emptyset$ for some $i \in [q]$);
(2) $(r_1, ..., r_{q-1})$ is a linear subextension of G containing all release points;
(3) for all $(s_1, ..., s_q) \in S_1 \times \cdots \times S_q$, $(s_1, r_1, ..., r_{q-1}, s_q)$ is a linear subextension of G.

The first step of the algorithm is to enumerate all linear subextensions of release points. This is actually equivalent to the enumeration of all topological orderings of the partial order restricted to R, and can be done using a BFS-based recursive algorithm (although more involved and efficient algorithms exist, see *e.g.* [17, 20, 22, 24]). Hence, in the following, we fix such a linear extension[3] $(r_1, ..., r_{q-1})$.

For the sake of readability, we will now restrict ourselves to steps only: we first assume that G does not contain release points, by considering the restriction of the partial order to $V \setminus R$. In addition, we will consider orchestration points as normal steps. In order to obtain execution arrangements containing "concrete" steps only, simply remove the orchestration points once an execution arrangement is returned. Hence, we now assume $V = S$.

Our procedure is described in detail in Algorithm 2, and consists in constructing the partition $S_1, ... S_q$ step by step. Also, it takes as input a partial partition $S_1, ..., S_q$ of a subset of S. It takes as input the subset $S_{rem} \subseteq S$ of remaining steps that have to be assigned to some set of the partition $\{S_1, ..., S_q\}$ of $S \setminus S_{rem}$. For the first call, simply set $S_{rem} = S$ and $S_i = \emptyset$ for all $i \in [q]$.

Once a step s has been chosen (line 4), we need to decide to which set it can belong to. To do so, we determine two indices i_{min} and i_{max} such that for all $i \in \{i_{min}, ..., i_{max}\}$, s can be put in S_i. Roughly speaking, we cannot put s to the left of a set S_j such that $s' < s$ for some $s' \in S_j$, or to the left of some release point r_j such that $r_j < s$ (and, similarly, to the right of a set S_j or a release point r_j such that $s < r_j$ or $s < s'$ for some $s' \in S_j$). This is illustrated in Figure 5.

LEMMA 3.3. *Every output of Algorithm 2 is an execution arrangement, and every execution arrangement is an output of Algorithm 2.*

---

[3]We could incorporate the enumeration of sequences of release points inside Algorithm 2. However, for the sake of readability, we choose to separate this step.

Algorithm 2 Enumeration of execution arrangements given a linear extension $(r_1, ..., r_{q-1})$ of release points

Input: $S_{rem} \subseteq S$, $\{S_1, ..., S_q\}$ partition of $S \setminus S_{rem}$
1: **if** $S_{rem} = \emptyset$ **then**
2:     output $(S_1, r_1, S_2, r_2, ..., r_{q-1}, S_q)$
3: **else**
4:     $s \leftarrow$ source of $G[S_{rem}]$ (arbitrarily chosen)
5:     $i_{min} \leftarrow \max(\{i \in \{2, ..., q\} : r_{i-1} < s$ or $s' < s$ for some $s' \in S_i\} \cup \{1\})$
6:     $i_{max} \leftarrow \min(\{i \in \{1, ..., q-1\} : s < r_i$ or $s < s'$ for some $s' \in S_i\} \cup \{q\})$
7:     **for all** $i \in \{i_{min}, ..., i_{max}\}$ **do**
8:         make a recursive call with input $S_{rem} \setminus \{s\}$, $\{S_1, ..., S_i \cup \{s\}, ..., S_q\}$
9:     **end for**
10: **end if**

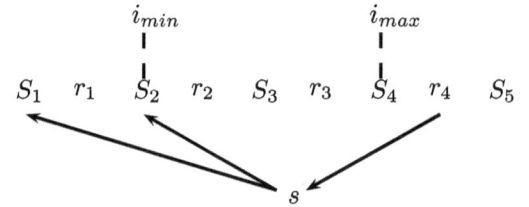

Figure 5: Illustration of i_{max} and i_{min}. Arrows indicate that $s < r_4$ and that there exists $s'_1 \in S_1$ and $s'_2 \in S_2$ such that $s'_1 < s$ and $s'_2 < s$. Hence, s may belong to S_2, S_3 or S_4.

PROOF. Let $\Sigma = (S_1^*, r_1, S_2^*, ..., r_{q-1}, S_q^*)$ be an output of our algorithm, and let us show it is indeed an execution arrangement. First, $(r_1, ..., r_{q-1})$ is a fixed linear extension of R, and the algorithm only stops when all steps have been assigned to a set S_i, thus properties (2) and (1) are obviously satisfied. For all inputs $(S_1, ..., S_q)$ of the algorithm, we prove that for all $(s_1, ..., s_q) \in S_1 \times \cdots \times S_q$, $(s_1, r_1, ..., r_{q-1}, s_q)$ satisfies property 3, by induction on $|\bigcup_{i \in [q]} S_i|$. The property is obviously true at the first call since $(r_1, ..., r_{q-1})$ is a linear subextension of R. Then, let $(S_1, ..., S_q)$ be an input satisfying the property, and s chosen at line 4. Let $i \in \{i_{min}, ..., i_{max}\}$. For all $j < i$, by definition of i_{min}, it holds that $s \not< r_j$, and $s \not< s'$ for all $s' \in S_j$. Similarly, for all $j \geq i$ we have $r_j \not< s$, and, for all $j > i$ and all $s' \in S_j$, we have $s' \not< s$. This proves that $(s_1, r_1, ..., r_{q-1}, s_q)$ is a linear subextension of G for all $(s_1, ..., s_q) \in S_1 \times \cdots \times S_i \cup \{s\} \times \cdots \times S_q$.

Conversely, let $\Sigma = (S_1^*, r_1, ..., r_{q-1}, S_q^*)$ be an execution arrangement. We now show that Σ is an output of the algorithm. To do so, assume that there is a call of the algorithm with input $\{S_1, ..., S_q\}$ such that $S_i \subseteq S_i^*$ for all $i \in [q]$ (this is obviously true at the first call). Let s be the step chosen at line 4, and i^* such that $s \in S_{i^*}^*$. We need to show that $i_{min} \leq i^* \leq i_{max}$. If $i_{min} = 1$ then the first inequality obviously holds. Otherwise, the definition of i_{min} implies that we have $r_{i_{min}-1} < s$ or $s' < s$ for some $s' \in S_{i_{min}}$. In both cases, having $i^* < i_{min}$ would break property 3 and Σ would not be an execution arrangement. Similarly, the second inequality holds trivially if $i_{max} = q$, and $i_{max} < i^*$ together with the definition of i_{max} would imply that Σ is not an execution arrangement.   □

3.4 Reduction to WSP

It now remains to test the satisfiability of an execution arrangement. Indeed, as we saw in Lemma 3.1, all execution sequences of the same execution arrangement behave the same with respect to satisfiability. To do so, we show that satisfiability of an execution arrangement reduces to the satisfiability of a finite number of "classical" WSP instances. We recall the formal definition of WSP [25].

> WORKFLOW SATISFIABILITY PROBLEM (WSP)
> *Input*: A constrained workflow authorization schema
> $\qquad W = (G = (S, E), U, A, C)$
> *Question*: Is there a valid plan $\pi : S \to U$?

Let $\Sigma = (S_1, r_1, S_2, r_2, ..., r_{q-1}, S_q)$ be an execution arrangement (*i.e.* an output of Algorithm, line 2), and $c = (T, \Theta, P)$ be a constraint with release points $P = \{r_{p_1}, \dots, r_{p_{|P|}}\}$ (*w.l.o.g.* we assume $p_i \leq p_j$ whenever $i \leq j$, *i.e.* this ordering is a linear extension of $R(\Sigma)$). As in Section 2.3, for all $i \in \{1, \dots, |P| - 1\}$, define $T_i = T \cap S(\text{btw}(r_{p_i}, r_{p_{i+1}}))$, $T_0 = T \cap S(\text{left}(r_{p_0}))$, $T_{|P|} = T \cap S(\text{right}(r_{p_{|P|}}))$, and the "classical" constraint $c_i = (T_i, \Theta|_{T_i})$. Recall that c is satisfied by an execution sequence σ iff there exists a plan π such that $\pi|_{T_i}$ satisfies c_i for every $i \in \{0, \dots, q\}$. Thus, for each $i \in [|P|]$, it makes sense to define the WSP instance $W_i = (G_i = (S_i, E_i), U, A_i, C_i)$, which defines the partial order of G restricted to S_i, $A_i = A \cap (S_i \times U)$ and $C_i = \{c_i | c \in C\}$. By the foregoing, we obtain the following result:

LEMMA 3.4. Σ *is satisfiable (for WSP WITH RELEASE POINTS) if and only if W_i is satisfiable (for WSP) for every $i \in [|P|]$.*

Using this result, we are thus able to use any state-of-the-art solver for WSP as a black box in order to obtain the general algorithm. There are several papers describing the design and evaluation of practical WSP algorithms, see, e.g., [7, 18, 19, 25]. Some of these algorithms are bespoke, while others use SAT solvers.

3.5 Analysis of the algorithm

We now analyze the running time and space of our algorithm with respect to the different parameters of an instance: the number of users $|U|$, the number of constraints $|C|$, the number of steps $|S|$, the number of release points $|R|$ and the number of orchestration points $|O|$. We denote by $|W|$ the total size of an instance. First, observe that we always have $|O| = O(|R| + |S|)$ by construction (in practice, $|O|$ will be much smaller than $|S| + |R|$ because of the simplification mentioned at the end of Section 2.1). We will also consider the number $|\mathcal{B}|$ of xor branchings in a problem instance. (Clearly $|\mathcal{B}| \leq |O|$.)

Most techniques we use in this algorithm are based on *recursive procedures*. Given an input I, such a recursive procedure applies various operations (dependent on I), and then makes one or several recursive calls with inputs $I_1, \dots, I_w$. In order for such a procedure to terminate, there must exist an integer-valued *measure* $\ell(I)$ which strictly decreases with each recursive call, *i.e.* such that $\ell(I_j) < \ell(I)$ for all $j \in [w]$. For instance, the measure of the recursive procedure of Section 3.2 is the number of xor branchings in the input, which

decreases by one at each new call, while the measure of Algorithm 2 is the number of steps, which also decreases by one at each new call.

The *width* of a recursive algorithm is the maximum number of recursive calls at each step (*i.e.* w in the previous notation), while the *depth* is the measure $\ell(I)$ of the first input of the algorithm. Then a recursive algorithm has a running time of $O(w^{\ell(I)} T(I))$, where $T(I)$ is the running time of a single call, and a space complexity of $O(\ell(I) Sp(I))$, where $Sp(I)$ is the space complexity of a single call.

The worst case complexity (time or space) of our algorithm is the product of the respective complexity of the algorithms for solving the three subproblems:

(1) enumeration of all xor-free subinstances;
(2) given a xor-free instance, enumeration of all execution arrangements;
(3) given an execution arrangement, reduction to WSP and satisfiability test.

The first step, described in Section 3.2, uses a recursive algorithm. Its branching width is 2, its depth is $|\mathcal{B}|$ (the number of xor-branchings of the instance), and every step takes polynomial time and space, since it simply consists in removing some vertices of the workflow specification. Thus, the algorithm uses polynomial space and its running time is $O(2^{|\mathcal{B}|} \cdot |W|^{O(1)})$.

Given a xor-free instance of the previous step, the next task is to enumerate all execution arrangements (Section 3.3). To do so, we first enumerate all linear extensions of release points. This can be done in time linear in the number of such linear extensions [22], which is at most $|R|!$. Then, given a linear extension of the release points, we can apply Algorithm 2, which is a recursive algorithm, whose branching width is at most q, the number of release points plus one (see line 7), and depth is $|S|$ (since we remove an element of S_{rem} at each recursive call). Moreover, each call takes polynomial time and space. Hence Algorithm 2 takes time $O(q^{|S|} \cdot |W|^{O(1)})$. Thus subproblem 2 uses polynomial space and its running time is

$$O(|R|! q^{|S|} |W|^{O(1)}) = O(|R|!(|R| + 1)^{|S|} |W|^{O(1)}).$$

Finally, the last step contains a reduction to several instances of WSP, and a satisfiability test for each of them. More precisely, given an execution arrangement Σ, we construct, in polynomial time, $|R(\Sigma)| + 1 = O(|R|)$ instances of WSP. Then, the running-time of the satisfiability test of each WSP instance depends on the chosen algorithm. Let $wsp(\alpha, \beta, \gamma)$ be the running time of an algorithm solving a WSP instance with α users, β steps and γ constraints. The running time of this step is thus $O(|R|) wsp(|U|, |S|, |C|)$, while the space complexity is the one of the chosen algorithm for WSP. If all constraints are user-independent, then the algorithm of [18] runs in time $wsp(|U|, |S|, |C|) = O(2^{|S| \log_2 |S|} |W|^{O(1)})$ and polynomial space. Thus, this step takes time $O(2^{|S| \log_2 |S|} |W|^{O(1)})$ and polynomial space.

In total, the running-time of our algorithm is thus

$$O(2^{|\mathcal{B}|} |R|!(|R| + 1)^{|S|} wsp(|U|, |S|, |C|) |W|^{O(1)}).$$

If all constraints are user-independent, this becomes

$$O(2^{|\mathcal{B}|} |R|!(|R| + 1)^{|S|} 2^{|S| \log_2 |S|} |W|^{O(1)}),$$

which is an FPT running time parameterized by the number of vertices of the workflow specification. Moreover, the algorithm uses polynomial space. Thus, we obtain the following result.

THEOREM 3.5. *If all constraints are user-independent, WSP WITH RELEASE POINTS can be solved in time*

$$O(2^{|\mathcal{B}|}|R|!(|R|+1)^{|S|}2^{|S|\log_2(|S|)}|W|^{O(1)})$$

and polynomial space.

As long as the values of $|\mathcal{B}|$ and $|R|$ are small, our algorithm may well be efficient in practice since the branch-and-bound algorithm of [18] has proved to be very efficient in practice and was further improved in [19]. For instance, in the particular case where $|R| = 0$, we obtain the same running time as for WSP. Observe that this algorithm scales polynomially with the number of users which is likely to be, in practice, the largest parameter of a workflow. Finally, our algorithm is deterministic, *i.e.* does not produce false positive or false negative answers, contrary to the algorithm of Basin *et al.* [3]. It also uses polynomial space, contrary to the algorithm of Crampton and Gutin [10].

4 RELATED WORK

Research on workflow satisfiability began with the seminal work of Bertino, Ferrari and Atluri [4] and Crampton [8]. Wang and Li were the first to demonstrate that WSP, subject to specific and limiting restrictions, was fixed-parameter tractable [25]. A substantial body of work now exists on the fixed-parameter tractability of WSP [6, 9, 11]. In particular, it is known that WSP is fixed-parameter tractable (parameterized by the number of steps) when all constraints are regular [11] or user-independent [6].

Basin, Burri and Karjoth introduced the notion of release points [3] in order to model workflows in which the set of steps that are executed may vary and for which constraints only apply to certain sets of steps. They modeled workflows using a process algebra and define the notion of an *enforcement process*, which corresponds to a valid plan in our model of workflow satisfiability. They showed that the enforcement process existence (EPE) problem, which corresponds to the workflow satisfiability problem, is NP-hard, and developed a polynomial-time heuristic to solve the EPE problem. Their algorithm achieves good results under the assumption that the user population is large and "the static authorizations are equally distributed between them".

We believe it is reasonable to assume the user population is large, at least relative to the number of steps in the workflow. Indeed, our FPT algorithms are of interest provided this assumption holds. However, it is unclear whether it is reasonable to assume that static authorizations are equally distributed. We adopt a different approach by extending an existing model for compositional workflows, due to Crampton and Gutin [10], to accommodate release points, and modifying the definition of constraint satisfaction and workflow satisfiability accordingly. By making use of existing work on WSP we are able to provide the first FPT algorithm for WSP with release points. Moreover, this algorithm is exact and may be used for any workflow specification containing user-independent constraints. This is in contrast to the work by Basin *et al.*, which yields a non exact algorithm, in the sense that it may produce false

negatives (although it does run in polynomial time) and only applies to specific SoD and BoD constraints. However, it should also be noted that the approach of Basin *et al.* can model more complex workflow specifications, such as ones containing loops. In other words, their approach is applicable to more workflow patterns than ours, but to fewer types of workflow constraints.

On the other hand, there exists work on workflow satisfiability with more complex control flow patterns that does not consider release points [5, 10, 27], of which only the work of Crampton and Gutin [10] considers fixed-parameter tractability of WSP. One contribution of this paper is to extend the model due to Crampton and Gutin [10], but we also introduce the notion of execution arrangements and an algorithm which considers execution arrangements (rather than execution sequences). Thus we provide techniques that can usefully be applied to WSP for compositional workflows without release points.

5 CONCLUDING REMARKS

In this paper, we have extended recent work on FPT algorithms for the workflow satisfiability problem by introducing release points. Release points allow constraints to be defined for a workflow specification in which the set of steps that is executed may vary from one workflow instance to another. In particular, a constraint can be "switched on" when certain steps are executed in a certain sequence and "switched off" otherwise. The typical use case is when there is non-deterministic branching in the specification and the constraint should apply when one branch is executed but not the other. As such, this work allows us to further close the gap between the workflow specifications that are required in practice and those for which we can provide algorithms to solve the workflow satisfiability problem. In particular, our algorithms can be used as the basis for an on-line reference monitor for workflows containing xor branching (applying methods described by Crampton and Gutin [10, Section 2.2]).

We plan to extend our model to include sub-workflows that can be repeated. A purchase order workflow, for example, might include a sub-workflow containing a single step that creates an item in a purchase order. We expect that some care will be required to integrate looping constructs and release points.

In Section 3.5 we noted that we reduce WSP WITH RELEASE POINTS to WSP and use existing WSP solvers. The performance of such solvers has improved dramatically in recent years [7, 18, 19, 25]. We plan to use state-of-the-art solvers to test the hypothesis that strong satisfiability for real-world workflow specifications with xor branching and release points can be solved efficiently in practice.

It may also be interesting to consider the workflow satisfiability problem when the authorization policy changes over the lifetime of a workflow instance. Such changes might occur, for example, if some users are unavailable at certain times. Some related prior work exists on workflow resiliency [21, 25]. It is also possible to model certain constraints with release points by modifying the authorization policy. Indeed, this is essentially how Basin *et al.* define enforcement processes for their SoD and BoD constraints [3].

Finally, recent work has shown that WSP is FPT for class-independent constraints [9], a generalization of user-independent constraints that allow for the specification of constraints over groups of users. Such constraints are useful for specifying requirements determined by organizational structures. It would be interesting to investigate whether WSP with release points remains FPT when we allow class-independent constraints in the workflow specification.

Aknowledgement. Gregory Gutin's research was supported by Royal Society Wolfson Research Merit Award.

REFERENCES

[1] AMERICAN NATIONAL STANDARDS INSTITUTE. *ANSI INCITS 359-2004 for Role Based Access Control*, 2004.

[2] BANG-JENSEN, J., AND GUTIN, G. *Digraphs - theory, algorithms and applications.* Springer, 2002.

[3] BASIN, D. A., BURRI, S. J., AND KARJOTH, G. Obstruction-free authorization enforcement: Aligning security and business objectives. *Journal of Computer Security 22*, 5 (2014), 661–698.

[4] BERTINO, E., FERRARI, E., AND ATLURI, V. The specification and enforcement of authorization constraints in workflow management systems. *ACM Trans. Inf. Syst. Secur. 2*, 1 (1999), 65–104.

[5] BERTOLISSI, C., SANTOS, D. R. D., AND RANISE, S. Automated synthesis of run-time monitors to enforce authorization policies in business processes. In *Proceedings of the 10th ACM Symposium on Information, Computer and Communications Security, ASIA CCS '15, Singapore, April 14-17, 2015* (2015), F. Bao, S. Miller, J. Zhou, and G. Ahn, Eds., ACM, pp. 297–308.

[6] COHEN, D., CRAMPTON, J., GAGARIN, A., GUTIN, G., AND JONES, M. Iterative plan construction for the workflow satisfiability problem. *J. Artif. Intell. Res. (JAIR) 51* (2014), 555–577.

[7] COHEN, D. A., CRAMPTON, J., GAGARIN, A., GUTIN, G., AND JONES, M. Algorithms for the workflow satisfiability problem engineered for counting constraints. *J. Comb. Optim. 32*, 1 (2016), 3–24.

[8] CRAMPTON, J. A reference monitor for workflow systems with constrained task execution. In *10th ACM Symposium on Access Control Models and Technologies, SACMAT 2005, Stockholm, Sweden, June 1-3, 2005, Proceedings* (2005), E. Ferrari and G. Ahn, Eds., ACM, pp. 38–47.

[9] CRAMPTON, J., GAGARIN, A., GUTIN, G., JONES, M., AND WAHLSTRÖM, M. On the workflow satisfiability problem with class-independent constraints for hierarchical organizations. *ACM Trans. Priv. Secur. 19*, 3 (2016), 8:1–8:29.

[10] CRAMPTON, J., AND GUTIN, G. Constraint expressions and workflow satisfiability. In *18th ACM Symposium on Access Control Models and Technologies, SACMAT '13, Amsterdam, The Netherlands, June 12-14, 2013* (2013), M. Conti, J. Vaidya, and A. Schaad, Eds., ACM, pp. 73–84.

[11] CRAMPTON, J., GUTIN, G., AND YEO, A. On the parameterized complexity and kernelization of the workflow satisfiability problem. *ACM Trans. Inf. Syst. Secur. 16*, 1 (2013), 4:1–4:31.

[12] CYGAN, M., FOMIN, F. V., KOWALIK, L., LOKSHTANOV, D., MARX, D., PILIPCZUK, M., PILIPCZUK, M., AND SAURABH, S. *Parameterized Algorithms.* Springer, 2015.

[13] DIESTEL, R. *Graph Theory, 4th Edition*, vol. 173 of *Graduate texts in mathematics.* Springer, 2012.

[14] DOWNEY, R. G., AND FELLOWS, M. R. *Fundamentals of Parameterized Complexity.* Texts in Computer Science. Springer, 2013.

[15] GUTIN, G., AND WAHLSTRÖM, M. Tight lower bounds for the workflow satisfiability problem based on the strong exponential time hypothesis. *Inf. Process. Lett. 116*, 3 (2016), 223–226.

[16] IMPAGLIAZZO, R., AND PATURI, R. On the complexity of k-SAT. *J. Comput. Syst. Sci. 62*, 2 (2001), 367–375.

[17] KALVIN, A. D., AND VAROL, Y. L. On the generation of all topological sortings. *Journal of Algorithms 4*, 2 (1983), 150 – 162.

[18] KARAPETYAN, D., GAGARIN, A. V., AND GUTIN, G. Pattern backtracking algorithm for the workflow satisfiability problem with user-independent constraints. In *Frontiers in Algorithmics - 9th International Workshop, FAW 2015, Guilin, China, July 3-5, 2015, Proceedings* (2015), J. Wang and C. Yap, Eds., vol. 9130 of *Lecture Notes in Computer Science*, Springer, pp. 138–149.

[19] KARAPETYAN, D., PARKES, A. J., GUTIN, G., AND GAGARIN, A. Pattern-based approach to the workflow satisfiability problem with user-independent constraints. *CoRR abs/1604.05636* (2016).

[20] KNUTH, D. E., AND SZWARCFITER, J. L. A structured program to generate all topological sorting arrangements. *Inf. Process. Lett. 2*, 6 (1974), 153–157.

[21] MACE, J. C., MORISSET, C., AND VAN MOORSEL, A. P. A. Quantitative workflow resiliency. In *Computer Security - ESORICS 2014 - 19th European Symposium on Research in Computer Security, Wroclaw, Poland, September 7-11, 2014. Proceedings, Part I* (2014), M. Kutylowski and J. Vaidya, Eds., vol. 8712 of *Lecture Notes in Computer Science*, Springer, pp. 344–361.

[22] PRUESSE, G., AND RUSKEY, F. Generating linear extensions fast. *SIAM J. Comput. 23*, 2 (1994), 373–386.

[23] VAN DER AALST, W. M. P., TER HOFSTEDE, A. H. M., KIEPUSZEWSKI, B., AND BARROS, A. P. Workflow patterns. *Distributed and Parallel Databases 14*, 1 (2003), 5–51.

[24] VAROL, Y. L., AND ROTEM, D. An algorithm to generate all topological sorting arrangements. *Comput. J. 24*, 1 (1981), 83–84.

[25] WANG, Q., AND LI, N. Satisfiability and resiliency in workflow authorization systems. *ACM Trans. Inf. Syst. Secur. 13*, 4 (2010), 40.

[26] WHITE, S., AND MIERS, D. *BPMN Modeling and Reference Guide: Understanding and Using BPMN.* Future Strategies Incorporated, 2008.

[27] YANG, P., XIE, X., RAY, I., AND LU, S. Satisfiability analysis of workflows with control-flow patterns and authorization constraints. *IEEE Trans. Services Computing 7*, 2 (2014), 237–251.

A Secure Sum Protocol and Its Application to Privacy-preserving Multi-party Analytics

Shagufta Mehnaz
Dept. of Computer Science,
Purdue University
West Lafayette, IN, USA
smehnaz@purdue.edu

Gowtham Bellala*
C3 IoT
Redwood City, CA, USA
gowtham.bellala@c3iot.com

Elisa Bertino
Dept. of Computer Science,
Purdue University
West Lafayette, IN, USA
bertino@purdue.edu

ABSTRACT

Many enterprises are transitioning towards data-driven business processes. There are numerous situations where multiple parties would like to share data towards a common goal if it were possible to simultaneously protect the privacy and security of the individuals and organizations described in the data. Existing solutions for multi-party analytics that follow the so called Data Lake paradigm have parties transfer their raw data to a trusted third-party (i.e., mediator), which then performs the desired analysis on the global data, and shares the results with the parties. However, such a solution does not fit many applications such as Healthcare, Finance, and the Internet-of-Things, where privacy is a strong concern. Motivated by the increasing demands for data privacy, we study the problem of privacy-preserving multi-party data analytics, where the goal is to enable analytics on multi-party data without compromising the data privacy of each individual party. In this paper, we first propose a secure sum protocol with strong security guarantees. The proposed secure sum protocol is resistant to collusion attacks even with $N - 2$ parties colluding, where N denotes the total number of collaborating parties. We then use this protocol to propose two secure gradient descent algorithms, one for horizontally partitioned data, and the other for vertically partitioned data. The proposed framework is generic and applies to a wide class of machine learning problems. We demonstrate our solution for two popular use-cases, regression and classification, and evaluate the performance of the proposed solution in terms of the obtained model accuracy, latency and communication cost. In addition, we perform a scalability analysis to evaluate the performance of the proposed solution as the data size and the number of parties increase.

ACM Reference format:

Shagufta Mehnaz, Gowtham Bellala, and Elisa Bertino. 2017. A Secure Sum Protocol and Its Application to Privacy-preserving Multi-party Analytics. In *Proceedings of SACMAT'17, June 21–23, 2017, Indianapolis, IN, USA, ,* 12 pages.
DOI: http://dx.doi.org/10.1145/3078861.3078869

---

*This work was done while the author was at Hewlett Packard Labs.

---

1 INTRODUCTION

An important challenge for today's data-driven enterprises is how to extract information from a dataset that can facilitate good business decisions, without sacrificing the privacy of the individuals or organizations whose sensitive details may be contained in the dataset. This challenge is compounded when the analysis involves multiple organizations (or parties) wishing to collaborate, in order to obtain a broader understanding of a topic of mutual interest.

As a motivating example, consider a scenario where a group of hospitals wish to collaborate to improve their collective quality of healthcare. Each hospital already collects a lot of data about its patients, including their demographics, past medical history, lab results, current diagnosis, and prescribed treatment and outcomes. This data contains a wealth of information that if shared across the group could mutually benefit all parties by enabling faster diagnosis and effective treatment for similar cases. However, this data contains extremely sensitive and private information both about the patients and the hospitals. Thus, for a variety of reasons (including regulatory[1]), sharing this sort of data can be problematic. This hinders the desire of the organizations to become more data-driven.

This general class of problem arises when multiple parties, each owning a privacy-sensitive dataset, would like to collectively perform analytics on the union of the datasets while respecting the privacy and security concerns of each individual party. Current commercial solutions require each party to share their raw data or local aggregates with a trusted third party or a mediator under an appropriate confidential agreement, and have the mediator compute and share the results. However, for reasons such as the recent cyber attacks and resulting massive privacy breaches, many organizations are understandably hesitant to share either raw or aggregate data with third parties [1, 2].

In this paper, we introduce a generalized framework that enables training of machine learning models on multi-party, distributed data in a privacy-preserving manner. **The proposed framework assumes an *untrusted mediator*. Under our framework, each party shares only encrypted local results, and then the mediator aggregates these results to obtain the global result.** The encrypted local results are also anonymized so that the mediator cannot associate a local result with the party to which the local result belongs. The proposed framework is generic and applies to several machine learning algorithms.

We first propose a secure sum protocol that serves as a key building block in this framework. While secure sum protocols for

---

[1]https://www.congress.gov/bill/105th-congress/senate-bill/1368

multiple parties have been widely investigated and applied [3, 4], they are not secure when two or more parties collude. In contrast, our proposed protocol is secure under the honest-but-curious model, and to collusion attacks. We show theoretically that the proposed secure sum protocol is secure with up to $N - 2$ parties colluding, where N denotes the total number of parties collaborating in the analysis. We then use the proposed secure sum protocol to develop two secure gradient descent algorithms, one for horizontally partitioned data and the other for vertically partitioned data. This secure gradient descent solution applies to a broad class of machine learning problems.

The proposed solution has several advantages over existing methods for privacy-preserving multi-party analytics, as described below. Most of the existing approaches for Secure Multi-party Computation (SMC) are either theoretical or based on complicated techniques, such as Yao's garbled circuits [5] and oblivious transfer, that do not scale to large datasets. In contrast, our proposed approach uses simple crypto protocols that are practical, efficient, and scale to large datasets while providing strong security guarantees. In addition, most existing SMC based approaches avoid the use of a mediator and rely on peer-to-peer communication. As a result, the communication cost and latency overhead increase significantly (sometimes exponentially) as the number of parties increase. In contrast, our approach can be easily extended to multiple parties. Finally, most existing approaches for privacy preserving data mining and SMC propose secure protocols that are designed to support a specific analytic functionality. For example, a secure protocol, known as additive data perturbation [6], is designed only to support secure clustering and does not apply to other analytic functionality. In contrast, our proposed framework is generic and applies to a wide range of analytic functionality including regression, classification, and clustering. Below are the main contributions of this paper.

- We propose a secure sum protocol that is secure under collusion attacks (even with $N - 2$ parties colluding).
- We design two secure gradient descent algorithms, one for horizontally partitioned data, and the other for vertically partitioned data using the proposed secure sum protocol. These algorithms enable privacy-preserving multi-party analytics. Moreover, they are generic and apply to a wide class of machine learning problems such as regression, classification and clustering.
- We have implemented and tested the proposed solution for two analytic use-cases, linear regression and binary classification, using both real-world and synthetic datasets. We evaluate the performance of the proposed approach in terms of accuracy of the resulting model, communication cost, and latency, and compare it with two baseline approaches that use a trusted mediator. We also perform a scalability analysis to determine the performance of the proposed approach as the size of the data, and the number of parties are increased.

2 RELATED WORK

Secure sum protocols are a key building block in privacy-preserving data mining and have been widely studied in the literature. Clifton et al. [3] proposed a round-robin based secure sum protocol under the honest-but-curious model that is based on randomization.

However, this solution is not secure when the parties collude. To overcome this limitation, Sheikh et al. [4] proposed an extension that is secure under two colluding parties. However, such a protocol is not secure when more than two parties collude. In contrast, our proposed protocol is secure under the honest-but-curious model with at most $N - 2$ colluding parties.

The problem of privacy-preserving, multi-party analytics has been extensively investigated in the areas of privacy-preserving data mining (PPDM) [7] and secure multi-party computation (SMC). Privacy-preserving algorithms for data mining tasks, such as clustering, classification and association rule mining, have been proposed for both horizontally partitioned datasets [8–11] and vertically partitioned datasets [8, 12, 13]. However, these approaches have several drawbacks: they are designed for a specific machine learning algorithm and do not easily generalize to others; they do not scale well to large datasets or multiple parties; they do not provide strong security guarantees. Below, we provide a brief overview of existing approaches broadly classified into three categories.

(1) **Anonymization-based strategies [8]:** These approaches partition attributes in a given database table into two sets – those containing Personally Identifiable Information (PII) and the rest that do not, and remove the set of PII (e.g., 'Name', 'Social Security Number'). Attributes such as "Zip code", "Age", "Gender", etc. which can identify an individual when used in combination are anonymized using techniques such as k-anonymity [14], l-diversity, etc. However, numerous studies have shown that distinction of an attribute into "identifying" and "non-identifying" is difficult and non-trivial as this distinction may change depending on what prior or external information is available to the attacker [15]. One famous example of de-anonymization attack is the Netflix fiasco, where attackers were able to de-anonymize the Netflix dataset based on the published movie ratings, and externally available datasets. Similar attacks have been demonstrated on several anonymized databases [16].

(2) **Secure Multi-party Computation (SMC)-based strategies [9]:** These approaches typically consider the entire data (all attributes) as private, and use cryptographic protocols such as homomorphic encryption, Yao's garbled circuits, etc. Most SMC-based strategies rely on peer-to-peer communication and are usually defined in 2-party scenarios, with extension to multi-party scenarios often resulting in significant communication overhead. While SMC-based strategies provide strong security guarantees, they are based on complicated techniques that are slow and do not scale for large datasets. Similarly, while the recent results on fully homomorphic encryption are promising, they are far from practical [17].

(3) **Randomization-based strategies [8]:** These approaches are based on randomization techniques, such as additive data perturbation and random subspace projection, that masks the underlying data while preserving the statistical properties of the overall dataset [18]. While these approaches are fast and efficient, they do not provide strong security guarantees, and are often susceptible to attacks [19].

Our proposed solution belongs to the second category. It is secure under the honest-but-curious model and against collusion attacks. It uses an untrusted mediator and leverages a simple, and efficient secure sum protocol that scales well to both large datasets and multiple parties. In addition, the proposed framework is applicable to a wide range of machine learning problems.

3 PRELIMINARIES

3.1 Data Partitioning

Let $\{X^{(i)}, y^{(i)}\}_{i=1}^{m}$ denote a dataset consisting of m data samples where $\{X^{(i)}, y^{(i)}\}$ corresponds to the ith sample, $X^{(i)} = (x_1, \cdots, x_n)$ represents an attribute vector with n explanatory (or independent) variables and $y^{(i)}$ represents the dependent variable. Let $X_j^{(i)}$ denote the jth attribute (column) in $X^{(i)}$. In this paper, we consider the setting where the dataset is partitioned across multiple parties (> 2). We consider two scenarios. In the first, the data is horizontally partitioned across parties, i.e., each party owns all the attributes for a subset of data samples. In the second, the data is vertically partitioned across parties, i.e., each party owns a subset of attributes for all data samples.

Figure 1 shows a toy example consisting of two independent attributes x_1, x_2, and a dependent variable y. Figure 1(a) shows an example of horizontal partitioning where each party owns a subset of data samples, while Figure 1(b) shows an example of vertical partitioning where each party owns a subset of attributes for all data samples.

Heart rate (x_1)	Calcium score (x_2)	Length of stay (y)
78	408	20
72	159	8
89	211	13
77	190	9

Heart rate (x_1)	Calcium score (x_2)	Length of stay (y)
78	408	20
72	159	8
89	211	13
77	190	9

(a)   (b)

Figure 1: (a) Horizontal, and (b) Vertical partitioning

3.2 ElGamal Cryptosystem

The ElGamal cryptosystem [20] consists of the following key generation, encryption and decryption algorithms:

- Key generation: Given a security parameter k, it publishes a multiplicative cyclic group G of prime order q with a generator g, such that discrete logarithm problem over the group G is hard. As a next step, it selects a secret key r randomly from $\mathbf{Z}_q^* = \{1, 2, \ldots, q-1\}$ and computes a public key $y = g^r$. The secret key r is kept private while the public key y can be known to everyone.

- Encryption: Given a message $m \in$ G and a public key y, it selects an integer d randomly from $\mathbf{Z}_q^*$ and outputs a ciphertext $C = E_y[m] = (A, B)$, where $A = g^d$, $B = my^d$.

- Decryption: Given a ciphertext (A, B), and a secret key r, it outputs the plain text $m = D_r[C] = D_r[(A, B)] = \frac{B}{A^r}$.

Since the encryption algorithm selects integer d randomly, ElGamal is a non-deterministic cryptosystem.

4 SECURE SUM PROTOCOL

A secure sum protocol enables multiple parties to compute the sum of their individual values while preserving these values' privacy. Our proposed protocol leverages collusion-resistant anonymization [21] in order to provide privacy to the values of the parties. In the following, we outline the threat model, present the protocol, discuss the performance of the protocol in terms of accuracy and communication cost, and explain some of its important properties.

4.1 Threat Model

We consider an honest-but-curious adversary model, i.e., an adversary will follow the protocol but will try to acquire as much information as possible about the private values during the sum computation. The adversary has control over the untrusted mediator

and at most $N - 2$ parties. The collusion-resistant anonymization is achieved by randomly permuting the input values (or, the segments of the input values) submitted by the parties. This anonymization guarantees that the mediator along with the $N - 2$ colluding parties will not be able to breach the anonymity of an honest party's value. Note that, at the end of our secure sum protocol, the sum value is shared across all the parties including the mediator.

4.2 Protocol

The following is the list of our assumptions on the parties and the mediator:

i. Each party P_i has a secret key and a public key, i.e., R_i, and Y_i, respectively. Also, the mediator M's secret and public keys are R_M and Y_M, respectively. The public keys of all parties and the mediator are known to all entities.

ii. The encryption and decryption operations performed by the parties always follow a particular order. For simplicity, we assume that the order is the same as the order of the parties' public keys in the list that is shared by all.

Overview of the protocol: The proposed protocol has three distinct phases: (I) input preparation, (II) anonymization and (III) sum computation. In phase (I), each party prepares its input values for submission to the mediator. The first step of this phase is to shard the individual values into a number of segments, while in the second step the value segments are recursively encrypted with the public keys of the mediator and the N parties. In phase (II), the mediator sends the set of all prepared value segments to the Nth party (the party to which the last shared public key belongs to). The Nth party performs decryption and shuffling (i.e., re-ordering of the segments) on the value segments prepared in phase (I) and sends the randomly shuffled segments to the $(N-1)th$ party. The $(N-1)th$ party then further decrypts and shuffles the value segments, and this process continues until the segments are decrypted and shuffled by the $1st$ party. Finally, the mediator receives anonymized value segments from the $1st$ party with only one layer of encryption with the mediator's public key. In phase (III), the mediator decrypts the value segments using its own secret key and computes the sum.

The following is a formal representation of the protocol phases:

(I) **Input Preparation:** This phase consists of two steps-

(a) Segmentation: Each party P_i shards its input value into a number of segments. For instance, in order to shard its value S_i into s segments, P_i generates secret shares $\alpha_{i1}, \alpha_{i2}, \ldots, \alpha_{is}$ uniformly randomly such that $\sum_{j=1}^{s} \alpha_{ij} = 1$ and for $1 \leq j \leq s$, $\alpha_{ij} > 0$. These shares are used to divide P_i's value S_i into s segments $\alpha_{i1}.S_i, \alpha_{i2}.S_i, \ldots, \alpha_{is}.S_i$ (denoted by elements of set $\mathbf{S_i} = \{S_{i1}, S_{i2}, \ldots, S_{is}\}$, respectively) such that $S_i = \sum_{j=1}^{s} S_{ij}$.

(b) Encryption: Each party P_i encrypts elements in set $\mathbf{S_i}$.

    i. At first, P_i encrypts the elements in $\mathbf{S_i}$ using the mediator's public key that results in $\mathbf{S_i'} = \{S_{i1}', S_{i2}', \ldots, S_{is}'\}$ where $S_{ij}' = E_{Y_M}[S_{ij}]$ or, $\mathbf{S_i'}[j] = E_{Y_M}\mathbf{S_i}[j]$.

    ii. As the next step, P_i employs the public keys of all the parties to the elements in $\mathbf{S_i'}$ and generates $\mathbf{S_i''}$ such that $\mathbf{S_i''}[j] = [E_{Y_k}[\mathbf{S_i'}[j]]]_{k=1 to N}$.

At the end of this phase, each party P_i sends the prepared value segments $\mathbf{S_i''}$ to the mediator M.

(II) **Anonymization:** The mediator M receives all prepared value segments $\Psi = \{\mathbf{S_1''}, \mathbf{S_2''}, \ldots, \mathbf{S_N''}\}$. Note that the size of the set Ψ is $(N * s)$ since each party shards its value into s segments. Since the encryption order is from 1 to N, the appropriate decryption order is from N to 1. Therefore, the mediator M sends the set Ψ to party P_N at the first iteration, which then updates Ψ by decrypting and randomly shuffling and sends the updated Ψ to party P_{N-1} for the next iteration. The iterations terminate when the mediator M receives the updated value segments from party P_1. The following explains the steps in the $(N-i+1)th$ iteration of the anonymization phase.

(a) Party P_i receives Ψ either from mediator (if $i = N$), or from party P_{i+1} (otherwise).

(b) P_i strips off one layer of encryption from Ψ as follows: $\Psi[k] = D_{R_i}[\Psi[k]]$ for $1 \leq k \leq (N * s)$.

(c) P_i randomly re-orders the elements in Ψ by using a random shuffle function π and obtains a randomized set of value segments $\Psi = \Psi[\pi(k)]$ for $1 \leq k \leq (N * s)$.

(d) P_i sends decrypted and shuffled Ψ to the mediator M (if $i = 1$) or to the party P_{i-1} (otherwise).

At the end of N iterations, the mediator M receives the anonymized value segments that has only one layer of encryption with public key Y_M.

(III) **Sum Computation**: M computes the sum as follows:

(a) M decrypts the value segments as $\Psi[k] = D_{R_M}[\Psi[k]]$ for $1 \leq k \leq (N * s)$.

(b) M computes the sum of the elements in set Ψ to obtain the global sum S_G.

(c) M sends the global sum S_G to all the parties.

4.3 Performance

4.3.1 Accuracy. This protocol does not compromise the accuracy of the resulting sum, i.e., the securely computed sum is same as the sum computed over the plain text values.

4.3.2 Communication cost. In phase (I), each party sends its prepared input which results in a number N of communications. In phase (II), the value segments are sent from the mediator to the Nth party and then to the other parties sequentially which results in a number $(N + 1)$ of communications. In phase (III), the mediator sends the global sum S_G to all the parties which results in N additional communications. Therefore, the number of communications required for each global sum computation is $(3N + 1)$, i.e., $O(N)$.

4.4 Advantage of Value Segmentation

In phase (I), each party P_i shards its value S_i into s number of segments. In order to understand the advantage of value segmentation, consider the case where there are only two honest parties (let those be P_1 and P_2) among N, and the rest $N-2$ parties are colluding with the mediator M. With an ordinary background knowledge that P_1's value should be larger than that of P_2's, it is easy to identify S_1 and S_2 from the honest parties' values. However, with value segmentation, the task of extracting exact input values of the honest parties becomes more complex (see Section 5.2 for more details).

4.5 Protocol Parallelization

Note that, in phase (II), the value segments are anonymized sequentially, i.e., while one party is anonymizing the value segments, the other $(N - 1)$ parties are not able to work on the same segments

simultaneously. However, if the parties want to compute D sums at a time, i.e., their input for sum computation has D dimensions, the protocol is N-parallelizable provided that $D \geq N$. For example, if $N = 4$, and $D = 40$, we can form a unique order of parties for each 10 dimensions, and the value segments in those 10 dimensions can be encrypted and decrypted according to a particular order. In the above example, the four unique orders could be $[P_1, P_2, P_3, P_4]$, $[P_2, P_3, P_4, P_1]$, $[P_3, P_4, P_1, P_2]$, and $[P_4, P_1, P_2, P_3]$ so that at a given time all the parties can parallelly take part in anonymizing 10 dimensions without any collision.

5 SECURITY ANALYSIS OF THE PROPOSED SECURE SUM PROTOCOL

5.1 Privacy Guarantee

In phase (I), each party submits the encrypted value segments to the mediator. In phase (II), each party has access to a set of encrypted value segments which have N layers to 1 layer of encryption(s) (in N iterations, respectively) even after striping off one layer of encryption with its own secret key. Therefore, it is not possible for a party to reveal the plain text of a value segment even if $(N - 1)$ parties collude - which ensures confidentiality during the anonymization phase. In phase (III), the mediator has access to the plain text of the value segments. However, it is not possible for the mediator to identify any association between a value segment and an honest party as long as at most $(N - 2)$ parties collude with the mediator.

5.2 Collusion Resistance

Proposition: The anonymized value segments Ψ that the mediator M receives from party P_1 at the end of phase (II) is computationally indistinguishable as long as there are H honest parties such that $H \geq 2$.

Proof: Let us assume a scenario where the mediator M collaborates with malicious parties $P_{MAL} \subseteq P$ such that $|P| - |P_{MAL}| = H$. To distinguish honest parties' value segments from the anonymized set, parties in P_{MAL} could assist the mediator M by excluding their value segments Ψ_{MAL}. However, if the number of value segments for each party is s, and there are H honest parties, the probability that the mediator M is able to associate a value segment $S_D \in \{\Psi - \Psi_{MAL}\}$ with an honest party is $\frac{s}{s*H}$, or $1/H$. Since $H \geq 2$, $1/H$ is at most $1/2$. This implies that value segments in $\{\Psi - \Psi_{MAL}\}$ are indistinguishable, i.e., each segment is equally likely to belong to each non-colluding party.

6 PRIVACY-PRESERVING MULTI-PARTY ANALYTICS ON HORIZONTALLY PARTITIONED DATA

6.1 Problem Setup

In this section, we consider the set-up where the data is horizontally partitioned across multiple parties, and the goal is to train a machine learning model on the global data while ensuring the data privacy of each individual party.

At the end of the analytics, the final model is shared across all the parties including the mediator. However, the mediator along with the colluding parties is unable to learn the data or local results of the honest parties.

6.2 Key Observations

We begin by noting that most machine learning algorithms can be formulated as an optimization problem, with the goal of minimizing a cost (or objective) function as shown below:

$$\min_{\theta_0, \theta_1, \ldots, \theta_n} J(\theta_0, \theta_1, \ldots, \theta_n) \tag{1}$$

While some optimization problems may have a closed form solution, most optimization problems rely on gradient descent, which sometimes tends to be more efficient than a closed form solution. As an example, the linear regression problem has a closed form solution that involves matrix inversion, which is a costly operation when the size of the dataset is large, and hence gradient descent is commonly used to solve the linear regression problem. Gradient descent is a simple, iterative algorithm as described below.

- Initialize the model parameters $\{\theta_0^0, \theta_1^0, \cdots, \theta_n^0\}$.
- In each iteration $t + 1$, update parameter $\theta_j^{(t+1)}$, for $j = 1, 2, \cdots, n$ until termination criteria is satisfied.

$$\theta_j^{(t+1)} = \theta_j^t - \alpha \frac{\partial}{\partial \theta_j^t} J(\theta_0, \theta_1, \cdots, \theta_n) \tag{2}$$

Each step in the gradient descent algorithm involves updating all the parameters based on the current gradient value, where α in (2) denotes the learning rate that controls the rate of convergence. The update step is terminated upon convergence.

In most machine learning algorithms, the cost function J in (1) and its partial derivative $\frac{\partial J}{\partial \theta_j}$ in (2) involve a summation over the training data $\{X^{(i)}, y^{(i)}\}_{i=1}^m$ as shown below.

$$J(\theta_0, \theta_1, \cdots, \theta_n) = \frac{1}{m} \sum_{i=1}^m J(\theta_0, \theta_1, \cdots, \theta_n | \{X^{(i)}, y^{(i)}\}) \tag{3}$$

$$\frac{\partial}{\partial \theta_j^t} J(\theta_0, \theta_1, \cdots, \theta_n) = \frac{1}{m} \sum_{i=1}^m \frac{\partial}{\partial \theta_j^t} J(\theta_0, \theta_1, \cdots, \theta_n | \{X^{(i)}, y^{(i)}\}) \tag{4}$$

Below, we provide two examples to demonstrate this.

(1) *Linear Regression:* In linear regression, given n independent variables (or attributes), the hypothesis function to estimate the dependent variable is given by

$$h_\theta(X) = \sum_{j=1}^n \theta_j x_j, \tag{5}$$

where $X = (x_1, \cdots, x_n)$ denotes the feature vector with the first feature typically corresponding to a constant (or 1). The goal of linear regression is to estimate the parameters θ_j that best fit the training data. The cost function J and its partial derivative $\frac{\partial J}{\partial \theta}$ for linear regression are given by:

$$J(\theta_0, \theta_1, \ldots, \theta_n) = \frac{1}{2m} \sum_{i=1}^m (h_\theta(X^{(i)}) - y^{(i)})^2 \tag{6}$$

$$\frac{\partial}{\partial \theta_j} J(\theta_0, \theta_1, \ldots \theta_n) = \frac{1}{m} \sum_{i=1}^m (h_\theta(X^{(i)}) - y^{(i)}) X_j^{(i)} \tag{7}$$

(2) *Binary Classification:* Logistic regression is widely used for binary classification, where given a data sample $X = (x_1, x_2, \cdots, x_n)$, the output variable is modeled as

$$h_\theta(X) = \frac{1}{1 + e^{-\sum_{j=1}^n \theta_j x_j}} \tag{8}$$

The cost function J and its partial derivative $\frac{\partial J}{\partial \theta}$ for logistic regression are given by:

$$J(\theta_0, \theta_1, \ldots, \theta_n) = -\frac{1}{m} \sum_{i=1}^m [y^{(i)} log(h_\theta(X^{(i)}))$$
$$+ (1 - y^{(i)}) log(1 - h_\theta(X^{(i)}))] \tag{9}$$

$$\frac{\partial}{\partial \theta_j} J(\theta_0, \theta_1, \ldots \theta_n) = \frac{1}{m} \sum_{i=1}^m (h_\theta(X^{(i)}) - y^{(i)}) X_j^{(i)} \tag{10}$$

As noted in the above two examples, and as shown in Equations (3) and (4), both the objective function J and the partial derivative $\frac{\partial J}{\partial \theta}$ in the gradient descent algorithm are evaluated on the training data $\{X^{(i)}, y^{(i)}\}_{i=1}^m$. In the case of horizontally partitioned data, the m samples are distributed across multiple parties. Let m_i denote the number of samples with party P_i, where $\sum_{i=1}^N m_i = m$. Equations 3 and 4 can then be re-written as:

$$J(\theta_0, \theta_1, \cdots, \theta_n) = \frac{1}{m} \sum_{i=1}^m J(\theta_0, \theta_1, \cdots, \theta_n | \{X^{(i)}, y^{(i)}\})$$
$$= \frac{1}{m} \sum_{i=1}^N \sum_{k=1}^{m_i} J(\theta_0, \theta_1, \cdots, \theta_n | \{X^{(k)}, y^{(k)}\}) \tag{11}$$

and

$$\frac{\partial}{\partial \theta_j^t} J(\theta_0, \theta_1, \cdots, \theta_n) = \frac{1}{m} \sum_{i=1}^m \frac{\partial}{\partial \theta_j^t} J(\theta_0, \theta_1, \cdots, \theta_n | \{X^{(i)}, y^{(i)}\})$$
$$= \frac{1}{m} \sum_{i=1}^N \sum_{k=1}^{m_i} \frac{\partial}{\partial \theta_j^t} J(\theta_0, \theta_1, \cdots, \theta_n | \{X^{(k)}, y^{(k)}\}) \tag{12}$$

Note that the inner summation $\sum_{k=1}^{m_i} J(\theta_0, \theta_1, \cdots, \theta_n | \{X^{(k)}, y^{(k)}\})$ and $\sum_{k=1}^{m_i} \frac{\partial}{\partial \theta_j^t} J(\theta_0, \theta_1, \cdots, \theta_n | \{X^{(k)}, y^{(k)}\})$ in each of those equations denote computations that are based on data belonging to a single party, and thus can be completely evaluated by the party. On the other hand, the outer summation involves data across parties, and thus this summation should be computed in a secure, privacy-preserving manner. Moreover, note that while the inner summation may involve complex and non-linear functions, the outer summation is simply over N scalars, each generated by a party. **In other words, irrespective of the machine learning algorithm and its cost function, the outer summation always involves a simple sum over N scalars, which can be computed using a secure sum protocol.**

6.3 Secure Gradient Descent Algorithm

Algorithm 1 describes our privacy-preserving horizontally partitioned multi-party data optimization algorithm for a generic machine learning problem with a cost function J and gradient function $\frac{\partial J}{\partial \theta}$.

At the end of the gradient descent algorithm, each party has the model parameters $\{\theta_1, \theta_2, \cdots, \theta_n\}$, which can be used by the party to predict/classify any new data samples it collects. Finally, Algorithm 1 can be naturally extended to other variants of gradient descent such as the mini-batch and stochastic gradient descent.

1: M initializes $\{ \theta_1, \cdots, \theta_n \}$
2: M sets convergence to false
3: M sets J to ∞
4: **for** each gradient descent iteration until convergence is true **do**
5:      M sends $\{ \theta_1, \ldots, \theta_n \}$ to all parties
6:      **for** $i = 1, \cdots, N$ **do**
7:          **for** each dimension $j = 1, \ldots, n$ **do**
8:              P_i computes local gradient $LG_{ij} = \sum_{k=1}^{m_i} \frac{\partial}{\partial \theta_j} J(\theta_0, \theta_1, \cdots, \theta_n | \{X^{(k)}, y^{(k)}\})$
9:          **end for**
10:         P_i computes local cost value $LJ_i = \sum_{k=1}^{m_i} J(\theta_0, \theta_1, \cdots, \theta_n | \{X^{(k)}, y^{(k)}\})$
11:         P_i shards each element in $\{LJ_i, LG_{i1}, \cdots, LG_{in}\}$ into two segments
12:         P_i encrypts the shards $\{\{LJ_i\}_1, \{LJ_i\}_2, \{LG_{i1}\}_1, \{LG_{i1}\}_2, \cdots, \{LG_{in}\}_1, \{LG_{in}\}_2\}$ with the public keys of M, and P_is in order of $i = 1, \ldots, N$
13:         P_i sends $\{E[\{LJ_i\}_1], E[\{LJ_i\}_2], E[\{LG_{i1}\}_1], E[\{LG_{i1}\}_2], \cdots, E[\{LG_{in}\}_1], E[\{LG_{in}\}_2]\}$ to mediator M
14:     **end for**
15:     M receives $\{E[\{LJ_i\}_1], E[\{LJ_i\}_2], E[\{LG_{i1}\}_1], E[\{LG_{i1}\}_2], \cdots, E[\{LG_{in}\}_1], E[\{LG_{in}\}_2]\}$ from all P_i
16:     M sends the encrypted shards to party P_N
17:     **for** $i = N, N-1, \cdots, 2$ **do**
18:         P_i decrypts and shuffles the shards
19:         P_i sends the decrypted and shuffled shards to party P_{i-1}
20:     **end for**
21:     P_1 decrypts and shuffles the shards
22:     P_1 sends the anonymized shards to mediator M
23:     M decrypts and extracts local gradients for each dimension $j = 1, \ldots, n$
24:     M computes global gradient $G_j = \sum_{i=1}^{N} \sum_{k=1}^{2} \{LG_{ij}\}_k$ for each dimension $j = 1, \ldots, n$
25:     **for** each dimension $j = 1, \cdots, n$ **do**
26:         M updates $\theta_j = \theta_j - \alpha G_j$
27:     **end for**
28:     M computes $J_{new} = \sum_{i=1}^{N} \sum_{k=1}^{2} \{LJ_i\}_k$
29:     **if** $J - J_{new} \le \epsilon$ **then**
30:         convergence is true
31:     **end if**
32: **end for**

Algorithm 1: Algorithm for privacy-preserving horizontally partitioned multi-party data optimization for a generic machine learning algorithm.

7 PRIVACY-PRESERVING MULTI-PARTY ANALYTICS ON VERTICALLY PARTITIONED DATA

7.1 Problem Setup

The complexity of privacy-preserving analytics greatly increases when dealing with vertically partitioned data. In contrast to horizontal partitioning of data, vertical partitioning raises several unique questions with respect to the way data is processed, and results are obtained and shared. Below, we discuss two such questions and our assumptions.

i. In problems like classification and regression, there is a dependent variable y, i.e., the variable to be modeled. An important question in these problems is the location of this dependent variable. There are two possibilities: the dependent variable y is known to all parties, or it is private and belongs to some party. This impacts the

way the model is built and evaluated. Both cases are realistic and model different situations. In this paper, we focus on the former where the dependent variable y is known to all parties.

ii. The second question concerns how the final model is shared among parties. One possibility is to let all the parties know the obtained model - but this may often reveal too much information and fail to comply with the privacy constraints. An alternate fully secure solution is to split the model among the parties. We design our protocol for the latter (fully secure) approach, but it can be easily extended to the former approach. Specifically, we split the model among parties, where each participant has model parameters only for the attributes it owns. However, the downside to this approach is that a secure protocol has to be run each time the model needs to be used on a new data point. If this performance penalty has to be avoided, one can resort to the former approach by sharing the global model with all the parties at the end of our secure optimization protocol.

7.2 Key Observations

Our proposed secure solution is based on two key observations. First, we note that several popular machine learning models, such as linear regression, ridge regression, LASSO, SVM and logistic regression, model the dependent variable y as $h_\theta(X) = f(\langle \Theta, X \rangle)$, i.e., as a function of the inner product between the model parameters $\Theta = (\theta_1, \theta_2, \cdots, \theta_n)$ and the attribute vector $X = (x_1, x_2, \cdots, x_n)$. In vertically partitioned data, since the attributes are distributed across multiple parties, we can use a secure sum protocol to compute $\langle \Theta, X \rangle$. Second, note from Equations 6, 7, 9, and 10 that given the value of $h_\theta(X^{(i)})$ for all training samples $i \in [1, m]$, the objective function can be evaluated by each party independently (as we assumed the dependent variable $y^{(i)}$ to be known to all parties). Similarly, each parameter θ_j can be updated by the party that owns the jth attribute. Hence, both the cost function and the update step can be computed independently by the parties once $h_\theta(X^{(i)})$ is known, which in turn can be computed using a secure sum protocol.

7.3 Secure Gradient Descent Algorithm

Algorithm 2 describes our privacy-preserving vertically partitioned multi-party data optimization algorithm for a generic machine learning problem which models the dependent variable as a function of $\langle \Theta, X \rangle$, and has a cost function J with gradient function $\frac{\partial J}{\partial \theta}$.

At the end of the proposed algorithm, each party learns the final model parameters only for the attributes it owns. Hence, in order to use the learned model to predict/classify any new data samples, the parties should initiate a secure sum protocol.

Algorithm 2 can be extended to other variants of gradient descent. For example, in the case of mini-batch gradient descent, the parties may decide a-priori on the batch size b, and random seed values. Then, in Steps 8-10, each party will compute the local h_θ only for a small subset of size b from their data (rather than the entire dataset). Also, in Steps 28 and 31, the parties will compute the gradient value and the objective function only using the selected sub-samples, and normalize it accordingly (i.e., normalize with b rather than m). Note that the use of mini-batch gradient descent will significantly improve the overall performance of our algorithm. We could similarly use stochastic gradient descent where only one random sample is used in each iteration of the gradient descent.

```
1:  for i = 1,. . ., N do
2:      P_i initializes θ_js for the jth attributes that belong to P_i
3:      P_i sets convergence to false
4:      P_i sets J to ∞
5:  end for
6:  for each gradient descent iteration until convergence is true do
7:      for i = 1,. . ., N do
8:          for r = 1,. . ., m do
9:              P_i computes local h_θ, Lh_i^r = Σ_{j=1}^{n_i} θ_j x_j for each training
                sample r
10:         end for
11:         P_i shards each element in {Lh_i^1, Lh_i^2, · · · , Lh_i^m} into two
            segments
12:         P_i encrypts the shards {Lh_i^1}_1, {Lh_i^1}_2, · · · , {Lh_i^m}_1, {Lh_i^m}_2}
            with the public keys of M, and P_is in order of i = 1,. . ., N
13:         P_i sends E[{Lh_i^1}_1], E[{Lh_i^1}_2], · · · , E[{Lh_i^m}_1], E[{Lh_i^m}_2]}
            to the mediator M
14:     end for
15:     M receives E[{Lh_i^1}_1], E[{Lh_i^1}_2], . . ., E[{Lh_i^m}_1], E[{Lh_i^m}_2]}
        from all P_i
16:     M sends the encrypted shards to party P_N
17:     for i = N, N − 1,. . ., 2 do
18:         P_i decrypts and shuffles the shards
19:         P_i sends the decrypted and shuffled shards to party P_{i−1}
20:     end for
21:     P_1 decrypts and shuffles the shards
22:     P_1 sends the anonymized shards to mediator M
23:     M decrypts and extracts local h_θ for each row i = 1,. . ., m
24:     M computes h_θ for each row i = 1,. . ., m
25:     M sends h_θ values to all P_i
26:     for i = 1,. . ., N do
27:         for each dimension j that belongs to P_i do
28:             P_i updates
                θ_j = θ_j − α (1/m) Σ_{k=1}^{m} (∂/∂θ_j) J(θ_0, θ_1, · · · , θ_n | {X^{(k)}, y^{(k)}})
29:         end for
30:     end for
31:     P_i computes J_new = (1/m) Σ_{k=1}^{m} J(θ_1, θ_2, · · · , θ_n | {X^{(k)}, y^{(k)}}),
        using the h_θ values
32:     if J − J_new ≤ ε then
33:         convergence is true
34:     end if
35: end for
```

Algorithm 2: Algorithm for privacy-preserving vertically partitioned multi-party data optimization for a generic machine learning algorithm.

8 DISCUSSION ON SECURE GRADIENT DESCENT ALGORITHMS

This section discusses some key properties of the Algorithms 1 and 2 in the following:

(1) In Step 11 of the algorithms, we shard the data into two segments. In general, one may shard the data into s segments, where $s > 1$.

(2) Steps 17-22 of the algorithms involve a sequential process, where each party decrypts the shards, shuffles them, and sends them to the next party. This results in only one party being active at any given time, with the remaining $N − 1$ parties being idle (idle CPU cycles). However, we can parallelize the gradient descent operation to improve the overall CPU usage, by using a

different encryption ordering for each dimension in Step 12 of the algorithms.

• In Algorithm 1, rather than encrypting all the local gradients using the same encryption order, say we encrypt all $\{LG_{i1}\}_1$, $\{LG_{i1}\}_2$ using the parties' public keys in order $i = 1, \cdots, N$; all $\{LG_{i2}\}_1$, $\{LG_{i2}\}_2$ using order $i = 2, \cdots, N, 1$; all $\{LG_{i3}\}_1$, $\{LG_{i3}\}_2$ using order $i = 3, \cdots, N, 1, 2$, etc. Then, the mediator can invoke parallel decryption cycles in Steps 17-22 by sending $E[\{LG_{i1}\}_1]$, $E[\{LG_{i1}\}_2]$ to party N first; $E[\{LG_{i2}\}_1]$, $E[\{LG_{i2}\}_2]$ to party 1 first, $E[\{LG_{i3}\}_1]$, $E[\{LG_{i3}\}_2]$ to party 2 first etc.

• In Algorithm 2, rather than encrypting all the local $h_θ$'s using the same encryption order, say we encrypt the local sum of first data sample of all parties $\{Lh_i^1\}_1$, $\{Lh_i^1\}_2$ using the parties' public keys in order $i = 1, \cdots, N$; the local sum of second data sample $\{Lh_i^2\}_1$, $\{Lh_i^2\}_2$ using order $i = 2, \cdots, N, 1$; the third data sample $\{Lh_i^3\}_1$, $\{Lh_i^3\}_2$ using order $i = 3, \cdots, N, 1, 2$, etc. Then, the mediator can invoke parallel decryption cycles in Steps 17-22 by sending $E[\{Lh_i^1\}_1]$, $E[\{Lh_i^1\}_2]$ to party N first; $E[\{Lh_i^2\}_1]$, $E[\{Lh_i^2\}_2]$ to party 1 first, $E[\{Lh_i^3\}_1]$, $E[\{Lh_i^3\}_2]$ to party 2 first etc. This improves the CPU utilization of all the parties, thereby reducing the overall execution time.

(3) Data segmentation (or data sharding) used in Step 11 of the algorithms makes the protocols robust to prior knowledge attacks. We could replace the data sharding solution with alternate approaches that mask the structure of the data. An alternate approach is to have the parties determine a-priori a large random number R, so that each party P_i generates s random numbers $\{r_{i1}, r_{i2}, \cdots, r_{is}\}$ from $[−R, R]$ such that $\sum_{j=1}^{s} r_{ij} = Lh_i^r$ (in Algorithm 2). The local $h_θ$ for all other data samples $r \in [1, m]$ can also be masked using a similar approach.

9 PERFORMANCE EVALUATION

9.1 Experiment Setup

We used two testbeds in this analysis. The first testbed is a cluster of 9 Virtual Machines (VM) on a HPE Cloud openstack instance. Each VM is a single core, Intel Xeon machine with 8GB of RAM and 60GB storage running Debian GNU/Linux. The second testbed is an Amazon AWS EC2 cluster of 4 *t2.micro* instances with 1 GB of RAM and EBS-only storage. We implemented our solution in Python v2.7.3, where we used ZeroMQ for communication between parties/machines. We used an open source implementation of the ElGamal cryptosystem[2].

We performed three sets of experimental analysis. In Section 9.2, we evaluate the computational performance of the proposed secure sum protocol, measured by the latency (total wall-clock time) and the total communication cost. We evaluate and compare non-parallelized and parallelized versions of this protocol.

In Section 9.3, we evaluate our secure gradient descent protocol for two analytic use-cases: linear regression and binary classification (logistic regression) with horizontal data partitioning. We also evaluate our protocol with vertically partitioned data for the linear regression use-case. We compare the proposed solution scenario, i.e., distributed untrusted (DU) (where parties execute gradient descent locally and share encrypted intermediate results with an

---

[2]https://github.com/RyanRiddle/elgamal

untrusted mediator) with two baselines: (i) centralized trusted (CT), where the parties transfer their entire raw data to a trusted mediator to perform the analysis, and (ii) distributed trusted (DT), where parties execute gradient descent locally and share intermediate results with a trusted mediator to aggregate. We evaluate these solutions on several real datasets under three different metrics: accuracy or quality of the resulting machine learning model, latency, and total communication cost.

Finally, in Section 9.4, we perform a scalability analysis to evaluate the computational performance of the proposed gradient descent solution and compare it with the two baselines. We use a synthetic dataset for this analysis, where we vary the number of instances as 1K, 10K, 100K, and the number of parties as 2, 4, and 8.

All the results shown in this section are averaged over 5 repetitions of each experiment. While the experiments presented in Section 9.3 are performed on Amazon AWS EC2 instances, the HPE Cloud openstack cluster has been used for the experiments in Sections 9.2 and 9.4. Independent of testbeds and analytic use-cases, the experiments demonstrate that the DU scenario outperforms the baseline CT scenario for large datasets. Although the DT scenario results in lower communication cost than that of the DU scenario, the DT scenario has weak privacy guarantees as the parties share their intermediate results with a trusted mediator in plain text. Moreover, as the dataset size increases, the difference between the latencies of the DT and DU scenarios reduces as shown later in this section.

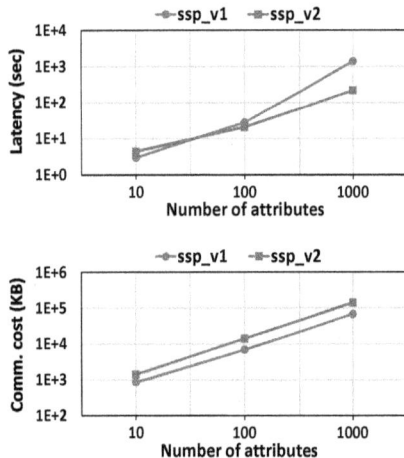

Figure 2: Latency and communication cost comparison between non-parallelized (ssp_{v1}) and parallelized (ssp_{v2}) secure sum

9.2 Experimental Analysis of Secure Sum Protocol

We implement non-parallelized and parallelized versions of the proposed secure sum protocol, and evaluate their performance measured by latency and communication cost. For all the experiments in this section, we perform secure linear regression on a dataset consisting of 100K instances, and partitioned horizontally between 2 parties. As noted in Section 4.5, the secure sum protocol

Dataset name	# of Instances	# of Attributes	Use-case
Bike Sharing [22]	17389	16	Linear Regression
YearPredictionMSD [23]	515345	90	Linear Regression
Phishing Websites [23]	2456	30	Binary Classification
SUSY [24]	5000000	18	Binary Classification

Table 1: Datasets from UCI repository

can be parallelized to compute D secure sums at the same time. This parallelization is useful for secure gradient descent solutions as such solutions require to compute the global gradient for each independent attribute. In this experiment, we compare the latency and communication cost between the non-parallelized (ssp_{v1}) and the parallelized (ssp_{v2}) versions of our secure sum protocol, where we vary the number of attributes as 10, 100, and 1000. In the case of ssp_{v2}, the order of public keys' used for secure global gradient computation of half of the attributes is $[P_1, P_2]$ whereas the order $[P_2, P_1]$ is used for the rest half attributes. As shown in Figure. 2, the parallelized version improves the latency significantly when compared to the non-parallelized version as the number of attributes increases. However, the parallelized version incurs a higher communication overhead as the number of communications increases due to parallelization. Note that, in the following experiments, the results with the DU scenario represent the non-parallelized version of the secure sum protocol.

9.3 Experimental Analysis of Secure Gradient Descent Algorithms

We present the simulation results on four datasets from the UCI repository as shown in Table 1. We use 500,000 randomly selected instances from the SUSY dataset while all the instances from the other datasets are used. For each dataset, we assume 70% of the data as training data, which is distributed uniformly across 3 parties. For example, in the case of the YearPredictionMSD dataset, each party owns 120,247 instances under horizontal partitioning and 30 columns under vertical partitioning.

9.3.1 Linear Regression on Horizontally Partitioned Data. The number of gradient descent iterations for linear regression on the horizontally partitioned Bike Sharing and YearPredictionMSD datasets are 150 and 25, respectively. Figure 3(a) and 3(b) show comparisons among the CT, DT, and DU scenarios in terms of their latency and communication cost, respectively. Though the latency of the CT scenario is minimum for the smaller Bike Sharing dataset, regression analysis on the larger YearPredictionMSD dataset results in the maximum latency for this scenario. The latency in the CT scenario consists of both the communication time to transfer all the data to the mediator, and the computation time to execute linear regression centrally. In contrast to CT, the cost of the DT and DU scenarios depend mostly on the number of iterations and less on the size of the dataset. In the case of large datasets like YearPredictionMSD, the difference between the latencies of the DT and DU scenarios decrease since in both scenarios the local gradient computation takes significant amount of time (due to the size of dataset) and the latency for running the secure sum protocol in the DU scenario becomes insignificant. The communication cost for the CT scenario is also the maximum among all for the YearPredictionMSD dataset.

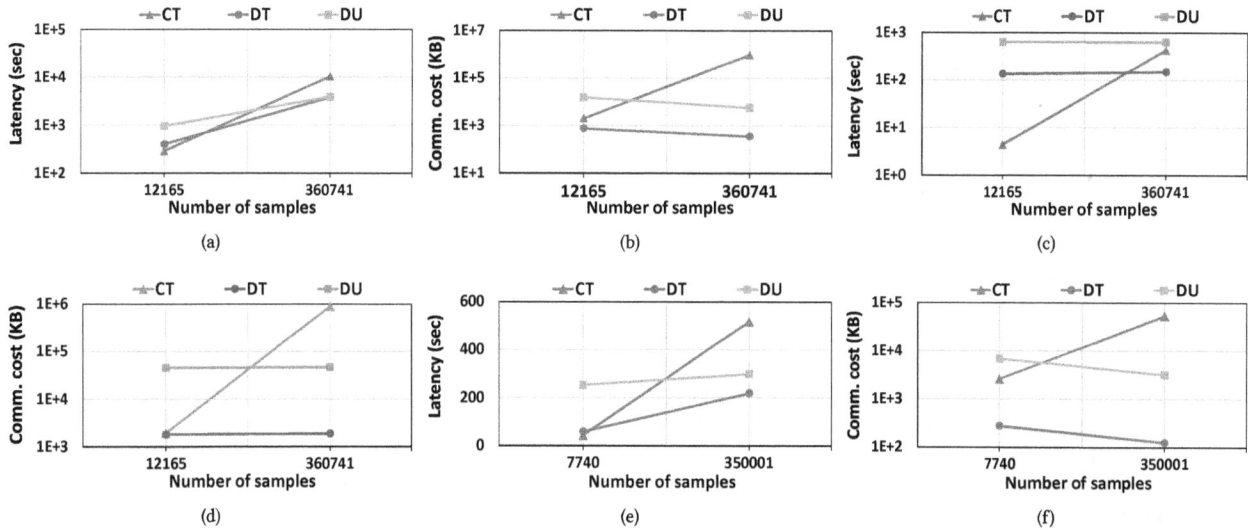

Figure 3: Comparison among the CT, DT, and DU scenarios for analytics on real datasets: (a), (b) latency and communication cost for linear regression on horizontally partitioned data; (c), (d) latency and communication cost for linear regression on vertically partitioned data; (e), (f) latency and communication cost for logistic regression on horizontally partitioned data

We assess the accuracy of the CT, DT, and DU scenarios using the Root Mean Square Error (RMSE) measure. The experiment shows that the DU scenario has the same accuracy as the two baselines. For example, the RMSE calculated for YearPredictionMSD test dataset is 1040.9 for all the scenarios. Since all the scenarios have same accuracy, we omit the accuracy comparison in later experiments.

9.3.2 Linear Regression on Vertically Partitioned Data. In the case of vertical partitioning, we would need a secure sum for each sample as described in Section 7.2. In order to reduce the overhead in latency and communication cost, we randomly select a set of subsamples from the large dataset. In other words, we implement mini-batch gradient descent. For both the Bike Sharing and YearPredictionMSD datasets, a mini-batch of 100 samples is used for computing the gradients in each step. The number of gradient descent iterations for both datasets is 100. Figure 3(c) and 3(d) show that while the latency and communication cost for the DT and DU scenarios are similar for both datasets, these metrics increase linearly with the increase in the size of the dataset for the CT scenario.

9.3.3 Logistic Regression on Horizontally Partitioned Data. The number of gradient descent iterations for logistic regression on the horizontally partitioned Phishing Websites and SUSY datasets are 38 and 25, respectively. As shown in Figure 3(e), the CT scenario result in the highest latency for the large SUSY dataset while the difference between the latencies of the DT and DU scenarios decreases. Figure 3(f) shows the results of the comparison among the CT, DT, and DU scenarios in terms of communication cost which are similar to the results in Figure 3(b).

9.4　Scalability Analysis of Secure Gradient Descent Algorithms

In order to perform the scalability analysis, we use synthetic datasets for the linear regression use-case. The datasets are generated using

the make_regression[3] function. We use a life sciences dataset[4] for the binary classification use-case.

9.4.1 Linear Regression on Horizontally Partitioned Data. In the following, we present experiment results for linear regression on horizontally partitioned data with variable number of samples and parties.

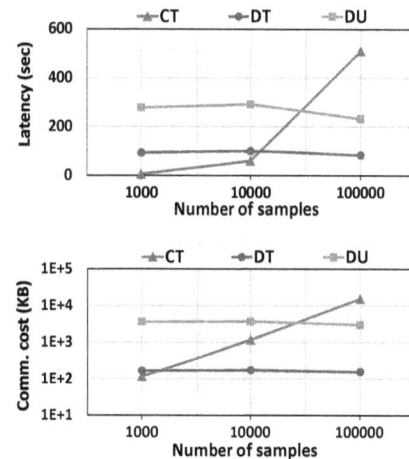

Figure 4: Comparison among the CT, DT, and DU scenarios in terms of latency and communication cost for linear regression on horizontally partitioned data (variable number of samples)

---

[3] http://scikit-learn.org/stable/modules/generated/sklearn. datasets.make_regression.html

[4] ds1.10, http://komarix.org/ac/ds/)

• *Variable Number of Samples:* Figure 4 shows the comparison among the CT, DT, and DU scenarios in terms of latency and communication cost for linear regression on horizontally partitioned data with variable number of samples. The experiment is with three sets of data of sample sizes 1K, 10K, and 100K, where each sample consists of 5 input attributes. Two parties participate in the analytics (each owns half of the samples) and the numbers of gradient descent iterations required for convergence for the three datasets are 91, 94, and 85, respectively, and are equal for all the CT, DT, and DU scenarios.

As shown in Figure 4, the latency of the CT scenario increases as the dataset size increases. The latency of the DU scenario for all sample sizes is higher than the DT scenario and that is attributed to the cryptographic operations in the secure sum protocol of Section 4, i.e., onions of encryprion, and decryption. The communication cost of the CT scenario also increases linearly with the dataset size which is not true for the DT and DU scenarios. Again, the communication cost of the DT and DU scenarios depend on the number of iterations. From this experiment, it is clear that using the CT scenario for larger datasets (in most practical cases datasets are large) is not cost effective. Moreover, even though the DT scenario has lower latency and communication cost when compared with the DU scenario, the latter provides stronger security guarantees.

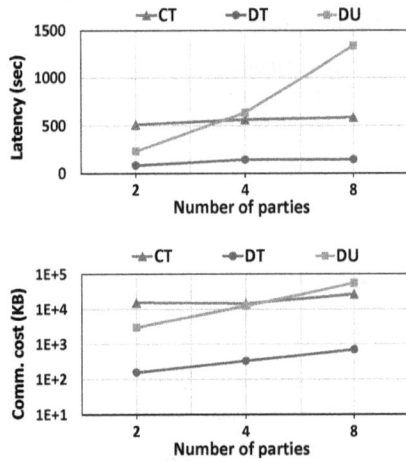

Figure 5: Comparison among the CT, DT, and DU scenarios in terms of latency and communication cost for linear regression on horizontally partitioned data (variable number of parties)

• *Variable Number of Parties:* This experiment has a similar setting as above but varies the number of parties as 2, 4, and 8 instead of varying the number of samples. The experiment is with a dataset of sample size 100K, where each sample consists of 5 input attributes. Two, four, and eight parties participate in the analytics (each owns 50K, 25K, and 12.5K samples, respectively) and the number of gradient descent iterations required for convergence is 85.

As shown in Figure 5, the latency of the DU scenario grows faster than that of the CT and DT scenarios. This is attributed to the increased number of encryptions and decryptions required by

the increased number of parties. However, the growth of communication cost is slower than that of latency. Moreover, for larger datasets, e.g., the dataset with 1M samples, the DU scenario would outperform the CT scenario in terms of communication cost even in the case of 8 parties.

9.4.2 Linear Regression on Vertically Partitioned Data. While performing multi-party analytics on vertically partitioned datasets, we use mini-batch gradient descent. In the following, we present experiment results for variable size of mini-batch, variable number of samples, and variable number of parties.

• *Variable Number of Mini-batch Size:* In the following, we assess how the size of mini-batch affects the latency and communication cost of the CT and DT scenarios. The experiment is with a dataset of sample size 100K, where each sample consists of 8 input attributes. Two parties participate in the analytics (each owns 4 input attributes) and the number of gradient descent iterations required for convergence is 89.

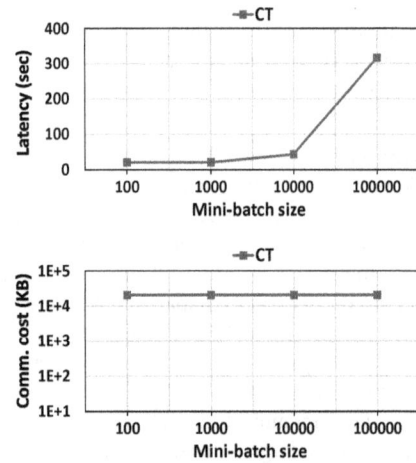

Figure 6: Linear regression on vertically partitioned data for the CT scenario: latency and communication cost comparison for variable mini-batch size

(a) *CT Scenario:* We vary the mini-batch size with 0.1K, 1K, 10K, and compare these with the case of 100K. Figure 6 shows comparisons among different mini-batch sizes in terms of latency and communication cost.

The latency increases with the increasing mini-batch size. This is because in the case of 0.1K subsamples, the mediator randomly selects 0.1K samples for each iteration of gradient descent and updates the θ values according to only those subsamples. However, in the case of 10K subsamples, the mediator needs to run analysis on 10K rows in each iteration which increases the computation time significantly. The communication costs for all mini-batch sizes are similar as the most significant cost component is the initial communication cost to transfer the data to the mediator.

(b) *DT Scenario:* We vary the mini-batch size with 0.1K, 1K, 10K, and compare those with the case of 100K. Figure 7 shows comparisons among different mini-batch sizes in terms of latency and communication cost.

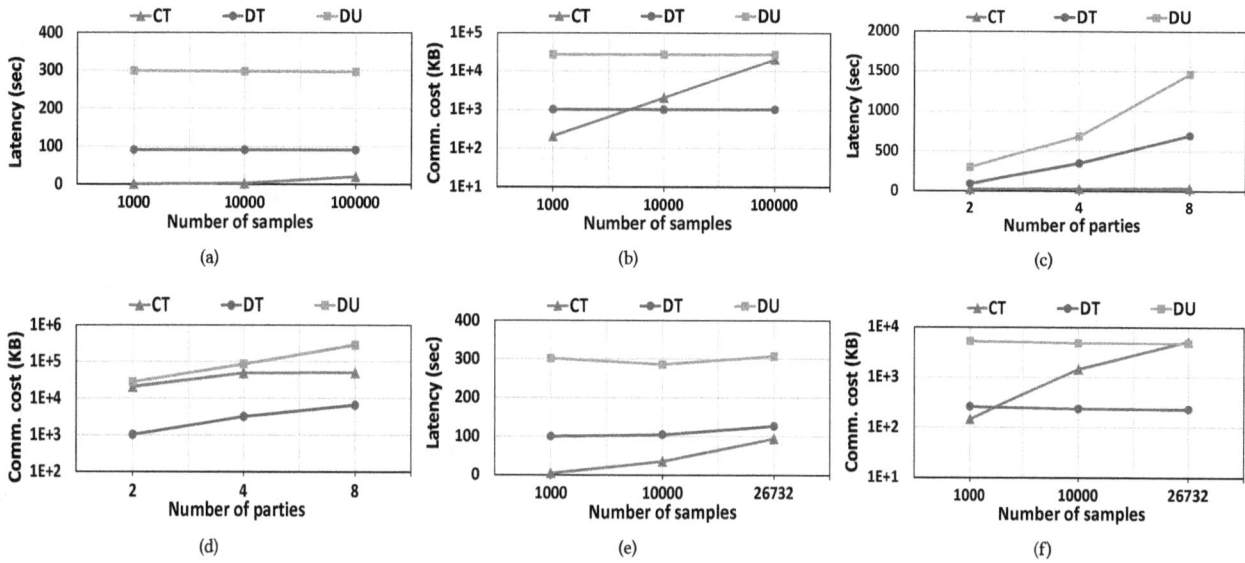

Figure 8: Comparison among the CT, DT, and DU scenarios for scalability experiments: (a), (b) latency and communication cost for variable number of samples [linear regression on vertically partitioned data]; (c), (d) latency and communication cost for variable number of parties [linear regression on vertically partitioned data]; (e), (f) latency and communication cost for variable number of samples [logistic regression on horizontally partitioned data]

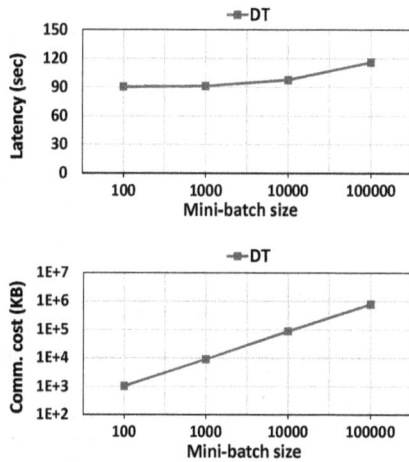

Figure 7: Linear regression on vertically partitioned data for DT scenario: latency and communication cost comparison for variable mini-batch size

The communication cost increases with the increasing mini-batch size. This is because in the case of 0.1K subsamples, the parties need to randomly select 0.1K rows and send the 0.1K local h_θ sums to the mediator at each iteration. The mediator then computes 0.1K sums and updates the θ values accordingly. However, in the case of 10K subsamples, the parties need to send 10K local h_θ sums which increases the communication cost significantly. The increasing number of bytes being transferred with increasing size of mini-batch results in higher latency though the number of gradient descent iterations is fixed for all the cases.

- *Variable Number of Samples:* Figure 8(a) and 8(b) show comparisons among the CT, DT, and DU scenarios in terms of latency and communication cost for variable number of samples. The experiment is with three sets of data of sample sizes 1K, 10K, and 100K, where each sample consists of 8 input attributes. Two parties participate in the analytics (each owns 4 input attributes), the size of mini-batch is 0.1K, and the number of gradient descent iterations required for convergence is 89.

As shown in Figure 8(a), the latency of the CT scenario is less in comparison with both the DT and DU scenarios. The computation time at the mediator is significantly reduced in the CT scenario since the analysis runs on only 0.1K randomly selected subsamples in each iteration. The increase in the latency with increasing size of dataset in the CT scenario is due to the increase in communication time for transferring the data to mediator. Since the latency of the DT and DU scenarios depend on the number of iterations, it remains similar for all sample sizes. However, in terms of communication cost, the CT scenario performs worse with increasing number of samples as shown in Figure 8(b). Therefore, for larger datasets, e.g., dataset with 1M samples, the DU scenario would outperform the CT scenario in terms of communication cost.

- *Variable Number of Parties:* Figure 8(c) and 8(d) show comparisons among the CT, DT, and DU scenarios in terms of latency and communication cost for 2, 4, and 8 parties. The experiment is with a dataset of sample size 100K, where each sample consists of 8 input attributes. Two, four, and eight parties participate in the analytics (each owns 4, 2, and 1 input attribute(s), respectively) and the number of gradient descent iterations required for convergence is 89.

As shown in Figure 8(c), the latency of the DU scenario grows faster than that of the CT and DT scenarios. This is attributed to the increased number of encryptions and decryptions required by the increased number of parties. The latency of the CT scenario is significantly less in comparison with the latency of both the DT and DU scenarios for the reason mentioned for the previous experiment. The growth of communication cost for the DU scenario is slower than that of latency (Figure 8(d)). For larger datasets, e.g., dataset with 1M samples, the DU scenario would perform the CT scenario in terms of communication cost even in the case of 8 parties.

9.4.3 Logistic Regression on Horizontally Partitioned Data. In the following, we present experiment results for logistic regression on horizontally partitioned data.

- *Variable Number of Samples:* Figure 8(e) and 8(f) show comparisons among the CT, DT, and DU scenarios in terms of latency and communication cost for variable number of samples. The experiment is with three sets of life sciences datasets- one consisting of ~27K samples, and the two other consisting of randomly selected samples from these ~27K samples and of sizes 1K and 10K, where each sample consists of 10 input attributes. Two parties participate in the analytics (each owns half of the samples) and the numbers of gradient descent iterations required for convergence are 98, 89, and 88, respectively, for the 1K, 10K, and ~27K datasets.

As shown in Figure 8(e), the latency of the CT scenario increases as the dataset size increases. Although the numbers of iterations for sample sizes 10K, and ~27K are almost similar, the increase in the latency for the ~27K case is due to the local gradient computation time. The communication cost of the CT scenario increases linearly with the dataset size which is not true for the DT and DU scenarios (Figure 8(f)). Even with a dataset of ~27K samples, the DU scenario outperforms the CT scenario in terms of communication cost.

10 CONCLUSION AND FUTURE WORK

In this paper, we introduce a generalized framework for privacy-preserving multi-party analytics. We first propose a secure sum protocol that is secure under the honest-but-curious model, and is resistant to collusion attacks as long as there are at least two honest (non-colluding) parties. We then use this protocol to propose two secure gradient descent solutions, one for horizontally paritioned data and the other for vertically partitioned data. The proposed framework is generic and applies to a broad class of machine learning problems. We demonstrate our solution for two popular analytic use-cases, regression and classification, and evaluate its performance with respect to the accuracy of the obtained model, latency and communication cost, on both real and synthetic datasets. We also assess the scalability properties of the proposed solution as the size of the data or the number of parties increase. We compare the proposed solution with two baselines that use a trusted mediator. Our experimental results demonstrate that while the proposed solution does not compromise on the accuracy of the obtained model, it is secure, scales well, and achieves better computational performance (latency and communication cost) compared to the centralized trusted mediator solution as the size of the data increases. As part of the future work we plan to expand our study to evaluate the proposed solution for other machine learning algorithms such as LASSO and SVM, and also extend the scalability analysis to study the effect of increasing data dimensionality on the solution complexity.

11 ACKNOWLEDGMENTS

The work reported in this paper has been partially supported by the Schlumberger Foundation under the Faculty For The Future (FFTF) Fellowship.

REFERENCES

[1] Third-Party Vendors a Weak Link in Security Chain. http://www.esecurityplanet.com/network-security/third-party-vendors-a-weak-link-in-security-chain.html

[2] Recent Data Security Breaches Involving Third-Party Vendors. https://www.privacyandsecurityforum.com/wp-content/uploads/2015/10/25092-Privacy-and-Data-Security-Breach.pdf.

[3] Clifton, C., Kantarcioglu, M., Vaidya, J., Lin, X., Zhu, Michael Y.: Tools for privacy preserving distributed data mining. ACM Sigkdd Explorations Newsletter 4.2, pp. 28–34 (2002)

[4] Sheikh, R., Kumar, B., Mishra, D. K.: A distributed k-secure sum protocol for secure multi-party computations. arXiv preprint arXiv:1003.4071 (2010)

[5] Yao, Andrew C.: How to generate and exchange secrets. In Proceedings of the 27th Annual Symposium on Foundations of Computer Science. IEEE Computer Society, Washington, DC, USA, 162-167 (1986)

[6] Muralidhar, K., Parsa, R., Sarathy, R.: A General Additive Data Perturbation Method for Database Security. Manage. Sci. 45, 10, 1399-1415 (1999)

[7] Verykios, Vassilios S., Bertino, E., Fovino, Igor N., Provenza, Loredana P., Saygin, Y., Theodoridis, Y.: State-of-the-art in privacy preserving data mining. SIGMOD Rec. 33, 1 , 50-57 (2004)

[8] Aggarwal, C. C., Yu, P. S.: A general survey of privacy-preserving data mining models and algorithms, Privacy-Preserving Data Mining, Advances in Database Systems, vol. 34, Springer, US, pp. 11-52 (2008)

[9] Lindell, Y., Pinkas, B.: Secure Multiparty Computation for Privacy-Preserving Data Mining, Journal of Privacy and Confidentiality: Vol. 1: Iss. 1, Article 5 (2009)

[10] Lindell, Y., Pinkas, B.: Privacy Preserving Data Mining. In Proceedings of the 20th Annual International Cryptology Conference on Advances in Cryptology, Mihir Bellare (Ed.). Springer-Verlag, London, UK, 36-54 (2000)

[11] Kantarcioglu, M., Clifton, C.: Privacy-Preserving Distributed Mining of Association Rules on Horizontally Partitioned Data. IEEE Trans. on Knowl. and Data Eng. 16, 9, 1026-1037 (2004)

[12] Vaidya, J., Clifton, C.: Privacy preserving association rule mining in vertically partitioned data. In Proceedings of the eighth ACM SIGKDD international conference on Knowledge discovery and data mining. ACM, New York, NY, USA, 639-644 (2002)

[13] Vaidya, J.: Privacy preserving data mining over vertically partitioned data, Ph.D. dissertation, Purdue University, West Lafayette, Indiana. http://www.cs.purdue.edu/ homes/jsvaidya/thesis.pdf (2004)

[14] Sweeney, L.: k-anonymity: a model for protecting privacy. Int. J. Uncertain. Fuzziness Knowl.-Based Syst. 10, 5, 557-570 (2002)

[15] Narayanan, A., Shmatikov, V.: Myths and fallacies of Personally Identifiable Information. Commun. ACM 53, 6, 24-26 (2010)

[16] Narayanan, A., Shmatikov, V.: De-anonymizing Social Networks. In Proceedings of the 2009 30th IEEE Symposium on Security and Privacy. IEEE Computer Society, Washington, DC, USA, 173-187 (2009)

[17] Gentry, C.: A Fully Homomorphic Encryption Scheme. Ph.D. Dissertation. Stanford University, Stanford, CA, USA (2009)

[18] Evfimievski, A., Srikant, R., Agrawal, R., Gehrke, J.: Privacy preserving mining of association rules. In Proceedings of the eighth ACM SIGKDD international conference on Knowledge discovery and data mining. ACM, New York, NY, USA, 217-228 (2002)

[19] Huang, Z., Du, W., Chen, B.: Deriving private information from randomized data. In Proceedings of the ACM SIGMOD international conference on Management of data. ACM, New York, NY, USA, 37-48 (2005)

[20] El Gamal, T.: A Public Key Cryptosystem and a Signature Scheme Based on Discrete Logarithms. IEEE Transactions on Information Theory, 31(4), pp. 469–472 (1985)

[21] Ashrafi, Mafruz Z., Ng, See K.: Collusion-resistant Anonymous Data Collection Method. Proceedings of the 15th ACM SIGKDD International Conference on Knowledge Discovery and Data Mining, pp. 69–78 (2009)

[22] Fanaee-T, H., Gama, J.: Event labeling combining ensemble detectors and background knowledge, Progress in Artificial Intelligence: pp. 1-15, Springer Berlin Heidelberg (2013)

[23] Lichman, M.: UCI Machine Learning Repository [http://archive.ics.uci.edu/ml]. Irvine, CA: University of California, School of Information and Computer Science (2013)

[24] Baldi, P., Sadowski, P., Whiteson, D.: Searching for Exotic Particles in High-energy Physics with Deep Learning. Nature Communications 5, (2014)

Enabling Data Sharing in Contextual Environments: Policy Representation and Analysis

Erisa Karafili
Imperial College London
180 Queen's Gate, SW7 2AZ, London, UK
e.karafili@imperial.ac.uk

Emil C. Lupu
Imperial College London
180 Queen's Gate, SW7 2AZ, London, UK
e.c.lupu@imperial.ac.uk

ABSTRACT

Internet of Things environments enable us to capture more and more data about the physical environment we live in and about ourselves. The data enable us to optimise resources, personalise services and offer unprecedented insights into our lives. However, to achieve these insights data need to be shared (and sometimes sold) between organisations imposing rights and obligations upon the sharing parties and in accordance with multiple layers of sometimes conflicting legislation at international, national and organisational levels. In this work, we show how such rules can be captured in a formal representation called "Data Sharing Agreements". We introduce the use of abductive reasoning and argumentation based techniques to work with context dependent rules, detect inconsistencies between them, and resolve the inconsistencies by assigning priorities to the rules. We show how through the use of argumentation based techniques use-cases taken from real life application are handled flexibly addressing trade-offs between confidentiality, privacy, availability and safety.

CCS CONCEPTS

• **Security and privacy → Security services; Access control; Information accountability and usage control;** • **Social and professional topics** → *Medical information policy;*

KEYWORDS

Data Sharing; Data Access; Usage Control; Cloud; Policy Language; Abductive Reasoning; Argumentation Reasoning

ACM Reference format:
Erisa Karafili and Emil C. Lupu. 2017. Enabling Data Sharing in Contextual Environments: Policy Representation and Analysis. In *Proceedings of SACMAT'17, June 21–23, 2017, Indianapolis, IN, USA, , 8 pages.*
DOI: http://dx.doi.org/10.1145/3078861.3078876

1 INTRODUCTION

Data services are increasing popularity, especially with the rise of Big Data and IoT devices, where data are shared, stored, used and transformed by different entities. A serious issue in data services is the necessity of protecting and ensuring security properties of

shared data. During the exchange of the latter, the entities involved should agree on the rules related to the data. These agreements are composed of data access and usage rules that ensure the security and privacy of the data, but also of user preferences, business and legislative rules. The above rules are applied to the same set of shared data in contextual environments. Therefore, conflicts between rules can be easily produced. Due to the legislative and context dependent nature of the rules, there is a need for the conflicting rules to co-exists, e.g., conflicting rules can have different priorities depending on the applied context. Furthermore, all the above rules need to be analyzed.

We propose a novel technique based on argumentation and abductive reasoning that uses a high-expressive policy analysis language [4] for representing and analyzing data sharing agreements rules, for Cloud environments. To the best of our knowledge, this is the first attempt where argumentation based reasoning is used for detecting and solving conflicts between policies, in particular for data sharing. Argumentation reasoning permits: the co-existence of conflicting rules due to its non-monotonic nature; the analysis made to the rules, where the integration with abductive reasoning increases the efficiency of the rules; and the conflict resolution through the use of priorities between rules. Our technique best accommodates the legislative and context dependent nature of the rules thanks to the expressive power of the used language and the argumentation reasoning that provides the rules with different priorities for different contexts.

Different techniques [21, 32, 34] have been introduced for data services in order to solve part of the security problems related to them. A good part of these techniques focuses on permitting a correct data access and an efficient usage control [8, 33], suitable for data at rest and not for data that migrate and cross between multiple parties. The problem of access and usage control is a well studied one [20, 28], but the existing solutions do not permit a fine grained representation of the different types of rules, their conflicts detection and resolution.

When an exchange of data occurs the parties should agree on the rules related to the data and create the *data sharing agreements* [30] (DSA) that describe how data should be treated. The agreement can be seen as a contract, between two or more parties, and the different rules are the terms of the contract. The terms express how and who is permitted/denied/obliged to access, delete, use, and share the data, along with the different constraints that should be respected. Representing and stipulating the various rules of the DSAs is not trivial, due to the heterogeneity of the rules and the conflicts generated between them, e.g., different rules, legislations, and contexts can be applied to the same shared data.

Our proposed technique, thanks to the high-expressivity of the used policy language, permits the representation of different access and usage rules together with their constraints, as well as the user preferences, business and legislation rules applied to the data. Some of the represented constraints are the temporal ones, e.g., a given piece of data can be accessed only for 30 minutes; geographical constraints, e.g., the data can be accessed only from the office; cardinality constraints, e.g., the data can be accessed at most three times; event-defined constraints, e.g., if the data is revoked by the author, the data cannot be further shared; purpose use constraints, e.g., the data can be used just for statistical use.

The DSAs rules are represented as policies that can permit, deny or oblige the execution of certain actions. Given their diverse type, it is common that different rules can lead to conflicting actions, e.g., we can have a permit policy to access a given piece of data and a deny access policy for the same piece of data (for the same user with the same constraints), or policies that oblige and deny the same action with identical constraints. The policies can lead to other types of conflicts with respect to the context that can be applied, called *conceptual conflicts*, e.g., for the same data two different and conflicting legislation rules can be applied. Deciding the rules that will be part of the DSAs is important, as DSAs should be composed of correct and non conflicting rules. Thus, it is essential that both of the above conflicts are detected and solved. The conflict resolution is not a trivial task because the rules can have exceptions, be used in specific contexts, or be incomparable.

To capture and solve the various conflicts, we base our technique on abductive and argumentation reasoning. We use an abductive constraints system, called A-system[1] [23] for finding the various conflicts between policies, together with redundancies and gaps between them. The conceptual conflicts cannot be captured by simply using the abductive system, as they are context dependent, and not easily spotted.

We use argumentation based reasoning to permit the co-existence of conflicting rules and to detect and solve the conceptual conflicts. Argumentation based reasoning is a well suited technique for implementing decision making mechanisms under conflicting, incomplete and context dependant knowledge. We use *GorgiasB*[2] [9], a tool based on abductive and argumentation reasoning, which easily accommodate the various policies and discover the conceptual conflicts. The latter are solved by introducing priorities/hierarchies between policies that state which policies have precedence over the others for particular contexts. The use of priorities between rules permits the co-existence of conflicting rules which best describe realistic rules, especially legislative ones where different laws can be applied to the same case but depending on the environment circumstances some rules might take precedence.

We start by giving a brief introduction to our main use case in Section 2. An overview of the related work regarding the data protection techniques is given in Section 3. In Section 4, we present briefly the used policy language, how it can represent data sharing agreements, and the performed analysis tasks. We introduce a novel policy analysis for conflict detection and resolution through an argumentation based decision process in Section 5. Finally, we go

back to our use case and show its DSAs representation and conflict resolution in Section 6. In Section 7, we conclude and present some future works.

2 INTRODUCTION TO THE USE CASE

In this section, we introduce a real use case, where data sharing agreements need to be represented and stipulated. The use case is taken from an e-health scenario of an European Project (Coco Cloud project[3]). The main actors are the data subject, data controller, recipients, and data processor. For constructing the data sharing agreements the various rules are represented, and decisions about the rules that apply to the particular cases are made. Deciding the rules of DSAs is not trivial, as conflicts arises. The conflicts between the DSAs rules need to be captured, and solved.

In our use case, the patient is the *data subject*, some of his rights are to access to his medical data, to know who is processing his data, to ask for the deletion of his personal data. The *data controller* is an entity (public authority, agency, legal person), which determines the purpose and means of processing the data of the data subject. In our use case, the hospital is the data controller of the patient's data and determines the purpose for which the data are processed (e.g., administrative purpose or treatment purpose). The doctors of the hospital are the *data recipients* that need to comply to the data controller rules. The data recipients are considered as part of the data controller, the employees within the hospital do not stand as separate entities than the hospital itself. The hospital that is the data controller has various rules of how the doctors can access the patient's data, e.g., a doctor needs to be inside the hospital for accessing the patient's data (geographical constraint), he needs to be during his office hours (temporal constraint), and he needs to be the patient's treating doctor (role-based constraint). The above described rules are mainly business rules.

The *data processor* is an entity (public authority, agency, legal person) that is processing the data on behalf of the controller. In our use case, the cloud provider is considered the data processor as far as it respects the instructions of the controller. The controller rules that should be respected by the processor can also have a legal nature, e.g., if the controller is in an EU country, the cloud provider should as well be in an EU country and cannot send the data to countries outside the EU and EEA.

A *third party* is an entity (public authority, agency, legal person) that is not the data subject, data controller or processor, and that under the direct authority of the controller or processor is authorized to process the data. In our use case, a doctor outside the controller hospital is considered a third party. Once access is obtained, the third party becomes a data controller and has to comply with the data protection principals. Another third party can be an insurance company that asks for the patient's data to the hospital.

Some of the rules applied to the data are related to the type of data or the data subject. For example, the patient, as the data subject, has the permission to access his medical data. The legislation says that the patient cannot temporally access his private medical records, in case they are of a high emotional impact to him, e.g., suspects of a terminal illness that can effect the well-being of the patient. In this case, the patient is temporally denied the access to his data, until

[1]A-system http://dtai.cs.kuleuven.be/krr/Asystem/
[2]GorgiasB http://gorgiasb.tuc.gr/
[3]http://www.coco-cloud.eu/

the final results are issued. Thus, the rule that permits the patient to access his data is in conflict with the legislation because of the type of data.

The patient can be in different situations, e.g., intensive treatment, unconscious, emergency, that affect how the data are shared and used. For sake of simplicity we assume that the situation where the patient is involved, which describes the environment circumstances, is already given to the system by a trusted entity/agent. Usually the patient gives the permission to the doctor to access his sensitive data. In case the patient is unconscious, he is not able to grant this access. Thus, the doctor can access to the patient's personal data for contacting a family member and getting their permission to access the patient's sensitive data. The unconscious state does not give directly to the doctor the permission to access to all the patient's data. If the family member is not able to give this permission and the patient is in intensive treatment, the legislation permits a commission of the family doctor and hospital director to grant the access. In this case, there are various rules that are in conflict and different contexts are applied to the same case, e.g., unconscious, family member permission, intensive treatment. Thus, deciding the rules to be applied becomes more difficult.

The territory where the data are generated is another constraint added to the rules. The doctor can share the patient's data with a doctor of another hospital (third party), to ask for a second opinion. EU regulations state that data generated in EU can be shared just with EU and EEA countries. In case the third party doctor is not in an EU country, the data cannot be shared. Suppose now that the patient wants to take his medical data, generated in an EU country, outside an EU and EEA country. Also in this case, the patient cannot share his data.

Let's see another example where different contexts are applied and the data cross borders is more evident. Suppose that while the data subject is on vacation in a non EU and EEA country, he has an accident, and is in a critical situation for his life (e.g., an emergency situation). In this case, depending on the legal agreements EU has with that country, and because the data subject is in an emergency situation, part of the medical data of the patient can be shared. In this example, different rules create conflicts and the problem of deciding the rules to be applied is more difficult. In the coming sections, we will explain how these conflicts can be solved by introducing priorities between rules.

3 RELATED WORK

Nowadays, the solutions for protecting the used and shared data, aside from focusing on protecting the databases where they are stored [7] and the network used for their transfer [14], or constructing coordination techniques for data re-use [11], are also working on protecting the data themselves, by using data-centric solutions. The change of focus is due to the increase of connectivity between users, and with that also the increase of the various attacks. Protecting and ensuring the security of all the environments where the data are transferred/stored/used is becoming challenging. Therefore, data-centric security solutions that focus on protecting the data wherever they go, are taking hold [2, 17, 21, 32, 34].

In the data-centric security solutions persist two main challenges: the control of data access and the usage of data. Both of them,

together with their own issues, have been widely studied. Different solutions are developed for solving their problems [6, 19]. The role-based access control [6] is a well known technique to ensure the data access depending on the user roles. Our solution can represent the different users roles and their specific policies for accessing and using the data.

UCON (Usage control) is a well studied concepts [25]. In [24], the authors introduce the usage control for controlling the access and usage of digital information. They put emphasis on the problem of delegation of rights that should be covered by UCON. In [27], the authors introduce the problem of usage control, by proposing a two level policy language that is expressive enough to represent the basic usage control notions, as prohibition and obligation, and to represent a generic server-side architecture that can implement usage control. The Obligation Specification Language (OSL) [8] expresses requirements for usage control, like obligations, permission-like statement, and constraints of the duration of a usage. This language is used by a mechanism for usage control [28]. Another work [15] focuses on using data usage control in distributed systems, in particular, when having a data flow in-between different connected systems. Fully decentralised infrastructure for enforcement of global usage control is introduced in [16], where the data as well as the events for the data usage occur in multiple distributed systems. Our work is taking into account all the above issues, faced by the usage control literature, as it permits policies that represent permissions, denials, obligations and delegations of rights.

Another interesting approach for sharing and accessing data is the use of sticky policies [21, 22]. Sticky polices are machine readable policies that contains conditions and constraints attached to data that describe how the data should be treated, as the latter cross multiple parties. In [13], the authors introduce the *sticky policy paradigm* and technologies for enterprise privacy enforcement and exchange of customer data. The promised privacy rights and obligations are specified through a privacy control language [12], for authorization management and access control, that includes user consents, obligations and distributed administration. The sticky policies are widely used in the cloud environment [26, 31]. Our policy language can represent the various policies represented by the sticky policies.

The data usage problems concern different entities that are using the data and the agreements they make regarding the different rules that describe how the data should be treated, called data sharing agreements [30]. The DSAs describe not only the agreements between the data subject, controller, and processor, but also the different business and legislation rules complaint to the contexts of data sharing. The authors of [20] introduce a language that represents the different rules of data sharing agreements. This approach though, suffers from the lack of expressivity, which does not permit the representation of complex DSAs, as well as the absence of analysis for the DSAs. Moreover, it does not permit dealing with the co-existence of conflicting rules and the problem of deciding the rules to be applied in particular cases.

All the above represented approaches, from the data access and usage control, to the sticky policies and finally the DSAs representation, suffer from the problem of deciding the rules that should apply to the shared data. For solving this problem, we propose an analysis to be made to the rules together with a conflict resolution technique. The proposed analysis is based on the abductive [10] and argumentation based reasoning [3, 5]. Argumentation reasoning is a suitable technique for implementing decision making mechanisms [1, 9] under conflicting knowledge.

4 DATA SHARING AGREEMENTS: REPRESENTATION AND ANALYSIS

In this section, we give a brief introduction of the used policy language. We show how it can represent the different DSAs rules, together with their constraints and the data access and usage control rules [8, 28]. The policy language enables various analysis tasks performed to the rules and permits their efficiency and soundness. For performing the analysis, we use an abductive constraint logic programming system, A-system.

4.1 A policy analysis language

Our model is based on the policy analysis language [4]. This policy language, through its high expressive power, naturally represents the various rules and constraints that should be applied during the access, usage and sharing of data. It defines policies that represent in their structure *subject*, *targets*, and *actions*. It is composed of predicates, domain description predicates and policy regulations rules. The policy regulation rules are composed of predicates and domain description ones, and represent authorization and obligation rules. Some of the predicates of the policy language are introduced below.

$$req(Sub, Tar, Act, T)$$
$$permitted(Sub, Tar, Act, T) \quad denied(Sub, Tar, Act, T)$$
$$do(Sub, Tar, Act, T) \quad deny(Sub, Tar, Act, T)$$
$$obl(Sub, Tar, Act, T_s, T_e, T)$$

The predicate $req(Sub, Tar, Act, T)$ represents the request that a given subject, Sub, is doing at the instant of time T, for performing a given action, Act, to the target, Tar. The predicates $permitted(Sub, Tar, Act, T)$ and $denied(Sub, Tar, Act, T)$ represent respectively that to a given subject is permitted/denied at the instant of time T, to perform a certain action to the target. The predicates $do(Sub, Tar, Act, T)$ and $deny(Sub, Tar, Act, T)$ record respectively whether an action is permitted to occur or not. The predicate $obl(Sub, Tar, Act, T_s, T_e, T)$ denotes that at the instance of time T, a given subject is placed under an *obligation* to perform a certain action to the target between the interval of time from T_s to T_e, where T_s is the starting time when the obligation holds and T_e is the ending time of the obligation.

The domain description predicates represent changed/unchanged properties of the system regulated by policies. The unchanged properties, are static and usually defined by the user. The dynamic properties are defined using the Event Calculus [18], and represent a set of properties that define system events regulated or not by policies.

Some of the domain description predicates are *initiates*, *terminates*, *holdsAt*, *happens*. The *initiates* predicate describes the state properties that hold due to an event, while *terminates* describes which properties stop holding after an event. The *holdsAt* predicates means that a given property is true in a state, while the *happens* predicates indicates the event that occurs in a given instant of time.

4.2 Data Sharing Agreements Representation

The used policy language can represent the permission, denial and obligation concepts for the DSAs. In the following examples, we introduce the representation of various DSAs rules of our use case.

Example 4.1. Bob (B) is the family doctor ($fDoc$) of the patient Alice. The family doctor has the permission to access to Alice's prescriptions[4], (A_presc), at the instant of time T.

$$permitted(B, A\_presc, access, T) \leftarrow holdsAt(fDoc(B, Alice), T),$$
$$holdsAt(owner(Alice, A\_presc), T).$$

Every time, the family doctor Bob writes a prescription to Alice, he needs to send a notification, ($send\_n$), in less than 30 minutes.

$$obl(B, Alice, send\_n, T, T + 30, T) \leftarrow holdsAt(fDoc(B, Alice), T),$$
$$do(B, A\_presc, write, T),$$
$$holdsAt(owner(Alice, A\_presc), T).$$

We can represent DSAs rules with different types of constraints.

Example 4.2. Suppose that our patient, Alice, wants to give the permission (*perm*) to a family member to read her data. The family member, Faust (F), can read the data, after Alice has given the permission.

$$permitted(F, A\_presc, read, T) \leftarrow T \geq T1,$$
$$holdsAt(owner(Alice, A\_presc), T_1),$$
$$do(Alice, F, perm(A\_presc, read), T_1).$$

Faust, Alice's family member, cannot read her prescriptions more than 4 times, where N is a number in this case.

$$permitted(F, A\_presc, read, T) \leftarrow N \leq 4, T \geq T_1,$$
$$holdsAt(readD(F, A\_presc, N), T),$$
$$do(Alice, F, perm(A\_presc, read), T_1),$$
$$holdsAt(owner(Alice, A\_presc), T_1).$$

Example 4.3. Bob can access Alice's prescriptions just during his working hours (*shift*).

$$permitted(B, A\_presc, access, T) \leftarrow holdsAt(fDoc(B, Alice), T),$$
$$holdsAt(owner(Alice, A\_presc), T),$$
$$holdsAt(shift(B), T).$$

$$denied(B, A\_presc, access, T) \leftarrow holdsAt(fDoc(B, Alice), T),$$
$$holdsAt(owner(Alice, A\_presc), T),$$
$$\textbf{not } holdsAt(shift(B), T).$$

4.3 DSAs analysis

The used policy analysis language enables a wide range of analysis tasks that can be performed to the DSAs rules. Below we introduce briefly some of the performed analysis tasks that permit the construction of sound, complete and efficient DSAs.

The *modality conflicts* analysis task finds conflicts between policies regulation rules, and permits to have sound DSAs. In particular, it can capture the case when an action is both permitted/obliged and denied on the same instant of time. More complex conflicts can be constructed, where constraints about events occurrences and/or subject roles are added. All the above conflicts and inconsistencies between predicates are captured by our modality conflicts, which helps correcting them.

---

[4]We use the *owner* property for relating the patient to his data.

The *coverage of gaps* analysis finds the different gaps (cases) that are not covered by the DSAs rules, and permits the construction of a complete list of rules that should be part of the DSAs. One type of gap that can be found is when there is an explicit request for performing a certain action to a certain object, and there is no authorization policy rule that neither permits nor denies this request. Another type of gap that can be found is when there is an explicit request for performing a certain action to a certain object, and this permission is given not as an authorization policy rule, but as a consequence of a default permission of the system.

The *policies comparison* analysis checks whether a policy is included/equivalent/implied by another one. This analysis improves the efficiency of the DSAs, by identifying redundant rules, that can be easily removed from the DSAs.

5 CONFLICT RESOLUTION THROUGH ARGUMENTATION REASONING

The above introduced analysis, implemented through an abductive system, is not able to capture the conceptual conflicts, as the latter are not direct conflicts between predicates (e.g., permitted/obliged and denied predicates), or they are context dependent. To find and solve the conceptual conflicts, we propose a technique based on non-monotonic reasoning [5], in particular, argumentation reasoning [3, 9]. We introduce an analysis that uses argumentation reasoning together with the abductive one, as the latter alone cannot capture the conceptual conflicts. The rules can be in conflict between each other, as they can hold for general domain description predicates but not for specific ones, or vice versa. The resolution of the conceptual conflicts is a decision making problem, and is solved by introducing priorities between rules [1]. We use argumentation reasoning, as it is a well suited technique for implementing decision making mechanisms for conflicting rules that have priorities/preferences between them and that are strongly context dependent. Argumentation reasoning permits to represent the various conflicting rules, the context where they are valid and the preferences between them. The priorities between rules permits us to work with conflicting policies and to analyze them.

Abductive and argumentation reasoning gives us the expressive power to work with strict, defeasible and conflicting rules, along with, exceptions and priorities between them. To apply the abductive and argumentation reasoning, we use the GorgiasB [29] tool. GorgiasB is a tool for preference-based argumentation with a graphical user interface. Its graphical interface helps to structure and model the knowledge and the decision making by preferences.

Our decision making technique has as input the various rules together with the domain description predicates that can be facts or defeasible knowledge, and finds the conflicts between rules, if there is any, and solves them. The resolution of the conflicts is done step by step, by putting priorities between rules[5] and explicitly specifying when a particular rule has to be considered stronger than another one. A preference/priority relation, denoted by >, is used to indicate preferences between rules. Given two conflicting rules r_1 and r_2, where for the context and the information we have, r_1 should be applied instead of r_2, we denote it with $r_1 > r_2$. The introduced

priority rules together with the existing rules are checked, and if any conflict is found, other priorities rules are introduced.

Below we give an example of DSAs representation, where the analysis is performed for capturing the conflicting rules. The identified conflicts are solved by introducing priority rules.

Example 5.1. Following our use case, the family doctor can access the patients' prescriptions (*Presc*) and private information (*PInfo*). On the other hand, the treating doctor (*tDoc*) has a more restrictive access, as he is permitted to access just the patients' prescriptions, and not the private information[6]. Below, we represent the rules in a semi-natural language, where P and D denote respectively the patient and the doctor.

$(i) Access(data, D, permitted) \leftarrow fDoc(D, P) \land Owner(P, data) \land Presc(data)$
$(ii) Access(data, D, permitted) \leftarrow fDoc(D, P) \land Owner(P, data) \land PInfo(data)$
$(iii) Access(data, D, permitted) \leftarrow tDoc(D, P) \land Owner(P, data) \land Presc(data)$
$(iv) Access(data, D, denied) \leftarrow tDoc(D, P) \land Owner(P, data) \land PInfo(data)$

The last rule is represented with the policy language as follows:

$denied(Sub, Tar, access, T) \leftarrow req(Sub, Tar, access, T),$
$holdsAt(tDoc(Sub, P), T),$
$pInfo(Tar),$
$holdsAt(owner(P, Tar), T),$
$holdsAt(work(D, H), T),$
$holdsAt(hosp(P, H), T).$

When the patient is an emergency situation (*Emerg*) (where his life is at risk) the doctor has access to the patient's private information, e.g., for contacting a family member of the patient. This exception is represented as below.

$(v) Access(data, D, permitted) \leftarrow Emerg(P, H) \land tDoc(D, P) \land Owner(P, data) \land PInfo(data)$

The above predicate is written in policy language as follows:

$permitted(Sub, Tar, access, T) \leftarrow req(Sub, Tar, access, T),$
$holdsAt(Emerg(P, H), T),$
$holdsAt(tDoc(Sub, P), T),$
$pInfo(Tar),$
$holdsAt(owner(P, Tar), T),$
$holdsAt(work(D, H), T),$
$holdsAt(hosp(P, H), T).$

Conflicts are found for the above rules. The two last rules, (iv) and (v), are in conflict with each other, as one says that generally treating doctors cannot access the private information of a patient, while the other one gives permission to the treating doctor to access the information, in case of an emergency. A preference relation between rules is added in this case, stating that rule (v) is preferred over rule (iv), $(v) > (iv)$, in case there is an emergency. After the preference is introduced and no other conflict is found, the scenario can be tested.

[5]For sake of understandability, we call the priorities between rules, *priority rules*.

[6]The treating doctor should work ($work(D, H)$) in the same hospital (H) where his patient is hospitalized ($hosp(P, H)$).

6 USE CASE: DSAS REPRESENTATION AND ANALYSIS

In this section, we continue with our use case that was already introduced in the previous sections. First, we describe the various entities involved in the DSAs and the types of data. We continue by showing some DSAs rules and their analysis, where the conflicts are detected and solved by introducing priorities between rules.

As described in the above sections, we want to model the data sharing agreements between different entities, for sharing and using the data. In our case, we give a special focus on the use of the cloud environment. Our solution can be used independently from the applied environment. The different actors are the patients (sometimes we call them clients) $\mathcal{P} = \{P_1, P_2, \cdots\}$, the service providers that are the different hospitals and medical centers $\mathcal{H} = \{H_1, H_2, \cdots\}$, and the doctors $\mathcal{D} = \{D_1, D_2, \cdots\}$, that work in various hospitals or medical centers.

Every patient has his associated *data* that can be of three types:

- prescriptions: $Presc(data)$, e.g., blood pressure, analyses, medicine prescriptions, x-rays, etc.;
- private prescriptions: $PData(data)$, e.g., anti-depressive treatments;
- personal information: $PInfo(data)$, e.g., contact information and family member contacts.

A further division, based on the notion of type $TypeD(data, type)$ that describe the medical data, is made to the prescription data, e.g., the otolaryngology and the dental information are of the same type, the orthopaedic data and the different x-rays data are of the same type, while food allergy data and x-rays data have different types. General analyses and blood pressure are considered general medical information, thus, we include them in all types of data.

Usually, in EU countries, every patient (P) has a *family doctor*: $FDoc(D, P)$. When the patient is treated/examined/hospitalized in an hospital, he has also the *treating doctors*: $TDoc(D, P)$. In this case, for D to be the treating doctor of P, then D should work in the same hospital where P is treated/examined/hospitalized, as follows:

$$TDoc(D, P) \text{ when } Hosp(P, H) \wedge Work(D, H).$$

The doctors usually have a specialisation. Thus, we divide them by their specialisation, called types[7]: $Spec(D, type)$.

The patient's data are used, accessed, and shared between different entities by respecting their DSAs. The first step is to agree on the terms of the DSAs, where some terms, usually legal ones, are irrefutable. Let us give some of the DSAs terms for our scenario.

(1) The family doctor can access to all the data of the patient.
(2) The patient can access to all his data.
(3) The treating doctor can access to the prescription data related to his specialisation.
(4) The hospital regulation says that the treating doctor can access to the patient's data during his working time, and while he is in the hospital.
(5) The treating doctor cannot access to the patient's data when he is not in the hospital, or not during his shift, or the data are not related to his specialisation.
(6) Nobody else can access the data.

---

[7]For sake of simplicity, we assume that the types of the specialisations of the doctors are the same as the types that the prescriptions data are divided.

The family doctor accesses to all the patient's data, described as follows:

$$Access(data, P, permitted) \leftarrow FDoc(D, P) \wedge Owner(P, data) \quad (1)$$

Rule 2 states that the patient can access to all of his data, represented as below:

$$Access(data, P, permitted) \leftarrow Owner(P, data) \quad (2)$$

Rule 3 states that the treating doctor is permitted to access the prescriptions, in particular, just the prescriptions that deal with his specialisation, e.g., an orthopaedic doctor accesses to the x-ray of the patient, but does not access to his food allergies data. Rule 4 states that the treating doctor can access to the patient's data just during his shift, $shift(Doctor)$, and while he is in the hospital. For ensuring the latter, we compare the position of the hospital where the doctor is working, $hospP(Hospital, Location)$ with the position of the doctor, $position(D, Location)$. All the other accesses, e.g., while the doctor is not in the hospital, not during his working hours, or not relevant prescription to his specialisation, are not allowed, rule 5. Below, we introduce the representation of rule 3 and 4 together, and rule 5.

$$
\begin{aligned}
Access(data, D, permitted) \leftarrow & \ TDoc(D, P) \wedge Owner(P, data) \wedge \\
& Presc(data) \wedge TypeD(data, t_1) \wedge \\
& Spec(D, t_2) \wedge t_1 = t_2 \wedge shift(D) \\
& \wedge position(D, L_1) \wedge hospP(H, L_2) \\
& \wedge same(L_1, L_2)
\end{aligned}
$$
$$(3)$$

$$
\begin{aligned}
Access(data, D, denied) \leftarrow & \ TDoc(D, P) \wedge Owner(P, data) \wedge \\
& (PData(data) \vee PInfo(data) \vee \textbf{not } shift(D) \vee \\
& (position(D, L_1) \wedge hospP(H, L_2) \wedge \textbf{not } same(L_1, L_2)) \vee \\
& (TypeD(data, t_1) \wedge Spec(D, t_2) \wedge t_1 \neq t_2 \wedge Presc(data)))
\end{aligned}
$$
$$(5)$$

There are some cases, in EU legislation, where the patient cannot access his data, e.g., when the patient's medical data can be of high emotional impact $Emot(P, data)$ (e.g., suspects of a terminal illness that if revealed early to the patient can effect his well-being and life). The rule in this case is:

(7) If the medical data are of high emotional impact (as described by law), then the patient is not allowed to access his private prescription.

$$
\begin{aligned}
Access(data, P, denied) \leftarrow & \ Emot(P, data) \wedge PData(data) \wedge \\
& Owner(P, data)
\end{aligned}
$$
$$(7)$$

The above rule 7 is in conflict with rule 2. The latter permits the patient to access his data. The conflict is solved by putting priorities between them. We state that the last rule is stronger than the previous one, in case of high emotional impact data: rule 7 > rule 2.

An interesting rule is the one dealing with the intensive treatment, $Intens(P, H)$[8]. The treating doctor can access to the patient's private prescription when the patient grants access to him.

(8) When the patient is in intensive treatment the treating doctor can access to all the normal prescription of the patient, despite his specialisation.
(9) The doctor can access to the patient's private prescription when the patient grants $Grant(P, data, D)$ access to him.

---

[8]$Intens(P, H)$ means that patient P is in intensive treatment in hospital H.

(10) All the rest of the data accesses are denied.

$$Access(data, D, permitted) \leftarrow Intens(P, H) \land TDoc(D, P) \land \\ Presc(data) \land Owner(P, data) \land \quad (8) \\ position(D, L_1) \land hospP(H, L_2) \land same(L_1, L_2) \land shift(D)$$

$$Access(data, D, permitted) \leftarrow TDoc(D, P) \land PData(data) \land \\ Owner(P, data) \land Grant(P, data, D) \land \\ hospP(H, L_2) \land position(D, L_1) \land same(L_1, L_2) \land shift(D) \\ (9)$$

$$Access(data, D, denied) \leftarrow Intens(P, H) \land Owner(P, data) \\ \land TDoc(D, P) \land (PInfo(data) \lor \quad (10) \\ (PData(data) \land \textbf{not } Grant(P, data, D)))$$

In this case, rule 8 and 9 are in conflict with rule 5, as the latter is denying the access to not related and private prescriptions, while the two new rules are permitting it. The cases of being in an intensive treatment and granting the access to the treating doctor have higher priority. Thus, rule 8 > rule 5 and rule 9 > rule 5.

Sometimes, patients can be unconscious when they are in intensive treatment. In this case, we have the following rules.

(11) When the patient is in intensive treatment and unconscious $Uncon(P)$, the doctor can access to the patient's private information, for contacting a family member.

(12) In the above case, the doctor can access the private prescription when a patient's family member grant access to them, $FGrant(P, data, D)$.

$$Access(data, D, permitted) \leftarrow \quad Intens(P, H) \land TDoc(D, P) \land \\ PInfo(data) \land Owner(P, data) \\ \land Uncon(P) \land hospP(H, L_2) \land \\ position(D, L_1) \land same(L_1, L_2) \\ \land shift(D) \\ (11)$$

$$Access(data, D, permitted) \leftarrow Intens(P, H) \land TDoc(D, P) \land \\ PData(data) \land Owner(P, data) \\ \land Uncon(P) \land FGrant(P, data, D) \\ \land hospP(H, L_2) \land position(D, L_1) \\ \land same(L_1, L_2) \land shift(D) \\ (12)$$

Also in this case, we have conflicts between policies. In particular, rule 11 and 12 are in conflict with both rule 5 and 10. Again, the exception rules have higher priority, as being unconscious and in intensive treatment is stronger then being hospitalized or just in intensive treatment. Thus, rule 11 > rule 5, rule 11 > rule 10, rule 12 > rule 5 and rule 12 > rule 10.

Sometimes, the family members are not able to grant the access. In such case, the hospital and law regulations state that the access can be granted from the family doctor and the ward director ($director(D, H)$), by using the $Grant^*$ predicate.

(13) When the patient is in intensive treatment, unconscious, and the family member cannot grant access to the private prescription, the doctor can access the patient's private prescription, when the family doctor and ward/hospital director grant the access to him.

$$Access(data, D, permitted) \leftarrow Intens(P, H) \land TDoc(D, P) \land \\ PData(data) \land Owner(P, data) \land Uncon(P) \land \\ fDoc(P, D_1) \land director(D_2, H) \land hospP(H, L_2) \land \\ Grant^*(D_1, D_2, data, D) \land \textbf{not } FGrant(P, data, D) \land \\ shift(D) \land position(D, L_1) \land same(L_1, L_2) \\ (13)$$

In this case, we have conflicts between rules 13 and rule 5 and 10, where rules 13 has higher priority: rule 13 > rule 5, rule 13 > rule 10.

The medical data of the patient are shared between hospitals inside the EU or EEA, e.g., for asking for a second opinion, or when the patient is staying in another country. The medical data cannot be shared outside the EU and EEA. Suppose that while the patient is on vacation in a non EU or EEA country, e.g., Canada, he has an accident, and is in a critical situation for his life (e.g., an emergency situation). When the patient is in an emergency situation, the patient's prescriptions can be shared to another hospital outside the EU and EEA, in case that country has legal agreements with the EU. In this case, Canada is part of a "white-list" of countries, where the cross borders flow of information is permitted.

(14) The data can be shared inside the EU and EEA.

(15) The data cannot be shared outside EU or EEA.

(16) In case, the patient is in an emergency situation in a non EU or EEA country, then the patient's prescriptions can be shared with that country, if that country has legal agreements for cross borders flow of information with EU.

We represent rules 14 and 15, when a second opinion ($SecondOp$) is requested by the treating doctor D_1 to another doctor D. To decide if the access is permitted or denied, we check the location of the hospital where D is working. $EU^*(Hospital)$ indicates if the given hospital is located in an EU or EAA country or not.

$$Access(data, D, permitted) \leftarrow Owner(P, data) \land TDoc(D_1, P) \land \\ SecondOp(D_1, D) \land Work(D, H) \land EU^*(H) \\ (14)$$

$$Access(data, D, denied) \leftarrow \quad Owner(P, data) \land Work(D, H) \land \\ \textbf{not } EU^*(H) \\ (15)$$

We represent below rule 16, where the predicate $Agreement$ indicates that the country where the hospital is located has legal agreement with EU for cross border flow information.

$$Access(data, D, permitted) \leftarrow Emerg(P, H) \land Owner(P, data) \land \\ Presc(data) \land Work(D, H) \land \\ \textbf{not } EU^*(H) \land Agreement(H) \\ (16)$$

In this case, rule 16 is in conflict with rule 15, where the emergency situation and the legal agreements prevails. Thus, rule 16 is stronger than rule 15, represented as rule 16 > rule 15.

7 CONCLUSION AND FUTURE WORK

Data sharing agreements are a useful abstraction to group together references to the rules governing the sharing of data which regard legislation and constraints on data usage. Such rules are often conflicting and naturally have different priorities according to the context of application. The conflicts between rules arise from conflicts between business needs and privacy considerations and between security and safety, in particular in medical applications. To represent the rules of the data sharing agreements an expressive policy notation is needed. In this work, we presented a new technique for representing and working with data sharing agreements, based on a policy language and argumentation reasoning, that allows to express context dependent rules regarding data usage and obligations.

Analysis of the DSAs rules for inconsistencies is necessary, as the inconsistencies generate conflicts between rules. We showed how this analysis can be done through abduction and argumentation. We performed the analysis that capture conflicts between DSAs rules with the help of an abductive based tool (A-system). Furthermore, we performed other two tasks analysis that find redundant rules, and gaps between them, by giving as result correspondingly the redundant rules and the missing cases. To handle the context dependent nature of the priorities between policies and the co-existence of conflicting ones we use an argumentation based techniques. We showed how the introduced argumentation based analysis handles naturally a variety of use cases and how systems such as GorgiasB can be used for its implementation. Our analysis captures the conceptual conflicts and solves them by introducing priorities between the conflicting rules. The introduced analysis is applied offline to the rules, and improves the efficiency and correctness of the DSAs. We showed the DSAs representation together with the analysis and conflict resolution through a real use case scenario, taken from an e-health scenario.

A future challenge is to work with policies that deal with data integrity and availability. Currently the priority rules are introduced manually, due also to the complexity of the involved rules. An interesting future work is to automate this process and use online learning to gather information and learn automatically the priorities between rules, depending on the contexts. Data quality characteristics like timeliness, interpretation and relevance, are interesting to be analyzed in further works, by bridging the gap that exists between data access/usage control and security and information systems.

ACKNOWLEDGMENTS

Supported by FP7 EU-funded project Coco Cloud grant no.: 610853, and EPSRC Project CIPART grant no. EP/L022729/1.

REFERENCES

[1] Arosha K. Bandara, Antonis C. Kakas, Emil C. Lupu, and Alessandra Russo. 2009. Using argumentation logic for firewall configuration management. In *Integrated Network Management, IM 2009. 11th IFIP/IEEE International Symposium on Integrated Network Management.* IEEE, 180–187.

[2] Jennifer Bayuk. 2009. Data-centric security. *Computer Fraud & Security* 2009, 3 (2009), 7–11.

[3] Andrei Bondarenko, Phan Minh Dung, Robert A. Kowalski, and Francesca Toni. 1997. An Abstract, Argumentation-Theoretic Approach to Default Reasoning. *Artif. Intell.* 93 (1997), 63–101.

[4] Robert Craven, Jorge Lobo, Jiefei Ma, Alessandra Russo, Emil C. Lupu, and Arosha K. Bandara. 2009. Expressive policy analysis with enhanced system dynamicity. In *Proceedings of the 2009 ACM Symposium on Information, Computer and Communications Security, ASIACCS.* ACM, 239–250.

[5] Phan Minh Dung. 1995. On the Acceptability of Arguments and its Fundamental Role in Nonmonotonic Reasoning, Logic Programming and n-Person Games. *Artif. Intell.* 77, 2 (1995), 321–358.

[6] David F. Ferraiolo and D. Richard Kuhn. 1992. Role-Based Access Controls. In *15th National Computer Security Conference.*

[7] Michael Gertz and Sushil Jajodia. 2007. *Handbook of database security: applications and trends.* Springer Science & Business Media.

[8] Manuel Hilty, Alexander Pretschner, David A. Basin, Christian Schaefer, and Thomas Walter. 2007. A Policy Language for Distributed Usage Control. In *Computer Security - ESORICS.* Springer, 531–546.

[9] Antonis Kakas and Pavlos Moraitis. 2003. Argumentation Based Decision Making for Autonomous Agents. In *AAMAS.* ACM, 883–890.

[10] Antonis C. Kakas, Robert A. Kowalski, and Francesca Toni. 1992. Abductive Logic Programming. *J. Log. Comput.* 2, 6 (1992), 719–770.

[11] Erisa Karafili, Hanne Riis Nielson, and Flemming Nielson. 2015. How to Trust the Re-use of Data. In *Security and Trust Management - 11th International Workshop, STM.* Springer, 72–88.

[12] Günter Karjoth and Matthias Schunter. 2002. A privacy policy model for enterprises. In *Proceedings 15th IEEE Computer Security Foundations Workshop (CSFW-15).* IEEE Computer Society, 271–281.

[13] Günter Karjoth, Matthias Schunter, and Michael Waidner. 2003. Platform for Enterprise Privacy Practices: Privacy-Enabled Management of Customer Data. In *Privacy Enhancing Technologies: Second International Workshop, (PET),* Roger Dingledine and Paul Syverson (Eds.). Springer, 69–84.

[14] Charlie Kaufman, Radia Perlman, and Mike Speciner. 2002. *Network Security: Private Communication in a Public World, Second Edition* (second ed.). Prentice Hall Press, Upper Saddle River, NJ, USA.

[15] Florian Kelbert and Alexander Pretschner. 2013. Data usage control enforcement in distributed systems. In *Third ACM Conference on Data and Application Security and Privacy, CODASPY'13.* ACM, 71–82.

[16] Florian Kelbert and Alexander Pretschner. 2015. A Fully Decentralized Data Usage Control Enforcement Infrastructure. In *Applied Cryptography and Network Security - 13th International Conference, ACNS.* Springer, 409–430.

[17] Young-Jin Kim, Marina Thottan, Vladimir Kolesnikov, and Wonsuck Lee. 2010. A secure decentralized data-centric information infrastructure for smart grid. *IEEE Communications Magazine* 48, 11 (2010), 58–65.

[18] Robert A. Kowalski and Marek J. Sergot. 1986. A Logic-based Calculus of Events. *New Generation Comput.* 4, 1 (1986), 67–95.

[19] Aliaksandr Lazouski, Fabio Martinelli, and Paolo Mori. 2012. A Prototype for Enforcing Usage Control Policies Based on XACML. In *Trust, Privacy and Security in Digital Business - 9th International Conference, TrustBus.* Springer, 79–92.

[20] Ilaria Matteucci, Marinella Petrocchi, and Marco Luca Sbodio. 2010. CNL4DSA: a controlled natural language for data sharing agreements. In *Proceedings of ACM Symposium on Applied Computing (SAC).* ACM, 616–620.

[21] Marco Casassa Mont and Siani Pearson. 2011. Sticky Policies: An Approach for Managing Privacy across Multiple Parties. *Computer* 44 (2011), 60–68.

[22] Marco Casassa Mont, Siani Pearson, and Pete Bramhall. 2003. Towards accountable management of identity and privacy: sticky policies and enforceable tracing services. In *14th International Workshop on Database and Expert Systems Applications, 2003. Proceedings.* IEEE Computer Society, 377–382.

[23] Bert Van Nuffelen and Antonis C. Kakas. 2001. A-system: Declarative Programming with Abduction. In *Logic Programming and Nonmonotonic Reasoning, 6th International Conference, LPNMR, Proceedings.* Springer, 393–396.

[24] Jaehong Park and Ravi S. Sandhu. 2002. Towards usage control models: beyond traditional access control. In *SACMAT.* ACM, 57–64.

[25] Jaehong Park and Ravi S. Sandhu. 2004. The $UCON_{ABC}$ usage control model. *ACM Trans. Inf. Syst. Secur.* 7, 1 (2004), 128–174.

[26] Siani Pearson, Marco Casassa Mont, Liqun Chen, and Archie Reed. 2011. End-to-End Policy-Based Encryption and Management of Data in the Cloud. In *2011 IEEE Third International Conference on Cloud Computing Technology and Science.* IEEE Computer Society, 764–771.

[27] Alexander Pretschner, Manuel Hilty, and David A. Basin. 2006. Distributed usage control. *Commun. ACM* 49, 9 (2006), 39–44.

[28] Alexander Pretschner, Manuel Hilty, David A. Basin, Christian Schaefer, and Thomas Walter. 2008. Mechanisms for usage control. In *Proceedings of the 2008 ACM Symposium on Information, Computer and Communications Security, ASIACCS.* ACM, 240–244.

[29] Nikolaos I. Spanoudakis, Antonis C. Kakas, and Pavlos Moraitis. 2016. Gorgias-B: Argumentation in Practice. In *Computational Models of Argument - Proceedings of COMMA.* IOS Press, 477–478.

[30] Vipin Swarup, Len Seligman, and Arnon Rosenthal. 2006. Specifying Data Sharing Agreements. In *7th IEEE International Workshop on Policies for Distributed Systems and Networks (POLICY).* IEEE Computer Society, 157–162.

[31] Slim Trabelsi and Jakub Sendor. 2012. Sticky Policies for Data Control in the Cloud. In *Proceedings of the 2012 Tenth Annual International Conference on Privacy, Security and Trust (PST '12).* IEEE Computer Society, 75–80.

[32] Cong Wang, Qian Wang, Kui Ren, and Wenjing Lou. 2010. Privacy-Preserving Public Auditing for Data Storage Security in Cloud Computing. In *INFOCOM, 2010 Proceedings IEEE.* IEEE, 1–9.

[33] Xinwen Zhang, Francesco Parisi-Presicce, Ravi Sandhu, and Jaehong Park. 2005. Formal Model and Policy Specification of Usage Control. *ACM Trans. Inf. Syst. Secur.* 8 (2005), 351–387.

[34] Wenchao Zhou, Micah Sherr, William R. Marczak, Zhuoyao Zhang, Tao Tao, Boon Thau Loo, and Insup Lee. 2010. Towards a Data-centric View of Cloud Security. In *Proceedings of the Second International Workshop on Cloud Data Management (CloudDB '10).* ACM, 25–32.

Mining Relationship-Based Access Control Policies

Thang Bui
Stony Brook University
thang.bui@stonybrook.edu

Scott D. Stoller
Stony Brook University
stoller@cs.stonybrook.edu

Jiajie Li
Stony Brook University
jiajie.li@stonybrook.edu

ABSTRACT

Relationship-based access control (ReBAC) provides a high level of expressiveness and flexibility that promotes security and information sharing. We formulate ReBAC as an object-oriented extension of attribute-based access control (ABAC) in which relationships are expressed using fields that refer to other objects, and path expressions are used to follow chains of relationships between objects.

ReBAC policy mining algorithms have potential to significantly reduce the cost of migration from legacy access control systems to ReBAC, by partially automating the development of a ReBAC policy from an existing access control policy and attribute data. This paper presents an algorithm for mining ReBAC policies from access control lists (ACLs) and attribute data represented as an object model, and an evaluation of the algorithm on four sample policies and two large case studies. Our algorithm can be adapted to mine ReBAC policies from access logs and object models. It is the first algorithm for these problems.

ACM Reference format:
Thang Bui, Scott D. Stoller, and Jiajie Li. 2017. Mining Relationship-Based Access Control Policies. In *Proceedings of SACMAT '17, Indianapolis, IN, USA, June 21–23, 2017,* 8 pages.
DOI: http://dx.doi.org/10.1145/3078861.3078878

1 INTRODUCTION

The term *relationship-based access control* (ReBAC) was introduced to describe access control policies expressed in terms of interpersonal relationships in social network systems (SNSs). The underlying principle of expressing access control policies in terms of chains of relationships between entities is equally applicable and beneficial in general computing systems: it increases expressiveness and often allows more natural policies. This paper presents ORAL (Object-oriented Relationship-based Access-control Language), a ReBAC language formulated as an object-oriented extension of ABAC. Relationships are expressed using attributes that refer to other objects, including subjects and resources, and path expressions are used to follow chains of relationships between objects. In ORAL, a ReBAC policy consists of a class model, an object model, and access control rules. Section 6 compares ORAL with previous ReBAC models.

This material is based on work supported in part by NSF Grants CNS-1421893, and CCF-1414078, ONR Grant N00014-15-1-2208, AFOSR Grant FA9550-14-1-0261, and DARPA Contract FA8650-15-C-7561. Any opinions, findings, and conclusions or recommendations expressed in this material are those of the authors and do not necessarily reflect the views of these agencies.

The cost of manually developing an initial high-level policy is a barrier to adoption of high-level policy models. *Policy mining* algorithms promise to drastically reduce this cost, by partially automating the process. There is a significant amount of research on role mining and some recent research on ABAC policy mining [11, 13–15]. There is no prior work on mining of ReBAC policies (or object-oriented ABAC policies with path expressions).

This paper defines the ReBAC policy mining problem and presents the first algorithm for mining ReBAC policies from ACLs and attribute data represented as object models. It is easy to show that the problem is NP-hard, based on the Xu and Stoller's proof that ABAC policy mining is NP-hard [15]. Since we desire an efficient and practical algorithm, our algorithm incorporates greedy heuristics and is not guaranteed to generate an optimal policy. Our algorithm has three phases. In the first phase, it iterates over tuples in the subject-permission relation, uses selected tuples as seeds for constructing candidate rules, and attempts to generalize each candidate rule to cover additional tuples in the subject-permission relation by replacing conditions on user attributes or resource attributes with constraints that relate user attributes with resource attributes. The algorithm greedily selects the highest-quality generalization according to a rule quality metric based primarily on the ratio of the number of previously uncovered subject-permission tuples covered by the rule to the rule's WSC. The first phase ends when the set of candidate rules covers the entire subject-permission relation. The second phase attempts to improve the policy by merging and simplifying candidate rules. The third phase selects the highest-quality candidate rules for inclusion in the mined policy. This high-level algorithm structure is based on Xu and Stoller's algorithm for mining ABAC policies from ACLs [15], but there are also many differences between the algorithms, as discussed in detail in Section 6.

Our algorithm can be adapted to mine ReBAC policies from access logs and object models, in a similar way as Xu and Stoller's algorithm [15] was adapted to mine ABAC policies from access logs and attribute data [13].

We evaluate our algorithm on four relatively small but non-trivial sample policies and on two much larger and more complex case studies developed by Decat, Bogaerts, Lagaisse, and Joosen based on the access control requirements for Software-as-a-Service (SaaS) applications offered real companies [7, 8]. We translate Decat *et al.*'s detailed natural-language descriptions of the policies into class models and ReBAC rules, omitting a few aspects left for future work, mainly temporal conditions, obligations, and policy administration. To the best of our knowledge, these two case studies are the largest rule-based policies (as measured by the number and complexity of the rules) on which any policy mining algorithm has been evaluated.

Our evaluation methodology is to start with a ReBAC policy, generate ACLs representing the subject-permission relation, run our algorithm, and compare the ReBAC policy mined from ACLs with the original ReBAC policy. For the four sample policies, the mined policy is identical to the original policy, except for one minor syntactic variation in one conjunct of one condition of one rule of one sample policy (the variant is semantically equivalent to and equally simple as the original conjunct). For the e-document case study, our algorithm achieves roughly 80% to 90% similarity between the original and mined policies, depending on details of the comparison metric. For the workforce management case study, the mined policy is simpler than the original policy, and our algorithm achieves roughly 70% to 90% similarity between the original and mined policies, depending on the metric.

2 POLICY LANGUAGE

This section presents our policy language, ORAL. It contains common ABAC constructs, similar to those in [15], plus path expressions.

A *ReBAC policy* is a tuple $\pi = \langle CM, OM, Act, Rules \rangle$, where CM is a class model, OM is an object model, Act is a set of actions, and $Rules$ is a set of rules.

A *class model* is a set of class declarations. A *class declaration* is a tuple $\langle className, parent, fields \rangle$ where $parent$ is a class name or the empty string (indicating that the class does not have a parent), and *fields* is a set of field declarations. A *field declaration* is a tuple $\langle fieldName, type, multiplicity \rangle$, where $type$ is a class name or Boolean, and *multiplicity* is optional, one, or many. The *multiplicity* specifies how many values of the specified type may be stored in the field and is "one" (also denoted "1", meaning exactly one), "optional" (also denoted "?", meaning zero or one), or "many" (also denoted "*", meaning any natural number). Boolean fields always have multiplicity 1. Every class implicitly contains a field "id" with type String. We keep the language minimal by not allowing user-defined fields with type string. However, their effect can be achieved using a field that refers to an object having the desired string as its id. Thus, the set of types in a policy contains Boolean, String, and the names of the declared classes. A *reference type* is any class name (used as a type).

An *object model* is a set of objects whose types are consistent with the class model and with unique values in the "id's . An *object* is a tuple $\langle className, fieldVals \rangle$, where *fieldVals* is a function that maps the names of fields of the specified class, including the id field and inherited fields, to values consistent with the types and multiplicities of the fields. The value of a field with multiplicity many is a set. The value of a field with multiplicity one or optional is a single value; the special placeholder $\perp$ is used when a field with multiplicity optional lacks an actual value. For an object $o = \langle c, fv \rangle$, let type($o$) = c and fVal(o) = fv.

A *condition* is a set, interpreted as a conjunction, of atomic conditions. We often refer to the atomic conditions as conjuncts. Informally, an atomic condition is a condition on the value of one field of one object. An *atomic condition* is a tuple $\langle p, op, val \rangle$, where p is a non-empty path, op is an operator, either "in" or "contains", and val is a constant value, either an atomic value or a set of atomic values. Note that val cannot equal or contain the placeholder $\perp$. A *path* is a sequence of field names. In examples, we usually write conditions with a logic-based syntax, for readability, using "∈" for "in" and "∋" for "contains". For example, we may write $\langle dept.id, in, \{CompSci\} \rangle$ as dept.id ∈ {CompSci}. We may use "=" as syntactic sugar for "in"

when the constant is a singleton set; thus, the previous example may be written as dept.id=CompSci. Note that a condition may contain multiple atomic conditions on the same path.

A *constraint* is a set, interpreted as a conjunction, of atomic constraints. Informally, an atomic constraint expresses a relationship between the value of one field of one object (the subject issuing the request) and the value of one field of another object (the requested resource). An *atomic constraint* is a tuple $\langle p_1, op, p_2 \rangle$, where p_1 and p_2 are paths (possibly the empty sequence), and op is one of the following four operators: equal, in, contains, supseteq. The "contains" operator is the transpose of the "in" operator. Implicitly, the first path is relative to the requesting subject, and the second path is relative to the requested resource. The empty path represents the subject or resource itself. In examples, we usually write constraints with a logic-based syntax, for readability, using "=" for "equal" and "⊇" for "supseteq", and we prefix the subject path p_1 and resource path p_2 with "subject" and "resource", respectively. For example, $\langle specialties, contains, topic \rangle$ may be written as subject.specialties ∋ resource.topic. Other relational operators, such as ⊆, could also be added; we omit them for now, since they are not needed for our case studies.

A *rule* is a tuple $\langle subjectType, subjectCondition, resourceType, resourceCondition, constraint, actions \rangle$, where $subjectType$ and $resourceType$ are class names, $subjectCondition$ and $resourceCondition$ are conditions, $constraint$ is a constraint, $actions$ is a set of actions, and the following well-formedness requirements are satisfied. Implicitly, the paths in $subjectCondition$ and $resourceCondition$ are relative to the requesting subject and requested resource, respectively. The *type of a path p* (relative to a specified class), denoted type(p), is the type of the last field in the path. The *multiplicity of a path p* (relative to a specified class), denoted multiplicity(p), is one if all fields on the path have multiplicity one, is many if any field on the path has multiplicity many, and is optional otherwise.

Well-formedness requirements on rules are as follows. (1) All paths are type-correct, assuming the subject and resource have type $subjectType$ and $resourceType$, respectively. (2) (a) The two paths in the constraint have the same type, and (b) this type is not String. Part (a) reflects the assumption that comparing objects of different types is either meaningless or useless (since it would be equivalent to "false"). Part (b) prohibits constraints that compare identifiers of objects with different types, which would be meaningless. It does not reduce the expressiveness of the model, because a constraint violating it, such as specialties.id ∋ topic.id, can be written more simply as specialties ∋ topic. (3) The path in the condition does not have reference type. This reflects the fact that our language does not allow constants with reference type. (4) In conditions with operator "in", the path has multiplicity optional or one, and the constant is a set. This excludes sets of sets from the model. (5) In conditions with operator "contains", the path has multiplicity many, and the constant is an atomic value. (6) In constraints with operator "equal", both paths have multiplicity optional or one. (7) In constraints with operator "in", the first path has multiplicity optional or one, and the second path has multiplicity many. (8) In constraints with operator "contains", the first path has multiplicity many, and the second path has multiplicity optional or one. (9) In constraints with operator "supseteq", both paths have multiplicity many.

In examples, we prefix the path in the subject condition and resource condition with "subject" and "resource", respectively, for readability. For example, our project management policy contains the rule: A contractor working on a project can read and request to work on a non-proprietary task of the project whose required areas of expertise are among his/her areas of expertise. This is expressed as $\langle$Contractor, true, Task, resource.isProprietary=false, subject.projects $\ni$ resource.project $\wedge$ subject.expertise $\supseteq$ resource.expertise, {read, request}$\rangle$.

For a rule $\rho = \langle st, sc, rt, rc, c, A \rangle$, let $sType(\rho) = st$, $sCond(\rho) = sc$, $rType(\rho) = rt$, $rCond(\rho) = rc$, $con(\rho) = c$, and $acts(\rho) = A$.

An *subject-permission* tuple is a tuple $\langle s, r, a \rangle$, where s and r are objects, and a is an action. This tuple means that subject s is permitted to perform action a on resource r. A *subject-permission relation* is a set of such tuples.

Given an class model, object model, object o, and path p, let $nav(o, p)$ be the result of navigating (a.k.a. following or dereferencing) path p starting from object o. The class model and object model are implicit arguments to this relation and the following relations. We elide these arguments, because in our setting, they are unchanging in the context of a given policy, so making them explicit arguments would just add clutter. The result might be no value, represented by $\perp$, an atomic value, or a set. A set may be obtained if any field along the path (not necessarily the last field) has multiplicity many. This is like the semantics of path navigation in UML's Object Constraint Language (OCL) (http://www.omg.org/spec/OCL/).

An object o *satisfies* an atomic condition $c = \langle p, op, val \rangle$, denoted $o \models c$, if $(op = in \wedge nav(o, p) \in val) \vee (op = contains \wedge nav(o, p) \ni val)$. The *meaning* of a condition c relative to a class C, denoted $[\![c]\!]_C$ is the set of instances of C (in the implicitly given object model) that satisfy c. A condition c *characterizes* a set O of objects of class C if O is the meaning of c relative to C.

Objects o_1 and o_2 *satisfy* an atomic constraint $c = \langle p_1, op, p_2 \rangle$, denoted $\langle o_1, o_2 \rangle \models c$, if $(op = equal \wedge nav(o_1, p_1) = nav(o_2, p_2)) \vee (op = in \wedge nav(o_1, p_1) \in nav(o_2, p_2)) \vee (op = contains \wedge nav(o_1, p_1) \ni nav(o_2, p_2)) \vee (op = supseteq \wedge nav(o_1, p_1) \supseteq nav(o_2, p_2))$.

A subject-permission tuple $\langle s, r, a \rangle$ satisfies a rule $\rho = \langle st, sc, rt, rc, c, A \rangle$, denoted $\langle s, r, o \rangle \models \rho$, if $type(s) = st \wedge s \models sc \wedge type(r) = rt \wedge r \models rc \wedge \langle s, r \rangle \models c \wedge a \in A$.

The *meaning* of a rule ρ, denoted $[\![\rho]\!]$, is the subject-permission relation it induces, defined as $[\![\rho]\!] = \{\langle s, r, a \rangle \in OM \times OM \times Act \mid \langle s, r, a \rangle \models \rho\}$.

The *meaning* of a ReBAC policy π, denoted $[\![\pi]\!]$, is the subject-permission relation it induces, defined as the union of the meanings of its rules.

3 PROBLEM DEFINITION

An *access control list (ACL) policy* is a tuple $\langle CM, OM, Act, SP_0 \rangle$, where CM is a class model, OM is an object model, Act is a set of actions, and $SP_0 \subseteq OM \times OM \times Act$ is a subject-permission relation. Conceptually, SP_0 is the union of the resources' access control lists.

An ReBAC policy π is *consistent* with an ACL policy $\langle CM, OM, Act, SP_0 \rangle$ if they have the same class model, object model, and actions and $[\![\pi]\!] = SP_0$.

An ReBAC policy consistent with a given ACL policy can be trivially constructed, by creating a separate rule corresponding to

each subject-permission tuple in the ACL policy, using a condition "id=..." to identify the relevant subject and resource. Of course, such a ReBAC policy is as verbose and hard to manage as the original ACL policy. Therefore, we must decide: among ReBAC policies consistent with a given ACL policy π_0, which ones are preferable? We adopt two criteria.

One criterion is that the "id' field should be avoided when possible, because policies that use this field are (to that extent) identity-based, not attribute-based or relationship-based. Therefore, our definition of ReBAC policy mining requires that these attributes are used only when necessary, i.e., only when every ReBAC policy consistent with π_0 contains rules that use them.

The other criterion is to maximize a policy quality metric. A *policy quality metric* is a function Q_{pol} from ReBAC policies to a totally-ordered set, such as the natural numbers. The ordering is chosen so that small values indicate high quality; this is natural for metrics based on policy size. For generality, we parameterize the policy mining problem by the policy quality metric.

The *ReBAC policy mining problem* is: given an ACL policy $\pi_0 = \langle CM, OM, Act, SP_0 \rangle$ and a policy quality metric Q_{pol}, find a set *Rules* of rules such that the ReBAC policy $\pi = \langle CM, OM, Act, Rules \rangle$ is consistent with π_0, uses the "id" field only when necessary, and has the best quality, according to Q_{pol}, among such policies.

The policy quality metric that our algorithm aims to optimize is *weighted structural complexity* (WSC), a generalization of policy size first introduced for RBAC policies [12] and later extended to ABAC [15]. Minimizing policy size is consistent with prior work on ABAC mining and role mining and with usability studies showing that more concise access control policies are more manageable [1]. Informally, the WSC of a ReBAC policy is a weighted sum of the numbers of elements of each kind in the policy. Formally, the WSC of a ReBAC policy π, denoted WSC(π), is the sum of the WSC of its rules, defined bottom-up as follows. The WSC of an atomic condition $\langle p, op, val \rangle$ is $|p| + |val|$, where $|p|$ is the length of path p, and $|val|$ is 1 if val is an atomic value and is the cardinality of val if val is a set. The WSC of an atomic constraint $\langle p_1, op, p_2 \rangle$ is $|p_1| + |p_2|$. The WSC of a condition c, denoted WSC$_{cndn}(c)$, is the sum of the WSC of the constituent atomic conditions. The WSC of a constraint c, denoted WSC$_{cnst}(c)$, is the sum of the WSC of the constituent atomic constraints. The WSC of a rule is WSC($\langle st, sc, rt, rc, c, A \rangle$) = w_1WSC$_{cndn}(sc) + w_1WSC_{cndn}(rc) + w_2WSC_{cnst}(c) + w_3|A|$, where $|A|$ is the cardinality of set A, and the w_i are user-specified weights.

4 ALGORITHM

This section presents our algorithm. It is based on the ABAC policy mining algorithm in [15]. The main differences are summarized in Section 6.

Top-level pseudocode appears in Figure 1. It reflects the high-level structure described in Section 1. We refer to the tuples selected in the first statement of the first while loop as *seeds*. The top-level pseudocode is explained by embedded comments. It calls several functions, described next. Function names hyperlink to pseudocode for the function, if it is included in the paper, otherwise to the description of the function.

// Phase 1: Create a set Rules of candidate rules that covers SP_0.
$Rules = \emptyset$
// uncovSP contains tuples in SP_0 that are not covered by Rules
$uncovSP = SP_0.copy()$
while $\neg uncovSP.isEmpty()$
  // Select an uncovered tuple as a "seed".
  $\langle s, r, a \rangle$ = some tuple in $uncovSP$
  $cc = candidateConstraint(s, r)$
  // s_s contains subjects with permission $\langle r, a \rangle$ and that have
  // the same candidate constraint for r as s
  $s_s = \{s' \in OM \mid \text{type}(s') = \text{type}(s) \wedge \langle s', r, a \rangle \in SP_0$
                $\wedge\ candidateConstraint(s', r) = cc\}$
  $addCandidateRule(\text{type}(s), s_s, \text{type}(r), \{r\}, cc, \{a\}, uncovSP, Rules)$
  // s_a is set of actions that s can perform on r
  $s_a = \{a' \in Act \mid \langle s, r, a' \rangle \in SP_0\}$
  $addCandidateRule(\text{type}(s), \{s\}, \text{type}(r), \{r\}, cc, s_a, uncovSP, Rules)$
end while
// Phase 2: Combine rules using least upper bound and inheritance.
// Also, simplify them and remove redundant rules.
$mergeRulesLUBandSimplify(Rules)$
$mergeRulesInheritance(Rules)$
$mergeRulesLUBandSimplify(Rules)$
// Remove redundant rules
while $Rules$ contains rules ρ and ρ' such that $[\![\rho]\!] \subseteq [\![\rho']\!]$
  $Rules.remove(\rho)$
end while
// Phase 3: Select high quality rules into Rules'.
$Rules' = \emptyset$
Repeatedly move highest-quality rule from $Rules$ to $Rules'$ until
$\sum_{\rho \in Rules'} [\![\rho]\!] \supseteq SP_0$, using $SP_0 \setminus [\![Rules']\!]$ as second argument
to Q_{rul}, and discarding a rule if it does not cover any tuples in
SP_0 currently uncovered by $Rules'$.
return $Rules'$

// Repeatedly merge rules using least upper bound and
// simplify them, until this has no effect
function $mergeRulesLUBandSimplify(Rules)$
$mergeRulesLUB(Rules)$
while $simplifyRules(Rules)$ && $mergeRulesLUB(Rules)$
  skip
end while

Figure 1: Policy mining algorithm.

The workset $uncovSP$ in Figure 1 is a priority queue sorted in descending lexicographic order by the quality Q_{sp} of the subject-permission tuple. Informally, $Q_{\text{sp}}(\langle s, r, a \rangle)$ is a triple whose first two components are the frequency of permission $\langle r, a \rangle$ and subject s, respectively, i.e., their numbers of occurrences in SP_0, and whose third component (included as a tie-breaker to ensure a total order) is the string representation of the tuple.

$$
\begin{aligned}
\text{freq}(\langle r, a \rangle) &= |\{\langle s', r', a' \rangle \in SP_0 \mid r' = r \wedge a' = a\}| \\
\text{freq}(s) &= |\{\langle s', r', a' \rangle \in SP_0 \mid s' = s\}| \\
Q_{\text{sp}}(\langle s, r, a \rangle) &= \langle \text{freq}(\langle r, a \rangle), \text{freq}(s), \text{toString}(\langle s, r, a \rangle) \rangle
\end{aligned}
$$

function $candidateConstraint(s, r)$
// cc is the set of type-correct candidate constraints
$cc = \emptyset$
for T **in** $(\text{reach}(\text{type}(s)) \cap \text{reach}(\text{type}(r)))$
  // add candidate constraints where the paths have type T
  for p_1 **in** $\text{paths}(\text{type}(s), T)$
    for p_2 **in** $\text{paths}(\text{type}(r), T)$
      $cc.\text{add}(\langle p_1, \text{opFromMul}(\text{multiplicity}(p_1), \text{multiplicity}(p_2)), p_2 \rangle)$
    end for
  end for
end for
return $\{c \in cc \mid \langle s, r \rangle \models c\}$

Figure 2: Compute candidate constraints for subject s and resource r

The function $candidateConstraint(s, r)$ in Figure 2 returns a set containing all the atomic constraints that hold between resource r and subject s. It first computes a set cc of candidate constraints using type-correct shortest paths to each type T reachable from both $\text{type}(s)$ and $\text{type}(r)$ in the graph $\text{graph}(CM)$, which has a vertex for each class, and an edge from c_1 to c_2 if c_1 has a field with type c_2. It then selects and returns the candidate constraints satisfied by $\langle s, r \rangle$. This algorithm infers only constraints where the paths have reference types. It could easily be extended to infer constraints where the paths have type Boolean, but such constraints do not arise in our current case studies. It uses the following auxiliary functions. $\text{reach}(T)$ returns the set of classes reachable from T in $\text{graph}(CM)$, including their superclasses. **function** $\text{paths}(T, T')$ returns the set of shortest paths from T to T' in $\text{graph}(CM)$. **function** $\text{opFromMul}(m, m')$ returns the relational operator suitable for left and right operands with multiplicity m and m', respectively, defined by the following case statement on $\langle m, m' \rangle$: $\langle \text{many}, \text{many} \rangle \Rightarrow \text{supseteq} \mid \langle \text{many}, \_ \rangle \Rightarrow \text{contains} \mid \langle \_, \text{many} \rangle \Rightarrow \text{in} \mid \langle \_, \_ \rangle \Rightarrow \text{equal}$.

We extend this function to also produce non-shortest paths. These extensions are not reflected in the pseudo-code. Specifically, we extend $\text{paths}(T, T')$ to return paths with length at most $\text{dist}(T, T') + \text{SPED}$ and $\text{dist}(T, T') + \text{RPED}$ when $T = \text{type}(s)$ and $T = \text{type}(r)$, respectively, where $\text{dist}(T, T')$ is the length of shortest paths from T to T' in $\text{graph}(CM)$, and SPED (mnemonic for "subject path extra distance") and RPED (mnemonic for "resource path extra distance") are parameters of the algorithm. In order to limit the overall complexity of a candidate constraint, we also introduce a parameter MTPL (mnemonic for "maximum total path length") that limits the sum of the path lengths in a constraint; specifically, in the inner loop, a candidate constraint is constructed only if $|p_1| + |p_2| \leq \text{MTPL}$.

The function $addCandidateRule(st, s_s, rt, s_r, cc, s_a, uncovSP, Rules)$ in Figure 3 calls $computeCondition$ to compute conditions sc and rc that characterizes s_s and s_r, respectively. MSPL and MRPL are the maximum path length for paths in the subject condition and resource condition, respectively; they are parameters of the algorithm. $addCandidateRule$ then constructs a rule $\rho = \langle st, sc, rt, rc, \emptyset, s_a \rangle$, calls $generalizeRule$ to generalize ρ to ρ' and adds ρ' to candidate

function addCandidateRule($st, s_s, rt, s_r, cc, s_a, uncovSP, Rules$)
// *Construct a rule ρ that covers subject-permission tuples*
// $\{\langle s, r, a \rangle \mid s \in s_s \wedge r \in s_r \wedge a \in s_a\}$.
$sc = $ computeCondition($s_s, st,$ MSPL);
$rc = $ computeCondition($s_r, rt,$ MRPL)
$\rho = \langle st, sc, rt, rc, \emptyset, s_a \rangle$
$\rho' = $ generalizeRule($\rho, cc, uncovSP, Rules$)
$Rules$.add(ρ')
$uncovSP$.removeAll($[\![\rho']\!]$)

Figure 3: Compute a candidate rule and add it to *Rules*

rule set *Rules*. The details of the functions called by addCandidateRule are described next.

The function computeCondition(O, C, L) computes a condition C that characterizes the set O of objects of type C using paths of length at most L. A path with multiplicity optional or one appears in at most one conjunct, of the form $\langle p, \text{in}, V \rangle$ where V is the collected values of $o.p$ for o in O. A path with multiplicity may appear in multiple conjuncts, of the form $\langle p, \text{contains}, val \rangle$ where *val* is in the intersection of the values of $o.p$ for o in O. First, paths not containing the id field are considered. If the resulting condition does not characterize O, then (by construction) it is an over-approximation, and a conjunct using the "id" field is added to ensure that the resulting condition characterizes O. The condition returned by computeCondition might not be minimum-sized among conditions that characterize O: possibly some conjuncts can be deleted without changing the condition's meaning. We defer minimization of the condition until after the call to generalizeRule (described below), because minimizing the condition before that would reduce opportunities to find constraints in generalizeRule.

A rule ρ' is *valid* if $[\![\rho']\!] \subseteq SP_0$.

The function generalizeRule($\rho, cc, uncovSP, Rules$) attempts to generalize rule ρ by adding some of the atomic constraints in cc to ρ and eliminating the conjuncts of the subject condition and resource condition that use the same paths as those constraints. A rule obtained in this way is called a *generalization* of ρ. It is more general in the sense that it refers to relationships instead of specific values. The meaning of a generalization of ρ is a superset of the meaning of ρ. In more detail, generalizeRule sorts cc in the order described below, tries to add the constraints in every subsequence of cc to ρ, and if any of the resulting generalized rules is valid, it returns the highest-quality rule among them according to the rule quality metric described below, otherwise it returns ρ. When trying to add a constraint c in cc to a rule ρ, generalizeRule first tries removing the conjuncts of the subject condition and resource condition that use the same paths as c. If the resulting rule is invalid, it attempts a more conservative generalization by removing only the conjunct in the subject condition that uses the same path as c. If that rule is also invalid, it instead removes only the conjunct in the resource condition that uses the same path as c. If that rule is also valid, then there is no valid generalization of ρ using c.

generalizeRule sorts cc because the order in which candidate constraints are considered can affect the resulting generalized rule. For example, suppose adding candidate constraint c_1 keeps the rule valid and removes a conjunct in the subject condition, and that

adding candidate constraint c_2 removes a conjunct in the subject condition and a conjunct in the resource condition, and yields a higher-quality resulting rule if the resulting rule is valid. Suppose, further, that adding c_2 keeps the rule valid only if c_1 has already been added. In this case, the highest-quality generalization will be created only if c_1 is considered before c_2. To sort cc, we temporarily add each constraint c in cc to ρ (in the same way as described above) and, if this leads to a valid generalization of ρ, compute the number of subject-permission tuples in *uncovSP* covered by the resulting rule, and then sort cc in descending order by these values. If adding c does not lead to a valid generalization of ρ, c is useless and can be removed from cc.

A *rule quality metric* is a function $Q_{\text{rul}}(\rho, SP)$ that maps a rule ρ to a totally-ordered set, with the order chosen such that larger values indicate higher quality. The second argument SP is a set of subject-permission tuples. Based on our primary goal of minimizing the mined policy's WSC, a secondary preference for rules with more constraints, and a tertiary preference for rules with shorter paths in constraints, we define

$$Q_{\text{rul}}(\rho, SP) = \langle |[\![\rho]\!] \cap SP|/\text{WSC}(\rho), |\text{con}(\rho)|, 1/\text{TCPL}(\rho) \rangle$$

where $\text{TCPL}(\rho)$ ("total constraint path length") is the sum of the lengths of the paths used in the constraints of ρ.

The preference for more constraints is a heuristic, based on the observation that rules with more constraints tend to be more general than other rules with the same $|[\![\rho]\!] \cap SP|/\text{WSC}(\rho)$ (such rules typically have more conjuncts) and hence lead to lower WSC for the policy. In generalizeRule, *uncovSP* is the second argument to Q_{rul}, so $[\![\rho]\!] \cap SP$ is the set of subject-permission tuples in SP_0 that are covered by ρ and not covered by existing rules.

The function mergeRulesLUB(*Rules*) attempts to improve the quality of *Rules* by merging pairs of rules that have the same subject type, resource type, and constraint by taking the least upper bound of their subject conditions, the least upper bound of their resource conditions, and the union of their sets of actions. The *least upper bound* of conditions c_1 and c_2, denoted $c_1 \sqcup c_2$, is

$$\{\langle p, \text{in}, val \rangle \mid (\exists val_1, val_2. \langle p, \text{in}, val_1 \rangle \in c_1 \wedge \langle p, \text{in}, val_2 \rangle \in c_2$$
$$\wedge\ val = val_1 \cup val_2)\}$$
$$\cup\ \{\langle p, \text{contains}, val \rangle \mid \langle p, \text{contains}, val \rangle \in c_1$$
$$\wedge\ \langle p, \text{contains}, val \rangle \in c_2)\}.$$

Note that the meaning of the merged rule ρ_{mrg} is a superset of the meanings of the rules ρ_1 and ρ_2 being merged. If the merged rule ρ_{mrg} is valid, then it replaces ρ_1 and ρ_2 in *Rules*. mergeRulesLUB(*Rules*) updates its argument *Rules* in place, and it returns a Boolean indicating whether any rules were merged.

The function simplifyRules(*Rules*) attempts to simplify all of the rules in *Rules*. It updates its argument *Rules* in place, replacing rules in *Rules* with simplified versions when simplification succeeds. It returns a Boolean indicating whether any rules were simplified. It attempts to simplify each rule in the following ways.

(1) It eliminates conjuncts from the subject and resource conditions when this preserves validity. Since removing one conjunct might prevent removal of another conjunct, it searches for a set of conjuncts that maximizes the quality of the resulting rule. To limit the cost, we introduce a parameter MCSE (mnemonic

for "maximum conjuncts to simplify exhaustively"). If the number of conjuncts is at most MCSE, the algorithm tries removing every subset of conjuncts. If the number of conjuncts exceeds MCSE, the algorithm sorts the conjuncts in descending lexicographic order by Q_{ac} (quality metric for atomic conditions) and then attempts to remove them linearly in the sorted order, where $Q_{ac}(\langle p, op, val \rangle) = \langle |val|, |p|, \text{isId}(p), \text{toString}(p) \rangle$, where $|val|$ is 1 if val is an atomic value and is the cardinality if val is a set, and $\text{isId}(p)$ is 1 if p is "id" and is 0 otherwise. The last component of Q_{ac} is included as a tie-breaker to ensure a total order. (2) It eliminates atomic constraints when this preserves validity. It searches for the set of atomic constraints to remove that maximizes the quality of the resulting rule, while preserving validity. (3) It eliminates overlapping actions between rules. Specifically, an action a in a rule ρ is removed if there is another rule ρ' in the policy such that $\text{sCond}(\rho') \subseteq \text{sCond}(\rho) \wedge \text{rCond}(\rho') \subseteq \text{rCond}(\rho) \wedge \text{con}(\rho') \subseteq \text{con}(\rho) \wedge a \in \text{acts}(\rho')$. (4) It eliminates actions when this preserves the meaning of the policy. In other words, it removes an action a in rule ρ if all the subject-permission tuple covered by a in ρ are covered by other rules in the policy. Note that (3) is a special case of (4), listed separately to ensure that this special case takes precedence.

The function mergeRulesInheritance(*Rules*) attempts to merge a set of rules if their subject types or resource types have a common superclass and all the other components of the rule are the same. In this case, it replaces that set of rules with a single rule whose subject type or resource type is the most general superclass for which the merged rule is valid. For example, rules $\langle st_1, sc, rt, rc, c, A \rangle$ and $\langle st_2, sc, rt, rc, c, A \rangle$ are replaced with $\rho_{mrg} = \langle st', sc, rt, rc, c, A \rangle$ if ρ_{mrg} is valid, and st' is a superclass of st_1 and st_2, and these conditions do not hold for any superclass of st'.

4.1 Sample Policies and Case Studies

We developed six ReBAC policies: four sample policies, which have non-trivial and realistic rules, but are smaller and not directly based on the policy of a particular organization, and two large case studies, based on the policies of real (but anonymous) companies, as described by Decat *et al.* [7, 8]. Each policy has handwritten class model and rules, and a pseudorandom synthetic object model generated by a policy-specific algorithm. Each object model generation algorithm is parameterized by a size parameter N.

The *Electronic Medical Record (EMR) sample policy*, based on the EBAC policy in [2], controls access by physicians and patients to electronic medical records. The numbers of physicians, patients, medical records, and hospitals are proportional to N. A sample rule is "A physician at a facility can view a medical record for a consultation with any physician at that facility by a patient still registered at the facility", expressed as ⟨ Physician, true, MedicalRecord, true, subject.affiliation = resource.consultation.physician.affiliation ∧ subject.affiliation ∈ resource.consultation.patient.registrations, {view}⟩.

The *healthcare sample policy*, based on the ABAC policy in [15], controls access by nurses, doctors, patients, and agents (e.g., a patient's spouse) to electronic health records (HRs) and HR items (i.e., entries in health records). The numbers of wards, teams, doctors, nurses, teams, patients, and agents are proportional to

N. A sample rule is "A doctor can read an item in a HR for a patient treated by one of the teams of which he/she is a member, if the topics of the item are among his/her specialties", expressed as ⟨ Doctor, true, HealthRecordItem, true, subject.teams contains resource.record.patient.treatingTeam ∧ subject.specialties ⊇ resource.topics, {read}⟩, where HealthRecordItem.record is the health record containing the HR item.

The *project management sample policy*, based on the ABAC policy in [15], controls access by department managers, project leaders, employees, contractors, auditors, accountants, and planners to budgets, schedules, and tasks associated with projects. The numbers of departments, projects, tasks, and users of each type are proportional to N. A sample rule appears in Section 2.

The *university sample policy*, based on the ABAC policy in [15], controls access by students, instructors, teaching assistants (TAs), department chairs, and staff in the registrar's office and admissions office to applications (for admission), gradebooks, transcripts, and course schedules. The numbers of departments, students, faculty, and applicants for admission are proportional to N.

The *e-document case study*, based on [7], is for a SaaS multi-tenant e-document processing application. The application allows tenants to distribute documents to their customers, either digitally or physically (by printing them and employing postal mail). The overall policy contains rules governing document access and administrative operations by employees of the e-document company, such as helpdesk operators and application administrators. It also contains specific policies for some sample tenants. The numbers of employees of each tenant, registered users of each customer organization, and documents are proportional to N.

The *workforce management case study*, based on [8], is for a SaaS workforce management application provided by a company called eWorkforce which handles the workflow planning and supply management for product or service appointments (e.g., install or repair jobs). Tenants (i.e., eWorkforce customers) can create tasks on behalf of their customers. Technicians working for eWorkforce, one of its workforce suppliers, or one of the subcontractors of one of the workforce supplies receive work orders to work on those tasks, and an appointment is scheduled if appropriate. The numbers of helpdesk suppliers, workforce providers, sub-contractors, helpdesk operators, contracts, work orders, etc., are proportional to N.

The algorithm parameters are set as follows in our experiments. For all policies, MCSE = 5. For EMR, MSPL = 3, MRPL = 4, SPED = 0, RPED = 1, and MTPL = 4. For healthcare, project management, and university, MSPL = 3, MRPL = 3, SPED = 0, RPED = 0, and MTPL = 4. For e-document, MSPL = 4, MRPL = 4, SPED = 0, RPED = 0, and MTPL = 4. For workforce management, MSPL = 3, MRPL = 3, SPED = 0, RPED = 2, and MTPL = 5.

5 EVALUATION

To evaluate the effectiveness of our algorithm, we start with a ReBAC policy, generate ACLs representing the subject-permission relation, run our algorithm on the ACLs along with the class model and object model, and compare the mined ReBAC policy with the original ReBAC policy. If the mined policy is similar to the original policy, the algorithm succeeded in discovering the rules that are implicit in the ACLs.

We compare the mined policy with the original policy and with a simplified version of the original policy, obtained by applying simplifyRules. When the algorithm fails to produce high-level rules, the mined policy differs from both the original and simplified original. When it produces high-level rules that have similar or lower WSC than the original handwritten rules, but express some aspects in a different high-level way, the mined policy differs from the original but agrees with the simplified original. Thus, comparison with the simplified original policy is a more robust measure of the algorithm's ability to discover high-level rules.

5.1 Policy Similarity Metrics

Both of our policy similarity metrics are normalized to range from 0 (completely different) to 1 (identical).

Syntactic Similarity. Syntactic similarity measures the fraction of atomic conditions, atomic constraints, and actions that rules or policies have in common. The Jaccard similarity of sets is $J(S_1, S_2) = |S_1 \cap S_2| / |S_1 \cup S_2|$. The *syntactic similarity of rules* $\rho_1 = \langle st_1, sc_1, rt_1, rc_1, c_1, A_1 \rangle$ and $\rho_2 = \langle st_2, sc_2, rt_2, rc_2, c_2, A_2 \rangle$ is 0 if $st_1 \neq st_2 \lor rt_1 \neq rt_2$ and is the average of $J(sc_1, sc_2)$, $J(rc_1, rc_2)$, $J(c_1, c_2)$ and $J(A_1, A_2)$ otherwise. The *syntactic similarity of rule sets* $Rules_1$ and $Rules_2$ is the average, over rules ρ in $Rules_1$, of the syntactic similarity between ρ and the most similar rule in $Rules_2$. The *syntactic similarity* of policies π_1 and π_2 is the maximum of the syntactic similarities of the sets of rules in the policies, considered in both orders.

Semantic Similarity. *Semantic similarity* measures the fraction of granted entitlements that rules or policies have in common. The *semantic similarity of rules* ρ_1 and ρ_2 is $J(\llbracket \rho_1 \rrbracket, \llbracket \rho_2 \rrbracket)$. We extend this to *per-rule semantic similarity of policies* in exactly the same way that syntactic similarity of rules is extended to syntactic similarity of policies. Note that this metric measures similarity of the meanings of the rules in the policies, not similarity of the overall meanings of the policies.

5.2 Policy Similarity Results

Figure 4 shows the sizes of the policies and the results of policy similarity measurements. Each data point is the average over 30 pseudo-random object models. We set all weights w_i in the definition of WSC to 1.

For the *healthcare policy*, *project management policy*, and *university policy*, the original, simplified original, and mined policies are identical. For the *EMR policy*, the original and simplified original policies are identical, and the mined policy has perfect per-rule semantic similarity with them and nearly perfect (0.98) average syntactic similarity with them.

The *e-document case study* is the most difficult for our algorithm. The algorithm does well on 37 of the 39 input rules, achieving an average syntactic similarity of 0.90 and an average semantic similarity of 0.92 with the simplified original policy. The mined policy's WSC is significantly higher than the WSC of the original policy, mostly due to the algorithm's difficulty with two rules.

For the *workforce management case study*, the algorithm achieves an average syntactic similarity of 0.74 and an average semantic similarity of 0.93 with the simplified original policy. The mined

policy's WSC is lower than the WSC of the original policy, although higher than the WSC of the simplified original policy.

5.3 Performance Results

Figure 5 shows the running time as a function of ACL policy size $|SP_0|$ on an Intel i7-6700HQ CPU for both case studies and some sample policies. Each data point is the average over 10 pseudo-random object models. Error bars show 95% confidence intervals using Student's t-distribution. The running times on these policies are low-order polynomials in $|SP_0|$: the slopes of the best-fit lines on a log-log plot of the data are 1.4 for workforce management, 1.5 for e-document, 2.7 for project management, and 3.2 for healthcare.

The results for the two case studies are encouraging indicators of the algorithm's scalability: the algorithm can mine dozens of complex rules from ACLs with several thousand entries in several minutes, and the running time grows roughly proportional to $|SP_0| \times \sqrt{|SP_0|}$.

6 RELATED WORK

6.1 Policy Models

Entity-Based Access Control (EBAC) [2] is the policy model most closely related to ours. EBAC is quite similar to ORAL, except that it is based on entity-relationship models, instead of object-oriented models, and hence lacks the concept of inheritance, which ORAL includes. EBAC's expression language includes quantifiers, and ORAL does not, although some conditions that require quantifiers in their language can be expressed in ORAL using the built-in binary relations on sets, such as $\supseteq$.

Several ReBAC models have been proposed, by Carminati, Ferrari, and Perego [4], Fong [9], Cheng, Park, and Sandhu [5], Hu, Ahn, and Jorgensen [10], Crampton and Sellwood [6], and others. Some are designed specifically for OSNs, while others are designed for general use. Our model differs from all of them because it is designed as a (nearly) minimal extension of a typical ABAC language, and the extension is achieved by adopting an object-oriented model and incorporating standard object-oriented concepts, notably path expressions, like in UML's Object Constraint Language (OCL) (http://www.omg.org/spec/OCL/). None of these ReBAC models are based on general object-oriented data models. None of these ReBAC models can express constraints between fields (a.k.a. attributes) of different entities, such as the constraint "subject.expertise $\supseteq$ resource.expertise" in the sample rule in Section 2. In this regard, ORAL is significantly more expressive.

On the other hand, ORAL lacks some features found in these ReBAC models. For example, all of the languages cited above include some form of transitive closure, and ORAL does not. The languages in [2, 3, 5, 9] include some form of negation, and ORAL does not, although some conditions expressed with negation in other frameworks can be expressed in ORAL using atomic conditions of the form $\langle p, in, \emptyset \rangle$. The modal-logic-based policy languages in [3, 9] include formulas that specify graph patterns, not merely paths. Many realistic applications do not require these language features, but they are useful for some applications. These features can easily be added to our policy language. However, developing policy mining algorithms that fully exploit them may be difficult. We leave that challenge for future work.

Policy	#rules	N	#obj	#field	$|SP_0|$	WSC			Mined vs Orig		Mined vs. SimpOrig	
						Orig.	SimpOrig	Mined	SynSim	SemSim	SynSim	SemSim
EMR	6	15	344	854	708	49	49	49	0.98	1	0.98	1
healthcare	9	5	737	1806	2207	54	54	54	1	1	1	1
project mgmt.	13	5	181	300	322	76	76	76	1	1	1	1
university	10	5	731	908	2439	54	54	54	1	1	1	1
e-document	39	125	421	2045	2687	359	250	463	0.85	0.79	0.90	0.92
workforce mgmt.	27	10	411	1123	1739	262	208	223	0.68	0.92	0.74	0.93

Figure 4: Policy sizes and policy similarities. For the given value of N, #obj is the average number of objects in the object model, #field is the average sum of the number of instances of each class times the number of fields in that class, SynSim is syntactic similarity, and SemSim is per-rule semantic similarity.

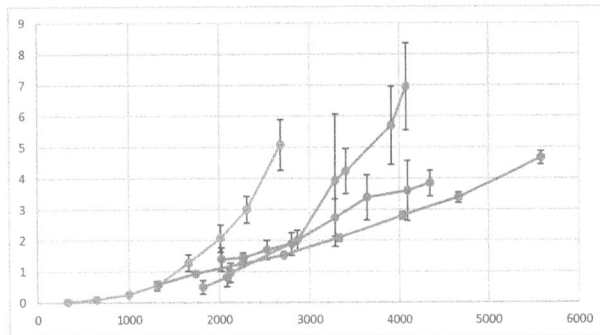

Figure 5: Running time, in minutes, as a function of $|SP_0|$ for project management (gray), healthcare (orange), e-document (blue), and workforce management (green).

The languages in [3, 5, 6, 9] allow every relation to be traversed in reverse. ORAL, like EBAC and OCL, does not; instead, the policy designer explicitly enables reverse traversal where appropriate by including a field in the reverse direction (this corresponds to using a bidirectional association in the UML class model).

6.2 Policy Mining

The most closely related prior work on policy mining is for ABAC policies without path expressions. Xu and Stoller developed the first algorithms for mining ABAC policies, from attribute data plus ACLs [15], roles [14], or access logs [13]. Our algorithm is based on their algorithm for mining ABAC policies from ACLs [15]. Adapting their algorithm to be suitable for ReBAC mining required many changes, most notably generalization of loops over attributes to iterate over paths when generating conditions and constraints; specifically, we introduce the idea of generating constraints based on shortest paths and nearly-shortest paths between classes in the graph representation of the class model. The technique for merging rules for sibling classes into a rule for an ancestor class is also new. We also modified the algorithm to accommodate changes in the supported relational operators: in conditions, we allow "in" and "contains", instead of "equal" and "supseteq" in [15]; in constraints, we allow "in" in addition to "equal", "contains", and "supseteq" allowed in [15]. We also introduced several techniques to limit and prioritize the paths being considered.

REFERENCES

[1] Matthias Beckerle and Leonardo A. Martucci. 2013. Formal Definitions for Usable Access Control Rule Sets—From Goals to Metrics. In *Proceedings of the Ninth Symposium on Usable Privacy and Security (SOUPS)*. ACM, Article 2, 11 pages.

[2] Jasper Bogaerts, Maarten Decat, Bert Lagaisse, and Wouter Joosen. 2015. Entity-Based Access Control: supporting more expressive access control policies. In *Proceedings of the 31st Annual Computer Security Applications Conference (ACSAC 2015)*. ACM, 291–300. https://lirias.kuleuven.be/handle/123456789/521795

[3] Glenn Bruns, Michael Huth, Philip Fong, and Ida Siahaan. 2012. Relationship-Based Access Control: Its Expression and Enforcement Through Hybrid Logic. In *Proc. Second ACM Conference on Data and Application Security and Privacy (CODASPY)*. ACM, 117–124.

[4] Barbara Carminati, Elena Ferrari, and Andrea Perego. 2009. Enforcing access control in Web-based social networks. *ACM Transactions on Information and System Security* 13, 1 (2009), 1–38.

[5] Yuan Cheng, Jaehong Park, and Ravi S. Sandhu. 2012. A User-to-User Relationship-Based Access Control Model for Online Social Networks. In *Proc. 26th Annual IFIP WG 11.3 Conference on Data and Applications Security and Privacy (DBSec) (Lecture Notes in Computer Science)*, Vol. 7371. Springer, 8–24.

[6] Jason Crampton and James Sellwood. 2014. Path conditions and principal matching: a new approach to access control. In *Proc. 19th ACM Symposium on Access Control Models and Technologies (SACMAT)*. ACM, 187–198.

[7] Maarten Decat, Jasper Bogaerts, Bert Lagaisse, and Wouter Joosen. 2014. The e-document case study: functional analysis and access control requirements. CW Reports CW654. Department of Computer Science, KU Leuven. https://lirias.kuleuven.be/handle/123456789/440202

[8] Maarten Decat, Jasper Bogaerts, Bert Lagaisse, and Wouter Joosen. 2014. The workforce management case study: functional analysis and access control requirements. CW Reports CW655. Department of Computer Science, KU Leuven. https://lirias.kuleuven.be/handle/123456789/440203

[9] Philip W. L. Fong. 2011. Relationship-based access control: protection model and policy language. In *Proc. First ACM Conference on Data and Application Security and Privacy (CODASPY)*. ACM, 191–202.

[10] Hongxin Hu, Gail-Joon Ahn, and Jan Jorgensen. 2013. Multiparty access control for online social networks: model and mechanisms. *IEEE Transactions on Knowledge and Data Engineering* 25, 7 (2013), 1614–1627.

[11] Eric Medvet, Alberto Bartoli, Barbara Carminati, and Elena Ferrari. 2015. Evolutionary Inference of Attribute-based Access Control Policies. In *Proceedings of the 8th International Conference on Evolutionary Multi-Criterion Optimization (EMO): Part I (Lecture Notes in Computer Science)*, Vol. 9018. Springer, 351–365.

[12] Ian Molloy, Hong Chen, Tiancheng Li, Qihua Wang, Ninghui Li, Elisa Bertino, Seraphin B. Calo, and Jorge Lobo. 2010. Mining Roles with Multiple Objectives. *ACM Trans. Inf. Syst. Secur.* 13, 4, Article 36 (2010), 36:1–36:35 pages.

[13] Zhongyuan Xu and Scott D. Stoller. 2014. Mining Attribute-Based Access Control Policies from Logs. In *Proceedings of the 28th Annual IFIP WG 11.3 Working Conference on Data and Applications Security and Privacy (DBSec 2014) (Lecture Notes in Computer Science)*, Vijay Atluri and Guenther Pernul (Eds.), Vol. 8566. Springer-Verlag, 276–291.

[14] Zhongyuan Xu and Scott D. Stoller. 2014. Mining Attribute-Based Access Control Policies from Role-Based Policies. In *Proceedings of the 10th International Conference & Expo on Emerging Technologies for a Smarter World (CEWIT 2013)*. IEEE Press.

[15] Zhongyuan Xu and Scott D. Stoller. 2015. Mining Attribute-based Access Control Policies. *IEEE Transactions on Dependable and Secure Computing* 12, 5 (September–October 2015), 533–545.

Security Analysis and Legal Compliance Checking for the Design of Privacy-friendly Information Systems

Paolo Guarda
Faculty of Law, University of Trento
Trento, Italy
paolo.guarda@unitn.it

Silvio Ranise
Security & Trust, FBK-Irst
Trento, Italy
ranise@fbk.eu

Hari Siswantoro
Security & Trust, FBK-Irst
DISI, University of Trento
Trento, Italy
siswantoro@fbk.eu

ABSTRACT

Nowadays, most of business practices involve personal data processing of customers and employees. This is strictly regulated by legislation to protect the rights of the data subject. Enforcing regulation into enterprise information system is a non-trivial task that requires an interdisciplinary approach. This paper presents a declarative framework to support the specification of information system designs, purpose-aware access control policies, and the legal requirements derived from the European Data Protection Directive. This allows for compliance checking via a reduction to policy refinement that is supported by available automated tools. We briefly discuss the results of the compliance analysis with a prototype tool on a simple but realistic scenario about the processing of personal data to produce salary slips of employees in an Italian organization.

CCS CONCEPTS

• **Security and privacy** → *Formal security models*; • **Applied computing** → *Law*;

KEYWORDS

EU DPD; Legal compliance; Access Control Policies

ACM Reference format:
Paolo Guarda, Silvio Ranise, and Hari Siswantoro. 2017. Security Analysis and Legal Compliance Checking for the Design of Privacy-friendly Information Systems. In *Proceedings of SACMAT'17, Indianapolis, IN, USA, June 21-23, 2017,* 8 pages.
DOI: http://dx.doi.org/10.1145/3078861.3078879

1 INTRODUCTION

In today's interconnected world, the security of IT systems is a continuously evolving endeavour as the threat landscape changes in real time making inadequate—shortly after their deployments—security policies, mechanisms, and tools. This fast moving situation requires that organizations be constantly vigilant to ensure that their security posture remains strong by keeping their controls up-to-date. To add complexity, legal requirements protecting specific types of data must also be taken into account and suitably enforced

in order to comply with existing laws and regulations. The most important class of legal requirements concern privacy and data protection as they constitute core values of individuals. Several legislations concern these values: the EU Data Protection Directive (EU DPD),[1] the HIPAA,[2] and the Sarbanes-Oxley[3].

The ultimate goal of an effort to integrate legal compliance and security solutions is to protect data appropriately (including those subject to regulations) and to guarantee the privacy of users. For this to become possible, it is crucial to develop methodologies and techniques that support the specification and automated analyses of regulations for data protection and privacy together with security solutions in a coherent and uniform way. Automation is essential to command the complexity of today's (and future's) digital information systems and allow for quick updates to security and privacy solutions for countering new threats. There are *three main desiderata* that such methodologies and techniques should satisfy to unfold their full benefit for privacy and data protection: (**D1**) they should be applicable at the very beginning of the design process so as to facilitate the embedding of security solutions and Privacy Enhancing Technologies (PETs) as recommended by Security- and Privacy-by-Design approaches; see, e.g., [11]; (**D2**) they should document which simplifying assumptions about the regulations are being made to resolve the ambiguities of natural language, give them a precise meaning, and permit the application of automated techniques for security analysis and compliance checking; and (**D3**) they should present system designers with detailed results about the reasons for which a security analysis or a compliance check is failing. In other words, it is not enough that the tools return a yes/no answer and should include scenarios (e.g., authorization queries) violating the property under consideration.

(D1) implies that standard specification languages at design time (such as Message Sequence Charts or Business Process Notation) should be supported by the techniques. Because of (D2), the mathematical model and the document describing the simplifying assumptions that relate it to the text of the regulation should be the results of an interdisciplinary approach involving legal experts, computer scientists, and IT security experts. This would promote a deeper understanding of the regulation, its corner cases, and those parts that are applicable to digital information systems formalized in a mathematical model. This, in turn, would facilitate the interpretation of the results returned by the tools for security analysis and legal compliance. (D3) would simplify the process of patching designs and policies even in face of evolving security and legal

[1] http://eur-lex.europa.eu/legal-content/EN/TXT/?uri=celex:31995L0046
[2] https://www.hhs.gov/hipaa/
[3] http://www.soxlaw.com

requirements. To the best of our knowledge, no available approach addresses the three desiderata above.

The main contributions of the paper are a methodology and a technique to integrate legal compliance and security checks fulfilling the desiderata above. These are based on three building blocks: (1) a declarative framework to specify the processing of data for certain purposes together with legal requirements and security policies at design-time (Section 3.1), (2) an interdisciplinary approach to derive a formal specification—expressed in the declarative framework—from regulations or laws written in natural language (Section 3.2), and (3) automated techniques to solve security analysis and compliance checking problems (Section 3.3).

The declarative framework (1) supports the specification of digital information system designs and permits the expression of legal requirements in a scenario independent way and of security policies abstracting away the details of the enforcement mechanisms—cf. (D1). The framework (1) and the interdisciplinary approach (2) allow one to make explicit the simplifying assumptions that lead to the formalization of (parts of) the regulation—cf. (D2). An important by-product of (1) and (2) is the capability of instantiating legal requirements derived from legislations to the scenario under consideration by defining few key notions (such as the legal roles played by the entities in the system and how these are empowered or mandated with selected capabilities) without the need to consider the regulation in its entirety (with all the subtleties related to the use of legal jargon) every time a new scenario is considered. Following an established tradition in policy verification, security analyses are reduced to logical problems whose solution is possible by using (off-the-shelf) Satisfiability Modulo Theories (SMT) solvers. Given the use of a common framework to express both security and legal requirements, another contribution of the paper is to show that similar reductions to logical problems can be done to support also compliance checking. The use of state-of-the-art theorem provers permit to provide policy designers with authorization queries that violate the property under consideration—cf. (D3). Since reducing security policy analyses to logical problems is well-known (see, e.g., [3]), in this paper we mainly focus on compliance.

We apply the approach to the EU Data Protection Directive (DPD) since the utility of the proposed techniques can be evaluated in the context of the EU DPD whose implications have been thoroughly studied. We use a simple scenario to illustrate the key ideas underlying our work (Section 2).

2 OVERVIEW

We illustrate our approach to integrate security analysis and compliance checking on a simple scenario, namely the processing of personal data to produce the salary slips of employees in an Italian organization, named ITOrg. The process is described by the Message Sequence Chart (MSC) of Figure 1. ITOrg asks each Employee to fill in a form with profile information such as name, surname, address, number of kids, type of car, etc. The Employee can send the filled in form to ITOrg (message 'profile') and give her consent for some of the purposes for which (parts of) the data in the form can be used. ITOrg delegates the processing of selected parts of the profile to its departments. For producing salary slips, after checking that the employee has given the consent for processing information

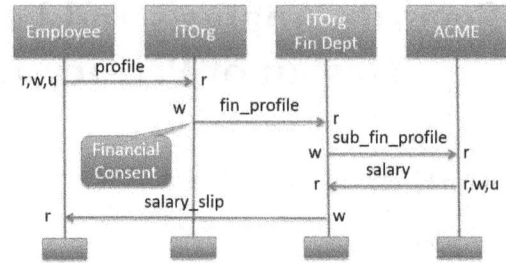

Figure 1: Semantics of the purpose 'salary_comp'

that are used to compute the salary slips—the callout in the figure, ITOrg forwards the pertinent information in the profile to its Fin(ancial) Dep(ar)t(ement)—message 'fin_profile'. In turn, ITOrg Fin Dept sends (possibly a sub-set of) the received information to ACME (message 'sub_fin_profile') that performs the actual computations to produce the salary slip. Once the computations have been performed, ACME sends the salary slip to ITOrg Fin Dept (message 'salary') that can be further processed (if the case) and finally send the salary slip to the Employee (message 'salary_slip'). Notice that each send and receive event in the MSC is decorated with permissions: r for read, w for write, and u for update. The meaning of such decorations is the following: the entity sending or receiving a message with payload p must have (one of) the permissions in the decoration close to it. For instance, an Employee should be granted the permission to w(rite) or u(pdate) her profile in order to send a message containing it. The fact that an entity has (or not) the permissions specified in the decorations is specified by an access control policy (see, e.g., [12]). There are several ways to describe such a policy, one of which is the access control matrix in Table 1 characterizing the rights of each subject (row) with respect to every object (column) in the system (for brevity, profile has been shortened to pro, salary to sal, and ITOrg has been dropped from ITOrg Fin Dept). An entry in the table marked with an asterisk means that the right can only be exercised in the context of the process to achieve the given purpose 'salary_comp.' (For example, the ITOrg Fin Dept can read the content of a message containing the 'salary' of an employee if this action is performed in the process described by the MSC of Figure 1.) This implies that we consider access control policies that are purpose-aware (see, e.g., [1]). We assign the meaning to a purpose by associating it with a plan to achieve certain goals since "an action is for a purpose if it is part of a plan for achieving that purpose;" see, e.g., [25]. Among the many possible ways to describe plans, one of the most popular is to use MSCs (especially at design-time) as we did for the scenario above. The use of MSCs allows us also to specify the contextual conditions

Table 1: Access control policy to produce salary slips

	pro	fin_pro	sub_fin_pro	sal	sal_slip
Employee	r,w,u				r
ITOrg	r	w			
Fin Dept		r*	w*	r*	w*
ACME			r*	r,w,u*	

under which the process (purpose) should be executed, as it is required to specify security policies in almost all modern information systems; see, e.g., [18]. To illustrate, consider the MSC in Figure 1: ITOrg can send the message 'fin_profile' only if the Employee has given her consent (call-out in the figure marked Financial Consent) to the processing of financial data.

The problem of legal compliance. Are the personal information of employees processed in a way which is compliant with the EU DPD? In order to answer this question, we need the availability of three main ingredients: (i) a formalization of the EU DPD, (ii) a mean to instantiate it to the information system under consideration, and (iii) techniques to check compliance.

To derive (i), several challenges must be addressed because of the generality and comprehensiveness of the set of rules introduced to protect EU citizens against the uncontrolled collection and use of personal data with the ultimate goal of respecting individual privacy. For instance, not all the rules in the regulation can be expressed (and enforced) as (purpose-aware) access control policies because of their complexity and broad spectrum of applicability. An essential part of this work consisted in a careful analysis of the text of the regulation in order to identify the parts which are amenable to be specified by (purpose-aware) access control policies. We describe how we derive a formalization of the EU DPD in Section 3.2 below. Here, we just present an excerpt of the EU DPD, shown in Table 2, which is relevant to check the compliance of the system described by the MSC in Figure 1 and the access control policy in Table 1. Column Eff(ect) reports when p(ermitting) and d(enying) to *Process* some Personal Data (*PD*) by some entity under the control of the Data Subject (*DS*), Data Controller (*DC*), or the Data Processor (*DP*) for a certain *Purpose* (when needed) according to what is described in the column Condition. *PD* are information relating to an identified or identifiable natural person (e.g., the profile information of an employee). *DC* is a natural or legal person which alone or jointly with others determines the purposes and means of the processing of PD (e.g., ITOrg is the DC in the system considered above). *DS* is an individual that is the subject of the PD held by a DC (e.g., an employee is the DS). *DP* is any individual or organization that processes PD on behalf of DC (e.g., both ITOrg Fin Dept and ACME are DPs). The first three lines of Table 2 contains the conditions permitting an action to be performed while the last three lines shows the conditions denying the action the right to be executed. More precisely, the condition in the first line of the table specifies that a *DS* can *Process* the *PD* provided that a *DC* has *Emp*owered her with the possibility to do so. While the EU DPD stipulates that—regardless of the purpose—a DS can perform any action on her PD,

Table 2: Formalization of the EU DPD (excerpt)

Eff	Condition
p	$DS \wedge Proc \wedge PD \wedge Emp$
p	$DC \wedge Proc \wedge PD \wedge Pur \wedge Cons$
p	$DP \wedge Proc \wedge PD \wedge Pur \wedge Man$
d	$DS \wedge Proc \wedge PD \wedge \neg\, Emp$
d	$DC \wedge Proc \wedge PD \wedge \neg\, Pur \wedge Cons$
d	$DP \wedge Proc \wedge PD \wedge Pur \wedge \neg\, Man$

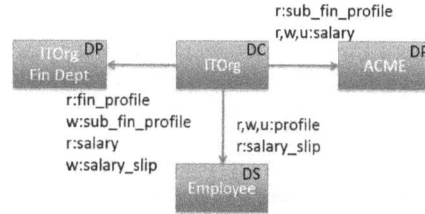

Figure 2: A bridge structure for salary slips

an information system is usually designed to provide only a sub-set of all possible actions that a DS is entitled to do. For this reason, we introduced *Emp* to express which actions the DS can perform when interacting with the system. The condition in the second line of the table specifies that a *DC* can *Process PD* for a given *Purpose* provided that the *DS* has given her *Cons*ent. The condition in the third line of the table specifies that a *DP* can *Process PD* for a given *Purpose* provided that a *DC* has *Man*dated it to do so. This formalizes one of the principles stated in the EU DPD that a *DC* can delegate (part of) the operations to one or more *DP*s in order to carry out the processing required to achieve a given purpose. The conditions in the last three lines of the table correspond to (some of) the negative versions of those in the first three. In the case of a *DS* trying to *Process* her *PD* if a *DC* has not empowered her to do so, this is sufficient to deny access (fourth line). Similarly, a *DC* cannot *Process PD* if the *DS* has not given her consent (fifth line) and a *DP* cannot *Process PD* if a *DC* has not mandated it to do so (last line). Since the EU DPD describes only the provisions permitting access, we have developed an approach to derive negative rules that we explain in Section 3.2 below.

We are now left with the problem to instantiate the formal rules in Table 2 to the system under consideration—ingredient (ii) above. We do this by using a labeled directed graph, called bridge structure, mapping the legal roles (namely, *DS*, *DC*, and *DP*) to the entities in the system (e.g., Employee and ITOrg) and describing the *Emp*ower and *Man*date relationships between *DC* and *DS* or *DP*, respectively. The bridge structure for the system described by the MSC in Figure 1 and the policy in Table 1, is shown in Figure 2. Each node is identified by an entity in the MSC and is labeled by a legal role: an Employee is a *DS*, ITOrg is a *DC*, ITOrg Fin Dept and ACME are two *DP*s. The *Emp*ower relation is identified by the arrow from ITOrg to Employee which is labeled by the pairs 'r,w,u:profile' and 'r:salary_slip' saying that an Employee is entitled to r(ead), w(rite) and u(pdate) the profile and to r(ead) the salary_slip. The *Man*date relation is identified by the two arrows from ITOrg to ITOrg Fin Dept and ACME which are labeled by 'r:fin_profile,' 'w:sub_fin_profile', 'r:salary' and 'w:salary_slip' for the former and 'r:sub_fin_profile' with 'r,w,u:salary' for the latter saying that ITOrg Fin Dept is delegated the permissions to r(ead) the fin_profile and the salary as well as to w(rite) the sub_fin_profile and salary_slip, that ACME is delegated to r(ead) sub_fin_profile and to r(ead), w(rite) and u(pdate) the salary.

With the information in the bridge structure of Figure 2, it is easy to instantiate the abstract EU DPD rules of Table 2 to the information system for producing salary slips. In fact, it is sufficient to define the various notions in the (abstract) conditions in terms of the notions introduced in the (concrete) access control policy of Table 1 by using the mapping from entities in the system to legal roles (i.e. *DS* is an Employee, *DC* is ITOrg, *DP* is either ITOrg Fin Dept or ACME) and the *Emp*ower (e.g., Employee is entitled to write and update the profile) and *Man*date (e.g., ACME is delegated to read sub_fin_profile by ITOrg) relationships. By doing this, it is possible to interpret the abstract rules in Table 2 as access control policies involving the same entities of the concrete ones in Table 1. For instance, the first line of Table 2 can be read as an Employee is permitted to read, write and update the profile or to read the salary_slip. As another example, the third line of Table 2 can be read as follows: ACME can read sub_fin_profile or read, write and update salary for the purpose of salary_comp.

As a last step—ingredient (iii) above, we are required to check the compliance of the access control policy of Table 1 against the EU DPD rules in Table 2. For this, we leverage the fact that the bridge structure in Figure 2 allowed us to derive a version of the EU DPD rules instantiated to the system under consideration as discussed above. It is easy to see that such an instantiation can be seen as an access control policy (denoted π_{iDPD} below) expressed in the same terms used by the access control matrix in Table 1 (denoted π_{acm} below). Based on this observation and the availability of several automated techniques to check for policy refinement (see, e.g., [3, 26]), we recast the problem of checking the compliance of the access control policy against the EU DPD as the problem of verifying that the π_{acm} refines π_{iDPD} or, equivalently, that every authorization requests permitted or negated by π_{acm} is also so by π_{iDPD}. An available tool for policy analysis, such us those described in [3, 26], can automatically perform this check with the results summarized in Table 3. The lines marked with R_3 and R_4 refer to the cases in which both policies return P(ermit) and D(eny), respectively. Since only these two cases are reported by the tool, we are entitled to conclude that there exist no sources of non-compliance as it is never the case that an authorization query is permitted by π_{iDPD} and denied or left undetermined by π_{acm}, neither that a query is left undetermined by π_{iDPD} and granted or denied by π_{acm}. Notice that the tools show some (concrete) queries that are permitted and some that are denied. For instance, the first line implies that an Employee can u(pdate) her pro(file) even if she has not given the consent to process the personal data concerning her. As another example, the fifth line implies that ITOrg cannot write the salary_slip if the employee has not given her consent to the processing.

We describe the formal framework to express the (abstract) EU DPD rules, the (concrete) access control policies, and the bridge

Table 3: Results of refinement checking (excerpt)

		s	a	o	Fin Consent
R_3	Employee	u	pro		False
R_3	ITOrg	w	sub_fin_pro		True
R_3	Fin Dept	r	sub_fin_pro		True
R_3	ACME	w	sal_slip		True
R_4	ITOrg	w	sal_slip		False
R_4	Fin Dept	w	sal		False
R_4	ACME	r	sal		False

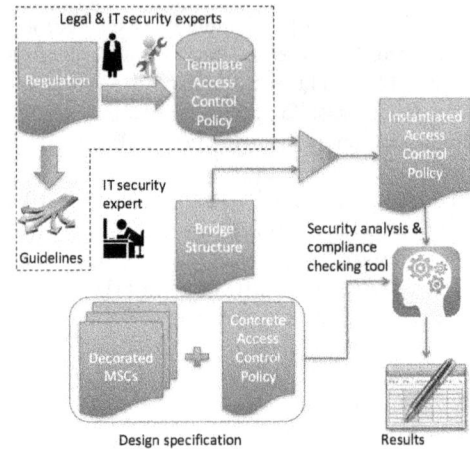

Figure 3: Our approach

structures in Section 3.1. We explain how these notions can be used to implement compliance checking on top of available techniques for the analysis of access control policies in Section 3.3.

3 THE THREE BUILDING BLOCKS

Figure 3 shows an overview of our approach to compliance checking. We start by considering the L-shaped (dashed) box at the top-left corner of the picture. Legal and IT security experts collaborate to identify the parts of the regulation (in our case the EU DPD) that are amenable to formalization, make it explicit any simplifying assumptions restricting the scope of applicability of the rules, use the declarative framework to derive a mathematical model, and compile a set of guidelines (in natural language) that should help IT system designers to bridge the gap between technical and legal levels. This process is time consuming, requires a lot of ingenuity and interdisciplinary skills but it is done once for each regulation of interest. The remaining of the figure shows what an IT security experts (possibly complementing the designs of IT system architects) should do in order to come up with a privacy-friendly IT system design. First of all, she produces a (decorated version) of the MSCs describing the main processes in the system and associates each one of them with a purpose. Second, she designs the (concrete) access control policies that the various entities in the MSC should respect in order to send or receive messages. Third, by using the guidelines made available by the group of experts that produced the formal model of the regulation, she specifies the bridge structure in order to instantiate the (formal) model to the system under consideration. Afterwards, she can use the automated tool for security analysis and compliance checking to answer several questions about the system design: is this authorization query permitted or denied? Do the (concrete) access control policy enable the execution of the scenarios described by the MSCs in the design? And, most importantly for this paper, is the (concrete) access control policy compliant with the (formalization of the) regulation? The results returned by the tool can be used by the IT system expert to revise the system design or the bridge structure when security or compliance issues are detected.

3.1 Declarative framework

We take First Order Logic (FOL) [13] as the declarative framework underlying our approach. The reason for this choice is three-fold. First, FOL seems to be expressive enough according to our experience with the formalization of the EU DPD reported below and the long line of works on specifying access control policies with logic (see, e.g., [23]). Second, there is a well-known set of techniques to reduce policy analysis problems to logical ones that can be solved by using off-the-shelf available reasoning tools, called Satisfiability Modulo Theories (SMT) solvers (see, e.g., [3, 26]). Third, there is a cornucopia of techniques available in the literature to model the dynamic behavior of IT systems and verify their properties, which use FOL and SMT solvers, that can be exploited to model the (decorated versions of the) MSCs adopted in our approach and verify basic properties such as their feasibility (see, e.g., [9]). For lack of space, we discuss here only the most relevant notions underlying the formalization of policies.

Access Control Policies. We take Attribute Based Access Control (ABAC) [18] as the model underlying our policies. The choice is motivated by the observation (made in [20]) that ABAC supports, not only, the simulation and combination of a wide range of classical access control models but also their refinement so as to supplement rather than supplanting the classical models. In this way, we are free to specify a wide range of access control policy idioms together with their combinations.

In ABAC, access rights are permitted or denied depending on the security-relevant characteristics—called attributes—of the entities involved in access control: a *subject* (e.g., a user or an application) asking to perform an *action* (e.g., read, write, update) on a *resource* (e.g., a file, a document, or a database record) in an *environment*, i.e. a collection of contextual information (e.g., location, time of day). The tension between the specification of access rights (i.e. actions that subjects can perform on resources) and safety (i.e. no subject can get permissions that compromise some security goals) requires to identify the authorization queries known to be permitted, denied, and unregulated (i.e. neither permitted nor prohibited) [19]. We formalize this as follows.

Let S, A, R, and E be sets of subjects, actions, resources, and environments, respectively. Following [2], we regard these entities as records whose fields are their attributes; an entity is uniquely identified by the values associated to its attributes. Thus, S, A, R, and E are the Cartesian products of the set of possible values of each attribute (this is uniquely determined according to an arbitrary order over the attributes). An *access control policy* is a tuple (S, A, R, E, P, D) where S, A, R, E are as defined above while P and D are sub-sets of $AQ = S \times A \times R \times E$, whose elements are called *authorization queries*. P is the set of *permitted* authorization queries—i.e. s is allowed to perform a on r in e when (s, a, r, e) is in P—and D is the set of *denied* ones—i.e. s is not allowed to perform a on r in e when (s, a, r, e) is in D.

A group of subjects is a sub-set of the set S and a resource (environment) class is a sub-set of the set R (E, respectively). We assume that actions have just one attribute that ranges over the set of possible action identifiers and that environments have (at least) the following two attributes: *purpose* ranging over the (finite) set of possible purpose identifiers and *consent* ranging over the set

of Boolean functions from the set of resource identifiers. For any policy (P, D), we assume that P and D are non-empty and disjoint. It may be the case that the union of P and D do not contain all possible authorization queries, i.e. $(P \cup D) \subset AQ$ (this is known as the open-world assumption [12]). An authorization query in the set $U = AQ \setminus (P \cup D)$ is *unregulated*. When complementing a set X w.r.t. AQ, we write X^c; e.g., $U = (P \cup D)^c$.

The sets P and D of permitted and denied authorization queries are given as set-comprehensions of the form $\{(s, a, r, e) \mid \varphi(s, a, r, e)\}$ where s, a, r, and e denote the tuples of attributes of subjects, actions, resources, and environments, respectively, and φ is a FOL expression constraining (at most) the attributes in s, a, r, and e. In the same way, we can specify a group of users as $\{s \mid v(s)\}$, a resource class as $\{r \mid \rho(s)\}$, and an environment class as $\{e \mid \gamma(e)\}$ for v, ρ, and γ FOL expressions constraining (at most) the attributes in s, r, and e, respectively.

3.2 From regulations to template policies

The EU DPD identifies the general principles (including consent, specification of purpose, minimal disclosure, and data quality [17]) that regulate how data shall be performed and organize them in a set of legal provisions. Given our focus on (purpose-aware) access control policies, we have considered only those provisions directly related to such policies. In other words, we have discarded provisions (a) from which it was impossible to derive access control rules and (b) those requiring substantial human interpretation. An example of (a) is art. 1: "*Object of the Directive: 1. In accordance with this Directive, Member States shall protect the fundamental rights and freedoms of natural persons, and in particular their right to privacy with respect to the processing of personal data. 2. Member States shall neither restrict nor prohibit the free flow of personal data between Member States for reasons connected with the protection afforded under paragraph 1.*" An example of (b) is art. 6(1): "*Member States shall provide that personal data must be: (a) processed fairly and lawfully.*" We were able to consider some of the provisions involving human judgement when an authorization condition could be identified. Examples of this are the consent given (or not) by the data subject (art. 7(a)) and the quality of data that should be "*adequate, relevant and not excessive in relation to the purposes for which they are collected and/or further processed*" (art. 6(1)). To keep track of the simplifying assumptions—desideratum (*D2*) in the introduction—resulting from the ideas stated above, we produced an annotated version of the EU DPD[4] with the hope of clarifying the results obtained by the compliance checking technique (to be described in Section 3.3 below). The document aims to simplify the task of deriving template access control policies from the natural language.

Below, we describe how we have identified the possible types of information that shall be protected, the set of legal roles involved in the processing of data, a set of auxiliary notions that are crucial to express authorization conditions and specify the possible relationships among the various roles or contextual conditions, and a bridge structure for the instantiation of the template policy to an ABAC policy for the system under consideration.

---

[4]The annotated version of the EU DPD with supplementary material including the guidelines for system designers, the prototype tool, benchmarks, and experimental results are available on-line at https://sites.google.com/view/eu-dpd-gdpr-compliance.

Data classes. From our annotated version of the EU DPD, we have identified the following three classes of data: (1) Personal Data (*PD*) "*shall mean any information relating to an identified or identifiable natural person ('data subject'); an identifiable person is one who can be identified, directly or indirectly, in particular by reference to an identification number or to one or more factors specific to his physical, physiological, mental, economic, cultural or social identity*" (art. 2(a)); (2) Sensitive Data (*SD*) is "*personal data revealing racial or ethnic origin, political opinions, religious or philosophical beliefs, trade-union membership, and the processing of data concerning health or sex life*" (art. 8(1)); and (3) Non-Personal Data (*NPD*) is information that, either in origin or on account of its having been processed, cannot be associated with any identified or identifiable data subject; hence, the EU DPD may not be applied.

Legal roles. We have defined the following three legal roles: (1) Data Controller (*DC*) "*shall mean the natural or legal person, public authority, agency or any other body which alone or jointly with others determines the purposes and means of the processing of personal data; where the purposes and means of processing are determined by national or Community laws or regulations, the controller or the specific criteria for his nomination may be designated by national or Community law*" (art. 2(d)); (2) Data Processor (*DP*) "*shall mean a natural or legal person, public authority, agency or any other body which processes personal data on behalf of the controller*" (art. 2(e)); (3) Data Subject (*DS*) "*shall mean any natural person that is the subject of the personal data*" (art. 2(a)).

Auxiliary notions. We have singled out the following four recurring conditions for the specification of access control policies to preserve privacy: (1) Purpose (*Pur*), (2) Consent (*Cons*), (3) Data Quality (*DQ*), and (4) Member State Requirement (*MSReq*). For *Pur*, observe that "*PD shall be collected for specified, lawful and legitimate purposes and not processed in ways that are incompatible with the purposes for which the data have been collected*" (art. 6(1)(b)). The view adopted in this work (recall Section 3.1) is to associate a purpose with a MSC defining a set of plans to achieve certain goals so that an action is carried out in the context of a plan. For *Cons*, *PD* "*shall be collected and processed only if the data subjects have given their explicit consent to data processing*" (art. 7(a)). This means a clear affirmative act establishing a freely given, specific, informed and unambiguous indication of the data subject's agreement to the processing of *PD*, such as by a written statement, including by electronic means. For *DQ*, *PD* "*shall be adequate, relevant, and not excessive with respect to the purposes for which they are collected and processed; accurate and, where necessary, kept up to date; retained no longer than necessary for the purposes for which the data were collected*" (art. 6(c, d, e)). This requirement ensures that the data processed are always those which are strictly necessary to achieve a certain purpose and represents a variation of the Privacy-by-default principle[5]. For *MSReq*, Member States (MSs) "*shall, within the limits of the provisions analysed, determine more precisely the conditions under which the processing of personal data is lawful*" (art. 5). The EU DPD sets the 'lowest common denominator' with respect to

the legal provisions about data protection and privacy; MSs may indicate additional ones in order to align the EU DPD to their legal systems. This allows us to impose additional regulatory constraints when considering scenarios in which national legislations may be more restrictive than the EU DPD.

We have also identified two main relationships between *DC*s and *DS*s or *DP*s: (1) Mandate (*Man*) and (2) Empower (*Emp*). The former specifies which operations the *DC* delegates to the *DP*s (see art. 2(e), art. 16, art. 17(2,3)). A *DP* can further delegate some of the operations to other *DP*s. When the *DC* mandates an action to a *DP*, it can perform the action. The relation *Emp* specifies which operations the *DC* gives the possibility to execute to the *DS* when interacting with the system being designed. Indeed, art. 12 states that the *DS* has unrestricted access to the data related to her. However, an information system typically provides only a sub-set of all possible operations on some data. The relation *Emp* allows us to specify which actions the system being designed will support and to which the EU DPD shall apply. The *DS* should still be able to execute the operations not mentioned in *Emp*, albeit in ways which are not supported by the system (e.g., by manual intervention of system administrators).

Template policies. To derive the formal rules of the template access control policies, we have replaced the natural language text with the corresponding data classes, legal roles, and auxiliary notions identified above in the tabular format of the selected articles (overall we have selected 8 out of 34 articles in the EU DPD) and used the standard Boolean connectives to combine them and form expressions of Boolean algebra. To illustrate, consider a rule taken from art. 7(a). From this, we are able to derive the following Boolean expression:

$$(DC \wedge Proc \wedge PD \wedge Pur \wedge Cons) \qquad \vee \qquad (DP \wedge Man \wedge Proc \wedge PD \wedge Pur \wedge Cons) \qquad (1)$$

where $\vee$ is disjunction and $\wedge$ is conjunction. Such expression can be read as the Data Controller (*DC*) or a Data Processor (*DP*) mandated by the Data Controller (*Man*) can process (*Proc*) Personal Data (*PD*) for an allowed purpose (*Pur*) and an explicit consent has been given by the Data subject (*Cons*). Formally, the abbreviations *DC*, *DP*, *DS*, etc introduced above are considered as Boolean variables that act as placeholders and await to be instantiated to every system under consideration by means of a bridge structure, such as the graph depicted in Figure 2 (see also below). We let $\mathbb{V}$ be the set of Boolean variables corresponding to the abbreviations of the notions introduced above, $\mathbb{P}$ the disjunction of the (27) conjunctions of variables in $\mathbb{V}$ derived from the EU DPD as described above, and $\mathbb{D}$ the disjunction of the (82) conjunctions of (possibly negated) variables in $\mathbb{V}$ obtained by negating only those variables that form the "mandatory" part of each authorization condition in $\mathbb{P}$. To illustrate, two of the disjuncts in $\mathbb{D}$ corresponding to (1) are $DC \wedge Proc \wedge PD \wedge \neg Pur \wedge Cons$ and $DC \wedge Proc \wedge PD \wedge Pur \wedge \neg Cons$ where $\neg$ denotes negation. The meaning of the disjuncts above is as follows: a *DC* cannot process *PD* for a purpose which is not the appropriate one even if the *DS* has given her consent (first disjunct), a *DC* cannot process *PD* for an appropriate purpose when the *DS* has not given her consent (second disjunct), a *DP* cannot process *PD* if it has not received the mandate to do so (¬*Man*) even if the

---

[5]This principle, implicit in the EU DPD text, was made explicit in the General Data Protection Regulation, that will come into force in 2018. In particular, art. 25(2) says that the *controller shall implement appropriate technical and organisational measures for ensuring that, by default, only personal data which are necessary for each specific purpose of the processing are processed.*

DS has given her consent and the processing is for a legitimate purpose (third disjunct). This is our approach to address the problem that the EU DPD lists only the positive provisions, i.e. conditions permitting access. A template policy is the pair $(\mathbb{P}, \mathbb{D})$ of Boolean expressions over the set $\mathbb{V}$ of Boolean variables.

We observe that some disjuncts in $\mathbb{P}$ and $\mathbb{D}$ have been obtained by considering not only a given letter of a selected article but also some additional articles defining some notions that should be ubiquitously taken into account. To illustrate, consider art. 7(a); expression (1) was obtained by including also articles 2(a), 16, and 17(2,3) that introduce the notion of mandate from a *DC* to a *DP*; this is why the second disjunct in (1) contains the condition *Man*.

Bridge structures. The last artifact supported by our framework is the bridge structure whose goal is to specify how the template policy should be instantiated to the system under consideration. Roughly, the idea is to describe how the legal roles map to the groups of user, the data classes to the resource classes, the mandate and empower relation are implemented in the system. More precisely, one needs to identify the sets $\mathcal{G}, \mathcal{R}, \mathcal{N}$ corresponding to the users groups, resource classes, and environment classes in the system design. Then, a bridge structure is a tuple $(lr, dc, dq, msr, ma, em)$ where lr is a mapping from $\mathbb{S} = \{DS, DC, DP\}$ to a FOL formula representing user groups in $\mathcal{G}$, dc is a mapping from $\mathbb{D} = \{PD, SD, NPD\}$ to a FOL formula representing resource classes in $\mathcal{R}$, dq is a mapping from $\{DQ\}$ to a FOL formula representing resource classes in $\mathcal{R}$, msr is a mapping from $\{MSReq\}$ to a FOL formula constraining the attributes of subjects, actions, resources, and environments, ma is a mapping from $\{Man\}$ to a FOL formula constraining the attributes of an entity corresponding to a DC or a DP, another entity corresponding to a DP, a resource, and an action, and em is a mapping from $\{Emp\}$ to a FOL formula constraining the attributes of an entity corresponding to a DC, another entity corresponding to a DS, a resource, and an action.

Example 3.1. Let us consider again the system for producing salary slips described in Section 2. We explain how (most of) the functions in the bridge structure can be derived from the labeled graph in Figure 2 and the MSC in Figure 1. lr can be derived from the annotations (in black) of the nodes; e.g., $lr(DS) = $ Employee, $lr(DC) = $ ITOrg, $lr(DP) = $ ITOrg Fin Dept $\lor$ ACME. dc is implicitly defined by the superscripts of messages in the MSC; when they are omitted (as in Figure 1), it means that all resource classes are considered PD, i.e. dc maps PD to the disjunction of the formulae representing all resource classes mentioned in the MSC. For the sake of simplicity, we omitted considerations concerning the data quality and further legal requirements imposed by MSs. As a consequence, both dq and msr maps the single variable in their domains to *True*. The mappings ma and em can be read from the labeled arrows in the graph of Figure 2. For example, $em(Emp)$ returns the formula

$$(\text{ITOrg} \land a = r \land \text{profile} \land \text{Employee}) \quad \lor$$
$$(\text{ITOrg} \land a = w \land \text{profile} \land \text{Employee}) \quad \lor$$
$$(\text{ITOrg} \land a = u \land \text{profile} \land \text{Employee}) \quad \lor$$
$$(\text{ITOrg} \land a = r \land \text{salary\_slip} \land \text{Employee})$$

meaning that ITOrg (the data controller) empowers the Employee (the data subject) with the capabilities of reading ($a = r$), writing

($a = w$) or updating ($a = u$) her profile and to read ($a = r$) her salary slips. □

Given a system design and a bridge structure B, we define the instantiated template policy as the ABAC policy $(\iota_B(\mathbb{P}), \iota_B(\mathbb{D}))$ where ι_B is the instantiation function defined (by recursion) on the structure of the Boolean formulae in the obvious way.

3.3 Security and Compliance

We assume that a design specification is given for a given ABAC policy $\pi = (P, D)$ together with a bridge structure β. It is possible to reduce several policy analysis problems to satisfiability problems [3, 26]. Here, for lack of space, we consider only the policy refinement problem.

This consists of verifying which authorization queries are permitted by a policy and denied or left undetermined by another. Formally, this can be stated as follows: a policy (P, D) refines a policy (P', D') iff $P \subseteq P'$ and $D \subseteq D'$. Assuming that $P' = \{(s, a, r, e) | \varphi'_P(s, a, r, e)\}$ and $D' = \{(s, a, r, e) | \varphi'_D(s, a, r, e)\}$, it is possible to reduce the two set-inclusions above as the validity of the following two formulae: $\varphi_P \Rightarrow \varphi'_P$ and $\varphi_D \Rightarrow \varphi'_D$. By refutation these are equivalent to check that

$$\varphi_P \land \neg \varphi'_P \text{ and } \varphi_D \land \neg \varphi'_D \text{ are both unsatisfiable.} \quad (2)$$

While the reduction of policy analysis problems to satisfiability problems in FOL considered above is well-known (see, e.g., [3, 26]) and we omit it here, a contribution of this paper is to use the encoding of refinement between policies to support legal compliance checking. This is possible by using the bridge structure B that induces an instantiation function ι_B that allows us to derive an ABAC policy $(\iota_B(\mathbb{P}), \iota_B(\mathbb{D}))$ from the template policy $(\mathbb{P}, \mathbb{D})$, as observed at the end of Section 3.2. The idea is then to define that a design specification for an ABAC policy (P, D) is compliant with the (EU DPD) template policy $(\mathbb{P}, \mathbb{D})$ under the bridge structure B iff (P, D) refines $(\iota_B(\mathbb{P}), \iota_B(\mathbb{D}))$. In turn, the refinement test can be reduced to two satisfiability checking problems by using (2), i.e.

$$\varphi_P \land \neg \iota_B(\mathbb{P}) \text{ and } \varphi_D \land \neg \iota_B(\mathbb{D}) \text{ are both unsatisfiable.} \quad (3)$$

Mechanizing compliance. The first step toward mechanization is to identify sufficient conditions to guarantee the decidability of the satisfiability problem (3) above. Following [3, 26], we assume the types of the attributes of the various entities may range over the integers and the reals with Linear Arithmetic operations and the usual ordering relations, enumerated data-types, abstract sets with total functions, tuples, and records. There are two advantages in adopting this set τ of types. First, it is expressive enough to specify a wide variety of situations as witnessed by its adoption in popular, generic, model-based specification languages such as B and Z. Second, it is well-known how to model the types in τ as a theory T_τ of first-order logic whose satisfiability problem for quantifier-free formulae (i.e. arbitrary Boolean combinations of constraints on the attributes that can be expressed in the theory T_τ) is decidable; see, e.g., [3] for details.

THEOREM 3.2. *Checking policy compliance is decidable and NP-complete if (A1) the types of the attributes of an ABAC policy are in τ and (A2) the FOL expressions defining permitted and denied authorization queries of the ABAC policy, user groups, classes of resources* *and environments, and the formulae returned by the bridge structure are quantifier-free.*

This is a corollary of results in [3]. NP-completeness, in our experience, is not a hindrance to the practical applicability of our approach because of the efficiency of state-of-the-art SMT solvers.

4   DISCUSSION

We have introduced a declarative framework—based on FOL—to support the specification of information system designs, purpose-aware access control policies, and legal requirements. We have shown how to instantiate the legal requirements to a particular system for checking compliance via a reduction to policy refinement. We have presented techniques, using SMT solvers, supporting the integration of the standard policy analysis problem with compliance checking. Our experience with an implementation of the proposed technique confirms its utility and scalability on realistic and synthetic compliance problems.[6]

Since policy analysis problems have been thoroughly studied in the literature about access control (see, e.g., [3, 26] for an overview), here we focus on closely related works about legal compliance. Lam et al. [22] propose a privacy policy specification language based on Datalog capable of encoding some parts of HIPAA and show the decidability of the language. Barth et al. [4] present a framework—based on Temporal Logic—for specifying privacy regulations like HIPAA and introduce two notions of compliance that take into account the past computations and their impact on the future to allow a given purpose to be achieved. The work in [8] elaborates on the formalism proposed by Barth et al. and presents a decidability result for compliance checking. It is possible to incorporate such constraints in our framework by adapting techniques for solving the Workflow Satisfiability Problem in security-sensitive business processes (see, e.g., [10]). As future work, we plan to compare the expressiveness of our (extended) framework and the one in [8].

Garg et al. [16] propose an expressive, first-order logic-based privacy policy specification language in which HIPAA can be completely encoded. They present an auditing algorithm that incrementally inspects the system log against a policy and detects violations. Chowdhury et al. [7] propose extensions of XACML for specifying HIPAA and enforcing compliance at run-time. A similar approach is developed in [14, 15] for the EU DPD. Our approach differs from these because it focus on design time, uses simpler specification languages, and use static analysis techniques to ensure compliance by construction.

In requirement engineering, some approaches (e.g., [5, 6, 24]) have been proposed to ensure legal compliance by extending software requirements. Such works focus on the specification of legal provisions with little (or no) support to checking compliance.

As future work, we plan to derive a template policy for the General Data Protection Regulation (GDPR) that is going to be adopted in the various EU MSs starting May 2018. We believe our approach may help organizations to speed up the compliance process. We also plan to study the relevance of some of the notions introduced in our framework, such as the Mandate and Empower relations, with the strategy for data governance that an organization may adopt [21]. This should permit the alignment of the data governance strategy with the privacy and data protection policies as early as possible during system development.

REFERENCES

[1] C.A. Ardagna, M. Cremonini, S. De Capitani di Vimercati, and P. Samarati. 2008. A Privacy-Aware Access Control System. *JCS* 16, 4 (2008), 369–392.

[2] A. Armando, S. Oudkerk, S. Ranise, and K. Wrona. 2014. Formal Modelling of Content-Based Protection and Release for Access Control in NATO Operations. In *FPS 2013 (LNCS)*, Vol. 8352. 227–244.

[3] A. Armando, S. Ranise, R. Traverso, and K. Wrona. 2016. SMT-based Enforcement and Analysis of NATO Content-based Protection and Release Policies. In *ABAC@CODASPY*. ACM, 35–46.

[4] A. Datta Barth, J. C. Mitchell, and H. Nissenbaum. 2006. Privacy and contextual integrity: Framework and applications. In *IEEE Symp. on S&P*.

[5] Travis D Breaux and Annie I Antón. 2008. Analyzing regulatory rules for privacy and security requirements. *Software Engineering, IEEE Transactions on* 34, 1 (2008), 5–20.

[6] Travis D Breaux, Matthew W Vail, Annie Antón, and others. 2006. Towards regulatory compliance: Extracting rights and obligations to align requirements with regulations. In *Req. Eng., 14th Int. Conf.* IEEE, 49–58.

[7] Omar Chowdhury, Haining Chen, Jianwei Niu, Ninghui Li, and Elisa Bertino. 2012. On XACML's adequacy to specify and to enforce HIPAA. In *USENIX Ws. on Health S&P*.

[8] Omar Chowdhury, Andreas Gampe, Jianwei Niu, Jeffery von Ronne, Jared Bennatt, Anupam Datta, Limin Jia, and William H Winsborough. 2013. Privacy promises that can be kept: A policy analysis method with application to the HIPAA privacy rule. In *SACMAT*. ACM, 3–14.

[9] A. Cimatti, S. Mover, and S. Tonetta. 2011. Proving and explaining the unfeasibility of message sequence charts for hybrid systems. In *FMCAD*. 54–62.

[10] J. Crampton. 2005. A reference monitor for workflow systems with constrained task execution. In *SACMAT*.

[11] G. Danezis, J. Domingo-Ferrer, M. Hansen, J.-H. Hoepman, D. Le Métayer, R. Tirtea, and S. Schiffner. 2014. Privacy and Data Protection by Design—from policy to engineering. ENISA. (2014).

[12] S. De Capitani di Vimercati, S. Foresti, S. Jajodia, and P. Samarati. 2007. Access Control Policies and Languages. *IJCSE* 3, 2 (2007), 94–102.

[13] Herbert Enderton and Herbert B Enderton. 2001. *A mathematical introduction to logic.* Academic press.

[14] K. Fatema, D. W Chadwick, and B. Van Alsenoy. 2012. Extracting Access Control and Conflict Resolution Policies from European Data Protection Law. In *Privacy and Identity Management for Life.* 59–72.

[15] K. Fatema, C. Debruyne, D. Lewis, D. OSullivan, J. P Morrison, and A. Mazed. 2016. A Semi-Automated Methodology for Extracting access control rules from the European Data Protection Directive. In *SPW, 2016 IEEE*. 25–32.

[16] D. Garg, L. Jia, and A. Datta. 2011. Policy auditing over incomplete logs: theory, implementation and applications. In *ACM CCS*.

[17] P. Guarda and N. Zannone. 2009. Towards the development of privacy-aware systems. *Inf. and Sw. Tech.* 51, 2 (2009), 337–350.

[18] V. C Hu, D. Ferraiolo, R. Kuhn, A. R. Friedman, A. J Lang, M. M Cogdell, A. Schnitzer, K. Sandlin, R. Miller, and K. Scarfone. 2013. Guide to Attribute Based Access Control (ABAC) Definition and Considerations (Draft). Number 800-162 in NIST.

[19] T. Jaeger and J. E. Tidswell. 2001. Practical Safety in Flexible Access Control Models. *ACM Trans. Inf. Syst. Secur.* 4, 2 (May 2001), 158–190.

[20] X. Jin, R. Krishnan, and R. Sandhu. 2012. A Unified Attribute-Based Access Control Model Covering DAC, MAC and RBAC. In *DBSec (LNCS)*. 41–55.

[21] V. Khatri and C. V. Brown. 2010. Designing Data Governance. *Comm. of the ACM* 53, 1 (2010), 148–152.

[22] E. Lam, J. C. Mitchell, A. Scedrov, S. Sundaram, and F. Wang. 2012. Declarative privacy policy: finite models and attribute-based encryption. In *ACM IHI.*

[23] N. Li and J.C. Mitchell. 2003. Datalog with constraints: a foundation for trust management languages. In *Proc. of PADL*. 58–73.

[24] A. Siena, I. Jureta, S. Ingolfo, A. Susi, A. Perini, and J. Mylopoulos. 2012. *Capturing Variability of Law with Nómos 2.* Springer, 383–396.

[25] M. C. Tschantz, A. Datta, and J. M. Wing. 2012. Formalizing and enforcing purpose restrictions in privacy policies. In *IEEE Symp. on S&P*. 176–190.

[26] F. Turkmen, J. den Hartog, S. Ranise, and N. Zannone. 2015. *Analysis of XACML Policies with SMT.* Springer, 115–134.

---

[6]For lack of space, we omit a report of our findings that can be found on-line at https://sites.google.com/view/eu-dpd-gdpr-compliance.

A Distributed Multi-Authority Attribute Based Encryption Scheme for Secure Sharing of Personal Health Records

Harsha S. Gardiyawasam Pussewalage
Department of ICT, University of Agder
N-4898, Grimstad, Norway
harsha.sandaruwan@uia.no

Vladimir A. Oleshchuk
Department of ICT, University of Agder
N-4898, Grimstad, Norway
vladimir.oleshchuk@uia.no

ABSTRACT

Personal health records (PHR) are an emerging health information exchange model, which facilitates PHR owners to efficiently manage their health data. Typically, PHRs are outsourced and stored in third-party cloud platforms. Although, outsourcing private health data to third party platforms is an appealing solution for PHR owners, it may lead to significant privacy concerns, because there is a higher risk of leaking private data to unauthorized parties. As a way of ensuring PHR owners' control of their outsourced PHR data, attribute based encryption (ABE) mechanisms have been considered due to the fact that such schemes facilitate a mechanism of sharing encrypted data among a set of intended recipients. However, such existing PHR solutions suffer from inflexibility and scalability issues due to the limitations associated with the adopted ABE mechanisms. To address these issues, we propose a distributed multi-authority ABE scheme and thereby we show how a patient-centric, attribute based PHR sharing scheme which can provide flexible access for both professional users such as doctors as well as personal users such as family and friends is realized. We have shown that the proposed scheme supports on-demand user revocation as well as secure under standard security assumptions. In addition, the simulation results provide evidence for the fact that our scheme can function efficiently in practice. Furthermore, we have shown that the proposed scheme can cater the access requirements associated with distributed multi-user PHR sharing environments as well as more realistic and scalable compared with similar existing PHR sharing schemes.

KEYWORDS

Access control, Attribute based encryption, Security, Personal health records

1 INTRODUCTION

Personal health records (PHR) are health information of patients, which are maintained and kept under the control of themselves. There are several advantages of using PHRs from the patients' perspective. PHRs induce patient-centric health information sharing capability given that the private health data is always under the

SACMAT'17, June 21-23, 2017, Indianapolis, IN, USA
© 2017 ACM. ACM ISBN 978-1-4503-4702-0/17/06...$15.00
DOI: http://dx.doi.org/10.1145/3078861.3078880

control of the patient. In addition, there are practical restrictions with regard to sharing of health information of patients between healthcare deliverers due to privacy and legal constraints. Hence, it would be an advantage to have a PHR which is shareable with different care deliverers.

The use of PHRs is an attractive option, however the difficulty associated with management of health information induces a significant management overhead to the owners of health records. But the utilization of cloud platforms for management of health information helps to resolve the aforementioned issue since it allows the PHRs to be outsourced to cloud infrastructures instead of storing them locally. This approach potentially leads to a better availability of health data as well as relieving the patients from the burden of maintaining them. However, considering the fact that cloud infrastructures are managed by third-parties who may be curious about the data being stored, privacy concerns have been raised on the stored data [6][11]. Also, such storage servers could become targets for various malicious activities and may lead to illegal exposure of sensitive data belonging to patients [14]. Therefore, it is crucial to adopt necessary privacy preserving mechanisms to ensure the security and privacy of outsourced PHRs of patients.

A promising approach would be to encrypt the PHR data before being outsourced to a cloud platform, so that the confidentiality of private health data is kept preserved. To achieve this, incorporation of attribute based encryption (ABE) schemes have been considered lately [15]. ABE schemes can be divided into two categories based on their functionality, as key-policy attribute based encryption (KP-ABE) schemes and ciphertext policy attribute based encryption (CP-ABE) schemes. In a KP-ABE scheme the ciphertext is associated with a set of attributes and users' secret keys are encoded with attribute based access structures [10]. If the access structure associated with a user's secret key satisfies the set of attributes which is used to generate a specific ciphertext, the user will be able to decrypt the ciphertext with the help of his secret key. CP-ABE can be considered as the dual of KP-ABE, where the ciphertext is encoded with the access structure while the users' secret keys are encoded with attributes [5]. In relation to a PHR sharing application, CP-ABE schemes seem to be more conducive compared to KP-ABE schemes, given that the PHR owner will be able to specify the intended recipients through an attribute based access structure while a user who possesses a set of attributes that satisfies the access structure could potentially decrypt the encrypted PHR data using his relevant secret keys.

Another important fact that must be considered is the access requirements for a PHR sharing scenario would be complex in nature where potential recipients may come from different domains such as the patients' relatives and healthcare professionals from different care providers. Hence, the flexibility of the underlying access control mechanism is of paramount importance to cater the demands of access requirements. CP-ABE schemes do have the potential as we have mentioned above, but the existing schemes have some drawbacks which hinder the effectiveness and applicability with respect to secure sharing of PHRs.

The remainder of this paper is organized as follows. A brief description of related work is presented in Sec. 2 followed by the contributions of this paper in Sec. 3. In Sec. 4, we present the case that we have addressed along with the security requirements to be maintained in the proposed scheme. Preliminary knowledge corresponding to the proposed scheme is presented in Sec. 5. An overview of the proposed PHR sharing scheme is given in Sec. 6 while the phases of the proposed scheme are presented in detail in Sec. 7. In Sec. 8, we analyze the security of our scheme whereas in Sec. 9, we evaluate the performance and efficiency in terms of associated computational cost. Finally, we compare the proposed PHR sharing scheme with similar existing schemes in Sec. 10 before the paper is concluded in Sec. 11.

2 RELATED WORK

In this section, we summarize the most prominent existing research work on utilizing CP-ABE methods for secure sharing of PHRs while discussing associated weaknesses of the considered solutions.

Ibraimi et al. [12] have proposed a secure PHR sharing scheme using the CP-ABE scheme in [13] while introducing the concept of personal and public domains. The solution consists with a trusted authority (TA) for managing attributes in the public domain while the PHR owner himself acting as the TA for the personal domain for the purpose of issuing attributes relevant for the personal domain. Thus, the PHR owner can encrypt the private health data using an attribute based access structure, allowing only the users who have attributes that satisfy the associated access structure can successfully decrypt the data. Although this is a patient-centric solution, it has some drawbacks as well. The main issue is the use of a single TA for administrating the user attributes of the public domain. This approach could not only lead to a single point of failure but also may cause key-escrow problems given the fact that the TA can access all the encrypted files. In addition, the adoption of a single TA for managing all attributes in the public domain may also not be a realistic assumption with respect to an e-health environment which is (generally) inherently distributed. For instance, consider a scenario where a user's PHR requires to be encoded with attributes belonging to two healthcare providers. In such a situation, it is not realistic to assume that the attributes related to both organizations are handled by the same central TA, while it is more realistic to think of a scenario where each organization acts as an attribute authority to issue own attributes. We have noticed that cloud based personal health information sharing schemes for a similar setting but with a central TA are proposed in [1, 3, 4, 8, 16].

In the quest of dealing with the aforementioned issue, Li et al. [14] proposed an ABE based PHR sharing scheme using multiple authorities such that each authority administrates a disjoint set of attributes. Thus, users belonging to the public domain can ascertain required attributes from the relevant attribute authority (AA) while users in the private domain ascertain the attributes from the PHR owner similar to [12]. In this solution, the authors have utilized the multi-authority attribute based encryption (MA-ABE) scheme proposed by Chase and Chow [7] to achieve the secure sharing of PHRs. However, the main drawback of this MA-ABE scheme is that it requires users to obtain at least one attribute from each AA for the proper functioning of the encryption scheme. Due to this restriction in the utilized encryption scheme, the PHR sharing scheme in [14] is far from being effective in practice.

3 OUR CONTRIBUTIONS

In order to realize a flexible cloud based PHR sharing scheme, it is necessary to utilize a flexible and scalable multi-authority ABE scheme. As we have pointed out in Sec. 2, the lack of scalability and flexibility in existing distributed multi-authority ABE schemes have affected the evolution of such systems. Thus, the main contribution of this paper is constructing a novel distributed multi-authority CP-ABE scheme and propose a flexible cloud based PHR sharing scheme utilizing the proposed multi-authority CP-ABE construction.

In the proposed PHR sharing scheme, we define two user domains (as in [14]) public and private where public domain consists of healthcare professionals and personal domain consists with family and friends. We use a set of distributed, public attribute authorities (AAs) to manage public attributes while the PHR owner manages the private attributes. With the proposed multi-authority CP-ABE scheme, we are able to provide fine-grained PHR access for the users from both domains without requiring attributes from each existing AA, as it was in [14]. The proposed multi-authority CP-ABE scheme is collusion resistant, hence two or more users will not be able to collude their attributes and gain access to PHR data, given that it is not possible on their own. Furthermore, the proposed scheme supports on-demand revocation, which ensures that a user will not be able to use a revoked attribute for further access.

We also show that the proposed CP-ABE scheme is secure and thereby it can enforce the intended security and privacy requirements associated with the PHR sharing scenario. In addition, we also provide evidence for the feasibility and scalability of the proposed PHR sharing scheme in terms of associated computational cost based on simulation results.

4 CASE DESCRIPTION AND SECURITY REQUIREMENTS

In this section, we describe the PHR sharing scenario for which the multi-authority CP-ABE scheme is proposed. We also present the system model corresponding to the considered case while stating the security and privacy requirements that must be satisfied.

4.1 Case Description

We consider a cloud based PHR system which involves multiple PHR owners and PHR users. PHR owner is a patient who is interested in outsourcing his private health data while having the full control of outsourced data. PHR owner is capable of uploading, deleting PHR information along with sharing them among a set of PHR users based on user attributes. PHR users include both users from the professional domain such as healthcare professionals, insurance companies, etc. and users from the personal domain such as family and friends. PHRs are stored in a central cloud repository which

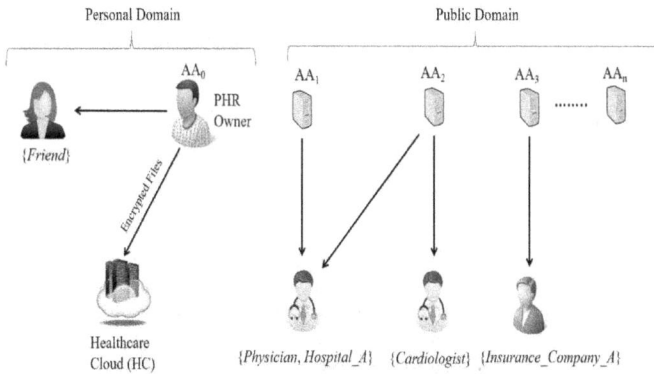

Figure 1: System model

we denote here on in as the healthcare cloud (HC). Users should be allowed to access the PHR data of patients as long as they satisfy the (attribute based) access requirements specified by the PHR owner.

We assume that the healthcare cloud is semi-trusted, which means that it will follow the specified operational protocol while being curious on the data being stored. We further assume that the users may also be curious on the stored data, hence they may want to extract more information than what they are allowed through colluding attributes with fellow users.

As shown in Figure 1, we use a set of distributed public attribute authorities (AAs) with each AA is responsible for managing a disjoint set of attributes and issuing PHR users with relevant attributes (in the form of secret keys) upon validating attribute requirements for the requested attributes. PHR owner also acts as an AA for providing secret keys relevant for the attributes of the personal domain for personal domain users.

4.2 Security Requirements

The main security requirements that we intend to achieve through the proposed scheme are outlined below.

- *Confidentiality of PHR data*: PHR data of patients must be kept secret from unauthorized parties.
- *Patient-centric access control*: PHR owners should have the full control of the outsourced health data, allowing them to determine who are eligible to access them.
- *Resistant to attribute collusion*: Multiple users should not be able to collude their attributes and decrypt PHR data.
- *Efficient on-demand user revocation*: Whenever an attribute of a certain user is no longer valid, the user should not be able to decrypt PHR data using the secret keys associated with the revoked attribute.

5 PRELIMINARIES

This section is dedicated to provide the required background details associated with the proposed PHR sharing scheme.

5.1 PHR Access Structure

We associate each PHR with a unique PHR identification PHR_{id}. Each PHR can have many information categories such as personal information, diagnosis, medications, allergies, emergency data, etc.

and we define them as PHR objects (PHR_{obj}) of a PHR. Hence, each PHR can have many different PHR objects. Moreover, we associate each PHR_{obj} with an access structure ($\mathcal{T}$) which governs the attribute requirement for accessing the PHR_{obj}. We define an access structure as a Boolean statement with disjunction ($\vee$) and conjunction ($\wedge$) operations combining subject attributes. An example access structure $\mathcal{T}(P_k, CD)$ relevant for the PHR_{obj} cardiac diagnosis (CD) corresponding to $PHR_{id} = P_k$ is shown below.

$$\mathcal{T}(P_k, CD) : (Cardiologist \wedge (Hospital\_A \vee Hospital\_B)) \vee Family$$

This statement states that any user who is a family member of the PHR owner or work as a cardiologist at hospital A or hospital B is authorized to access the cardiac diagnosis PHR_{obj} associated with the PHR identification P_k.

5.2 Access Sub-structures

We represent an access structure $\mathcal{T}$ as the disjunction of a set of sub-structures $\{\mathcal{T}_i\}_{i=1,2,...,q}$ such that, $\mathcal{T} = \mathcal{T}_1 \vee \mathcal{T}_2 \vee ... \vee \mathcal{T}_q$, where each $\mathcal{T}_i$ is a conjunction of some subject attributes (Boolean statement of $\wedge$ operations). We call each $\mathcal{T}_i$ as an access sub-structure of $\mathcal{T}$.

6 OVERVIEW OF THE PHR SHARING SCHEME

As explained in Sec. 4, our system consists with multiple distributed public AAs. Each AA manages a disjoint set of attributes and issues attributes for the users belonging to the public domain. In addition, PHR owner acts as a private AA to provide attributes that specify personal relationships such as for example *Family* for the personal domain users. During initialization of the system, every AA first defines a set of secret exponents and public exponents in such a way that each administered attribute is associated with a distinct secret attribute exponent and a corresponding public attribute exponent. Initialization of AAs can function independently without requiring any global coordination.

PHR users can obtain attributes from the relevant AAs by providing evidence that they are eligible for the requested attributes. If the AA responsible for the requested attribute is satisfied with regard to the eligibility of the attribute requesting user to ascertain the requested attribute, the AA will issue the relevant secret keys for the user. We assume that the secret keys are securely handed over to the corresponding user.

When a PHR owner wants to outsource a PHR_{obj} to HC, he should first construct the access structure $\mathcal{T}$. Note that the attributes in $\mathcal{T}$ can have a combination of attributes from both personal and public domains. Then, the PHR_{obj} is encrypted with the help of public attribute keys corresponding to the attributes in $\mathcal{T}$ defined by the relevant AA (details will be given in the following sections). The generated ciphertext along with $\mathcal{T}$ is sent to the HC to be stored. When a user is required to access a specific PHR_{obj}, he can request for the required PHR_{obj} from the HC by sending a PHR access request indicating the PHR_{id} and the relevant PHR_{obj}. However, the user will only be able to decrypt the encrypted PHR_{obj}, if and only if the user has a set of secret keys corresponding to a set of attributes which satisfies the $\mathcal{T}$ associated with the encrypted PHR_{obj}.

7 MULTI-AUTHORITY CP-ABE (MA-CP-ABE) SCHEME

In this section, we present the proposed multi-authority CP-ABE (MA-CP-ABE) scheme in detail. Our scheme is influenced by the single authority CP-ABE scheme of L. Ibraimi et al. [13]. We describe the functionality of the proposed MA-CP-ABE scheme by dividing it into five main phases: system initialization, key distribution, PHR encryption, PHR decryption and user revocation.

7.1 System Initialization

To initialize the system, first a set of global public parameters are generated which are shared among all AAs. AAs agree on two multiplicative cyclic groups $\mathbb{G}_0, \mathbb{G}_1$ of prime order p with g being a generator of $\mathbb{G}_0$ and a bi-linear map [9] $e : \mathbb{G}_0 \times \mathbb{G}_0 \rightarrow \mathbb{G}_1$ along with a secure hash function $H : \{0, 1\}^* \rightarrow \mathbb{Z}_p^*$ that maps each user identity string to a unique value in $\mathbb{Z}_p^*$. The user identity should be a unique identifier for a given user such as for example an E-mail address. Then, AAs publish the set of global public parameters of $(\mathbb{G}_0, \mathbb{G}_1, H, e, g, p)$. Therefore, any new AA can be globally initialized by acquiring the set of global parameters which are shared by the existing AAs. Then, each AA (including PHR owner) is locally initialized, and the initialization procedure is described below. We assume that k^{th} AA is denoted with AA_k while the attribute set administered by AA_k is denoted by AT^k.

- AA_k chooses two random exponents $\alpha_k, \beta_k \in \mathbb{Z}_p^*$ and computes $X_k = g^{\beta_k}, Y_k = e(g, g)^{\alpha_k}$. Then a unique random identifier $t_{k,i} \in \mathbb{Z}_p^*$ for each element i in AT^k is selected. In addition, each attribute administered by AA_k is also associated with a public attribute exponent $T_{k,i}$, where $T_{k,i} = g^{t_{k,i}}$.
- AA_k will keep $\{\alpha_k, \beta_k, t_{k,i}\}_{i=1,2,...,|AT^k|}$ as the master secret (MK_k) and publish $\{X_k, Y_k, T_{k,i}\}_{i=1,2,...,|AT^k|}$ as the authority's public key denoted by PK_k.

7.2 Attribute Key Distribution

Let us assume that user U_m wants to acquire attribute keys for the set of attributes AT_m. In addition, assume that AT_m^k denotes the subset of attributes in AT_m which should be acquired from AA_k. Suppose that AA_k has already validated the eligibility of U_m for ascertaining the requested attributes. The process of attribute key distribution is as follows.

- AA_k first maps the identity of U_m (we use the E-mail address as the user identity) to a unique identifier $r_m \in \mathbb{Z}_p^*$ with the use of the secure hash function H.
- Then, a secret key for each requesting attribute is generated as described below. If the secret key set is denoted by SK_m^k,

$$SK_m^k = \{sk_0^k, sk_i^k\}_{i=1,2,...,|AT_m^k|}$$

and,

$$sk_0^k = g^{\frac{\alpha_k - r_m}{\beta_k}}, \quad (1)$$

$$sk_i^k = g^{\frac{r_m}{t_{k,i}}}, \quad (2)$$

where $t_{k,i}$ is the MK component of the ith attribute in AT_m^k defined by AA_k. Note that secret key component sk_0^k

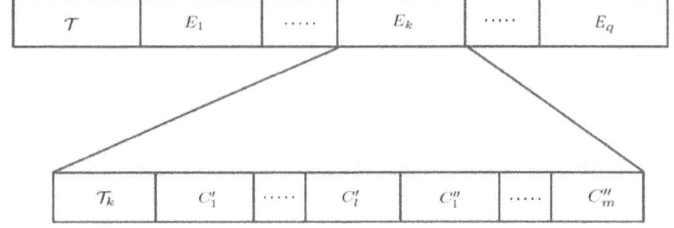

Figure 2: Structure of the ciphertext $E(M)$

relates the user identity to the identity of issuing authority AA_k whereas the secret key component sk_i^k relates the user identity to the attribute itself.

- The generated secret key set is securely transferred to U_m.

7.3 PHR Encryption

Let us assume that the PHR owner wants to encrypt PHR data $M \in \mathbb{G}_1$, which includes information on his *allergies*. First, he generates the access structure $\mathcal{T}$ and deduce a set of access sub-structures $\{\mathcal{T}_k\}_{k=1,2,...,q}$ as mentioned in Sec. 5.2. Thus the ciphertext of M encoded with $\mathcal{T}$ is given by $E(M)$,

$$E(M) = (\mathcal{T}, \{E_k\}_{k=1,2...,q}),$$

where E_k denotes the ciphertext of M encoded with access sub-structure $\mathcal{T}_k$. The structure of the ciphertext $E(M)$ is illustrated in Figure 2 and the process of computing E_k is described below.

Let us assume that k^{th} sub-structure $\mathcal{T}_k$ contains m attributes and they are administered by l AAs such that, $l \leq n$, where n is the total number of AAs in the system. Note that any AA may administrate more than one attribute of the considered m attributes. Then, we can represent the ciphertext E_k using ciphertext components $C_0, \{C_i'\}_{i=1,2,...,l}$ and $\{C_i''\}_{i=1,2,...,m}$ such that,

$$E_k = (\mathcal{T}_k, C_0, \{C_i'\}_{i=1,2,...,l}, \{C_i''\}_{i=1,2,...,m}).$$

The computation of the aforementioned ciphertext components of E_k is as follows. PHR owner first generates a random exponent $s \in \mathbb{Z}_p^*$ and using the public keys of l AAs, he computes ciphertext components C_0 and $\{C_i'\}_{i=1,2,...,l}$ such that,

$$C_0 = M \prod_{i=1}^{l} Y_i^s = Me(g,g)^{s \sum_{i=1}^{l} \alpha_i}, \quad (3)$$

$$C_i' = X_i^s = g^{\beta_i s}. \quad (4)$$

To compute $\{C_i''\}$ a secret share of s is assigned for each attribute in $\mathcal{T}_k$ by following the steps given below.

- For each attribute in $\mathcal{T}_k$ except the last, a random exponent $s_i \in \mathbb{Z}_p^*$ is assigned while the last element is assigned the value equals to $ls - \sum_{i=1}^{m-1} s_i$.
- Then, the PHR owner computes $\{C_i''\}_{i=1,2,...,m}$ such that,

$$C_i'' = T_i^{s_i} \quad (5)$$

where T_i corresponds to the public attribute exponent of the ith attribute in $\mathcal{T}_k$.

Similarly, PHR owner generates ciphertexts relevant for all the sub-structures of $\mathcal{T}$. Finally, the PHR owner sends the ciphertext of M, $E(M)$ along with PHR identification (PHR_{id}) and PHR_{obj} information ($PHR_{obj} = allergies$) to the HC to be stored as a part of his PHR.

7.4 PHR Decryption

Suppose U_m wants to access a specific PHR_{obj} stored in the HC. U_m should first send an access request indicating the PHR_{id} and PHR_{obj} corresponding to the access required PHR information to the HC. Then, the HC fetches the corresponding $\mathcal{T}$ associated with the requested PHR_{obj} and sends it back to U_m. Let us assume that the attribute set owned by U_m is denoted with AT_m. Then, U_m determines the smallest subset of attributes AT_m' which he owns that satisfies the received $\mathcal{T}$. Based on AT_m', U_m generates a sub-structure $\mathcal{T}'$ and sends it to the HC. According to the received $\mathcal{T}'$, HC fetches the corresponding PHR ciphertext E' and sends it back to U_m which enables him to decrypt the encrypted data using the relevant attribute secret keys. The decryption process is as follows.

For illustrative purposes, let us assume that the received ciphertext E' is encoded with m attributes which are administered by l AAs. Then,

$$E' = (\mathcal{T}', C_0, \{C_i'\}_{i=1,2,\ldots,l}, \{C_i''\}_{i=1,2,\ldots,m}),$$

where C_0, C_i' and C_i'' are given in (3) - (5) respectively. Further assume that $\{sk_i\}_{i=1,2\ldots,m}$ denotes the relevant attribute secret key set owned by U_m for the attribute subset AT_m' and $\{sk_0^i\}_{i=1,2,\ldots,l}$ refers to the set of secret key components which relates the identity of U_m to the l AAs who issued the m attributes. According to (1) and (2) $sk_i = g^{\frac{r_m}{t_i}}$ and $sk_0^i = g^{\frac{\alpha_i - r_m}{\beta_i}}$, where t_i denotes the MK component defined by the AA who administrates the corresponding attribute. In order to decrypt E', U_m first computes,

$$\prod_{i=1}^{m} e(C_i'', sk_i) = \prod_{i=1}^{m} e(T_i^{s_i}, g^{r_m/t_i}) = e(g,g)^{ls(r_m)}. \quad (6)$$

Thereafter U_m computes,

$$\prod_{i=1}^{l} e(C_i', sk_0^i) = \prod_{i=1}^{l} e(g^{s\beta_i}, g^{\frac{\alpha_i - r_m}{\beta_i}}) = e(g,g)^{s \sum_{i=1}^{l} \alpha_i - ls(r_m)}. \quad (7)$$

From (6) and (7) U_m can compute the support string Ω such that,

$$\Omega = e(g,g)^{ls(r_m)} e(g,g)^{s \sum_{i=1}^{l} \alpha_i - ls(r_m)} = e(g,g)^{s \sum_{i=1}^{l} \alpha_i}. \quad (8)$$

Then, U_m will be able to discover M using (3) and (8) as follows.

$$\frac{C_0}{e(g,g)^{s \sum_{i=1}^{l} \alpha_i}} = \frac{Me(g,g)^{s \sum_{i=1}^{l} \alpha_i}}{e(g,g)^{s \sum_{i=1}^{l} \alpha_i}} = M$$

7.5 On-demand User Revocation

When a particular attribute belonging to a specific user is revoked, the user should not be able to use the secret keys related to the revoked attribute in any further transactions. In our proposed scheme, the revocation process is handled by the AA which is responsible for the attribute to be revoked. We summarize the revocation process as follows. Suppose AA_k requires to revoke the attribute ω from U_m. In addition, assume that the secret exponent associated with the attribute ω defined by AA_k is given by t_ω.

- First of all, a new random secret exponent t_ω' for the attribute to be revoked ω is selected and based on the new secret, the associated public attribute exponent $g^{t_\omega'}$ is generated and published.
- According to (2), it is evident that modification to the secret attribute exponent of a given attribute affects the secret keys associated with the considered attribute. Hence, the

relevant secret keys need to be updated accordingly. Therefore, new secret keys are generated (using the new secret exponent t_ω') and sent to the users who obtained the attribute ω previously except the user to be revoked (U_m).

- Given that the public attribute exponent related to the revoked attribute is modified, messages encoded with the attribute ω will be contaminated. We elaborate this further through the following example.

Consider the encryption of message M, with a sub-structure $\mathcal{T}_1 = \omega$. Let us assume that $E(M)$ represents the encryption of M prior to the revocation of attribute ω. Then, according to Sec. 7.3, $E(M) = (\mathcal{T}_1, C_0, C', C'')$, where $C_0 = MY_k^s$, $C' = X_k^s$ and $C'' = g^{t_\omega s}$. Note that the alteration of the public attribute exponent of attribute ω will only contaminate the ciphertext component C'' given that C_0, C' ciphertext components are independent of the public attribute exponent of attribute ω (revoking attribute). We use a re-encryption mechanism to update the contaminated ciphertext component. The process is described below using the aforementioned example.

- AA_k first generates a re-encryption key $RE_{key} = t_\omega'/t_\omega$.
- Then, AA_k sends RE_{key} to HC which enables the HC to re-encrypt the contaminated ciphertext components. If the corresponding updated ciphertext component is given by C_{new}'' then,
$$C_{new}'' = C'' RE_{key} = g^{t_\omega s \frac{t_\omega'}{t_\omega}} = g^{t_\omega' s}.$$
- Thus, the ciphertext corresponding to the encryption of M after the revocation is given by $E_{new}(M)$, then
$$E_{new}(M) = (\mathcal{T}_1, C_0, C', C_{new}'').$$

After the revocation, the revoked user (U_m) will not be able to use his old secret keys corresponding to attribute ω due to the fact that the public attribute exponent related to the attribute ω is already modified. Given that other users who have ascertained the attribute ω from AA_k are issued with new secret keys, they will be able to use the new secret keys for future transactions.

8 SECURITY ANALYSIS

In this section, we evaluate the security of the proposed MA-CP-ABE scheme and discuss some important security properties of the proposed scheme. First, we introduce the following assumptions on which the security of the proposed scheme is based upon.

Discrete Logarithm (DL) Assumption: Suppose $\mathbb{G}$ is a cyclic group of order p with g being the generator. Given (g, g^a) there is no probabilistic polynomial time algorithm which can compute $a \in \mathbb{Z}_p^*$ with non-negligible probability.

Decisional Bi-linear Diffie-Hellman (DBDH) Assumption: Suppose $\mathbb{G}$ is a cyclic group of order p with a generator g and e being a bi-linear map. Given that $a, b, c, z \in \mathbb{Z}_p^*$, there is no polynomial-time adversary can distinguish the tuple $(g^a, g^b, g^c, e(g,g)^{abc})$ from the tuple $(g^a, g^b, g^c, e(g,g)^z)$ with non-negligible probability.

8.1 Resistant Against Chosen Plaintext Attacks

Our intention is to demonstrate that the proposed MA-CP-ABE scheme is indistinguishable under chosen plaintext attacks (IND-CPA secure), given that the DBDH assumption is held. Suppose there exist a polynomial-time adversary $\mathcal{A}$ that can break the MA-CP-ABE scheme with a non-negligible advantage ϵ. We show that it is possible to build a simulator $\mathcal{S}$ that can play the DBDH game with an advantage $\epsilon/2$ as follows.

Let us assume that $\mathbb{G}_0$ and $\mathbb{G}_1$ are two cyclic groups with g being a generator of $\mathbb{G}_0$. Further assume that e is an efficiently computable bi-linear map and $a, b, c, z \in \mathbb{Z}_p^*$ are randomly chosen. Suppose, the simulator $\mathcal{S}$ is fed with a DBDH instance $(g, g^a, g^b, g^c, R_\delta)$ in which R_δ is set through flipping a fair coin δ where,

$$R_\delta = e(g,g)^{abc}, \quad if \quad \delta = 0$$
$$= e(g,g)^z, \quad if \quad \delta = 1.$$

The game proceeds as follows.

Initialization phase: The adversary $\mathcal{A}$ selects a challenge access sub-structure $\mathcal{T}'$ with attributes from l out of n AAs, and sends it to $\mathcal{S}$. Note that we denote the attribute set in $\mathcal{T}'$ by AT'.

Setup: We assume that the simulator $\mathcal{S}$ simulates on-behalf of all n AAs. For each attribute ω_i in AT', the simulator $\mathcal{S}$ chooses a random element $q_i \in \mathbb{Z}_p^*$ and thereby sets the public attribute exponent for each element in AT' as $T_i = g^{q_i}$. For all the other attributes (which are not elements in AT'), the simulator $\mathcal{S}$ sets $T_i = g^{b/q_i}$. Furthermore, $\mathcal{S}$ selects a set of n random exponents $\{d_i, \beta_i\}_{i=1,2,..,n} \in \mathbb{Z}_p^*$ and by allowing, $e(g,g)^{\alpha_i} = e(g,g)^{ab/l}e(g,g)^{d_i}$, $\mathcal{S}$ implicitly sets each AA's secret key $\alpha_i = \frac{ab}{l} + d_i$. Then, all the public parameters of the simulator are forwarded to the adversary $\mathcal{A}$.

Phase 1: The adversary $\mathcal{A}$ sends attribute key requests to the simulator $\mathcal{S}$ for the attributes which are not elements in AT'. For the adversary $\mathcal{A}$, the simulator selects a random exponent $\hat{r} \in \mathbb{Z}_p^*$ and generates the secret key sk_0^i which relates the identity of the issuing authority and the identity of the adversary as follows.

$$sk_0^i = g^{\frac{d_i - \hat{r}b}{\beta_i}} = g^{\frac{\alpha_i - (\hat{r}b + \frac{ab}{l})}{\beta_i}}$$

Then, the Simulator $\mathcal{S}$ should generate the attribute secret keys sk_i corresponding to the each requested attribute. To have a valid simulation of attribute secret keys, sk_i must be in the form,

$$sk_i = g^{\frac{(\hat{r}b + \frac{ab}{l})}{t_i}} = g^{\frac{(\hat{r}b + \frac{ab}{l})q_i}{b}}.$$

Hence, $\mathcal{S}$ sets $sk_i = g^{\hat{r}q_i}g^{\frac{aq_i}{l}}$. It is evident that this is a valid simulation of secret keys, since, $sk_i = g^{\frac{(\hat{r}b + \frac{ab}{l})q_i}{b}} = g^{\hat{r}q_i}g^{\frac{aq_i}{l}}$. Then, $\mathcal{S}$ sends the secret keys (sk_0^i, sk_i) for the attributes that are not elements of the challenge access sub-structure $\mathcal{T}'$ to $\mathcal{A}$.

Challenge phase: $\mathcal{A}$ sends two plaintexts $M_0, M_1 \in \mathbb{G}_1$ to $\mathcal{S}$. Then $\mathcal{S}$ will encrypt one of M_0, M_1 according to $\mathcal{T}'$ by flipping a fair binary coin v. To encrypt M_v, the simulator $\mathcal{S}$ first computes C_0 and $\{C_i'\}_{i=1,2,...,l}$ such that,

$$C_0 = M_v \prod_{i=1}^{l} Y_i^c = M_v e(g,g)^{\sum_{i=1}^l (\alpha_i)c} = M_v e(g,g)^{\sum_{i=1}^l (\frac{ab}{l} + d_i)c}$$

$$= M_v e(g,g)^{abc} e(g,g)^{\sum_{i=1}^l (d_i)c} = M_v R_\delta e(g,g)^{\sum_{i=1}^l (d_i)c}$$

$$C_i' = X_i^c = g^{\beta_i c}.$$

For each attribute in AT' except the last, a random exponent $h_i \in \mathbb{Z}_p^*$ is assigned while the last element is assigned the value equals to

$lc - \sum_{i=1}^{m-1} h_i$. Then, $\mathcal{S}$ computes $\{C_i''\}_{i=1,2,...,m}$ such that, $C_i'' = T_i^{h_i}$. Then, $\mathcal{S}$ forwards the resulting ciphertext E_v to $\mathcal{A}$.

$$E_v = (\mathcal{T}', C_0, \{C_i'\}_{i=1,2,...,l}, \{C_i''\}_{i=1,2,...,m})$$

Phase 2: The simulator $\mathcal{S}$ acts exactly as it did in Phase 1.

Guess: The adversary $\mathcal{A}$ submits a guess $v' \in \{0,1\}$. If $v' = v$ the simulator $\mathcal{S}$ will guess that $\delta = 0$ and outputs a 0 indicating that $R_\delta = e(g,g)^{abc}$. This will simulate a valid random encryption of the message M_v under the access structure $\mathcal{T}'$. If $v' \neq v$, simulator $\mathcal{S}$ outputs a 1 indicating $R_\delta = e(g,g)^z$, meaning that the adversary gains no information about the plaintext M_v. Thus, we can come to the following conclusions.

- If $v' \neq v$, then the advantage of $\mathcal{A}$ is given by, $Pr[v' \neq v | R_\delta = e(g,g)^z] = \frac{1}{2}$.
- We assumed that the advantage of the adversary $\mathcal{A}$ to break the MA-CP-ABE scheme is given by ϵ. Hence, the advantage of the adversary $\mathcal{A}$ in the DBDH game when $v' = v$ is given by, $Pr[v' = v | R_\delta = e(g,g)^{abc}] = \frac{1}{2} + \epsilon$.
- Given that the simulator $\mathcal{S}$ guesses $\delta = 0$ when $v' = v$ and $\delta = 1$ when $v' \neq v$, the total advantage of the simulator $\mathcal{S}$ in the DBDH game is given by,

$$\frac{1}{2}(Pr[v' \neq v | R_\delta = e(g,g)^z] + Pr[v' = v | R_\delta = e(g,g)^{abc}]) - \frac{1}{2} = \frac{\epsilon}{2}.$$

Therefore, we can conclude that the proposed MA-CP-ABE scheme is IND-CPA secure given that the DBDH assumption is held.

8.2 Resistant Against Attribute Collusion

For any attribute based system, it is crucial to prevent attribute collusion which may potentially leads to illegitimate access of resources. We ensure the prevention of collusion attacks via infusing identity related characteristic to each obtained secret key relevant for a given attribute. Suppose two PHR users U_1 and U_2 wish to collude secret keys of two attributes ω_1, ω_2 which are owned by U_1 and U_2 respectively. Further assume that ω_1 is administered by AA_1 and ω_2 is administered by AA_2 while t_1, t_2 denote the corresponding attribute secret exponents defined by the respective AA. Then, according to (3) - (5) the ciphertext E for the plaintext M encoded with the access sub-structure $\mathcal{T}' = \omega_1 \wedge \omega_2$ is given by,

$$E = (\mathcal{T}', C_0, \{C_i'\}_{i=1,2}, \{C_i''\}_{i=1,2}),$$

where $C_0 = Me(g,g)^{(\alpha_1+\alpha_2)s}, C_i' = g^{\beta_i s}$ and $C_i'' = g^{t_i s_i}$. In addition, the secret keys of U_1 and U_2 corresponding to attributes ω_1 and ω_2 are given by $(g^{r_1/t_1}, g^{\frac{\alpha_1 - r_1}{\beta_1}})$ and $(g^{r_2/t_2}, g^{\frac{\alpha_2 - r_2}{\beta_2}})$ respectively. In the attempt to decrypt E, according to (6) - (7) U_1 and U_2 can compute,

$$temp_1 = e(g^{t_1 s_1}, g^{r_1/t_1})e(g^{t_2(2s-s_1)}, g^{r_2/t_2}), \tag{9}$$

$$temp_2 = e(g^{\frac{\alpha_1 - r_1}{\beta_1}}, g^{\beta_1 s})e(g^{\frac{\alpha_2 - r_2}{\beta_2}}, g^{\beta_2 s}). \tag{10}$$

From (9) and (10) users can compute the helper string Ω such that,

$$\Omega = temp_1 \cdot temp_2$$
$$= e(g,g)^{(\alpha_1+\alpha_2)s}e(g,g)^{r_1 s_1}e(g,g)^{r_2(2s-s_1)}e(g,g)^{-(r_1+r_2)s}. \tag{11}$$

In order to recover M from C_0, the computation result in (11) must be equivalent to $e(g,g)^{(\alpha_1+\alpha_2)s}$. The aforementioned equivalence will only be possible if the following condition is held.

$$e(g,g)^{r_1 s_1}e(g,g)^{r_2(2s-s_1)}e(g,g)^{-(r_1+r_2)s} = 1 \tag{12}$$

The relation in (12) can only be maintained if and only of $r_1 = r_2$. Hence, it is infeasible to achieve a successful decryption via colluding attribute secret keys of more than one user.

8.3 Enforcing Confidentiality of PHR Data

In the proposed PHR sharing scheme, PHR data are encoded with an attribute based access structure specified by the PHR owner himself, which is only decryptable by a user who possesses a set of attributes that satisfies the associated access structure. Furthermore, we have shown that the proposed MA-CP-ABE scheme is secure against chosen plaintext attacks and attacks mounted via attribute collusion. Thus, the scheme can guard against the possibility of illegal disclosure of patient's private health data and thereby the confidentiality of data is maintained.

9 PERFORMANCE EVALUATION

In this section, we evaluate the performance of the utilized MA-CP-ABE scheme which functions as the underlying access control mechanism for the proposed PHR sharing scheme.

Computational overhead of the proposed MA-CP-ABE scheme heavily depends upon the overhead associated with encryption and decryption operations given that they require exponentiation and pairing operations in $\mathbb{G}_0$. Thus, we conduct simulations on determining approximated computational cost for the above mentioned two processes. The simulations were run on a Core i5, 2.5 GHz PC with 8 GB of RAM. In order to generate the necessary cyclic groups, we used the elliptic curve $y^2 = x^3 + x$ over a 512 bit finite field having a group order of 160 bits. We choose this parameter setting by considering the fact that it can generate keys having the equivalence security of 1024 bit RSA keys [2].

For the analysis, we simulated a simple multi-authority environment with 5 AAs each managing 10 attributes. We conducted simulations to determine the behavior of encryption time and decryption time with the number of attributes in a given access sub-structure $\mathcal{T}'$ under the following four cases.

- Case 1: All the attributes in $\mathcal{T}'$ belong to the same AA.
- Case 2: Attributes in $\mathcal{T}'$ belong to 2 AAs.
- Case 3: Attributes in $\mathcal{T}'$ belong to 3 AAs.
- Case 4: Attributes in $\mathcal{T}'$ belong to 4 AAs.

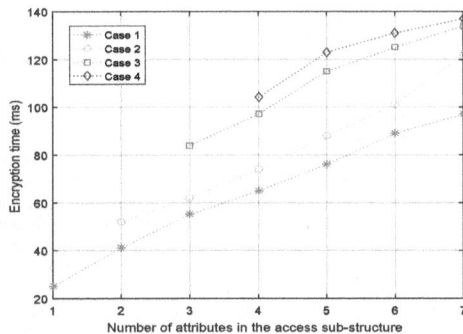

The obtained results are illustrated in Figure 3(a) and Figure 3(b). Figure 3(a) represents the variation of encryption time with respect to the four aforementioned cases while Figure 3(b) represents the variation of decryption time. Note that the corresponding encryption and decryption time values are average approximations obtained after 100 iterations. According to the results, it is obvious that both encryption time and the decryption time increase with the number of attributes in $\mathcal{T}'$. However, the variations exhibit nearly linear characteristics which speak for the scalability of the proposed MA-CP-ABE scheme. In addition, we can also observe that the decryption time is slightly lower than the encryption time since the decryption process requires less number of exponentiation operations compared to the process of encryption in the proposed MA-CP-ABE scheme. Note that we considered a maximum of 7 attributes in the access sub-structure $\mathcal{T}'$, since we rarely come across a sub-structure having more than 5 attributes in practice. However, given that the variation of computational cost is almost linear, it is fair to conclude that the proposed scheme is realistic and will function effectively under access sub-structures with a larger number of attributes as well.

Along with the computational cost, it is also important to analyze the size of an encrypted message when utilizing the proposed scheme under the considered parameter setting. Suppose a message $M \in \mathbb{G}_1$ is encrypted with a sub-structure $\mathcal{T}'$ such that the number of attributes in $\mathcal{T}'$ is m and they are administered by l AAs. Given that we use a 512 bit finite field to generate cyclic groups, each ciphertext component (C_0, C', C'') will be of 1024 bits. Hence, the size of the ciphertext is $1024(m + l + 1)$ bits. Although we assumed that $M \in \mathbb{G}_1$ (1024 bits), message sizes of health information could be much larger in practice, especially considering medical images. Thus, we can use an AES symmetric key K to encrypt the message M and then encrypt K with the proposed MA-CP-ABE scheme.

10 DISCUSSION

In this section, we compare our proposed PHR sharing scheme with similar schemes found in the literature. A comparison between our scheme and identified related works are tabulated in Table 1.

The PHR sharing scheme in [1] uses the CP-ABE scheme of J. Bethencourt et al. [5] as the underlying access control mechanism while the PHR sharing schemes proposed in [12, 16] use the CP-ABE scheme of L. Ibraimi et al. [13] and B. Waters [17] respectively.

(a) Variation of encryption time with number of attributes in $\mathcal{T}'$

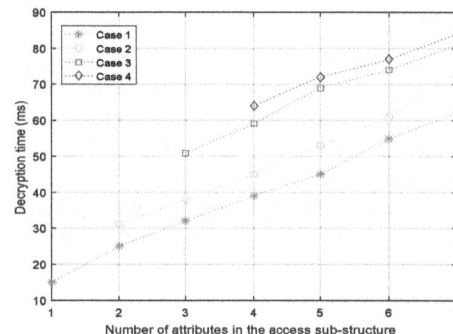

(b) Variation of decryption time with number of attributes in $\mathcal{T}'$

Figure 3: Variation of computational cost

Table 1: Comparison of PHR sharing schemes

Scheme	Access control mechanism	Attribute management	User domain	Drawbacks
L. Ibraimi et al. [12]	CP-ABE [13]	Centralized	Public & Personal	Central TA to manage all attributes in the public domain
S. Alshehri et al. [1]	CP-ABE [5]	Centralized	Public	"
C. Wang et al. [16]	CP-ABE [17]	Centralized	Public & Personal	"
M. Li et al. [14]	MA-ABE [7]	Distributed	Public & Personal	Not Scalable
Proposed Scheme	Proposed MA-CP-ABE	Distributed	Public & Personal	-

All of the above mentioned CP-ABE schemes use a centralized TA to manage and issue attributes to all users in the system. Such a centralized approach is not suitable for PHR sharing application in consideration with the associated access requirements. For instance, a PHR owner may want to share a specific PHR file with users having attributes from more than one organizational entity (ex: allowing access for any physician from hospital A or hospital B). In such a scenario, it is not realistic to assume that attributes specific for each organizational entity is issued by a centralized TA. In our solution, we adopt a fully distributed system architecture such that each entity have the capability of operating as an AA.

In contrast to the aforementioned solutions with a centralized TA, M. Li et al. [14] proposed a PHR sharing scheme supporting a distributed attribute architecture by utilizing the MA-ABE scheme of Chase and Chow [7]. This MA-ABE scheme in [7] requires a user to have at least one attribute from each of the available AAs and therefore the PHR sharing scheme in [14] is not scalable and far from being effective in practice. For instance, let us consider the following scenario. Assume that there are 100 AAs in the system and a PHR owner wants to encrypt a PHR_{obj} with only one attribute which belongs to a specific AA. However, for the proper operation of the utilized MA-ABE scheme in [14], the PHR_{obj} must be encrypted with at least one attribute from each AA (which can be achieved via dummy attributes). This applies for the decryption as well. Thus, the computation cost increases significantly with the number of AAs in the system, although the number of real attributes used for the encryption is significantly low. In our solution, we overcome this issue, and a PHR owner only needs the public keys of AAs corresponding to the attributes he uses to encrypt PHR data while decrypting user only needs secret keys corresponding to the attributes used during the encryption process (not necessary to have secret keys from all AAs in the system).

11 CONCLUSION

In this paper, we have proposed a distributed, multi-authority CP-ABE scheme (denoted as MA-CP-ABE) and thereby proposed a secure and scalable attribute based PHR sharing scheme using cloud computing which allows a PHR owner to flexibly share his private PHR data with users from both public and personal domains. Our scheme addresses the challenges brought by multiple PHR owners and users (who may come from different domains) while overcoming the practicality and scalability limitations associated with the existing PHR sharing frameworks. Our MA-CP-ABE scheme is more scalable, since it facilitates a PHR owner to encrypt private data with a set of attributes (from one or more AAs) in such a way that a user who possesses secret keys corresponding to the aforementioned attributes can successfully decrypt the data (i.e.

the scheme does not require a user to have secret keys from all AAs). We have also shown that the proposed scheme is resistant against chosen plaintext attacks and attacks mounted via attribute collusion under standard security assumptions. Furthermore, the scheme can handle on-demand user revocation which helps in preventing illegitimate access via already revoked attributes. With the help of simulation results, we have shown that the proposed scheme is both efficient and realistic.

REFERENCES

[1] S. Alshehri, S. P. Radziszowski, and R. K. Raj. 2012. Secure Access for Healthcare Data in the Cloud Using Ciphertext-Policy Attribute-Based Encryption. In *Proc. of the 28th International Conference on Data Engineering Workshops*. IEEE, 143–146.

[2] E. Barker, W. Barker, W. Burr, W. Polk, and M. Smid. 2012. Recommendation for Key Management – Part 1: General (Revision 3). *NIST Spec. Publ.* 800-57 (2012).

[3] M. Barua, X. Liang, R. Lu, and X. Shen. 2011. ESPAC: Enabling Security and Patient-Centric Access Control for eHealth in Cloud Computing. *International Journal of Security and Networks* 6, 2/3 (2011), 67–76.

[4] M. Barua, X. Liang, R. Lu, and X. Shen. 2011. PEACE: An Efficient and Secure Patient-Centric Access Control Scheme for eHealth Care System. In *Proc. of the IEEE Conference on Computer Communications Workshops*. IEEE, 970–975.

[5] J. Bethencourt, A. Sahai, and B. Waters. 2007. Ciphertext-Policy Attribute-Based Encryption. In *Proc. of the IEEE Symp. on Security and Privacy*. IEEE, 321–334.

[6] S. Bleikertz, M. Schunter, C. W. Probst, D. Pendarakis, and K. Eriksson. 2010. Security Audits of Multi-tier Virtual Infrastructures in Public Infrastructure Clouds. In *Proc. of the Workshop on Cloud Computing Security*. ACM, 93–102.

[7] M. Chase and S. S. M. Chow. 2009. Improving Privacy and Security in Multi-authority Attribute-based Encryption. In *Proc. of the 16th ACM Conference on Computer and Communications Security*. ACM, 121–130.

[8] D. Chen, L. Chen, X. Fan, L. He, S. Pan, and R. Hu. 2014. Securing Patient-Centric Personal Health Records Sharing System in Cloud Computing. *China Communications* 11, 13 (2014), 121–127.

[9] H. Cohen, G. Frey, R. Avanzi, C. Doche, T. Lange, K. Nguyen, and F. Vercauteren. 2005. *Handbook of Elliptic and Hyperelliptic Curve Cryptography*. Chapman & Hall/CRC.

[10] V. Goyal, O. Pandey, A. Sahai, and B. Waters. 2006. Attribute-based Encryption for Fine-grained Access Control of Encrypted Data. In *Proceedings of the 13th ACM Conference on Computer and Communications Security*. ACM, 89–98.

[11] B. Grobauer, T. Walloschek, and E. Stocker. 2011. Understanding Cloud Computing Vulnerabilities. *IEEE Security & Privacy* 9, 2 (2011), 50–57.

[12] L. Ibraimi, M. Asim, and M. Petkovic. 2009. Secure Management of Personal Health Records by Applying Attribute-Based Encryption. In *Proc. of the 6th International Workshop on Wearable Micro and Nano Technologies for Personalized Health*. IEEE, 71–74.

[13] L. Ibraimi, Q. Tang, P. Hartel, and W. Jonker. 2009. Efficient and Provable Secure Ciphertext-Policy Attribute-Based Encryption Schemes. In *Information Security Practice and Experience*. Springer Berlin Heidelberg, 1–12.

[14] M. Li, S. Yu, Y. Zheng, K. Ren, and W. Lou. 2013. Scalable and Secure Sharing of Personal Health Records in Cloud Computing Using Attribute-Based Encryption. *IEEE Transactions on Parallel and Distributed Systems* 24, 1 (2013), 131–143.

[15] H. S. G. Pussewalage and V. A. Oleshchuk. 2016. Privacy preserving mechanisms for enforcing security and privacy requirements in E-health solutions. *International Journal of Information Management* 36, 6, Part B (2016), 1161–1173.

[16] C. J. Wang, X. L. Xu, D. Y. Shi, and W. L. Lin. 2014. An Efficient Cloud-Based Personal Health Records System Using Attribute-Based Encryption and Anonymous Multi-receiver Identity-Based Encryption. In *Proc. 9th International Conference on P2P, Parallel, Grid, Cloud and Internet Computing*. IEEE, 74–81.

[17] B. Waters. 2011. Ciphertext-Policy Attribute-Based Encryption: An Expressive, Efficient, and Provably Secure Realization. In *Public Key Cryptography – PKC 2011*. Springer Berlin Heidelberg, 53–70.

Author Index

NOTES

www.ingramcontent.com/pod-product-compliance
Lightning Source LLC
Chambersburg PA
CBHW061352210326
41598CB00035B/5962